DANIEL KOLLÁR
JÁN LACIKA
PETER PODOLÁK

SLOVAKIA

TRAVELLING AROUND REGIONS

COMPILED BY: DANIEL KOLLÁR

SLOVAKIA – travelling around regions
1st edition, 2003

Authors:	Daniel Kollár, Ján Lacika, Peter Podolák, Mária Bizubová, Tibor Kollár, Ján Szöllös and Gabriel Zubriczký
Editors:	Peter Augustini and Daniel Kollár
Responsible editor:	Daniel Kollár
Technical editor:	Tibor Kollár
Translation:	HACON
Photographs:	Karol Kállay and Ján Lacika
Cartography:	Ján Lacika
Ilustrations of castles:	Matúšovo kráľovstvo (Matthias' Kingdom)
Recommendations:	Tibor Kollár
Cover:	JAGUS DTP
Design and layout:	JAGUS DTP
Print:	Kníhtlačiareň Svornosť, a. s., Bratislava

This guidebook is also available in the Slovak, English, German and Polish languages.

© DAJAMA, Ľubľanská 2, 831 02 Bratislava

ISBN 80-88975-58-1

Introduction

Although the Slovak Republic is one of the youngest European states, the settlement of its territory dates to the remote history. Its inhabitants, the Slovaks, have lived long centuries in the shade of the Hungarian nation, as part of the Kingdom of Hungary and did not decide on their fate or future. About hundred years ago there were few that knew anything about Slovaks or Slovakia. And if so, they were often considered some ethnicity living in the Kingdom of Hungary. Slovakia did not exist as an independent country and it was mostly referred to as anything between the Tatra Mts. and the Danube. Only the 20th century brought realisation of dreams and endeavours of several generations of Slovaks in the form of an independent State. Slovaks now have their own state and joined the countries standing on the threshold of the European Union.

In case of Slovakia, the above mentioned efforts were always determined by its geographical position. Slovakia lies in the centre of Europe. Its northern and north-western boundaries run along the ridges of the Carpathian Arch while in the south and south-west they coincide with the rivers of Morava, Danube and Ipeľ. The natural barriers and relatively large distance from the sea have protected Slovakia to some extent from different influences. It was the reason why Slovakia acquired the character of an oasis of silence and tranquillity in the past and maintained those features until the present. The pace of Time was always somewhat slower in Slovakia and the grace of many of its places lies precisely in their tranquillity and relative isolation.

Dear readers,

This is the tourist guidebook, the aim of which is to present you Slovakia as an interesting country for its natural setting, history, architecture, culture, arts, recreation and sport opportunities. The introduction to the guidebook offers the general characteristics interesting for visitor of any country. The guidebook will lead you across the individual regions of Slovakia describing their natural and historical assets. The travel in each of its regions follows the general presentation of the area, its situation within Slovakia, map displaying its interesting places and communities marked in yellow, it continues by presenting the centre of the region and all interesting localities. Our recommendations of the most attractive parts and landmarks of the particular region conclude the chapters. The guidebook also contains a brief survey of the basic practical and useful tourist information.

The varied beauties of Slovakia guarantee the visitors that they will find here everything needed for relaxation and holidaymaking in a wonderful mostly well conserved nature, decent standard of tourist facilities and what is also important, cordial and hospitable people. We are confident that our guidebook will contribute to your satisfaction and joy of having chosen Slovakia for your holiday.

Daniel Kollár and Peter Augustini

Content

MAIN AUTHORS:

RNDr. Daniel Kollár, CSc. (born on 13 September 1963 in Trnava) – human geographer working at the Institute of Geography, Slovak Academy of Sciences in Bratislava. Involved with studies in social geography and geography of tourism. Author of numerous scientific articles, science popularising books, homeland studies, author of guidebooks (Slovak-Austrian region of Pomoravie, Slovak-Polish Tatras, Slovak-Austrian-Hungarian Danubeland, Liptov, Orava) and compiler of the series Regions Without Frontiers, Visiting Slovakia, and Knapsacked Travel in Slovakia. His hobbies are history, tourism, sport and travel.

RNDr. Ján Lacika, CSc. (born on 11 March 1956 in Prague) – physical geographer and geomorphologist working at the Institute of Geography, Slovak Academy of Sciences in Bratislava. University teacher, recognised Slovak traveller, participated in several expeditions and he is the editor of the journal *Geografia*. Author of several specialised articles, science popularising books (for example Slovakia, Slovak-Polish Tatras, Slovak-Austrian-Hungarian Danubeland, High Tatras, Spiš, Bratislava, Nitra and its environs) and tourist guidebooks (for instance, Nízke Tatry, High Tatras, Environs of Bratislava, etc.). He is interested in photography, travel and tourism.

RNDr. Peter Podolák, CSc. (born on 8 November 1955 in Žilina) – human geographer working at the Institute of Geography, Slovak Academy of Sciences in Bratislava. He is involved in geography of population and settlements. Author of several specialised articles and guidebooks (for example, Malá Fatra, Veľká Fatra, etc.). He is interested in geography, history, tourism and travel.

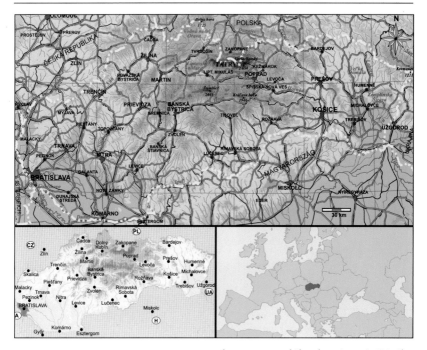

Situation

The Slovak Republic is a small inland country in the centre of Europe. The geographical centre of the Old Continent is, as matter of fact, the St. John church in Kremnické bane, the village in district Žiar nad Hronom. With total area of 49,038 square kilometres Slovakia is rather a small country. It is only a bit larger, than for instance, Netherlands, Denmark or Switzerland. Its territory stretching in the direction of the geographic parallel can be flown over by plane in half an hour, as the distance between its eastern and western extremes is only 429 kilometres. The width of the territory from the north to the south moves between eighty and two hundred kilometres. In fact, Slovakia fills the space between Poland and Hungary seen from the north-south direction while in the west it borders on Czechia and Austria. Slovakia's shortest border is that with Ukraine in the east which is only 96 kilometres long. Slovakia has no sea and the closest sea to it is the Adriatic Sea, 361 km far away from the south-western border of Slovakia. The Slovaks who want to bath in the Baltic Sea must travel 440 km in air.

Nature

In spite of being such a small country, Slovakia boasts a large diversity of natural assets. Tall mountain peaks alternate with deep valleys and gorges. Extensive forests, meadows and pastures form an eye-catching patchwork neighbouring with fertile lowlands, and the mountain torrents gradually change into calm rivers and all that is adorned by marvellously rich flora and fauna. There are also extinguished volcanoes, canyons, caves and abysses, grand rivers and waterfalls, mineral springs, medicinal and poisonous plants, shy animals and predators.

The varied natural landscape types are typical for Slovakia where many almost virgin areas still survive. One only has to

visit the mysterious valleys and ravines of central and northern Slovakia to find there everything that is missing to the modern world. This is the reason why many of the natural nooks of Slovakia are so much sought out by the national and foreign visitors. They offer unique experience seldom occurring in other parts of the world.

Surface

Many songs and poems present Slovakia as the land between the Tatras and the Danube. The Tatras are considered the gem of the West Carpathian Arch, which occupies a great part of the Slovak territory. They consist of the Western and Eastern parts and their most visited and most popular range is that of the **High Tatras**. They are "built" of the resistant granite and crystalline shale rocks. It is also the tallest mountain range in Slovakia (25 of its tops are taller than 2,500 m).

Left: Gerlachovský štít peak
Right: Veľké Hincovo pleso lake

The High Tatras were modelled by glacier and represent a wonderful set of natural beauties with glacier valleys, cirques, lakes, waterfalls and peaks. Rightly they are often referred to as the "miniature Alps", as on a small area of 341 square kilometres (260 square kilometres on the Slovak side of the border with Poland) they offer the everything what the Alps have got with the exception of glaciers. The peaks of the High Tatras are also the tallest in the whole Carpathian Arch and the tallest mountains north and east of the Alps.

Slovakia is typical for its altitudinal dissection. The difference between the highest (the Gerlachovský štít peak 2,654 m) and the lowest situated spots (Streda nad Bodrogom 94 m above sea level) also presumes great differences in climate and consequently flora, fauna and soil types. The Carpathian Arch falls into several more or less parallel mountain ranges (for instance Nízke Tatry, Malá and Veľká Fatra, so popular among trippers), which are separated by brief depressions. The depressed areas form a belt of valleys sometimes connected by narrow passes and sometimes by wider river valleys. The varied surface of Slovakia also displays three lowlands: Záhorská in the west, Podunajská in the south-west and the Východoslovenská nížina lowland in the south-east of Slovakia.

Caves, some of them of world importance, constitute very attractive phenomena of the Slovak landscape. The first natural locality entered in the UNESCO List of World Heritage was the underground cave system of the **Slovak and Aggteleg karsts.**

Waters

From the hydrological point of view surface of Slovakia can be compared to a roof. The rivers spring in its territory and flow to the neighbouring states. Part of the European water divide, which divides the watersheds of the Baltic and Black Seas, is in the territory of Slovakia. The **Danube**, which flows here from Germany and Austria, is one of the symbols of this country. Only a short stretch (22.5 km) of the river flows by Bratislava and 149.5 km of it coincides with the state Austrian and Hungarian frontier. When in summer ice thaws in the Austrian Alps its discharge reaches the highest intensity, that of the majority of other Slovakian rivers (Váh, Hron, Ipel) peaks in springtime.

The majority of lakes in Slovakia are of glacier origin and almost all of them are situated in the Tatra Mountains. The glacier lakes called here „plesá" represent the remains of the glacier activity which took place in the last stage of the Ice Age when the water of the thawing glaciers filled the surface depressions. There is about a hundred of them in the High Tatras and in combination with peaks they add an extra charm to the mountainous landscape. Each of the lakes has its specific colour determined by its location and shades of the surrounding mountains. The largest (20 hectares) and deepest (53 m) of them is the **Veľké Hincovo pleso** lake. The glacier activity in the Tatras is also responsible for

the origin of waterfalls. The tallest of them is the **Kmeťov vodopád** waterfall in the valley of Nefcerka and its individual cascades are about 80 meters tall. Many of the local waterfalls are arranged in step-like manner and their cascades adorn several valleys.

Slovakia also boasts numerous mineral springs and abundant groundwater reserves. While the mineral springs are dispersed all over the territory, the largest groundwater reserves are in the river sediments of the Danube and above all those of the Žitný ostrov, river island in the south of Slovakia where there is approximately 10 billion cubic metres of high quality groundwater. However, the attractions, which invite visitors, are the graceful nooks of vegetation on the banks of the Danube and its network of arms where time and life pace has apparently stopped.

Climate and weather

Slovakia lies in the moderate climatic zone on the divide of the Atlantic and Con-

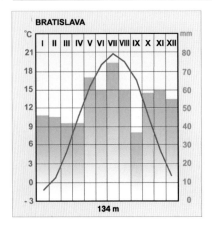

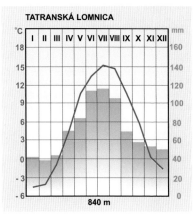

tinental parts of Europe. There are different climates in the lowlands and the mountains. The lowlands are dry and warm with stable character of weather, while the mountains are wetter and colder with changeable weather. The warmest part of Slovakia is the Podunajská nížina lowland in contrast to the coldest part of the country, the Tatra Mts. The mean annual temperature in the Podunajská nížina lowland is more than +10 °C while in the Tatras it drops below -3 °C. The warmest and the coldest months are July and September respectively. Tropical days, when the air temperature exceeds 30 °C during the day and does not decrease below 20 °C in the night, occur in summer months.

Distribution of atmospheric precipitation is also influenced, apart from sea level altitude of a particular locality, by other factors. Some mountain ranges constitute something referred to as „the precipitation shade" – it means that the rains or snow falls only on the windward side of the range which is facing the prevailing western and north-western winds bringing moisture from the Atlantic Ocean. The most conspicuous precipitation shade is observable in the region of Spiš, which lies on the leeward side of the Tatras. The precipitation total of Levoča, the centre of the

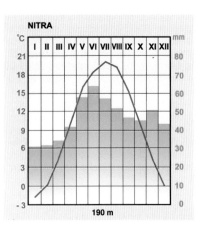

region, equals to less than 600 mm, the value typical for lowlands. The driest area of Slovakia is the Podunajská nížina lowland with the annual precipitation total of 500-600 mm. The Tatras in turn and its valleys in particular are the wettest parts of the country where the same parameter amounts to more than 2,000 mm a year, though mostly in the form of snow. Snowing in summer is in no way unusual in the Tatras and the snow cover in higher altitude keeps from November to May. The rainiest months are June and July and the driest months are those of autumn.

Instability of weather is something one has to count with in Slovakia. Weather changes determined by frontal disturbances appear in average every three days and they mostly arrive from the west. But the variations across the year do display some regularity. One of them is the colloquially referred to as **Medard's drop** in line with the proverb „Medard's drop drops forty days" – and it denotes the rainy period occurring in the end of June

and the beginning of July. Another regular phenomenon, quite contrary to the above described, is **Indian summer** which appears by the end of September and beginning of October. It is characterised by the steady sunny and dry spell, ideal for high-mountain hiking. Thunderstorms are quite common in summertime and their occurrence has been increasing in recent years. Inversion is the climatic phenomenon typical for autumn and winter seasons in the Carpathian basins. The cold air accompanied by fog maintains in basins and valleys while the tops of the surrounding mountain ranges bathe in sunshine. They mostly occur in the Oravská and Zvolenská kotlina basins.

Flora, fauna and nature conservation

Although man has changed vegetation and deforested lowlands and basins in Slovakia, its mountain ranges withheld large forest complexes. Slovakia, com-

Right: Autumn in the Carpathians

pared to other European countries is densely forested (forests occupy 36% of the total territory). In the consequence of the varied ecological conditions Slovakia is extremely rich in plant and animal species. About 2,400 original vascular plants, and even more species of mushrooms, lichens, and mosses occur here and it is more than compared to, say Poland, area of which is six-fold largest. Some of these species exist only in Slovakia. The fauna amounting to more than 40 thousand species is also varied. The majority of them live in the forest zone. It includes boar, red deer, and bear. The speciality of Slovakia is the **European bison**, the biggest European mammal living in the reserve near Topoľčianky and **chamois**, occurring in the top parts of the Tatra Mts. Water streams and bodies, lakes and ponds are used for fish breeding. Attractive fishing ranges are in the

central and northern Slovakia with abundant the trout-bearing streams.

Many plants and animals are protected under legal provisions. Entire territories, which include the National Parks, Landscape Areas and Nature Reserves, are likewise legally protected. In total there are more than thousand protected territories on the area exceeding 9,500 square kilometres. Here belong 9 National Parks and 16 Protected Landscape Areas. The National Parks (NP) are mostly situated in the Carpathian mountain area. The oldest of them is the **Tatranský National Park** (TANAP) designated as early as 1948. The **NP of Pieniny** is the smallest and the **NP of Nízke Tatry** is the largest of them. In its territory the **NP of Slovenský raj** protects the remarkable karstic plain landscape with deep gorges and one of the largest ice caves in the world. The **NP of Malá Fatra** is the westernmost situated of the Slovak high-mountain ranges. The **NP of Muránska planina** with its wild and by man least affected mountain and karstic landscape

Left: Bears in Tatras
Right: Svätopluk. Maria Theresa

is in turn the southernmost situated of them. The **NP of Poloniny** protects the virgin East Carpathian beech and fir-beech woods and it is situated in the extreme east of the country. So far the two most recently established National Parks (in 2002) are the **NP of Slovenský kras** and **NP of Veľká Fatra**. The lesser level of protection is applied to 16 **Protected Landscape Areas** which in contrast to NP's are also in lowland parts of Slovakia where the rare floodplain woods are the subjects of protection.

History

The territory of Slovakia has been settled from the oldest times. Several cultures inhabited its territory until they were dominated by the expanding **Celts** in the 4th century BC followed by the German-Roman rivalry at the turn of the Eras. In time of Migration of Nations the first Slavs arrived here. The Samo's Domain existing in the mid-7th century was followed by establishment of the Nitra Principality at the beginning of the 9th century and finally by the **Great Moravian Empire** in 833 AD – the first common state of the Slovak and Czechs ancestors. After the fall of Great Moravia the Old Hungarian tribes who finally dominated the original population haunted the territory of Slovakia, and it became part of the Kingdom of Hungary for the long thousand years.

The Hungarian state consolidated after centuries of internal struggle between the nobility and the ruler and

reached a considerable prosperity, which was also the result of the thriving mining towns, above all in the territory of Slovakia – Banská Štiavnica, Banská Bystrica, and Kremnica where gold, silver and copper were mined or the trade centres such as Bratislava, Trnava, Košice, Levoča, and Bardejov. In what is now the city of Bratislava, the first university of Slovakia, **Istropolitana University** was opened in 1467. The royal house, which ruled the country after the raid the Turks undertook in Europe, was that of Habsburgs which withheld the throne until 1918.

From the point of view of Slovaks, the crucial period in their history was the nineteenth century when they formulated their first political programme. The promising development of their matter though, was mutilated by the Austrian-Hungarian Compromise signed in 1867 and the following period of Magyarisation of all Kingdom's other than Hungarian member nations which lasted full 50 years. Only the First World War activated

Historical dates

approx. 100 000 BC

Neanderthal man lived next to hot springs in today's region of Spiš, northern Slovakia. The cast of brain cavity of female individual was found in the travertine hill in Gánovce.

approx. 5 000 BC

The first farmers arrived at the territory of Slovakia and built their settlements.

16th century BC

Expansion followed by a rapid decline of the oldest stone town was discovered at Myšia hôrka near Spišský Štvrtok.

5th -1st century BC

Celts lived in the territory of Slovakia. They built *oppidums* (towns), smelted iron, struck coins, and represented the first advanced civilisation of its kind in Slovakia.

9th century AD

The Roman legions passed over the Danube and entered our territory.

179 AD

The Roman legionaries carved the inscription celebrating victory over the German tribe of Marcomans in the castle rock in Trenčín.

5th century

The first Slavs crossed the mountain passes of the Carpathians and appeared in the territory of today's Slovakia.

623-658

The Frankish merchant Samo assumed leadership of the Slave tribe union. Founded and headed Samo's Dominion - the first state of the Western Slavs.

833

The Moravian Prince Mojmír III drove out Prince Pribina of Nitra and founded the Great Moravian Empire by annexation of the Moravian Principality.

863

Sts. Constantine and Methodius from the Greek town of Thesaloniki arrived at the Great Moravian Empire with the mission to Christianise the local people. The Great Moravian Prince Rastislav invited them.

907

Old Hungarians defeated the Bavarian army below the Brezaulaspurc (now Bratislava) Castle on the banks of the Dunaj (Danube) river.

1000

Hungarian state ruled by King Stephen I was founded. The territory of what is today Slovakia was included.

1111

Inventory of the Zobor Abbey was compiled in Nitra. The Documents of Zobor are the oldest document existing in territory of Slovakia.

1238

Trnava acquired the privileges of free royal borough as the first town in Slovakia granted by King Belo IV.

1241-1242

The Tartar hordes attacked the Kingdom of Hungary. Many stone castles were built then and King Belo IV invited settlers from Germany to colonise the depopulated country.

1296-1321

The powerful magnate Matúš Čák Trenčiansky also referred to as the Lord of the Váh and Tatras assumed control over the great part of Slovakia.

1412-1769

King Sigigmund pawned 16 towns of Spiš to the Polish ruler Vladislav II. The towns were recovered only during the reign of Empress Maria Theresa.

1428-1443

Ján Jiskra of Brandýs gathered the warriors, former Hussites, into the mercenary army called „bratríci" after the defeat of the Hussite Rebellion in Bohemia and invaded the Kingdom of Hungary.

1467-1490

The first university Istropolitana in the territory of Slovakia existed in Pressburg (today Bratislava).

1517

Majster Pavol finished the main altar of the parish church of St. James in Levoča.

1526

The army of the Kingdom of Hungary suffered an absolute defeat in battle at Mohács on 29 August. In fight against the Turks also King Louis II was killed.

1536

The Parliament of the Kingdom of Hungary promoted Pressburg (now Bratislava) to Capital of the Kingdom.

1604-1711

Six consecutive Rebellions of Estates swept the Kingdom of Hungary.

1635
Cardinal Peter Pázmány founded the university in Trnava.

1683
Imperial troops assisted by the army of the Polish King Jan Sobieski defeated the Turks at the battle of Vienna. The memorable battle definitely stopped the expansion of the Ottoman Empire.

1722
Count Mikuláš Pálffy founded the first manufacture producing wool cloth in Malacky.

1740-1780
The rule of the enlightened Empress Maria Theresa. Her son Joseph II continued in reforms, which meant revolutionary changes for the Kingdom.

1787
Anton Bernolák codified the first literary form of the Slovak. However, it did not catch on.

1805-1809
Slovakia did not escape the Napoleon's war. The Pressburg Peace was signed in Bratislava on 26 December 1809 after the battle of three Emperors at Austerlitz.

1843
The second codification of the Slovak literary language authored by Ľudovít Štúr was more successful than that of Bernolák. It was generally accepted and it is still used at the present time.

1848-1849
The Slovak Voluntary Corps organised the first armed uprising of Slovaks. Three campaigns of the Corps fighting side by side with the Imperial troops though, did not succeed in bringing freedom to the Slovak nation.

1860-1863
The National Assembly of Slovaks in Martin adopted the Memorandum of the Slovak Nation in Martin in 1861. Two years later Matica slovenská, the first national institution involved in promotion of education and culture of Slovaks was founded in Martin.

1867
Austrian-Hungarian Compromise meant increased oppression of Slovaks by Hungarians.

1918
Slovakia became part of the newly established Czechoslovak Republic declared on 28 October in Prague. The Slovak National Council confirmed the act on 30 October in Martin. Bratislava joined the state only on 1 January 1919.

1939
The independent Slovak State was declared on 14 March 1939 in Bratislava. Priest Jozef Tiso became the President of this new state practically established by the Nazi Germany.

1944
Slovak National Uprising broke in central Slovakia. It was announced on 29 August in Banská Bystrica. After the first successful operations of the rebels, the German army occupied the centres of uprising and the Slovak soldiers and partisans had to retreat to the mountains.

1944-1945
The Red Army entered Slovakia through the Dukla mountain pass on 6 October 1944 and started to liberate Slovakia from the Nazi occupation. Bratislava was liberated on 4 April 1945.

1947-1948
In contrast to Czechia, the communist party did not win the 1947 elections in Slovakia. Nevertheless, after the communist coup in February 1948 Slovakia also fell under the control of communists and the Soviet Union.

1968
Slovak politicians led by Alexander Dubček actively participated in the process of the Prague Spring. The expectations of democratic change though, were truncated by the troops of the Warsaw Pact, which entered and occupied the country in August 1968.

1898
The Velvet Revolution brought about the essential political change, deprived the communists of power and opened the way to democracy and plurality. Massive demonstrations supporting the change took place all over Slovakia.

1993
Slovakia became the independent and sovereign state on 1 January and entered the UNO on 19 January. The Slovak National Council elected Michal Kováč the first president of the new democratic state.

Economy

The economy of Slovakia is now passing a difficult moment mostly due to the transformation process. Its ultimate aim is to prepare the country for the access to the European Union. Many industries in Slovakia enjoy a long historical tradition. Slovakia was one of the most developed, industrially speaking, parts of the Kingdom of Hungary. Mining and metallurgy concentrated in the regions of central Slovakia, Spiš and Gemer, machinery, glass production, food processing industry were the best developed branches. In time between the two World Wars part of the arm industry was moved from Czechia to the region in the valley of the Váh river. Wide industrialisation was one of the assets achieved in the after-War era when the originally agricultural character of Slovakia changed to industrial. However, the heavy industry with low share of finished products was promoted. Huge companies such as the metallurgical compound of what is now the **US Steel** in Košice or the gigantic chemical complex of **Slovnaft** in Bratislava are the best examples. As the young state has inherited unfavourable industrial structure its priority now is to restructure and attract foreign capital, which would also contribute to reduction of unemployment reaching currently as much as 25% in some regions. The industries with the best outlooks are those related to car manufacturing, construction material, glass, footwear, electrical engineering, paper and wood processing branches. Slovakia is also a perspective country in the area of travel and tourism and its great potential and predisposition for this industry is not fully exploited yet.

the anti-Austrian-Hungarian resistance, which culminated in 1918 by disintegration of the Monarchy and declaration of **Czechoslovakia**, the common state of Czechs and Slovaks.

Historically the first independent **Slovak State** was established in 1939 under the pressure of the Nazi German international policy. The end of the Second World War brought about restoration of **Czechoslovakia**, under the hegemony of the communist party, which lost its power after more than forty years and was replaced by the democratic system through the Velvet Revolution in 1989. The democratic process exposed the long-simmering economic, social and ethnic problems, which were finally resolved by the peaceful division of Czechoslovakian into two independent states. The independent **Slovak Republic** was established on 1 January 1993.

Left: Port of Bratislava
Right: Presidential Palace

Political orientation and administrative division

Slovakia is parliamentary democracy. The head of the state is President with 5-year functional period. He shares his powers with the Parliament, the official name

of which is the **National Council of the Slovak Republic**. This top legal authority of the Slovak Republic is single-chambered and it has 150 members. The deputies are elected for 4-year functional period. The most important legal document is the **Constitution of the Slovak Republic** from 1992. The executive power is in hands of the Government of the Slovak Republic presided by the Prime Minister. The President, Parliament, and the Government seat in the Capital of Slovakia - Bratislava.

Slovakia has been divided into 8 administrative regions and 79 districts in July 1996. The reform of public administration, which should strengthen the position of self-government, was started in 2001. Eight higher territorial units coinciding with the administrative units at the level of regions were established and headed by their chairmen denoted here by the historical term „zhupans".

Population and settlements

Population

Population of Slovakia amounts to more than 5,379,000 inhabitants and ranks at the 22nd position among the European nations. Similar populations are those of the Scandinavian countries, such as Denmark or Finland. The density of population is the average 109 inhabitants per 1 square kilometre. The majority adhere to the Slovak nationality (85.8%) and the largest minority is that of Hungarians living in the southern districts stretching from Bratislava in the south-west to Trebišov in the south-east of the country. The official share of Gypsies is about 1.7%, which obviously is not altogether true, because many of them declare themselves either Slovaks or Hungarians. Demographers estimate the more realistic number of Gypsies living in Slovakia at 380 thousand individuals. They mostly inhabit the

ers (7%). The Greek-Catholic and the Orthodox Churches have its representatives amounting to 270,194 (5%) believers and they inhabit eastern Slovakia. The number of all persons adhering to some denomination is 4,521,000 (84%) while the people with no religion (697,308 individuals or 13%) constitute another large group.

Slovaks abroad

Slovakia lived through several emigration waves when its people left their homeland from different reasons. In the 19th and the first half of the 20th centuries the reasons were unemployment and poverty. The people emigrated from the poorest regions above all to the USA in search of better life. After the Second World war, in the years 1945, 1948, and 1968 there were three emigration waves for political reasons. Currently about 2.7 million Slovaks live beyond the frontiers of Slovakia. The majority of them are in the USA (1.8 million). There are also large Slovak minorities in Hungary, Romania, Yugoslavia, Czechia, Canada, Australia, and Argentina. Many of Slovaks living abroad reached considerable success in their lives and some of them even became world-famous. **Andy Warhol**, the founder of Pop-Art, whose parents were Slovaks is one of them. Such movie stars like Pola Negri and Peter Lorre, the main protagonist of the famous film Casablanca, have their roots in Slovakia. Among more recent generations of actors are Paul Newman whose mother was Slovak and Steve McQueen whose original name was Štefan Ihnačák before he was adopted by Irish parents. The parents of **Eugene Andrew Cernan**, the last man to walk on the Moon in 1972, were of Slovak and Czech origin.

southern and eastern districts. The Czech minority (0.8%) is dispersed all over the country and the majority of them live in Bratislava. The Ruthenian and Ukrainian minorities (24 thousand and 11 thousand persons respectively) live in the north-east next to the border on Ukraine. The legislation provides for the rights of the minorities by granting them the right to bilingual road signs in the communities with more than 20% representation of a particular ethnicity. This is the primary guide for visitors for identification of the presence of ethnic minorities in region.

Slovakia can be characterised as a Catholic country. The most recent census carried out in 2001 revealed that about 3,708,120 persons adhere to the Roman Catholic religion. It is 69% of total population. The second numerous denomination in Slovakia is the Evangelical Church of Augsburg confession with 372,858 followers.

Towns

The first towns of Slovakia are historically and archaeologically dated to the 11th and 12th centuries. German settlers strengthened their role in the country after the Tartar invasion and the following colonisation. Many of them acquired royal privileges and by the end of the 13th centu-

Left: Woman from Orava
Right: Veľký Lipník in Spiš

ry there were about 30 royal boroughs in the territory of Slovakia. The towns became centres of trade and crafts. Boom came in the 14th and 15th centuries when mining and crafts fully developed into an amazing prosperity. The most important of them were Bratislava, Trnava, Košice, Prešov, Bardejov and the mining towns of Banská Štiavnica, Banská Bystrica, and Kremnica. The number of towns progressively increased until there were 25 royal boroughs and 227 little towns in the second half of the 19th century. Some of them declined while other flourished in the era of industrialisation and the arrival of railway.

The rich history of towns has left some admirable traces in their appearance and architecture. Many of them are classified as Town Monument Reserves and form a significant part of the national cultural heritage. Their shape and way they are set amidst the natural environment make many of the Slovak towns original and perfect places worth to visit. Now there are 138 towns in Slovakia, the majority of population live in towns (57%) and they represent the economic, social, and cultural potential of the country. The largest of them is **Bratislava**, where 429,000 inhabitants live on the area of 367 square kilometres. In terms of size and population, it is followed by Košice with 236,000 inhabitants and another 9 towns with more than 50 thousand inhabitants (Prešov, Nitra, Žilina, Banská Bystrica, Trnava, Martin, Trenčín, Poprad, and Prievidza).

Villages

The majority of the Slovak villages were founded in the Middle Ages. The people living in them were involved in farming, forestry, fishing and these activities have influenced their development and appearance. The densest settlement was in what is referred to as the old cultural territory of Slovakia in the south-west of the country above all along the lower reaches of the Váh, Nitra, and Hron rivers. The communities generally developed around a small core and division of property led to con-

struction of new houses. As the population grew, the groups of houses gradually acquired regular shapes creating streets, which normally eventually met in the central square with the church, the most typical dominant of the Slovak villages, and the building of the municipal office. Many villages concentrated around castles. The rural settlement of Slovakia is characterised by compact villages such as those in the Podunajská, Záhorská or Východoslovoenská nížina lowlands and they are comparatively large (sometimes with 5,000 inhabitants) in contrast to the dispersed settlement typical for the villages of the north-western and central Slovakia. These mostly developed in time between the 16th and 19th centuries when people left the overpopulated villages to move in remoter and higher situated parts of the territory. These dispersed settlements are now gradually changing into holiday communities.

Left: Spišský hrad Castle
Right: St. Michael the Archangel church in Nitra

Monuments and architecture

Castles and castle ruins

Slovakia has got abundant cultural and historical, fortified and stately buildings. There are more than 100 castles and at least a double number of manor houses built in different historical eras. They all were repeatedly modified and reconstructed. In the past they were the protagonists of history and their owners controlled the life of the country and its people.

The fortified settlements and yards preceded castles for the 9th and 10th centuries in Slovakia. The next two centuries brought progress in form of the changed building technology and the castles were built of stone (Spišský hrad and Nitriansky hrad Castles). The number of new castles rapidly increased under the Tartar threat and after their attack in the years 1241 and 1242. King Belo IV decided to strengthen the boundaries of the Kingdom of Hungary by having built stone sentry castles along important roads, cross-roads or next to the fords (Pajštún, Plavecký hrad, Podbranč, Strečno, Oravský hrad, Liptovský hrad, Ľubovniansky hrad, to name the best known of them). Some of them were seats of the **county** head, „zhupan", the representative of the ruler and administrator of the adjacent area. Castles were mostly built as forts and stood on strategic places with difficult access. Other castles were the town castles (Zvolen, Kremnica, Banská Bystrica) built by rich towns in defence against the possible assaults.

Some castles were reconstructed in the 14th-15th centuries. Their Romanesque architecture was replaced by many Gothic architectural and artistic details and within the castle fortification new palaces were built. The Renaissance style brought a substantial change in architecture. The forts were equipped with more dweller-friendly elements, comfort and smart details. The majority of castles started to fall in decay and many of them were burnt at the order of rulers and changed into ruins. As a matter of fact, the sovereigns considered the castles centres of anti-Habsburg rebels which meant their end. But many of them survive and now shelter museums and exhibitions illustrating the history of the individual regions (castles of Bratislava, Devín, Trenčín, Orava, Kežmarok, Ľubovňa, Spiš, etc.) The **Spišský hrad** Castle and the monuments, which surround it, was inscribed in the UNESCO List of the World Cultural and Natural Heritage.

Manor houses and chateaux

Some castles and forts were rebuilt in the course of the 16th and 17th centuries into more comfortable and elegant structures inhabited by their owners until the 20th century. They were denoted chateaux. This is the reason why the Oravský hrad Castle or Zvolenský hrad Castle are sometimes referred to as chateaux. The result of adaptation of many of them was a fairly romantic appearance (chateaux of Bojnice or Smolenice) inspiring fairy-tale impressions in visitors.

Manor houses, which replaced the medieval castles and chateaux, were mostly built in flat terrain and assumed the historical role of the Gothic little castles. Originally their defensive purpose prevailed but the emphasis on their representative function and comfort was laid after the 16th century. There are manor houses built in different architectural styles in Slovakia. The manor houses in Bytča and Strážky are the most frequently visited manor houses in the Renaissance style, in turn the builders of castles in Svätý Anton, Bernolákovo and Orlové followed the Baroque fashion. Rococo style is obvious in manor houses in Topoľčianky, Dolná Krupá, and Betliar. Part of every manor house area was also a garden or park. The Baroque style was applied to the arrangement of parks next to the manor houses in Bernolákovo, Betliar, and Veľký Biel.

Many of surviving manor houses changed into museums with valuable artistic collections (Svätý Anton, Betliar, Markušovce, Strážky, and Topoľčianky),

some of them are used by artists or musicians (Budmerice, Dolná Krupá, Moravany) or they acquired social function and provide home to elderly or sick people. The special type of a simpler rural mansion which existed in Slovakia in the 19th century is „curia" and it normally stood in the centre of the village. The curias once owned by petty gentry can be seen almost in every village of Slovakia.

Churches

Construction of churches as the buildings serving to public Christian services started comparatively late in Slovakia. Although some archaeological investigations point to older traditions of sacral architectures, the first churches in the territory of Slovakia were most probably built only in time of the Great Moravian Empire in the 9th century. Foundations of the single-nave Great Moravian church

Left: Wooden church in Matysová
Right: Log house in museum of Stará Ľubovňa

were found at the Nitriansky hrad Castle and those of the three-nave basilica are south of the Castle of Bratislava.

Regardless the finds of the Great Moravian churches, the pre-Romanesque church of **St. George** in **Kostoľany pod Tribečom**, probably from the first half of the 11th century is considered one of the oldest sacral architectures in Slovakia. The Romanesque period was typical for construction of basilicas (Banská Štiavnica, Bíňa, Diakovce, Spišská Kapitula) and small single-nave churches (Dražovce, Hamuliakovo). The Gothic style concentrated in two important architectural centres, Bratislava and Košice. The classical example of the Gothic style in Bratislava influenced by the Viennese artists is the **St. Martin Minster** in Bratislava and the best example of the east Slovakian Gothic is the **St. Elisabeth Minster** in Košice. Gothic architecture can be contemplated in many sacral buildings in eastern Slovakia (St. Egidius church in Bardejov, the chapel of Zápoľský family in Spišský Štvrtok, St. Martin Minster in Spišská Kapitula, St. Nicholas church in Prešov, etc.). Likewise, other building styles are evident in architecture of Slovak churches. Traces of the Renaissance style can be seen on the parish church in Sabinov, those of Baroque characterise the University church in Trnava and monastic church in Jasov, while the Classicist style is represented above all by the Evangelical churches in Banská Bystrica, Levoča, and Kremnica.

The thousand-year history is also imprinted in the interior of churches. The austere and modest Romanesque decoration was progressively replaced by the Gothic artistic and architectural details, later enriched by paintings and graffito ornamentation in time of the Renaissance. The Baroque contributed by generous interiors with wall paintings, altar pictures and sculptures and other artefacts with artistic flair such as pews, candelabras, etc. Rococo, Classicism in fact only finished the interiors of Slovak churches and some of them are indeed remarkable for varied and rich ornamentation.

Wooden churches

Specific samples of sacral architecture in Slovakia are the wooden churches. Their folk builders expressed the perfect harmony of human soul with nature and the effort to disengage from the earthly worries. Among the oldest are the Gothic wooden churches and the most valuable of them are, for example, in Hervartov (region of Spiš) or Tvrdošín (Orava).

The „articled" churches are those built under the article of the law issued by Emperor Leopold I at the end of the 17th century. They were built in time of expansion of the Reformed movement and the Emperor's bill allowed for construction of two Evangelical churches in some counties of the Kingdom. The articled churches had to be built outside the settlements, they had to be without a tower with bell and their entrance had to be made in the wall turned away from the settlement. Such churches are for instance, in Sv. Kríž (Liptov), Leštiny (Orava), Kežmarok (Spiš), and in Hronsek (Pohronie).

There is also a third type of wooden churches, which were normally built in eastern Slovakia. First they were Greek Catholic later some of them were changed to Orthodox churches. The majority of them is from the 18th century. The special features of the East Christian rite are reflected in their interior decoration and furniture where the unique Carpathian **icons** dominate.

Folk architecture

The houses in Slovak villages usually faced the street or square of the community. The entrance was located in the yard. Wood, clay, and stone were the traditional materials used for their construction. As Slovakia was always rich in forests, wood was the most popular material for building of houses and farm buildings. Log constructions were typical for central and northern Slovakia, while frame construction with various types of filling was applied in eastern Slovakia. Stone was used in mining towns and com-

munities and in the southern part of central Slovakia. Clay was typical for the houses in the south-western and south-eastern Slovakia. The log houses in northern Slovakia were not plastered and decorated by ornamental elements. Whitewashed houses, sometimes with blue paint added were typical for southern regions. Shingle roofs were usual in the north and centre while straw or even reed roofs were normal in the south.   Unburned and later burnt clay bricks started to dominate in the beginning of the 20th century. The wooden architecture is still typical for the sub-mountainous and mountainous areas of Slovakia. Although the original wooden buildings in the Slovak countryside are rather rare now, there are still some wonderful examples of this type of architecture in some regions of central and eastern Slovakia.

Left: Ornamentation of Čičmany
Right: Maximilian fountain

Open-air museums

Folk architecture can be contemplated in numerous open-air museums. The best known of them include those in Martin, Nová Bystrica, Zuberec, Pribylina, Stará Ľubovňa, and Bardejov.   Such open-air museums also organise different types of cultural or social events in summer and they try to imitate the life, work or leisure activities of our ancestors. Apart from open-air museums there are also numerous town or village monument reserves, for instance Čičmany, which boasts several original log houses with white ornamentation, log houses and shingle roofs in Podbiel, dwellings carved into volcanic rocks in Brhlovce, etc. Perhaps the best known locality for folk architecture is **Vlkolínec** with an extra remarkable set of wooden buildings inscribed in the UNESCO List of World Cultural and Natural Heritage in 1993.

Culture and arts

Slovak culture and arts are as young as the Slovak nation. The beginnings of the cultural and artistic activities, which can be denoted Slovak, date to the second half of the 18th century. The first artists who adhered to the Slovak nation lived in time of rule of Empress Maria Theresa and her son King Joseph II. It must be emphasised that although the indigenous culture and art are young they did not spring out of nothing. Cultural awareness existed a long time before it manifested as Slovak, it existed amidst the ethnically mixed and multicultural environment in which all members of community contributed to the development of the local culture by their shares.

Fine arts

History of fine arts in Slovakia dates deep into remote past, including the primeval era. Perhaps it started with the Moravian Venus, the little statue carved in the mammoth tusk was made by some anonymous•artist 22 thousand years ago. The Bronze Age was especially rich in artistic artefacts. Wonderful jewels, ornamented pottery, cult objects, arms, toys and other objects were found in Nižná Myšľa, Barca and Spišský Štvrtok. The Celts left here the first coins, and the first Christian motifs appeared on the finds from the Roman period. Those of the time of the Great Moravian Empire include jewels and buttons of high artistic value. Medieval works of art represent mostly religious themes. They acquired the form of church wall paintings, altars carved in wood or wonderful illustrations in old books and documents. The Gothic **altar of St. James** carved in wood produced in the workshop of the genius **Majster Pavol of Levoča** (1460-1540) is one of the top artworks existing in Slovakia.

The Renaissance artists were the first to chose secular themes and their works also adorned streets and squares. The Renaissance **Maximilian fountain** from 1572 standing on the Hlavné námestie square in Bratislava is a good example. In the time when Baroque was fashionable several outstanding European artists lived and worked in Slovakia. One of them, was sculptor G. R. Donner (1693-1741) who created, apart from other excellent works of art, the **statue of St. Martin** in St. Martin Minster in Bratislava. J. Kupecký (1667-1740), born in family of Czech immigrants became one of the most important European Baroque painters. The first generation of artists who adhered to the Slovak nationality lived in the 19th century. The most important among them was P. M. Bohúň (1822-1879) who portrayed Slovaks active in fight for emancipation of the nation, he depicted important historic events and scenes of rural life. L. Mednyánsky (1852-1919) born in Beckov was also one of outstanding European painters who concentrated on landscapes. Three renowned sculptors were born in Pressburg (Bratislava) in the second half of the 19th century: V. Tilgner (1844-1896), J. Fadrusz (1858-1903), and A. Rigele (1879-1940).

The modern fine art in Slovakia dates in the period between the two world wars.

Its best-known representative is M. Galanda (1895-1938). His oil painting **Mother** from 1933 is part of the world's basic fund of modern fine art. Works of this strong generation of Slovak painters including M. Benka (1888-1971), Ľ. Fulla (1902-1980), J. Alexy (1894-1970), A. Bazovský (1899-1968), and K. Sokol (1902) can be characterised as very Slovak and simultaneously universal. Their paintings are gathered in the Slovak National Gallery in Bratislava. Regional galleries and museums often situated in some of the chateaux and manor houses (Bojnice, Červený Kameň, Svätý Anton, etc.) also contain valuable artistic heritage. Every second year one of the greatest world exhibition of children book illustrations, **Biennial**, is held in Bratislava.

Music

Medieval music developed in Slovakia almost exclusively in churches and monasteries. Music ensembles composed of monks were active in the Benedictine

monasteries as early as 11th century. Music became part of secular life in the period of Renaissance and it was sung in national languages. The Baroque music resounded in residences of nobility in the 18th century. Aristocrats considered part of good manners to have an orchestra of their own or at least have musician invited to their palaces from time to time.

The **Baroque, Romantic or Classicist music** has enchanted above all the top aristocracy living in the Capital, then Pressburg. The greatest musicians of that time performed in the town, among them W. A. Mozart (1762), J. Haydn (1767 and 1722), and L. v. Beethoven (1796), who also visited the family residence of aristocrat Brunswick in Dolná Krupá. Moreover, the composer of European importance, J. N. Hummel was born here in 1778. F. Liszt started his career in Pressburg in 1820 and later regularly returned

to give concerts. In 1886 he performed in St. Martin Minster where he presented his **Coronation Mass.** Another important representative of Romanticism in music was F. Schubert who visited Želiezovce in 1818. Three famous Hungarian composers: the author of operettas, native of Komárno, F. Lehár, E. Dohnány, native of Bratislava, and B. Bartók (1906-1918), enthusiast collector of the Slovak folk songs also had close links to Slovakia.

Original Slovak music can be talked about only at the beginning of the 20th century. The first Slovak composer who achieved recognition in musical Europe was J. L. Bella (1843-1936), native of Liptovský Mikuláš. In 1926 his opera *Kováč Vieland* or the Blacksmith Vieland was the first work of the Slovak author on the repertory of the Slovak National Theatre, which was opened six year before it. Slovakia also had its own interpreters of opera who became known in the world (for instance, the singers P. Dvorský, E. Grúberová or L. Poppová). Authors of

Left: Slovak National Theatre in Bratislava
Right: Jozef Ignác Bajza. Hugolín Gavlovič

classical music of international significance were M. Sch. Trnavský (1881-1958), J. Cikker (1911-1989) and E. Suchoň (1980-1993) whose opera **Krútňava** (The Whirl) became the national opera. The pioneer of the Slovak popular music was G. Dusík (1907-1988) the unforgettable author of the Slovak tango. The Reduta of Bratislava is the seat of the Slovak Philharmonic Orchestra since 1949. The Slovak Chamber orchestra was founded in 1960, its founder and long-year art director was the outstanding Slovak violinist B. Warchal (1930-2001). The top season of the Slovak musical scene is the event **Bratislavské hudobné slávnosti** (The Music Feast of Bratislava), while **Bratislavské džezové dni** (Jazz Festival of Bratislava) takes place in autumn and the most important pop music festival in Slovakia is **Bratislavská lýra** organised every year since 1966.

Literature

The author of what is probably the oldest literary work written in the territory of Slovakia is the Roman Emperor Marcus Aurelius. During his campaign against the Quads in 172 AD he wrote his philosophical book *Ta eis heauton*

(Conversations with oneself) on the banks of the Granus (Hron) river. The first literary expressions originated in time of the Great Moravian Empire thanks to priests Sts. Constantine and Methodius, who created the first Slav alphabet and gave stimulus to the development of indigenous literature. Methodius' follower Gorazd, the author of biography Methodius' Life was also very creative. **Monasteries** became the centres of learning where the books were copied and documents gathered in the Middle Ages. Apart from Latin the local language was also used for writing after the 15th century. The Spiš Prayers written by the local provost G. Baka in 1479 are the examples. The first poems and dramas appeared in Slovakia in the 16th century. Pavol Rubigall the native of Kremnica published *Opis cesty do Konštantínopla* (Description of journey to Constantinople), the first travel book in verse in 1544. Slovak literature written by the Slovak authors appeared for the first time only in the second half of the 18th century. In 1783 the book *René mládenca príhody a skúsenosti* (Adventures of René the Youth) by the Catholic priest J. I. Bajza (1755-1836) was the first Slovak novel.

The book *Valaská škola – mravov stodola* (The Wallachian school) in verse by priest Hugolín Gavlovič written in the west Slovakian dialect is of high artistic value. The development of literature called for codification of the Slovak literary language. A. Bernolák (1762-1813) made the first attempt but this literary Slovak based on the west Slovakia dialect did not find wide support. The recognised authorities of that time J. Kollár (1793-1852) and P. J. Šafárik who promoted the Czech-Slovak solidarity preferred the Czech language in their work. J. Hollý (1785-1849) – the author of the epic *Svätopluk* – defended Bernolák's Slovak and later also supported **codification of the Slovak language,** which was eventually realised by Ľ. Štúr (1815-1856) in 1843.

In the revolutionary years 1984-1985 a group of romantic poets was formed and started to write in Štúr's Slovak. The

group consisted of J. Kráľ (1822-1876), S. Chalupka (1812-1883), J. Botto (1829-1881), and A. Sládkovič (1820-1872). P. Dobšinský (1828-1885) who collected folk fairy tales also adhered to the group. Younger generation of Slovak authors including the greatest Slovak poet P. O. Hviezdoslav (1849-1921) continued in what the Štúr's generation started. S. H. Vajanský (1847-1916), M. Kukučín (1860-1928) and the trio of first women in the Slovak literature, B. S. Timrava (1867-1951), E. Maróthy-Šoltésová (1855-1939), and T. Vansová (1857-1942) were all active in prose. The most outstanding names connected with the beginnings of the Slovak modern literature are J. Jesenský (1874-1945), J. Cíger-Hronský (1896-1960), and M. Rázus (1888-1937). The next generation consisted of many talented poets such as J. Smrek (1898-1982), J. Kostra (1910-1975), M. Válek (1927-1991), V. Mihálik (1926-2001), and M. Rúfus (1928) and writers like V. Mináč (1922-1996), F. Hečko (1905-1960), V.

Left: Illustrations of Ľudovít Fulla
Right: Ľudovít Štúr

Šikula (1936-2001), and J. Jaroš (1940) for instance. Many gifted authors were opposed to the totalitarian regime and were not permitted to publish their works. The authors who joined the dissent were for instance, D. Tatarka, L. Mňačko, H. Ponická, L. Ťažký, M. Bútora or M. Šimečka who published abroad or even had to emigrate.

Theatre and film

The first permanent theatrical scene, the Slovak National Theatre was founded in Bratislava in 1920. Later more of them followed: Nová scéna in Bratislava and theatres in Košice, Prešov, Nitra, Trnava, Martin, Banská Bystrica and Zvolen. The first professional actors were personalities like J. Borodáč, A. Bagar, J. Jamnický, and H. Meličková. Slovakia had then several generations of excellent actors such as L. Chudík, M. Huba, V. Záborský, J. Budský, J. Króner, F. Dibarbora, K. Machata, and Š. Kvietik and among those currently active are M. Labuda or J. Kukura. Small and unconventional forms of theatre developed along the traditional ones. The **Divadlo na Korze** in Bratislava was one of the most popular. It was founded in 1962 and their stars were M. Lasica and J. Satinský. The theatre was closed in 1971 by the then state administrators for its progressive and responding character which did not convene to the communist cultural dictate. Theatre Astorka resumed its tradition and continues performing in more favourable political atmosphere following 1989. Radošinské naivné divadlo led by S. Štepka is also one of the most successful theatres in Bratislava.

The Slovak pantomime, with its famous protagonist M. Sládek who founded the theatre Arena in Bratislava is the one that won international recognition. Slovak theatres often present the dramas of Slovak playwrights such as J. Chalupka (1791-1871), author of the comedy Kocúrkovo, P. O. Hviezdoslav, J. Záborský, Š. Králik, I. Stodola, I. Bukovčan, O. Záhradník, and R. Sloboda. The young generation is represented by V. Klimáček

who founded the semi-professional theatre GUNAGU in Bratislava.

The first feature film made in Slovakia was *Jánošík* shot by the American-Slovak company and directed by the brothers Siakeľ. It was presented on 21 November 1921. Only an incomplete copy of this silent film exists. The attractive theme about the national hero, the robber Jánošík was shot again twic. P. Bielik (1910-1983) was the main protagonist in the film of 1936 and directed the next film about Jánošík in1963. The Czech photographer K. Plicka (1894-1987) greatly contributed to the development of film in Slovakia. He has shot unique documents on life in Slovak villages and an exceptional feature *Zem spieva* (The Singing Country). The majority of successful Slovak films were made after the Second World War. The older films were mostly dedicated to the theme of the Slovak National Uprising and the comedies and criminal films were made later in more consolidated atmosphere. Animated films created by the director and artist V. Kubala are very well known to the Slovak audience. So far the most successful film was *Obchod na korze* (The Shop on the Main Street) shot by J. Kádar, which won Oscar in 1965. The outstanding Slovak actor J. Króner represented the main protagonist of this

film. Among the best film directors in Slovakia are M. Ťapák, M. Hollý, Š. Uher, D. Hanák, M. Luther and J. Jakubisko. M. Šulík is the young director of the most successful film of the last years Záhrada (Garden). P. Barnabáš is another famous director who mostly shoots documents about extreme sports.

Folk Art

Common people living in countryside and mostly involved with farming have preserved their specific costumes almost to the present time. Their dominant and typical ornamental element was **embroidery**. There were many regional and local specialities depending on pattern and composition of garments. **Wood carving** was also part of typical activities of rural areas. Wood-carved jugs used in sheep keeping and drinking of sour sheep milk are still used above all in the northern re-

Left: Woman from Detva
Right: Little dancers from central Slovakia

gions of Slovakia. Folk art created the basis for the professional art existing in Slovakia. Statues of the saints and figures of Bethlehem, paintings on glass and ornamented Easter eggs were typical manifestations of fine art in Slovakia. Pottery specialised in jugs was spread in the southern and western Slovakia. The jugs, plates, and other kitchenware produced by the folk artists were decorated by motifs proper to every region and to the taste of the locals.

Traditions and usage

In the sphere of spiritual culture Slovaks have maintained a lot of traditions and customs which characterise their daily lives. Seasonal usage was linked mostly to important ecclesiastic dates. The winter cycle started by the Advent, the first Sunday following the 25th November, saint's day of Catharine, and lasted until the end of Shrovetide. The end of November meant an end to the dancing parties until the saint's day of Steven (26th December) and this was the reason the „Catharine" parties were very gay. The feast of **St. Nicholas** was among very popular feasts when St. Nicholas groomed in fur coat accompanied by the devil and angel visited every house where there were some children. They scared the „bad" ones and brought candies, fruit or honey cookies to the good. On the name day of **Lucy** (13th December) groups of women roaming around the village scared the local men. In the second half of December everybody lived in expectation of Christmas. The **Christmas Day** (24th December) was also interpreted as the crucial date when traditional meals and foodstuffs, symbols of Christmas, had to be on the festive table. If there was abundance of everything in the house, people believed that there would be a good harvest in the forthcoming year. In the evenings the carol singers visited the houses and wished happy and blessed Christmas. They returned again on the **Three Magi Day** (6th January) which was followed by the gayest season of the year - Shrovetide.

It was time of parties and weddings, which lasted until Ash Wednesday - which was the beginning of the 40-day fast.

The cycle of customs of spring and summer seasons was limited by the fast before the Easter and the summer harvest. People scarcely left their houses and their food was very simple during the period of fast. The last Flower Sunday before Easter was celebrated in the spirit of the approximating spring. The villagers carried Morena and Dedko (puppies, which were symbols of the leaving winter). The strictest fast was observed on **Good Friday**. On the following Saturday also denoted White Saturday the youths fashioned their whips of osier and girls prepared painted eggs for the next Monday when whipping and bathing started – the typical way of celebrating **Easter** in Slovakia. Another typical custom which still lives is the erection of May Poles on the eve of the 1ˢᵗ May. The holiday of the **Cor-pus Christi** was the following Christian feast when processions were held on the roads with scattered flowers and green twigs. Summer was dedicated to field works and the only important feast was celebration of harvest at the end of the season.

All these important dates were always connected with special songs and dances. Every region possesses its different and typical style of songs and dances linked to the local environment. Shepherd or robber songs are typical for the central and north-western parts of the country. Folk festivals held in different parts of Slovakia are the best opportunities to know the local usage. Slovaks and foreigners abundantly visit them. The most important of them are annually organised in Východná, Myjava, Detva, Zuberec and Červený Kláštor. Normally they take place in summer months and each of them is special and different.

BRATISLAVA

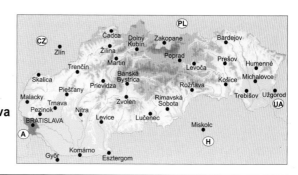

History of Bratislava

Old Town

Urban districts

The geographical position of Bratislava is very similar to that of the neighbouring Vienna or Budapest. These three Central European metropolises lie on the banks of the river Danube in places, where the great river leaves behind mountain ranges. Bratislava is only 65 kilometres from Vienna and only 50 from the Vienna's international airport of Schwechat. The distance between Bratislava and Budapest is 180 km, and that between Bratislava and Prague is 330 km.

The position of Bratislava is eccentric with regard to the territory of the Slovak

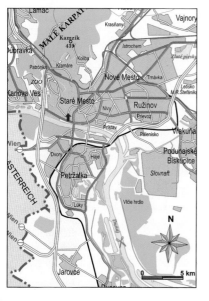

Republic. It is situated in its extreme south-western corner. A comparatively long section of the city border coincides with the frontier, a rare phenomenon in comparison to other European capitals. Bratislava is one of the youngest European capitals. It was capital during the short existence of the Slovak State in the years 1939-1945. Later in 1993 it again became the capital of the independent Slovak Republic. The territory also referred to as Greater Bratislava has an area of 367.5 square kilometres with population 429,000 (to December 31st 2001) equalling to about eight per cent of Slovakia's total population. Pursuing the new administrative arrangement of 1996 Bratislava became the part of province Bratislava.

History of Bratislava

The history of creative presence of man in the territory of today's Bratislava goes back several thousand years. To know the first inhabitants of the town, we should go back as far as the **Older Stone Age**.

The **Celts** brought a revolutionary change in the history of Bratislava. The Celtic tribes, which subdued a substantial part of the northern half of Europe, also settled in the territory of modern Bratislava. They maintained contacts with more civilized southern half of the Old Continent. They were often inspired by progressive elements of Classical times, imitating especially the Romans. The towns were one of them. They built up a large settle-

DANVBIVS

FLV.

ment which the experts call the **Oppidum of Bratislava**, the nature of which was undoubtedly urban as the Celtic finds testify. It means that Bratislava with its two thousand years old municipal tradition is one of the oldest towns in Central Europe.

After a short Dacian episode, which took place short before the arrival of new era, another important period of Bratislava's history started, which can be called after the prevailing ethnicities the **German-Roman period**. As the Romans were not able to push the frontiers of the Empire up to the crests of the Carpathians, the territory of Bratislava became part of the turbulent contact zone separating often hostile Romans living south of the Danube and Germans ruling over the areas north of this great European river. For approximately four centuries the area immediately neighbouring the Danube found itself on the border between two different worlds, which

meant permanent political and economic instability. The part of modern Bratislava lying south of the Danube belonged to the Roman province of Pannonia administered by the Roman legions settled nearby in *Carnuntum* (today Bad Deutsch Altenburg in Austria). There were (within the territory administered now by the village of Rusovce) a Roman fort called **Gerulata** with a settlement bigger than usual and a market place.

The fall of the Roman Empire was followed by a cultural, economic and political vacuum. Several waves of migration passed over the territory of Bratislava during the **migration period** of the 4th to 6th centuries.

Agitated Europe politically calmed down in the 8th and 9th centuries. The fact that the eastern frontier of the Frankish realm united by Charles the Great stabilized amidst the territory inhabited mostly by the Slavs was especially important for Bratislava. Now it was in a boundary position. Charles´ descendants fighting between them for the crown of the successor

Left: Pressburg in 16th century
Right: Document with coat of arms

state of the Western Roman Empire tried to conquer this territory. But they met with resistance from the Slav princes Mojmír and Pribina, who were not on particularly good terms with each other either. When the Moravian prince defeated his rival Pribina from Nitra and drove him out of the country, he built the stable foundations of the powerful though not long existing **Empire of Great Moravia**. A large portion of the populations of this new state formation, which reached its apex in the second half of the 9th century, inhabited forts, and two of them were constructed in the territory of Bratislava. One was situated below the Devín castle rock, and the second occupied the castle hill of Bratislava.

The local fort was included into the settlement structure of the arising early feudal **Hungarian Kingdom**. Arpád's direct descendant **Stephen I** elected as the first King of Hungary in 1000 was even seated at the Bratislava castle for some time.

The date of **December 2nd 1291** is not the date of birth of Pressburg. One should take it rather as the date of its school leaving certificate, which confirms the aptness of its inhabitants to become the free citizens of a royal borough. Important group of privileges provided for the economic development of the town. It concerned **trade and the crafts**. Another municipal privilege worth mentioning concerned the defence of the town. Only the royal boroughs were allowed to have **municipal fortifications**. The town walls of Pressburg restricted a comparatively small medieval town. Between the 14th and 16th centuries inside the fortifications a **Gothic town** had developed, from which much more had survived than from its Romanesque predecessor.

A special and above-standard relation originated between Pressburg and the **King Sigismund of Luxembourg** who ascended to the throne in 1387 and reigned for fifty years, longer than any other Hungarian ruler. In 1430 Pressburg received another privilege, the **right to strike coins** in its own mint. The prestige of the town grew with the granting of a coat of arms in 1436.

Ladislav's successor was Hunyady's son **Matthias Corvinus**. Traditional sympathy of the Hungarian sovereigns to Pressburg also continued during his thirty-year reign. Ceremonious confirmation of the privileged position of the town by **The Golden bull of King Matthias** in 1464 and the addition of a new **privilege**, that of **the sword**, in 1468 manifested it. The name of King Matthias is connected with the penetration of humanistic ideas into Central Europe. The result of one such inspiration was the opening of university, which followed the example of the oldest university at Bologna. Pressburg was chosen for the seat of this university and its name was **Universitas Istropolitana** (often and incorrectly referred to as Academia Istropolitana). In spite of its short duration, Pressburg became known in the cultural Europe of that time.

The defeat of combined Hungarian forces at the **battle of Mohács** in 1526 was disastrous for the country. The army of the Ottoman Sultan Süleyman II first

deprived the country of its king and then of its freedom. But Pressburg paradoxically benefited from the situation.

Ferdinand of Habsburg, confirmed by repeated coronation in Székesfehérvar a year after the Pressburg congress, compensated the town for its goodwill and promoted it to the capital of Hungary by the law approved by the Hungarian Parliament in 1536. It was a temporary act. It would be in force only until the entire territory was won back from the Turks.

The fall of Székesfehérvar meant that Hungary lost its traditional coronation town. This is how Pressburg won another **privilege, the one of coronation of the Hungarian kings** and their spouses. It was another, though temporary function to be kept until 1830 and used nineteen times.

The period of greatest prosperity and expansion is connected with the forty-year rule of **Maria Theresia** on the Hungarian

Left: Coronation of Carolina Augusta
Right: Coronation of Maria Theresa

throne. Her indeed unusually positive relation to Pressburg may have originated on the day of her pompous coronation on June 25th 1741. After this she used every occasion to visit the beloved town. Thanks to the queen's favour the life of the town became more varied and refreshed by various attractive events and feasts. For the sake of comfort, many aristocrats decided to own residences or fashionable **palaces in Pressburg**.

The queen also wanted to make her stays in Pressburg more pleasant and decided to **reconstruct the castle**. The Renaissance palace of Pálffy was adjusted and the style adapted to the most recent trends of fashion. New buildings in castle area and a big Baroque garden of French type were added to it. The castle almost entirely lost is defensive function and its residential and prestige functions were emphasised. In 1766 a Rococo palace called the **Theresianum** next to the eastern wing of the castle was constructed.

Maria Theresia's wars with Prussia luckily did not affect Pressburg at all. A long period of peace similar to that in the 14th century was repeated. All areas of human activity throve in such a favourable: Trade, crafts, learning, education, arts, and spiritual life. The spirit of **enlightenment and tolerance** entered Pressburg. Number of its population increased more than three-fold. The town sheltered 33 thousand inhabitants and it meant that Pressburg was the largest city in Hungary. Pressburg was larger than Buda, Pest or Debrecen. The town was expanding and new suburbs were originating outside the inner walls. The municipal fortifications again became the principal obstacle to the further urbanistic development of Pressburg. It was obvious that the town had to be liberated from its **restraining ring of the town walls**. Son of Maria Theresia, Emperor **Joseph II** was much less interested in Pressburg than his mother. The political position of Pressburg weakened during the reign of Joseph II although the city still had good conditions for economic growth.

The economic growth of Pressburg was slowed down by the **Napoleonic Wars** at the beginning of the 19th century. French troops came close to Pressburg twice. The first time was in 1805, when they easily took the town. A squad of thirty cavalrymen occupied the shuttle bridge over the Danube and opened the way to three hundred cavalrymen and 9,000 infantry soldiers. Shortly after the Battle of Austerlitz (today Slavkov) took place. The peace treaty that entered history as the **Peace of Pressburg** confirmed Napoleon's famous victory. The documents were signed on December 26th 1805 in the Hall of Mirrors of the Primatial Palace (→ 112). The treaty brought about great losses of territory for the defeated kingdom.

The second half of the 19th century is characterized by the onset of the **industrial revolution**. The number of industrial plants working in the city jumped up to forty-one in the sixties. In 1869 there were 2,392 firms employing 5,293 workers. And before the end of the 19th century another

19 factories giving jobs to additional 1,700 people were founded. The biggest factories of Pressburg originated in the years 1873 to 1911. Dynamit-Nobel (1873), Stein Brewery (1873) Apolo Refinery (1895), Cvernovka (textile factory) (1900) and Gumonka (rubber factory) (1911) are worth mentioning.

The development of industry was accompanied by that of modern transport. The introduction of **steam engine in river navigation** in 1818 meant a revolutionary progress in the industry. Travelling to the right bank of the Danube by the **Pressburg "propeller"** was a favourite pastime of the citizens. The following year they even could walk to the Petržalka park via the first fixed bridge over the Danube, later called after the Emperor Franz Joseph. In 1840 the **first train on the horse railway** left Pressburg for Svätý Jur. Pressburg did not lag too much behind the rest of the world in the sphere of steam engines. **The first steam locomotive** entered its railway station on August 30th 1848. The railway track of the trains

going to Marcheg was later extended to Vienna, and this track is linked with the oldest railway bridge and tunnel in the former territory of Hungary. When in 1895 the **first tram** set out on a journey across the city, it meant the beginnings of the modern municipal transport. **Trolley buses** were introduced in 1911.

Pressburg was spared the direct impact of the **First World War**. The population suffered from the war only indirectly. Nevertheless, the war lasted longer for the citizens of Pressburg. When the arms stopped firing on all the fronts, the battle for Pressburg only began. When the Czechoslovak Republic was declared on the ruins of the Monarchy on October 28th 1918 and two days later was confirmed in Martin by the Slovak National Council, the destiny of Pressburg was unclear.

On February 2nd 1919 the Slovak Government led by Vavro Šrobár moved from Žilina to Pressburg, which became the

Left: Hotel Carlton on a postcard

capital of Slovakia. Pressburg lasted only for another month, because on March 6th 1919 its **name was changed to Bratislava**. The first years of Bratislava in interwar Czechoslovakia were the ones of establishment of numerous national institutions, such as the Slovak National Theatre, Comenius University, etc. The population increased from 83,000 in 1919 to 124,000 in 1938. Bratislava remained a city of three nationalities also after the disintegration of Monarchy, only in different ratios. The share of Slovaks (and Czechs) increased from 33% in 1919 to 59% in 1938 (Czechs were represented by 17%). The share of Germans dropped in the same period from 36 to 22%, and in case of Hungarians it was from 29 to 13%.

When on March 14th 1939 the independent Slovak State was declared, **Bratislava became its capital**. President Jozef Tiso had his seat in Grassalkowich's Palace. The state created under the pressure of Nazi Germany did not last long. It practically disappeared in April 1945 with the entry of the Red Army accompanied by the Romanian troops. Bratislava was also expanding during the Second World War. In four decades the population of the city quadrupled. **The extreme population increase** was attributed to in-migration from the whole of Slovakia. People were coming in search of jobs and possibility to obtain flats. The post-war city was experiencing an unusual boom. But it has to be said that the development was extensive. Mass construction of housing estates started. Flats were built but the basic amenities lagged behind. In 1978 construction of flads continued on the right bank of the Danube, in Petržalka. Petržalka with its 120,000 inhabitants became in ten years the biggest housing estate in Czechoslovakia. This extensive growth stopped after the November 1989 revolution and the population stabilized for the whole following decade at about 450,000. **Bratislava became again the capital of the independent Slovak Republic** after the division of the Czech and Slovak Federal Republic on January 1st 1993.

Old Town

The centre of Bratislava is also referred to as the Staré Mesto or Old Town (134 m above sea level, population 44,800). It became the district of Bratislava I in 1996 and its area 9.6 square kilometres makes it the smallest one of Slovakia. It is simultaneously the most densely populated district (4,790 inhabitants per square km). The Old Town includes the historic core of the city and adjacent quarters, originally medieval suburbs. The eastern part of the Old Town is flat and covered by dense urban fabric. The western part lies on the hills with greater part of urban greenery compared to the rest of the city. The southern limit of the Old Town coincides with the channel of the Danube.

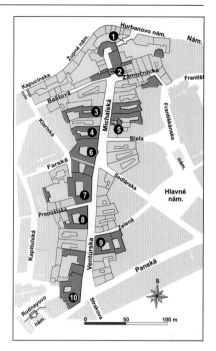

Michalská and Ventúrska streets

You should start at Hviezdoslavovo námestie square with a wonderful view of the slender silhouette of Michalská veža tower with its typical onion-shaped roof. The view of this traditional landmark is framed on the left by the modern building of the **Dom obuvi** (House of Shoes) colloquially called by the natives Veľký Baťa. The beginning of Michalská street runs along the old stone **bridge of St. Michael ❶** over the former water moat. It was built in the first half of the 18th century and replaced the original wooden drawbridge. On the left side of the bridge the passersby get a nice view of the rest of the former **town moat**. Left from the Michalská veža tower the parts of the double **town walls** have been preserved. The preserved and visible part of the walls consists of higher and lower parts. The lower part was added to the original higher part in the time of Turkish wars, approximately in the mid-16th century. It stands on the foundations of older medieval fortifications. If you bend a little over the railing of the bridge at the extreme left, the half-circle of the **Prašná bašta** bastion appears. It was preserved in the back part of house No. 11 standing at the bend of Zámočnicka ulica street. It was first referred to in 1520. The

upper section of Michalská ulica passes through the preserved remains of **barbican**, which protected the entry into the inner town from 15th century. The curve of the street was intentional as it prevented the direct artillery attacks on the actual Michalská brána gate.

The Baroque house built into the barbican in the second half of the 18th century shelters the **At the Red Crab pharmacy** which contains the original furnishing of one of the oldest pharmacies in Bratislava and also the Museum of Pharmacy. Before passing under the Michalská brána gate do not forget to look at the narrow house on its right side. It is **house** with the narrowest facade in the city (1.6 m), which documents the skills of Bratislava's medieval builders when they had to come on terms with the limited space inside the town walls. The width of this extremely narrow house corresponds to that of the moat and its peripheral walls coincide with those of the fortifications.

The **Michalská veža** ❷ tower constitutes one of the symbols of the city. It is the only one preserved out of four providing for the entry into the fortified medieval town. It provided for the passage into the town from the north, coming from the Záhorie or Moravian regions. In the night it was closed. Its name derives from the village that existed in early Middle Ages beyond the gate and around the long before demolished church of St. Michael. The tower has seven floors now. One can identify several architectural styles from Gothic to Baroque. The lowest part is the passage with a brick cross vault and five floors of a massive four-sided tower. The part from the second floor down to the ground is the oldest. It originated as a Gothic fortified gate sometime in the first half of the 14ᵗʰ century. The rest of the prism with another three floors was added in the first third of the 16ᵗʰ century when

Left: Michalská ulica street
Right: Gate of the Pállfy Palace

Turkish attacks were expected and the city was more thoroughly fortified. Under the tower is the **zero kilometre**, from which the distances of the individual world settlements are calculated.

Ascent to the gallery of Michalská tower is worthwhile as you can also see an **exhibition of historic arms** from the Town Museum deposited in the tower. The panoramic view from the top of the tower is superb. The view of the near Zámočnícka and Baštová streets deserves special attention. These two streets originated as narrow castle lanes in the immediate vicinity of the town walls. On the left there is **Zámočnícka ulica** street. Its name (Smith's street) reveals that there were workshops of craftsmen here in the past. The fire of 1590 destroyed its original Gothic buildings. On the right of the tower is **Baštová ulica** street. Its name derives from the bastions, which used to be part of the defensive system north of the street. The headsman used to live in this street and that is why the name of the street before 1879 was Katova or Headsman's street.

Standing at Michalská tower one gets a view of the whole of **Michalská ulica** street, which is one of the oldest in the city. Its lower part existed as early as the Romanesque period of Pressburg. Later it was widened by the addition of more houses along the road used by merchants on their way from the north to Bratislava's ford over the Danube. The builders of the inner town walls set its present length sometime in the 14ᵗʰ century. The modern urban fabric of Michalská street is varied in styles with preserved or restored Renaissance houses prevailing.

Let us stop first at **Segner's curia** ❸ (house No. 7) in the western row of houses, which attracts attention with its two two-storied oriels. It is also the house where his grand-grandson **Johann Andreas Segner** (1704-1777), a scientist of European rank was born.

Jeszenák Palace ❹ (house No. 3), built in 1730 as a city palace, is the second oldest of Bratislava. Only Esterházy's palace in Kapitulská street is older. The royal counsellor Pavol Jeszenák built it in the 17th century. It is similar to Hillebrandt's palace of Daun-Kinsky in Vienna.

A comparatively modest building with simple Neo Classical facade standing on the eastern side of Michalská street hides one a pleasant surprise: the wonderful Gothic interior of the **Chapel of St. Catharine** ❺. The charm of the remote past breathes from the white walls with tender arches. The chapel is one of the oldest surviving buildings of Bratislava. The Cistercian Francis de Columba, the chaplain of the Pope's ambassador Cardinal Gentile, built it. The chapel was consecrated in 1325.

The most magnificent building of Michalská street is at its lower end. It is **Palác Uhorskej kráľovskej dvorskej komory** ❻ (the palace of the Hungarian Royal Court Chamber), today the University Library. In its central hall the lower council of the **Hungarian Parliament** formed by the county deputies, free royal borough, and chapters, had its sessions in the years 1802-1848. This is the place, where the manifests of the followers of the radical wing of the Hungarian nobility against the obsolete social system in the country were read and where the passionate speeches of Juraj Palkovič and Ľudovít Štúr concerning national and social rights were heard. This body adopted social laws, including the one on abolition of serfdom in 1848. The building was adapted to the needs of the **University Library**, its present purpose, in the years 1951-1953.

Ventúrska ulica street, continuing Michalská, bears the name of the family Ventura from Italy. Ventúrska street is connected with Michalská by a short tapered section caused by close proximity of the facing houses. One of the buildings forming this bottle neck is the **Palace of Leopold de Pauli** ❼ (house No. 13). It was built in the years 1777-1776 for the main administrator of the royal property on the former royal plot. Gothic houses probably occupied the site before this. The chamber architect F. K. Römisch, who probably followed the design of Hille-

brandt, built it. De Pauli's city palace is a nice sample of the new trend in the architecture of Pressburg's city palaces applied in the last quarter of the 18th century. This palace has got all that is absent in other palaces. In its interior there is a garden with a graceful Rococo **music pavilion**. Some sources assert that in 1820 **Franz Liszt** gave a concert there.

The corner of Ventúrska and Prepoštská streets is occupied by **Zichy Palace** ❽ (house No. 11) with its smart and strictly Neo Classical facade. Its builder was F. Feline. It was built on the site of three older medieval houses as a four-wing building with inner gallery-rimmed courtyard. Count Franz Zichy had it build in 1775. The palace was restored for the purpose of ceremonies and feasts in the 1980's. **Pálffy Palace** ❾ (house No. 10) which was reconstructed in 1747 stands on corner of Ventúrska and Zelená streets. The tablet on the facade of Pálffy's palace facing Ventúrska street announces that it was presumably the venue of the concert of the

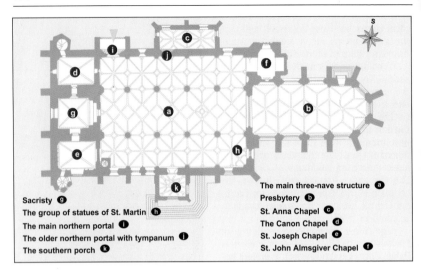

Sacristy **g**
The group of statues of St. Martin **h**
The main northern portal **i**
The older northern portal with tympanum **j**
The southern porch **k**

The main three-nave structure **a**
Presbytery **b**
St. Anna Chapel **c**
The Canon Chapel **d**
St. Joseph Chapel **e**
St. John Almsgiver Chapel **f**

then six year old child known by the whole world as **Wolfgang Amadeus Mozart** (1756-1791). In two venerable looking **houses** opposite Pálffy's palace the history of university education in Pressburg started more than 500 years ago. It includes the thirty-year lasting activity of the first humanistic university in Hungary known as the Academia Istropolitana.

Ventúrska street slightly widens in its lower part. The narrow triangle is very probably the remnant of an old market place from the beginnings of the medieval settlement below the castle. Its western part is occupied by **Erdödy's palace ⑩** (house No. 1) The former private seat of the state judge Count Juraj Erdödy is the last palace built in Pressburg from the second generation of the city palaces. The local architect Matej Walch finished it in 1770. Originally there were two floors and in the first half of the 20th century a third floor was built on top of them.

St. Martin's Minster and Kapitulská street

The pride of every Christian city is its parish church. This is undoubtedly the case with **St. Martin's Minster ❶**,

Left: St. Martin's Minster

Bratislava's biggest, oldest and most spectacular church. First the Pope's approval was needed to move the provost's church dedicated to the Most Holy Saviour from the castle into the settlement below the castle Pope Innocent III approved the request of the King Emerich of Hungary. Reconstruction, which was carried out since the 14th century under the patronage of the ruler and the town council, was in the Gothic taste. St. Martin's Minster was a **coronation church** in the years 1563-1830. The first ruler to be crowned here was Maximillian II. The coronation ceremony took place on September 8th 1563. It was followed by eighteen other coronations including that of Maria Theresia on June 25th 1741. The last king who received St. Stephen's royal crown below the lead statue of St. Martin was Ferdinand V on September 28th 1830. An incomplete **list of eleven kings and eight royal spouses** crowned in Pressburg's Minster is on the board placed on the inside northern wall.

Reconstruction in the Baroque taste first concentrated on the interior and later on the construction of the fourth chapel. In the years 1732-1734 the ground plan of the church was widened by the **chapel of St. John the**

Almsgiver one of the most valuable artistic monuments of Bratislava. The Baroque chapel was probably built according to the **George Raphael Donner's** design (1693-1741).

The recognized artist Georg Rafael Donner was entrusted with more works in the interior of the church. The new bulky Baroque altar with Donner's monumental **group of statues of St. Martin** replaced the removed Gothic one. This wonderful sculpture made in 1744 from lead represents a Roman soldier from Transdanubian Pannonia, who cuts his cape in two in a mighty movement of sabre to give half of it to a beggar suffering from cold.

The Baroque **tower** was destroyed by fire caused by lightning in 1833. It was only three years after the last coronation was held in the Minster. Reconstruction was entrusted to an important Pressburg Classicist architect Ignác Feigler senior. He chose the fashionable **romanticizing style**. The tower was given the Neo Gothic face, which has survived until today. The tower of the Minster is 85 metres tall. At its top is a gilded 2x2 m cushion bearing the **copy of the Hungarian royal crown**. The imitation is one metre tall and weighs 300 kilograms.

The visitors of Bratislava Minster's monumental interior of 70x23 metres can admire there many remarkable works of art, and others are deposited in the parts of the church closed to the public.

South of the St. Martin's Minster is the rectangular **Rudnayovo námestie** square. Its position in the neighbourhood of the Minster predestined the older names of this square: *Domplatz* in German or *Dómske námestie* in Slovak. The name of the square used since 1939 commemorates **Alexander Rudnay** (1760-1831), the first Slovak who achieved the title of Cardinal.

The street leading northward from presbytery of the Minster is called **Kapitulská**. Its length was determined by the town fortifications at its northern end. This is one of the oldest streets of

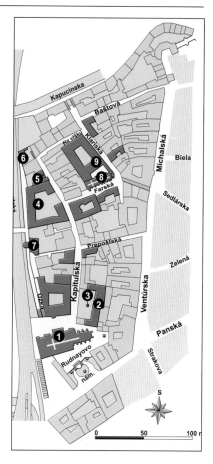

the town and the Church dignitaries, who were moved from the castle to the settlement below the castle by the beginning of the 13th century, created it. The houses of provost, canons and priests formed the street. It used to be the main street of the Romanesque Pressburg. It ran further to Zámocká ulica and the castle. Expansion of the town in the 14th century pushed the street to the western edge of the town.

In the right corner, at the end of the eastern row of houses of Kapitulská ulica street stands a big building with a comparatively large forecourt. It originated in 1632 by reconstruction of an

older house as ordered by the then provost Juraj Draškovič. The provost used it and this is the reason why it is called **Prepoštský palác ❷** or the Provost's Palace. The present Provost's Palace though, is a two-storied Renaissance building with short lateral wings, which close the mentioned forecourt or rather a garden. The **Late Renaissance portal** in the wall of the courtyard of honour of the Palace from 1632 is quite different from the simple facade. It is a unique architectural element in Slovakia. The **statue of St. Elisabeth of Hungary ❸** by sculptor Alojz Rigele from 1907 standing in the courtyard represents the Saint allegedly born in Pressburg Castle in 1207. The Provost's Palace is today the seminary for priests.

The **Esterházy Palace ❹** (house Nos. 6-10) is the only secular building on Kapitulská street. It is one of the old-est palaces in the city, as it was built almost a century before the city was seized by building frenzy in time of Maria Theresia, which gave origin to plenty of wonderful Baroque, Rococo, and Neo Classical palaces. It was built in the mid-17th century and restored in the Baroque style in the following century. The Listh family owned the original house. Later Count Esterházy bought it. The governor Albert, son-in-law of Queen Maria Theresia also lived in the house for some time.

The venerable looking **Gothic house No. 4** in the northern part of Kapitulská street called **Malý prepoštský dom ❺** or the Small Provost's House will certainly attract the visitor's attention. It consists of two Gothic houses from the 15th century. Behind the eastern row of the houses of Kapitulská ulica are the **western town fortifications ❻**, which were subject to extensive reconstruction, when the New Bridge over the Danube was constructed in the early 1970's.

Left: Kapitulská ulica street
Right: I. Esterházy statue by G. R. Donner

The massive **Vtáčia bašta** ❼ (Bird's Bastion), which was the defensive counterpart of the Luginsland bastion at the opposite slope of the castle hill, stands outside of the fortifications.

The dominating building of **Klariská ulica** street is the **St. Clara church** ❽ and monastery. Monastic building have stood here since the 13th century. They were originally Cistercian nuns, who along with Franciscan monks, were the first to come to Pressburg. By the end of the 13th century the **Gothic nave of the church** was started and it was finished in 1375. The vault of the church had to be restored again after fire in 1515. **Presbytery** was added to the nave and both are vaulted with ribbed cross vaults. In the early 15th century a five-sided **Gothic tower** lavishly adorned by pinnacles, gargoyles and little statues in what is called the Beautiful Style was added on the side of Farská ulica street. Today there are true copies of four statues on the tower. The original statues are kept inside the church. This Bratislava's landmark is impressive not only for its beauty, but also for its bold architectural solution. The builder decided for an unconventional approach when he did not build the tower on the foundations buried in earth. He rather built it on the lateral wall of the church nave.

The original Gothic **monastery of St. Clara** ❾ became dilapidated, when the nuns left Pressburg fleeing from the Turks in 1526. The order moved to Trnava. Later they came back only to face ownership problems with the city and the consequences of another fire. Finally it was Archbishop Peter Pázmány who decided for a deep change of architecture of the monastery. He supported all Catholic institutions within the framework of the Re-Catholicizing program of the Church and also helped to the nuns of St. Clara's order. The **new monastery** was built on the foundations of the old. The former monastery was reconstructed in the years 1957-1961 and it became the seat of the Slovak Pedagogic

Library. The monastery now shelters the **Office of the European Council**.

Panská and Laurinská streets

Panská and Laurinská streets form together the longest long street line in the historical centre of Bratislava with total length of 700 m. In the past they bore the common name of Dlhá or Long street. The more easterly-situated Laurinská is busier with more shops and less luxurious houses. Panská (or Lordly) street is what its name suggests, as there are many city palaces, which used to belong to the nobility and rich burgers.

Panská ulica street starts at the former Vydrická brána gate and ends at the crossroads with Rybárska brána. The Neo Classical **Csáky Palace** ❶ stands at the point, where Panská ulica street opens to the rectangular area of Rudnay's square. The domestic builder Matúš Walch built it for Count Juraj Csáky in 1775.

The **Keglevich Palace** ❷ stands on the corner of Panská and Strakova street.

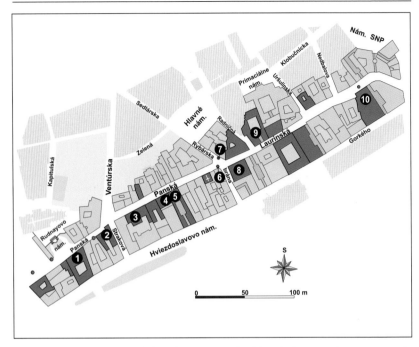

Side by side the proud Erdödy Palace it looks like a country mansion of some yeoman from the north of Slovakia. The short facade of the single floor house compensated by the tall red roof typical of old village mansions causes this rustic impression. The Baroque palace originated by rebuilding an older burgher house.

The **Pálffy Palace ❸** at Panská No. 19-21 revealed some pleasant surprises to the historians and archaeologists in recent years. The oldest written documents relating to this palace on today's Panská street are from 1415 to 1516. The Pálffy family bought the house in 1715. Count Pálffy was later nominated palatine and state judge. He paid thirty thousand guldens for the house. In the first half of the 19th century the Pálffys unified the original building in the Neo Classical style with the facade preserved up to now. In 1885 the rear parts of the palace were pulled down and a new palace was built facing the Prome-

nade (Hviezdoslavovo námestie square). Extensive reconstruction of the interior of the palace carried out in the 1980's adjusted the palace for the purpose of **Art Gallery of the city of Bratislava**.

A defensive tower occupied the site of **house No. 17**, now used by the *British Council*, in the 13th century. The Gothic house from the 15th century belonged to palatine Rozgoň, the protagonist of the civil war between the castle and the town. The owners of the house alternated until the Pauline monks from Marianka bought it. The Paulines wore typical white gowns and that is why the house was called **The House of the White Monks.** In the second half of the 17th century the Paulines changed the back part of the house into a **chapel of the Most Holy Trinity**. The later owners of the house pulled down the chapel of which only the Early Baroque portal with the year 1671 carved in it has survived.

Let us go back to the southern part of Panská. In its middle there are two palaces. It is good they are standing side

Right: Schöner Nazi

by side because we can compare the heavy, majestic Baroque building with the light and graceful Rococo house. **Esterházy Palace ❹** (No. 13) on the left was built in 1743 for Count Ján Esterházy, a member of one of the richest noble families in Hungary. The palace was one of the most luxurious in the city, though its exterior does not confirm it. The Rococo **Balassa Palace ❺** standing on the right (No. 15) is quite different from its neighbour. The three-storied house is lower, less massive and the ornamentation of the facade is considerably finer and more elaborate. The Rococo sculptured ornamentation of the facade is full of symbols and allegories of the Classical deities.

The crossroads of Rybárska brána, Panská and Laurinská street is certainly the liveliest spot of the city. People like to stop here to listen to the street musicians and the tourists love to have a snap made with **Čumil ❻** in background.

Rybárska brána street is a short street in the historic centre of Bratislava and part of the already mentioned *Corso*. It is a pedestrian zone between Hlavné námestie and Hviezdoslavovo námestie squares.

Next to house No. 1 stands a life-size statue with a top hat in his hand and a welcoming gesture. In contrast to the statue of Čumil this one painted in gleaming silver paint represents a real person, a native of Bratislava nicknamed **Schöner Nazi ❼** (Fair Nazi). His real name was Ignác Lamar, and he was born on August 12th, 1897 into the family of a shoemaker in Petržalka. Schöner Nazi frequented Bratislava's pubs and coffee houses and became an inseparable part of the city's folklore.

Laurinská ulica street is the prolongation of Panská. It starts at Rybárska brána and ends in Štúrova.

The first (No. 1) in the northern row of houses on Laurinská is a four-storied house with a Neo Classical facade. It was built after design of Ignác Feigler Senior in 1846. First of all it was the seat of the **Prvá prešporská sporiteľňa** or the First Pressburg Saving Bank founded in 1842 as the oldest bank institution in the city.

Opposite the First Pressburg Savings Bank is a modern corner building, **Dom slovenských spisovateľov ❽** (House of the Slovak Writers). There is a bookshop in its ground floor. On the corner of Laurinská and Radničná the Neo Classical **house of Baron Walterskirchen ❾** (No. 3) was built in the 19th century.

At the eastern end of Laurinská street stands the theatre building of **Divadlo P. O. Hviezdoslava ❿**. **A copy of bars** hangs across the street and above the heads of passers by just to remind us that it is the place where **Laurinská brána** gate used to stand. The first reference to the gate is from 1412, and it even quotes the salary of the gatekeeper. Contemporary drawings show that the two towers, Michalská and Laurinská were very similar. Both were protected by barbicans, and the curve of the upper part of the streets was the same. The tower of the gate had a shingle roof ending in a ball with a banner. For some time it was used as a jail. Laurinská brána was pulled down in 1778.

The Hlavné námestie square (The Main Square)

Out of the three central areas in the historic centre of Bratislava the **Hlavné námestie** square (The Main Square) with its squarish ground plan is the most impressive one. Through the history it was the stage and witness to practically every important event, which took place in the town. It used to be the main market place, stage for the Passion plays, gatherings, and the place, where the rulers were greeted and welcomed, but also where executions or public punishments were carried out. The splendid coronation trail headed by a new King of Hungary always attracted the crowds to Hlavné námestie. The affection of Bratislava's citizens toward their square survived. They still like to go to traditional Christmas fair, performances of musical bands, tower concerts of trumpeters or simply to relax next to the Renaissance fountain or under the sunshades of cafés.

People often meet next to **Maximilian's fountain ❶** in the western part of the square perhaps the same as Londoners meet at Piccadilly Circus under Cupid's statue. The square lacked a public water source until the second half of the 16th century. Only in 1572 the financial contribution of King Maximilian II made it possible to finish the fountain, which now bears his name and portrait.

Every building at Hlavné námestie deserves attention. The most important of them is the **Stará radnica ❷** or the Old Town Hall. Its appearance is owed to a complicated architectural development marked by numerous changes of style and reconstruction. The history of this wonderful building started in the remote past, when the city was founded. If we leave out the Celtic, Roman or Slav settlement of this locality, we can say that the oldest predecessor of the Old Town Hall was **Mayor Jacob's fortified house** built on the north-eastern side of the new central square.

Left: View from the tower of town hall

Pressburg was the first town in the Upper Hungary to acquire the building of Town Hall of its own. The municipal council had its sessions in Jacob's house even before the town bought it. The rebuilt Pressburg Town Hall on Hlavné námestie was fully used only after 1434. A new **passage** opening the entry into the Town Hall from the square was made before 1442. This remarkable architectural element has been preserved in its full beauty up till now. The original segmental quadripartite vault has five **bosses** with figural-heraldic ornamentation.

The Town Hall of Pressburg entered the 16th century in a new Late Gothic shell and became the dominant building of the square and an important part of the city's silhouette. In the second half of the 16th century the tower of the Town Hall was slightly adjusted to the principles of the Renaissance style. Six identical **Renaissance windows** were put into the facade facing the square; Unger's house had another two from 1581. **Renaissance arcades** on pillars, preserved up to now, and made by the stonemason Bartolomej from Wolfstahl were added in 1581.

But the most beautiful thing that happened to the Town Hall came at the end of the 17th century when Bastiano Corati Orsati made the lavish stucco ornamentation of the rooms: rims of the vaults and frames in which the painter Johann Jonas Drentwett from Augsburg placed beautiful **wall paintings**. He followed in style the Italian and Flemish patterns of the 17th century. The painting placed in the middle of the vault represents the theme of the Last Judgement.

The project was completed in 1912 and it involved construction of the eastern and southern wings of the Town Hall. All later interventions were mere repairs and reconstruction of some hidden valuable architectural details. While restoring the facade the **cannon ball** stuck in the facade, which commemorates the attacks of Napoleon's army in 1809 was also preserved. There is also a **board with a line** marking the water level of the Danube at

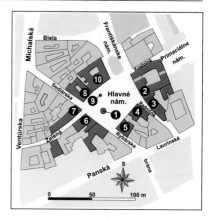

the time of the disastrous floods on February 5th 1850.

The **Apponyi Palace** ❸ next to Unger's house is out of the Hlavné námestie square in a short **Radničná ulica** street. It was build in the years 1761-1762 for count Juraj Apponyi, a member of a rich Hungarian noble family from Oponice near Topoľčany. At present the Apponyi Palace shelters the **Viticultural Museum** and regional library. The collections displayed on the ground floor and basement of the palace document the rich history of wine growing in the traditional viticultural region of the Little Carpathians. An original press used in wine production is placed in the courtyard.

The **house** (No. 2) standing opposite the Apponyi Palace with its main entrance from the Hlavné námestie square is one of the oldest in the city. Due to remarkable discoveries of very old architectural elements from the last third of the 13th century the citizens of Pressburg know it as a **house with a tower** ❹. Extensive renovation of the building in the 1980's of the 20th century led to discovery of the remains of an original burgher house with tower which was, like the predecessor of the Old Town Hall, made for living. The last of the trio of houses at the southern part of Hlavné námestie is the **Jeszenák Palace** ❺. The Baroque building on the corner of Hlavné námestie and Rybárska brána was built in the 18th century at the

site of an older house. The stone cartouche on corner bears the coat of arms of the original owner of the palace, Baron Ján Jeszenák. Recently the stylish and in the past very popular **café** and **sweet shop Café Mayer** returned to the ground floor of the palace.

The western row of houses at Hlavné námestie is the youngest one. **House No. 5** is especially interesting. It was built in 1906 on the site of an older medieval house of the Auer family from the 15th century. Queen Mary, the widow of King Louis II lived in it for some time. Today it is the seat of bank, but it has also the **café U Rolanda** on its ground floor. The interior of the café was refreshed by a true imitation of Kempelen's chess automate. The **Palugyay Palace ❻** (No. 6) standing on the corner of Hlavné námestie and Zelená Ulica street acquired its Neo Baroque appearance in 1880. The style is based on the traditions of the French Baroque. It was built for an

Left: Frenchman' statue on the Main Square

important businessman trading in wine, František Palugyay.

The opposite corner of **Zelená ulica** street is occupied by the **Zelený dom ❼** or the Green House (Sedlárska street No. 12). The name derives from the green painted facade and in its ground floor was a popular tavern and restaurant.

The front wing of the Zelený dom overlooks the **Sedlárska ulica** street. This medieval street, along with Rybárska brána, connects Michalská and Laurinská streets. Its name (The Saddler's street) suggests that in the past it was inhabited above all by saddlers. Today this street is the favourite route of walks of the citizens and a most lively part of what is called the **Bratislava Corso**. In the sixties of the 20th century the avant-garde theatre of *Divadlo na korze* (now the building of the Hungarian embassy) attracted the young audience, while today it is rather the Irish pub **The Dubliner**.

Let us go back to the Hlavné námestie square along the western wing of the **Kutscherfeld Palace ❽** turned to Sedlárska street. The windows of the palace (No. 7) overlook Maximilian's fountain. The corner two-storied palace is one of the most beautiful Rococo buildings in the city. It was built in 1762 on the site of several medieval plots. Today the Kutscherfeld Palace houses the **French embassy** and the **French Institute**. The presence of the French on Hlavné námestie square is suggested also by a recently installed bronze **statue of an Frenchman ❾** of a man in uniform wearing a typical three-horn Napoleon hat. The soldier looking like Napoleon himself leans on a bench, a favourite spot of the tourists making snapshots.

When in 1723 **Palác miestodržiteľskej rady ❿** (the Palace of royal governing council) was established, Pressburg was chosen as its seat. It was placed in the house in the north-eastern corner of Hlavné námestie. The city obtained this top office which represented the ruler in Hungary seated in Vienna. It was not entitled to take final decisions as it had to have them approved by the ruler represented by the

Hungarian Office in Vienna. In 1762 the office also bought the neighbouring house. The two buildings were connected and rebuilt as the palace of the royal governing council. The eastern facade of the palace faces Františkánske námestie square and its southern side overlooks the Hlavné námestie square. The two-storied building with interior courtyard was reconstructed in Rococo style. The carriages entered the yard from the Hlavné námestie square and left it by the exit to Františkánske námestie square or vice versa. There is again a top governmental body seated in the palace: the **Office of the Government of the Slovak Republic**.

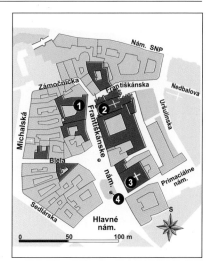

The Františkánske námestie square
Františkánske námestie square is a kind of counterpart to busy Hlavné námestie or the Main square. It offers a much quieter, almost chamber ambience amidst antique historic houses. Františkánske námestie originated some time in the 13th century, hence it is one of the oldest in the town. Its present name is linked to the presence of the church and monastery of the Franciscan order.

The **Mirbach Palace ❶** is the architectural gem of the upper part of Františkánske námestie square. It is rightly admired along with the Primatial Palace as one of the most beautiful sights offered by Bratislava. This Rococo building was built by Matej Hörlligl in years 1768-1770 on the site of the former Weitenhof house (Wide Yard House). It was a city property bought from the Franciscans.

The Mirbach Palace was presumably built for a rich brewer of Pressburg, M. Spech. However, he sold it immediately after it was finished to Imrich Csáky. The owners of the palace alternated until Count Emil Mirbach bought it and eventually donated it to the city in his last will, with the conditions that it would become an art gallery. The city fulfilled the principal condition of the testament. The **Art Gallery of Bratislava** is located in the palace and offers valuable occasional fine art expositions along with standing collec-

tions of the Baroque artists whose work or life was connected with Bratislava. There are, for instance the famous heads by František Xaver Messerschmidt and canvasses by František Xaver Palko.

Opposite to the Mirbach Palace is the Franciscan church. Let us stop first at the neighbouring building of the monastery, the history of which is closely connected with this church. It used to belong to the monks, who settled in the town in 1238. Inside the monastic complex the original **arcade stations of cross-corridor** built around the squarish cloister has survived. The present **facade** of the main monastic building facing Františkánske námestie dates from the latter half of the 19th century.

The **Franciscan church ❷** consecrated to the **Annunciation of the Virgin Mary** is very old. It is the oldest preserved sacral building in Bratislava. Unconfirmed sources have that it was built by the King of Hungary Ladislav IV Kumánsky in honour of the victory over the King Přemysl Otakar II of Bohemia in the famous battle on the Marchfeld in 1278. It was built in Gothic taste as a simple single-naved church. The earthquake of 1590 caused the fall of the Gothic cross vault. It was replaced by a new **Renaissance vault**. The

original Gothic **presbytery** and the **lateral walls** of the nave were preserved and today are the oldest part of the church. The **main altar** is from the mid-18th century and bears the painting of glass of the Assumption of the Virgin Mary from the end of the 19th century made according to the original painting from the 18th century. The **side altars** are also in the Baroque style, all of them are from the mid-18th century. The pulpit from 1756 is in the Rococo style and it is adorned with several notable reliefs. One of traditional ceremonies of the Pressburg coronations took place in the Franciscan church. It was the promotion of selected aristocrats to the **Knights of the Golden Spur**.

The **Jesuit Church ❸** in the lower part of the square was not always owned by the Jesuits. The German Evangelicals of Pressburg built the church following the royal consent in 1636. The re-Catholiciz-

ing pressure became stronger during the reign of King Leopold I and Archbishop Szelepcsényi took away the temple of the Evangelicals. The German **church** was given to the **Jesuits** who dedicated it to **the Most Holy Saviour**. The new administrators of the church started its reconstruction. The facade remained almost intact, except for the original Renaissance **portal**. Jesuits installed a lavishly ornamented and multi-coloured **symbol of their order** on it. **The main altar** from the 19th century bears the picture of Christ on the Mountain of Tábor by S. Majsch.

Sightseeing of the square ends under the **pillar of the Virgin Mary the Victorious ❹** which the oldest of the kind in the Kingdom of Hungary. It belongs to the group of pillars built by the Habsburg's all over the country in honour of their military successes. The one of Františkánske námestie stands here since 1675.

The Primaciálne námestie square (The Primatial square)

Comparatively young buildings surround **Primaciálne námestie** square (The Primatial square), with the oldest house counting not more than four hundred years. But that does not mean that the square is young.

The **Primatial Palace ❶**, which with his bulky building occupies the whole southern side of the Primatial square, is considered the most beautiful in Bratislava. It was built in the years 1778-1781 on the site of an older Archbishop's palace. The front wing overlooking the Primatial square is strictly Neo Classical.

One enters the Primatial Palace through a three-axial vestibule where a wide flight of stairs leads to the main halls on the first floor or Piano nobile. It overlooks the square and is directly connected with the main representative hall of the palace in its eastern wing. The huge hall looks even bigger because of the numerous mirrors on its walls. It is called the **Zrkadlová sieň** or the Hall of Mirrors. The role of the mirrors was to make the hall look bigger but above all to improve the

lighting. The 1805 Christmas season was a time celebrated by the French as one of their historic moments. After the battle at Austerlitz representatives of the countries which took part in it met in the Primatial Palace. The victorious Napoleon Bonaparte was represented by his Minister of Foreign Affairs Maurice Talleyrand and Prince John of Liechtenstein represented the defeated Emperor Francis. The treaty, later called the **Peace of Pressburg** was signed on December 26th 1805 in the Hall of Mirrors. Austria lost the territories of Tyrol, Istria, Dalmatia, and Venice and her access to the sea. France gained self-assurance and greed. The memory of the Peace of Pressburg was expressed by giving the name of the city to one of the Paris streets: *Rue de Presbourg* still existing near the Arc de Triomphe.

The city bought the palace in 1903 with the intention to expand the Town Hall. During reconstruction of the palace some folded pieces of cloth were found. When they were spread on the floor of the

corridor, the astounded custodian of the Municipal Museum August Heimar found out that it was a series of precious tapestries now known as the **Bratislava tapestries**. The Archbishop as owner of the palace gave up the precious find in favour of the city with the particular that they would be displayed in public. But first they had to be restored in the artistic workshops of Belmonte in Hungarian town of Gödöllő. The German expert and connoisseur of tapestries W. Zisch from Berlin estimated that the tapestries of Bratislava were made at the royal weaving workshop at Mortlake near London. The trade mark woven into the edge used by this particular workshop in the years 1616-1688 is the proof. The series of tapestries was made after the cartoons painted by Francis Cleyn from Rozstock. Tapestries were woven on wool and silk and the style of this true work of art is called mannerism.

In the vestibule there is also a passage to the inner square courtyard. In its centre is the **fountain of St. George ❷**.

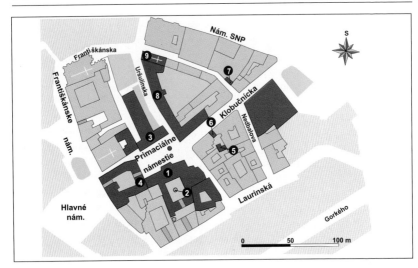

The group of statues made of sandstone represents the legendary knight fighting against a dragon.

Opposite the Primatial Palace is **Nová radnica ❸** (the New Town Hall). This modern building replaced the 17th century Jesuit monastery demolished in 1948.

The eastern side of today's Primatial Palace is closed by the buildings, which have their entrances from Uršulinska and Klobúčnícka streets. **Klobučnícka ulica** street as we see it now, is a comparatively young street. The dominating building of Klobučnícka street is the Neo Baroque tenement house No. 2 from 1910. In the yard of the smart four-storied house with attic roof is what is called **Hummel's house ❺**. It is a small and picturesque Renaissance house often denoted as the native house of **Johann Nepomuk Hummel** (1778-1837). This world famous composer and pianist though, was born in the house, which existed there before. Hummel's house contains now part of the **musical exhibition ❻** of the Municipal Museum, which documents the life and work of the composer, and the musical history of Bratislava.

Around today's **Nedbalova ulica** street, perpendicular to Klobučnícka, was

Right: Fire in 1811

the **Jewish ghetto** with a synagogue. Nedbalova ulica, as we know it now, originated as the street skirting the town walls of the medieval town. It followed the eastern section of the fortifications. Opposite the school standing near the crossroads with Klobučnícka street there is a preserved section of the **town walls ❼** from the 15th century. The inner part of the stone wall reaching the height of the neighbouring two-storied house is visible here.

Uršulínska ulica street connects Laurinská street with Primatial square and the square of the SNP. The **Ursuline church ❾** and **monastery ❽** unifies the eastern row of the Ursuline Street. The Evangelicals built the church in 1640 for their Slovak and Hungarian believers. The Ursulines consecrated the church to the **Virgin Mary of Loretto**.

The Bratislava Castle

The monumental building of **Bratislava Castle ❶** that cannot be confused with any other building in the city is visible from a great distance. Certainly every visitor of Bratislava notices the pronounced silhouette similar to an overturned table. The majestic impression is enhanced by the hill it stands on some eighty-five metres above the water level of the Danube.

The castle hill had a special function within the system of **Great Moravian fortified settlements**. It was an important fortified settlement in the last third of the 9th century as it is mentioned in the Salzburg annals in relation to a bloody battle between the Bavarians and early Magyars. On the western side of the hill where a medieval castle was later built there was a seat of some noble. The Church with a three-nave **stone basilica** ❷ and a cemetery occupied the eastern part of the hill top. The whole settlement was skirted by a defensive wall made of thick oak logs connected into chambers filled with earth and stones.

Building activity documented by archaeology took place on the castle hill of Bratislava as early as the 10th century. First there was a pre-Romanesque **stone palace** in the 11th and 12th centuries. The fortification of the castle hill made use of the defensive system of the previous fortified settlement. In the second half of the 13th century the castle progressively gained the shape of the Romanesque **Arpád period castle,** which it kept until the Gothic reconstruction carried out in time of King Sigismund in the first half of the 15th century. Generous reconstruction of the castle started in 1423 during the rule of Sigismund of Luxembourg, but it was not finished in time of his death in 1437. The result of this reconstruction was a Gothic castle referred to in literature as a **Sigismund's castle**. Two semicircular cannon **bastions** reinforced the castle walls. The northern bastion was called **Luginsland** ❸. Even today it is the dominant architectural element of Bratislava's castle well visible from the Hodžovo or Župné squares. A new entrance to the castle via **Žigmundova brána** ❹ (Sigismund's Gate) was built on the steep slope of the castle hill above the Danube.

Reconstruction of the castle generally referred to as **Pálffy's** was carried out in the period of the fading Renaissance style. Pálffy's luxurious castle palace was a part of ambitious plan for reconstruction of the whole castle hill, with the settlement

below it included in a massive fort with a complicated system of bastions and ramparts arranged in an irregular seven-pointed star. Out of this extensive project led by the Italian builder Jozef Priami only a tiny part was made reality. Only two cannon bastions were added to the castle. A long tunnel was drilled under the southwestern one. The tunnel was used as an entrance gate and its name was **Leopoldova brána** ❺ (Leopold's Gate). However, it proved to be an error as it was not conveniently situated and moreover it was rather unattractive from the architectural point of view. A new and more pompous entrance gate was started. Since it was situated on the western edge of the castle hill and as it was on the road from Vienna it acquired the name **Viedenská brána** ❻ (Vienna gate). This gate similar to Antique triumphal arches was ceremoniously opened on the occasion of Charles III's coronation in 1712. It has remained the main entrance to the area of Bratislava Castle until today.

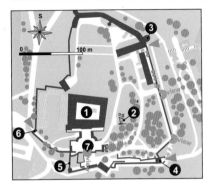

The last stage of big building adjustments of the Pressburg Castle was accomplished under the orders of Queen Maria Theresia. The ruler tried to rid the castle of any outdated functions of the former military fort as the political climate of the 18th century was that of relative peace. She had all fortifying elements removed and simultaneously improved or widened its residential function complying with the criteria of what was considered the utmost luxury. The works pursuing the project of reconstruction as presented by the imperial architects Jean Nicolas Jadot, Giovanni Batista Martinelli and Nicolas Pacassi started in 1755. The castle now called **Theresian** was prepared to serve the royal court in 1765. The obvious and intentional disproportion between the dreary exterior and impressive interior was again applied. Money not spent on the outer appearance was invested in the interior of the castle. The simplicity of the outer facades complied with the canons of Classicising Baroque. In front of the southern facade a couple of Baroque guard houses were built and on the southern terrace a kind of **čestné nádvorie ❼** (courtyard of honour) was created. The most interesting building though was that of the **Theresianum** built next to the eastern side of the palace in 1768. This lovely Rococo palace was the seat of the Governor, Prince Albert, who acquired the

Left: The Bratislava Castle
Right: House of the Good Shepherd. The emblem of artisan exhibition

office after he married Archduchess Maria Christina, daughter of Queen Maria Theresia. In May 1811, a devastating fire burst out in the castle and soon spread to the Podhradie or the settlement below the castle. For the next hundred and fifty years the people had to tolerate the sad picture of the destroyed castle on top of the hill, a vanishing symbol of the city's past glory.

Some parts of the castle are open to the public. They contain permanent exhibitions of the **Slovak National Museum**. There is an exhibition of **historical furniture** in the main palace and a remarkable collection of exhibits called the **Jewels of Slovakia's Remote Past**. Exhibits documenting the **history of musical instruments** are displayed in Luginsland bastion.

The western part of the Old Town

The western part of the Old Town is quite different from the other parts. It spreads over the foothills of the Little Carpathians and its urban fabric consists predominantly of family houses. On a flat hill at its south-eastern edge is the **Bratislava Castle** and on its eastern and southern slopes is **Podhradie**, the historic settlement below the castle.

Several buildings in Beblavá, Židovská, Mikulášska streets and at the stairway called Zámocké schody deserve attention. Let us look at them and start with the house at the lower end of **Židovská ulica** street, which is rightly, considered one of the most beautiful in Bratislava. It is the impressive **Dom u dobrého pastiera** (House of the Good Shepherd) (Židovská ulica street No 1) and its conspicuously slender construction makes it the best specimen of small-scale Rococo architecture in Bratislava. Its name derives from a tiny statue of Christ – Good Shepherd – standing on its corner. It was built in 1760. Since 1975 the House of the Good Shepherd has sheltered the **exposition of historic clocks** of the Municipal Museum. Also the collection of portable sun dials from the 16th – 18th centuries is interesting. **Zsigray's curia** standing at the opposite end of Ži-

dovská street (No 17) offers the opportunity to see the exhibits of the **Museum of Jewish Culture in Slovakia** explaining the history of the Jewish community of Bratislava and Slovakia. On the slope of the castle hill above **Mikulášska ulica** street there stands the **St. Nicholas'** (Sv. Mikuláš) **church**. The church has belonged to the followers of the Eastern Orthodox Church since 1950.

Beblavého ulica street climbs the castle hill from the corner of the House of the Good Shepherd. It was the shortest possible connection between the castle and St. Martin's Minster. As the famous Hungarian poet Sándor Petöfi lived in its upper part the street bore his name for some time. Today it offers an opportunity to sit and chat in pleasant stylish little cafés and restaurants in venerable houses from the 18th century. At the lower end of Beblavého street stands the Late Baroque **house No 1** from the late 18th century. It contains the **Museum of crafts** exhibiting works of artisans made of

glass, porcelain, various types of jewels, toys and liturgical objects. In the upper part of **Zámocké schody** stairs are two Renaissance houses from the beginning of the 17th century. The house on the corner of Beblavého was once the **Town Hall** of Podhradie. After Podhradie obtained municipal privileges in 1713 the magistrate consisting of six aldermen and a notary used to have sessions in the house. The former Town Hall is now the **Arkadia restaurant**, a smart place, the name of which derives from its main architectural feature – an open pillar arcade passing through two of its wings.

The round hills of Bratislava spreading from Štefánikova ulica street up to Dolná Mlynská dolina valley were for centuries a viticultural landscape with scattered little huts. This attractive locality acquired a new function only in the first half of the 20th century. The footpaths between the plots changed to streets built up with elegant villas; the property of the Bratislava's privileged class and social

elite. The locality is the most expensive and most luxurious quarter of the city. It main street is **Mudroňova ulica** street, originally called *Kaiserweg* or the Emperor's Road. Next to the castle on the Vodný vrch hill is the modern **building of the National Council of the Slovak Republic**. It was opened in May 1994 and the Slovak Parliament moved here from its old seat in Župné námestie. The new buildings of Parliament also include the popular **Parlamentka restaurant** with a terrace above the Danube offering a wide view of the city.

At the upper end of Mudroňova in the north-east is **Murmannova výšina** hill with the **House of Ekoiuventa** built in 1952, colloquially called "Michurin" (surname of Soviet scientist known for bold experimentation with plants). The building is a perfect sample of what is called Stalinist architecture. It is still serving its original purpose – it provides space for children's leisure activities. Stará vinárska ulica street starting nearby leads to the neighbouring height (252 m) with the **monument Slavín** and military cemetery where 6,845 Soviet soldiers who died while liberating Bratislava by the end of April of 1945 are buried.

The northern part of the Old Town

The quarters in the north of the historic centre of Bratislava are full of contrasts. There are busy wide streets and romantic narrow alleys. One can walk in wide squares and pleasant parks. Venerable buildings breathing with history stand side by side with modern buildings. In the northern part of the centre are the buildings of the government, ministries, the Presidential Palace and the seats of many other central administrative bodies and institutions. The main railway station in the northern centre is the place of the first contact with the city for visitors to Bratislava.

Left: The Bratislava Castle
Right: Interior of the Trinitarian church

Several squares originated around the disappeared town walls. One of them is **Župné námestie** square connected with the contiguous Hurbanovo square in the east. In the Middle Ages it was the site of the settlement of St. Michael, which later developed into a suburb. In time of Turkish wars the aldermen themselves decided to demolish the suburbs for the sake of better control over the immediate space beyond the town walls. Such was the destiny of the St. Michael suburb including its Gothic church bearing the name of the same patron saint. It was pulled down in 1529. The **Trinitarian order** later built one of the most beautiful Baroque **churches** in the town on its ruins.

In the time when this church was consecrated, construction of the **Trinitarian monastery** on the neighbouring plot of the disappeared cemetery was going on. When the Trinitarians left, the building was given to the county administration. But it was not suitable for the offices. It was pulled down and in its place a new **Župný dom** (County House) for the Pressburg county administration office was built in 1844.

In the years 1939-1994 the Slovak legislative bodies held their sessions in the Župný dom and after 1945 it became the seat of the Slovak National Council (in 1992 renamed to the National Council of the Slovak Republic). Since 1994 the sessions of the Slovak Parliament are held in a new building on the Vodný vrch hill. The shortest western side of the triangular Župné námestie coincides with the facade of the **Capuchin church** consecrated to **St. Stephen of Hungary**. The Capuchin church was consecrated by Bishop L. A. Erdödy of Nitra in 1717. Part of the church was pulled down and rebuilt in 1735. The space in front of the Capuchin church is adorned by the **Morový stĺp** (Plaque pillar).

The environs of **Panenská ulica** street belonged to the Pressburg Evangelicals or Lutherans since the late 17th century. They lost their two churches in the town centre in 1672 and a special imperial

commission prohibited the Evangelical service in the inner town. They were ordered out to the northern suburb, a scarcely built area between the Suché mýto and Kozia gates. Construction of the **Large Evangelical Church** on Panenská ulica took place in years 1774-1777. The architect M. Walch tried to imitate the original German Evangelical Church, which used to stand near the Old Town Hall. It is built in the Neo-Classical style. The building is divided into three naves by prismoid pillars. The interior has got excellent acoustics, an asset appreciated by music lovers, who attend concerts held in this church. The **altar** from 1776 forms a whole with the **pulpit**. A. F. Oeser, a Pressburg native, painted the **painting of the altar**: *Christ in Emaus*. A year after opening of the Large Evangelical Church the Slovak and Hungarian Evangelicals also built theirs. The **small Evangelical Church** on Panenská stands on the site of the former wooden articled church from 1682. It is again Walch's design and it is

equally simple. The interior of the church on an irregular ground plan was modernized in the 1970's. The original furniture from the 18th century with the exception of the altar and pulpit was not preserved.

Konventná ulica street is closely associated with Evangelical schooling in Pressburg, the beginnings of which date to 1606. The Evangelical community of Pressburg was one of the largest in Hungary in the early 18th century. It associated about seven thousand believers of the three nationalities. The community invited to its Lycée in Pressburg **Matej Bel** (1684-1749), the former student of this institution in 1714, immediately after the retreat of the plague epidemic. It soon became obvious that it was a good move. Matej Bel was not only a scientist of world importance, but also a good teacher and educator. He wrote and published text books, adapted the Latin grammar and

Left: Presidential Palace
Right: Manderla and the Castle

initiated the publishing of the newspaper *Nova Posoniensia* (Pressburg Newspaper) in Latin. He became the first priest of the German Evangelical Church and the chancellor of the Lycée. For his scientific achievements he was referred to as *Magnum Decu Hungariae* (The Great Ornament of Hungary).

Suché mýto square appeared in the historic documents in 1375 under the name *Dauermauth*. It was the medieval toll entrance into the inner suburbs through the gate and bridge over the moat. The modern Suché mýto is completely different in comparison with the past. Demolition of old houses and reconstruction of the transport system connected Suché mýto with what is now **Hodžovo námestie** square into one big open space framed by modern buildings. One of them is the **Forum Hotel** on the south-eastern side of the square. The hotel built according to design of the architect J. Hauskrecht has a capacity of 450 beds and was opened in 1988.

The dominant building of Hodžovo námestie square is the **Presidential Palace** built after 1760 as the **garden palace of Anton Grassalkovich**. The building of this wonderful Rococo palace was outside the town and it was placed between the garden of the summer Archbishop's Palace and the town. The Chairman of the Hungarian Royal Court Chamber, the guard of the crown, comes of the Novohrad County, Anton Grassalkovich had it built. The central architectural element of the palace is the **pavilion** in its middle from which **two palace wings** spread. In front of the palace is a **courtyard** skirted by an impressive fence with a pair of gilded metal gates.

The buildings on **Štefánikova ulica** street and the contiguous streets are mainly smart residential houses, which document the wide range of architectural styles, used in the city. On the eastern side of the street and neighbouring with Grassalkovich's garden is **Karácsony Palace** (house No. 2) with the Neo Baroque facade. It was built by the end of the 19th century and later rebuilt into an administrative building. Between Spojná and Leškova streets on the eastern side of Štefánikova ulica are several **luxurious family villas**, which sprang up in the 19ᵗʰ century on the western edge of the former Archbishop's garden. One of the most beautiful was built for the physician B. Tauscher in 1891. **Tauscher's villa** on the corner of Spojná and Štefánikova is a nice example of Pseudo Rococo architecture.

Villas cover the view of an extensive **park**, which is closed to the public. It belongs **to the area of The Office of the Government** of the Slovak Republic. The park occupies the site of the former Archbishop's garden, which stretched from today's Štefánikova up to Námestie slobody square. The **letný arcibiskupský palác** (summer Archbishop's Palace) on the upper part of Námestie slobody square lived through the good and bad times together with the garden. Today it is the seat of the **Office of the Government of the Slovak Republic**.

The eastern part of the Old Town

This part of the centre attracts the shoppers and visitors of Bratislava, because it has the majority of shops, shopping centres, and department stores. The busiest spot is the **Námestie Slovenského národného povstania** (SNP) or Square of the Slovak National Uprising. It commemorates one of the biggest national anti-Nazi uprisings in Europe which burst out in Central Slovakia at the end of August 1944. **The monument to the SNP** with a trio of big bronze statues by Ján Kulich is associated with this significant event of the modern Slovak history.

In the upper part of the square is the spacious building of the **Old** or **Main Post Office** (houses No. 34-36). A bit lower, on the corner of Uršulínska street, is the building of the **Tatrabanka** (No. 33) built in the years 1922-1925. The last building of the SNP square on the lower end of the side bordering with historical part of the city is the building known under the name **Manderla** (No. 23). This eleven-storied house is the first of Bratislava's "skyscrapers", and

for long the tallest building in the city. It was built in 1935 for the rich businessman trading in meat Rudolf Manderla.

The dominating building of the north-western side of the triangle-shaped SNP square is the Neo Romanesque **Calvinist church** with a tall tower. It was designed by the architect F. Wimmer and built in 1913. The biggest building of the square though is the **church and monastery of the Merciful Brothers** (Milosrdných bratov) in the north-east.

The **Špitálska ulica** street starts in the SNP square and heads to the northeast. Its name is linked to the fact it has been the site of several hospitals since the Middle Ages. As early as 1307 the municipal council agreed with the Antonite Order about administration of the hospital built on plots east of the town. The municipal **hospital of St. Anton** stood opposite today's St. Ladislav's church. Next to the **hospital of St. Ladislav** was a cemetery with a chapel. The central architecture of the complex is **St. Ladislav's**

church. Some metres away from St. Ladislav's church are the **Elizabethan church and monastery**.

The new quarter lying next to Starý most bridge also got a new church in 1913 thanks to Countess G. M. Szapáryová. It was a beautiful one, still to be seen on **Bezručova ulica** street, and known by the natives as **Modrý kostolík** or the Blue Church. It is a wonderful example of the Art Noveau style in sacred architecture.

Šafárikovo námestie square originated after 1891, when the first fixed bridge was built over the Danube. Varied buildings frame Šafárikovo námestie square. One of the most recent is the **Comenius University** (house No. 5). Architect F. Krupka built it in 1930 for the stock exchange following the winning design. Today it is the seat of the vice chancellor's office, Faculty of Law and part of Faculty of Philosophy of Comenius University.

Left: Bratislava's embankment
Right: Coronation mound

Bratislava's embankment
Today the area around the embankment of the city between the historic centre and the left bank of the Danube are the favourite routes of walks, occasional visits to a museum or gallery or meetings in one of the boat hotel restaurants on the river. The route starting at the Old Town and heading up stream toward the Botanical Garden is perhaps the most popular one for a Sunday afternoon walk.

The first part of the route runs along **Fajnorovo nábrežie** embankment bearing the name of the Evangelical bishop and writer Dušan Fajnor (1876-1933). Even before the origin of embankment the oldest of the existing four Bratislava bridges over the Danube, now called the **Starý most** (Old Bridge), was built. The bridge opened a day before the New Year's Eve of 1890 and remained the only over the Danube in Bratislava for another 83 years. In the space between Fajnorovo and Vajanského nábrežie embankments is the **building of the Slovak National Museum** built in the years 1924-1928 for the branch of the Czech *Zemĕdĕlské museum* or Museum of Agriculture. Now the Museum contains exhibitions of natural history. The monument to the Czech and Slovak statehood adorns the space in front of the Museum. It was ceremoniously introduced to the public on October 28th of 1988. A bronze **statue of lion** leaning on the state symbol of the former Czechoslovakia stands on almost fifteen metres tall pylon.

Vajanského nábrežie embankment bears the name of the Slovak politician, journalist, and writer, **Svetozár Hurban Vajanský** (1847-1916). The most interesting building on Vajanského embankment from the architectural point of view is **Jurenák Palace** (house No. 4). In this Neo Classical house of burgher K. Jurenák, composer **Johannes Brahms** (1833-1897) stayed during his visit to Pressburg. Next to the building of the Slovak Philharmonic Orchestra the embankment opens onto **Námestie Ľudovíta Štúra** square skirted by elegant buildings. Until 1939 it bore the name *Coronation square* as it used to be the setting of the final **ceremony of coronations**.

Now there is the **monument of Ľudovít Štúr**, made by T. Bártfay and J. Salay and erected in 1972. On the eastern side of the square is **Lanfranconi Palace** (No. 1). It was built in the later half of the 19th century on the site of the former salt office. Successful Pressburg businessman E. Lanfranconi ordered construction of the Neo Renaissance house designed by Ignác Feigler junior. What is interesting about the building is its roof construction, which was moved here from the Viennese World Exhibition. The building now belongs to the Ministry of the Environment of the Slovak Republic. Opposite is the **Dessewffy Palace** (No. 2). It was built in the latter half of the 19th century and the name derives from its owner Count Dessewffy. It used to be one of the most elegant and luxurious palaces in the city. Original ornamentation and antique furnishing from the 17th and 18th centuries in its interior partially survived.

The short **Mostová** (The Bridge) **ulica** street connects Námestie Ľudovíta Štúra with Hviezdoslavovo námestie squares. The street originated after the regulation of the river. Originally it headed to the pontoon bridge of Carolina Augusta over the Danube what explains the name of the street. Historic documents quote that there used to be the *Zum König von Ungarn Hotel* (King of Hungary Hotel) on this street. Now the principal landmark of this street is the **Reduta** building. It was built in 1911-1915 as designed by the Budapest architects M. Komor and D. Jakab. The monumental silhouette of this elegant building tries to copy the basic shape of the older building of the **provincial granary** which was built here in the years 1773-1774. The Reduta is now the seat of the **Slovak Philharmonic Orchestra**. Occasionally it hosts the top domestic and foreign musical ensembles and outstanding soloists of classic music. The concert season culminates in the **Bratislava Music Festival** organized in Autumn every year.

Hviezdoslavovo námestie square is a wonderful and lively place. The most impressive building on Hviezdoslavovo námestie square is the **Slovak National Theatre**. The elegant eclectic theatre building has adorned the city since 1886. The SND put on dramas and operas until 1955 when the drama ensemble moved to a separate new building on Laurinská street leaving the stage of the SND to ballet and opera only. The SND hosted some important figures of world opera and ballet. It was also here where several opera stars of Slovak origin started their careers: Peter Dvorský, Edita Grúberová, and Lucia Poppová.

The space in front of the SND building is adorned by **Ganymedes' fountain**. The fountain is the present of the First Pressburg Savings Bank. Ganymedes' fountain is not the only artistic work on the rectangular area of Hviezdoslavovo námestie square. There is also the **monument to the poet P. O. Hviezdoslav with its fountain** standing here since 1937.

The south-eastern part of Hviezdoslavovo námestie square widens into a small squarish area with a park. This was the plot originally reserved for the church of the St. Augustín of Notre Dame female order. Only the chancel with a little porch added in the 19th century was built. In the interior of the **presbytery** a ceiling **fresco** by the Baroque painter P. Troger survived. In front of the unfinished building stands a little wooden tower. The former **monastery** of the Notre Dame order built in 1754 as the front wing of the building is now the **Church school of Mother Alexia**. The park with the adjacent area of Hviezdoslavovo námestie square was the place where the "candle demonstration" took place on March 25th 1988. The security units using water cannons cruelly attacked the calmly protesting and praying believers with lit candles.

Rázusovo nábrežie embankment running from Námestie Ľudovíta Štúra to the New Bridge was created in the 18th century in the place where there was a fishermen's village before. Building in this space started in the mid-19th century and the embankment was called Dunajské. Now it bears the mane of the Slovak poet, writer and politician **Martin Rázus** (1888-1937). The oldest building on Rázusovo embankment is the compound of former barracks called **Vodné kasárne**. The building was adapted in the years 1949-1951 for the **Slovak National Gallery** (SNG). The collections of the SNG include the most important works of the Slovak fine arts since the 13th century until the present time and examples of European arts from the 15th to 18th centuries. Beside the permanent collections, interesting temporary exhibitions are sometimes held.

Left: Detail of Ganymedes' fountain
Right: Monument of the victims of the Prussian-Austrian war at Kamzík

Urban districts

Closest to the centre is the urban district **KARLOVA VES** (population 32,850). The most visited places of Karlova Ves are the Botanical garden and the Zoo. The **Botanical garden** on Botanická ulica street is owned and administered by the Faculty of Nature Science of Comenius University. It lies close to the Danube, west from the Lafranconi bridge. It was founded in the years 1942-1943 on an area 50.7 hectares. When the green house was constructed the garden acquired many tropical plant species. The pride of the green house is a little lake with precious water plants and numerous collections of cactuses. Today there are about 5,000 foreign plant species including 650 wood species. The botanical garden is interesting in every season, but it is most beautiful in the spring when the flowers are in full bloom. In Mlynská dolina valley in the neighbourhood of the Slovak Television is the **Zoo** of Bratislava. It was opened to the public in 1960. Its original area was 9 hectares. Later it was enlarged to the present 90 hectares and contains more than 200 animal species.

North of Karlova Ves is the village of **DÚBRAVKA** (population 35,200). The Baroque Roman Catholic **Church of St. Cosma and Damian** built in 1723 on the foundations of an older building is Dúbravka's most important cultural and historic monument. The Late Baroque altar of this church is from the last third of the 18th century.

The glass factory **Slovenské závody technického skla** has stood in the northwest of Dúbravka since the 1960's. Behind the factory and in the middle of a field are the foundations of a **Roman building** of the *villa rustica* type. The villa rustica of Dúbravka was a well equipped farming and craft homestead building with living and servicing rooms, a bath and maybe a sanctuary. The dimensions of the known ground plan are 11.20x13.20 m. Outside the basic, almost square ground plan were four apsides.

In the east Dúbravka borders on the urban district **LAMAČ** (population 6,550). Lamač entered history in July 1866 with the last battle of the **Prussian-Austrian war**. **ZÁHORSKÁ BYSTRICA** (population 2,100) is the northernmost urban district of Bratislava. The Baroque-Neo Classical Roman Catholic **church of Sts. Peter and Paul the Apostles** is the historic monument, which survived in Záhorská Bystrica. It was built in the years 1830-1834 on older foundations. In the south-western end of the village is the modern complex of buildings of the private **TV station Markíza**.

The urban district **DEVÍNSKA NOVÁ VES** (population 15,500) lies on the northwestern edge of Bratislava. Its western border coincides with the state frontier with Austria that in fact is in the middle of the river Morava. The originally Renaissance Roman Catholic **Church of the Holy Spirit** built in the early 16th century and later adapted, is the cultural monument, which deserves attention. The Neo Classical structure of the **customs station**

from the 18th century was recently adapted to the town hall. The building of the **steam engine-operated brickyard** founded in 1891 is historically interesting.

The National Nature Reserve of **Devínska Kobyla** is a unique locality of special fauna and flora is. It lies in part of the Devínske Karpaty mountains on an area 101 hectares between Devínska Nová Ves, Dúbravka and Devín; 234 species of mushrooms, 110 species of lichens, 100 species of mosses, and 1,100 plant species confirm the originality of this place. Xerophytes and thermophiles with precious and protected plant species and animals live on the southern and south-western slopes of Devínska Kobyla. The forests on the south-western slopes are the remains of the original thermopile oak growths. An **instructive path** leading through the reserve provides visitors with information about the occurrence of special vegetation

and wild life. It has got seven stops with information panels. The most interesting locality of the National Nature Reserve Devínska Kobyla is the sand profile on the **Sandberg** mountain. There are rock remains of the Tertiary sea with horizontal layers, the age of which is estimated at 14 to 16 million years. Another **instructive route** was prepared in 1996 over the flood plain of the Morava which runs along the river Morava from Devín to Devínska Nová Ves and ends in Vysoká pri Morave (outside Bratislava). The 23 km long route has 16 information boards.

The urban district **DEVÍN** (population 900) lies below the Devín Castle at the confluence of the Danube and Morava. Devín is ten kilometres away from Bratislava. The village with castle lies on the spot where the Danube enters the Devínska brána (Devín Gate).

Devín Castle standing on a massive rock hill above the confluence of the Danube and Morava is an unusually impressive landmark. Its ground plan is very

Left: Devínska Kobyla
Right: Devín Castle

irregular. Today we enter the castle through the western **Moravian Gate**. The southern gate protected by a pair of semicircular bastions was built in the 15th century on an older Great Moravian rampart. Close behind the gate and on the right side of the path is a precious archaeological monument from the Roman period of Devín's history. The ground plan of the **remains of a bulky stone building** from the 4th century suggests a Classical tomb. Fragments of wall with preserved plasters up to 85 cm tall and the original floor were found there. Left from the path and near the Moravská brána gate Old Slavic graves from the 10th and 11th centuries were found. The path divides into two on the ridge of the castle hill. The left branch leads to the place where stood a **Great Moravian church** in the 9th century. One can see its rectangular ground plan with an apsid. The first branch of the path leads to the conserved ruins of the middle and upper part of the **medieval castle**, which was smaller than the Great Moravian fort. In the first half of the 15th century the Gothic **Garay palace** with two stories was built and the **Renaissance palace** and fortifications were added in the 16th century. Some vaulted spaces of this palace are today used for exhibitions. The origin of the 55 metres deep **castle well**, which is on the courtyard of the middle castle. Near the well is also a terrace with view of the abandoned **amphitheatre**, the Danube and the mountain of Braunsberg in Austria. In the wonderful setting above the bicolour confluence of the Danube and Morava an elegant tower with battlements stands out. It is the **Virgin tower**. A bridge over a moat and stairs lead to the top platform with remnants of a guard tower from the 13th century rebuilt in the 15th century with panoramic view of the surroundings.

The urban district of **NOVÉ MESTO** (population 37,400) or the New Town links Rača and Vajnory with the city centre. It originated by building on agricultural land.

More than a half of the area of the urban district of Nové mesto is occupied by the landscape park called **Bratislavský**

lesný park. This indeed large (17 square kilometres) recreation area on the territory of Bratislava is the forested territory of the southern part of the Little Carpathians. This part consists mostly of meadows and broad-leaved forest, which offer possibilities of relaxing in a pleasant setting. The area has numerous marked hiking footpaths and tourist amenities.

The massive mountain of **Kamzík** (439 m) in the southern part of the Little Carpathians is a place frequently visited by Bratislava trippers. It is easily accessible by an asphalt road from Koliba. The name of the mountain originated from German *Gemsenberg*. At the crossroads next to its top is a **pillar** from 1683, which recalls the last stay of Turkish troops and their collaborators in the environs of the town immediately before the famous defeat at Vienna. Another **monument** standing below Kamzík in turn commemorates the last battle of the Prussian-Austrian war in 1866, which took place in the forests on the slopes of Kamzík. However,

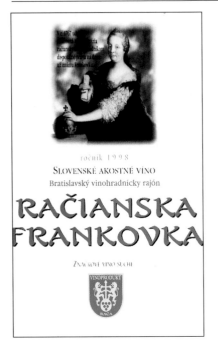

ročnik 1998

SLOVENSKÉ AKOSTNÉ VÍNO

Bratislavský vinohradnicky rajón

RAČIANSKA FRANKOVKA

ZNAČKOVÉ VÍNO SUCHÉ

VINOPRODUKT

the main tourist attraction of Kamzík is the 200 metres tall **TV tower** built in 1974 on its top. The revolving restaurant on top of the tower offers panoramic view of the environs reaching, in fair weather as far as the Neusiedel lake and the Alps in Austria. On the eastern side of Kamzík is the meadow called **Cvičná lúka** or the Exercise Meadow. Standing near the stalls with refreshments one gets a fine view of the wide plains of the Danube lowland. Cvičná lúka with its ski track is an ideal slope for the beginner skiers and sledders. The summer sled bob track attracts the trippers in summer.

North of Nové Mesto is the urban district **RAČA** (population 20,150). It is about 8 kilometre away from the city centre. In the west it includes part of the forested massive of the Little Carpathians and in the east it borders on Vajnory.

Left: Label of vine from Rača
Right: Church of St. Philip and St. James in Rača. Tavern in Vajnory

The history of Rača is closely linked to its **viticultural traditions**. The local vineyards are referred to in the oldest historic document from 1237. The medieval prosperity of viticulture can be attributed to favourable climatic conditions. Warmer climate supported expansion of vineyards even to elevated positions in the Little Carpathians.

A visit to Rača is an excellent opportunity to see a typical Little Carpathian viticultural village in its almost intact form. The oldest core of the village extends from Námestie hrdinov square to Evangelical church. Right in the square and on Alstrova ulica street are several **yeoman curias**. Historically the most valuable building in Rača is the **Roman-Catholic parish church of St. Philip and St. James** with a massive rectangular tower ending in a tall prismoid roof. The church was built before 1390 in the Gothic style. It was given Renaissance form in 1629 and Baroque reconstruction was carried out in 1732.

There are also typical **rural houses** in Rača. They are mostly concentrated on Alstrova street. When the street row of houses was full, the new houses were built behind with entrances from long yards. In some yards one can see five or six houses built in a row. The peasant houses of Rača were adapted to their main occupation – wine production. They had to have enough room for pressing and storage of wine. Some vintners emptied the front room of the house to use it as a tavern. Rača is rich in various folk traditions. It is rare to meet people wearing folk costumes, but they do put them on at the time of the traditional vintage.

The urban district **VAJNORY** (population 3,850) is on the north-western edge of Bratislava, about 10 km away from the city centre. Although Vajnory became part of the city, it preserved its traditional rural character. The oldest peasant houses of Vajnory are from the early 19th century. One of the Vajnory houses on Roľnícka ulica street was adapted as an ethnographic exhibition in 1966. The **Vajnorský ľudový dom** (The Folk House of

Vajnory) (No. 185) is not only a representative example of a traditional dwelling of a vintner of Vajnory, it also offers wonderful products of folk painters in its interior. One can see there various folk paintings with varied patterns of ornament. The colourful local folk costume is also the pride of Vajnory. In spite of its close proximity to the metropolis, the village still preserves many folk customs. Vajnory also has **Vajnorák**, the oldest **brass band** in Slovakia founded in 1866.

RUŽINOV (population 70,000) is the second largest urban district as far as the area and population are concerned. The cultural monument of Prievoz is the **Csáky's manor house** built around 1900. Part of it is a later built **oratory of The Sacred Heart of Jesus** administered by the female congregation of St. Francis of Assisi and today it is the parish church. At present the manor house is the hospital and Franciscan female monastery.

The biggest urbanistic project realized in the territory of the urban district **Ruži-**

nov was the series of Greater Bratislava housing estates: Štrkovec, Ostredky, Trávniky and Pošeň which took in about fifty thousand inhabitants. They were built between the years 1962 and 1970. Recreational activities of the quarter concentrate around **Štrkovecké jazero** pond, known for its swans. In June every year the race of unconventional vessels is organized on the pond.

The urban district **VRAKUŇA** (population 18,400) spreads on the eastern edge of Greater Bratislava. The urban fabric connected Vrakuňa with the contiguous urban district of **PODUNAJSKÉ BISKUPICE** (population 19,750).

The urban district **PETRŽALKA** (population 117,250) if it was independent settlement, would represent the third largest city in Slovakia. The result of enormous building activity on the right bank of the Danube can be best appreciated from the southern terrace of Bratislava Castle. This "concrete jungle" is home of every fourth Bratislavian.

The first houses of the gigantic **housing estate Petržalka** were started in 1976. Since then every year about 6,000 new flats were added to the vast area on the right bank of the Danube. About 10,000 workers were employed in its construction. Gradually 120,000 inhabitants moved onto the right bank of the Danube. There is probably no housing estate of comparable size in the whole of Europe.

RUSOVCE (population 1,900) is the biggest of the three urban districts of the other bank of the Danube lying south of Petržalka. Rusovce is a very old community. Though its territory was settled already in the Older Bronze Age it became most notable in the first four centuries when the northern frontiers of the Roman Empire moved to the middle section of the Danube. The territory of today's Rusovce found itself in the Roman province of Pannonia administered from Carnuntum. Romans built there the military camp of **Gerulata** as a

Left: Roman tombstone in Rusovce

part of the *Limes Romanus* defensive system, securing the northern limit of the Empire against the raids of German tribes.

The antique history of Rusovce is documented in the exhibition of the **Municipal Museum Múzeum antiky – Gerulata** (open only in summer).

The architectural feature of Rusovce is the Neo-Classical **manor house** built in 1840 on the site of an older manor house from 1521. The manor house acquired its attractive facade by application of the Romanticizing style of what is called the Windsor type imitating English Gothic. It has towers, battlements and a central risalite with terrace. In front of the manor house is the **statue of a lion** standing on a pillar. The manor house has got a big **park**, composition of its wood species is not especially varied but the trees are tall with big crowns. Oaks and plane trees prevail. The manor house serves the **folk ensemble SĽUK**, which moved here in 1951.

The village of **JAROVCE** (population 1,200) stretches along the south-west of the right bank of the Danube. The oldest documents referring to the village in connection with arrival of the Croatian immigrants are from the 16th century. The presence of Croatians in the village is obvious also from the older names *Horvátfalu* (1522) and *Kroatisch-Jahrendorf* used since the 18th century. **Folk architecture** from the 19th and the beginning of the 20th century survived on Mandľová ulica street. Years 1850, 1865, 1885, and 1895 are carved on the facades of the oldest houses.

ČUNOVO (population 900) is the remotest part of Bratislava on the right bank of the Danube. The most valuable historical monuments of the village is the Neo-Classical **curia** from the end of the 18th century and the Roman-Catholic **Church of St. Michael** built in 1783 in the Late Baroque taste. Attraction of the environs of Čunovo is the **Gabčíkovo dam** and a **modern water sport area**. **Danubiana** is a recently founded gallery containing miniature copies of the most important cultural and historical monuments existing in Slovakia.

BRATISLAVA
(dial: 02-)

Information

– **Bratislavská informačná služba**, Klobučnícka 2, ☎ 16186, 54433715, fax 54432708, bis@bratislava.sk, www.bratislava.sk/bis

Museums

– **Slovenské národné múzeum (SNM)**, Vajanského nábr. 2, ☎ 52961973, **Archeologické múzeum**, Žižkova 12, ☎ 54413680, 54416034, **Historické múzeum**, Bratislavský hrad, ☎ 54411444, 54414508, **Hudobné múzeum**, Bratislavský hrad, ☎ 54413349, **Múzeum kultúry karpatských Nemcov**, Žižkova 14, ☎ 54415570, 54415568, **Múzeum židovskej kultúry**, Židovská 17, ☎ 59349142-3, **Prírodovedné múzeum**, Vajanského nábr. 2, ☎ 52966623, 50349122, **Múzeum dopravy**, Šancová 1/A, ☎ 52494021, 52444163, **Mestské múzeum**, Primaciálne nám. 3, ☎ 54434742, 54435800, **Expozícia dejín mesta a feudálnej justície**, Primaciálne nám. 3, ☎ 59205130, **Expozícia vinohradníctva a vinárstva**, Radničná 1, ☎ 59205141, **Expozícia zbraní a mestského opevnenia**, Michalská 24, ☎ 54433044, **Hudobná expozícia**, Klobučnícka 2, ☎ 54433888, **Expozícia historických hodín**, Židovská 1, ☎ 54411940, **Expozícia umeleckých remesiel**, Beblavého 1, ☎ 54412784, **Literárna expozícia**, Somolického 2, ☎ 54434742, **Hrad Devín**, Muránska ul., ☎ 65730105, **Antická Gerulata**, Gerulatská 69, ☎ 62859332, **Múzeum polície SR**, Gunduličova 2, ☎ 0961/056096

Galleries

– **Slovenská národná galéria** – **Esterházyho palác**, Riečna 1, ☎ 54432081-2, **Vodné kasárne**, Rázusovo nábr. 2, ☎ 54434276, **Galéria mesta Bratislavy** – **Primaciálny palác**, Primaciálne nám. 1, **Mirbachov palác**, Františkánske nám. 11, ☎ 54431556, **Pálffyho palác**, Panská 19, ☎ 54433627, **MIRO**, Košická 56, ☎ 50702866, **Nova**, Baštová 2, ☎ 54433039, **Médium**, Hviezdoslavovo nám. 18, ☎ 54432251, **Galéria fotografie Profil**, Prepoštská 4, **Galéria Štefana Nemčoka**, Štefánikova 25, ☎ 52442777, **Dom umenia**, Nám. SNP 12, ☎ 52964458, **Umelecká beseda Slovenska**, Dostojevského rad 2,

K. F. A. Gallery, Karpatská 11, ☎ 52497030, **Perugia Gallery**, Zelená 5, ☎ 0903/773737, **Michalský dvor**, Michalská 3, ☎ 54411079, **Donner**, Klobučnícka 4, ☎ 54433753, **ÚĽUV**, Obchodná 64, ☎ 53332035, **SPP**, Drevená 4, ☎ 54131254, **Ardan**, Lermontovova 14, ☎ 52493235, **SFVU**, Michalská 7, ☎ 54433229, **Grémium**, Gorkého 11, ☎ 54430653, **X-Style**, Zámočnícka 5, **Gerulata**, Hodžovo nám. 3, **Café**, Panská 12, ☎ 54431228, **Bibiana** – **Medzinárodný dom umenia pre deti**, Panská 41, ☎ 54433550, **Danubiana**, Čunovo, ☎ 62528501

Atractiveness

– **Botanical garden**, Botanická 3, ☎ 65421311, **ZOO**, Mlynská dolina 1, ☎ 65422848, 65422823, **Michalská veža** tower, Michalská ul., **Chapel of St. Catharine**, Michalská ul., **Zichy Palace**, Ventúrska ul., **Pálffy Palace**, Ventúrska ul., **St. Martin's Minster**, Staromestská ul., **St. Clara church and monastery**, Klariská ul., **Pálffy Palace**, Panská ul., **Old Town Hall**, Hlavné nám., **Mirbach Palace**, Františkánske nám., **Primatial Palace**, Primaciálne nám., **Bratislava Castle**, Zámocká ul., ☎ 59341626, **House of the Good Shepherd**, Židovská ul., Monument **Slavín**, Na Slavíne, **Presidential Palace**, Hodžovo nám., **Slovak National Theatre**, Hviezdoslavovo nám., **Devínska Kobyla Mt.**, Devínska Nová Ves, **Devín Castle**, Devín, ☎ 54434742, **Manor house**, Rusovce

Swimming pools

– **DELFÍN**, Ružová dolina 18, ☎ 53415553, **KRYTÁ PLAVÁREŇ**, Junácka 4, ☎ 44256769, **ŠK ISKRA MATADORFIX**, Údernícka 20, ☎ 63830524, **ROSNIČKA**, Dolné Krčace, ☎ 64360960, **TEHELNÉ POLE**, Odbojárov 9, ☎ 44372828, **ZLATÉ PIESKY**, Senecká 2, ☎ 44257018

Luxurious hotels

– **DANUBE******, Rybné nám. 1, ☎ 59340000, **DEVÍN******, Riečna 4, ☎ 54433640, **FORUM******, Hodžovo nám. 2, ☎ 59348111, **MIVA******, Bzovícka 38, ☎ 63828021, **PERUGIA******, Zelená 5, ☎ 54431818, **RADISSON SAS CARLTON******, Hviezdoslavovo nám. 3, ☎ 59390000, **WEST******, Koliba-Kamzík, ☎ 54788692-5

High standard hotels

- **HOLLIDAY INN***, Bajkalská 25/A, ☎ 48245111, **ADONIS***, Vlčie hrdlo 1, ☎ 58597293, **BARÓNKA***, Mudrochova 2, ☎ 44882089, 44872324, **BRATISLAVA***, Seberíniho 9, ☎ 43411592, 43337980, **DUKLA***, Dulovo nám. 1, ☎ 55969815, **INCHEBA***, Viedenská cesta 7, ☎ 67273121, 67272000, **JUNIOR***, Drieňová 14, ☎ 43338000, **KYJEV***, Rajská 2, ☎ 59641111, **TATRA***, Nám. 1. mája 5, ☎ 59272111, 59272123, **Nº 16***, Partizánska 16a, ☎ 54411672, **BOTEL FAIRWAY***, Nábr. arm. gen. L. Svobodu, ☎ 54412090, 54412207, **BOTEL GRACIA***, Rázusovo nábr., ☎ 54432132, 54433430, **PENZIÓN GRÉMIUM***, Gorkého 11, ☎ 54131026

Standard hotels

- **ARCUS**, Moskovská 5, ☎ 55572522, **ASTRA**, Prievozská 14/A, ☎ 58238111, **ECHO**, Prešovská 39, ☎ 55569170, **NIVY**, Líščie Nivy 3, ☎ 55410390-5, **RAPID**, Telocvičná 11, ☎ 43410257-60, **REMY**, Stará Vajnorská 37A, ☎ 44455063, **SOREA**, Kráľovské údolie 6, ☎ 54414442, **TURIST**, Ondavská 5, ☎ 55410509, **DRUŽBA***, Botanická 25, ☎ 65420065, **FLÓRA***, Senecká 2, ☎ 44257988, **DOPRASTAV***, Košická 52, ☎ 55574313, **AVION**, Ivánska cesta 15, ☎ 43292206, **DANBAR**, Nejedlého 51, ☎ 64288710, **HYDRONIKA**, Vranovská 6, ☎ 63811166, **MORAVA**, Opletalova ul., ☎ 64777766, **SPIRIT**, Vančurova 1, ☎ 54777561, **KARPATIA**, Poľný mlyn 1, Záhorská Bystrica, ☎ 64776029, **MOTEL EVONA**, Senecká 2, ☎ 44456538

Restaurants

- **ALFA**, Jiráskova 1, ☎ 63812285, **ARKÁDIA**, Zámocké schody 3, ☎ 54435650, **AUŠPIC**, Viedenská cesta 24, ☎ 62250916, **BAMBUSOVÁ ZÁHRADA**, Prievozská 14/A, ☎ 54432426, **BIELA PANI**, Jozefská 11, ☎ 54435034, **CARIBIC´S**, Žižkova 1/A, ☎ 54418334, **ČÁRDA KORMORÁN**, Tematínska 7, ☎ 63828252, **ČERVENÝ RAK**, Michalská 26, ☎ 54431375, **DIVNÝ JANKO**, Jozefská 2, ☎ 54430418, **GANESHA**, Obchodná 42, ☎ 52731163, **HARMÓNIA**, Ventúrska 9, ☎ 54431683, **HRADNÁ VINÁREŇ**, Mudroňova 1, ☎ 59341358, **HYSTÉRIA PUB**, Odbojárov 9, ☎ 44454495, **CHEZ DAVID KOSHER**, Zámocká 13, ☎

54413824, **IZBA STAREJ MATERE**, Bajkalská 25, ☎ 53413731, **JADRAN**, Nevädzová 6, ☎ 43294722, **LA TRATTORIA**, Cintorínska 32, ☎ 52961620, **LEBERFINGER**, Viedenská cesta 257, ☎ 62317590, **MARIA THERESIA**, Palisády 50, ☎ 52925590, **MODRÁ KOLIBA**, Jasovská ul., ☎ 63813080, **MODRÝ DOM**, Roľnícka 56, Vajnory, ☎ 43711041, **MODUS-EXTRA**, Budyšínska 2, ☎ 44454052, **MS DANUBIUS**, Fajnorovo nábr. 2, ☎ 52922850, **OLYMPIA**, Živnostenská 1, ☎ 52961485, **PACIFIK**, Kutlíkova 17, ☎ 68286272, **PANDA**, Kvačalova 14, ☎ 55564696, **PARLAMENTKA**, Mudroňova 1, ☎ 54418433, **PIVOVARSKÁ REŠTAURÁCIA**, Krížna 59, ☎ 55572653, **PIZZERIA & GRILL**, Búdkova 4/A, ☎ 54413142, **PREŠPORSKÁ KÚRIA**, Dunajská 21, ☎ 52967981, **REDUTA**, Medená 3, ☎ 54435242, **REGIA**, Panenská cesta 14, ☎ 54416724, **RYBÁRSKY CECH**, Žižkova 1, ☎ 54413049, **SHANGHAI**, Prievozská 14/A, ☎ 53415079, **SLOVENSKÁ REŠTAURÁCIA**, Búdkova 39, ☎ 54775010, **SLOVENSKÁ REŠTAURÁCIA**, Hviezdoslavovo nám. 20, ☎ 54434883, **SLOVENSKÁ REŠTAURÁCIA**, Vlastenecké nám. 3, ☎ 62242170, **SMÍCHOVSKÁ PERLA**, Mariánska 11, ☎ 52966324, **STARÁ SLADOVŇA**, Cintorínska 32, ☎ 59322216, **TARPAN**, Májová 23, ☎ 62241585, **TERNO**, Nám. SNP 30, ☎ 54435389, **TOKYO**, Panská 27, ☎ 54434982, **TRAJA MUŠKETIERI**, Sládkovičova 7, ☎ 54430011, **U LISZTA**, Klariská 1, ☎ 54412540, **U VLADÁRA**, Palisády 40, ☎ 54434301, **YMCA**, Karpatská 2, ☎ 52499763

Pizzerias

- **PIZZA BOLERO**, Starohájska cesta 35, ☎ 624116 00, **PIZZA CAESAR**, Rovniankova 9, ☎ 63839839, **PIZZA DANO**, Hálova 5, ☎ 62242389, **PIZZA HOUSE**, Hviezdoslavovo nám. 15, ☎ 54431840, **PIZZA HUT**, Drevená 8, ☎ 54417666, **PIZZERIA ALVIANO**, Rybničná 13, ☎ 43711505, **PIZZERIA CIAO**, Trnavská cesta 37, ☎ 44373367, **PIZZERIA DIABOLINO**, Balkánska 150, ☎ 62859664, **PIZZERIA LA MAMMA**, Škultétyho 10, ☎ 44371938, **PIZZERIA ROMANTIKA**, Gaštanová 6, ☎ 54777674, **PIZZERIA SARANDA RISTORANTE**, Dr. V. Clementisa, ☎ 43335029

BELOW THE MALÉ KARPATY MTS.

Wine Route of the Malé Karpaty Mts.

Senec and its environs

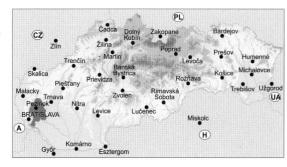

The landscape spreading east of the Malé Karpaty Mts. is characterised by two things - wine and water. In order to get the true image of this portion of Slovakia we should also add the sun. The chain of little towns and villages situated east of the mountain range are typical for vine growing. This is the largest viticultural region in Slovakia. Lovers of nature, folk culture and wine normally chose the route of their trips also referred to as the Malokarpatská vínna cesta (The Wine Route of the Malé Karpaty Mts.). It runs below the sunny slopes of the range skirted by fertile vineyards (on the area of more than 4,000 hectares) and wine cellars. All the towns and villages have their wine cellars, which offer pleasant sitting in the atmosphere typical for this region, administered by the district of Pezinok, which stretches from the ridge of the Malé Karpaty Mts. up to the Podunajská nížina lowland covering three towns and 14 villages.

Sun and water dominate in the Podunajská nížina lowland. The Slnečné jazerá lakes on the edge of the town Senec, the administrative centre of the district with similar area to that of Pezinok are the greatest attractiveness of this part of Slovakia. Senec is the favourite tourist centre where both the domestic and foreign visitors concentrate who prefer to pass the summer bathing.

Wine Route of the Malé Karpaty Mts.

SVÄTÝ JUR (population 4,250) is situated close to the Capital of Slovakia. It is an old settlement and its viticultural tradition is more than 700 years old. The settlement existing in the territory of what is today Svätý Jur was first mentioned in 1209 when King Ondrej II promoted it to the free market town. The local vineyards were first mentioned in 1270 but their history is obviously older. Crafts and trade, which developed along with viticulture and acquisition of addi-

tional privileges, caused that the town thrived and expanded. At the beginning of the 17th century the town walls were built and another important date in the history of the town is the year 1647 when Svätý Jur became the **free royal borough**. The 18th and 19th century was the period of stagnation and the town even lost its previous favoured position. But it kept its historical character until the present time. Its core is the town monument reserve established here after its renovation in 2001. The local **viticultural houses** from the 17th to 19th centuries characterise the architecture of the town. Tall gates with passages allowing the entry of carts loaded with grapes into the yards are its typical features.

The parish Roman-Catholic **church of St. George** is one of its most important cultural and historical monuments. This originally Early Gothic church from

the 13th century was repeatedly restored and enlarged. After the Turkish raid in 1663 when its tower burnt an independent wooden **belfry** was built next to the church. In Slovakia unique Early Renaissance stone altar with the statue of St. George dominates in the interior of the church. The **Holy Trinity church** from the 17th century, the Evangelical **church** from the 18th century, and the reconstructed Piarist **monastery** from the 17th century, now the seat of the Codecon brewery with nice restaurant, complete the list of sacral monuments in Svätý Jur. The secular historic monuments of the town include the remains of **town fortifications** from the 17th century and the equally old Renaissance Pálffy **manor house**, later adapted in the Baroque style. It houses now Academia Istropolitana Nova. Fans of history will certainly stop at the local **town hall** (the former Zichy curia from 1547) with exhibition dedicated to the history of the town. There is also the **Museum of Homeland**

Left: The main street of Svätý Jur
Right: The wine press of the Malé Karpaty region

Studies and Literature, where documents proving the settlement of the town and the life of the local teacher and writer Peter Jilemnický can be contemplated.

The picturesque situation of Svätý Jur lying amidst the vineyards on the slopes of the Malé Karpaty Mts. with swamps and the peat bog in the Nature Reserve of **Šúr** make it also an ideal starting point for the hiking trips in the Pezinské Karpaty Mts. Two hiking routes run up the reconstructed Prostredná ulica St. They coincide up to the part of the town called **Neštich** and later separate from each other. The first route runs by the Old Slav fortified settlement with preserved ramparts and the second route ascends along the ruins of the **Biely Kamen** Castle, which was probably built in the 13th century. It was the seat of the estate of Svätý Jur until the beginning of the 17th century. Turkish troops destroyed it and it was never restored.

The village **LIMBACH** lies on the protuberance of the Podunajská nížina lowland. The series of the valleys of the Malé Karpaty Mts. converge precisely in the area of this small viticultural community, which now has a new quarter of luxurious houses. Marked hiking paths lead through the village to the karstic spring **Limbašská vyvieračka** or to the mountain peat bog in the Nature Reserve of **Nad Šenkárkou**. Unmarked asphalt road leads from Limbach to the recreation centre **Slnečné údolie** with perfect conditions for camping. The lovers of wine often visit Limbach. The typical wine cellar offers the speciality of the place, the local wine **Limbašský silván** which made it famous also outside Slovakia.

The town of **PEZINOK** (population 21,000) with many churches, wine cellars, the wine producing enterprise and the Malokarpatské Museum also lies on the foothills of the Malé Karpaty Mts. It was first mentioned as the property of Bratislava Castle in 1208. Like in the neighbouring Svätý Jur, the first references to Pezinok linked to the viticulture

are from the 13th century. This activity fully developed thanks to different privileges in the 14th to 16th centuries. However, it was dominated by the Counts of Svätý Jur until it obtained the privilege of the **free royal borough** in 1647. Reformation and German colonists in the 16th and 17th century brought social and commercial prosperity to Pezinok as the result of full development of different crafts. Guilds and manufactures were founded. Paper processing factory and a brickyard were thriving here in the 18th and 19th century and the territory around Pezinok was an important **mining area** where pyrite, gold and antimony were extracted. Construction of railway connecting Pezinok with Bratislava and Trnava contributed to its prosperity. Wine is still the main symbol of the town. Especially the events held here every year attract visitors. Among them the most popular are the April **wine market**, **vintage** and **blessing of young wine** (Svätomartinské požehnanie mladého

vína) in September and the **Day of Open Wine Cellars** in November.

The town has several monuments. One of the oldest is the **chateau** built on the foundations of an older castle from the 13th century. This originally Renaissance chateau was reconstructed in the Baroque style in 1718 and later again in the 20th century when it was adapted to the new purpose - storage of wine with the stylish **Zámocká vináreň** wine cellar. A large park with precious trees surrounds the chateau. The pride of the town though, is the old Renaissance **town hall** built around 1600 and later rebuilt. The partially preserved **town walls** from the 17th century were important in anti-Turkish defence. Several **burgher houses**, special type of viticultural houses with U-shaped ground plan also characterise the architecture of the town. One of them houses the **Malokarpatské**

Left: Church in Pezinok
Right: Horná brána gate in Modra

múzeum (The Museum of the Malé Karpaty Mts.) focused on history of the town and viticulture. The complex also contains the native house of Ján Kupecký with the **commemorative room** of this important painter from the Baroque era. The house referred to as Schaubmar Mill with conserved milling technology contains the unique **Galéria insitného umenia** (Gallery of Naive Art).

Sacral monuments of Pezinok include the Roman-Catholic parish **church of Ascension of the Virgin Mary** from the 14th century, repeatedly adapted and the originally Renaissance **church of Lord's Transformation** from the 17th century later rebuilt in the Baroque style and referred to as the "Lower Church" The **monastery** and the **church of the Most Holy Trinity**, as well as the Evangelical **church** complete the list of the sacral buildings in the town.

Pezinok is the most popular salient point for the trips to the Malé Karpaty Mts. Car drivers use the mountain road leading to the mountain pass **Baba** (527 m), besides other, the venue of car competition. The adjacent recreation centre **Pezinská Baba** with the mountain hotel, downhill ski track and ski lift is also a very popular place. It is the starting point for the ridge tour in the Malé Karpaty Mts.

The town of **MODRA** (population 8,550) is another viticultural town also known for its pottery. Compared to Pezinok it is situated closer to the mountains. The tourist centre of **Zochova chata-Piesok** provides contact with the nature of the Malé Karpaty Mts. This tourist community with numerous private and public tourist cottages is crisscrossed by hiking trails. One of them leads to the top of the **Veľká Homoľa Mt.** (709 m) where the view tower was built in 2001, and further on to the group of quartz rocks called **Traja jazdci** (687 m). Along the road from Modra to Zochova chata cottage is another important holiday centre, **Harmónia** where the inhabitants of Bratislava relax. It is a good salient point for the trips heading to the

Zochova chata cottage, including the trail leading to the **Zámčisko Mt.** (468 m) with visible traces of what was once Old Slav fortified settlement and the symbolical **Štúrova lavička**, the bench dedicated to the important Slovak figure in the sphere of literature and politics.

However, Modra, first referred to in historical documents in 1158 is one of the five west Slovakian towns important for its viticultural traditions (so-called Pentapolitana, five towns including Modra, Bratislava, Pezinok, Trnava and Svätý Jur). Modra developed, despite its town privileges from 1361, as a serf town until it was promoted to **free royal borough** in 1607. That period was connected with high prosperity and Modra was one of the most important towns of Slovakia. Among the crafts, which developed in the town, pottery made Modra famous. Although the town was not one of those connected with railway it maintained the two main activities - vine growing and pottery at a good level. In 1883 the workshop and school of ceramics and factory **Slovenská ľudová majolika** (Slovak Folk Majolica) were opened here. Majolica of Modra with its typical decor, which can be bought in the local factory is much in demand even abroad.

Modra has also always been an important centre of culture. Among many personalities who lived here was **Ľudovít Štúr** who codified Slovak literary language. The **Museum** dedicated to him commemorates his life and activities and it is installed in the building of the former town hall. His **statue** carved in white marble stands in the square. Not far away from it is the Roman Catholic **church of St. Steven the King** from 1876. Another of Catholic **churches** consecrated to **St. John the Baptist** from the second half of the 14th century stands near the **cemetery** where several important Slovak personalities are buried including Ľudovít Štúr. Evangelicals built two **churches** here, one German and another Slovak in the beginning of the 18th century.

The secular monuments of the town include **burgher houses** on the square and on the Dolná ulica St. The oldest of them are from the 17th century. Parts of the **town walls** constructed in the first half of the 17th century also survive in Modra. Its most interesting part is the only preserved town gate of the original three, called **Horná brána** on the northern end of the town and the **sentry tower** with loopholes on the western side of town fortifications. The local **manor house** stands on the site of an old castle. It was adapted and the more than hundred years old gardening and viticultural school was moved there in 1957. The school has its own tavern where the brands of local wines, such as Veltlínske zelené, Rizling rýnsky, Rulandské biele or typical Frankovka modrá can be tasted. But there are more taverns and wine cellars in Modra and they are especially frequented in time of vintage (every even year in September), **Deň otvorených pivníc** (Day of Open Cellars) in Novem-

ber or the **Svätokatarínsky krst mladého vína** (Christening of the Young Wine) also in November.

ČASTÁ is the village situated north of Modra. It has a wonderful natural setting, which offers ideal hiking. Its main attractiveness, apart from the **Fugger House**, the largest wine cellar in the region, is one of the best preserved castles in Slovakia. It is the **Červený Kameň** Castle. Although Fugger family originally built it in the first half of the 16th century, its history is connected with the noble family of Pálffy. This important aristocratic family has gradually reconstructed the old castle into a stately residence with rich stucco ornamentation and frescos. Today it shelters **museum**, which contains historical furniture, arms, castle chapel and gallery with old paintings.

Visitors can also see the ground cellars and fortification system of the castle.

BUDMERICE also is a historical village with wonderful **manor house** built by the same Pálffy family in romantic style. This building from 1889 stands in a large park, which is, like the manor house perfectly cared after. The **manor house** serves to **the Slovak writers** as the calm haven for their creative activity. The largest village on the route is **ŠENKVICE**. Wine fans know the name of this village and its most important monument is the originally Gothic **church of St. Anna** from the 16th century fenced by a wall with corner bastions.

Senec and its environs

SENEC (population 14,650) is situated further in east, compared to Svätý Jur, Pezinok, and Modra, in the territory of the Podunajská nížina lowland. The first written reference to the settlement in the territory of what is now the town of Senec is from 1252. It received it first privileges in the end of the 15th century and since then it developed as a yeoman town. Progressively it became the trade centre of its environs with markets, among which the cattle market was the notable one. The year 1763 when Empress Maria Theresa founded one of the first economic schools in the Kingdom of Hungary and situated it in Senec was an important one. The town had its brickyard, distillery and several small industrial firms. Production of building materials and food-processing industry dominate in the present day Senec.

But it is above all the centre of summer recreation. Several artificial lakes in Senec, which originated by extraction of

Left: Slnečné jazerá lakes in Senec.
Červený Kameň Castle
Right: Manor house in Bernolákovo.
Statue of the Virgin Mary in Dunajská Lužná

gravel, compose the complex called Slnečné jazerá (Sun Lakes) on an area of 116 hectares. Their denomination expresses the fact that Senec enjoys more than average 2000 hours of sunshine a year, which makes it the most "sunny" town of Slovakia. Apart for bathing and water sport the recreation area offers excellent accommodation at different levels, camping sites and sport facilities. The local tennis hall for instance, is also very attractive for fans of this sport.

Senec has also some historical monuments. The former Renaissance curia **Turecký dom** (Turkish House) is one of the most beautiful buildings in this style in Slovakia. Its stands on the Mierové námestie square and it was built in the years 1556-1560. The oldest sacral building of the town is the Roman Catholic **church of St. Nicolas the Bishop**. This originally Gothic church was adapted in the Renaissance taste in the 17th century and it acquired the present shape in 18th century.

In environs of Senec there are several monuments such as the Baroque **manor house** in **VEĽKÝ BIEL** built in the 18th century, once residence of Archbishop Emerich Csáky. Today it houses home for elderly people. In the neighbouring **BERNOLÁKOVO** there is also a wonderful Baroque **manor house** of noble family Esterházy from the 18th century. In its area the first **golf ground** in Slovakia with nine holes was made in 1994. It is 1,723 metres long. The originally Rococo **manor house** from the 18th century is in the neighbouring village **IVANKA PRI DUNAJI** with the **monument** dedicated to **General M. R. Štefánik**, who perished here after air crash in 1919.

Fans of bathing will certainly visit the village **KRÁĽOVÁ PRI SENCI** and its pool with thermal spring with temperature of 52 degrees of Celsius. The local open-air museum of bee keeping with historical beehives is also intriguing. Bathing is possible near the village **DUNAJSKÁ LUŽNÁ**. The most important historical monument of this village is the Roman Catholic **church of Ascension of the Holy Cross** from the 18th century. Its main altar boasts the **statue of the Virgin Mary** carved in pear wood. It is one of the oldest preserved wooden medieval statues in Slovakia and as it inspired many legends it attracts pilgrims.

The village **SLOVENSKÝ GROB** attracts the lovers of good meals as this is the best place to taste the **baked goose** offered almost in every house, served here with "lokše", the typical local dumplings and the local wine.

WINE ROUTE OF THE MALÉ KARPATY MTS.
(dial: 02-, 033-)

Information
– **Informačné centrum**, Radničné nám. 9, Pezinok, ☎ 033/6901107, fax 033/6412303, **Malokarpatská turistická informačná kancelária**, Štúrova 84, Modra, ☎/fax 033/6474302, tik@post.sk, www.tik.sk

Museums
– **Slovenské národné múzeum – Múzeum Červený Kameň**, Častá, ☎ 033/6495132, 6495342, **Vlastivedné a literárne múzeum**, Prostredná 32, Svätý Jur, ☎ 02/44970476, **Malokarpatské múzeum**, M. R. Štefánika 4, Pezinok, ☎ 033/6412057, **Múzeum Ľudovíta Štúra**, Štúrova 54, Modra, ☎ 033/6472765, 6472944, **Izba ľudových tradícií**, Slovenský Grob, ☎ 033/6478222, **Obecné múzeum**, Šenkvice, ☎ 033/6496311

Galleries
– **Slovenská národná galéria – Galéria insitného umenia**, Schaubmarov mlyn, Cajlanská 255, Pezinok, ☎ 033/6404035, **Arias & Vanda Gallery**, Štúrova 108, Modra, ☎ 033/6474100, **Harmónia**, Štúrova 103, Modra, ☎ 033/6474220

Atractiveness
– **Červený Kameň** Castle, Častá, ☎ 033/6495132, 6495342, **Manor house**, Budmerice, ☎ 033/6448209, **Biely Kameň** Castle, Svätý Jur

Hotels
– **POD LIPOU***, Modra-Harmónia, ☎ 033/6407790, **ZOCHOVA CHATA**, Piesok 3715, Modra, ☎ 033/6470131, **LIPA**, Kollárova 20, Pezinok, ☎ 033/6412402, **ISTOTA**, Kučišdorfská dolina, Pezinok, ☎ 033/6402937, **NA VRCHU BABA**, Pezinok, ☎ 033/6403636, **LIMBACH**, SNP 18, Limbach, ☎ 033/6477281, **JELEŇ***, Holubyho 25, Pezinok, ☎ 033/6412361, **HYDROSTAV***, Píla, ☎ 033/6495204, **LEONARD**, Píla, ☎ 033/6495212, **HOTEL 1**, Kučišdorfská dolina, Pezinok, ☎ 033/6402176, **GALBOV MLYN**, Pri Mlyne 607/3, Viničné, ☎ 033/6476205, **EVA**, Jozefkovo údolie, Svätý Jur, ☎ 02/44970507, **HAFFNER**, Piesok 3773, Modra, ☎ 033/6470199, **MODRA**, Štúrova 111, Modra, ☎ 033/6472266, **KAMILA**, Čierna Voda 611, ☎ 45943611

Restaurants
– **PEZINSKÝ DVOR**, Kollárova 3, Pezinok, ☎ 0903/216930, **PREŠ**, Kollárova 20, Pezinok, ☎ 033/6413394, **U JELEŇA**, Štúrova ul., Modra, ☎ 033/6472264, **SLOVENSKÁ KOLIBA**, Modra-Piesok, ☎ 033/6470131, **VINOHRADNÍCKY DOM**, Štúrova 108, Modra, ☎ 033/6474100, **TAVERNA POD BAŠTOU**, Červený Kameň, Častá, ☎ 033/6495316, **PIVNICA U ZLATEJ HUSI**, Pezinská 2, Slovenský Grob, ☎ 033/6478225

SENEC AND ITS ENVIRONS
(dial: 02-)

Information
– **Turistická informačná kancelária – SCR**, Mierové nám. 19, Senec, ☎/fax 45928224, scr@senec.sk, www.senec.sk

Atractiveness
– **Sun Lakes**, Senec, ☎ 45923080, **Golf ground**, Dunajská ul., Bernolákovo, ☎ 45994332, **Monument of the General M. R. Štefánik**, Ivanka pri Dunaji

Hotels
– **LÚČ***, Nám. 1. mája 1, Senec, ☎ 45927336, **SENEC***, Slnečné jazerá – sever, Senec, ☎ 45927255, 45927266, **ZÁTOKA***, Slnečné jazerá – sever, Senec, ☎ 45922501-4, **HAVANA***, Šamorínska 41, Senec, ☎ 40202310, **DRUŽBA**, Slnečné jazerá – juh, Senec, ☎ 45915391-2, **FORTUNA**, Slnečné jazerá – juh, Senec, ☎ 45915194, **AMÚR**, Slnečné jazerá – juh 440, Senec, ☎ 45924081, 45923080, **ISTROCHEM**, Slnečné jazerá – sever, Senec, ☎ 45924522, **HYDROSTAV**, Slnečné jazerá – sever, Senec, ☎ 45923413

Restaurants
– **LUCULLUS**, Hviezdoslavova 2, Senec, ☎ 45923127, **NOSTALGIA**, Lichnerova 28, Senec, ☎ 45923367, **TURECKÝ DOM**, Nám. 1. mája 1, Senec, ☎ 45922184, **ZELENÝ DVOR**, Šamorínska 1, Senec, ☎ 45923540, **PARK**, Vlntčná 5, Bernolákovo, ☎ 45993932, **FÚZAČ**, Štefánikova 2, Ivanka pri Dunaji, ☎ 45943380

ZÁHORIE

**Senica and
its environs**

Below Malé Karpaty

**The Borská
nížina lowland**

**The Chvojnická and
Myjavská hill lands**

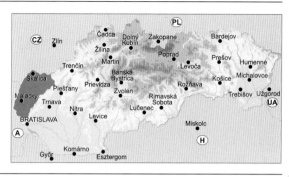

The name Záhorie (Transmountain region) appeared for the first time in the 17th century and it is based in the Latin name *Processus transmontanus*, which referred to the area situated beyond the Malé Karpaty Mts. or the Little Carpathians. Other names often used for this region were the Moravské pole (Moravian Field in Slovakia) or Pomoravie, Moravská nížina lowland or the Moravský dol lowland. Finally the name Záhorie was adopted for the region situated in the western part of the Slovak Republic next to the frontier

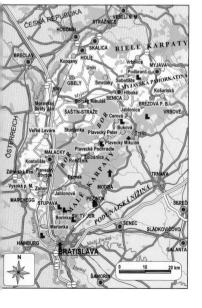

with Austria and Czech Republic. Historically and geographically it includes the districts of Senica, Malacky, Senica, and Myjava. The territory is limited in the west by the state frontier with Austria and it runs along the river Morava while in the north-west and south-east its borders coincide with the frontier with the Czech Republic and the ridge of the Malé Karpaty Mts. respectively.

The territory consists of the Záhorská nížina lowland, which borders on the Dolnomoravský úval dell and the Biele Karpaty Mts. in the north. The north-eastern part and the eastern parts are filled by the Myjavská pahorkatina hill land and the Malé Karpaty Mts. respectively. The north-south axis is about 75 kilometres long and its west-east axis is 35 km long.

Záhorie, due to its favoured geographical position and friendly climatic conditions is one of the territories with the earliest settlement in Slovakia. Its position was especially important in the Celtic and Germanic periods, as well as in time of the Great Moravian Empire. After establishing of the Kingdom of Hungary, Záhorie found itself in the periphery and lost its privileged position. After the Second World War when numerous industrial firms sprang here and farmers joined the newly founded co-operatives, Záhorie experienced a period of development which, however, did not include the villages and towns lying along the Czechoslovak-Austrian frontier because of the effects of Iron Curtain.

Senica and its environs

The administrative and economic centre of Záhorie is the town of **SENICA** (population 21,300). It was first mentioned in 1217. The town acquired its privileges and the right of fairs in 1396. In the 18th century Senica was one of the three most developed towns in the County of Nitra. The wool-cloth manufacturers especially thrived. After the First World War the plant producing synthetic fabric was built here and has influenced the economic life of the region ever since. Senica has got abundant sacral and profane architectural monuments. One of them is the Late Baroque **manor house** standing outside the historic centre. It was built to design of F. A. Hillebrand in 1760. It is the typical Theresian two-floor and three-wing building with attic roof, a conspicuous

Left: The manor house in Senica
Right: The square in Senica.
The manor house in Sobotište. Branč Castle

portal and large courtyard with pillars. The manor house was restored in the 1970s and it houses the **Záhorská galéria** gallery since 1985. The Late Classicist **manor house**, work of I. Feigler JR is from the first half of the 1860s. The Classicist curia from the first half of the 19th century completes the set of the former residences of aristocratic families of Senica. The most interesting sacral monument is the Roman-Catholic **church of Visitation of the Virgin Mary**. It was built as a Protestant church in 1631 on the site of an old Gothic parish church. After 1654 it served to Catholics. Next to the church stands the Gothic **chapel**. The Evangelical **church** is from the years 1783-1784. It was built as a Classicist Toleration church without tower, which was added to it in 1794. The **synagogue** of Senica built in 1864-1866 in oriental style commemorates the Jewish community, which used to live in the town. Senica is an important centre of cultural activity of its wide environs. It concentrates in the **Dom kultúry**

(House of Culture) where theatre shows, dance competitions or concerts are regularly held. The **Kunovská priehrada** water reservoir attracts lovers of summer recreation with its maintained sand beach and good accommodation and catering offer situated in pleasant forest setting.

SOBOTIŠTE, the village not far away from Senica also has an interesting background. It was settled by the radical sect of Anabaptists, called Habans in 1547, which built here their yards separated from the rest of the community in the 16th and 17th centuries and greatly influenced the economic and cultural development of the whole territory. Sobotište had its important figure, teacher Samuel Jurkovič who moved here in 1833. He founded **Gazdovský spolok**, the self-relying credit co-operative as the second on the European continent (only three months after the first co-operative was founded in Rochdale in England). One of remarkable monuments of Sobotište is the Renaissance-Baroque **manor house** with corner towers on the square. It was rebuilt from the original castle and acquired its present appearance after the Rococo-Classicist reconstruction in the second third of the 18th century. The manor house contains **Múzeum Samuela Jurkoviča** with exhibition of the history of the co-operative movement in Slovakia. Remains of one of the yards, typical **Haban structures** including the town hall, chapel, school, pottery work-

shop, a mill and seven houses also survive in the village. Fans of history will certainly visit the ruins of the **Branč** Castle towering on the easily discernible cone-shaped hill at the altitude of 475 m above the village **PODBRANČ** north-east of Senica. Branč was one in the network of frontier castles, which cared for the security of the roads heading from Moravia to the Carpathian passes. It was built in the 13th century and became the centre of administration of an extensive estate. The castle burnt by the end of the 17th century, furniture was moved out, its fortifications were pulled down and the castle fell in decay. Remains of walls of the individual buildings and some parts of the lower castle are all that is left. The short and undemanding ascent to the castle hill is worth the toil because it offers a wonderful panoramic view of the Myjavská pahorkatina hills and the Biele Karpaty Mts.

SMRDÁKY lying in the west became famous for its sulphurous medicinal springs known here since the 16th century. Baron Joseph Vietoris founded the spa in the years 1832-1833. He built the first spa building and manor house for well-to-do visitors. The repeatedly reconstructed and modernised manor house is still used. Due to the composition of the local medicinal water and excellent therapeutic results, the spa concentrated to therapy of skin diseases in the 20th century. Composition of

medicinal water of Smrdáky is indeed unique. One litre of the local water contains more than 3,100 mg of mineral components. The hydrogen sulphide content is especially high (more than 600 mg/l), which makes the Smrdáky water the most sulphurous water in Europe. Sulphurous mud is also highly curative. The spa consists of several empirical buildings. Although they were repeatedly reconstructed they kept the original appearance.

Four kilometres southward of Senica is the village **HLBOKÉ** where **Jozef Miloslav Hurban** lived in the years 1843-1888. He was one of the leading personalities of emancipation of the Slovak nation. The writer, poet and politician, Hurban was one of the initiators of enacting of the literary Slovak language and co-founder of Matica slovenská (along with Ľ. Štúr and M. M. Hodža). There is the **commemorative room** of J. M. Hurban in Hlboké.

Below the Malé Karpaty Mts.

The first village south of Senica and below the Malé Karpaty Mts. is **JABLONI-CA** with the originally Renaissance manor house from the beginning of the 17th century and the Roman Catholic Baroque **church of St. Stephen the King** rebuilt from an older church in the years 1750-1752. The neighbouring village **CEROVÁ** is one of the starting points for the trip to

the ruins of the **Korlátka** Castle built in the mid-13th century. As a royal castle it protected the western frontier of the Kingdom of Hungary. It is in decay since the 18th century. Only the outer walls of the upper castle and several stretches of lower fortifications were preserved. Apart from the castle ruins the village has also the Renaissance-Baroque **manor house** built in 1700. The manor house surrounded with a park is now used as a charity home of female order of the Holy Cross. Ruins of the **Ostrý Kameň** Castle towering on a rock at the height of 576 m bears witness of the history of the place. It was built at the end of the 12th century as a sentry castle on the trade route referred to as the Czech Road. Only ruins of the original Gothic upper castle and the lower situated Renaissance fortifications survive. They provide a fine view of the Záhorská nížina lowland.

If you continue further south-eastward you will pass through three villages bearing some form of the word "plavecký" in their names. They are **PLAVECKÝ PETER, PLAVECKÝ MIKULÁŠ**, and **PLAVECKÉ PODHRADIE**. The first word of the names stems in that of the warrior tribe of Polovci (or Plavci) invited here by King of the Kingdom of Hungary after the invasion Tartars in 1241. Their task

Left: Smrdáky. Ostrý Kameň. Korlátka
Right: Plavecký hrad Castle

was to protect the frontiers of the Kingdom. Plavecký Peter is a typical **farming settlement** of western Slovakia with distinct examples of folk architecture. Part of the **monument reserve** is also the originally Renaissance Roman Catholic church of Sts. Peter and Paul the Apostles from 1600. It was rebuilt in the Baroque style in 1712. It stands on the site of an older church and fortifying walls skirt it. The archaeological site of **Pohanská** from the Upper Bronze Age and the Lower Iron Age in the administrative territory is also of great historical value. Fortified settlement from the Hallstatt period with comparatively well discernible ramparts and settlement holes were discovered here. They are the remains of a Celtic *oppidum*, one of the largest in Slovakia. It was a large town, and its population outnumbered that of medieval Bratislava. The natural landmark of the area is the **Plavecký kras** karst spreading on an area of 39 square kilometres with numerous karstic springs, abysses, sink holes and cave attics. The

Deravá skala cave near Plavecký Mikuláš is especially interesting as it bears traces of *Homo sapiens* from the Upper Palaeolithic Era. However, the **Plavecký hrad** Castle, subject of many legends is the most important attractiveness. It used to serve as the royal frontier fort built in the years 1256-1273. Imperial troops damaged the castle in 1707 and it gradually changed into ruins. Its tower, the remains of the palace of the upper castle and large bastions of the lower castle survive. The ruins of the castle standing on steep hill (400 m) at the foothills of the Malé Karpaty Mts. represent an impressive silhouette and favourite destination of trippers. **JABLONOVÉ** is another of the villages lying below the Malé Karpaty Mts. which offers remains of folk architecture and the **Sviatok Pomoravia** Feast when folk ensembles and popular artists from Austria, Czechia and the Slovak part of the Pomoravie region meet here.

The town of **STUPAVA** (population 8,050), situated only several kilometres away from Bratislava, dominates in the

southern part of the region of Záhorie. One of the important events in its history was the arrival of Romans at the beginning of the 1st century. Romans built here the military station as documented by the inscription on the pillar of triumph of Emperor Marcus Aurelius in Rome from 180 AD. Stupava developed as a little town with right to fairs and markets in the Middle Ages. At the beginning of the 18th century the crafts of ceramics and pottery spread in Stupava, which are now represented by the famous artisan Ferdiš Kostka. He lived and worked in Stupava in the years 1878-1951. **Múzeum Ferdiša Kostku** is situated in his native house with the original interior of the workshop and furnace, which is the only original Haban furnace in Europe. But the symbol of modern Stupava is the local speciality - *sauerkraut* or acid cabbage. The September Days of Cabbage or as the locals say "Dni zelá" are abundantly visited also thanks to a wide offer of tasty local meals and "zelovica", the beverage made of cabbage juice. Stupava boasts the Baroque **manor house** standing on the edge of historical **park** in the centre of the town. It was built on the site of what was originally a water castle reconstructed by the aristocratic Pálffy family into the Early Baroque fortified manor house in mid-17th century. Today it is a social facility. Part of the plot with manor house is the park

with unique wood species. The Renaissance Roman Catholic **church of St. Stephen** from the first half of the 17th century is also an interesting cultural monument. It was adapted in the Baroque style by the beginning of the 18th century.

The ideal starting point for a walk to the **Pajštún** Castle is the village **BORINKA**. The castle was first mentioned in the document from 1273. In the past it was one of the frontier castles, which were built in the Malé Karpaty Mts. in the 13th century to protect the north-western frontiers of the Kingdom of Hungary. In the mid-18th century the castle burnt and in 1810 the Napoleon's troops destroyed it definitely. Only its ruins remained on the limestone rock at the height of 486 m. Now it is the favourite destination of trippers. The top plain of the ruins offers an impressing view of the Borská nížina lowland and the valley of the Stupavský potok brook. On sunny days the sight of the ridges of the Austrian Alps beyond the frontier refreshes the panorama. The village Borinka is known above all as the salient point for the trips in

Left: The manor house of Stupava. The view from Pajštún. The chapel in Marianka
Right: Above Medené Hámre. The Borská nížina lowland. The manor house in Malacky

the Malé Karpaty Mts. There are several landmarks in its vicinity making it the recreation settlement. On an area of 14.6 hectares stretches the karstic territory of the **Borinský kras** with Zbojnícka jaskyňa cave (closed to public), Pajštúnska and Borinská springs and the valley of Prepadlé and Medené Hámre. The Borinský potok brook, water of which used to drive the hammer mills, which processed the copper extracted in local mines, flows through the deep canyon-like valley of the Medené Hámre.

The neighbouring **MARIANKA** with the church and monastery from the 14th century became the most visited pilgrim site of Slovakia. The believers from Austria also know it under the name Marienthal. The most important sacral building here is the Roman Catholic **church of Nativity of the Virgin Mary**. It was built in 1377 in the Gothic style, it was widened in the 17th century and reconstructed in the Baroque style in the 18th century. J. Lippert reconstructed the presbytery of the church in the Neo-Gothic style in 1877 but the

Baroque stucco ornamentation of the nave with the motif of the Pauline order (two lions next a palm tree) survives. The statue of the sitting Madonna from the end of the 14th century, allegedly cut from a pear tree wood by some hermit, adorns the altar. As there are few Romanesque monuments preserved in Slovakia, Madonna of Marianka with the Romanesque flair is highly appreciated. In front of the church the Late Baroque **statue of St. John Nepomuk** stands and west of the church is the older building of the Paulist **monastery** from the 14th century, which was widened in 1593. The monastery was rebuilt into the summer residence of Archbishop Kristián August Saský of Esztergom in the years 1711-1717 and today it serves again to the male order of Brothers Comforters. The pilgrims mostly head to what is referred to as a miraculous spring. The road runs along six **chapels** built in the years 1710-1729. On the slope is the **Way of Cross** consisting of fourteen chapels.

The Borská nížina lowland

The central part of the Borská nížina lowland is Bor, a continuous area of blown sands and dunes which are situated north-east of Lozorno and Malacky. The main settlement in this part of the region of Záhorie is the town **MALACKY** (population 17,800) which developed from the sentry settlement on the frontier of the Kingdom of Hungary where the royal family of Árpads invited the tribe of Secules

from Transylvania to guard the frontier. Malacky developed as a yeoman town with rights to markets and fairs after 1573. Foundation of the first manufacture producing wool cloth owned by Count Mikuláš Pálffy also contributed to the development of the town. New industrial firms established after the Second World War was the impetus, which increased population of Malacky by more than ten thousand. The architectural monuments of the town include the originally Renaissance **manor house** from 1624. It was rebuilt into a luxurious aristocratic residence with English park at the end of the 19th century. The manor house is now used as a health care establishment. The **church of the Immaculate Conception of the Virgin Mary** and the **Franciscan monastery** with protecting walls and four towers are from 1653. The area between

the individual wings of the monastery and the church is a kind of inner yard, also referred to as the Paradise garden. Fans of art will certainly appreciate the main wooden altar of the Virgin Mary from 1720. Interesting items of the church include the Holy Stairs, a masterly imitation of the stairs Jesus had to climb on his last way. Similar copies are only in Vatican and Jerusalem. The Holy Stairs are in a separate chapel. One has to climb the stairs on knees because there are allegedly bones of saints deposited under each of them. The originally Late Renaissance Roman Catholic **church of the Most Holy Trinity** from 1653 was rebuilt in the years 1731-1741 in the Baroque style. The **synagogue** of Malacky situated in the centre of the town served to the large Jewish community which lived in Malacky at the turn of the 19th and 20th centuries. **Museum of Michal Tillner** situated on the road to Kostolište in the vicinity of a romantic water mill from the beginning of the 18th century is also interesting. One can contemplate paintings of M. Tiller exhibited in the mill. Malacky is the cultural centre of the region of Záhorie. Exhibitions, concerts of brass music, folk events are held here all the year round and the **Záhorácke ľudové slávnosti** (Folk Festival of Záhorie) is the best known of them.

Further south of Malacky, not far away from Plavecký Štvrtok, amidst the pine woods is the popular **Kamenný mlyn**, recreation area with cottages and a lake. **ZOHOR** is the village which has an interesting Roman Catholic Church of St. Margita of Antioch built on older foundations in 1893. **VYSOKÁ PRI MORAVE** is known to cyclists, as the lane for cyclists runs through this village along the Morava river as far as the Castle of Devín, while there is also an option to cross the river by ferry to Anger in Austria, a stop on the nice cycling circle along the Morava. **KOSTOLIŠTE** is almost part of Malacky and there is the **commemorative room** of one of the best Slovak painters, expressionist and illustrator, **Martin Benka** (1888-1971).

Left: The synagogue in Malacky
Right: Haban house in Veľké Leváre.
Church in Šaštín

Further north situated **VEĽKÉ LEVÁRE** was settled by the Habans, also referred to as the Hutter brothers, Anabaptists or neophytes. In 1592 the **Haban yard** was built around the local square. It is the largest surviving locality of the original dwelling of Habans in Europe. It was designated the **monument reserve of folk architecture** for its uniqueness and value. Habans tried to imitate the way of life of the primeval Christians based on common property and production of tools and consumer goods. They addressed each other brother and sister and were headed by the spiritual leader, preacher who was simultaneously the judge and administrator. The yard was involved in crafts and none of its members was allowed to own private property. Only the Christian Haban community could own the property and it was community, which was entitled and obliged to satisfy the needs of its members. Habans did not marry after their own choice of partner. Any individual with such intention was supposed to apply to the oldest member of the community and was presented three potential brides to choose from. New born children stayed with their mothers until 2 years and then they passed to a school where they were brought up by school sisters. Such community was still living in this village in the first half of the 20th century. In 1972 the **Habánske múzeum** (Museum of Habans) was opened in the village and it contains interesting items documenting the way life of the sect. The dominant of the village is the Baroque Roman Catholic **church of the Virgin Mary** with a monumental frontal facade. It was built in the memory of the 50th anniversary of defeat of Turkish troops at Vienna by the Viennese Archbishop and Cardinal Sigismund Kollonitz in 1729. It stands on the site of a wooden church and it is a single-nave Baroque building with two towers, rather unusual structure in Slovakia.

ŠAŠTÍN-STRÁŽE (population 4,950) situated not far away from Veľké Leváre is also known abroad as a pilgrim site where

people came to see the statue of the Virgin Mary. Pope Urban VIII confirmed the statutes of the place. The Pauline order acquired the statue in 1733 and decided to built the pilgrim **church** and **monastery** in Šaštín. The church was built in the Baroque style and consecrated at the presence of Empress Maria Theresa, Emperor Franz I of Lotharingia. The statue of the Virgin Mary of Seven Grievances was moved to the main altar made of red marble. The church has six side altars with paintings of J. L. Kracker, it is 62 m long, and 23 m wide. The building of the monastery has three tracts and on the fourth side there is basilica. In 1950 the Salesian order which resided here was driven out and the church passed under administration of the diocese priests. Pope Paul VI promoted the **church of the Virgin Mary of Seven Grievances** to *basilica minor*, the first in

Left: The statue of the Virgin Mary in Šaštín
Right: Chapel in Skalica

Slovakia which is now together with the monastic complex the National Cultural Monument. The economy of the place was influenced by the calico factory founded by Franz of Lotharingia in 1736. It was one of the first and largest textile factories in the Monarchy. The area now is rather known for the deposits of oil in the locality **GBELY** (population 5,250) which also has **Naftárske múzeum** (Museum of Crude Oil). Examples and exhibits of traditional tools used in industry are also exhibited outside the Museum.

The Chvojnická and Myjavská hill lands

In the northernmost protuberance of the Chvojnická pahorkatina hill land is the town **SKALICA** (population 15,000), which was first mentioned as a settlement in 1217. It became the free market settlement in the 14th century and free royal borough in 1372. Gradually it matched in significance towns like Bratislava, Trnava or Košice. At the turn of the 18th and 19th centuries the period of growth and prosperity of the town continued and in the second half of the 19th century Skalica became one of the centres of cultural life and centre of typography in the 20th century. The most valuable building and symbol of Skalica is the Romanesque **St. George chapel**. It stands on top of a small hill on the edge of the town and is one of the most beautiful Romanesque structures in Slovakia. It was built as a castle church probably in the 12th century. It is a half-circle shaped sanctuary with a round nave which survive in their original forms. At the beginning of the 15th century it was adapted and included into the town walls. Inside the rotunda are Gothic wall paintings representing St. George struggling with a dragon. Parts of the Gothic town wall still stand near the rotunda. It was designated the National Cultural Monument in 1970. Remains of **town walls** around the town built after promotion of Skalica to free royal borough

in 1372 survive. The best preserved sections are next to the Franciscan monastery, below the rotunda and in the area of hospital. The dominant of the square of Skalica is the parish **church of St. Michael.** This Roman Catholic Gothic church was built in 1372. It was repeatedly adapted and reconstructed but several Gothic elements were preserved along with the Renaissance tower with arcades. The chapel and ossuary of St. Ann from the 15th century stands by the church on the square. The originally Gothic **church of the Virgin Mary** and the **Franciscan monastery** are from the second half of the 15th century. They were built next to the town walls where the poor lived in the Middle Ages. The **church** and the **monastery** form a complex around the garden. Evangelicals built their church and monastery in the mid-17th century, which was rebuilt to hospital in the early 19th century. Je-

suits and Paulines also have their **churches** and **monasteries** in Skalica. The Evangelical church of Skalica used now by this denomination is an example of the Classicist style with Baroque elements. It was built in 1796 as a Toleration church lacking tower, which was added to it as late as 1938. Sacral monuments of this town also include the Classicist **Calvary** from 1823 situated near rotunda, the **Lady's Pillar** on the square and the building of **synagogue**, which is part of town walls. As far as the profane buildings are concerned, the Late Renaissance **town hall** from the first third of the 17th century deserves attention. In the second half of the 19th century another floor with Classicist facade was added to it. The Renaissance building of **Gvadányi curia**, now the municipal library and several burgher houses standing on the square are interesting. One of the most beautiful buildings in the town is the that of house of culture in Art Nouveau style where the **Záhorské múzeum** (Museum of Záhorie) with historical and archae-

Left: Záhorské Museum in Skalica
Right: The manor house in Holíč

ological exhibits seats. It is the building of the former House of Associations and one of the most original in Slovakia. This single-floor house was built in 1905 to design of D. Jurkovič. Its front is adorned by mosaics inspired by the painter M. Aleš. Viticulture has been an inseparable part of life of people in Skalica. Every visitor should taste the well-known local red wine *Skalický rubín*. Vineyards with remarkable little houses and wine cellars surround the town. Another typical feature of Skalica is its pastry, known to locals as *skalický trdelník*.

Seven kilometres south-west of Skalica is the town **HOLÍČ** (population 11,400) which developed next to the medieval water castle in the mid-11th century. It became the seat of the castle estate, which included the territory of the north-western part of Záhorie. Favourable position facilitated development of the town as trade centre more so when the estate fell in hands of the royal family of Habsburgs in 1736. Holíč was the second largest town in Záhorie in the second half of the 19th century. The most important building monument of Holíč is the National Cultural Monument, the Baroque-Classicist **manor house** with fortifications. It was built on old foundations of the water castle and its current appearance is the result of reconstruction of the old counter-Turkish fort from the 16th century. The Habsburgs had the original four-wing fort rebuilt into a luxurious imperial summer residence in the years 1749-1754. The most admired part of the interior was the Chinese Hall with walls decorated by painted leather tapestry. Underground corridors constructed for the royal sentry guarding the castle form part of fortifications. The manor house with the former French park, the Baroque walls fence pheasantry and pond. The manor house is owned by the state since 1918 and it is under reconstruction since 1974. Monuments of

Holíč include a **wind mill**, the only in Slovakia from the 19th century and the structure of **factory**. The factory producing porcelain was founded in the area of the Habsburg summer residence by Franz I of Lotharingia and it was here where the famous majolica of Holíč was made. It was the first factory of the kind in Austria-Hungary. The single-floor building of the factory houses is now **Museum of ceramics**. Among the sacral monuments the Roman Catholic Baroque-Classicist **church of the Divine Heart of Jesus** from 1755 is worth mentioning. By its side, the Capuchin **monastery** with square ground plan and simple facade was built. The oldest church of Holíč is the Gothic **church of St. Martin** from 1387, which was adapted by the end of the 17th century. Evangelicals had the Toleration Classicist **church** with a school and

parsonage built in the town in 1787. Sacral monuments include the Baroque **chapel of the Virgin Mary**, Baroque-Classicist **chapel of St. Florian** and the Classicist Jewish **synagogue** from the last third of the 18th century.

The symbol of **KOPČANY**, the village not far away from Holíč is the **chapel of St. Margita** built on the foundations of the original Romanesque church which used to stand next to the fortifications in time of the Great Moravian settlement. As the settlement gradually withdrew from the riverbed of the Morava to safety, the chapel remained isolated amidst the fields. Another interesting landmark of the village is the Baroque building of the local **stud** built as an imitation of manor house with adjacent tracts consisting of stables for horses of the Spanish riding style. The area of stud included surrounding meadows and forest, which was used

by the Habsburgs for ostentatious hunting parties. The imperial court travelled from Vienna to Kopčany through Moravská Nová Ves and the ford in Kopčany.

Folk tradition is maintained in **UNÍN** where the local people still stick to their beautiful local costume and in **MYJAVA** (population 13,100) where the Myjavské folklórne slávnosti (Folk Festival of Myjava) is held every year in June. This event full of folk music, dances and old customs is abundantly visited. The local ensemble **Kopaničiar** is well known even abroad. Myjava is the centre of the typical area with scattered settlement. The hilly and originally densely forested territory slowed down its settlement. Myjava was founded at the end of the 16th century and as the local people were involved in sheep keeping, wool was used for making wool-cloth and production of sacks used in mills. As far as wool-cloth is concerned, its producers and merchants from Myjava dominated in the Austrian-Hungarian market in the 18th and 19th centuries. In the 1840's Myjava became the centre of the Slovak emancipating movement. The newly established Slovak National Council had its session here in 1848 and the first national uprising of Slovaks against the Monarchy broke here. The local **Múzeum Slovenských národných rád** (Museum of Slovak National Councils) opened in 1968 after reconstruction of an older house commemorates the events. The oldest surviving building in the territory of the town is the originally Evangelical **church**, finished in 1729. It was built in the Baroque style and fenced by tall stone wall with the Classicist gate. Emperor Charles IV ordered to lower the wall and gave the church to the Catholics in 1731, who rebuilt it in 1732. Evangelicals built a new **church** in 1785. The **monument of the General Milan Rastislav Štefánik** from 1921 inscribed in the UNESCO list of monuments is also an interesting architectural work. Visitors frequent the **water reservoir of Stará Myjava** with ski centre, accommodation and catering facilities both in summer and winter.

Left: Folk costume of Myjava
Right: The Bradlo Mt.

Ten kilometres south of Myjava is the town **BREZOVÁ POD BRADLOM** (population 5,500), centre of the region since the 17th century. The local people were mostly involved in farming, cattle trade and crafts (shoe-making, weaving, and leather-dressing). They sold their products mostly in Morava and Silesia. The legendary **Uncle Ragan** was one of the famous tanners of Brezová pod Bradlom. His life symbolises the cunning and humorous character of the locals as described by the writer, local native Elo Šándor. This popular figure has been immortalised in the film made according to the Šándor's novel and the local inn bearing the name of the protagonist. One of the dominant sacral monuments of the town is the Evangelical Classicist **church** from the years 1783-1784, one of the biggest in Slovakia. It was built as the Toleration church lacking tower, which was added to it in 1795. The **church of the Most Holy Trinity** was built in 1590 as a Protestant church with fortifications.

The **Pamätný dom Samuela Jurkoviča** (Commemorative House of Samuel Jurkovič) is one of the profane monuments of the town. It is the native house of the founder of the first Slovak co-operative in Sobotište (1845). **Národný dom** (National House) on the square and **Mohyla** (Barrow) on top of the Bradlo Mt., the tallest mountain of the Myjavská pahorkatina Hills (543 m) commemorate M. R. Štefánik, Slovak astronomer, general and politician, who greatly contributed to the foundation of the 1st Czechoslovak Republic in 1918. Mohyla was built to design of D. Jurkovič and it consists of two stone tetrahedrons and a three-step pyramid with monumental sarcophagus inspired by old Egyptian architecture. In the corners of the barrow four 12 m tall obelisks stand. General M. R. Štefánik was born in the village **KOŠARISKÁ** where there is also the **museum** situated in the building of the Evangelical parsonage dedicated to this outstanding personality of the Slovak history.

SENICA AND ITS ENVIRONS
(dial: 034-)

Information
- **INFOSEN - Informačná kancelária mesta Senica**, Autobusová stanica, Senica, ☎/fax 6516459, infosen@stonline.sk, www.senica.sk

Museums
- **Múzeum Samuela Jurkoviča**, Sobotište, ☎ 6282102

Galleries
- **Záhorská galéria**, Sadová 619/3, Senica, ☎ 6512937-8

Atractiveness
- **Spa Prírodné liečebné kúpele Smrdáky**, Smrdáky, ☎ 6575101-5

Hotels
- **SENICA****, Hviezdoslavova 1417/62, Senica, ☎ 6517236

Restaurants
- **GASTROCENTRUM**, J.Kráľa 727, Senica, ☎ 6513031-2, **U JAKUBA**, Robotnícka 74, Senica, ☎ 6517921, **ARCADIA**, Námestie oslobodenia 16, Senica, ☎ 6518124, **BRANČ**, Námestie oslobodenia 11, Senica, ☎ 6512624, 651 43 60

BELOW THE MALÉ KARPATY MTS.
(dial: 02-, 034-)

Museums
- **Múzeum Ferdiša Kostku**, F. Kostku 25, Stupava, ☎ 02/65934882

Hotels
- **STUPAVA*****, Nová 1588, Stupava, ☎ 02/65934108, **PARK*****, Stupava, ☎ 02/65934268, 65934768

Restaurants
- **STUPAVSKÁ KRČMA**, SNP 68/1, Stupava, ☎ 02/65934073, **STUPAVA**, Hlavná 942, Stupava, ☎ 02/65934442

THE BORSKÁ NÍŽINA LOWLAND
(dial: 02-, 034-)

Information
- **Inforeg Záhorie - Euregio-Service-Center**, Na dieloch 67, Zohor, ☎/fax 02/65961552, jan.hladik@stonline.sk, www.inforeg-zahorie sk

Galleries
- **Galéria Ars Humanus**, Domkárska 9,

Zohor, ☎ 02/65961580, **Alojz Drahoš**, Lozornianska 25, Zohor, ☎ 02/65961617

Atractiveness
- **Church of the Virgin Mary of Seven Grievances**, Šaštín-Stráže, ☎ 034/6592714-6

Hotels
- **ATRIUM****, Zámocká 1, Malacky, ☎ 034/7723161, 7724559, **KAMENNÝ MLYN****, Plavecký Štvrtok, ☎ 034/7793269

Restaurants
- **U PAPOUŠKU**, Mierové nám., Malacky, ☎ 034/7723846, **ŠTADIÓN**, Zámocký park, Malacky, ☎ 034/7725576, **MACEK**, M. R. Štefánika 2760, Malacky, ☎ 034/7731630

THE CHVOJNICKÁ AND MYJAVSKÁ HILL LANDS
(dial: 034-)

Information
- **Turistická informačná kancelária mesta Skalica**, Námestie Slobody 10, Skalica, ☎ 6645341, fax 6600241, skalica@ba.telecom.sk, www.vino-zahorie.sk, www.skalica.sk, **Turisticko-informačná kancelária CK MALKO POLO**, M. R. Štefánika 524/19, Myjava, ☎/fax 6214064, info@ckmalkopolo.sk, www.myjava.sk/tik

Museums
- **Záhorské múzeum**, Námestie Slobody 13, Skalica, ☎ 6644230, **Múzeum holíčskej fajansy**, Holíč, ☎ 6682255, **Múzeum SNR**, Štúrova 276/2, Myjava, ☎ 6212256, **Múzeum Milana Rastislava Štefánika**, Košariská 92, ☎ 6242626

Atractiveness
- **St. George chapel**, Skalica, **Monument of the General M. R. Štefánik**, Košariská

Hotels
- **SV. MICHAL*****, Potočná 40, Skalica, ☎ 6960111, **TATRAN**, Nám. Slobody 98, Skalica, ☎ 6644491, 6644503, **SAN****, Bernolákova 12, Holíč, ☎ 6684187, **BANÍK****, Nám. 1. mája 5, Holíč, ☎ 6683523

Restaurants
- **ASTÓRIA**, Potočná 54, Skalica, ☎ 6648365, **VALO**, Sasinkova 1, Holíč, ☎ 6685500, **U SVÁKA RAGANA**, D. Jurkoviča 415, Brezová pod Bradlom, ☎ 6242161

DANUBELAND

Komárno and its environs

The Žitný ostrov island

Nové Zámky and its environs

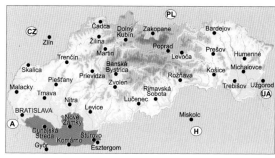

The Danube region, with its special landscape is situated in the south of Slovakia. The south-western and southern limits of the region follow the Slovak-Hungarian frontier running along the stream of the Danube. The western limit of this territory borders on the city of Bratislava; the northern limit coincides first with the Malý Dunaj river then with the northern border of the districts of Komárno and Nové Zámky. The territory of the Slovak part of the Danube region is administratively part of the regions of Trnava and Nitra, and it consists of the districts of Dunajská Streda, Komárno, and Nové Zámky.

The historical development and favourable natural conditions of the area contributed to the fact that the Danube region is the most densely populated area of Slovakia. The territory was settled since the oldest times and it became the scene of migration of various tribes and ethnicities.

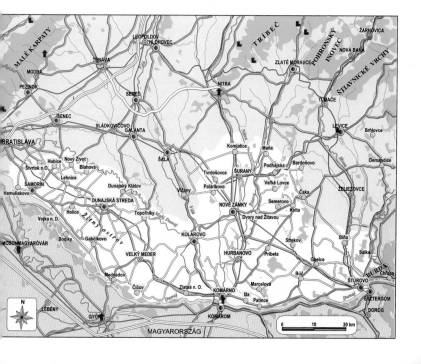

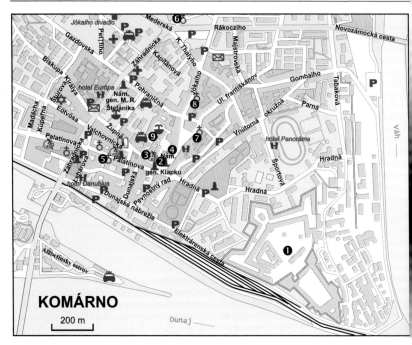

KOMÁRNO

200 m

From the point of view of nationality structure, the Hungarian nationality predominates at present. The highest number of Hungarians in terms of districts of Slovakia lives in the districts of Dunajská Streda (more than 80%) and Komárno (70%). Tourism is the industry, which markedly develops in the Danube region at present. The Danube, in turn, invites to navigation on boats and fishing. The dike of the Danube has a marked bike-route running from Bratislava to Komárno and it is the part of the International Danube bike route starting at Passau in Germany and leads to Budapest in Hungary.

Komárno and its environs

The centre of the Slovak part of the Danubeland, the town of **KOMÁRNO** (population 37,700) lies on the confluence of the Váh and Dunaj. It is one of the oldest

Right: The Courtyard of Europe.
The bastion of the fortification system

towns in Slovakia. A primeval settlement existed on the territory of the town as early as the Lower Stone Age. Three market settlements originated around the castle which stood on the site of the existing fort, a piece of land squeezed between the arms of the Váh and Danube: *villa Camarum, villa Kezw*, and *villa St. Andrae*. The oldest written reference to Komárno from 1037 comments collection of fees in the port of Komárno and fishing carried out in the area. Other sources from 1075 mention Komárno as the village with market, called *Camarum*. The medieval town lived its greatest prosperity in the 15th century when the rulers and court of Kingdom of Hungary frequently stayed in Komárno. The castle of Komárno became the main supporting point of the defensive system constructed against the Turks, after they occupied Buda and Esztergom in the years 1541-1543. The **fort ❶** of Komárno is the largest bastion fortification in Central Europe. It originated in the years 1546-1557 by reconstruction of the 13th century castle. A new pentagonal fort with star-shaped fortifications widened the old fort in the years 1663-1673. A bridge connected the forts over the moat and along with bridgeheads of St. Nicholas and St. Peter they formed a compact defensive system. The fort resisted practically all Turkish attacks. Only the 1783 earthquake damaged it to such an extent that it lost its strategic significance. However, this system of forts was again rebuilt in the early 19th century as the result of the Napoleonic wars. An outer defensive ring consisting of two bastion lines – called the Váh and Palatine lines – and four little advanced forts were added to it. The fort also played an active role in the years 1848-1849 when it resisted the siege and attacks of the Imperial troops led by General J. Klapka. It is a historic monument of European significance and the National Cultural Monument. Komárno obtained the privileges of free royal borough from Empress Maria Theresa in 1745. It ranked then among the five largest towns in the Kingdom of Hungary with approximately ten thousand inhabitants, and well-developed trade and crafts.

You can start sightseeing in Komárno at the centre near the former **Zichy Palace** ❷, which is one of the dominant features of the Námestie gen. J. Klapku square. Count Zichy had the palace built in the late 17th century. The palace was restored in 1989 and one part serves as the **Museum of Danubeland** ❸. There is a **permanent exhibition of the modern history of the town** in the rooms on the first floor of the palace. The disasters accompanying the town in its history also struck the Late Baroque Roman Catholic parish **church of St. Andrew** ❹ built in the years 1748-1756 now standing on Palatínova ulica street. Sightseeing of other churches of Komárno may start as well by the Roman Catholic **church of St. Rozália** ❻, a Neo-Classical building from 1848 situated on what used to be the mar-

ket place, now Námestie sv. Rozálie square. Closer to the town centre on Jókai street is the Neo-Classical **Reformed church** ❼ built in 1788 without a tower. The tower was added to it in 1832. Not far from this church the former **military church** stands in the Ulica františkánov street. Another important sacred monument is the originally Baroque **church of the Serbian Orthodox Church** from 1754. It stands on Palatínova street and was restored in the years 1849-1851. Its interior contains a collection of 23 Orthodox icons from the 17th and 18th centuries and a voluptuous iconostasis from 1770. The Late Baroque **chapel of St. Joseph**

from the second half of the 18th century, later adapted in the Neo-Classical style and the Baroque **group of statues of the Most Holy Trinity** built in 1715 as a reminder of the plague epidemic and anti-Habsburg wars complement the sacred monuments of the town. The **Courtyard of Europe ❾** is the name of a unique project of the architects grouped in the studio Europa in Komárno. It is in fact the intention, now implemented, to build historic architecture typical for the individual regions of Europe in a styled form on a new square of Komárno.

Komárno is widely known as a town with rich cultural and social life. Every two years in April **International Competition of Singers of F. Lehár**, as well as the **Lehár Festival** staging musicals and the June **Days of Jókai** (survey of amateur theatre ensembles) are organized. Cultural events include the **Days of Constantine and Methodius** held in July, **Days of European Heritage** in September and **Days of Matica** in October. In Bastion VI Jokai's theatre presents a survey

of theatre ensembles under the title **Theatre Bastion**. By the end of April and beginning of May **Days of Komárno** jointly organized by the towns of Komárno and Komárom in Hungary attract numerous visitors. Komárno is the native town of many famous figures. The two best known are the writer **Mór Jókai** and the composer **Franz Lehár**. The water sports area and boathouse is on the dead arm of the Váh. The visitors to the town are attracted by its **thermal swimming pool**. It exploits two hot springs with water temperature of 37 degrees of Celsius. They are 1,224 m and 1,040 m deep. The water is beneficial for the therapy of rheumatic diseases and overall recreation.

ČÍČOV is the village interesting for archaeologists with its finds from the La Téne, Roman and Roman-Barbarian eras. Visitors can also use the **instructive path** along the **Číčovské mŕtve rameno** (The Dead Arm of Číčov). Instructive path is 6 km long and it has 12 stops. It leads around the Lion lake and it takes about 5 hours to see it all. The arm is one of the

best conserved and most precious places, from the point of view of natural history, of Žitný ostrov. The National Nature Reserve is situated 2 kilometres west of Číčov and stretches along the bank of the Danube up to the village of Kľúčovec.

An alternative route runs eastward, along the Danube. The first village on the route, **IŽA**, 7 km away from Komárno is an attractive tourist point. The Roman fort called *Celemantia* is situated on the left bank of the Danube. Up to 2.2 m thick peripheral walls of the fort of rectangular shape survive in this archaeological site. The corners of the walls are rounded. In the middle of each wall there was a double gate guarded by towers. Sulphurous hot springs were discovered in **PATINCE** almost 50 years ago. Hot spring Héviz with temperature 27 degrees of Celsius, which springs up from the depth 200 m created a 650 square metres sized lake. Additional and richer springs were found near the old hot spring, which gave origin to the car camping site and

recreation centre with swimming pools fed by thermal water, suitable for bathing and boating.

The destinations of the tourists roaming in the Danube area should perhaps also comprise the town of **HURBANOVO** (population 8,000). The finds of a disappeared Romanesque church from the 12th century with burial place and 11th to 13th century medieval village are unique. Sacred monuments are represented by two churches. The Roman Catholic **church of St. Ladislav** was built in the years 1912-1913 on the site of an old Baroque church from 1718, which was restored after the earthquake in 1763. The Reformed **church** is from 1796, it was later rebuilt and a built-in tower was added to it along with new Late Neo-Classical facade. Opening of the planetarium in 1983 contributed to promotion of astronomy

*Left: Číčov. The thermal swimming pool in Patince. Celemantia - Iža. Golden Pheasant
Right: The observatory of Hurbanovo*

Zlatý bažant or Golden Pheasant exported to numerous countries of the world.

The town of **KOLÁROVO** (population 11,000) lies on the confluence of the Váh and Malý Dunaj. It is 18 km away from Komárno. A castle mentioned in 1349 – the Frog Castle – existed in the territory of the village. Now there are only its ruins left above the confluence of the Malý Dunaj and Váh. The sacred monuments of the town are represented by the Baroque Roman Catholic **church of Ascension of the Virgin Mary** from 1724. It originated on the site of an older Gothic church, which burnt in 1715. Advantageous position of the town at the confluence of two rivers makes it an ideal centre of water sports and fishing. The floating **water mill** on the Malý Dunaj river with preserved equipment from the early 20th century is the only technical monument of its kind in Slovakia. The town also has the **longest log bridge** in Central Europe and remains of a Baroque fort housing the **Museum of water milling** (Múzeum vodného mlynárstva).

among the public. Since 1962 it has been called **Slovenská ústredná hvezdáreň** (Slovak Central Observatory). It co-ordinates 15 observatories, seven astronomic cabinets, and six planetariums. The observatory is a multi-storied building with large and small glass domes, a communication tract and single-storied wings. The small dome was built at the same time when the summer-house, the large one was built in the thirties. There is a wonderful protected **park** around the observatory from the mid-19th century. The **manor house** built in historicizing style and inspired by the French Baroque-Neo-Classical style is from the beginning of the 20th century. The brewery existing in Hurbanovo also became famous. Now it is a part of the multinational company Heineken, but it still produces the beer

The Žitný ostrov island

The cultural and economic centre of Žitný ostrov is the district town of **DUNAJSKÁ STREDA** (population 24,000) situated 49 km from the capital Bratislava. Some sources assert that the oldest written reference to the settlement is from 1162. It was probably King Belo III who founded a market place there, which be-

Left: The water mill in Kolárovo.
Shops in Dunajská Streda
Right: Dunajský Klátov.
Thermal swimming pool in Veľký Meder.

came the core of the later town of Szerda-hely. An important period of development of the settlement was the 15th century. The decree of King Sigismund promoted it to a yeoman town in 1405. In the 16th century it was a town with market and fair privi-leges. Annexation of the settlements Újfal, Nemesszeg and Elötejed to Szerdahely in 1874 gave origin to the town, which be-came the centre of trade and crafts in Žitný ostrov. Sightseeing of the town can start at the rare sacred monument of the Roman Catholic **church of Assumption of the Virgin Mary**. This was originally a Gothic church from the 14th century dedi-cated to St. George. It was repeatedly adopted. Its chancel contains the painting of St. Nicolas the Bishop and on the southern facade is the painting of Calvary from the late 14th century restored in 1955. The church is an example of the Late Gothic sacred architecture. The Evangelical **church** built in the Neo-Gothic style in 1883 is also worthy of at-tention. The **Žitnoostrovné múzeum** with a permanent ethnographic and ar-chaeological exhibition is now in what is called the **Žltý kaštieľ** or Yellow Manor House. Bishop Mikuláš Kondé had this originally Baroque building built in the first half of the 18th century. It was adapt-ed in the Neo-Classical style in the early 19th century. The Museum was placed in this structure in the years 1970-1972. The Museum seated from 1964 in what was called **Biely kaštieľ** or White Manor House, which was built in romantic Neo-Classical taste in the late 19th century. This two-storied building was demolished

after the Museum was moved. The Slovak National gallery has exhibitions in the. **Vermes Villa** built at the turn of the 19th and 20th centuries. Fine arts exhibitions are usually organized in the exhibition pavilion of Žitnoostrovné Museum, in the Gallery of the Contemporary Hungarian Artists and in the private Gallery **ART-MA**. By the beginning of the 1970's the town became popular as a summer tourist centre. It was the time when the area of thermal swimming pools was opened. The area offers seven swimming pools with medicinal thermal water with proved effects on the locomotion appara-tus. The area also contains a natural lake suitable for boating. There is the car-camping site available nearby.

DUNAJSKÝ KLÁTOV is the village next to the Malý Dunaj river. The 25 km long Klátovské rameno arm flows through the village and it is one of the natural landmarks of the Danube region. Along its stream stretches the National Nature Re-serve of **Klátovské rameno**, which repre-sents an oasis of conserved nature with typical floodplain forest, abundant water and swamp flora and protected water wild life amidst the agricultural landscape. A remarkable **technical monument** stands of the bank of the Klátovské rameno arm. It is **Klátovský mlyn** or the Mill of Klátov. It is a brick building of, as experts say, the Anglo-American type. Today it contains a permanent **exhibition** and it is part of the Žitnoostrovné Museum. It is a favourite stop of tourists. Next to the confluence of the Malý Dunaj and its Klátovské rameno arm in the eastern part of Žitný ostrov is

the village of **TOPOĽNÍKY**. Thanks to the local hot springs and three **thermal swimming pools** with water temperature of 36 degrees Celsius, Topoľníky became one of the most visited places of Žitný ostrov. The quality of this medicinal water is comparable to that of Piešťany. Many visitors to the Danubeland choose the town of **VEĽKÝ MEDER** (population 9,200) as their destination. It lies in the south-eastern part of Žitný ostrov, only 12 km from the border with Hungary and 20 km from Dunajská Streda. The biggest tourist attraction of this little town is the **thermal swimming pool**. It makes use of natural mineral hot spring with the temperature of 54 degrees Celsius emanating from a well 1,500 m deep. The 100 ha large area of swimming pool is situated amidst forests. A combined indoor pool connected with outdoor pool is open all the year round. It has a toboggan, playing grounds and minigolf. The chemical composition of the local hot spring is suitable for the therapy of diseases of joints, muscles and back and it contributes to overall regeneration of the human organism.

GABČÍKOVO is 12 km away from the district town. It is situated on the banks of the Čilížsky potok brook. The little town recently became famous for its **water works Gabčíkovo**. The Danube always played an important role, and often a negative one, in its history. This was the rea-

son why the local people founded an association with the mission of protecting it against floods. As the floods occurred almost regularly, the gigantic water works were built in Gabčíkovo in 1980-1990 and became its new symbol. However, the town also has other attractions. It contains numerous cultural monuments. The former **Amade manor house** was built in its outskirts. Before there was a Gothic water castle surrounded by a moat. The palace was situated on the site of today's south-eastern wing of the manor house and castle walls fortified it. The old castle was reconstructed into a Renaissance manor house in the 17th century. Visiting Gabčíkovo one cannot miss the church standing in the centre of the town. It was originally the Gothic Roman Catholic **church of St. Margaret of Antioch** church reconstructed by the end of the 18th century in the Late Baroque style. The original Gothic window and the Late Gothic portal are worth seeing. A hot spring with a temperature 51 degrees Celsius feeds the local swimming pool. Two tree trunks 8,000 years old conserved under a 10 m thick alluvium of gravel were found here, when the Gabčíkovo dam was constructed. Today these tree trunks together with other natural and historic exhibits are part of the permanent exhibition of the local **Vlastivedný dom ľudovej architecture** (House of Natural History and Folk Architecture).

The village **HOLICE** is known by the Roman Catholic **church of Sts. Peter and Paul** built in the first half of the 13th century in the Late Romanesque style.

Left: The lock chamber in Gabčíkovo.
The town hall in Šamorín
Right: The square in Šamorín.
The manor house in Lehnice

The church contains unique remains of exterior wall paintings from the Late Middle Ages. In the last third of the 14th century, the church was rebuilt in the Gothic style. Renaissance adaptations were made in the 17th century. The town of **ŠAMORÍN** (population 12,300) is the centre of the western part of Žitný ostrov (The Rye Island). It is only 24 km away from Bratislava, near the Danube, the access to which was cut off by the canal of the Gabčíkovo Dam. Visitors who are interested in cultural monuments should start with the unique Reformed **church** which is one of the most beautiful Gothic churches in Žitný ostrov. Emperor Joseph II's resolution abolished the religious orders and this also concerned Franciscan monastery in Šamorín. The chancel contains unique and thoroughly restored Gothic wall paintings from the 13th century depicting various events from Bible. The second **church**, which is Evangelical or Lutheran, is from 1784-1785. It is Neo-Classical, but its interior

bears traits of the Baroque style. The Roman Catholic **church of the Virgin Mary's Ascension** built in the Late Baroque style is also one of the gems of the local sacred architecture. A unique type of sacred architecture can be seen at the **church of St. Margita**, which is to be found outside the town in a little settlement called **Šamot**. Originally it was built in the Romanesque style in 1260. It is a single-nave church with flat ceiling. The Jewish community living in Šamorín built their **synagogue** in 1912 in the romanticizing and historicizing style. Its interior is used as a fine art gallery, concert and theatre hall since 1996. The former **town hall**, now the municipal office, was originally a Renaissance structure, which was repeatedly adapted. ory can be seen in the **Mestský vlastivedný dom** (The Municipal House of Homeland Studies). Every year the event called the **Days of old Samária** becomes the summer attraction of the town. If you are a fan of fine arts then you should visit the private art

gallery called AT HOME. The **House of Arts** or Dom umenia of Šamorín originated by joining the restored old Jewish school with a big garden existing not far from the synagogue. The village of **Čilistov** was annexed to Šamorín in 1960. Čilistov is now better known for its recreation area with thermal **swimming pool** called **Lagúna** near the Hrušov dam.

Northeast from Šamorín is village **NOVÝ ŽIVOT**. An important sacred monument of the village is originally Gothic Roman Catholic **church of St. Peter and Paul** from the second half of the 15th century, adapted in the Neo-Classical taste in the 18th century. One of the interesting monuments of the village is the single-floor **curia** and the originally Baroque **manor house** from the early 18th century. Another **manor house** was built in the second half of the 18th century and rebuilt by the end of the 19th century in a roma-

Left: The church in Hamuliakovo
Right: The fort in Nové Zámky

ticizing historicist style. Now it houses the House of International School Relations. This extensive building with two lateral wings stands in the local park. The village of **LEHNICE** is famous for the Late Renaissance **manor house** from the early 17th century. Today it houses a hospital. **BLAHOVÁ** originated in 1951 by separation from the village of Lehnice. Next to the village and in a pleasant setting of the Malý Dunaj river is the popular recreation place **Madarász** with a swimming pool, mini-golf course and tennis courts.

Cultural monument enthusiasts should turn off the main road between Šamorín and Zlaté Klasy and visit the village of **ŠTVRTOK NA OSTROVE**. The unique Roman Catholic **church of St. James** is a Romanesque building with Gothic bell from the 13th century with two towers, which was adapted in the 16th century in the Renaissance style. The most valuable part of the building is the Romanesque portal of the western group of three towers and the Renaissance epitaphs from 1572. There are fragments of Gothic wall paintings in the interior of the church.

The village of **HUBICE** is situated 12 km north-east of Šamorín. The most important sacred monument of the village is the Romanesque Roman Catholic **church of the Visitation of the Virgin Mary** from the 13th century. It was rebuilt in the Gothic style in the 15th century and adapted in the Baroque taste in the 17th century. The stay of the aristocrats and Archbishops of Esztergom is testified to by numerous important secular monuments. The older and bigger manor house was built in 1830 probably on older foundations. In the 17th century the Archbishop of Esztergom György Szelepcsényi founded here the factory of Dutch type for production of wool cloth in the original building and introduced sheep raising. He also founded ponds and a game enclosure. The manor house is now private property. Better conserved and kept is the younger and "smaller" manor house from the first third of the 19th century built in the Neo-Classical style with two ground floor lateral wings. It originated by reconstruction of a horse stable. The burial **chapel** of the Wiener-Welten family from the end of the 19th century is worth to mention. The **curia** of the Kempelen family is also an interesting building. The inventor Wolfgang Kempelen lived in this curia in his older age. The most important sacred monument of the most western part of Žitný ostrov is the local Roman Catholic **church of the Holy Cross** from the 13th century in the village of **HAMULIAKOVO**. It is one of the most important brick Romanesque sacred buildings in Slovakia. Its present appearance is the result of repeated reconstruction in the period of Baroque and in the 19th and 20th centuries. The fresco decoration from the second half of the 14th century is unique. It consists of Gothic wall paintings inspired in old Church symbols.

VOJKA NAD DUNAJOM is 9 km south-east of Šamorín, in the western part of the island limited by the old channel of the Danube and the new feeding channel. The old village architecture of **earthen houses** with saddle reed roofs and original furniture is now represented by the **Vlastivedný dom** house. The Neo-Classical Roman Catholic **church of St. Michael** the Archangel is the most significant sacred monument in the village. It was built in the early 18th century on the site of an older church from the 13th century. One can also see a part of the **system of arms of the Danube** with surrounding floodplain woods in the village. Especially the fans of water sports, fishermen and lovers of cycling will find the natural setting ideal for their hobbies. The ferry connecting Vojka with Kyselica operated free of charge by the company running the basin of the Danube is also one of the attractions for tourists.

Nové Zámky and its environs

The town **NOVÉ ZÁMKY** (population 42,250) is the largest town of the region of Podunajsko. It was founded in the 16th century on the site of four villages destroyed by the Turks. It was first referred to in 1545 when on the left bank of the Nitra river a counter-Turkish fort with ramparts and wooden palisades was built. However, on the right bank of the river a new hexagonal **fort** was built of stone, which was one of the most advanced fortifying structures of Europe of that time. The new fort was built to design of Italian architects Ottavio and Guilio Baldigari. Apart from walls, it also had a water dike connected with the river Nitra and its main task was to impede the Turks to advance towards Vienna. The black year for Nové Zámky was 1663 when the Turkish army counting 200,000 warriors conquered the fort. Imperial troops liberated the fort only after 22-year Turkish occupation. Liberation of Nové Zámky was an important event and it was celebrated by bells tolling in whole Europe. However, the fort gradually lost its importance and King Charles III had it pulled down in the years 1724-1726. The form of the majority of its bastions is still recognisable, as the network of streets is arranged in hexagonal shape. One of the most beautiful cultural monuments of the town today is the **Calvary** from 1779 situated on the site of hexagonal foundations of the disappeared town walls near Forchách's bastion. Sacral monuments of

Nové Zámky include the Evangelical **church** from 1905, the Reformed **church** from 1924 and above all the Franciscan **monastery** with **church** from the 17th century. The monastery was built following the pattern of medieval monasteries. The dominant of the square now is the Roman Catholic **church of Holy Cross** built in the years 1584-1585. The original simple Late Gothic building was repeatedly reconstructed. The last adaptation was made in 1877 when the church acquired the Neo-Classical facade. The pride of the town is the Baroque **group of statues of the Most Holy Trinity** from 1749, the reminder of plague epidemic, which stroke the town in 1740. Anton Bernolák, important Slovak linguist who was the first to codify the Slovak language is buried in the Baroque **chapel of the Most Holy Trinity** from 1722. Bernolák's commemorative room is part of the local **museum of nat-**

Left: Group of statues of the Most Holy Trinity
Right: Venus of Hrádok

ural history, which also contains archaeological, historical and ethnographic collections. In what is now the building of municipal council is the **Gallery XC** open to public, which is focused on Central European fine arts of the 18th to 20th centuries. Nové Zámky has also rich cultural life. From March to May, the series of concerts in the framework of Novozámocká hudobná jar (Musical Spring of Nové Zámky) are organised, in March the cultural-literary days of G. Czuczor invite fans of literature, International Festival of Alternative Arts or the Days of the European Cultural Heritage are both held in September, while the October Festival of Jazz is also worth to visit. The centre of relaxation and recreation is the landscape part of **Berek** with more than 200-year old oaks including the area of the **thermal pool Štrand.**

North of Nové Zámky lies the town of **ŠURANY** (population 10,500). Its history was closely tied with that of the Šuriansky hrad castle, great part of which was pulled down in 1725. Emperor Francis II promoted Šurany to royal borough with market and fair rights in 1832. Šurany boast the oldest **sugar refinery** in Slovakia from 1854, now technical monument. As far as monuments of Šurany concern, there is also the two-towered, originally Baroque, Roman Catholic **church of St. Steven the First Martyr** from the 17th century rebuilt at the beginning of the 20th century, **manor house** in the Art Nouveau style from the beginning of the 20th century, and the Classicist **curia** from 1820. The town is also known for fine wines and thermal springs exploited in several pools and above all the **recreation area of TONA**. At Nitriansky Hrádok, now part of the town, with unique archaeological finds (sometimes referred to as the "Slovak Troy"), the magnified copy of the famous Venus of Hrádok, the clay original 4,800 years old, stands in the middle of the village. Small **viticultural huts** called here "**hajlochy**" represent the picturesque detail of the local landscape.

Further in south situated **DVORY NAD ŽITAVOU**, one of the oldest settlements in southern Slovakia, along with village **MAŇA** are archaeological localities. Remarkable stone artefacts can be seen here. They were not always considered products of human activity by the locals. In Middle Ages they were referred as "the thunder stones" and people believed that they were sent here as messengers from heaven and used to deposit them under the roofs of houses in order to protect their dwellings against lightning. Typical folk architecture of local houses and the Classicist **water mill** from the beginning of the 19th century are the landmarks of this village. The park surrounding the local Late Baroque **manor house** from the second third of the 18th century contains several rare wood species. But the tourist mostly concentrate on **Požitavské folklórne slávnosti** (Folk Festival of the region of Požitavie) held here every year in May. The route continues to the village **VEĽKÉ LOVCE**. The order of Paulines built in the locality of Máriačalád a large

HRADOCKÁ VENUŠA

monastery with church and thoroughly constructed cellars and hidings in 1512 . Only remains with fragments of this monument of wall paintings by J. Bergl from 1776 survive now.

An attractive place for relaxation during hot summer days is the village **PODHÁJSKA**. The local thermal pool was constructed here in 1973 when geothermal spring was discovered in the depth of 1,900 m. The water temperature is 83 degrees of Celsius and its yield is 50 litres per second. It is highly mineralised and its effects are allegedly similar to those of the Dead Sea water. There are two swimming pools, two pools for sitting only, and one pool for children, relaxation area, pearl baths, terraced solaria and other sophisticated supplementary facilities serving to full recreation or sport of visitors. The area of thermal swimming pool is decorated by the works of sculptors who attended the symposium "Prameň 98". Wonderful forests surrounding the village also offer interesting hiking routes. One of

them leads eastward to **BARDOŇOVO** with its local **manor house** currently under reconstruction. It is the National Cultural Monument.

There are several villages with well-preserved folk architecture and manor house in the vicinity of Šurany and Nové Zámky. In **TVRDOŠOVCE houses made of unburned clay bricks** and with straw roofs from the 19th century and the Renaissance **manor house** from the 17th century can be seen. **KOMJATICE** is the village represented by the Late Baroque **manor house** from the mid-18th century, rebuilt in 1872 in style of romantic French castles can be admired. Sacral monuments of the village include the Baroque Roman Catholic **church of Sts. Peter and Paul the Apostles** from the beginning of the 17th century with the Baroque wooden pulpit and epitaph of Count F. Forgách,

the Hungarian primate, from 1615 in its interior. Nature reserve of **Torozlín**, part of the administrative territory of the village situated next to the old arm of the Nitra river protects the swamp and hygrophile plant associations. The rare **swamp tortoise** was also spotted here. The whole local country was coated with forests alternating with swamps and marshy meadows in the past. Farming and other human activities caused gradual disappearance of swamps, and fertile soil is what is left. **PALÁRIKOVO** especially boasts fertile fields and its profane monument, which is the originally Baroque **manor house**, rebuilt in the Classicist style. It stands in the middle of large English park with valuable wood species on an area of 52 hectares.

The territory east of Nové Zámky is also rich in historical landmarks. Attractiveness of the village **SEMEROVO** is the never freezing **mineral spring** with a little lake, which was allegedly already known by the Roman soldiers who erected here a military

Left: Thermal swimming pool in Podhájska
Right: The view of Ostrihom from Štúrovo.
Kováčovské kopce hills

camp. A tablet inserted in the southern walls of the local church also mentioning Marcus Aurelius, the Roman Emperor commemorates the stay of the Romans in the area. One of the most important archaeological localities of Slovakia though, is in the village **BÍŇA**. It stretches on the site of what was a Great Moravian fort on an area 107 hectares with extensive still discernible earthen fortifications. The most valuable finds discovered here include 108 gold coins from the 5th century. The local **Chapel of Twelve Apostles**, originally the Romanesque rotunda with wall paintings from the beginning of the 12th century, adapted in the Baroque style in 1755 and the Roman Catholic **church of the Virgin Mary** built before 1217 are the sacral monuments of the village. The latter mentioned, originally monastic church from the beginning of the 13th century, is now the Late Baroque building with unique Romanesque and Early Gothic elements of European significance.

The centre of the eastern part of the Danubeland is **ŠTÚROVO** (population 13,300). It is situated on the left bank of the Danube, in the southern part of the Danube Hill land. Its rich history is closely connected with that of Esztergom lying on the opposite bank of the Danube in Hungary. The Turks built a fort in 1546 on the site of castle documented in 1304. Parkan became along with Esztergom an important starting point for the Turkish raids and efforts to obtain new territories. The settlement was promoted to a town with market right in 1724. Queen Maria Theresa endowed Parkan

with municipal privileges in 1740. The bridge connecting Parkan with Esztergom was finished in 1895. The bridge was named by Maria Theresa and reconstructed in 2001. Cultural monuments worth seeing include the Late Baroque Roman Catholic **church of St. Emerich** from the end of the 18th century. New side chapels were added to the main nave. Seeing the interior the visitor must notice the valuable paintings on the main and side altars, the Late Baroque pulpit with paintings of four Evangelists on a windowsill from 1760 and a Rococo organ from 1790. The Late Baroque Calvary from 1760 is also interesting.

Štúrovo is the southernmost town of Slovakia, which hosts many visitors from home and from abroad attracted here by its beautiful natural setting. The meander of the Danube starts here and provides a wonderful view of the dominant feature of the surrounding landscape: the Neo-Classical basilica of Esztergom from 1856. The gorge-like reach of the Danube between the Slovak mountain range of Burda and the Hungarian mountain range of Pilis is called the Vyšehradská brána Gate. The nature of Burda is protected by two National Nature Reserves. One of them is the **Kováčovské kopce – juh** (Kováčovské hills-south). Štúrovo also has one of the biggest bathing complexes of Slovakia, **Vadaš**, its area is 24 hectares, and it uses the natural hot spring with a temperature of 38 degrees Celsius. There are four swimming pools, toboggan, playground for children and various sport facilities. The area also has its car camping.

KOMÁRNO AND ITS ENVIRONS
(dial: 035-)

Information

– **TIK** – **Turistická informačná kancelária**, Župná 5, Komárno, ☎/fax 7730063, tik@komarno.sk, **IC** – **Informačné centrum**, Župná 14, Komárno, ☎ 7730295, **EIC** – **Európske informačné centrum**, Nádvorie Európy, Komárno, ☎ 7902018

Museums

– **Múzeum maďarskej kultúry a Podunajska**, Palatínova 13, Komárno, ☎ 7731476, **Podunajské múzeum**, Nám. gen. Klapku 9, Komárno, ☎ 7730055

Galleries

– **Galéria národov**, Okružná ul., Komárno, ☎ 7710004, **Galéria Limes** – **Vojenský kostol**, ul. Františkánov, Komárno, ☎ 7701143, **Galéria Lilla**, Hlavná ul., Chotín, ☎ 7786118, **Výstavná sien Csemadok**, Kossuthovo nám. 3, Komárno, ☎ 7702715

Hotels

– **EURÓPA*****, M. R. Štefánika 1, Komárno, ☎ 7731349, 7731350, **PANORÁMA****, Športová 1, Komárno, ☎ 7713113, **STARÝ ORECH**, Novozámocká 107, Hurbanovo, ☎ 7610051

Restaurants

– **BANDÉRIUM**, Nám. M. R. Štefánika, Komárno, ☎ 7731930, **KLAPKA**, Nám. gen. Klapku, Komárno, ☎ 7730053

Thermal swimming pools

– **Termálne kúpalisko**, Komárno, Vnútorná okružná ul., ☎ 7713014, **Termálne kúpalisko**, Patince, ☎ 7787764

ŽITNÝ OSTROV ISLAND
(dial: 031-)

Information

– **Turistická informačná kancelária**, Hlavná 50, Dunajská Streda, ☎ 5516521

Museums

– **Žitnoostrovné múzeum**, Muzejná ul., Dunajská Streda, ☎ 5522402

Galleries

– **Vermesova vila**, Gy. Szabóa 2, Dunajská Streda, ☎ 5522169, **Galéria súčasných maďarských umelcov**, Trhovisko, Dunajská Streda, ☎ 5529384, **ART-MA**, Bacsákova 10, Dunajská Streda, ☎ 5527871, **AT**

HOME GALLERY, Mliečanská 6, Šamorín, ☎ 5623225

Thermal swimming pools

– **Termálne kúpalisko**, Dunajská Streda, ☎ 5524091, **Termálne kúpalisko**, Veľký Meder, ☎ 5552809, **Termálne kúpalisko**, Topoľníky, ☎ 0905/112148, **Termálne kúpalisko**, Gabčíkovo, ☎ 5594101

Hotels

– **BONBÓN*****, Alžbetínske nám. 1, Dunajská Streda, ☎ 5522319, **BIHARI****, Poštová 1, Dunajská Streda, ☎ 5522347, **KORMORÁN***, Čilistov 1, Šamorín, ☎ 5626033

Restaurants

– **FONTÁNA**, Hlavná 677, Dunajská Streda, ☎ 5529507, **HUBERTUS**, Kračanská cesta, Dunajská Streda, ☎ 5522452

NOVÉ ZÁMKY AND ITS ENVIRONS
(dial: 035-, 036-)

Information

– **VADAŠ**, Hlavná 76, Štúrovo, ☎ 036/7511410, 7511091, www.vadas.sk

Museums

– **Vlastivedné múzeum**, Pribinova 5, Nové Zámky, ☎ 035/6400032

Galleries

– **Galéria umenia**, Baldigariovcov 18, Nové Zámky, ☎ 035/6400224, 6400239

Hotels

– **STARDUST*****, Komárňanská 3, Nové Zámky, ☎ 035/6400427-8, **KORZO****, Rákocziho 12, Nové Zámky, ☎ 035/6400432-3, **ZAHOVAY***, Námestie Slobody 10, Štúrovo, ☎ 036/7511137, **GUEST CENTRE**, Hlavná 78, Štúrovo, ☎ 036/7511023, **MONTANARA*****, Mužla 713, ☎ 036/7583200

Restaurants

– **ROYAL RESTAURANT**, T. G. Masaryka 31, Nové Zámky, ☎ 035/6421770, **BAŠTA**, Radničná 1, Nové Zámky, ☎ 035/6400252, **ZLATÝ LEV**, Gúgska 91, Nové Zámky, ☎ 035/6430109, **ATRIUM**, Hlavná 51, Štúrovo, ☎ 036/7512507

Thermal swimming pools

– **VADAŠ**, Hlavná 76, Štúrovo, ☎ 036/7511410, 7511091, **Termálne kúpalisko**, Podhájska, ☎ 035/6586130, **ŠTRAND**, Bezručova 21, Nové Zámky, ☎ 035/6424251

DOLNÉ POVAŽIE

Trnava

Environs of Trnava

Galanta and its environs

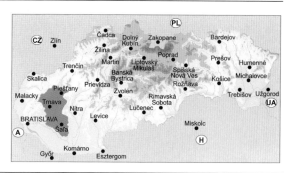

The region of Dolné Považie (Lower part of the Váh Basin) has assumed the name of the Váh river flowing through the territory from the north to south. The Váh separates the Trnavská pahorkatina hill land from the Považský Inovec Mts., enters the Podunajská nížina lowland and flows into the Danube near Komárno. Dolné Považie is one of the earliest settled territory of Slovakia. Its fertile loess Trnavská tabuľa table with slightly undulated surface and great amount of streams flowing down from the Malé Karpaty Mts. has always attracted settlers. The territo-

ry protected by the Malé Karpaty Mts. in the west and protuberance of the Považský Inovec Mts. in the east, favourable climatic properties, quality soil, thermal springs near Piešťany, and the Váh river with its tributaries, represented an environment inviting settlers since primeval times. Continuous settlement of the territory is testified to by numerous archaeological finds.

Dolné Považie seen from the tourist point of view is likewise frequented area. Trnava with numerous sacral monuments and Piešťany with world famous spa are topped off by the charming forests of the Malé Karpaty Mts. In the past an important trade route referred to as the Czech Road, which connected Czechia, Moravia with the Kingdom of Hungary led through this territory. Many castles were built along it in the 13th century. Now they are destinations of trippers. Dolné Považie includes the districts of Trnava, Piešťany, Hlohovec, and Galanta, which are part of the administrative region of Trnava and the district Šaľa administered by the region of Nitra.

Trnava

TRNAVA (population 70,300) also referred to as the Slovak Rome is thanks to its architectural gems and sacral monuments above all, the pearl among Slovak towns. Today's Trnava is the natural centre of Dolné Považie, seat of district and regional administration and the seventh largest town of Slovakia. It was probably

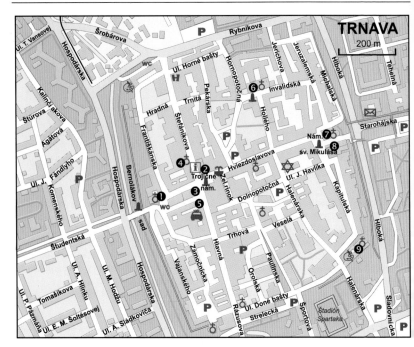

founded around the 9th century on the crossroads of long distant trade routes as a small market settlement and its name Sobota (Saturday) derived of the day on which market was held. Trnava developed at the beginning from several separate settlements, which thrived on trade related with the Czech Road and the influx of German colonists. The first trustworthy written reference to Trnava is from 1211, but the document issued by King Belo IV in 1238 which contained privileges of the **free royal borough** for Trnava as the first Slovak town is much more important in respect.

Trnava flourished in the 16th century when it became the centre of commerce. The town partially assumed the function of other trade centres of the Kingdom of Hungary in time when the Turks occupied them. While other towns of the Kingdom declined Trnava's population was steadily increasing. Crafts and trade were the

main occupations of its inhabitants while only a third of them were involved in farming and vine growing. In 1543 when Turks assaulted and occupied Esztergom, the Archbishop of Esztergom along with the chapter moved to Trnava and the town became the centre of cultural and ecclesiastical life the Kingdom for almost 300 years. The culminating period of the economic development of Trnava was the last third of the 16th century, when its prosperity attracted immigrants from all over the Kingdom of Hungary.

The 17th century in Trnava, like other parts of land, is characterised by war incidents, fire, and repeated plague epidemics. Despite of it the year 1635 became the milestone because it was when Cardinal Peter Pázmány founded **university** in Trnava. The majority of teachers and students of the university, which only taught philosophy and theology were Slovaks. In 1667 also the faculty of law and in 1769 the faculty of medicine were opened. University had its own printing

Right: The town tower

house, archives, library, botanical garden, pharmacy, collection of musical works, as well as observatory. University was eventually moved to Buda in 1777.

At the end of the 18th and beginning of the 19th century Catholic scholars, representatives of the emancipated Slovak nationalist concentrated in Trnava. Anton Bernolák who codified the Slovak literary language based on the West Slovakian dialect was among them. He was active in Slovak literature and along with Juraj Fándly founded the Slovak scholarly association in Trnava in 1792, which spread emancipating ideas of the national movement. The 19th century also brought about economic revival to Trnava. Population increased and agricultural firms were prospering. Horse railway connecting Trnava with Bratislava was finished in 1846, which was later reconstructed into the steam driven railway and in 1868 construction of **sugar refinery** started. In time of national oppression the **Association of St. Adalbert** was founded here in 1870 and replaced the activities of the then closed Matica slovenská giving courage and spirit to Slovaks to survive hard times. In time between the World Wars Trnava was the third biggest town of Slovakia. Its importance as an economic and cultural centre of Western Slovakia with strong agricultural background increased and it maintained this position until now. At present, Trnava is the seat of **the Trnava University** and the University of Sts. Constantine and Methodius, and since 1978 the Slovak metropolitan seat of **archbishop**. The centre of the town has been designated the **Town Monument Reserve** in 1987.

The walk around the historical centre of Trnava can start at **town walls**, lives and destinies of the local people often depended on. Only several towns of central Europe can boast such large section of castle walls as that surviving in the eastern and western parts of the town core. For their high level of preservation the walls are unique and significant monuments of the kind in terms of Europe. For-

tifications are from the 13th to 16th centuries and their repeated reconstruction testify to the fact the inhabitants of Trnava always cared after safety of their town. The town had originally four town gates and small gates for pedestrians in the Middle Ages. Entering the town through the western Bernolák's gate one can stop at the **St. James church ❶** (Franciscan) with **monastery** built in the years 1633-1640 on the site of the original Gothic church with monastery and cemetery. At the turn of the 17th and 18th centuries the church was reconstructed in the Baroque style. Walking down the Divadelná ulica St. arrives one to the central **Trojičné námestie** square, which is the traditional meeting point of people of Trnava and centre of the majority of cultural and social events. The dominant of the square and in fact of the town, is the **town tower ❷**. Majster Jakub built it in 1574 on Gothic foundations and its view terrace provides a perfect view of Trnava and its environs. The western edge of the square

consists of the building of one of the oldest theatres in Slovakia – **Divadlo Jána Palárika ❸** built in 1831. The original Empirical building with capacity of 548 chairs was the sixth theatre building in the framework of the Kingdom of Hungary. Opposite the theatre in the centre of the Trojičné námestie square stands the Baroque **group of statues of the Most Holy Trinity** from 1695, work of sculptor J. K. Klein. It was dismantled during the communist era but renewed in 1993. The set of monuments of the central square includes several Renaissance **burgher houses** skirting its northern side. Short detour from the square to the Štefánikova ulica St. leads to the Jesuit Baroque **church of the Most Holy Trinity ❹** built in 1710-1729 by the Trinity male order. The adjacent building of monastery housed the royal grammar school from 1784 after abolition of the Jesuit order.

Left: Ulica M. Sch.-Trnavského St.
Right: St. Nicholas Minster

Jesuits became owners of the whole complex after 1853. Continuing from the Trojičné námestie square and walking on the pedestrian zone of the Hlavná ulica St. it is possible to contemplate the building of town hall on the right side of the street. Contrary to other Slovak towns, the **town hall ❺** of Trnava stands outside its main square. This originally medieval building is now the complex of three independent architectures (town hall, Baroque corner house, and chapel in the courtyard). It was reconstructed in 1791 in Classicist style when the town hall acquired smart appearance and became the symbol of the town. Burgher houses built in the Renaissance style surround the town hall. Turning into the Trhová ulica St. one can arrive at the **St. Joseph Church** (Pauline order), the hall type of Protestant churches lacking tower. If you continue on the Paulínska ulica St, and turn left to the Dolnopotočná ulica St. you can see another interesting building, that of **synagogue**. It is from the 19th century and adorned by oriental features. A dome originally covered by glass is in the centre of the synagogue. The monument to Jewish victims of the Second World War stands in front of synagogue. The **Church of St. Ann** (Ursuline) standing on the Hviezdoslavova ulica St. not far away from the synagogue is from 1776.

The Early Baroque building of national significance, **university church of St. John the Baptist ❻** is one of the most valuable historical monuments of Trnava. The Italian builder Pietro Spazzo built it in 1637 and it formed part of the university complex. The monumental wooden main altar from 1640 by B. Knilling and V. Knoth dominates in its interior. However, its stucco ornamentation is also intriguing. Additional buildings, including the college, grammar school, university, seminars and refectories accompany the university church.

Among them the refectory for poor students – **Adalbertinum** and **refectory for nobility** built by Empress Marie Theresa are especially well known. Re-

markable structure is the Renaissance building of the former **Oláh's seminar**, today **Museum of Books**. It is part of the university complex and along with the university church was designated **National Cultural Monument**. Another Gothic monument, **St. Nicholas Minster ❼**, parish church stands on the square Námestie Sv. Mikuláša on the site of an older Romanesque church from the 14th century. It was a cathedral church of the Esztergom Archbishop in the years 1543-1820. An octagon chapel was added to the northern side of the church in the years 1739-1741, which now contains the painting of the Blessing Virgin Mary known as the Merciful Virgin Mary of Trnava. Close to the church is the Renaissance building of the **Archbishop's palace ❽** built by the Archbishop Mikuláš Oláh as his residence in 1562. The structure acquired the form of palace with closed courtyard by repeated reconstruction. Part of the square is also the **group of statues of St. Joseph** from

1731, the reminder of one of plague epidemics, which stroke Trnava. The Gothic **church of St. Helena** built in the mid-14th century next to southern town hall is also interesting. The Evangelical **church** and the Baroque **church of Assumption of the Virgin Mary** (Clare female order) with monastery, which was originally a Romanesque building from the 13th century conclude the list of important sacral monuments in Trnava. The **Západoslovenské múzeum** (West-Slovakian Museum) ❾ with archaeological, historical, artistic and ethnographic collections seats in the former monastery.

Fans of arts and music know the event bearing the name of important composer native of Trnava - Trnavská hudobná jar M. Sch. Trnavského (The Trnava Musical Spring of M. Sch. Trnavský). International country festival **Dobrofest Trnava** held here the last week of August every year has won special sympathies of people who love this type of music. Recreation zone of the town is **Kamenný mlyn**

with the **Koliba** hotel and bathing in the **pool** situated in the western part of the town. Every fan of sport in Slovakia knows that Trnava is above all the town of football. The local club Spartak was among the top European football clubs in the 1960's and 1970's. The atmosphere at the **Štadión Antona Malatinského** stadium becomes exciting and hilarious as soon as the hymn of the local club is played.

Environs of Trnava

Only several kilometres north of Trnava is the village **DOLNÁ KRUPÁ**. The Classicist manor house of the Brunswick family from 1793 built on the site of old **manor house** and on the edge of large **English Park** with precious trees is the pride of the village. Ludwig van Beethoven visited the manor house in the years 1800

and 1806 and found inspiration here for his Moonshine Sonata. There was also a little theatre building near the manor hose where L. van Beethoven performed but it does not exist anymore. The manor house is now used as the Home of the Slovak composers. The Rococo **Beethoven's Pavilion** with exhibition of the **Musical Museum** about life and work of L. van Beethoven stands by the manor house. The whole structure is one of the most significant Classicist monuments in Slovakia. North-west of Trnava at the foothills of the Malé Karpaty Mts. are the viticultural villages **DOLNÉ OREŠANY** and **HORNÉ OREŠANY** known for their excellent red wine. Both villages are connected by a busy asphalt road, part of the tourist route **Malokarpatská vínna cesta** (The Wine Route of the Malé Karpaty Mts.). The vine-growing and winemaking traditions and specialities of the local cuisine along with associated fun are attractive articles for wide audience. Further in the north lying village **SMOLENICE** also offers several landmarks. It is above all the **Smolenický zámok** Castle, one of the Romantic buildings in Slovakia. The castle was built on the site of an old sentry castle from the 14th century, which guarded the border mountain pass between Slovakia and the Czech lands. The Pálffy family owned it from 1777 and rebuilt it in the 19th century in the Romantic style. It has a conspicuous bulky tower with view terrace. Steep roofs, little towers, fortified courtyard with the chapel and bastions and the greenery are the components of the romantic image of this castle. Now it is the Home of Workers of the Slovak Academy of Sciences and it serves as the venue of symposia and conferences the

Left: The Driny cave. Smolenický zámok Castle
Right: Dobrá Voda Castle. Dobrovodský kras karst

whole year round. The castle is set amidst landscape park and thick forests. The local karstic landscape also offers the visit to the **Driny** cave. Part of the trip can be a walk along the **Instructive path of Smolenický kras**. The deep narrow of Hlboča and important archaeological locality Molpír on top of the hill opposite the Castle will intrigue fans of nature and history. The ascent to the tallest mountain of the Malé Karpaty Mts., **Záruby** (767 m) with four access paths is also an attractive part of the trip to Smolenice. The recreation centre **Jahodník** with yellow-marked hiking trail leading to the Driny cave is near the village.

North of Smolenice is the village **BUKOVÁ** with **water reservoir** and marked route, which leads southward to the romantic ruins of the **Ostrý Kameň** Castle from the 13th century. The Castle was a royal border fort guarding the Czech road in the past. It is in decay since the 18th century though part of its walls, bastion, and adjacent buildings are still observable. The top of the Castle provides a nice view of the Malé Karpaty Mts. and the Záhorská nížina lowland. Situation of the village **DOBRÁ VODA** in the inner-mountain basin is also picturesque. It is known as the place where the Slovak poet Ján Hollý lived and died. The main hiking route called Štefánikova magistrála passes through the village from the west to the north into the woods of the Brezovské Karpaty Mts. and by the ruins of the **Dobrá Voda** Castle towering above the area of the Dobrovodský kras karst. The Castle was built as a Gothic sentry castle in the 13th century on the site of an older fort. Its decay was topped by fire in 1762 and in the end of

the 18th century only prison existed here. History of the adjacent village **NAHÁČ** is connected with important representative of the Slovak literature, priest and writer Juraj Fándly. The local **museum** is dedicated to this personality. Blue-marked trail leads from the village northward to the ruins of the **Monastery of St. Catherine** from the beginning of the 17th century, which fell in decay at the end of the 18th century when Franciscan order was compelled to abandon it. **DECHTICE** is the village the history of which is connected with pottery and the Haban culture. Its Romanesque Roman Catholic **church** with unique fragments of Romanesque and Early Gothic wall paintings from the 12th and 14th centuries is from 1172.

East of Trnava is **BRESTOVANY**, made famous by writer Jozef Nižňánsky, author of popular historical and adventure novels. The dominant of the village is the Classicist manor house from the first half of the 19th century with a **park** and **monument** to composer Frederic Chopin.

Situated further in south is the village **KRIŽOVANY NAD DUDVÁHOM**, important archaeological locality. The oldest and most valuable monument in this village is the Romanesque **rotunda**, probably from before 1264. **MAJCICHOV** is another historical settlement, which is also known from the history of the Great Moravian Empire. **Great Moravian fort** with important trade and administrative function existed here. The most famous personality in the history of the village was the national revivalist Ján Palárik one of the founders of the Association of St. Adalbert in Trnava who is also buried in Majcichov. The local **commemorative room** contains documents of his life and work. **VODERADY** is the village with interesting architectural monument, the Late Baroque, Neo-Classicist **manor house** built in the mid-18th century, now school.

Left: The manor house in Hlohovec
Right: Napoleon's Bath in Piešťany

The route continues north-eastward from Trnava to **HLOHOVEC** (population 23,700), with attribute of "the town of roses" for its nice parks. History of Hlohovec is connected with existence of the original medieval castle Hlohovec built on site of an old Slav fort, which guarded the ford across the Váh river part of the important road connecting the regions of Považie and Ponitrie. The settlement, which became a serf town with town privileges, was founded below the castle. Hlohovec became the centre of trade in cattle of an extensive estate for long centuries. After the 1948-1949 revolution it also became the administrative centre of a wider region. Today the most important monument of the town is the Baroque manor house, originally the Hlohovec Castle mentioned in 1113. Reconstruction of the Castle into the Baroque **manor house** is connected with the family of Erdödy. It acquired its present appearance at the end of the 18th and 19th centuries. It has a large park with terraces and precious plane trees. Small

Empirical **theatre** building, the architectural gem of the region, stands in the area of the park. The centre of the town is the Námestie sv. Michala square with originally Gothic **parish church of St. Nicholas** from the 15th century. **St. Ann chapel** from 1748 stands by the church. Small **hospital** and **church** both from the 14th century are interesting monuments. In the northern part of the town the Franciscan **church** and **monastery** from 1492 can be seen. Part of the monastery is now used as a **museum** with several exhibitions documenting the nature and social development of the region of Považie. Fans of space and stars can visit the local **planetarium** with observatory.

Close to Hlohovec is an important railway junction of **LEOPOLDOV** (population 4,000). The original settlement was founded on the right bank of the Váh river opposite to the Castle of Hlohovec as ordered by Emperor Leopold I in 1664 whose intention was to build an anti-Turk fort. The fort was meant to replace the one

in Nové Zámky conquered a year before by the Turks. In the mid-19th century it was reconstructed into a prison and since then Leopoldov bears the nickname of a town of bars. The village **Červeník**, important archaeological site, today known for traditional Folk Festival of brass music neighbours with Leopoldov.

The most important centre of tourism and recreation of the northern part of the region of Dolné Považie situated below the protuberances of the Považský Inovec Mts. is the world famous spa of **PIEŠŤANY** (population 30,600). This **spa** is indicated for therapy of locomotion apparatus. Hot mineral springs (67-69 degrees of Celsius) and sulphurous medicinal mud were the basis for development of the spa and construction of its buildings. The self-restoring deposits of the medicinal mud as the product of the joint activity of mineral springs and river sediments of the Váh river is a remarkable phenomenon of this area. The mud and its therapeutic effects on inflammatory disorders is unique in Europe, and

probably in the world. Piešťany is the largest and most successful spa of Slovakia and as such has won the corresponding reputation. The first important owners of the spa was the family of Erdödy. Erdödy's had the first spa house built after the Napoleon's wars in 1822. It still stands and is referred to as the Old or Napoleon's Bath. However, it was the family of Winter who developed the spa to its full prosperity and fame. Hotels (Balnea Palace, Balnea Grand, Balnea Splendid, Balnea Esplanade) in the Art Nouveau style were built at the beginning of the 20th century. Today the spa offers 2,400 beds of medium and higher class. The spa spreads on an area of 40 hectares, partly in the centre of Piešťany and partly on the island formed by the Váh and its arm. The park of the **Kúpeľný ostrov** (the Spa Island) with its fonts and statues is an oasis of tranquillity

and refined taste, contributing to overall pleasant experience of visitors. Parts of the area are open-air thermal pools, network of sanatoriums, health care facilities. In the northern part of the island is the **social centre** of the spa, which provides cultural and artistic programmes of different nature, theatre festivals, and excursions to the local landmarks and monuments. In two halls of the centre international congresses and conferences are held.

History of the town is characterised by two surviving parts of the former Gothic **church** and **monastery** of Johanites, the Classicist **church of St. Steven**, built in the first half of the 19th century and the building of the old **Napoleon's Bath**. The history of balneology in Piešťany is documented by exhibits of the **Balneologické múzeum** situated in the wonderful building of Kursalon. The centre of the town is connected with the Spa Island by two bridges. The interesting **Kolonádový most** bridge serving to pedestrians was built in 1933 to design of an important Slovak architect Emil Belluš. The road bridge called Krajinský most stands further in south.

Piešťany has its famous symbol, **"barlolámač"**, the statue of man breaking the crutch over his knee, which is placed at the entrance of the roofed Kolonádový most bridge. Piešťany also offers a wide spectre of cultural and sport events to its visitors and patients, such as the Musical Summer of Piešťany, Country Boathouse, folk festivals, Grand Prix of Slovakia in water ski, international motorcycle and car races, etc.). The water reservoir of Sĺňava situated close to the town offers additional opportunities for bathing, yachting, surfing or water skiing.

On the left bank of the Váh, in the Považský Inovec Mts. the recreation centre of **Bezovec** attracts with its excellent ski slopes. Čertova pec is another place interesting for its bathing pool and game park. Travelling to these recreation centres one has to pass by the **MORAVANY NAD VÁHOM,** important archaeological site with Palaeolithic settlement of mammoth hunters. The oldest proof of a work of art

Left: The symbol of Piešťany
Right: Kúpeľný dom house in Piešťany. Fortified site in Ducové. The manor house in Vrbové

in Slovakia, the Neolithic **Venus of Mora-vany**, the statue of woman carved of mammoth bone, age of which is estimated at 22,800 years was found here. The local Renaissance **manor house** is also interesting. This originally medieval structure acquired its appearance as we know it now by the 16th century reconstruction. In the English park of the manor house statues by artists from all over the world are exhibited. Further north is the little village of **DUCOVÉ**, with another archaeological locality of **Kostelec** with the Great Moravian **fortified site** from the 9th century. Foundations of a little church, rotunda from around 850 AD and a small cemetery discovered here enhance significance of the place. **VR-BOVÉ** (population 6,180) the little town not far away from Dubové, is the native place of the traveller and adventurer **Móric Be-ňovský** who became

king of Madagascar in the 18th century, and the best Slovak football player **Jozef Adamec**. The most valuable historical monuments of Vrbové are the Gothic **church** from 1887 and the Baroque **curia** from the late 17th century with **commemorative tablet** of Móric Beňovský who was born here in 1746. The local **synagogue** built in the historicizing oriental style is from 1883. The town has its recreation centre on the shore of the **Čerenec** water reservoir.

Galanta and its environs

Although the territory of **GALANTA** (population 16,350) has been settled since the time immemorial the oldest written mention of it is from 1237. As much as three localities were mentioned in the oldest sources under the name *villa*

Galanta, which later joined into one. Acquisition of market right brought about an important change in the life of the settlement. Crafts and trade developed here in the 18th and 19th centuries and the town acquired a prospering and comfortable atmosphere where a gypsy band regularly welcomed the newcomers at the railway station. Galanta has not got plenty cultural or historic monuments but it still has something to offer to its visitors. They are mostly profane monuments including a couple of manor houses. The older Late Renaissance **manor house** with its own fortification was built in the first third of the 17th century. It was rebuilt in the second half of the 18th century in the Baroque and later in the Neo-Gothic styles. The younger and bigger Neo-Gothic **manor house** built on older foundations in 1633 was also rebuilt in the Baroque style in 1736. Another thorough reconstruction

Left: The manor house in Galanta
Right: Vincov les. The water castle of Šintava

followed in 1861. The present appearance of this large Neo-Gothic structure is one of the most eloquent examples of romantic buildings in Slovakia, which imitates the English Gothic style from time of Tudors. The manor house is surrounded by the **park** with 30 species of exotic wood species and bulky specimens of oak tree. The bust of composer **Zoltán Kodály** is placed in the park. Thanks to his composition *Dances of Galanta* the town is also known abroad. The most important cultural events include the festival of ensembles Kodályove dni (Kodály's Days) held in May every year. The Classicist Roman Catholic **church of St. Steven** in the Baroque style is from 1805. Interior of this monumental two-tower building contains the main altar from 1741. The unique building of **burgher house**, now sheltering the parish office, neighbours with the church, while in the building of the former bank from 1915 seats the **museum** now.

In the southern tip of the district of Galanta lies the village **TRSTICE** with typical **clay houses** from the 19th century and an interesting Roman Catholic **church of St. Steven** built in the years 1903-1908 in the Neo-Gothic style. In its interior two Renaissance chalices from 1600 can be seen. **TOMÁŠIKOVO**, the village situated further in north is interesting for its Baroque-Classicist **manor house** from 1760 built on older Renaissance foundations. It was an orphanage in the past, the first state institution of the kind in the Kingdom of Hungary. Today it serves as the health care facility. The contiguous **park** contains 22 species of exotic trees. The visit to the interesting technical monument, reconstructed and operating **water mill** from 1893, and known as Maticz's mill can be attractive for tourists. It is situated 2 kilometres away from the village on the spur of the Malý Dunaj and Suchý potok streams. Today the mill contains exhibition dedicated to **water milling.** Part of the river around the mill is the favourite bathing place of the locals and visitors.

North of Galanta on the right bank of the Váh river lies the town **SEREĎ** (population 17,400) known for production of sect, chocolate products and sweets. The oldest document mentioning the predecessor of this town is from 1313 referring to it as the settlement inhabited by the sentinels of the water castle situated in the administrative territory of the village Šintava. It was mentioned as an independent village in the 15th century when its territory also included the **water castle of Šintava** as the centre of the estate. The water castle of Šintava (remade into the manor house in the following centuries) was built in the 12th century as a fortress supervising the ford over the Váh river. In was reconstructed to the anti-Turkish fort in the 16th century and again in the 18th century, this time to the residence of the Esterházy family. On the site of the old water castle in the first half of the 19th century the Classicist manor house

was built which became the centre of the Sereď estate. In its interior is the exhibition of artefacts found here by archaeologists. The English park of the manor house contains exotic wood species. The town was known as the final station of the **first horse railway** in the territory of Slovakia built in the years 1837-1846 between Bratislava, Trnava and Sereď. It was reconstructed into the steam railway after 1872. The Baroque-Classicist Roman Catholic **church of St. John the Baptist** is from 1781. The **bridge** over the Váh is also an interesting technical monument as it is the only arched bridge in Slovakia made from pre-fabricated pieces standing on pillars, which bear the coats of arms of the Slovak towns.

SLÁDKOVIČOVO (population 6,100) is interesting for its romantic Neo-Gothic **manor house** built on older foun-

dations. It acquired its present appearance by the romanticising adaptation made in 1885. Now it is used as the educational centre. Its sacral monuments include the Baroque Roman Catholic **church of Assumption of the Virgin Mary** from the beginning of the 17th century. Visitors mostly head to the area of thermal swimming pools **Vincov les**. In the village **VEĽKÉ ÚĽANY** not far away from Sládkovičovo is a unique set of buildings of **Calvary** from the second half of the 18th century. The area is situated within a plastered brick fence from 1740 and contains 14 chapels built in 1900. The central chapel of the Virgin Mary of Seven Grievances was built in the years 1750-1756. The **house of folk dwelling** and the **swimming pool** Modrá Perla are also often visited. **JELKA**, the neighbouring village, boasts the Roman Catholic **church of the Nativity of St. John the**

Left: The manor house in Šaľa
Right: Church in Diakovce

Baptist with its Romanesque apse from the 13th century. The church was reconstructed in the 16th century and a new Baroque nave was added to it in the 18th century. Its most valuable part is the baptistery from the 18th century and mechanical organ from 1855. Beautiful nooks of the Malý Dunaj river were ideal for building of **water mills**. There used to be seven of them and one of them survives here with exhibition concerned with historical milling.

ŠAĽA (population 24,550) spreads south-east of Galanta on both banks of the Váh river. It is one of the oldest settlements in Slovakia. It acquired the first privilege in 1526 and became town in the 17th century with right of markets and fairs. Building of railway track between Vienna and Budapest in 1850 helped the town a lot. The oldest building and the dominant of Šaľa is the Renaissance **manor house**. Originally it was the water castle mentioned in old documents in the 15th century. The manor house was built in the second half of the 16th century and adapted in the 18th century in the Baroque style. It also served as a fort in wartime, which was the reason why the water dike was dug around it. The manor house is the true imitation of the palace of Thurzo family, which stands in Bytča. The Classicist Roman Catholic **church of St. Margaret Antioch** was built in the years 1828-1837 on the site of an older church from the 16th century. The dominant of the square in Šaľa is the Neo-Baroque **Trinity pillar** from 1895 with a group of statues of the Holy Trinity on its top. The **house of folk dwelling** in Šaľa from 1831, typical example of folk architecture in the south-western Slovakia, is also worth to see. In the modern part of the town there is also a sport hall, swimming pool and boatyard.

On the main road between Šaľa and Galanta is the village **KRÁĽOVÁ NAD VÁHOM** with typical **houses** made of clay bricks with saddle roofs and originally Baroque Roman Catholic **church of St. Elisabeth** from 1732. The **dam** of Kráľová protects the territory from floods. Its water is also used for irrigation and water transport between Komárno and Sereď. Geothermal springs in the village **DIAKOVCE** in turn provide opportunity for recreation. The local **thermal swimming pools** with water temperature 38 degrees of Celsius are well known to the locals. Sacral architecture of the village is represented by the Roman Catholic monastic **church of the Virgin Mary** from 1228,

which is along with the monastery in Hronský Beňadik the most remarkable and most valuable monastic architecture in Slovakia. Basilica is built of bricks and it is what is referred to as Lombard type of building. It was adapted at the end of the 19th century and the oldest structure built next to the southern side of the church is the **St. Steven chapel**, typical Early Romanesque building which is considered the primeval church for 1103.

TRNAVA
(dial: 033-)

Information
- **TINS - Trnavský informačný servis**, Trojičné námestie 1, Trnava, ☎/fax 5511022, ☎ 5505000, tins@extra.sk, www.trnava.sk

Museums
- **Západoslovenské múzeum**, Múzejné nám. 3, Trnava, ☎ 5512913-4, **Dom hudby**, M. Sch.-Trnavského 5, Trnava, ☎ 5512556, **Oláhov seminár**, Nám. sv. Mikuláša 10, Trnava, ☎ 5514421

Galleries
- **Galéria Jána Koniarka**, Zelený kríček 3, Trnava, ☎ 5511659, **Synagóga - Centrum súčasného umenia**, Halenárska 2, ☎ 5514657

Atractiveness
- **Church of St. John the Baptist**, Trnava, ☎ 5514586

Hotels
- **APOLLO***, Štefánikova 23, Trnava, ☎ 5511937, 5511939, **BARBAKAN***, Štefánikova 11, Trnava, ☎ 5514022, 5511847, **DREAM***, Kapitulská 12, Trnava, ☎ 5924111, **KOLIBA****, Kamenný mlyn 11, Trnava, ☎ 5334459, **INKA***, V. Clementisa 13, Trnava, ☎ 5905111, 5905200, **NUKLEON***, J. Bottu 2, Trnava, ☎ 5521095

Restaurants
- **AKROPOLIS**, Jeruzalemská 2, Trnava, ☎ 5514675, **POD BAŠTAMI**, Hlavná 45, Trnava, ☎ 5514049, **U MICHALA**, Orolská 5, Trnava, ☎ 5514538, **PRACHÁREŇ**, Radlinského 10, Trnava, ☎ 5511522

ENVIRONS OF TRNAVA
(dial: 033-)

Information
- **Informačné stredisko Piešťany**, Nálepkova 2, Piešťany, ☎/fax 7743355, ☎ 16186, incoming@ivco.sk, www.ivco.sk

Atractiveness
- **Smolenický zámok** Castle, Smolenice, ☎ 5586192-3, **Driny** cave, Smolenice, ☎ 5586200, **The manor house**, Dolná Krupá, ☎ 5577271, **Planetarium and observatory**, Sládkovičova 41, Hlohovec, ☎ 7301828, **Ostrý Kameň** Castle, Buková, **Dobrá Voda** Castle, Dobrá Voda, **Fortified site**, Ducové

Museums
- **Balneologické múzeum**, Beethovenova 5, Piešťany, ☎ 7722875, **Vlastivedné múzeum**, Komenského 15, Hlohovec, ☎ 7300337, **MOLPÍR**, Smolenice, ☎ 5586232

Galleries
- **NAMI**, Winterova 24, Piešťany, ☎ 7622592

Hotels
- **BALNEA ESPLANADE PALACE***, Kúpeľný ostrov 60, Piešťany, ☎ 7755211, **CITY***, Winterova 35, Piešťany, ☎ 7725454, **MAGNÓLIA***, Nálepkova 1, Piešťany, ☎ 7626251, **EDEN***, Winterova 60, Piešťany, ☎ 7624691, **SATELIT***, J. Murgaša 3, Piešťany, ☎ 7725833, **THERMIA PALACE***, Kúpeľný ostrov 1, Piešťany, ☎ 7756111, **BALNEA GRAND SPLENDID***, Kúpeľný ostrov, Piešťany, ☎ 7754111, **PATRÍCIA***, Červená veža 4089, Banka, ☎ 7724005

Restaurants
- **CENTRÁL**, Winterova 50, Piešťany, ☎ 7723157, **MAGURA**, Štefánikova 71, Piešťany, ☎ 7627979, **TOSCA**, Moyzesova 3, Piešťany, ☎ 7625468, **QUARTO**, Podzámska 2, Hlohovec, ☎ 7424743

GALANTA AND ITS ENVIRONS
(dial: 031-)

Museums
- **Vlastivedné múzeum**, Hlavná 21, Galanta, ☎ 7805535, **Dudvážske múzeum**, Hlavná 976/8, Galanta, ☎ 7806184

Atractiveness
- **Water mill**, Tomášikovo, **Water mill**, Jelka

Hotels
- **CENTRÁL***, Nám. sv. Trojice 4, Šaľa, ☎ 7704401, **CITY****, Vajanského 10, Galanta, ☎ 7802942, **HUTNÍK****, M. R. Štefánika 1151, Sereď, ☎ 7890435

Restaurants
- **LIMBA**, Hlavná 47, Galanta, ☎ 7808018, **HEPAJ**, Nitrianska 1, Šaľa, ☎ 7708810, **BIELY AGÁT**, Jesenského 6, Šaľa, ☎ 7704782, **TRIO**, Železničná 60, Sereď, ☎ 7892093

Thermal swimming pools
- **Termálne kúpalisko**, Diakovce, ☎ 7852250, **VINCOV LES**, Sládkovičovo, ☎ 7842830

STREDNÉ POVAŽIE

Trenčín

Environs of Trenčín

The country below the Javorina Mts.

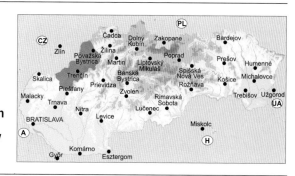

The longest Slovak river, Váh, which represents the central axis of this region, has endowed central Považie with its typical character. The Považské podolie valley stretches along the river Váh that flows through its centre. The mountain ranges of the Biele Karpaty, Malé Karpaty, Strážovské vrchy, Považský Inovec, and Myjavská pahorkatina, ideal for hiking, skiing, cycling and water sport, skirt the area.

The Váh river has always been an important transport route, which coincided with the Amber trade route in the past.

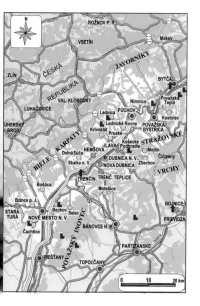

This fact has influenced the development of the region and the individual historical stages have left several valuable traces here in form of historical and cultural monuments. The traces of Roman legions, monuments from time of the Great Moravian Empire, archaeological sites, castles and manor houses, fortifications, sacral buildings and houses of rich burghers are part of the offer for tourists and visitors to the region. Mineral and thermal springs are represented in central Považie and its spas in Trenčianske Teplice and Nimnica are also fairly known and visited. The region consists of five administrative units: districts of Trenčín, Nové Mesto nad Váhom, Ilava, Púchov, and Považská Bystrica. Population of about 350 thousand lives on an area of 2,450 square kilometres, which makes the region one of the most densely populated in Slovakia. The recently delineated border with the Czech Republic and establishment of several border crossings represent another impetus to the development of the area, which became now transit territory.

Trenčín

Thanks to the strategic position in the valley of the Váh river **TRENČÍN** (population 58,000) has always been one of the most important towns in Slovakia. Archaeological finds testify to its settlement as early as Stone Age. When the Romans pushed the frontier of their Empire beyond the Danube and built the system of forts referred to as *Limes Romanus* (Bor-

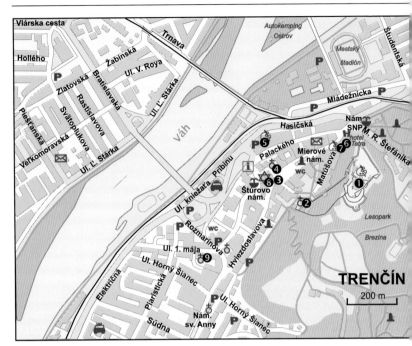

ders of the Roman Empire) they also founded several fortified camps north of the Danube. A unique authentic proof of presence of Roman legions in the territory of Trenčín exists. The Roman military settlement then called **Laugaricio** (today Trenčín) was the northernmost point of the Roman legions of Emperor Marcus Aurelius in the area of central Europe. The **inscription** on the steep face of the castle rock was carved in the memory of the victory over the Quads in 179 AD. The inscription is observable from the window of the view terrace of the restaurant in the local Tatra Hotel.

The prevailing part of the Central Považie became part of the Kingdom of Hungary at the beginning of the 11th century. Trenčín was the centre of the county, as well as of the later established territorial units. The first written mention of the settlement situated below a bulky castle next to the old trade route is from 1111. The

settlement was destroyed during the Tartar raid in 1241 though it fully developed again by the end of the 13th century when the Castle of Trenčín was acquired by the magnate Peter Čák. (1260-1321), who became practically the sovereign ruler of the whole territory of what is today Slovakia. He owned about 30 Slovak castles. Trenčín obtained various privileges and rights in the Middle Ages. King Sigismund promoted it to **free royal borough** in 1412 with similar rights as those, for instance, of Buda. The town suffered from Turkish raids and fighting during the Rebellion of Estates, fire and natural disasters. But it has always revived and was reconstructed into a more interesting and prospering form. In the second half of the 19th century Trenčín became an important commercial and industrial centre of the Central Považie when railway connection with Žilina was finished. In the second half of the 20th century the textile, food processing and machinery developed above all. Historical core of the town revived again after

Rights: The Castle of Trenčín

1989. Trenčín, the seat of the district and province, is now one of the most important towns of Slovakia with varied cultural and social life, and university.

The **Castle of Trenčín ❶** built on top of a steep rock is undoubtedly the dominant of the town and the region. It was the royal castle from the 11th century. The bulky fortifying system is the result of progressive perfection of an important boundary fort, later seat of the county. It had an important role above all in time of Turkish attacks. It was property of several aristocratic families. As the owners changed, the functions of the castle either changed or multiplied. The castle area, which is part of the Trenčianske múzeum consists of a set of palaces. Palaces Ľudovítov, Barborin or Zápoľského were gradually added to its basic structure consisting of the robust

Matúšova veža tower, Mlynská and Jeremiášová towers. However the castle fell in decay after fire in 1790 as its owners, the Illésházy family preferred to move to the more comfortable manor house in Dubník. Extensive reconstruction opened an access to the most valuable parts of it. Today it consists of a set of palaces and its characteristic Matúšova veža tower. Apart from them visitors also like to see the Delová bašta bastion, castle lapidary, and dungeon. Varied exhibitions, medieval games and attractive night sightseeing are organised at the castle throughout the year. Perhaps every child in Slovakia knows the 80-m deep **castle well** and the tale about Omar and Fatima. The legend has that the lord of the Castle, Štefan Zápoľský seized beautiful Turkish princess Fatima. One Turkish prince Omar who loved Fatima arrived with a

load of gold to buy Fatima off. But Zápoľský was only willing to release the girl if Omar dug a well at the courtyard of the Castle. It took three years to Omar to extract water from the hard castle rock but the couple was given freedom afterwards. The Castle, which is along with those of Spiš and Devín one of the largest in Europe, is the National Cultural Monument.

The fortified area called Mariánsky hrad or Mariánska hora spreads between the castle and town centre. It consists of the Roman Catholic parish **church of Nativity of the Virgin Mary ❷**, parsonage and ossuary built into the town walls. The originally Gothic church was built in the 14th century and rebuilt in the Renaissance style after fire in the 16th century. Valuable Gothic two-storied **ossuary** stands opposite the church. The structure

Left: At the Castle of Trenčín.
Water-sprite of Trenčín
Rights: The square in Trenčín

served as armoury in time of Turkish wars. More historic structures are situated in the town monument reserve, the historical centre of the town, particularly on the Mierové námestie square or close to it. It is accessible from the parish church by sheltered staircase built in 1568. **Farské schody**, as the locals call the staircase, was meant as a protected passage to the armoury. Fire severely damaged the staircase in the 18th century and its present appearance is the result of reconstruction made in the years 1978-1980.

Out of two town gates only the Horná brána or the Upper Gate also referred to as Turkish Gate survives. Now it is called **Mestská brána** (Town Gate) ❸. It is a six-storied tower-shaped structure with Gothic arch. There are inscriptions in Latin and the coat of arms of the town on it. The text: *If God does not guard the town, waking of the sentry is vain* has been the motto of Trenčín in the Middle Ages. The dominant of the Mierové námestie square is the **Holy Trinity Pillar** built in the

memory of plague, fire, and flood victims in 1712. The square is formed by prevailingly Renaissance **burgher houses** from the end of the 16th century and the beginning of the 17th century.

The originally Jesuit, later Piarist **monastery** and **church of St. František Xaverský ❹** were built in the Neo Baroque style in the 17th century. It was considerably damaged by the 1708 fire and its reconstruction finished in 1713 was made in the Baroque style. It represents an excellent synthesis of architecture, fine arts, sculpture, and stucco ornamentation. The paintings on its ceiling are among the most remarkable Baroque works in Slovakia. When the Jesuit order was abolished in 1773, the church and monastery passed to the Piarist order, which concentrated on education of youth above all. They widened the building in order to place the grammar school there. Now, apart from grammar school it also contains the **Galéria M. A. Bazovského ❺**. This gallery bears the name of the most original modern painter M. A. Bazovský (1899-1968) known for his expressive pictures.

The originally town palace of the Illésházy family was built in the 17th century. It served as the **County House ❻** from 1760 where the meetings of town councillors were held. It shelters now the **Trenčianske múzeum** (Museum of Trenčín) ❼ with expositions of history, nature, archaeology, ethnology, clothing, and arts related in some way or other to the local population. It is also sometimes used as the venue of concerts for its excellent acoustic characters. Not far away, on the ulica Ľudovíta Štúra St. is the local **synagogue ❽** from the 20th century. This romantic building contains features of Byzantine and Oriental architecture. Also the **Notre Dame Church ❾** is interesting. It is from the 20th century and in the Art Nouveau style. Sacral monuments also include the Classicist Evangelical church from 1794 and the Baroque chapel of St. Ann from 1789. In the urban district of

Trenčín, Záblatie is the Late Renaissance **manor house** from the 17th century, later baroquised with conspicuous cone-shaped tower and English **park** with precious wood species.

Fashion fair held here every year in summer may attract lady visitors while men will perhaps prefer to drop in some of the stylish little wine cellars below the Castle. The **instructive path** running through the landscape park of **Breziny** may be also a refreshing part of the trip to Trenčín. Marked trails to the Strážovské vrchy and the Biele Karpaty Mts. connected with a visit of some of the recreation centres in Krásna, Opatovská, Kubrická or Drietomská dolina valleys are somewhat longer hiking trips. **Zamarovské jamy** is the protected site situated in the administrative territory of Trenčín. It consists of small water reservoirs inhabited by waterfowl. The new initiative in

Left: Monastery in Skalka nad Váhom
Rights: Vršatské bralá cliffs

tourism bearing the name **Matúšovo kráľovstvo** (the Matthias' Kingdom) is an imaginary kingdom including about 1,100 towns and villages where an effort is made to revive Slovak history and to offer the opportunity to present it to visitors who can even acquire the passport of the Kingdom and travel around more than 50 castles, former estates of the magnate Matúš Čák Trenčiansky.

Environs of Trenčín

Immediately beyond Trenčín in the north, at the tapered part of the valley of the Váh river on its right bank next to the **SKALKA NAD VÁHOM** are the ruins of the old Benedictine Abbey. It was built in the 13th century on the site where monk Benedict from the Zobor Abbey lived. He was allegedly killed by robbers and thrown into the river. The legend has that his intact body was discovered a year after in the place indicated to people by an eagle. It was deposited in the Cathedral of

Nitra. In 1083 Benedict and his teacher Svorad were proclaimed saints in Rome. When the monastery was besieged by the imperial troops in the 16th century, it was fortified and a sentry tower was added to it. Today Skalka and the environs of the Baroque **church** from the 18th century are the **pilgrim locality.**

The village is also often used as the starting point for the trips to the **Súčanská dolina** valley, the northernmost locality of the hamlets in the Biele Karpaty Mts. The cliff Krasín with the remains of medieval castle towers above the valley. What was originally a single village separated into two, Dolná and Horná Súča in the 18th century. Its people were mostly living off farming, sheep keeping and production of linen. Slopes of the valley oriented to sun-bathed south-east were ideal for growing fruit, which was processed to distillates in Trenčín. **DOLNÁ SÚČA** has an originally Renaissance Roman Catholic **church** from the 16th century restored after fire in the Baroque style in the 18th century. The villagers still wear their typical folk costumes.

The tourist route continues on the right bank up the stream of the Váh to industrial town of **NEMŠOVÁ** (population 5,000) with tradition in glass production. Its monuments include the Late Baroque **church** from the first half of the 19th century and the Neo-Romanesque hunting **manor house** in locality Antonstal in the valley of the Ľuborča brook. Further in north is **PRUSKÉ** with the Renaissance **manor house** from the end of the 16th century, which was later adapted in the Baroque and Classicist styles. The manor house standing in the middle of English park is now used as a school. Sacral monuments of Pruské include the Franciscan **church** and **monastery** from the 17th century and the Baroque church of Sts. Peter and Paul from the 18th century. The landmark of the village is the group of 700-year old yew trees growing in the garden of the local parsonage. Trunks of some of them are more than 3.5 m in diameter. Not far from the village **KRIVOKLÁT** is

the protected natural phenomenon **Krivoklátska tiesňava** gorge, an impressing geomorphological form with occurrence of rare plants and animals. If you continue from Pruské north-westward, an imposing view of the **Vršatské bralá** cliffs opens in front of you. Remains of the royal sentry Castle **Vršatec** are on top of the rocks. The original Gothic castle from the 13th century at the height of 805 m was destroyed in time of Rákoczi's rebellion in 1706. The ruins provide an excellent view of the whole of central Považie. North-east of the Vršatecké bradlá cliffs is another rock massif **Červený kameň**, on top of which a primeval settlement was discovered.

On the other, left bank of the Váh is the mountain range of **Strážovské vrchy**, designated protected landscape area in 1989. It consists of several mountain belts and alternation of forests, meadows and rocks with views of nice valleys is typical for it. On one of its high plains with occurrence of numerous karstic forms there

is the mountain village **MOJTÍN** known for its excellent ski slopes. Another village situated in the middle of Strážovské vrchy Mts. is **ZLIECHOV** with typical folk architecture, log houses and brick houses with gabbles and saddle roofs. Environs of this village also offer numerous hiking opportunities including the ascent to the **Strážov Mt.** (1.213 m) the tallest mountain of the Strážovské vrchy Mts. In the west, above **KOŠECKÉ PODHRADIE** there are the ruins of the Košecký hrad Castle which was pulled down by the Imperial troops at the beginning of the 18th century. The route continues westward to the district town **ILAVA** (population 5,400). Its symbol is the originally Gothic castle rebuilt in the 16th century in an anti-Turk fort. The fort reconstructed in a monastery at the end of the 17th century is prison since the mid-19th century. Part of

the castle area is the Roman Catholic Baroque **church** from the 18th century with valuable interior and a crypt. In the local part Klobušice is the Classicist manor house with a park from 1840. Today it houses the **Museum of Commerce**, a restaurant and roadhouse.

In the middle of the Ilavská kotlina basin is the industrial town **DUBNICA NAD VÁHOM** (population 26,000). Its history is connected with the Renaissance **manor house** from the 16th century, adapted in the Baroque style at the beginning of the 18th century. It was the centre of the extensive Illésházy estate. Visitors like to stop at the **church of St. James** from the mid-18th century or the Baroque **manor house** from the 18th century with interesting stained glass windows from 1951 made to design of V. Hložník. Construction of the Škoda factory in 1928, now ZŤS which expanded especially after the Second World War provided employment to many locals. Simultaneously the town **NOVÁ DUBNICA** (population 12,500), in fact residential area for the employees of the giant industrial plant was founded. However, the formerly prospering region is now passing difficult times because of conversion of arm industry.

Lovers of walks in parks and landscape of spas will undoubtedly visit the spa of **TRENČIANSKE TEPLICE** (population 4,400) with wonderful setting in the Strážovské vrchy Mts. and the valley of the Teplička river. It is its situation amidst wonderful natural setting and its hot mineral springs, which won it the attribute of the pearl of the Carpathians. The spa was founded by the Paladin Štefan Zápoľský in the 16th century. It further developed under the administration of the Illésházy noble fam-

Left: Bridge of Glory in Trenčianske Teplice.
Košecký hrad Castle
Rights: Spa in Trenčianske Teplice

ily. The local medicinal water containing sulphur and gypsum are indicated for therapy of locomotion apparatus and nervous system. The spa offers several interesting landmarks and regular cultural events to its guests and visitors. One of them is the bath **Hamman** in the spa building Sina, which is decorated in oriental style of Turkish bath from the end of the 19th century. The English **park** of the area with a little swan lake and romantic nooks is well maintained and ideal for relaxation. The **church** from the beginning of the 20th century has a wooden carve ceiling. The traditional summer music festival, Biennial or Grand Prix of Slovakia in chorus singing, the area of thermal outdoor pool "Zelená žaba" and tennis courts, lighted ski slope, fishing, minigolf, horse riding, and cycling routes are included in the offer of the spa for all age groups of visitors. The spa also organises its own film festival **Art Film**, as a matter of fact, the most important in Slovakia which has won international recognition as testified to by the Bridge of Glory with tablets signed by movie stars like Gina Lolobrigida, Franco Nero and others. **MOTEŠICE** is the village very near to Trenčianske Teplice with famous stud which offers horse riding in the wonderful environs of the spa. Below the slopes of the Strážovské vrchy Mts. there is also an important archaeological site **SELEC** where examples of the local folk architecture still survive.

The dominant of the northern part of central Považie is the town **POVAŽSKÁ BYSTRICA** (population 43,000) with its famous **motorcycle racing track** near Sverepec, the venue of international races. The first written reference to the town is from 1316 and the destiny of the settlement was always closely connected with that of the **Považský hrad** Castle, picturesque silhouette of the region, towering on the steep mountain on the right bank of the Váh river. It was built in the second half of the 13th century and its mission was to protect the trade route passing by. It was rebuilt after fire in 1543

and after it was destroyed by Imperial army in 1698 it fell in decay. However, the ascent to its ruins can be a nice experience as the remains of its tower open a wonderful view of the landscape surrounding it. There are two small manor houses below the castle wanting restoration. In **Orlové**, which is part of the town there is the four-wing **manor house** with arcades. It was originally the Renaissance building from the 17th century and rebuilt in the 18th century in the Baroque style. Now it houses the museum of homeland studies specialised in archaeology, ethnography and nature history. It is frequently visited by families with children for its small zoo. The sacral dominant of the town is the originally Gothic church from the 14th century, later adapted in the Renaissance and Baroque styles. Považská Bystrica today is a modern town linked to the machinery industry.

One of the most beautiful valley in the region is next to the village **POVAŽSKÁ TEPLÁ** north of Považská Bystrica. Part of this valley is the **Manínska tiesňava** narrow, the narrowest canyon in Slovakia. It is attractive for its wild appearance and rare flora and fauna. Ascending up the stream of the brook it is possible to follow the **instructive path,** which leads to another natural landmark, which is the **Kostolecká tiesňava** narrow with the tallest rock hangover in Slovakia and impressive debris cone. Beyond the cone above the village **KOSTOLEC** is the cliff Bosmany which offers a nice open view of the environs. At the end of the valley is the hiking path, which runs over the flat saddle to the **Súľovské skaly** rocks, the largest rock town in Slovakia.

The twin town of Považská Bystrica is **PÚCHOV** (population 18,000) situated in the picturesque basin of the middle reach of the Váh. Although Púchov was first mentioned in historical documents as late as 1243, archaeological finds in its

Left: Horses in Motešice
Rights: The Manínska tiesňava narrow

immediate environs prove settlement from the Palaeolithic era. In time of the La Téne and Roman eras an important settlement existed here as well. Thanks to the favourable situation, Púchov soon became the natural commercial centre of the north of central Považie. Traditional crafts such as wool-cloth making, pottery and printing developed here. Today Púchov thrives on rubber and textile industries, it is also an important railway junction and seat of the Faculty of Industrial Technologies of the Trenčín University. Its profane monuments include the **County House** and the Baroque-Classicist manor house, originally the building of salt store from the 18th century, while sacral monuments are represented by two churches. Fans of history will certainly drop in the **Museum of the Púchov Culture**. The town organises the review of folk traditions Folklórny Púchov in June and the Fair of Púchov in September every year.

Považská Bystrica and Púchov are ideal starting points for trips to the southern part of the **Javorníky Mts.** This boundary mountain range between the north-western Slovakia and Moravia and its captivating romantic valleys were modelled by the right tributaries of the Váh on the Flysch rock basement. Wallachian colonisation in the 16th and 17th centuries endowed the region with special character. Deep forests were gradually transformed into terraced fields and pastures spreading to the highest positions above sea level. In the villages beautiful examples of the **folk log architecture** are still observable. Marked hiking trails pass through some nooks with attractive natural setting and perfect views. The whole area is rich in mushrooms and diverse forest fruits. The round ridges of the mountains offer interesting cycling and hiking routes in summer, while in winter the terrain is frequented by cross-country skiers. The most popular cross-country ski track is the one running along the main ridge of the Javorníky Mts. Winter is rich in snow and the ski centres of Lazy

pod Makytou, - Čertov, Papradno - Podjavorník, Maríková - Kátlina and Ráztoky are invaded by ski fans.

The stretch of Považské podolie valley between the towns of Považská Bystrica and Púchov tapers into the deep meandering valley flooded by the Nosice water reservoir also called Priehrada mládeže (The Dam of Youth). The spa **NIMNICA** is situated on its northern shore. During its construction in 1952 a spring was discovered there which gave origin to the local spa. It is indicated for diseases of respiratory and digestive systems. On the shore of the dam there is port of steamboats. Nimnica is a good salient point for trips to the Javorníky Mts. West of Púchov lies the village **LEDNICA** with the picturesque **Lednické bradlo** rock and castle **ruins** on its top, perhaps the most inaccessible one among the castles in Slovakia. The castle was built at the end of the 13th century and it was the seat of the Lednice estate. At the beginning of the 18th century Imperial troops destroyed it. Only the remains

of walls survive. The legend says that the spirit of beautiful lady of the castle Katarína walks on top of them in the night. The lord of the castle kidnapped her on the day of her wedding but Katarína wearing the white gown preferred to jump down from the castle walls. The wooden cross below the castle commemorates the place of her unfortunate death. South-west of Lednice is **LEDNICKÉ ROVNE**, village with glass-making traditions. The family of Schreiber founded the glass-producing manufacture here, one of the most advanced in central Europe, in 1892. The local **Slovenské sklárske múzeum** (Slovak Museum of Glass) is worth visiting. It seats in the reconstructed residence of the former owner of factory, Renaissance **manor house**. Collections of the Museum document the development of this craft in Slovakia from the oldest times until present.

Left: Lednica Castle
Rights: Tematín Castle. Beckovský hrad Castle

The country below the Javorina Mts.

Sightseeing of natural landmarks of the southern part of the region of central Považie starts in **NOVÉ MESTO NAD VÁHOM** (population 21,000). The core of the old settlement of what is today the town situated on the elevated terrace above the Váh river spreads around the local parish church. The centre of the town consists of rectangular square with a network of side lanes surrounded by town walls with gates. The dominant of the town is the Romanesque parish **church** from the 13th century rebuilt in the Baroque style with lavish decoration in the 17th century. The church is skirted by fortifications with gates. The Renaissance and Baroque burgher houses from the 16th and 17th centuries, the Lady 's Pillar from 1696 in the middle of the square and exhibitions of the **Podjavorinské**

múzeum (Museum of "the country below the Javorina Mts.") testify to the history of this former yeoman town. Visitors can also have a look at the Jewish cemetery with original tombstones from the 16th to 19th centuries. The **Zelená voda** recreation resort with excellent options of bathing, water sport and accommodation facility is situated east of the town.

The region of central Považie is the territory where sentry castles were systematically built from the 13th century. The system was meant to guard the western borders of the country. One of such castles is that of **Tematín**. Its romantic ruins standing on top of the side ridge of the Považský Inovec Mts. is visible from a large distance was destroyed by Imperial troops in 1710 and fell in decay afterward. Another castle within the system is the better known **Beckovský hrad** Castle situated on steep 50 m tall rock in the village **BECKOV**. The dominance of the rock and impression of invincibility it gave invited people to make use of these assets. The castle first mentioned in 1200 was originally owned by the king and later, at the end of the 13th century it fell in hands of Matúš Čák. Its owners alternated - at the end of the 14th century the family of Stibor of Stiborice bought it and the next owners, the Bánffy's who adapted the Gothic castle to the Renaissance residence, improved its fortifications preventing the Turks from conquering it at the end of the 16th century. When Bánffy's died out, the castle was owned by several noble families. It fell in decay after fire in 1759. The history of the castle is the subject of different legends. One of them narrates the origin of the name of castle derived from that of jester Becko for whom the Duke Stibor

had the castle built. Another legend has that the lord of the castle had his servant thrown down from the rock because he protected his child from the lord's favourite dog. Before his death, the servant pronounced a curse saying that they would meet in a year and day's time with his lord, and indeed precisely after that time the lord was bitten by a snake and fell down to the same abyss. The well-conserved ruins of the castle, the National Cultural Monument are frequently visited by tourists, above all in July when the castle festival takes place. The large village situated below the castle received town privileges in the 14th century. Several Late Renaissance **curias** (the former Ambro curia now shelters the exhibition of the local history) and sacral monuments are witnesses to famous history of Beckov. The Roman Catholic parish **church of St. Stephen the King** from 1424 and the Franciscan church and monastery from the end of the 17th century are the most interesting ones. The lime tree grove with specimens older than 150 years is the attraction of the centre of the village. Fans of nature and walks may appreciate three **instructive paths** running through the steppe and forest-steppe growths around the Beckov castle rock.

The territory west of Nové Mesto is referred to as **Podjavorinský kraj** or "the country below the Javorina Mts." Its dominant, of course, is the **Veľká Javorina Mt.** (970 m), popular destination of trippers. For its situation, the mountain is the venue of traditional meeting of Czechs and Slovaks. On its grassy top the **Holubyho chata** cottage stands. It is surrounded by excellent ski terrain with ski lifts. The pic-

turesque landscape between the regions of Považie and Záhorie, in the Czech-Slovak boundary area is characterised by small dispersed hamlets. One of the larger settlements is **BZINCE POD JAVORINOU**, with the **commemorative room** of the local native lady author Ľudmila Podjavorinská who made the region famous.

Further in south above the village of **ČACHTICE** the ruins of mysterious **Čachtický hrad** Castle stand. This also was one of the system of boundary royal castles defending the western border of the Kingdom of Hungary. It was built in the first half of the 13th century and widened in the 15th century. Ill-famed **Elizabeth Báthory** lived here at the turn of the 16th and 17th centuries. For her sadist habits she was called "the bloody countess" and allegedly killed 600 young girls in order to bath in their blood. The gadget used by the countess to obtain blood was a kind of iron maiden with knives incorporated in its lid. Once the unfortunate victim was laid in and the lid closed the knives pierced her chest and the blood was collected in the prepared tub. The countess was condemned to lifelong prison in 1611 by the Paladin Thurzo in Bytča and died in 1614. The story of the bloody countess became subject of numerous literary or theatre works. The castle was burnt during the Rebellion of Estates by the soldiers of Francis II Rákoczi and fell in decay. Today its pic-

turesque ruins offer a nice panoramic view. The Renaissance **manor house** of Čachtice from the end of the 17th century is the seat of exhibition of the Museum of Trenčín oriented to history and ethnography of the area. Čachtický kras karst is the area with numerous karstic phenomena, sinkholes and springs and the **cave** not accessible to public (protected natural phenomenon, fissure cave that originated by chemical action of water).

STARÁ TURÁ (population 10,000) and adjacent hamlets lies in the valley below the slopes of the Biele Karpaty Mts. Existence of this town was referred to for the first time in 1392. Stará Turá was the centre of the Slovak national revival in the regions and several important figures and writers live here. Sisters Mária and Kristína Royová (their **commemorative room** is in the building of the Evangelical parsonage), playwright Jozef Hollý, Augustín Roy are some examples. One can see the Roman Catholic Baroque church from 1748 and the Evangelical **church** in the Classicist style with Baroque details from 1784 in the town. The old **"Hussite tower**" and **the former communal house pillory,** and **Calvary** may be also interesting. The recreation area of **Dubník** with water reservoir, accommodation and catering facilities in the immediate vicinity of the town offer relaxation and bathing.

On the way up the Považie region one should not miss some of several wonderful valleys of the **Biele Karpaty Mts**. Examples of **folk architecture** (clay houses, log haylofts and water mills) survive in the valleys of Klanečnica or Bošáčka. The tri-

Left: Veľká Javorina Mt. Dubník
Rights: Čachtický hrad Castle

to Veľký Lopeník with captivating views of the environs or to **Haluzická súteska** (40 m deep canyon with the ruins of the Romanesque church above it) can be a pleasant hiking experience. The centre of the Bošácka dolina valley is the large village **BOŠÁCA**, an important ethnographic locality where the locals wear nice folk costumes. There are also well conserved **clay houses** with straw or shingle roofs from the 19th century and the Baroque **church** adapted in the Classicist style from the 18th century. In the part called

Zemianske Podhradie is the Renaissance **manor house** with a park from the 17th century. It was inhabited by Adela Ostrolúcka, the famous lover of the most important Slovak personality involved in national revival, Ľudovít Štúr. J. Ľ. Holuby, botanist and ethnography and V. Rizner, the founder of the Slovak bibliography also lived here and their **commemorative room** contains interesting documents to the fact. Some Slovaks rather know Bošáca from the label on the popular Slovak prune distillate *slivovica*, produced here.

TRENČÍN
(dial: 032-)

Information
- **Kultúrno-informačné centrum mesta Trenčín**, Štúrovo nám. 10, Trenčín, ☎/ fax 7433505, ☎ 16186, kic@trencin.sk, www.trencin.sk

Museums
- **Trenčianske múzeum**, Mierové nám. 46, Trenčín, ☎ 7434431, **Vojenské múzeum**, Martina Rázusa 7, Trenčín, ☎ 7435674

Galleries
- **Galéria M. A. Bazovského**, Palackého 27, Trenčín, ☎ 7436858

Atractiveness
- **The Castle of Trenčín**, Matúšova 19, Trenčín, ☎ 7435657

Hotels
- **TATRA*****, M. R. Štefánika 2, Trenčín, ☎ 6506111, 6506103, **BREZINA**, Lesopark Brezina, Trenčín, ☎ 6528171

Restaurants
- **LÁNIUS**, Mierové nám. 20, Trenčín, ☎ 7441978, **MARITIM**, Mládežnicka 4, Trenčín, ☎ 7443573, **ČIERNY KORZÁR**, J. Braneckého 12, Trenčín, ☎ 6529511, **DIAMANT**, Nám. sv. Anny 34, Trenčín, ☎ 6527437

ENVIRONS OF TRENČÍN
(dial: 032-, 042-)

Information
- **Turistická informačná kancelária**, Trenčianske Teplice, ☎ 032/6553066, **Turistická informačná kancelária**, Štúrova 5/9, Považská Bystrica, ☎ 042/16186, 4326222, fax 042/4326545, tik@px.psg.sk, www.povazska-bystrica.sk

Museums
- **Vlastivedné múzeum**, Orlové – kaštieľ, Považská Bystrica, ☎ 042/4323724, **Slovenské sklárske múzeum**, Lednické Rovne, ☎ 042/4601130, **Múzeum obchodu**, Klobušice, ☎ 042/4465638, **Mestské múzeum**, Ilava, ☎ 042/4465198, **Archeologické múzeum púchovskej kultúry**, Nábr. Slobody 522, Púchov, ☎ 042/4635538

Atractiveness
- Castle **Vršatec**, Vršatské Podhradie, **Považský hrad** Castle, Považská Bystrica, **Ma-**

nínska tiesňava narrow, Považská Teplá, **Kostolecká tiesňava** narrow, Kostolec

Hotels
- **VILA ANNA*****, 17. novembra 4, Trenčianske Teplice, ☎ 032/6553761, **FLÓRA****, 17. novembra 14, Trenčianske Teplice, ☎ 032/6552981-4, **GARNI VENEZIA****, 17. novembra 25, Trenčianske Teplice, ☎ 032/6552901, **SLOVAKIA****, T. G. Masaryka 3, Trenčianske Teplice, ☎ 032/6553501, **MARGIT****, T. G. Masaryka 2, Trenčianske Teplice, ☎ 032/6551028, **WILI*****, 1. mája 899, Púchov, ☎ 042/4631452, **MANÍN****, Štúrova 5/9, Považská Bystrica, ☎ 042/4326989

Restaurants
- **Q-CLUB**, Centrum 13/17, Považská Bystrica, ☎ 042/4327805, **LEGUÁN**, Športovcov 343, Považská Bystrica, ☎ 042/4325854, **ALFA**, Nová 134, Považská Bystrica, ☎ 042/4260260, **TRENČAN**, Sládkovičova 638, Považská Bystrica, ☎ 042/4321537

THE COUNTRY BELOW JAVORINA
(dial: 032-)

Information
- **INFOTUR – Informačná kancelária mesta Stará Turá**, Husitská cesta 253/3, Stará Turá, ☎/fax 7763893, e-mail: infotur@nm.psg.sk, www.staratura.sk

Museums
- **Podjavorinské múzeum**, Nám. Slobody 4, Nové Mesto n/V, ☎ 7712339

Atractiveness
- **Beckovský hrad** Castle, Beckov, **Čachtický hrad** Castle, Čachtice

Hotels
- **DIANA*****, Hviezdoslavova 19, Nové Mesto n/V, ☎ 7712215, **PERLA****, Zelená voda, Nové Mesto n/V, ☎ 7712487, **SANUS****, Dubník, Stará Turá, ☎ 7763528, **LIPA***, Husitská 5, Stará Turá, ☎ 032/7763891-2

Restaurants
- **IVANA**, Hviezdoslavova 19, Nové Mesto n/V, ☎ 7712215, **KRIŽAN**, Športová 23, Nové Mesto n/V, ☎ 7712920, **ELÁN**, Námestie Slobody 10, Nové Mesto n/V, ☎ 7713621, **SÁLOON RESTAURANT**, Kukučínova 103, Nové Mesto n/V, ☎ 7712570, **SALAMANDER**, SNP 41, Stará Turá, ☎ 7763024

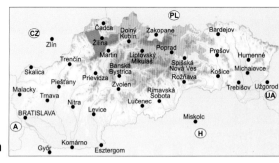

ŽILINA AND ITS ENVIRONS

Žilina

Environs of Žilina

Rajecká kotlina basin

The unique natural setting and abundant historic and cultural monuments make the region of Žilina very attractive. Mountains rich in forests cover most of its surface. The most valuable natural assets are protected in the National Park of Malá Fatra and the Protected Areas of Kysuce (part Javorníky) and the Strážovské vrchy Mts. Assets created by man are also valuable. The region boasts an unusual number of castles and buildings such as manor houses and curias from different historical periods, which can be found almost in every village. The most valuable castles are those of Budatín and Bytča. The oldest historic architectural monuments are the ruins of numerous medieval castles usually situated on top of hills. The Castles of Strečno, Starý hrad, Lietava, Hričovský or Súľovský inspire admiration of skills of old

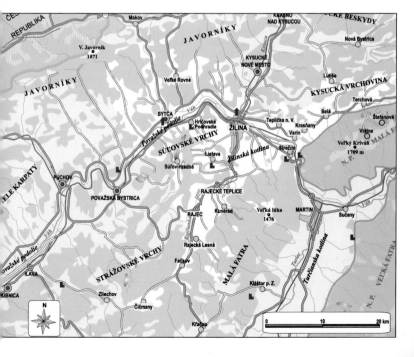

builders. The reconstructed squares of Žilina or Rajec are the town monument reserves and the compact old core of Žilina is also worth admiration.

Folk architecture can be seen in several villages of the region, which was famous for its craftsmen in the past mostly involved in peddling and the tinker's trade. The trade eventually developed into an art and its products can be admired in the unique museum dedicated to the subject. The wonderful natural setting of Rajecké Teplice provides not only therapeutic treatment to visitors of the local, spa but also relaxation and hiking in its environs. This region situated in the north-west of the Slovak Republic consists of two administrative districts, Žilina and Bytča. Population of about 187 thousand lives on an area of 1,097 square kilometres and it is one of the most densely populated parts of the country.

Left: Mariánske námestie square
Right: The Most Holy Trinity church

Žilina

ŽILINA (population 85,400) is no only the biggest town but also the me tropolis of the north-west of Slovakia. Ar chaeological finds confirm the settlemen of the Žilinská kotlina basin since the Ne olithic period. The territory of the contem porary town was first mentioned in th document of Tomáš, the Count of Nitr from about 1208 as *Terra de Selinan*. Th centre of this old Slav settlement lied i the vicinity of the still surviving church c St. Stephen the King in local part calle Závodie. Fighting between the feuda rulers by the end of the 13th century de stroyed the rest of the old core of th town. German colonists repopulated th area at the beginning of the 14th centur and built the new settlement on the ele vated terrace protected against the floo of the Váh river. The settlement wa planned beforehand and its ground pla in form of a regular chess board is th proof of it. Its centre was the main squar now the Mariánske námestie square). The first reference to Žilina as town is from 1312 though it probably possessed town privileges earlier. King Charles Robert promoted it to the royal borough in 1321. The town became the centre of trade and crafts and seat of administration for many villages around it. Many burghers of Žilina became founders of villages in the regions of Považie, Turiec and Kysuce. The documents from the 14th and 15th centuries contain numerous especially valuable and interesting references to Žilina. One of such documents, highly appreciated by Slovaks, is the **Privilegium pro Slavis** issued by King Louis I the Great in 1381. The King issued the document in an effort to solve the argument between the Slovaks and Germans living in Žilina. The cause was that the Germans did not admit Slovaks in the municipal council. Formerly, when Germans moved here from Tešín (Moravia) they shared the rule in the town with Slovaks but later when they got rich and powerful they tried to push the Slovaks out of the town council. Pursuing the King's decision both ethnicities were bound to have their representations in the council with their mayors alternating every year. This is how Žilina became the first town in Slovakia and the eastern part of central Europe where the trustworthy document about equality of rights of the native Slovak population and the richer German colonists was preserved. **Žilinská mestská kniha** (Town book of Žilina) is another valuable linguistic and historical document of European importance. It was started in 1378 when the series of municipal customs was laid down and listed in it. The first entry in Slovak language in this book is from 1451 and the whole book was translated into the Slovakized Czech several years later. This unique book contains the oldest written entry in our language in the territory of Slovakia.

At the end of the 15th and the beginning of the 16th century the estate of Strečno acquired the town and consequently it changed into the yeoman town.

Nevertheless, Žilina maintained its privileges of the free borough. In the following centuries Žilina became the centre of trade, crafts and education. Wool-cloth production made Žilina known in the whole central Europe in the 16th and 17th centuries. Several trade routes of international importance met next to the town. The road connecting Transylvania with Vienna then called *Via cursoris regii* or the Road of the Royal Courier passed through Žilina. The town suffered from repeated wars, fires, flood and epidemics at the end of the 18th and the beginning of the 19th century and economic decay followed. Žilina shrank into a small town in terms of population number, even smaller than Rajec or Bytča and stayed so for a long time. Revival came after construction of railway tracks between Košice - Bohumín, Žilina - Bratislava, and Žilina - Rajec at the end of the 19th century. The town became an important railway junction, which was the impetus for its development and growth of population. The plant

producing wool cloth used for military uniforms and blankets referred to as Uhorská továreň, then the largest in the Kingdom of Hungary brought again prosperity to Žilina. Development of the town continued after 1918 and above all after the Second World War when industry was restored. Due to continuous growth of population, extensive residential estates were built which accommodated thousands of immigrants from the villages. Adding of 15 adjacent villages to the territory of Žilina also increased its population and size. In the 1990's the historic core of the town was restored and Žilina became one of the best-reconstructed towns of Slovakia. Today it is the seat of many industries including chemical, paper, textile and food processing. Žilina also possesses its university and a number of secondary schools.

One of our best poets referred to Žilina as the pearl on the Váh. Its history is

Left: Burgher houses

unique as testified to by many of its historical and artistic monuments. The **Mariánske námestie** square is the core of the town monument reserve. Analogies of this square are to be seen in many towns of Slovakia, but that of Žilina is the only one complete with arcades surviving in contiguous lanes. It is square-shaped with typical Renaissance burgher houses from the 16th to 18th centuries with protruding second floor and arcades below them. Foundations of the square were laid down in the 14th century. The Baroque **Lady's Pillar** with the Immaculate Conception built at the end of the re-Catholicizing period in 1738 stands in the middle of the square. One of the dominants of the town is the Baroque **church of St. Paul the Apostle** ❶ with two towers and the Jesuit monastery from the mid-18th century on the western side of the square. The **town hall** ❷ in the corner of the square was repeatedly adapted. Its present appearance is from 1890. One of its attractive details is the chime on its front side. The current appearance of the building is the result of several adaptations in the Renaissance and Baroque styles. Although the appearance of the town has been changing in the course of centuries, it has preserved its original style and charming atmosphere. Its numerous cafe houses offer relaxation to the natives and visitors. Many of architectural monuments can be also seen in the closest vicinity of the Mariánske námestie square. The Roman Catholic parish **church of the Most Holy Trinity** ❸ was built around 1400 on the site of the disappeared Castle of Žilina. This three-nave church was originally built in the Gothic style and then rebuilt in the Renaissance style. The most valuable detail of the church is represented by its altar paintings. The **Burianova veža** ❹ tower standing near the church is one of the oldest Renaissance belfries in Slovakia. It is similar to the Italian town belfries called *campanillas*. The bulky square-shaped stone tower was built in the first half of the 16th century and it was meant to strengthen the defence of the town. It

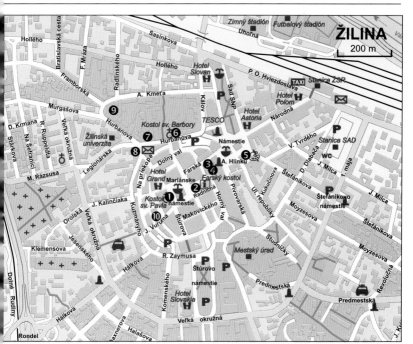

order to discern it from the old tower of the parish church it was given the name Nová veža (New Tower) and only later it acquired its present name. The top of the tower provides a beautiful view of the roofs and lanes of the historical town of Žilina and the panorama of the mountains around it. On the contrary, the panorama of the town seen from the Námestie Andreja Hlinku square is the most typical view and often reproduced on postcards of Žilina. The Mestské divadlo theatre stands there and it was built during the Second World War. It bears traits of the Italian Neo-Classicist style. The **Považská galéria ⑤** gallery with exhibitions of modern painting stands nearby.

The **church of St. Stephen** in the part of town called Závodie is the oldest surviving architectural monument in the territory of Žilina. The origin of this Late Romanesque church dates to 1200. Its inner ornamentation is especially valuable. A stone wall with entrance gate and a bastion from the 17th century fences the church. A small Renaissance chapel also stands next to the church. Other valuable cultural and historical monuments of Žilina include the **Franciscan church ⑥** and **monastery** from the beginning of the 18th century with very valuable Baroque decoration in their interior. The **Rosenfeld Palace ⑦**, in the past the most beautiful private building in the town, from the beginning of the 20th century is an important monument in the Art Nouveau style probably inspired by the Viennese castle of Belvedere. The **synagogue ⑧** of Žilina was built in the first half of the 19th century on the site of an old Jewish sanctuary. The functionalist architecture of the building with Moorish elements is unique also in the context of Slovakia. Today it is the cultural centre. The **Katolícky dom ⑨** with National Theatre on the Framborská ulica St. was built in the 1930's in the Neo-Classicist style. The large state emblem of Slovakia with statues of two eagles is placed on its facade. On 6 October 1938 representatives of seven political

parties signed an agreement on autonomy of Slovakia in this building. Not far from the Mariánske námestie square is an important Art Nouveau cinema building - **Grand Bio Universum** ⑩ from the 1920's. The first Slovak feature film Jánošik was presented here in 1921. It is now House of Arts. It has got excellent acoustic properties, ideal for musical performances. Žilina became one of the first towns in Slovakia with pedestrian zones as early as 1970. The zone stretches now from the railway station along the Národná ulica St., through the historical town as far as the housing estate of Hliny.

Budatín, now part of the town, was once an independent village. The **Castle of Budatín** with strategic position on the confluence of the Váh and Kysuca rivers is its dominant. In the past it was mentioned as the toll point. Construction of the Castle dates to the second half of the

13th century. Its oldest part is the bulky four-storied Romanesque tower with elements of Early Gothic architecture, which was later adapted in the Renaissance style. It stands on the site of disappeared water castle. It guarded the important trade road leading to Silesia. At the beginning it was the royal property, later it was owned by several noble families including the Csáky's who had it reconstructed in the years 1922-23. The Castle contains the collections of the **Považské múzeum** (Museum of Považie) and a **gallery** displaying unique **exhibition of tinker's trades products**. Tinker's trade was one of the typical occupations of the locals from the mid-18th century. Exhibition in the Castle of Budatín is the only of the kind in the world. It Castle **park** is also interesting. It was originally an English type of park founded probably in the mid-19th century. Currently it is abandoned though it still contains some exotic trees. The Žilinská kotlina basin is surrounded by charming nature with attrac-

Left: Castle of Budatín
Right: Church in Terchová

tive options of recreation and tourism. Immediately above the town is the mountain **Dubeň** (613 m), which offers wide views of the basin and the Kysucká vrchovina upland. The **landscape park of Chrásť** and the area of summer and winter recreation of Hradisko offer more options for hikers and holiday-makers. Water reservoirs of Hričov and Žilina near Mojšová Lúčka are also attractive. In Trnové, administratively part of Žilina, is the log Roman Catholic **church of St. George** from the 16ᵗʰ century with painted ceiling, one of the important representatives of folk sacral architecture in Slovakia.

Environs of Žilina

TERCHOVÁ lying north-east of Žilina is the typical representative of dispersed settlement on the border of the Malá Fatra Mts. and the Kysucká vrchovina upland. It was founded in time of the Wallachian colonisation. In the past it consisted of more than 120 hamlets. They are mostly depopulated today. At the present only about 70 of them are inhabited and many original cottages were adapted to holiday cottages. The village was first mentioned in 1580. Its inhabitants were involved in sheep raising, forest works, some of them worked in the local quarry, and other commuted to Czechia or south Slovakia. At the end of the Second World War it was burnt - 120 log houses with farm buildings were then destroyed. The village was restored after the war. Terchová is the birth place of Adam František Kollár, scholar and reformer in time of the Enlightenment, who worked at the Imperial court in Vienna. The village is known for its typical folk music. Original **folk log architecture** survives in the individual hamlets. The traditional **folk festival** of Terchová celebrated in summer annually attracts thousands of visitors. The **commemorative room** of the folk hero and legendary robber **Juraj Jánošík** situated in the building of the former school is also one of its most visited attractions. Ter-

chová is the ideal starting point for hiking the Malá Fatra Mts. and the contiguous Kysucká vrchovina upland. There is the road from Terchová to the **Vrátna** valley, the most attractive part of the region. The Vrátna valley has four points of access. Immediately beyond Terchová the road passes through impressing entrance to the valley, the canyon of **Tiesňavy**, with the Vrátňanka brook. It has many rock forms skirting the cascading brook. This National Nature Reserve consists of the proper canyon, the mountain ridge and the adjacent slopes of the Sokolie and Boboty Mts. There are numerous bizarre and attractive rock forms similar to different animals or human figures, such as Ťava (the Camel), Krokodíl (Crocodile) or Mních (the Monk). In the narrow gorge on the slope of the Boboty Mt. above the brook there stands the little statue of Madonna and a sign marks the level of water in 1948 floods when high water destroyed a large part of Štefanová killing 14 people. The **Zbojnícky chodník** (The Rob-

ber's Path) starts in Tiesňavy and leads through the very interesting parts of rock landscape. At the head of the **Stará dolina** valley is the tourist cottage **Chata Vrátna**. Not far away from the lower station of the chair lift to the Snilovské sedlo saddle is the **Symbolic cemetery** dedicated to victims of mountains. Hikers also like to stop at the Skok waterfall. The Chata Vrátna cottage serves as the salient point for trips to the main ridge of the Krivánska Fatra Mts. with its tallest mountain **Veľký Kriváň** (1,709 m). At the head of the **Nová dolina** valley on the foothill of the Veľký Rozsutec Mt. is the village Štefanová with numerous typical structures of folk architecture and modern buildings remade to tourist cottages and pensions offering accommodation. There are abundant options for hiking in more or less demanding terrain, which can be combined. They mostly start in

Štefanová, which is also a good place to start from if you want to climb the **Veľký Rozsutec Mt**. (1,610 m). The area of the Rozsutec Mt. is the National Nature Reserve where the complex consisting of several gorges, ravines, waterfalls, and rock faces are protected. The Reserve is known for great amount of rare plant and animal species including several endemic and relic ones. Part of the reserve is the system of gorges called **Diery**. It consists of three independent parts. The **Dolné diery** is the gorge accessible by ladders and footbridges. The **Horné diery** is another gorge between the Veľký and Malý Rozsutec Mts. characterised by spectacular rocks, waterfalls and rich flora. The **Nové diery** is the third gorge, which protrudes from the Dolné diery up the stream of one of the tributaries of the brook. The passage through the most attractive parts of the Dolné and Nové diery follows the **instructive path**, which starts in Štefanová. The locality **Starý Dvor** is the starting point for another part of the val-

Left: The canyon of Tiesňavy
Right: Nové diery gorge. Veľký Kriváň Mt.

ley, which is mostly visited by downhill skiers.

A continuous belt of villages lies along the road from Terchová to Žilina. All of them are good for start of hiking in both ranges but they also display some interesting monuments. In **BELÁ**, the remains of the local **folk architecture** and a remarkable building of belfry survive. **KRASŇANY** has been attractive until recently for its two Late Renaissance manor houses which exhibited collections of the Považské Museum. However, they were moved to Budatín after the two manor houses were returned to heirs of their original owners. In the neighbouring **GBEĽANY** is the Baroque **manor house** from the mid-18th century and the Classicist **curia**. In **TEPLIČKA NAD VÁHOM** the tourist can admire the close to the road standing building of the originally Renaissance manor house, now enlarged and rebuilt. It is a monumental three-storied building with two corner towers. The local, also originally Renaissance **church** is from the 16th century and later the Baroque chapel was added to it. The chapel contains the embalmed body of the last lady of the Strečno Castle, Žofia Bosniaková, wife of Paladin František Wesselényi. Perhaps the best mountain for views in the whole area, the **Straník Mt.**, of the Kysucká vrchovina upland, towers above the village. Ski lifts are on its northern and western slopes. The mountain is known for its excellent wind conditions and it was the reason why the school of motorless flying was situated here. Now it is the main centre for rogalo flying. Its top offers a wonderful wide view of the Žilinská kotlina basin and the surrounding ranges. The village of **VARÍN** was a little town in the Middle ages with right to fairs. It was known for its trades and crafts, among which those of boot-making and fur-making were especially well-developed. The Gothic **church** from the first half of the 13th century with a portal and the Baroque chapel of St. Florian stand on its square. The village is also the seat of

the **Administration of the National Park of Malá Fatra**. Not far away of the village is the recreation centre Pod Jedľovinou with the Fatranka cottage, a ski lift, and additional options of accommodation.

On the left bank of the Váh ruins of the **Strečno** Castle tower on top of the limestone rock. It is the National Cultural Monument. The Castle was built in the mid-14th century as sentry and toll collecting castle. It acquired its present form at the turn of the 15th and 16th centuries. At the end of the 17th century after the defeat of the Thököly's rebellion Emperor Leopold had it pulled down. The Castle was reopened after a long reconstruction in 1995. It is an indivisible part of the local panorama and the castle rock offers a beautiful view of the pass of Strečno and a large part of the Žilinská kotlina basin. The deep river valley of the Váh separates

the southern part of the Malá Fatra Mts. from the north-easier part of the range. The river forms a typical cut in form of river relief, the **Domašínsky meander** in the area of the mountain pass of Strečno. The Váh flows here by three flanks of the flat and forested hill of Domašín. The Domašínsky meander is the protected natural phenomenon since 1978 as it is unique in the area of the Western Carpathians. The legendary rocks Margita and Besná, once dangerous for rafters flowing timber down the river, are also here. This part of

Left: Domašínsky meander. Strečno Castle
Right: Manor house in Bytča. Ferry below Strečno

the valley is best seen from the ruins of the Strečno or Starý hrad Castles. The **Starý hrad** Castle (original name Varín) was the centre of the estate, which also included Žilina in the 13th century. In the first half of the 16th century different yeoman fought from the Starý hrad Castle against that of Strečno, which finally assumed the guard functions of the first mentioned. The seat of the estate moved to Krasňany in the 16th century and the Castle fell in decay. The best conserved part of it is the tower. Monuments and tombstones commemorating the Slovak National Uprising and heavy fighting in time of the Second World War are also parts the Slovak history. Above all the **Mohyla francúzskych partizánov** (The Barrow of French Partisans) standing on the hill Zvonica near Strečno is often visited.

BYTČA (population 11,500) is also an important town lying south of Žilina. It was property of the Nitra Bishopric as a serf settlement lying next to water castle as early as 1234. After 14th century it developed as a yeoman town and centre of feudal estate of 23 villages. In the 16th to 19th centuries Bytča thrived on trade and crafts. Modern industry started to develop in the town after construction of railway. Visitors also like to see the local **manor house**, the product of the Renaissance architecture. It is one of the few Renaissance manor houses in Slovakia, which kept its original appearance free from any alterations or modifications. It was built in the years 1571-1574 on Gothic foundations of an old water castle. The bulky square-shaped building with central

courtyard and arcades has circular corner bastions. The walls of arcades on the courtyard are decorated by paintings and portrays of the dukes. The six-storied tower with the Renaissance graffiti decoration stands in the centre of the northern wing of the compound. Another building in the area is what is referred to as the **Wedding Palace**, the only of the kind in Slovakia. Its owner, Paladin Juraj Thurzo had it built in 1601 for wedding feasts of his seven daughters. Several Renaissance and Classicist **burgher houses** from the 19th and 20th centuries stand on the square in the centre of the town. The originally Gothic church was rebuilt in the Renaissance style and it has an interesting Baroque decoration in its interior.

Good transport connection facilitates interesting trips from Bytča to the Strážovské vrchy and Javorníky mountain ranges. The **Súľovské skaly** rocks forming an attractive rock town, are situated only several kilometres from Bytča southeastward. Interesting landforms in form of

rock towers, needles, windows and gates separated by deep waterless gorges, ravines and valleys are the results of action of rain, ice, and wind, in other words, chemical and mechanical weathering. Among the most beautiful forms here are the 13 metres tall **Gotická brána** (the Gothic Gate), rock mushroom and many other rocks with fancy names (for instance, Maria Theresa, Owl, Spruce Tree and the like. The 7.5 kilometres long **instructive path** in form of circle has 17 stops. Visitors can also contemplate here the richest site of orchids in Slovakia, the Súľovský vodopád waterfall and the ruins of the **Súľovský hrad** Castle. It dates to the 15th century and it was allegedly built by the Hussites on top of the Roháč Mt. with difficult access. It consists of two independent castles, the upper and the lower. Although they stand close to each

other, there is a difference in height between them and they are connected by a tunnel dug into the rock. The 1703 earthquake has damaged the building considerably and it was never restored.

In spite of the fact that the **Javorníky Mts**. are not among the most attractive ranges of Slovakia, they enjoy attention of hikers, who love beautiful views, romantic forest nooks with mountain torrents and bucolic valleys. The local forests are also rich in wildlife and forest fruit. The settlement here is dispersed what adds the landscape its special charm. Many local villages conserve specimens of folk architecture. Northwest of Bytča is the tallest mountain of the range, the **Veľký Javorník Mt.** (1,072 m). Part of the flat main ridge is deforested and used for grazing. Instructive path with information boards, marked in red passes along the main ridge and the 25 km long route runs alternatively in the Slovak and the Czech territories. The typical village of the area is the **VEĽKÉ ROVNÉ**. Its people were involved in sheep keeping and tinker's trade while this craft, so typical for areas with poor soil, was developed into an art. Many log houses dispersed all over the area are now reconstructed and used as holiday cottages. Ruins of the originally Romanesque **Hričovský hrad** Castle can be seen next to the Považská cesta road, south of Žilina. It is one of the oldest castles in the middle part of the region of Považie. The first written reference to the Castle is from 1265. First the crown owned then its owners alternated. It fell in decay in the 17th century and now only the palace walls and the tower remain. the beautiful view from the ruins of the

Left: Courtyard of manor house in Bytča.
Súľovský hrad Castle
Right: Hričovský hrad Castle. Rajecké Teplice

surrounding mountain ranges and the Váh valley enhances the pleasant experience of the trip. The imposing limestone rock called the **Hričovská skalná ihla** (The Rock Needle of Hričov) is also near the Castle.

Rajecká kotlina basin

RAJEC (population 6,100) lying in the central part of the Rajecká kotlina basin is one of the oldest settlements in this region. The first written mention of Rajec is from 1193. It developed as a little town after the 14th century, which obtained its privileges, including the rights to fairs and markets, in the 17th century. The people of Rajec lived off wool-cloth making and tannery. Special red leather called *rajčianka* or cordovan, exported to the rest of the Kingdom of Hungary used to be the typical local product in the past. Rajec was even larger and more important than Žilina until the 19th century. Its reconstructed old town was designated the Town Monument Reserve. Its rectangular central **square** with two-storied Renaissance and Baroque burgher houses and the building of the **town hall** from the 16th century standing in the centre is well conserved. The originally single-nave Gothic church was rebuilt in the 15th century while its original Late Gothic portal survived. The Roman Catholic **church of St. Ladislav** was later adapted in the Baroque style. Rajec also has the **Mestské múzeum** (Town Museum) with collections concentrated on nature history and ethnography. Among its most valuable exhibits is the document signed by Empress Maria Theresa in 1749 which granted exemption to people of

Rajec from paying toll in the whole territory of the Kingdom of Hungary.

Part of the Museum is the typical room of burgher house of Rajec from the beginning of the 20th century with practical examples of textile production, wicker, straw and leather products. Tourists seek out the area of the local thermal swimming pool with five pools in summer months as it provides pleasant relaxation in thermal water.

RAJECKÉ TEPLICE (population 2,700) was first mentioned as a settlement in 1376. The local alkaline thermal springs were known as early as 14th century. In the 17th century the spa was built here. Rajecké Teplice now is one of the most attractive spas in Slovakia. It is indicated for therapy of rheumatic disease of locomotion apparatus, neurosis and some occupational diseases. The newly constructed compound of **spa buildings Aphrodite** furnished in antique style and equipped with the most modern diagnostic and therapeutic apparatuses is especially

attractive. Thanks to composition and temperature (38 degrees of Celsius) the local medicinal water is highly curative. There is also a **public swimming pool** and beautiful park. The forested rocky mountain of Skalka rises above the spa. It is accessible by the well-maintained path and its top offers an all-encompassing view. The National Natural Reserve of **Slnečné skalky** with impressing tower and pillar-shaped rocks is also near the spa. The panels of the **instructive path** leading from Rajecké Teplice to Porúbka provide basic information on natural assets, history and human impact on nature. The **Kuneradský zámok** Castle stands several kilometres from Rajecké Teplice. It is the Art Nouveau building from 1916 imitating the Romanesque architecture with corner towers, terraces and arcades. It also serves to spa purpose.

The villages situated south of Rajec

are remarkable ethnographic localities. Precious folk architecture, maintained typical culture and usage invite tourists. The most visited village in this parts is **ČIČMANY**, the Monument Reserve of Folk Architecture. It contains **log peasant cottages** with the typical white ornamentation. The painting was intended to protect the logs against the effect of solar radiation. The Reserve consists of 136 houses. The best-preserved ones include the ground building of **Radenov dom** and the neighbouring Gregorov dom, which shelters the ethnographic exhibition. Visit to Čičmany, which is now also an important centre of summer and winter tourism, can be concluded by stopping at the attractive local restaurant in the building of the former Baroque **manor house** from the end of the 18th century.

The whole southern part of the Žilinská kotlina basin, the Rajecká kotlina basin, was an important centre of trade and crafts in the Middle Ages. Among the artisans of the region above all the wood-

Left: Radenov dom in Čičmany
Right: Bethlehem of Rajecká Lesná

carvers and carpenters were once famous. The proof of their art is the masterpiece of the locals of **RAJECKÁ LESNÁ**, the unique and extra large **Bethlehem** carved in wood, to which continuously new details and figures are added. Apart from biblical figures with their traditional stories one can see in this Bethlehem typical structures from all parts of Slovakia. In Rajecká Lesná the tourist can contemplate historical **log houses** with saddle shingle roofs. In the valley above the village there is a 10 metres tall **geyser**. The often-visited destination of tourists in this region is **Fačkovské sedlo** saddle (802 m), which offers excellent ski tracks with all accompanying facilities. The saddle also offers the shortest possible access to the dominant of the southern part of the Lúčanská Fatra Mts. the 1,352 metres tall **Kľak Mt**. This is one of the most beautiful mountains of Slovakia and it offers a wonderful panoramic view of the environs, unique flora and dissected landforms.

North of Rajecké Teplice is the ruin of the **Lietava** Castle, which also offers attractive view of wide environs. This medieval fort played an important role in the history of the north-western Slovakia. It was one of the largest and most important castles of Slovakia and considered unassailable. Its estate consisted of 35 communities. The Castle was built at the beginning of the 14th century and its first know owner was Matúš Čák Trenčiansky. Different noble families later owned it and when the family of Thurzo died out, it fell in decay. An often visited area is that of the ridge of the Lúčanská Malá Fatra Mts. The routes of ascent lead through the long forested valleys and they are rather demanding.

The tallest mountain of this part of the range is **Veľká lúka** (1,475 m) and along with the mountains Horná lúka and Minčol it offers a wonderful view. One of the villages for the possible start of the ascent is **VIŠŇOVÉ**. Immediately beyond the village is the karstic Višňová dolina valley. The neighbouring village **STRÁŇAVY** is within comfortable reach if you walk by the old gamekeeper's lodge, which houses the **Múzeum malofatranskej operácie** (Museum of the operation in Malá Fatra) with documents concerning the period of the Slovak National Uprising against the Nazi occupation. The village also has a **thermal pool**.

ŽILINA
(dial: 041-)

Information
- **SELINAN CK - Turisticko-informačná kancelária**, Burianova medzierka 4, Žilina, ☎ 5620789, 5621478, fax 5623171, selinanck@bb.telecom.sk, www.selinan.sk

Museums
- **Považské múzeum**, Topoľová 1, Žilina, ☎ 5001511, **Zámok Budatín**, Žilina-Budatín, ☎ 5620306, 5001511, **Múzeum židovskej kultúry**, Dlabačova ul., Žilina, ☎ 5620485

Galleries
- **Považská galéria**, Štefánikova 2, Žilina, ☎ 5622522, **Art Signum**, J. Vuruma 8, Žilina, ☎ 5626822, **Emócia**, Štefánikova 2, Žilina, ☎ 7634724, **Klasik**, Hurbanova ul., Žilina, ☎ 5111150

Atractiveness
- **Observatory**, Malý Diel 20, Žilina, ☎ 7634371, 5643200, **Burianova veža** tower, Žilina, **Church of St. Stephen**, Žilina-Závodie, **Church of St. George**, Žilina-Trnové

Hotels
- **ASTORIA*****, Národná 1, Žilina, ☎ 5624711-4, **GRAND*****, Sládkovičova 1, Žilina, ☎ 5643265, **SLOVAKIA*****, Nám. L. Štúra 2, Žilina, ☎ 5623265, **SLOVAN*****, Kmeťova 2, Žilina, ☎ 5620134, **GARNI***, Vysokoškolákov 4, Žilina, ☎ 7246153, **DOPRASTAV G**, Kragujevská 11, Žilina, ☎ 7342448, **POLOM**, Hviezdoslavova 22, Žilina, ☎ 5621151-2

Restaurants
- **GOLD WING**, Mariánske nám. 5, Žilina, ☎ 5640683, **VIX RESTAURANT**, Sládkovičova 164/3, Žilina, ☎ 5626401, **GMK CENTRUM**, Mariánske nám. 3, Žilina, ☎ 5622136, **HUBERT**, Framborská 10, Žilina, ☎ 5620175, **CHINA RESTAURANT**, Štúrova 5, Žilina, ☎ 5626674, **NA BRÁNE**, Bottova 10, Žilina, ☎ 5620832

ENVIRONS OF ŽILINA
(dial: 041-)

Information
- **Turistická informačná kancelária**, Ul. sv. Cyrila a Metoda 96, Terchová, ☎ 5993100, ☎/fax 5695307, ztt@terchova.sk, www.terchova.sk

Museums
- **Hrad Strečno**, Strečno, ☎ 5697400, 5001511, **Expozícia Jánošík a Terchová**, Ul. sv. Cyrila a Metoda 96, Terchová, ☎ 5620033, 5695508

Atractiveness
- **Thermal swimming pool**, Víťazstva 1, Stráňavy, ☎ 5966370, **Strečno** Castle, Strečno, ☎ 5697400, **Starý hrad** Castle, Varín, **Manor house**, Bytča, ☎ 5533311, **Súľovské skaly** rocks, Súľov-Hradná, **Hričovský hrad** Castle, Hričovské Podhradie

Hotels
- **BRÁNICA******, Bránica, Belá, ☎ 5693035-6, **BOBOTY***, Vrátna - Nový dvor, Terchová, ☎ 5695227-8, **MAK**, Holúbkova Roveň, Terchová, ☎ 5695937, **TERCHOVÁ**, Vrátňanská cesta, Terchová, ☎ 5993109, **DIERY**, Biely Potok, Terchová, ☎ 5695322

Restaurants
- **ZBOJNÍCKA PIVNICA**, Vyšné Kamence 12, Terchová, ☎ 5695385, **KOLIBA**, Vrátna, Terchová, ☎ 5695112, **STARÝ MAJER**, Vrátna, Terchová, ☎ 5695419, **GÓL**, Ul. S. Sakalovej, Bytča, ☎ 5532753, **AZIEL**, Štefánikova 216/2, Bytča, ☎ 5522544

RAJECKÁ KOTLINA BASIN
(dial: 041-)

Information
- **ZENITA**, Nám. SNP 1/29, Rajecké Teplice, ☎ 5494990-1, fax 5494057, zenit@nextra.sk, www.zenit-cr.sk

Museums
- **Mestské múzeum**, Rajec, ☎ 5422198, **Pamiatková rezervácia ľudovej architektúry**, Čičmany, ☎ 5492123, 5001511, **Slovenský betlehem**, Rajecká Lesná, ☎ 5488134

Atractiveness
- **Spa Rajecké Teplice**, Osloboditeľov 131/4, Rajecké Teplice, ☎ 5494256-7, **Spa building Aphrodite**, Osloboditeľov 131/4, Rajecké Teplice, ☎ 5494955-8, **Thermal swimming pool Laura**, Ul. 1. mája, Rajecké Teplice, ☎ 5493915, **Thermal swimming pool Veronika**, Bystrická ul., Rajec, ☎ 5422457, **Kuneradský zámok** Castle, Kunerad, ☎ 5493698, **Lietava** Castle, Lietava

Hotels
- **VEĽKÁ FATRA*****, Kuneradská 24, Rajecké Teplice, ☎ 5493727, **KĽAK**, Sládkovičova 685/12, Rajec, ☎ 5422248, **KAŠTIEĽ**, Čičmany, ☎ 5492197

Restaurants
- **TALIZMAN**, Súľovského 5, Rajecké Teplice, ☎ 5493294, **RYBÁRSKA BAŠTA**, Rajecké Teplice, ☎ 5494030, **PRI RADNICI**, Nám. SNP 4, Rajec, ☎ 5424445

KYSUCE

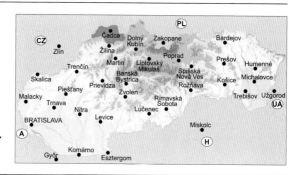

Čadca

Upper Kysuce

Eastern and Lower Kysuce

It is not sure what was first: the region of Kysuce or the Kysuca river. Did the river give the name to the region or was it the other way round? Difficult question! But the river certainly plays an important role in the life of the Kysuce people. It inspires them and gives them the feeling of patriotism. The most popular song of the region says: "Kysuca, Kysuca, cold water, when I drink of you, my head ails...". The Kysuca river is the unifying element of the landscape surrounding it. All ridges and valleys incline towards its wide basin, which turns around the ridge of the Javorníky Mts. The Kysuca river springs in the Kysuce region and flows practically in its middle. Its outlet into the Váh lies only three kilometres beyond the southern boundary of the region leaving it through the narrow in the belt of cliffs with the name the Gate of Kysuce.

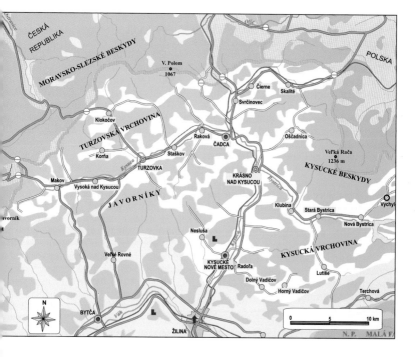

The region of Kysuce was always a bit remote from the centres and situated in the periphery of Slovakia. It suffered from its boundary position right on the Slovak-Moravian-Polish frontier. The western part of the region borders on the Czech Republic and the northern edge coincides with the Polish frontier. In the east Kysuce region stretches as far as the ridge of the Kysucká vrchovina Mts., which together with the Kysucká brána Gate forms its southern border. Industry and urbanisation came here only after the Second World War. Until then the people of Kysuce lived off the bad stony land and forests. Only after the railway was constructed they could commute to the mines and metallurgical plants in Ostrava on the Moravian side of the border. On the other side, underdeveloped industry and delayed urbanisation caused that the region has well conserved its original and natural appearance.

Left: Palárikova ulica St. in Čadca
Right: Church of St. Bartholomew in Čadca

Čadca

Although the new territorial and administrative division of Slovakia divided the region of Kysuce into two districts, its natural centre remained in **ČADCA** (population 26,700), which lies next to the confluence of the Kysuca river and the Čierňanka brook. The ground plan of the town is similar to human palm with five fingers, in reality, five side valleys. Čadca is in terms of Slovakia comparatively young town. The first written reference to the existence of a settlement in this place is from 1565. It has always benefited from its situation on the crossroads of trade routes running from the Kingdom of Hungary to Moravia and Silesia. At the moment when the seat of the Kysuce district of the estate of Strečno was established in Čadca in 1769, the town became the centre of the region. In the revolutionary year 1848 the Slovak National Council led by Jozef Miloslav Hurban and Ľudovít Štúr seated for a short time in the local parsonage and in December the same year the first mous summons to the Slovak nation were conceived here. Čadca was also the place where the volunteers gathered and fought against the Hungarian revolutionary guards side by side with the Imperial troops and defeated them on 11 December. In 1854 the famous revolutionary poet Janko Kráľ came to Čadca and stayed five years working as the employee of the local administration. The twentieth century brought the greatest changes to Čadca. New textile factory became the main employer of the inhabitants of the upper part of the Kysuce region. After the Second World War also the branch of the Tatra car factory was built here and for the growing number of population new housing estates were constructed.

The "young" town of Čadca contains "young" monuments. The oldest and also the most important though, is the Baroque **St. Bartholomew church** built in 1735 on the site of an older wooden church. Part of the main altar is the precious **altar painting** by an outstanding Slovak painter, Jozef Božetech Klemens from the second half of the 19th century. A group of 19 **protected lime trees** stands next to the church, which were planted here in the memory of the 1848 uprising. The most frequented area of the town and its centre is the **Námestie slobody** square with the dominating building of **Mestský dom** (Municipal House) built in 1932. The entrance of the **Information Centre** is next to it. Opposite the Municipal House is the busy **Palárikova ulica** street with excluded traffic. Next to the Palárikov dom house in Moyzesova ulica street is the **Kysucké múzeum** (Museum of Kysuce), which contains the exhibition of traditional folk artefacts of the region. It was financed from collection organised by Matica slovenská.

Hiking trips to the Javorníky Mts. and Turzovská vrchovina Mts. start directly from Čadca. The environs of the mountain hotel **Husárik** in the south offer nice landscape and ideal ski conditions in winter. In the valley below the Husárik Hotel is the spring called **Vojtovský prameň**. Its slightly mineralized water is salty and the locals

refer to it as the Salty Spring. On the opposite side of the town centre is another, sulphurous spring called **Bukovský prameň**. In the settlement Liškovci, above the spring, is the **tourist lookout tower**. Another interesting tourist destination near Čadca is the quarry situated in the locality **Milošová-Megoňky** where the unique stone balls of Kysuce can be seen. Čadca boasts a busy cultural and sport life during the whole year. In winter there is the traditional **passage over the Javorníky Mts. on skis**, the main event of June is the popular **marathon of Kysuce**. End of the summer is the time of festival of spiritual songs called **Magnificat**. The weekend following the St. Bartholomew name day (24 of August) is the term of the traditional **fair**.

Upper Kysuce

The Horné or Upper Kysuce is the picturesque landscape stretching around the upper reach of the Kysuca river. The region is squeezed between the Javorníky Mts. in

the south and the Turzovská vrchovina, which is the promontory of the Moravian-Silesian Beskydy Mts. The main valley stretches from Čadca as far as Makov and it is densely settled. The villages founded in time of the Wallachian colonisation are dispersed in a long chain and every next village starts where the previous ends. A different character of settlement is that in the surrounding highlands which consists of impressing mosaics of forests, meadows, strips of fields and a number of dispersed **hamlets**. More than two thirds of the Kysuce people lived in the above-described hamlets until mid-20th century. After the Second World War they started to move to the surrounding towns of Čadca, Turzovka and the villages in the valley of the Kysuca river which are now the largest rural settlements of Slovakia. Some of them, for instance, Oščadnica, Skalité, Raková have more than 4 thousand inhabitants.

Left: The group of statues in Turzovka
Right: Turzovka

The first village of the settled belt in the main valley of the upper reach of the Kysuca river going from Čadca is **RAKOVÁ**. It was founded in the late 16th century, and it was first mentioned in historical documents in 1635. The local Gothic **church of the Virgin Mary's Nativity** from 1874 is the work of architect Jozef Zítek, known for having designed the National Theatre of Prague. The author of the altar painting from 1879 is Jozef Božetech Klemens. Raková is the native place of the important Slovak playwright, writer and patriot **Ján Palárik** (1822-1870). In his memory every year the competition (Palárikova Raková) of the amateur theatre groups is held here. The administrative territory of the village reaches as far as the frontier with the Czech Republic, marked by the forested massive mountains of Zadné hory on the eastern edge of the Moravian-Silesian Beskydy Mts. On the slopes of the Veľký Polom (1,067 m) and Malý Polom (1,060 m) Mts. the original fir-beech and spruce woods survive. Also the neighbouring village of **STAŠKOV** has got its famous native. It is **Jozef Króner**, one of the most popular Slovak actors, and main protagonist of the famous Oscar film "The shop on the main street" who was born here in 1924. It was perhaps here, on the bank of the river Kysuca where the actor acquired his life-long passion for fishing.

The centre of the region of Upper Kysuce is **TURZOVKA** (population 7,900). It is a young town (since 1968) but its history started in 1598. The head of the county Juraj Thurzo, lord of the Bytča estate, gave it its name. Thurzovka counted twelve thousand inhabitants in 1954 and it was the largest village in Slovakia. Its people were involved in extraction and processing of wood of the surrounding forests. The wood industry is still the main economic branch of the town. In the centre of the town is the Baroque **church of Ascension of the Virgin Mary** from 1759. Its interior contains several paintings by **Jozef Božetech Klemens** painted in the years 1873-1882. The artist lived here around 1880 as the guest of his pa

...ron and friend Fraňo Tagáni, great patriot and founder of the Slovak cultural association Tatrín. Turzovka is also the birth place of the painter **Ondrej Zimka** and writer **Rudolf Jašík** who described the hard life in its native region.

At the occasion of the 400th anniversary of foundation of Turzovka the group of statues **Drotár a džarek** (Tinker and *džarek*) was made by sculptor and native of Kysuce Miroslav Cipár and placed here. It is the tribute to one of the most frequent crafts of Kysuce and Považie regions: **tinker's trade**. As the region of Kysuce was very poor the people were also compelled to seek other bread-winning activities than logging and farming, and tinker's trade was the one that spread here. The activity emerged in the 18th century when tinkers peddled in the surrounding villages and fixed the earthenware with wire. They carried a roll of wire, pieces of metal, awl, pliers, and hammer in their typical knapsacks made of wood. They made holes in vessels, pulled the wire through and made

a wire net to hold the broken plate or pot together. The craft developed into a rather sophisticated and artistic form in the course of time, while soldering, sticking, and wire stitching were also applied. People of more than 150 Slovakia villages were involved with the trade in the 19th century. However, most of them lived in the Kysuce region (Turzovka, Vysoká nad Kysucou, Staškov, Zákopčie, and Nesluša) and in central Považie (Kolárovice, Štiavnik, Dlhé Pole, and Veľké Rovné). The tinkers soon started to go ever further away from their native villages and hamlets. They undertook long journeys even abroad. Some were travelling on their own, some joined bigger groups led by a chief. The destinations were in Poland, Russia, Balkans and even the USA. The best and most skilled of them became rich and opened workshops of their own. They hired apprentice hands called here *džarek*. They had their workshops in Warsaw, St. Petersburg, Moscow, Zürich, Chicago and Boston. One of them was even in Siberian Irkuts. The Hunčík

dynasty of tinkers in Russia took over the production of samovars. Along with the original tinker's trade also the artistic branch thrived which was involved with production of works of art and jewellery made of wire. For instance, Štefan Hunčík from Vysoká nad Kysucou was awarded the gold medal at the 1903 London exhibition. The tinker's trade started to decline after the First World War as it could not compete with the mass machine production. The standing exhibition of the Považské Museum in Budatínsky zámok Castle situated in the northern suburb of the town of Žilina is specialised in tinker's trade.

Turzovka today is well known especially to Catholics. It is even referred to as the "Slovak Lourdes". Like in Lourdes, Medjugorie or Fatima the Virgin Mary appeared to the still living local native Matúš Lašut, on a hill called **Živčákova** (788 m) not far from Turzovka. It happened on 1 June 1958. The news about appearance of the Virgin Mary quickly spread and thousands of pilgrims from all over Slovakia and abroad started to arrive at Turzovka. On their way back home they carried water from the local spring which is allegedly medicinal. In 1992 Cardinal Ján Chryzostom Korec approved construction of a little **chapel of the Virgin Mary**, the **Queen of Peace** which was consecrated in October 1993. When Pope John Paul II visited Slovakia in 1992, he consecrated the founding stone of the new church of the Immaculate Heart of the Virgin Mary to be built on the sacred place near Turzovka in near future. The Živčákova Mt. is accessible on foot from Turzovka and from Vysoká nad Kysucou, or one can drive along the new asphalt road skirted by crosses of the **Cross Way**, which starts in the village of Korňa on the other side of the mountain. Two main pilgrimages to the Živčákova Mt. take place on the feast day of the Holiest Trinity and on the anniversary of consecration of the chapel (the nearest

Left: Pilgrim place Živčákova
Right: The stone ball of Kysuce in Klokočov

Sunday to 17 October). Mass assemblies of pilgrims also take place on the day of Ascension of the Virgin Mary (15 August) and on the day of the Immaculate Conception of the Virgin Mary (8 December). In 1998 at the occasion of the 40th anniversary of appearance celebrations were held with participation of more than 30 thousand believers including pilgrims from abroad. The **Beskydské slávnosti** (Beskydy Festival) held every year in August should be also mentioned as they are attractive parts of folklore of the region of Kysuce.

The village of **KORŇA** originated by joining several hamlets located in the administrative territory of Turzovka. On its lower end on the left side is the **Korniansky ropný prameň** (The oil spring of Korňa), a remarkable natural spring of crude oil linked to the rocks of the Carpathian Flysch. It is the only of the kind in Central Europe. Locals knew it from the time immemorial. They collected oil in buckets and used it for heating and lighting. When the great "fever" around crude oil broke in the 20th century the people of Kysuce dreamt about getting rich at least as the oil magnates of Texas. The probes made in Korňa after the First World War were accompanied by great expectations. The drill hole went to the depth of 300 m, but the yield was very poor, only about 10 tons of crude oil. Disappointment of local people culminated when natural gas broke in fire in May 1921. Today the local people need not seek wealth underground. Tourism is the new activity to pursue. The local **agro-tourist centre** near the boarding house of Mária proves it.

The road from Turzovka to the border crossing to the Czech Republic leads through the typical village of **KLOKOČOV**. This village originated in the same year as Korňa. Next to the settlement of Hrubý Buk is a remarkable natural reserve of **Klokočovské skálie**. It is one of the localities where the most important rarity of the region can be admired. They are the mysterious stone balls. The balls are located in the narrow strip of sandstone rocks and agglomerates between the settlement of Kor-

nica near Klokočov and the quarry Megoňky north-west of Čadca. This strip is about 15 km long and not wider than 500 m. The origin of mysterious stone balls is not completely clear. Their almost perfectly round shape tempts the people to think that it is the produce of the long extinguished civilisation or even extraterrestrials. Geologists though presume that they are the result of secondary spherical jointing of rocks caused by weathering. The stone balls of Kysuce are indeed a unique natural phenomenon, rare in the world. Similar balls were found in Costa Rica, Mexico, Brazil, and New Zealand. The balls of Kysuce match the ones found elsewhere at least by their size. The diameter of the largest of them called Mary found in the locality of Megoňky is 3 metres. There are several of them with diameter surpassing 1 m. People have carried away many smaller balls with diameter below 60 cm and use them for decoration of their gardens. One of the balls 55 cm in diameter is located in the lower end of Klokočov used as guard

stone. The territory administered by the commune Klokočov offers numerous excellent options of hiking, skiing and cross-country skiing. Ski lifts are below the mountain of **Konečná** (865 m) close to the border crossing Klokočov-Bílá and next to the commune Hlavice. Wonderful environs of the **mountain cottage Kysuce** are ideal for summer hiking. It is located directly on the state frontier in neighbourhood of the Czech tourist centre Súlov-Bílý Kříž.

The village **VYSOKÁ NAD KYSUCOU** like other villages of the Upper Kysuce consists apart from the chain-like colonisation villages along the valley of the Kysuca river of many isolated settlements scattered on the slopes of the Turzovská vrchovina highland and Javorníky Mts. The village lived an especially dramatic period at the end of the Second World War. In the Kysuce comparatively intensive anti-Nazi resistance existed in that time and Vysoká nad Kysucou paid

cruel tax for helping partisans. In April 1945 soldiers of German raiding squad broke in the village and carried all men they could find out of the village where they shot them. Out of 42 village men only one saved It was the father of sculptor Miroslav Cipár He freed himself from under a heap of dead bodies and crawled to safety and became the only eyewitness of this horrible crime Below the saddle of **Semeteš** (685 m) on the road from Turzovka to Bytča in the region of Považie a small stone monument was erected in memory of victims. Vysoká nad Kysucou is also mentioned in relation to the American astronaut **Eugene Andrew Cernan**, commander of spacecraft Apollo 17 and one of the last terrestrials who stepped the surface of the Moon on 12 December 1972. Although he was born in Chicago his grandfather's origin is in Vysoká nad Kysucou. The local school bears his name.

The highest situated village in the valley of the Kysuca river is **MAKOV**. It lie amidst wonderful landscape with prevalence of forests above fields and meadows

Left: Stone balls of Kysuce in locality Megoňky
Right: The main ridge of the Javorníky Mts.

It is part of the **Chránená krajinná oblasť (CHKO) Kysuce** (Protected Landscape Area of Kysuce). This also is the reason why the village and its people are mostly involved in tourism and recreation. The village was founded in the second half of the 17th century by Wallachian people from Těšín. It was the only village of Kysuce that had its own petty aristocrats but it did not maintain independence for long. In the document from 1720 Makov is mentioned as part of Vysoká nad Kysucou. The extensive territory of Makov as we know it now was formed by the end of the 19th century. Until then it was divided among seven contiguous villages. The first village magistrate was the well-known specialist in forestry Rudolf Matter from Čadca. Makov is the crossroads of important routes. The road leading to the west toward the frontier ridge of Turzovská vrchovina highland branches into two roads ascending to the border crossings to the Czech Republic. One of them heads over the **Makovské sedlo** saddle (801 m) to the valley of Vsetínska Bečva and the other

ascends the **Bumbálka Mt**. (870 m), to descend later to the valley of Rožnovská Bečva. The Bumbálka mountain cottage is a good starting point for hiking tours. It is also a favourite ski resort offering fine down-hill and cross-country ski conditions. There is another road leaving Makov and heading to the south which continues from the saddle of **Javorník** (818 m) to Bytča in the region of Považie. Scattered hamlets in the western part of the territory of Makov are an interesting tourist destination. In one of its settlements **Papajovci** grows what is often denoted as the oldest elm tree in Central Europe. Its age is estimated at 400 years and the circumference of its trunk at the height of man's shoulders reaches 625 cm. The river **Kysuca** springs below the top of the Hričovec Mt. in the main ridge of the Javorníky Mts. at the altitude of 825 m above sea level and flows 66 km to join the muddy water of the Váh river. The river Kysuca collects waters of the basin area of 1,038 square kilometres. The comparatively far away situated recreation centre of

Veľký Javorník-Kasárne is also situated in the administrative territory of Makov. Until recently it was accessible by car only from the Moravian side of the frontier. Today there is also available a new access road from Makov. At the guard point near the frontier the military barracks were constructed in 1833 for the soldiers who were here to prevent people crossing the border because of cholera epidemic in the territory of Moravia. The centre is now climatic spa. It is the starting point for the tours to the **Veľký Javorník Mt.** (1,071 m), the highest mountain of the Javorníky Mts.

Eastern
and Lower Kysuce

Kysuce is a comparatively uniform landscape. Apart from its southern edge

Left: Veľký Javorník - Kasárne
Right: At the Veľká Rača Mt.
Funicular to the Veľká Rača Mt.

crossed by the narrow strip of limestone cliffs the whole area consists of Flysch rocks. Before the landscape was altered by man is was entirely coated by forest. When shepherds and farmers came they replaced it by fields and meadows. Kysuce today is a picturesque mosaics harmoniously patched by natural and by man created landscape elements. The landscape of the eastern and lower parts of the Kysuce region is even more varied and interesting because of the tall Kysucké Beskydy Mts. and long forked valleys with charming cliffs in the south-east.

The special feature of the **Čierňanka** valley in the northernmost tip of the Kysuce region is the presence of the Goral ethnicity. The territory north of Čadca bordering on Poland was colonised by people whose language coincides with that of the people of Orava and northern Spiš – the Goral dialect. The **Goral Feasts** held in the natural amphitheatre in **SKALITÉ** offer an authentic meeting with the culture of Gorals living in Kysuce. The village Skalité spreads all over the valley as far as the road and railway border crossing to Poland next to the community **Serafínov**, which has four ski lifts available for ski fans. The massif of **Javorský Beskyd** (northern part of the Kysucké Beskydy Mts.) rising above the southern end of the village is also interesting for tourists. The best mountain for views is **Tri kopce** (824 m), which offers far-reaching views of the wonderful landscape with scattered hamlets. It lies on the route of the popular **Kysucká lyžiarska magistrála** (the main ski route of Kysuce). Passing through the neighbouring village of **ČIERNE**, which was also founded during the Wallachian colonisation one arrives to the village of **SVRČINOVEC**. Next to the hamlet called **U Dejov** is the school where Slovakian writer of Czech origin, **Peter Jilemnický** (1901-1949) taught in the years 1923-1926. He depicted the poverty of Kysuce in his novel *Pole neorané*. The road heading to the border crossing to the Czech Republic passes through Svrčinovec.

The village **OŠČADNICA** stretches in the valley of eponymous brook and it is the third largest village in Slovakia with population over 5,500. It was founded comparatively late, in the first half of the 19th century. The village has the Baroque-Classicist church of **Ascension of the Virgin Mary** built in 1804. On the hill Sivova Grapa not far away from it is **Calvary** with a small church where pilgrimages are held every year in August. At the lower end of the village is the **manor house** from the turn of the 19th and 20th centuries set into a nice park. It houses the **Kysucká galéria** (Gallery of Kysuce). In the village several surviving folk houses are to be seen and more of them still exist in the surrounding isolated hamlets dispersed all over the administrative territory of Oščadnica. Some of them are older than the village itself. High situated old Wallachian settlements below the Veľká Rača Mt. are considered the oldest. The document from 1540 mentions the community Diedova. The modern local names Dedovka, Dedová or Zádedová are all derived from this old name. Oščadnica is abundantly visited above all in winter. There are two ski centres **Dedovka** and **Lalíkovci**, known as ones of the best equipped in Slovakia. The **chair lift** in Lalíkovci can be used before the undemanding ascent to the top of the frontier mountain of **Veľká Rača** (1,236 m), the tallest mountain of the Kysucké Beskydy Mts. and the as a matter of fact, of the region of Kysuce. Another route of ascent is the **instructive path** starting in the Dedovka. **Skalné diery** caves are situated between the upper station of the lift and the mountain top. At the top part of the Veľká Rača Mt., which offers a wonderful panoramic view, comparatively rare species of spruce and extensive growths of blackberries grow. Tourist cottage stands on the other, Polish side of the frontier. The best time to visit Oščadnica is in May when there is **Oščadnická heligónka** i.e. competition in playing on concertina held.

In the neighbouring **Bystrická dolina** valley there are five, more or less connected in chain-like manner, colonised villages. **KLUBINY** lies near **Klubinská dolina** valley which maybe especially interesting locality for fans of botany. The valley also contains rich springs with drinking water. Higher situated community of **STARÁ BYSTRICA** originated during the Wallachian colonisation around 1585. Its people kept large herds of cattle in special summer stables called here *folvarky*. Count Windischgräz founded here a small iron processing plat in 1767, which disappeared before end of the 18th century. The original houses of Stará Bystrica did not survive. The most important historical monument here is the Late Baroque **curia** built at the beginning of the 19th century. The local **church of St. Michael the Archangel** and the synagogue are hundred years younger.

The environs of the village **NOVÁ BYSTRICA** with settlement Vychylovka are more interesting than the village itself. There are two attractions for tourists. The first of them, **Múzeum kysuckej dediny** (Museum of the Kysuce Village) was opened in 1981 in the Chmúrna valley. The region of Kysuce has not got many examples of original folk architecture, moreover the people of Kysuce built here many houses lacking any style after the war spending the money earned in the mines and metallurgical plants in the neighbouring Moravia. This is the reason why this open-air museum is in fact the only opportunity to learn about the architecture which existed in Kysuce in the past. There are 34 structures used for dwelling, sacral, technical or farming purposes brought here from different parts of region. They include, for instance, an original inn from Korňa,

which serves the same purpose in the open-air museum. Various attractive events are schemed here for tourists. An extra attraction is that of the **forest railway**, the unique technical monument and the only of the kind in Europe. Similar type of railway is known only in the Ands of Peru or the Rocky Mountains in the USA. The part of the railway, which survives now, is only an example of the former much longer railway track. Italian war captives started its construction in 1915. The original 61 km long track connected Oščadnica in Kysuce with Lokca in the region of Orava. The forest railway had to overcome the altitude difference of 217 m on the most difficult one and a half kilometre long track section. Three plowturns facilitated it. In the 1920 s the track was prolonged to as much as 100 km. Then it was gradually shortened until 1969 when it was completely closed because of financial reasons. The planned dismantling was not realised. On the contrary, restoration of its most valuable part was started in 1974.

Left: Railway of Kysuce
Right: Above Nová Bystrica. Church in Vychylovka. Log house in Vychylovka

Sporadic operation along the first reconstructed section was opened in 1980 and fifteen years later the section passing through the open-air museum as far as the first plowturn prolonged it. The train, which hauled timber to the sawing mills, is now transporting the tourists. It is pulled by steam engine on weekends, while on work days it is replaced by a small diesel engine. In the upper part of the Bystrická dolina valley above Nová Bystrica the **water reservoir of Nová Bystrica** was constructed in the years 1983-1989. Villages Hrvelka and Riečnica were covered by water of the reservoir with an area of 190 ha. Church of Riečica survives. The reservoir supplies 900 litres of potable water every second to the town of Čadca. However, the construction of reservoir caused the problem of road communication between the regions of Kysuce and Orava, now covered by water, which was not resolved yet.

The villages Stará Bystrica, Nová Bystrica, and Oščadnica are situated in the territory of the eastern part of the **CHKO Kysuce** (Protected Landscape Area). This large protected territory was designated in 1984 to an area of 654 square kilometres. The western part lies in the upper part of the valley of the Kysuca river, on the administrative territory of Klokočov, Korňa, and Makov. The eastern part of the CHKO is linked with the Polish Żywiecky Park Krajoobrazowy and the Slovak CHKO of Horná Orava. Its western part forms a whole with the Czech CHKO of Beskydy. Administration of the CHKO seats in the town of Čadca.

Although **KRÁSNO NAD KYSUCOU** (population 6,900) became town in 2002, it is one of the oldest communities of the region. It was mentioned as early as 1325. In the past it served as a transhipping point of timber hauled here from the Bystrická dolina valley. After the Second World War the wood and metal processing plants were constructed here.

The centre of the Lower Kysuce region is the district town **KYSUCKÉ NOVÉ MESTO** (population 16,300). It is much older

than Cadca. It is mentioned as Jesenín in the oldest document from 1244. The local toll station helped to the development of the primeval settlement, which obtained the town privileges in the years 1321 and 1325. Kysucké Nové Mesto was a yeoman town with frequently changing owners. One of them was also the Polish King Vladislav (1393) or an important aristocrat Ctibor of Beckov (1410). In the years 1431 to 1431 the town was in the power of Hussites. In 1698 the rebellion against the lords of the town led by Mikuláš Štrba took place there. The town has not got many historical or cultural monuments. Many of them, including the Gothic church from 1300 were damaged by extensive fire which afflicted a great part of the town in 1904. On the site of the burnt old church the new Romanesque **church of St. James** was built. Several original Renaissance **burger houses** from the 17th century survive on the central square. The Renaissance building of the former **brewery** from the 17th century stands on the Jesenského street. The interested thing about the village of **NESLUŠA** situated west of Kysucké Nové Mesto is that the ancestors of the famous actress Pola Negri lived there.

RADOĽA is probably the oldest village of Kysuce. Numerous archaeological finds prove a very old settlement of the area. Foundations of an old Romanesque church, part of a disappeared castle, are also a remarkable discovery. The Renaissance

manor house of Radoľa from the first half of the 16th century is an important monument of the village. It is the only of the kind in the region of Kysuce. Apart from the curia in Stará Bystrica and the manor house in Oščadnica there are no other aristocratic residences left in this traditionally very poor region. Perhaps the only exception were the petty yeoman families living in the village of Makov. The region was administered by lords of the castles of Strečno, Budatín and the manor house in Bytča. The manor house of Radoľa is now occupied by the **Museum of Kysuce** which exhibits here the artefacts documenting the oldest history of the region. A detour to the **Vadičovská dolina** valley offers nice landscape with picturesque cliffs. The dominant mountain towering above the villages **HORNÝ VADIČOV** and **DOLNÝ VADIČOV** is the **Ľadonhora Mt.** (999 m). One can leave the enchanting landscape of the Kysuce region through the **Kysucká brána** gate situated between two forested tops of the **Rochovica Mt.** (640 m) and **Brodnianka Mt.** (720 m).

Left: Burgher houses in Kysucké Nové Mesto.
Manor house in Radoľa. Ľadonhora Mt.
Right: Wooden Bethlehem of Kysuce

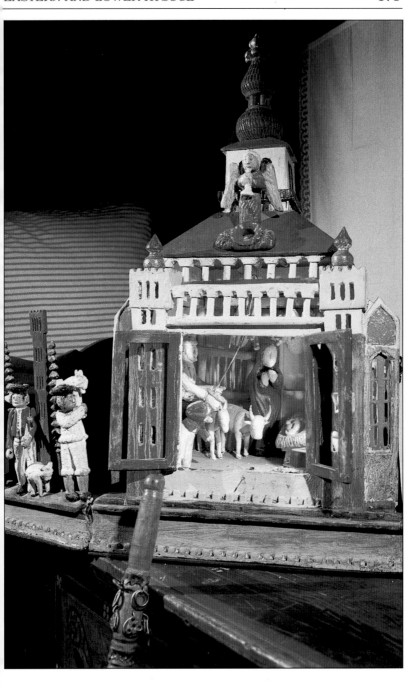

ČADCA
(dial: 041-)

Information
– **Informačné centrum**, Nám. slobody 30, Čadca, ☎ 16186, 4332611, fax 4332612, ikcadca@mail.viapvt.sk, www.ikcadca.pvt.sk

Museums
– **Kysucké múzeum**, Moyzesova 50, Čadca, ☎ 4321386, 4321389

Atractiveness
– **Stone balls of Kysuce**, Milošová-Megoňky, Čadca

Galleries
– **Kysucká galéria**, A. Hlinku 1, Čadca, ☎ 4332166

Hotels
– **LIPA**, Matičné nám. 1, Čadca, ☎ 4335091, **HUSÁRIK**, Čadca, ☎ 4321628, **KRIVÁŇ**, Čadca, ☎ 4323804, **PENZIÓN MEDEA**, Palárikova 1152, Čadca, ☎ 4331806

Restaurants
– **KYSUCKÁ REŠTAURÁCIA**, Horná 1223, Čadca, ☎ 4324186, **SLOVENSKÁ REŠTAURÁCIA**, Slovanská 210, Čadca, ☎ 4332132, **SAVARIN**, Matičné nám. 1, Čadca, ☎ 4331278, **TATRA**, Palárikova 99, Čadca, ☎ 4332400-3, **LAPEK**, Palárikova 1083, Čadca, ☎ 4333474, **GASTON**, Májova 2243, Čadca, ☎ 4323927, **MEDEA**, Palárikova 1152, Čadca, ☎ 4325565

UPPER KYSUCE
(dial: 041-)

Information
– **JAMPEX**, Makov 141, ☎ 4364636

Atractiveness
– **Palárikova Raková** – amateur theatre groups, Raková, ☎ 4341055, **Festival of the Beskydy**, Turzovka, ☎ 4352461, **Oil spring of Korňa**, Korňa, **Stone balls of Klokočov**, Klokočov

Hotels
– **FRAN****, Kasárne 290, Makov, ☎ 4364151, 4364171, **PANČAVA****, Pančava 162, Makov, ☎ 4364415, **BUMBÁLKA**, Makov, ☎ 4364305, **PENZIÓN POĽANA**, Makov 276, ☎ 4364306

Restaurants
– **ARTEMIS**, Stred 181, Turzovka, ☎ 4353913

EASTERN AND LOWER KYSUCE
(dial: 041-)

Information
– **Turisticko-informačná kancelária Rača**, Oščadnica, ☎/fax 4382101, tik@velka-raca.sk, www.velka-raca.sk

Museums
– **Múzeum kysuckej dediny**, Vychylovka, Nová Bystrica, ☎ 4397219, **Kysucké múzeum – kaštieľ**, Radoľa, ☎ 4212505

Galleries
– **Kysucká galéria – kaštieľ**, Oščadnica, ☎ 4332807

Atractiveness
– **Forest railway**, Vychylovka, Nová Bystrica, ☎ 4397219, **Observatory of Kysuce**, Dolinský potok 1278, Kysucké Nové Mesto, ☎ 4212946, **Goral Feasts**, Skalité, ☎ 4376106, **Folk festival**, Ochodnica, ☎ 4233121

Hotels
– **KRIVÁŇ***, Nám. slobody 104, Kysucké Nové Mesto, ☎ 4215385-6, **KYSUCA**, Litovelská 1331, Kysucké Nové Mesto, ☎ 4213571, 4212880, **KRIVÁŇ**, Nám. slobody 5, Kysucké Nové Mesto, ☎ 4215366, **RAČA**, Nám. Bernáta 275, Oščadnica, ☎ 4382143, **ACACIA**, Oščadnica, ☎ 4382177, **PENZIÓN FIESTA**, Oščadnica 873, ☎ 4382400, 4334090, **LES**, Neslušà 1059, ☎ 4281250, **KOLONIAL**, Centrum 1284, Skalité ☎ 4376405, **PENZIÓN SILVESTER**, Ústredie 912, Skalité, ☎ 4376206, **MAGISTRÁL**, Čierne 1033, ☎ 4373223, **RUDINA**, Rudina 147, ☎ 4214129, **MOTEL SKALKA**, Radoľa 392, ☎ 4212156

Restaurants
– **SLOVANSKÁ REŠTAURÁCIA**, Nám. slobody 19, Kysucké Nové Mesto, ☎ 4213171, **PIZZA**, Nám. slobody 23, Kysucké Nové Mesto, ☎ 4212417, **JELEŇ**, Nová Bystrica, ☎ 4397228

ORAVA

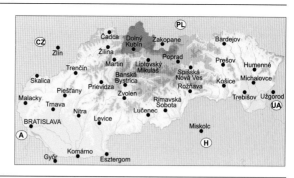

Upper Orava

White Orava

Lower Orava

The region of Orava lies in the north-western part of Slovakia, on the border with the Poland. The border point in environs of the village Oravská Polhora is also the northernmost point of Slovakia. The territory of Orava, area 1,661 square kilometres, is under the administration of the Žilina province and there are districts Dolný Kubín, Námestovo, and Tvrdošín. The northern and eastern limits of the region coincide with the state border, its south-eastern and southern limits coincide with the ridges of the West Tatras and of the Chočské vrchy Mts. respectively. The south-western frontier of the Orava region coincides with the northernmost protuberance of the Veľká Fatra Mts. with the Šíp Mt., and the western border of the region leads across the Veľký and Malý Rozsutec mountains in the Malá Fatra mountain range, Púpavový vrch Mt. in the Kysucká vrchovina

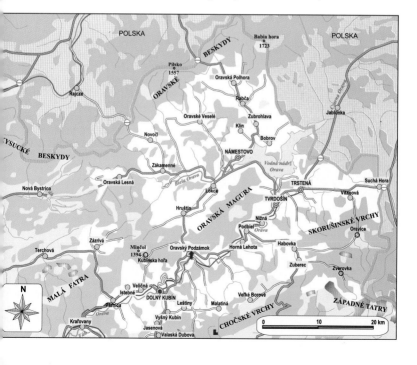

Mts. and ends on the contact of the Kysucké and Oravské Beskydy Mts. on the Slovak-Polish border.

Upper Orava

The administrative centre of the Upper Orava region has been recently established in the district town of **TVRDOŠÍN** (population 9,500). Tvrdošín was mentioned for the first time in 1265 in an act of the Old Hungarian king Belo IV as *Toardosina*, a customs point for the Old-Hungarian–Polish trade relations when salt, lead and linen was transported through the town. Also a fort belonging to the Orava estate probably existed there. Tvrdošín obtained the privilege of the royal borough from king Ľudovít I in 1369. The town preserved its freedoms and privileges also in the 15th century, but the precariousness of the political situation in the 16th century

caused the gradual decline of the custom office in Tvrdošín and a growing dependence on the Orava Castle landlords, especially of Juraj Thurzo and his descendants. The period of anti-Habsburg rebellions in the 17th century, and the presence of the Polish-Lithuanian troops of Jan Sobieski in 1683, caused enormous damage to Tvrdošín. Life settled down in the 18th century. In the 19th century Tvrdošín, with almost two thousand inhabitants, became the seat of the Upper Orava district, actively employed in wood manufacture, tannery, dyeing and button manufacturing. The period after the Second World War was the one of intense promotion and development and today Tvrdošín is the cultural and administrative centre of the Upper Orava region.

The pride of Tvrdošín and the oldest preserved building is the Gothic wooden Roman-Catholic **All Saints church** situated in the local cemetery. Its origins date back to the second half of the 15th century and it was rebuilt in Renaissance style in

Left: The All Saints church in Tvrdošín
Right: Square in Trstená

the 17th. The Baroque altar from the end of the 17th century, with the painting of All Saints, dominates the interior of the church. Formerly, there was a low Gothic altar of which one wing, with the paintings of St. Peter and St. Ján the Baptist was preserved. The original central part of the altar, a painting of Bemoaning the Death of Christ from the 15th century was moved in 1919 to a museum in Budapest. The interior of the church was finished in the mid-17th century. Viewing the church, especially the paintings of the Apostles, the Late Renaissance pulpit with figures of the Evangelists from 1654, and a painting of St. Juraj mounted on a horse fighting a dragon (a distemper painting on wood from 1653) will draw the attention of any visitor. The wonderful dome paintings (a sky with stars, angels and a panelled ceiling) complement the Gothic mysticism of the space. Highly artistic and expert reconstruction and restoration of the church was awarded a prize by EUROPA NOSTRA in 1993 and the church itself, as the National Cultural Monument, was included in the list of European cultural heritage. Among other important monuments in Tvrdošín is another Roman-Catholic church, the **St. Trinity church** built in 1766-1770 on the site of older foundations. The Late Baroque **Lady's Pillar** of the end of the 18th century, standing in front of the church, and the Baroque **chapel** from 1815 complete the list of sacral monuments. Among the secular ones the **municipal house**, built around 1811 in the square and several **curias, public buildings** and **the houses of linen-makers**, commemorating the lively trade and craft activities in the second half of the 19th century, are worth mentioning. However, the final destination for many visitors to the town, is the municipal quarter called Medvedzie, and especially the **Gallery of Mária Medvecká** – a permanent exposition of the Orava Gallery. It is a biographic exposition of the paintings of this remarkable painter who was born and grew up in Medvedzie, and after a period of sojourn came back to work in Orava. The

building of the curia where the exposition is installed dates back to the 19th century. The exposition with 261 artistic works occupies 583 m² and shows Mária Medvecká's (1914-1987) paintings of the landscape of Orava, including still life, portraits, floral and figural compositions.

Part of Tvrdošín also includes the present day suburbs of **Krásna Hôrka** and **Medvedzie**, which were independent communities in the past. Archaeological discoveries from the Lower Bronze Age prove that a pre-historic settlement once existed there. Krásna Hôrka originated at the beginning of the 15th century through Wallachian colonisation being a serf community of the Orava estate. Its population made their living by linen-making, glass manufacturing, trading in stone-masonry and seasonal work in the lower parts of Old Hungary. The Baroque **chapel**, the **belfry** and the **Lady's Pillar** recall the deep religiosity of the local population. Neighbouring Medvedzie originated in 1355 as a squire community which later belonged to the Medvecký family. Their origins are well preserved in the architecture of the Classicist curias from the end of the 18th and the beginning of the 19th centuries.

TRSTENÁ (population 7,100) lies in the lower part of the Oravica stream, only several kilometers north of Tvrdošín, its eternal rival in the battle for the prominent position in Upper Orava region. Trstená was founded in 1371 by German settlers as a market town under the name of *Bingenstadt*. Later it adopted the name Trstená because of the abundant occurrences of peat bogs and cane (tŕstie = cane) around the town. Though it was an agricultural community in the 17th century craftwork was developing rapidly. The guild of pottery manufactured a broad assortment of products which became famous abroad. Trstená ceramics were remarkable for their distinctive design, decoration and the very technology of its

---

Left: Bobrova roľa in Podbiel
Right: Open-air museum in Zuberec

manufacturing. The development of crafts and trade went on into the 18th and 19th centuries and there even was a petroleum refinery in Trstená.

A significant monument in the town is the Roman-Catholic **church of St. Martin**. Originally a Gothic church, probably from the 14th century, it was altered in 1641 into the Renaissance style and a century later it became Baroque. In the spacious main square another Roman-Catholic **St. George church** and a **Franciscan monastery** can be seen. Both Baroque buildings are from the 18th century and they close the southern side of the square. Extremely valuable are also the stone pillars – the **Pillar of St. Ján Nepomucký** in front of the church of St. George and the **Pillar of St. Florián** in front of the parish office (the oldest stone sculpture in Orava). Two **chapels** and a **rectory** from 1743 complement the sacral monuments of Trstená.

The road ends south-east of Trstená at **BREZOVICA**. The community lies on the northern foothills of the Skorušinské vrchy mountains, about five kilometres from Trstená. The only preserved examples of the old architecture are several **log houses** and a Roman-Catholic **church of the Virgin Mary** built between 1883-1884. The church stands along the green-marked and comfortable tourist route leading from Trstená across Brezovica to the Skorušinské vrchy mountains. After a mild ascent beyond the village and below the ski lift the first aim is the round top of the **Javorinky mountain** (1,123 m). The green path continues further along the ridge south-eastward and ends at the highest top of the Skorušinské vrchy mountains – **Skorušina** (1,314 m). It offers some attractive views of the Roháče mountains.

The last community before reaching the Slovak-Polish border crossing is **SUCHÁ HORA**. The customs of the local people are well preserved by the local folk group, who also present what is called the **Goral alternative** in folk costumes. The preserved **folk architecture** represented

by the log houses gives a true picture of the past life to the visitor.

The larger village of **NIŽNÁ** lies south of Tvrdošín, in the valley of the river Orava. While the southern part of the community, on the left bank of the river, is situated under the Skorušinské vrchy mountains, the northern part is under the slopes of the Ostražica mountain (765 m) belonging to the Oravská vrchovina mountain range. Now it is known to Slovaks mainly as the place where TV sets are made. The most important monument of Nižná is an originally Gothic Roman-Catholic **church of St. Gál** built between 1614-1620. By the end of the 17th century it was enclosed by a protecting wall and in 1715 it was styled in the Baroque. Among the most valuable items in the church are the golden chalice of Kraków (1570), two bells from 1629 and a painting of the Annunciation from the beginning of the 19th century.

Not far away from Nižná, at the mouth of the Studený potok brook which runs from the Roháč area to the Orava

river is a typical Orava village called **POD-BIEL**. Its name was derived from the Biel hill, eventually the Biela skala rock (750 m) where there was a castle in the Middle Ages, and legend has that there was also a Knights' Templar monastery here. At present the Biela skala rock is a protected nature locality with occurrences of valuable geologic, geomorphic, archaeological and botanic phenomena. At the present visitors focus their interest mainly upon the locality called **Bobrova roľa** where there is a compound of original **log houses** built in the 19th and early 20th centuries and declared a **monument reserve** in 1977. The old iron industry is exemplified by the ruins of the iron-mills of 1836 standing at the entry to the Studená dolina valley, on the left hand side of the road to Zuberec. In the hall of the iron mill a partially preserved blast furnace can also be seen.

The region of Zuberec is spread out in the north-western part of the Tatra region occupying the Orava part of the West Tatras, the Podtatranská brázda furrow and the Skorušinské vrchy mountains. In the south it is bordered by the ridge of the West Tatras, in the west and north by the ridge of the Skorušinské vrchy mountains and in the east by the Slovak-Polish state border. **ZUBEREC** is 12 km from Podbiel, lying on the main road from Dolný Kubín to the Polish border. It is situated in the furrow of Podtatranská brázda at the foothills of the West Tatras, in an area called Roháče. Zuberec is today a tourist centre in the Orava part of the West Tatras and the point of departure for the Sivý vrch mountain or otherwise to the region of the Roháče mountains.

Sacral cultural, historical monuments are represented by the Roman-Catholic **church of St. Valentine** built in 1933 and designed by the architect M. M. Harminc. The intense spiritual life of the people in Zuberec is manifested by 14 **crosses** dis

Left: The Goral room. Oravice
Right: Juráňova dolina valley

persed all over the community's environs. Especially valuable are the stone crosses and **tombstones** adorned with relieves in the local cemeteries, from the turn of the 19th and 20th centuries and a stone cross near the church bearing pictures of the life of St. Andrew and St. Florián from 1839.

However, three kilometers from Zuberec, at Brestová, a unique open-air **Museum of the Orava Village** can be visited. It is located in impressive mountain scenery overlooked by the peaks of the Pálenica, Sivý vrch and Brestová mountains in the south, the Osobitá mountain in the east and the massive Mních mountain in the west. Over an area of about 20 hectares, and on both sides of the Studený potok brook, is a village containing the typical folk buildings of the individual regions of Orava. Styles of all regions are represented here – the south-western part of the lower, central and upper Orava regions, the north-eastern Tatras, the Goral area and the north-western Beskydy region. The first example is a **forester's house** from the Zákamenné region with a typical village tavern, which was built in 1970, and the first part of the museum was opened to the public in 1975. A visitor can see here **all kinds of buildings** – peasant houses, larders, lumber rooms, farmsteads, shepherd's huts, haylofts, etc.); **sacral buildings** (a wooden church, cemetery and belfry) and the **craftsman's** and **linen-maker's houses** (a Wallachian mill, a sawmill, a potter's furnace and fulling mill, etc.). The Museum is thematically divided into five sections regarding each individual region. **The Market Place of the Lower Orava** exemplifies the richer side of the region with rather large, ostentatious houses. **The Mill** near the brook includes a water mill, sawmill and fulling mill with their common water-driven mechanism. **The Lane of the Zamagurie Region**, with houses and farmsteads of rich and medium rich farmers, represents the typical structure of an Orava village. **The Goral Settlement** represents the poorest part of Orava lying on south-eastern slopes of the Oravské Beskydy mountains. Here can be

seen the poor loggers', shepherds' and peasants' houses, and the house from Oravské Veselé with log walls, a clay floor and a open fire place stands out. The **cemetery** with the Late-Gothic **wooden church** from Zábrež from the 15th century, standing on an elevated location, dominates the area. The museum regularly organises ethnological expositions and the **Podroháčsky Folk Festival** is held in the local amphitheatre in August.

HABOVKA is situated only one kilometre south-west of Zuberec on the way to Podbiel, eleven kilometres distant. It is situated on the confluence of the Blatná brook and the Studený potok brook beside the Skorušinské vrchy mountains and the Podtatranská brázda furrow. Among the most important sacral monuments is the Roman-Catholic **church of the Virgin Mary** built in the Classicist style in the years 1817-1820 and reconstructed in 1952. Let us mention also the **chapel** of 1812, standing above the community with the folk sculpture of Madon-

na, and a Baroque organ of the second half of the 18th century.

North-east of Habovka lies the holiday community of **Oravice**. Its precise location is in the furrow Podtatranská brázda 10 km from Habovka and 6 km south of Vitanová in the valley of the Oravica brook and is a part of the territory of the town of Tvrdošín. The most attractive feature about Oravice is its geo-thermal water spring (the temperature of the water is 54°C and its yield is 120 l/sec). Progressively additional cottages, a swimming pool with thermal water, open all the year round, a ski lift, car-camping, and playgrounds now make of Oravice a favourite holiday and tourist resort. For lovers of hiking Oravice represents the starting point to the picturesque and secluded corners of the Tichá, Juráňova, Bobrovecká, Suchá and Mihulčia dolina valleys offering wonderful scenery full of multifarious gorges.

Left: Church in Námestovo
Right: The Orava dam

White Orava

The tourist centre of the Upper Orava region, called Biela Orava (White Orava) is the district city of **NÁMESTOVO** (population 8,000). Námestovo, a Wallachian-peasant community, originated in 1557 as a result of the efforts of the Orava Castle landlord, František Thurzo. The Thurzo family founded here an Evangelic parish and Námestovo was not only a market centre of this part of Orava but also a centre of religious life. The old trade road leading across Námestovo to Polish Žywiec, and the right to trade linen acquired by the town in 1776, helped its development. Linen manufacture and trade contributed to the progressive change of what was originally a farming community augmented by the Austro-Old Hungarian ruler Maria Theresa in 1776 when she granted the town a municipal market privilege. Námestovo obtained the right to run four annual fairs and a weekly market on Thursdays, which became the most popular in the Orava region. The linen-makers, tanners, leather-processing craftsmen and furriers from Námestovo were especially in great demand. One of the most important sources of income for the citizens of Námestovo in the course of the 18th and 19th centuries was also linen and textile trade, preceded by the growing of flax and hemp, which was typical female work, whereas men did linen weaving. Progressively the ornamentation of home-made linen with distinctive blue-print patterns, using mostly plant motifs, was created. In 1775 dyeing and mangling workshops were established where the linen was first mangled and afterwards manually printed with indigo. Throughout almost two centuries the blue-print linen cloth was typical for the decoration of Orava folk costumes. The decline of home-produced linen came in the period of the First World War, when it was drastically replaced by the manufacture and industrial production of textiles. The development of industry and the construction of the Orava Dam offered the

city opportunities in the form of travel and tourism and its importance has considerably grown since then.

The **Orava dam** became an important holiday and sport centre with lodging, catering facilities and the usual services to the holiday-makers. Sport and recreation facilities are concentrated on southern shore of the water reservoir in two centres: **Slanická osada** and the **hotel Goral**. Numerous restaurants, hostels, hotels, two car-camping sites, sport facilities and sport equipment rental services contribute to the satisfaction of visitors. The summer tourist season starts in the middle of June and ends in September. There is also the possibility of a sight-seeing tour by boat. There are four boats with regular departures every day during the summer season. A favourite point in the reservoir is the Nature Reserve **Slanický ostrov** island, which used to be the Slanica community. The church standing in the island is the Roman-Catholic **church of Ascension of the St. Cross** built in 1766-1769 first as a Baroque chapel. The chapel was reconstructed in 1843 in Classicist style into a church with two towers and a "locksmith's" chapel. The Baroque inventory of the church is deposited in the Orava Gallery, the church in turn shelters a permanent exposition of folk art.

The city itself has the Roman-Catholic **church of St. Simon and Jude**, built between 1656 to 1659 as an Evangelical church. It was enlarged in the first quarter of the 19th century and later repeatedly renewed. In the interior the altars, the pulpit from the 19th century and a painting of the Madonna in the style of an icon from 1758, a wooden cross from 1818, and the reconstructed **tomb** of the Murín family, one of the wealthiest in Námestovo in the 19th century, are of interest. The secular monuments include Classicist wooden and brick **houses of linen-makers** forming a row in a street that used to be the busiest part of the city in the 18th and 19th centuries. Symbols of the Slovak

National Revivalist movement are the **statue and a commemorating board of P. O. Hviezdoslav** and the **tomb** of M. Hamuljak at the local cemetery.

North-east of Námestovo, close to the Orava Dam are the three communities of **KLIN, ZUBROHLAVA** and **BOBROV.** Several typical brick **houses of linen-makers** are preserved in the centre of the village Klin, which date to the second half of the 18th and the beginning of the 19th centuries. Another place of interest is the national Nature Reserve of **Klinské rašelinisko** (The Peat Bog of Klin) extending over an area of 9.23 ha and situated between the city of Námestovo and Klin. It is the mountain type of peat bog with occurrences of specific forms of plant and animal life typical for waterlogged areas. The past glory of linen-making of the village Zubrohlava can be recalled in the **houses of craftsmen** of

the second half of the 18th and beginning of the 19th centuries with their Classicist facades. Only a few kilometres southward is the community of Bobrov. There are remarkable Classicist **houses of linen-makers** standing in the centre of the community bearing testimony to the wealthy past. The most important sacral building is the local Baroque Roman-Catholic **church of St. Jakub** built in 1753, later reconstructed and expanded with a lateral **chapel.** Another interesting monument is the **Calvary** with a central chapel from 1894 depicting Christ stopping on the Way to the Cross.

South-west of Námestovo, up to the confluence of the Hruštínka and Biela Orava rivers, along the north-eastern slopes of the Oravská Magura mountains, the visitor reaches **LOKCA.** The village has an original Renaissance Roman-Catholic **church of the Most Holy Trinity** from 1665, expanded and rebuilt in the Baroque style in the 18th century. Also the Baroque **stone pillar of St. Ján Nepomucký** of 1751 is of interest.

Left: Hviezdoslav's gamekeepers lodge
Right: The column bridge and square in Dolný Kubín

The largest community of the southern part of White Orava is **HRUŠTÍN**. The most important sacral monument is the Roman-Catholic **church of St. John the Baptist**, built in 1820 with an interior dating from the end of 19th century. The **chapel of St. Anna** dating from 1800, **statues of St. Florián** and **St. Ján Nepomucký**, as well as the **Trinity Pillar** and a **crucifix** standing by the road to Oravský Podzámok, depict the religious life of the village.

Lower Orava

The centre of the Lower Orava region is the city of **DOLNÝ KUBÍN** (population 19,600). The name Kubín (Kolbin) appears for the first time in a document dating back to 1325. The community originated in the territory of the Orava estate in the 14th century. In 1632 Dolný Kubín was promoted to a town. Since 1683 the town was the seat of the Orava county. The promising economic development of Dolný Kubín was interrupted in the second half of the 17th century, especially during the devastating presence of the Polish-Lithuanian troops moving to Vienna to help out against the Turks. Extensive reconstruction of Dolný Kubín was initiated after a fire in 1834. Its square acquired a typical urban character. The town as an economic and trading centre of the Orava region (with numerous trades, food producing plants, an iron-plant, saw-mill, mill, printers, money institutes, and a business school) also became the centre of the Slovak national life in the region. Numerous personalities of Slovak culture and enlightenment were active here: Vavrinec Čaplovič, founder of the library and the Society of Scholars, who donated to the Orava county his library of 45 thousand volumes, (1778-1853), Pavol Országh Hviezdoslav, the most important of all Slovak poets, (1849-1921), Janko Matuška, poet and writer whose poem *Nad Tatrou sa blýska, hromy divo bijú* (The Lightnings and Thunders over the Tatras...) became the Slovak national anthem (1821-1877), Andrej Radlinský, one of the founders of Matica slovenská and of the St. Vojtech Society (1817-1879), among others. The economic and cultural progress of the city continued also in the 20th century but in the 1930's it was hampered by big economic crisis and general unemployment. Many solved their difficult situation by emigration, above all to America. After the Second World War and the territorial reorganization in 1960, Dolný Kubín became again the most important administrative, economic and cultural centre of the entire Orava region. At present it is the entry gate to all of Orava's attractive corners offering numerous options for leisure and sport.

The oldest cultural and historical monument here is the Roman-Catholic **church of St. Catherine ❶** with the Gothic wall and tower from the 14th century, reconstructed in Neo-Gothic style in 1885-1886. In its interior is a Late-Gothic winged altar of the beginning of the 16th century and a Renaissance epitaph of the family Zmeškal from 1622 which are most interesting. The basic urbanistic Middle

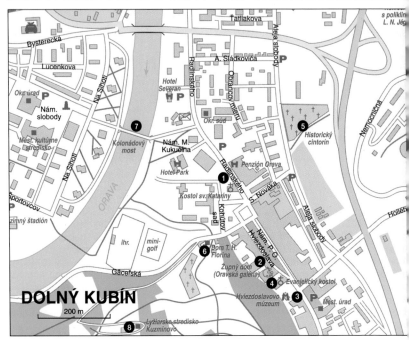

DOLNÝ KUBÍN

200 m

Age monument is the **Hviezdoslavovo ná-mestie** square (the Square of Hviez-doslav). It is the result of almost two hun-dred years' construction with numerous Renaissance and Baroque **burgher hous-es**. The dominant building of the square is **Župný dom ❷** (the County House) of the last third of the 17th century. On its facade the coat-of-arms of Orava of the 18th cen-tury can be seen. Nowadays it is the seat of **Oravská galéria** (Gallery of Orava) with permanent expositions of old, folk and modern arts related to Orava. In upper part of the square is **Hviezdoslavovo múzeum ❸** (Museum of Hviezdoslav). The building of the Museum was built at the beginning of the 20th century as a library for V. Čaplovič, whose book collections are there until now. There is also a literary museum of P. O. Hviezdoslav commemo-rating the life and artistic work of this ge-nius of Slovak poetry. In front of the Mu-seum stands the **statue of P. O. Hviez-**

doslav by F. Štefunko. Opposite is the house of the poet where he lived, worked and died. The facade of the building bears a **commemorative board**. Next to the Mu-seum is the **Evangelic church ❹** built in the years 1893-1894 as designed by B. Bulla. It stands on the site of the original church damaged by fire. Among the sacral monuments is also the nearby historical **cemetery ❺** with the tombs of important figures of the Slovak nation. As far as the secular buildings are concerned visitors should pay attention to the reconstructed **house of T. H. Florin ❻**. It was originally a house of a dyer occupied later by this globetrotter active in cultural life. At pre-sent it is used by the Orava Museum for its expositions. An admired object of the contemporary Dolný Kubín is the wooden **column bridge ❼** over the river Orava connecting the old part of the city with the local part Bysterec. Fans of skiing will ap-preciate the modern **ski centre Kuzmíno-vo ❽** almost in the centre of the city. This "ski paradise" offers to the visitor a 900 m

Right: Orava Castle

long ski track with three lifts, artificial snow and night illumination.

Dolný Kubín is also an ideal starting point to the most beautiful parts of the **Oravská Magura** mountain range. The most frequently visited mountain of Oravská Magura is the **Kubínska hoľa Mt.** (1,346 m). Its huge, denuded massive ridge offers some admirable panoramic views. But Kubínska hoľa is rather more visited in winter as a **ski resort**. Lovers of cross-country skiing prefer the ridge of the Kubínska hoľa mountain, while downhill skiers concentrate in the area with five ski lifts on the southern slopes of the mountain.

Nevertheless, the most attractive locality for the tourists is the nearby community of **ORAVSKÝ PODZÁMOK**, lying only several kilometers north-east of Dolný Kubín on the river Orava, under impressive cliffs. A decisive role in its past was played by the castle built on the cliff. There was also an agile trade and social life, and several crafts thrived. In the 20th century, however, the community partially lost some of its economic importance but one of the most interesting landmarks of northern Slovakia, the **Orava Castle**, still attracts thousands of tourists every year.

Construction of the castle, much like others in Slovakia was created on the site of old wooden forts after the Tartar invasion in 1241. In 1370 it became a county castle and the seat of the Orava Castle estate which included almost the whole of Orava. Originally it was built in the Romanesque and Gothic styles and later altered in Renaissance and Neo-Gothic styles. It consists of several buildings copying the shape of the castle rock. In 1556 the Castle fell into the hands of the Thurzos' who were the authors of the most extensive reconstruction of the castle's history. Orava castle acquired its present form in 1611. After the Thurzos' died

out the castle was owned by several landlords who did not take much care of it. The biggest disaster affected the castle in 1800 when it burnt down, and became useless. The most extensive reconstruction was made after the Second World War. Today the Castle is a remarkable compound of buildings of the lower, central and upper castles with palaces, fortifications and towers. Visitors are intrigued by its three entrance gates communicated by a tunnel, under which there is a dungeon. In the Castle itself **Oravské múzeum** (the Orava Museum) was established with numerous series of expositions. In the oldest part of the upper castle an archaeological exposition documenting the oldest history of the Orava settlement is installed. Natural history is represented on the bottom floors of the central castle with samples of

fauna and flora of the Roháče Mts., the Orava Dam and the Oravská kotlina basin. On the upper floor of the central castle an ethnographic exposition is placed. It displays the typical tools, garments and products of the rural people, describes their customs, their way of life and work. Historical exposition consists of a group of medieval and Renaissance buildings with their original furniture.

Two kilometres to the east and up the river stream, near the main Orava road and railway communications is the village of **HORNÁ LEHOTA**. The Baroque **manor house**, later reconstructed in Classicist style, is the pride of the community. After an ambitious reconstruction it is used nowadays as a **motel** with a stylish restaurant and a tavern that should satisfy the most particular clientele.

Left: Zázrivá
Right: Wooden church in Leštiny.
Native house of M. Kukučín in Jasenová.
Manor house in Horná Lehota

Going to the south under the slopes of the Choč mountains is the community of **LEŠTINY**. The most important monument in the community is the wooden Evangelic **church** of 1688 with wooden belfry. Visitors are attracted especially by the main altar from the beginning of the 18th century, church pews with coats of arms, Renaissance baptistery of the 17th century, a copy of the burial flag of J. Zmeškal and an epitaph of M. Meško of 1753. An important secular building in Leštiny is the Late-Baroque **manor house of the Zmeškals'** from the end of the 18th century, rebuilt in the Classicist style in 1840, and a **curia** of the 17th century, rebuilt in the first third of the 19th century.

West of Leštiny, under the Veľký Choč mountain and the cliffs of Ostrá and Tupá skala lies **VYŠNÝ KUBÍN**. Numerous important personalities of Slovak culture were born or lived in Vyšný Kubín: the poet P. O. Hviezdoslav, the writer A. V. Gazda, the teacher A. Medzihradský, the book collector A. Čaplovič, the lady writer

M. Figuli amongst others. P. O. Hviezdoslav is here commemorated by a **monument** at the site of the house where he was born, as the house itself was burnt down. In the community are several **squire houses** and **log buildings** from the 18th and 19th centuries. The **Kubínyis' manor house** from the end of the 18th century, rebuilt in the second half of the 19th century, the Classicist **squire curia** from the 19th century and an original Renaissance **manor house** from the 17th century, later rebuilt in Classicist style represent the squire traditions of the community.

In Vyšný Kubín begins a tourist path to the tallest mountain of the Chočské vrchy mountains – **Veľký Choč** (1,611 m). The green route continues first crossing the community by a field road with a magnificent view of the panorama of **Ostrá skala** and the **Tupá skala** rocks, which are protected rock areas. A wonderful open panoramic view comprises all the mountain ranges of northern Slovakia. Descent is possible to Liptov or to Orava by several footpaths.

Going to Orava is a comparably steep descent which ends either in Vyšný Kubín or in **JASENOVÁ**, situated more southward, and in **VALASKÁ DUBOVÁ**. The most famous native of the community Jasenová, besides the founder of the Orava library

V. Čaplovič, was the writer M. Kukučín (1860-1928). His **native house**, a typical Lower Orava homestead from the mid-19th century still exists in the community. An exposition installed in four rooms of the house commemorates by written and picture documents the life and work of the famous writer. The house is furnished with typical wooden furniture and its exterior is likewise an example of Orava wooden architecture.

Nearby Valaská Dubová is the southernmost village of Orava on the border of the region contiguous with Liptov. Valaská Dubová entered Slovak history mainly by capturing the Slovak national hero, Juraj Jánošík who robbed the rich to give to the poor. The old folk traditions of Jánošík's capture is commemorated in the local **tavern**, a simple brick building built at the beginning in the 19th century on the site of its wooden antecedent. Valaská Dubová is the starting point for tourists heading to the Veľký Choč mountain. The most important sacral building in the community is the Roman-Catholic Neo-Romanesque **church of St. Michael Archangel**, built between 1866-1872. The main altar with the painting of St. Michal Archangel is from the end of the 19th century and the wall paintings by J. Hanula are from 1904.

UPPER ORAVA
(dial: 043-)

Information
– **Turisticko-informačná kancelária CS-TOURs**, Vojtaššákova 496, Tvrdošín, ☎ 5323888, 5323111, fax 5323111, cstours@mail.viapvt.sk, www.cstours.sk, **Turisticko-informačná kancelária Zuberec**, Zuberec 289, ☎ 5320777, ☎/fax 5395197, tatrainfo@stonline.sk, www.zuberec.sk

Museums
– **Múzeum oravskej dediny**, Zuberec, ☎ 5395149

Galleries
– **Galéria Márie Medveckej**, Tvrdošín, ☎ 5322793, **ART-galéria**, Tvrdošín, ☎ 5322268

Atractiveness
– **All Saints church**, Tvrdošín, ☎ 5322452, 5322163, **Monument reserve**, Podbiel, **Observatory**, Podbiel, ☎ 0903/535832, **Iron mills**, Podbiel, ☎ 5382027, **Thermal swimming pool**, Oravice, Tvrdošín, ☎ 5394440, **Swimming pool**, Nižná, ☎ 5381712

Hotels
– **OSOBITÁ****, Roháčska dolina 378, Zuberec, ☎ 5395105, **RADAR***, Nižná Doba 506, Nižná, 5381219, **LIMBA**, Hviezdoslavova 185, Tvrdošín, ☎ 5322072, **PRIMULA**, Zuberec 373, ☎ 5395001, **TATRAWEST**, Zuberec, ☎ 5395210, **SKALKA**, Nám. M. R. Štefánika 12, Trstená, ☎ 5392786

Restaurants
– **KORUNA**, Vojtaššákova ul., Tvrdošín, ☎ 5322360, **ADRIA**, SNP 151, Trstená, ☎ 5392428, **LAHÔDKY**, Železničiarov 301, Trstená, ☎ 5393077

WHITE ORAVA
(dial: 043-)

Information
– **Informačné centrum Námestovo**, Nábrežie 1038, Námestovo, ☎ 5523777, icn@orava.sk, www.orava.sk

Museums
– **Hviezdoslavova hájovňa**, Oravská Polhora, ☎ 5864780, **Slanický ostrov umenia**, Oravská priehrada, Námestovo, ☎ 5863212

Hotels
– **TYRAPOL****, Oravská Lesná, ☎ 5593142, **HUTNÍK****, Oravská priehrada, Námestovo, ☎ 5522633, **SLANICA****, Slanická osada, Námestovo, ☎ 5522742, **PENZIÓN SLANICA****, Slanická osada, Námestovo, ☎ 5522741, **GORAL**, Oravská priehrada, Námestovo, ☎ 5522269, **STUDNIČKA**, Oravská priehrada, Námestovo, ☎ 5522366

Restaurants
– **MARÍNA**, Hviezdoslavovo nám. 1, Námestovo, ☎ 5581048, **ALEX**, Hviezdoslavova 50, Námestovo, ☎ 5524000, **FORTUNA**, Hviezdoslavova 15/9, Námestovo, ☎ 5522974

LOWER ORAVA
(dial: 043-)

Information
– **Turistická informačná kancelária Dolný Kubín – Slovakotour**, Gáceľská 1, Dolný Kubín, ☎/fax 5867299, tik@kubin.sk, www.kubin.sk

Museums
– **Oravské múzeum**, Hviezdoslavovo nám. 7, Dolný Kubín, ☎ 5864780, 5866239, **Literárne múzeum P. O. Hviezdoslava**, Hviezdoslavovo nám. 7, Dolný Kubín, ☎ 5864780, **Dom T. H. Florina**, Gáceľská ul., Dolný Kubín, ☎ 5865461, **Oravský hrad**, Oravský Podzámok, ☎ 5816111, 5820390, **Pamätná izba Martina Kukučína**, Jasenová, ☎ 5864780

Galleries
– **Oravská galéria**, Hviezdoslavovo nám. 11, Dolný Kubín, ☎ 5863212

Hotels
– **PARK*****, Radlinského 1739, Dolný Kubín, ☎ 5864110, **U ZELENEJ LIPY****, Okružná 1258/50, Dolný Kubín, ☎ 5885960, **VEĽKÁ HAVRANIA****, Veľká Havrania 81, Zázrivá, ☎ 5896362, **SEVERAN***, Radlinského 1729, Dolný Kubín, ☎ 5864666, **MARÍNA**, Hviezdoslavovo nám. 1667, Dolný Kubín, ☎ 5866751, **HUTNÍK***, Malá Lučivná, Istebné, ☎ 5891376, **ORAVAN**, Hviezdoslavovo nám., Oravský Podzámok, ☎ 5893115, **PLICHTA**, Párnica, ☎ 5892248

Restaurants
– **MARÍNA**, Hviezdoslavovo nám., Dolný Kubín, ☎ 5866751, **LUCIA**, Hviezdoslavovo nám., Dolný Kubín, ☎ 5863263, **TOLIAR**, Oravský Podzámok, ☎ 5893124

TURIEC

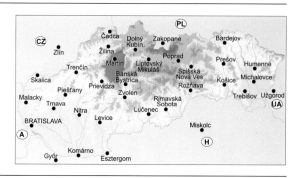

Martin

Northern Turiec

Southern Turiec

The region of Turiec spreads in the north-western part of Slovakia in the Turčianska kotlina basin surrounded by mountain ranges of Malá and Veľká Fatra, Kremnické vrchy, and Žiar. The axis of the valley is the Turiec river flowing north into the Váh river below the narrow of Strečno. The border separating Turiec from the neighbouring regions runs on the ridges of the surrounding mountain ranges. For its beauty and natural assets this region is one of the most picturesque in the territory of Slovakia.

The Malá and Veľká Fatra Mts. are ideal for hiking, cycling paragliding and mountaineering. Fans of hiking love the walks in the Gaderská and Blatnická dolina valleys with attractive setting and the exciting ascent to the main ridge of the Veľká Fatra Mts. The Malá Fatra Mts. also offers interesting spots with panoramic views, deep valleys and the Šútovský vodopád waterfall and there are numerous ski centres in both ranges.

The cultural heritage of this region comprises typical villages with folk architecture, stately rural manor houses from different historical periods. The linkage between the national and cultural history in the centre of Turiec, which is the town Martin, is more obvious here than whenever else in Slovakia. Martin concentrates several cultural institutions of national importance. The spa of Turčianske Teplice offers the complete spa cures. Turiec in general is known for abundance of mineral springs (for instance Fatra and Budiš). The region of Turiec consists of two administrative districts, Martin and Turčianske Teplice. On the area of more than 1,100 square kilometres population of about 115 thousand lives.

Martin

In the northern part of the Turčianska kotlina basin lies the town **MARTIN** (population 60,000), the administrative and cultural centre of the region. Martin for the majority of Slovaks is also the

centre of national life since the mid-19th century. The oldest archaeological finds document continuous settlement of its area from the time of the Lusatian culture, that is from 3,000 years ago. The first written mention of Martin is from 1284. King Charles Robert granted Martin town privileges in 1340. Martin developed into the yeoman town, which depended on the Sklabiňa estate and the family of Révay. The administration of the Turiec county seated in Martin from 1535. It was a small farming town with only 2000 inhabitants until the mid-19th century. The revolutionary year 1848 when it became the centre of emancipation and political life of the Slovak nation and simultaneously that of business activities meant the stimulus of its development. In 1861 the first programme of the emancipated Slovak politics, The **Memorandum of the Slovak Nation**

was prepared and presented here in 1861. The assembly, which met in front of the local Evangelical church formulated then the requests concerning the basic national rights of until then ignored Slovak nation in the Kingdom of Hungary. However, the mentioned requests were ignored and only fulfilled after 1918. The **relief** by Ján Koniarek from 1932 placed on the building of the Evangelical parsonage commemorates the event.

Nevertheless, one of the few achievements of the Memorandum was the foundation of **Matica slovenská** (an institution caring for the rights and spiritual welfare of Slovaks in sphere of ethnic emancipation) in 1863. Almost five thousand participants of the founding assembly met on 4 August 1863 in Martin. The first chairman of Matica slovenská, which was meant to concentrate the efforts and attempts in cultural and creative activities of the nation was the Catholic priest Štefan Moyzes. In spite of

Left: Námestie SNP square
Right: Divadlo SNP theatre

nterruption of the activity of Matica in 1875 when it was forced to close, it became the only scientific, literary and artistic, political and social centre of Slovaks. Thanks to voluntary contributions of private persons many valuable items and historical documents of the Slovak national life were then concentrated and partially made accessible to public in the building of Matica. Matica also edited and published books and periodicals, which greatly contributed to the educational, moral and economic progress of the nation. *Slovenské pohľady*, for instance, published since 1881, now the literary periodical with the longest history in Europe, was one of the titles published by Matica. Another success of the Memorandum was the opening of three secondary schools, called here gymnasiums imparting tuition in Slovak language. Two of them were situated in the region of Turiec, one in Martin opened in 1867 and another in Kláštor pod Znievom from 1869.

More institutions founded in Martin also played an important role for the nation. The printing association which later assumed the name Kníhkupecko-nakladateľký spolok (Association of booksellers and publishers), the women association Živena and editorials of several periodicals were seated in Martin. Closing of Matica slovenská 1875 by the Hungarian government has interrupted the emancipating efforts of the leading figures of the nation. Its re-opening is the result of endeavour of Andrej Kmeť and his followers. The then constructed **Národný dom** (National House) in Martin concentrated mineralogical, geological, and botanical collections which Andrej Kmeť donated to it. The Muzeálna slovenská spoločnosť (Slovak Museum Society) was founded in 1893 and it initiated collections and later construction of the first Slovak National Museum in the years 1906-1908. Martin was also the place where the Slovak theatre and musical life were born.

Left: The pedestrian zone in Martin

In spite of being such an important centre of culture, Martin entered the 20th century as a small town (population 3,551 in 1900). In October 1918 the Slovak National Council adopted and approved the document known as **Martinská deklarácia** (Declaration of Martin) in the building of the former Tatra bank, now Slovenská sporiteľňa. The document expressed the will of the Slovak nation to enter the common state with the Czech nation which was to be founded after disintegration of Austria-Hungary. Revived activity of the Matica in Martin after 1919 fully unfolded the cultural and artistic life in the town, while industrial, food-processing and wood-processing plants were put in operation after the Second World War giving work to the locals and the villagers.

The historical centre of Martin is small. It spreads around the pedestrian zone next to the church of St. Martin

and continues as far as the Memoranndové námestie square with the Evangelical **church**. As Martin was stricken by repeated fire, which destroyed the town twice in the 19th century, there are not many historical monuments left. Houses built in the Art Nouveau style from the turn of the 19th and 20th centuries prevail. The oldest building of the town is the Roman Catholic **church of St. Martin ❶** from the mid-13th century built on the site of an older temple from the 10th century. During reconstruction made here in the 19th century precious Gothic frescoes were discovered under the layer of paint. The church contains the tombs of the Révay family, rests of Gothic statues, the Cross Way by Fraňo Štefunko and the picture of the Virgin Mary by Martin Benka. The Evangelical **church ❷**, which also stands on the Memorandové námestie square, was built after the Toleration Patent was issued in 1784 and financed by collection of believers. The dominant building of the Námestie

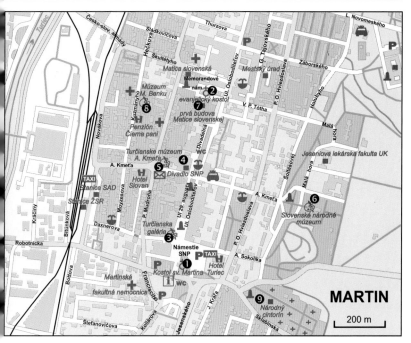

SNP square is that of the former **County House** from 1740. Originally it as a ground building, to which another floor was added and its facade adapted in the Classicist style. The County House became the seat of Turiec County administration after it was moved here from the Sklabiňa Castle in 1772. It was thoroughly reconstructed in 1983 and now it houses the **Turčianska galéria ❸** (Gallery of Turiec). It contains art works of the region from the Gothic period up to the present time with emphasis on the beginnings of the modern Slovak painting represented by artists like Martin Benka, Ľudovít Fulla, Janko Alexy, Miloš Alexander Bazovský, and the art legacy of the founder of the Slovak modern painting, Mikuláš Galanda.

The former **Národný dom ❹** (National House), built in 1889 financed by collections of common people, has always been the centre of cultural life. It sheltered the Slovak Choir and the collections of the Slovak Museum Society. After the Second World War, the Divadlo SNP (Theatre of the Slovak National Uprising) used the building. Reconstruction of this building started in 2001. In the former building of the first Slovak National Museum from 1908 which stands nearby is now the **Turčianske múzeum Andreja Kmeťa ❺** (Andrej Kmeťs Museum of Turiec). It is the National Cultural Monument since 1994. The second building of the Slovak National Museum at Malá hora is from 1933 and it houses the **Ethnographic Museum ❻**. The new building of the Slovak National Museum was built in the years 1929-1933 in order to place there the ever larger historical, ethnographic, nature-historical and numismatic collections. Parts of it are also a gallery and botanical garden. The Museum specialises in ethnography (for instance, it contains the largest collection of folk costumes in Slovakia), and a remarkable collection concerning the spheres of farming, bee-keeping, wood-carving, crafts, arts, etc.

The first building of Matica slovenská was opened at the third assembly of the institution in 1865. From its ban in 1875 until its reopening in 1919 it was owned and used by the government. Since its reconstruction in the 1980's it serves to the **Slovak National Literary Museum ❼** with exhibition of the oldest Slovak literature. Valuable documents and objects linked to the Slovak literature are gathered here. The courtyard of the Museum is the venue of different cultural activities in summer. The second building of **Matica slovenská** on Mudroňova ulica St. is from the 1930's and it houses several departments of the institution. Not far away from the Evangelical church is the old building of one of the original three "gymnasiums" of Matica slovenská, which offered secondary education to the Slovak youth in the years 1867-1875. Cultural institutions of Martin of

national importance include the **Museum of Martin Benka ❽** and the **Národná knižnica** (National Library). The Museum displays the paintings of this important Slovak artist in the authentic building where he lived and worked after 1958. The National Library contains more than three million of books and documents including literary legacy and correspondence of the most important figures of the Slovak cultural life. Many of them are also buried in the local **National Cemetery ❾**, which was designated the National Cultural Monument and its atmosphere is indeed impressing. Among the outstanding representatives of the Slovak literature, fine arts or drama buried here are the writers Svetozár Hurban Vajanský, Jozef Gregor Tajovský, Jozef Cíger Hronský, poets Janko Kráľ and Štefan Krčméry, painters Martin Benka, Miloš Alexander Bazovský and others.

Lovers of folk architecture will certainly stop at the **open-air Museum of**

Left: Museum of the Slovak Village
Right: Šútovský vodopád waterfall

the **Slovak Village** situated in the southern edge of the town in locality Jahodnícke háje. It is the largest exhibition of folk structures in Slovakia. Almost 100 examples of traditional folk buildings from the regions of Orava, Kysuce, Liptov, and Turiec are concentrated on the area of 28 hectares. Ethnographic summers are organised here when the local artisans bring their products and demonstrate their skills in all kinds of crafts. Typical refreshment is offered in the village inn, which is part of the area. On the road back to town there is also the option to stop at the mineral spring called Medokýš. On the western suburb of the town, Podstráne there is chair lift to **Martinské hole Mts**. that operates in winter seasons for skiers. This important centre of recreation, tourism and winter sports is also accessible by car. The Chata na Martinských holiach cottage is the favourite place for relaxation and an advantageous starting point for hiking trips to, for instance, Veľká Lúka and Minčol, easily accessible mountains.

Northern Turiec

Towns and villages of northern Turiec are the immediate starting points for the trips to the Malá Fatra Mts., above all to its Krivánska and Lúčanská parts. **VRÚTKY** (population 7,300) was first mentioned in 1255. During the whole of the Middle Ages it existed as a small farming village owned by different noble families. Its importance increased after the railway track connected it with the rest of the world by the end of the 19th century and Vrútky became the railway junction. The role of the town was also strengthened by construction of railway and repair workshops. Popular recreation centre **Piatrová** is situated in its southern edge.

The steep southern slopes of the Krivánska Fatra Mts. rise from the Turčianska kotlina basin and make the bulkiness of the range even more im-

pressing. The favourite salient point for the tops of the main ridge is the village **TURČIANSKE KĽAČANY** situated on the opposite bank of the Váh river. The hiking path, which starts in the village heads to the **Chata na Kľačianskej Magure** cottage with several ski facilities. There are several precious and important areas such as Suché, Krivé, Kľačianska Magura, and Hajasová protected by a stricter regime under nature conservation. The village **ŠÚTOVO** is another salient settlement for the trips to the Šútovská dolina valley. Parts of the eponymous National Nature Reserve are also the 38 m tall **Šútovský vodopád** waterfall, the tallest in the Malá Fatra Mts. and the attractive gorge of **Tesnô**.

SUČANY is the village situated in the southwest. It was continuously settled from the time of the Púchov culture. The first written mention of the village is from 1258. In the 14th century the local castle was mentioned. King Matthias had it pulled down after 1488. In the

mid-14th century Sučany acquired the town privilege with judicial autonomy and the market right. Sučany is now a large industrial settlement concentrated on wood-processing, production of building materials and it has the water power station. Another industrial village, **TURANY** is in its neighbourhood. It was a yeoman town in the past. One of the most valuable monuments in the region is situated in Turany. It is the Gothic **church** from the 13th century with wonderful wing altar from the end of the 15th century. In **TURČIANSKA ŠTIAVNIČKA** is the Renaissance **manor house** standing on the edge of the large park. If you continue down the nice valley of the Kantorský potok brook you will arrive at **SKLABINSKÝ PODZÁMOK**. The ruins of the Early Gothic **Sklabiňa Castle** from the 13th century stand above the village. The family of Révay had it adapted and a

Left: Sklabiňa Castle
Right: Necpaly

Renaissance manor house built in its courtyard. It was also fortified then. The Castle became the seat of the head of the County in time between the 14th and 18th centuries. The Renaissance manor house survived until the Second World War. After it burnt in 1944 it fell in decay together with the Castle. The next village **SKLABIŇA** was mentioned as early as 1258 and its history is linked to the eponymous castle. The people of Sklabiňa were nicknamed "môstkári" (bridge-builders) because every house had its own little footbridge over the brook which passes through the village.

TURČIANSKE JASENO is the place of origin of the famous family of Jesenský boasting the important scholar and physician known under the name **Ján Jesenius**. It was he, then the chancellor of the Prague University, who demonstrated the first public autopsy in Europe. He participated in the Rebellion of Estates in Czechia, which won him imprisonment and execution on the

Staromestské námestie square in Prague. At the 430th anniversary of his birth (in 1966) the Jesenius' **commemorative room** was opened in his native village. Another village, **KOŠŤANY NAD TURCOM** became famous for peddlers with medicinal oils and saffron, who travelled as far as Russia, Latvia or Netherlands with their goods. There are remains of **folk architecture** from the 19th century with typical arched gates and the Rococo-Classicist **manor house** from the second half of the 18th century.

In the eastern part of the Turčianska kotlina basin, below the slopes of the Veľká Fatra Mts. there are several villages interesting for tourists. **BELÁ-DULICE** is known thanks the **Jasenská dolina** valley with its ski centre, which offers options of accommodation. Going up the Belianska or Jasenská dolina valleys it is possible to climb the **Lysec Mt.** (1,381 m), which is the dominant of the area. Its top is good for views, which are indeed captivating. At the head of the

Belianska dolina valley is another natural dominant – the mountain **Borišov**, below which is the picturesque mountain cottage, the only of the kind in the Veľká Fatra Mts. At the point where the Necpalská dolina valley contacts with the Turčianska kotlina basin is the village **NECPALY** with interesting history. The hoard of bronze and golden objects found here some time ago testifies to the settlement of the area by people of Lusatian culture in the Bronze Age. The first written reference to the village is from 1266. The village has four manor houses but all of them are closed to public. The Early Gothic Roman Catholic **church** from the 13th century contains the Romanesque sanctuary and frescoes from the 14th century. Another dominant of the village is the Late Classicist Evangelical **church** built in the 19th century on the site of an old wooden church.

Further in south situated **BLATNICA** represents an old cultural village also known for medicinal oil and saffron

peddlers. The local folk architecture is well preserved. Not far away from the village are the ruins of the **Blatnický hrad** Castle, which dates to the 13th century. It was the centre of the Blatnica estate with 16 villages. The castle was inhabited until 1790 and then it fell in decay. Apart from its walls, remains of domes and loopholes survive. The environs of the village are the richest archaeological sites in this part of Slovakia. Settlements from the Upper Stone Age and the Roman Era were found in the cave **Na vyhni** above the Konský dol. At the beginning of the Gaderská dolina valley, on the slope of the Plešovica Mt. in turn, the fortified settlement from the Bronze Age and Roman Era is situated. In the centre of the village stands the Late Baroque **manor house** from the 18th century, which shelters the **Museum of Karol Plicka**, photographer. It is worth visiting

Left: Environs of the Mažarná cave
Right: Meander of the Turiec river

as it contains an original collection of historical photographs focused on Slovakia and its people, made with absolute mastery. Original **houses** of peddlers selling medicinal oils and saffron from the turn of the 18th and 19th centuries can be seen next to the Blatnický potok brook. The local Baroque-Classicist **curia** is from the first half of the 18th century and the evangelical **church** is from the 18th century. Many important personalities were born in this picturesque village, it was for instance the first Slovak lady-botanist, Izabela Textorisová (there is her **commemorative room** in the building of the former school) or brothers Siakeľ who chose precisely Blatnica to make here the first Slovak feature film in 1921. The people of Blatnica, mostly peddlers selling medicinal oils, travelled to Russia and supplied the region with tea imported from this country. Blatnica became part of history of the Slovak National Uprising against the Nazi invaders, as commemorates the **Park národov** (Park of Nations) situated at the point where Gaderská dolina valley crosses the Blatnická dolina valley. Historical stables, which were used for horse breeding in time of Empress Maria Theresa are also one of the attractions of the village. The horses bred here now are used for recreation riding and therapy of children.

Situation of Blatnica next to the **Gaderská dolina** and **Blatnická dolina** valleys is an ideal salient point for the trips to the most beautiful valleys of the Veľká Fatra Mts. Continuation of the Gaderská dolina valley in its upper end is the valley of **Dedošová** and together they are almost 18 kilometres long. It is in fact a canyon with bulky rocks, rock tower and other interestingly shaped rock formations. Its rich and rare flora and occurrence of rare animals enhance its attractiveness. The Blatnická dolina valley is somewhat shorter but also interesting. It is often use for the access to the areas of Krížna and Kráľova studňa Mts. in the main ridge of the Veľká Fatra

Mts. In the lower part of the valley is the conspicuous rock - Skalné okno (Rock Window). The marked hiking trail, which passes up in places deep and canyon-shaped Konský dol and leads to the imposing limestone massif of **Tlstá**, connects the Gaderská and Blatnická dolina valleys. The ascent to the Tlstá Mt. is rather demanding even for experienced hikers. Beyond the altitude of 700 m there are bulky rock terraces and tall rock faces visible from large distance. There is also one of the largest caves of the Veľká Fatra Mts., it is the **Mažarná** cave. Its particularity is the spring from limestone substratum, which is a rare phenomenon at this altitude above sea level. The spring was probably the cause of the fact that the cave was always used as the refuge for men and animals, as testified to by finds from the Neolithic periods. Nevertheless, the cave is not accessible to public so visitors have to limit themselves to contemplating of its impressing portal.

In the central part of the Turčianska kotlina basin near the Turiec rives is the Nature Reserve of **Kláštorské lúky**, important botanical site with occurrence of several rare plant and animal species and that of migrating fowl. The Turiec river is characterised by numerous **meanders**. If you climb the hill Stráž nad Socovcami with the 13th century church on its top, you will get a nice view of the meandering river. In the village of **PRÍBOVCE** the local Evangelical **church** attracts attention, as its tower from 1901 is considered the most beautiful in the region of Turiec. On the western side of the Turčianska kotlina basin there lye several communities which can be used for the access to the area of the Lúčanská Fatra Mts. In **VALČA** there is the Classicist **manor house** from the first half of the 19th century and the Early Renaissance **church** from the 16th century. Recently a new ski centre was established in this village situated next to the lower ends of the

Valčianska and Slovianska dolina valleys.

Further in south lying **KLÁŠTOR POD ZNIEVOM** is the village with the richest history in the region of Turiec. It was first referred to as early as 1113. It was situated next to the old trade road leading from the region of Ponitrie to Poland. In 1248 the Premonstratesian order moved here in their newly built church and monastery. A settlement then called Znievske podhradie formed around it. King Belo IV granted, as the first community in Turiec, the town privilege. The monastery played an important role in the political and economic life in the region of Turiec. Jesuits, who dedicated themselves to growing medicinal herbs and production of medicinal oils took over the monastery in 1586. One of the first three Slovak grammar

*Left: The former grammar school
in Kláštor pod Znievom
Right: Blue Bath in Turčianske Teplice*

schools existed here in the years 1869-1874. The **Premonstratesian monastery** from the 13th century and its **church**, the Early Gothic parish **church of St. Nicolas**, the former Classicist **town hall** and the **church** of top of Calvary are the historic monuments of Kláštor pod Znievom today. High above the village rise the ruins of the **Zniev** Castle. The original castle was first mentioned in 1243 as Turčiansky hrad Castle. In the 14th century a Gothic building and new fortifications were added to it. Thököly's soldiers set fire to the castle in 1688 and it was gradually abandoned and changed into ruins after the 18th century. The village **VRÍCKO**, which lies near originated in the 14th century and was owned by Jesuits. In the village some surviving remains of folk architecture can be seen. The village is good for starting the trips to the dominant of the southern part of the Lúčanská Fatra Mts., the **Kľak** Mt. top of which offers a wonderful panoramic view.

Southern Turiec

The centre of the southern part of the Turčianska kotlina basin is the spa **TURČIANSKE TEPLICE** (population 7,000). The local hot springs were first mentioned in 1281 while the existence of community dates to 1351. The legend has that King Sigismund of Luxembourg bathed in local springs in 1423. The town of Kremnica acquired the land with springs and invested in construction of the first spa buildings. The spa was especially popular and visited in time of wars with the Habsburgs when the noble rebels used it as a refuge. The spa buildings consist of several structures built in the Rococo-Classicist style, while the foundations of the oldest of them are from the 16th century. It expanded in 1885 when the remarkable Late Classicist polygonal domed building of **Modrý kúpeľ** (The Blue Bath) and a park were added to it. The spa still operates and it is indicated for the diseases of locomotive apparatus, urological and gynaecological disorders including skin diseases. The capacity of the spa is 500 beds, and about 7,000 patients a year. Experts recommend at least a 4-week stay to attain the full effect of the treatment although a fortnight stay also positively influences the bodily functions. The local medicinal water emanates in seven springs yielding up to 30 l/s with temperature between 38 and 47.5 degrees of Celsius. The spa area spreads in the southern part of the town and consists of several buildings. The large **park**, protected area, is 2 km long and it stretches as far as Dolná Štubňa. There are also two thermal swimming pools. The important Slovak painter Mikuláš **Galanda** (1895-1938) is the local native and **exhibition** of his paintings is installed in his native house. Part of the town is **DIVIAKY** with the Renaissance **manor house** from the second half of the 17th century and another Rococo-Classicist **manor house** built in the mid-18th century. The building of the

Classicist **belfry** with square ground plan is from 1833.

Several interesting landmarks can be seen in **MOŠOVCE** situated further in north. The village was first mentioned in 1233. Mošovce, originally privileged yeoman town, was later administered by the Sklabiňa estate and the Révay family. The typical occupation of the local people, like in the whole region of Turiec, was production of medicinal oils and trade in saffron. The home-pressed oils were exported to many foreign countries. In their best times as much as 900 peddlers with oil left Turiec and travelled as far as Ukraine, Poland, Russia, Netherlands or Germany. Normally they left when the farm work was finished in autumn and returned in springtime. **Ján Kollár**, (1793-1852) poet and historian, native of Mošovce, eager promoter of solidarity among the Slav nations, ranks among the most important Slovak figures in the area of culture. The place where his native house used to stand was adapted to a park with a **com-**

JAZERNICA, situated not far from Mošovce has the Gothic church with the Romanesque ground plan from the beginning of the 15th century. The interesting item in its interior is the Late Gothic wing altar from 1517 with paintings. The protected natural phenomenon called **Jazierko**, it is what the experts call the spring lake surrounded by rare marshy vegetation. West of Jazernica is the oldest village of the region, **SLOVENSKÉ PRAVNO**, mentioned for the first time in historical documents as early as 1113. The village acquired the market right in 1665 and its people were involved mostly in farming and pottery. The historical buildings of this village include the originally Renaissance **curia** from the beginning of the 17th century. The Rococo **manor house** was built in 1754 on older foundations. The originally Gothic **church** was adapted in the Renaissance style by the end of the 18th century. It is fenced by wall and next to its southern part is the **belfry** from the beginning of the 17th century.

JASENOVO lies further in south and it is known for surviving remains of folk architecture – log houses with carved gables. The village is a convenient starting locality for trips to the mountain range of Žiar. The most important mountain of this range is the conspicuous rocky **Vyšehrad Mt.** with far-reaching views from its top. It is also famous archaeological site, which was settled since the Upper Stone Age. On its top there are the ruins of once important castle from the 13th century. The village **BUDIŠ** is known for the local mineral water sold under the eponymous trademark. There are three springs and the bottling plant in the village. Some visitors will appreciate the architecture of the original log **houses** with wooden gables.

German colonists arriving here in the course of the 14th century significantly influenced the development of Turiec. The oldest settlements were founded here on the edge of the upper part of the Turčianska kotlina basin

memorative tablet. This village has an interesting Rococo-Classicist **manor house** from the second half of the 18th century, which stands on the edge of the large English **park** with several interesting structures. The garden pavilion from 1800 was built in the Classicist style. Mausoleum in the Art Nouveau style houses the **Museum of Guilds of Mošovce**. The Neo-Gothic Roman Catholic **church** has a valuable interior decoration, Gothic statues and paintings moved here from the original Gothic church. Mošovce are now popular for its recreation centre and the local manufacture of fur coats. Next to the thermal spring is the **sport area of Drienok** with swimming pools, playgrounds and accommodation facility. The system of tree rows and the river bank greenery, older than 100 years, is also among the prides of this village.

Left: Church in Mošovce
Right: Rock faces of the Tlstá Mt. in Veľká Fatra

(Horný Turček, Dolný Turček, Sklené, Horná Štubňa) and German colonists also settled in already existing communities such as Dolná Štubňa or Čremošné. The second wave of German colonisation arrived by the end of the 14th century to settle the western part of Turiec. Germans founded here Vrícko and also strengthened the original Slovak population in Jasenovo and Brieštie, while they avoided the central parts of the basin.

Among the most important cultural and historical monuments of the southern part of Turiec is the **church** in **HORNÁ ŠTUBŇA**. It was built in the mid-17th century on older foundation and later the tower was added to it. The Renaissance **church** in **SKLENÉ** is equally interesting. Natural and protected peat bog with occurrence of rare plant species is situated near the village **RAKŠA**.

DOLNÝ TURČEK was the village of colliers in the past and beehives carved in wood in form of male or female figures are the typical products of the locals. **HORNÝ TURČEK** in turn offers a remarkable technical monument, the old **water main** from the 14th century, which supplied the mines in Kremnické Bane. A modern water reservoir was built in Horný Turček which supplies water to the deficient areas around the towns of Prievidza and Žiar nad Hronom.

The oldest written reference to **ČREMOŠNÉ** is from 1340. Golden ore was once extracted in its environs. The attractive recreation area of Čremošnianske lazy with ski lifts and tourist cottages is situated on the meadows above the village. In the Žarnovická dolina valley, not far from the village the **cottage**, which commemorates the historical meeting of the then illegal Slovak National Council with the military leaders

of the country where it was decided on the start of the Slovak National Uprising against the German occupation. The spa of Turčianske Teplice along with the village Čremošné are ideal for starting trips to the southern part of the Veľká Fatra Mts. and the Kremnické vrchy Mts. **Veľká Fatra Mts.** is among the first large-area protected landscape territories designated in 1974. The result of the 30-year experience in nature conservation is that the most valuable natural assets are successfully surviving here. Among them is the concentration of **yew trees** in the southern part of the range, which is the largest in Europe in terms of tree number (more than 150 thousand specimens). The Veľká Fatra Mts. was designated the **National Park** in spring 2002.

MARTIN
(dial: 043-)

Information
- **Turisticko-informačná kancelária mesta Martin**, Divadelné nám. 1, Martin, ☎ 16186, 4238776, tik@martin.sk, www.martin.sk, **CK Stahlreisen**, Ul. 29. augusta 9, Martin, ☎ 4131407, 4221855, fax 4132994, info@stahl.sk, www.stahl.sk

Museums
- **Etnografické múzeum**, Malá hora 2, Martin, ☎ 4131011, **Turčianske múzeum Andreja Kmeťa**, A. Kmeťa 2, Martin, ☎ 4230639, **Múzeum slovenskej dediny**, Jahodnícke háje, Martin, ☎ 4132686, 4139491, **Múzeum Martina Benku**, Kuzmányho 34, Martin, ☎ 4133190, **Slovenské národné literárne múzeum Matice slovenskej**, Osloboditeľov 11, Martin, ☎ 4134152, **Národný cintorín**, Sklabinská ul., Martin, ☎ 4230377, **Dokumentačné centrum českej kultúry na Slovensku**, Moyzesova 11, Martin, ☎ 4230136, **Dokumentačné centrum rómskej kultúry**, Malá hora 2, Martin, ☎ 4131011

Galleries
- **Turčianska galéria**, Daxnerova 2, Martin, ☎ 4224448

Atractiveness
- **Church of St. Martin**, Martin, ☎ 4220794, **Swimming pool SUNNY**, Na Bystričku, Martin, ☎ 4133827

Hotels
- **GRANDIS***, Hrdinov SNP 90, Martin, ☎ 4220015, **TURIEC***, A. Sokolíka 2, Martin, ☎ 4221017, **LUNA***, A. Medňanského 18, Martin, ☎ 4281894, **SI****, Prieložtek 1, Martin, ☎ 4307101, 4134659, **OLYMP***, Kollárova 49, Martin, ☎ 4238275

Restaurants
- **MAJA**, Jesenského 10, Martin, ☎ 4230942, **ETNA**, Osloboditeľov 54, Martin, ☎ 4220886, **ČIERNA PANI**, Kuzmányho 24, Martin, ☎ 4131523, **TOSCA**, Na Bystričku 137, Martin, ☎ 4134786

NORTHERN TURIEC
(dial: 043-)

Information
- **Informačné centrum JASED Jasenská dolina**, Belá-Dulice 385, ☎/fax 4297717, jased@enelux.sk, www.jasenskadolina.sk, **Komunikačné centrum Združenia cestovného ruchu Veľká Fatra**, Belá-Dulice, ☎ 4297768, info@velkafatra.sk, www.velkafatra.sk, **TUR.I.EC – Turisticko-informačné ekocentrum**, Dom služieb, Blatnica, ☎ 4948284, turiecinfo@stonline.sk

Museums
- **Múzeum Karola Plicku**, Blatnica, ☎ 4948142

Atractiveness
- **Swimming pool**, Horná ul., Vrútky, ☎ 4284935, **Sklabiňa** Castle, Sklabinský Podzámok, **Šútovský vodopád** waterfall, Šútovo, **Blatnický hrad** Castle, Blatnica, **Zniev** Castle, Kláštor pod Znievom

Hotels
- **GADER****, Blatnica, ☎ 4948106, **PIATROVÁ***, Karvaša-Bláhovca, Vrútky, ☎ 4284298

Restaurants
- **NOSTALGIA**, Sládkovičova 9, Vrútky, ☎ 4285588, **GADER**, Blatnica 53, ☎ 4948194, **RANČ U BARTOŠA**, Žabokreky 140, ☎ 4388166

SOUTHERN TURIEC
(dial: 043-)

Information
- **Kultúrna a informačná agentúra**, Partizánska 1, Turčianske Teplice, ☎ 4923229

Museums
- **Rodný dom Mikuláša Galandu**, Kollárova ul., Turčianske Teplice, ☎ 4924270, **Múzeum mošovských cechov a remesiel**, Mošovce, ☎ 4944196

Thermal swimming pools
- **VIESKA**, Turčianske Teplice, ☎ 4923464, **V PARKU**, Turčianske Teplice, ☎ 4913369

Hotels
- **LESNÍK***, Kuzmányho 18, Turčianske Teplice, ☎ 4922543, **GEOSTROJ**, Banská 529, Turčianske Teplice, ☎ 4924275, **RELAXTOUR**, Partizánska 41, Turčianske Teplice, ☎ 4922650, **VYŠEHRAD**, Kollárova 501, Turčianske Teplice, ☎ 4922583

Restaurants
- **PANDA**, Slnečná 3, Turčianske Teplice, ☎ 4924169, **MILKA**, Partizánska 412, Turčianske Teplice, ☎ 4922631, **CORADDO**, Horná Štubňa 365, ☎ 4927004, **DRIENOK**, Na Drienok 460, Mošovce, ☎ 4944162

PONITRIE

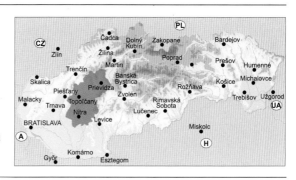

Nitra

Environs of Nitra

Upper Nitra

Ponitrie is one of the regions of Slovakia interesting not only for its natural beauty, but above all for its cultural-historical heritage. Ponitrie has attracted our ancestors who left their traces all over the area. Especially, the arrival of the Slav tribes at the territory of Slovakia, their concentration in the area of Nitra, and the foundation of the first Slav Principality increase importance of this territory. If we add the natural attractiveness of its landscape to the overall picture, it is indeed an interesting area.

The region spreads on the area of almost four thousand square kilometres and more than half million inhabitants live here. It consists of the districts of Nitra, Zlaté Moravce, Topoľčany, Partizánske, Bánovce nad Bebravou, and Prievidza, which are well connected by road and railway networks. The prevailing part of the territory is filled by the Podunajská pahorkatina hill land delimited by the Považský Inovec Mts., Strážovské vrchy Mts. Tribeč and the Pohronský Inovec Mts. In the north, the territory borders on the Hornonitrianska kotlina basin skirted by the mountain ranges of Vtáčnik, Kremnické vrchy and Žiar in the east.

Nitra

The itinerary pursuing the beauties and landmarks of Ponitrie starts at the very centre of the area, the town of **NITRA**. As far as population number is concerned (87,300), this is the largest town of the region and the fourth largest of Slovakia. Nitra is referred to as the oldest urban formation in Slovakia as it exists since the 870's AD. Nitra was especially attractive for settlers as great amount of finds from the Iron and Stone Ages and later Bronze Age testify to. It was settled by the Slavs in the 5th and 6th century and Nitra became the political, economic, and cultural centre of the Slav tribes north of the Danube in the 7th century. The **Principality of Nitra** ruled by **Prince Pribina** was formed here at the turn of the 8th and 9th centuries. Pribina was the first known ruler of the Slav tribe considered the predecessor of Slovaks. Pribina had the first Christian church built

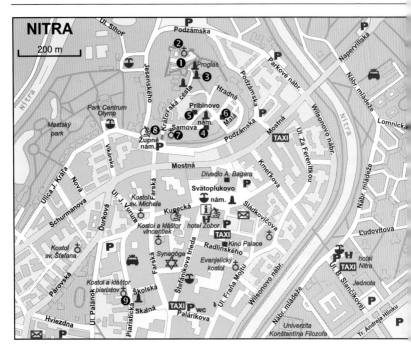

in the territory of what is now Slovakia, particularly in Nitra in 828, and the Archbishop Adalram of Salzburg consecrated it. Nitra progressively became part of the prosperous Great Moravian Empire with King Mojmír I at the head. The **Bishopric of Nitra** along with the first monastery in the territory of today's Slovakia originated in the 9th century. Great Moravia lived its best time in time of King Svätopluk I and Nitra was then the main centre of this realm. The famous legend about the **three rods of King Svätopluk** is also from this time. When King Svätopluk was dying he had his three sons invited to his bed and handed one rod to each of them. He asked them to break it. After his sons easily broke the rods, the King tied the three rods and again asked his sons to break the rods. This time it was not so easy. This was the way Svätopluk wanted to demonstrate his progeny the need of solidarity as the guarantee of invincibility and prosperity. How-

ever, his sons did not draw any lesson from their father's warning and divided the Kingdom of the Great Moravia after his death. Invasion of old Hungarian tribes finished with the Slav realm in 906.

The Principality of Nitra survived the following two centuries to become part of the **Kingdom of Hungary** afterwards. The Archbishopric of Esztergom was founded in 1000 and the area of Nitra became its Bishopric. Two valuable written documents known as the **Documents of Zobor** are still deposited in the archives of the Nitra Bishopric. They were written in the years 1111 and 1113. The younger of them is especially well-known. It is the list of the extensive monastic properties, which stretched from town of Trenčín to the Danube river. Nitra became the **free royal borough** on 2 September 1248 when King Belo IV granted privileges to the Lower Town of Nitra. The Castle of Nitra with the Upper Town remained property of the Bishopric, but the short history of Nitra as the free royal borough ended in 1288 when it became the

Right: Nitra

yeoman town, which in spite of it withheld certain autonomy. Bishops mostly respected the rights of the burghers who in turn guaranteed development of trade and crafts. War events such as conquering of Nitra by the troops of Ján Jiskra in 1440, Turkish raids and Rebellion of Estates decisively influenced further development of the town. Turks did not succeed to conquer Nitra in 1642 but they did occupy it in 1663 for one year. The last heavy blow for Nitra was the Rákoczi's rebellion at the beginning of the 18th century when Nitra has to be almost completely rebuilt. Restoration of the town was made in the Baroque style. It enriched the town by numerous architectural buildings, which are now its pride. The beginnings of the 19th century brought about the stages of Empire and Classicism, which also have left traces in the historical part of Nitra.

Nitra, now administrative centre of the region is also its important economic centre, seat of two universities and above all, centre of agricultural schooling and re-search. It has got varied cultural life (theatre festival Divadelná Nitra, Musical Spring of Nitra, etc.) and the trade activities involved in agriculture also concentrate here including the nation-wide agricultural exhibition Agrokomplex organised in August every year. Visitors of Nitra can stop at the **Slovenské poľnohospodárske múzem** (Slovak Agricultural Museum) with open-air expositions at the rear of the exhibition area or the **museum** with exhibition of historic motorcycles, Nitrianska galéria (The Gallery of Nitra), and **Ponitrianske múzeum** (Museum of Ponitrie) situated in the centre of the town. The latter mentioned Museum seats in the Neo-Renaissance building from 1880 and apart from standing collections it also prepares several thematic exhibitions throughout the year. Fans of theatre will certainly visit the **Divadlo Andreja Bagara** (Theatre of Andrej Bagar) in the centre. It is the liveliest part of the town, especially the pedestrian zone on Štefánikova trieda St. with numerous coffee-houses offers pleasant moments of relaxation.

The dominant of the town is the **Castle of Nitra ❶**. It was built in the 11th century on the site of a bulky Slav fort and it consists of several parts. The core of the Castle is the cathedral with adjacent Bishop's residence. The oldest surviving part of the cathedral is the Romanesque **church of St. Emeram ❷** from the 11th or 12th century. It was rebuilt after fire in the second half of the 13th century and after Matúš Čák's soldiers destroyed it, a new Gothic church was built next to it in 1317. From then it served as what is called the "trustworthy" place of chapter and later as the treasury of the cathedral. Today, it forms together with the Upper and Lower Churches the most valuable structure in the area of the Castle. The originally Gothic **Upper Church** was built in the years 1333-1335 and three centuries later the **Lower Church** was added to it. A wide staircase connects both of them. The appearance of the cathedral

as we know it now is from the years 1710-1736 and its interior is also from that time. Among the most valuable monuments of the interior is the main altar of the Lower Church made by the Austrian sculptor J. Pernegger who used the painting of D. Voltera as a model. The originally Gothic **Bishop's Palace** standing by these sacral buildings obtained its Late Baroque appearance in the second half of the 18th century. Its outer fortifications with the oldest parts from the Romanesque period are especially interesting. The legendary **Vazulova veža** tower with square ground plan was several times rebuilt and adapted in the Romantic style in the second half of the 19th century. Allegedly the Hungarian Prince Vazul was imprisoned in this tower. In the southern part of the Early Baroque fortifications with bastions and cellars is the **entrance gate of Bishop Pálffy** from 1673 and the bridge over the castle dike with stone ornamentation from the 18th century. The **Castle well** and the Baroque pillar with the statue of the **Immaculate Conception ❸** from 1750 made by the Austrian sculptor M. Vogerle are the reminders of plague epidemic of the first half of the 18th century.

The **Upper Town** was founded below the Castle and became part of its Gothic fortifications. Its present Baroque-Classicist appearance consists of Great Seminar, Franciscan monastery and the County House. Though the sacral monuments prevail one can also find here several wonderful burgher houses. Veľký seminár or the **Great Seminar ❹** is the most important Baroque building of the town. It was built in the 1770's while the Neo Renaissance part of the building was added to in 1877. This building houses the large and valuable Bishop's library. Malý seminár or the **Small Seminar ❺** stands opposite and it was built in the Neo-Classicist style in the second half of the 19th century following the design of K. Mayer. The bulky **statue of Prince Pribina**, the first known ruler of Slavs and the legendary figure of Nitra stands in front of it, Visitors of this part of the town will certainly stop at the

Empire **house of Bishop Kluch** (U Corgoňa) ❻ from 1818-1821 and at its corner the statue of Corgoň, which also gave name to the local beer, stands. Another important building of the Upper town is the Roman-Catholic **church** and **monastery** ❼ of Franciscan order. This Baroque structure was built in 1630 on the site of an older building. It was destroyed during Turkish occupation in the years 1663-1664 and practically decayed until the beginning of the 18th century. It acquired its present appearance in the 18th century and in its interior are interesting relieves of F. X. Seegen moved here from the monastery at Zobor. The historicizing Art Nouveau building of the former **Župný dom** (County House) ❽ built by the end of the 19th century stands nearby. Part of this two-storied house

with its southern facade turned towards the Lower Town is the underpass through which one can enter the Upper Town.

The **Lower Town** is situated south of the Upper Town and separated from it by the arm of the Nitra river. Only some remains are left of it apart from several 19th century houses and churches. Its most important sacral monuments include the Piarist monastery and church, and the Vincent monastery with church, synagogue and the church of St. Steven. The Roman Catholic **church of St. Steven** is one of the oldest buildings of the town, as its oldest parts date as early as 10th century. Its present appearance is the result of the 1720 reconstruction. In its interior are the remains of the Romanesque

frescoes. The extensive Baroque complex of the **monastery** and **church ❾** of Piarists was built by the male order on the site on the former Great Moravian fort. It was built in several stages in the 18th century and its interior is furnished with items from the same time and the most valuable is the Baroque main altar. The Vincent **monastery** and **church** from the years 1852 to 1865, as well as the **synagogue** from 1911 conclude the list of sacral monuments of this part of the town. The **monument dedicated to the victims of Holocaust** stands at the Jewish cemetery.

The trip by chair lift to the top of the **Zobor Mt.** offers a wonderful view of Nitra and its environs and pleasant walks in the landscape park which also contains the instructive path Zobor, which passes by the sanatorium built on the foundations of the Benedictine monastery of St. Hippolite from the 10th century, the oldest in Slova-

Left: Constantine and Methodius
Right: Church in Kostoľany. Castle Gýmeš

kia. Next to is the entrance to the **Svoradova jaskyňa** cave bearing the name of hermit St. Svorad who allegedly lived here in the 11th century. St. Svorad is buried in the Castle cathedral. The road from Zobor passes through the viticultural part of the town with little **taverns** inviting the passers-by to taste the exquisite local wine. Another interesting landmark of the town is **Calvary** with 14 chapels of Cross Way from the end of the 19th century.

Environs of Nitra

Leaving Nitra in the north-eastern direction along the eastern foothills of the Tribeč Mt. the road passes by the village of **JELENEC**. Jelenec has got several interesting houses built of earthen bricks from the 19th century, the Roman Catholic Baroque **church** from 1720 and the Baroque manor house from 1722 rebuilt in the 20th century. The recreation centre of **Jelenec-Remitáž** with water reservoir and a fishing pond is quite near. There is also the **Jelenská gaštanica** natural reserve with the oldest artificially planted stand of chestnut trees in Slovakia. The rich history and culture of this area is documented by the exceptionally valuable pre-Romanesque **church of St. George** from the 10th century in **KOSTOĽANY POD TRIBEČOM** which is the oldest complete pre-Romanesque architecture in the territory of Slovakia. Its interior contains the remains of the Romanesque and Gothic wall paintings from the 11th century (the oldest in Slovakia) and the Romanesque stone baptistery. Above the village, at the height of 514 m there are ruins of the originally Gothic Castle **Gýmeš,** built in the second half of the 13th century on the site of an older fort. The castle was the centre of the estate Jelenec or Gýmeš in the past owned by the Forgách family. Although Turks conquered and damaged it, it was renewed and inhabited until 1865. It fell in decay afterwards.

The state road E 571 continues from Jelenec by the village of **BELADICE** with the Baroque-Classicist manor house from the 18th century and rebuilt in 1874, sur-

rounded by valuable old lime and alder trees. It is now used as a school. The following town on the route is **ZLATÉ MO-RAVCE** (population 15,600) follows. It is the former centre town of the Tekov County, today the principal town of the region of Požitavie. The famous history of the town first mentioned in historical documents in 1113 is characterised by several historic monuments. The most interesting profane monuments include the original Renaissance **manor house** from 1630, rebuilt at the end of the 18th century in the Baroque style and widened in the 20th century, the Renaissance **County House** from the 17th century, and the **mausoleum** of the Migazzi family. The local manor house shelters Museum of natural history including the **commemorative room** of poet Janko Kráľ. The most important sacral

dominant of the town is the Classicist **church of St. Michael the Archange**l from 1785 rebuilt in 1823. The most famous citizen of Zlaté Moravce was the poet **Janko Kráľ** (1722-1876) whose grave here is only symbolical as he is in fact buried in the National Cemetery in Martin.

The village **TOPOLČIANKY** lying north of Zlaté Moravce in the valley of the Žitava river below the foothills of the Tribeč Mts. is especially attractive for tourists. The pride of the village is above all the extensive English park with picturesque Classicist **manor house**, the southern tract of an older castle. Originally there stood a Gothic water castle replaced by the Renaissance fort, which was the seat of the Tekov County in the 16th and 17th centuries and played an important role in defence against the Turks. By the beginning of the 19th century the then owner Count Ján Keglevich had the southern Renaissance

tract of the castle pulled down and built a Classicist one on its site, which is considered one of the purest and most beautiful architecture in Classicist style in Slovakia. In the past, the castle was the summer residence of the Habsburg royal house and after the Second World War it also served as such to Czechoslovak presidents. It was when also the last thorough adaptation of the structure was accomplished. The first president of the Czechoslovak Republic, T. G. Masaryk especially liked to relax and work at this place. The last of the presidents who dwelled here in 1951, was Antonín Zápotocký. The Classicist tract was progressively changed into a **museum**. Visitors today can admire the library with more than 14,000 volumes, one of the few fully conserved Castle libraries in Slovakia. The interior and valuable furniture from the 16th to 19th centuries with wonderful ornamentation and collections of porcelain and ceramics (one of the largest in Slovakia) also deserve attention. Three Renaissance tracts of the Castle are now used as a **hotel** with presidential apartments, beside other. The little hunting castle with a beautiful park full of precious imported wood species, national stud and horse racing track make of Topoľčianky is the favourite and frequently visited destination of trippers. One of its attractiveness is also the **game park** where on an area of 30 hectares several tens of European bison imported from Poland live. The local farms traditionally breed horses. Several kilometres north of Topoľčianky are the ruins of **Hrušov** Castle towering on top of the   Skalka

Left: The manor house in Topoľčianky
Right: Game park. Hrušov Castle

Mt. at the height of 488 m. This royal castle built in the 13th century guarded the trade road passing over the mountain range Tribeč. It was destroyed by the Imperial army in 1708 and is in decay since then. However, its surviving walls induce romantic atmosphere and provide a nice panoramic view of the Tribeč and Pohronský Inovec Mts.

The road continues from Zlaté Moravce southward and passes through the villages **VIESKA NAD ŽITAVOU** and **TESÁRSKE MLYŇANY** with **arboretum Mlyňany**, one of the most beautiful gardens of Central Europe. This master piece of gardening specialised in acclimatisation of foreign wood species enhanced by sophisticated garden architecture with the Neo-Classicist manor house will certainly satisfy any fan of gardening. Štefan Ambrózy founded it in 1892 when he bought a small forest on the slope of the valley of the Žitava river and started to plant imported exotic wood species. At the present time on an area of 67 hectares there grow more than 2,300 species of deciduous and coniferous trees. The park consists of the European, American, Chinese and Japanese parts with small ponds and lakes, and oriental arbours which supplement the scenery with great taste. After seeing the area the tourist also stop in the town of **VRÁBLE** (population 9,500), one of the farming centres of the region of Požitavie. **Ruins** of the Baroque counter-Turk fort from the first half of the 17th century testify to history of this originally market and yeoman town. The fort has repeatedly saved the locals from Turkish raids. Sacral monuments of the town include the Neo-Romanes-

que **church**, Late-Baroque **chapel** and the group of statues of **Calvary**. Fans of wine will not miss the **national archives of wines** in the locality Pod vinicami, which concentrates the wines of best quality from several viticultural regions of Slovakia. The local **water reservoir** offers possibilities of refreshment and water sport in hot summer months. Those who prefer bathing in thermal water will go southward of Nitra and stop at **POĽNÝ KESOV**, the village with two-open air pools with thermal water.

Going from Nitra straight to north, you will also find the western foothills of the Tribeč mountain range interesting. The first village after leaving Nitra behind is **DRAŽOVCE,** an important archaeological site with Slav settlement and cemetery from the time of the Great Moravian Empire. The well-preserved picturesque Romanesque **church of St. Michael** from

Left: The church in Dražovce
Right: The square in Topoľčany

the beginning of the 12th century is the historical attractiveness of the village. This repeatedly adapted church was built on the site of a fort from the Iron Age. A short walk leading to the church will also offer you an interesting view of the town of Nitra. Younger history of the area is documented by two **manor houses** from the 17th and 19th centuries in the village **HORNÉ LEFANTOVCE** situated not far away from Nitra. The older Renaissance manor house from 1618, originally medieval castle standing on elevated terrace above the village surrounded by park, was the residence of important noble family Elefanty and the younger manor house was adapted from the original monastery from the 14th century. Another important Hungarian noble family of Apponyi resided in the village **OPONICE**. The ruins of the **Oponický hrad** Castle witness to the famous history of the village. The Castle was built in the 13th century and it resisted the Turkish raids in the past. It was fortified in the 16th century and rebuilt in the Renaissance style. It burnt in 1645 and fell in decay. The Apponyi family built the Renaissance **manor house** in the village in the 17th century and rebuilt it in the mid-19th century in order to place there one of the largest **library** in the Kingdom of Hungary of that time. History of the area is also documented by the Renaissance **manor house** from the 17th century built on older foundations in **NOVÉ SADY** and **manor houses** from the 16th and 19th centuries in **NITRIANSKA STREDA** and **BOŠANY**, the centre of leather-processing industry in Slovakia.

The seat of district administration **TOPOĽČANY** (population 28,950) has not got such a rich history as Nitra, nevertheless it also possesses structures worth to see. The first written reference to the settlement in the territory of Topoľčany is from 1173. It was part of the royal property and in 1342 the King Charles Robert promoted it to royal borough. Fortifications from the 15th century reveal its importance. The town was granted the right of storage and

toll collection and it had a mail station on the imperial-royal road **Via Magna**, which was finished in 1550 as one of the longest mail and transport communications in the Kingdom of Hungary. It connected Vienna with Košice, Debrecen and Sibia in Romania. The Baroque **church** of Topoľčany from 1740 was reconstructed in 1779 and finished in 1802. The **manor house** in quarter Tovarníky built in the mid-18th century on the foundations of an older Renaissance building from the beginning of the 17th century surrounded by park is also in the Baroque style. The local **museum of nature history** offers an ideal chance to obtain more information on the town and its environs. Part of collections of the museum is dedicated to the history of brewery in Slovakia, as the modern symbol of Topoľčany is the beer **Topvar**, one of the best Slovakian beers. The Považský Inovec mountain range is the recreation hinterland of Topoľčany with the most frequented area of the **Duchonka** water reservoir offering bathing, water sports and fishing.

Fans of history will perhaps climb the hill towering above the village **PODHRADIE** with the **Topoľčiansky hrad** Castle on its top. This royal castle from the 13th century became the centre of the castle estate of Topoľčany. In the 15th century it was occupied by the Hussites and later it fulfilled an important task in defence against the Turks. During Rákoczi's rebellion it was severely damaged by the imperial troops and although it was later reconstructed it fell in decay. Today its main tower in Romantic style with well preserved fortifications dominates in the horizon.

Upper Nitra

The route continues from Topoľčany north-eastward and after a short time there is the next district town **PARTIZÁNSKE** (population 24,900) known as the "capital of footwear" and centre of shoe-making industry in Slovakia. Its history is young as it is linked to the Bata company and the plant producing foot-

wear was built here in the years 1938-1942. The former settlement Baťovany (renamed to Partizánske in the memory of partisans fighting here during the Slovak National Uprising) has grown and widened to a small town. Now it represents an interesting complex of after-war architecture. The Roman Catholic **church of the Divine Heart of Jesus**, a pure example of architectural functionalism dominates to the centre of the town. The Gothic-Renaissance **manor house** in the part called Šimonovany built on the site of an old water castle from the 13th century (adapted in the 16th century and restored in the 19th century) and the originally Late Romanesque **church** from the 13th century Baroquised in 1750 are the reminders of remote history of the settlement. Visitors also like to visit the local **Hornonitrianska hvezdáreň** observatory, which offers lectures, discussions and observation of night sky.

Several **manor houses** in the environs of the town, for instance in Brodzany, Malé Bielice, Klátová Nová Ves, Veľké Uherce, Chalmová, Čereňany, Zemianske Kostoľany, Diviacka Nová Ves are the reminders of history of the region. The majority of them are from the first half of the 17th century when the progressing decadence of castles was the impetus for their construction. The best known **manor house** is the Renaissance building from the 17th century and park in **BRODZANY**. It houses now the **Museum of A. S. Puškin** (in the past Puškin's wife with children liked to stay here as the owner of the manor house, Baron G. Friesenhof married her sister) and the originally Renaissance **manor house** in **VEĽKÉ UHERCE** rebuilt in the 19th century in the Neo-Gothic style imitating English medieval castles. Some of them though, are in decay or are used as schools.

Another stop of trippers might be as well in **NOVÁKY** (population 4,400), industrial town known above all for its

Left: The manor house in Brodzany
Right: Bojnický zámok Castle

chemical plant. As Nováky was also the seat of the castle estate owned by the family Majthényi, there existed several aristocratic residences and manor houses. The **curia** from the 16th century and two **manor houses** from the 18th century still survive in Nováky. The curia houses the municipal council and the manor house serves to the Notre Dame female order. The sacral dominant of the town is the Roman Catholic church from the 18th century built on older foundations of the Romanesque-Gothic church. But Nováky of today are better known for the water polo team, the best in Slovakia, and the local open-air and in-door swimming pools or the thermal pools in Chalmová, which is not far away from Nováky. Ideal for recreation is the **thermal swimming pool** of Čajka in **BOJNICE** (population 5,000), the world famous spa. History of this town is connected with sulphurous hot springs, which occur here. The spa also has one of the oldest and most beautiful spa parks in Slovakia. The springs are used for therapy of nervous disorders and those of locomotion apparatus. The water temperature is from 28 to 52 degrees of Celsius.

However, the gem of Bojnice is its "fairy-tale" **Bojnický zámok** Castle, one of the most visited and most beautiful cultural-historical monuments in Slovakia. The Castle stands on a large travertine mound on the site of medieval castle from the 11th century. In the past the most famous Hungarian noble families owned it and the last of them was the family of Pálffy. Count Ján Pálffy had the structure reconstructed by the Budapest architect J. Hubert at the end of the 19th century following the pattern of romantic castles of the Loire in central France. The typical silhouette of the romantic image of medieval castle is enhanced by steep roofs of the palace, chapel and towers. Collections of artistic and historical **museum** are concentrated in the interior of the castle. Among them is the original furniture and the artistic collection of the Pálffy's from the turn of the 19th and 20th centuries and the most valuable item of national impor-

tance is the Late-Gothic **altar of Bojnice** made by Nardo di Cione Ortagna, artist from Florence in the mid-14th century. The visit to the castle includes that of dripstone **cave** under the Castle connected with it by the 26-m deep castle well. **International Festival of Ghosts and Spooks** in held here regularly by the end of April and beginning of May. The Bojnický zámok Castle becomes then the meeting point of ghosts, spooks, witches, and vampires from all over the world. Shrieks and yells are heard here for several days and nights. This event full of scaring atmosphere and pleasant fear takes several days, but eventually the evil powers surrender and leave the castle.

An extensive park and landscape park are the inseparable parts of the castle area. The 600-year old **lime tree of Bojnice** of the King Matthias with 12.5-m trunk circumference stands in front the castle entrance. Children appreciate the **castle zoo** above all. This zoo was founded in 1955 on an area of more than 40

hectares. It houses 280 animal species where African elephants and Persian leopards can be contemplated. The most interesting item of the zoo visited annually by more than half million visitors is the complete collection of doves and that of high-mountain ungulates, though the pavilions of elephants, monkeys or bears are also among the favourites of visitors. Another attractiveness is the performance of the local **group of historical fencing Bojník** and those of **Aquila**, the association of **falconers**. Bojnice also boasts the Gothic Roman Catholic Church of St. Martin from the 14th century and below it is the Prepoštská jaskyňa cave, important archaeological site of the remains of Neanderthal man, Renaissance and Baroque burgher houses and remains of the town fortifications from the 17th century.

Left: The park of Bojnický zámok Castle
Right: Burgher houses in Prievidza.
Uhrovecký hrad Castle

In the immediate vicinity of Bojnice is the district town **PRIEVIDŽA** (population 53,100). It was first mentioned in Documents of Zobor in 1113. Its development was favoured by town privileges granted to the settlement by Queen Mary of Anjou in 1383, which guaranteed freedom and better economic chances to the locals. In spite of privileges though, the town did not get rid of dependence on the castle estate of Bojnice. The 17th and 18th centuries brought about to Prievidza favourable conditions for the development of crafts and trade. The new impetus for development of the town was construction of the railway track at the end of the 19th century accompanied by opening of several factories. The dominant economic activity in the town in the second half of the 20th century was mining and it determined the modern character of the town. Today, Prievidza is the economic and administrative centre of the area of Upper Nitra and the second largest town in the region of Ponitrie. Abundant urban greenery makes it one of the "greenest" towns of Slovakia. The visit of the **Hornonitrianske vlastivedné múzeum** (Museum of Natural History of Upper Nitra) in the **monastery** from the 18th century offers information on history of the town. The monastery with its **church** is one of the most beautiful Baroque complexes in Central Europe. It was originally a fort from the 15th century, which was rebuilt by the end of the 16th century in the Renaissance style and again reconstructed into a two-storied structure in the 18th century. The oldest sacral monument of the town is the originally Romanesque **church** from the 13th century in the cemetery and the originally Gothic Roman Catholic **church of St. Bartholomew** stands in the centre of the town.

HANDLOVÁ (population 18,000) the town lying in the north-east of it is also the mining centre. Its interesting **houses**, examples of folk architecture are from the end of the 19th century. The Gothic Roman Catholic **church of St. Katherine** from the 14th century which was bombed in the Second World War is the interesting sacral monument of the town. It was built again in 1958. Today the pride of the town is its abundant urban greenery. Recreation area **Remata** in the Žiar mountain range with excellent ski terrain provides relaxation zone for the town.

The centre of the western part of the region Upper Nitra is the town **BÁNOVCE NAD BEBRAVOU** (population 20,900) known for production of Tatra trucks which won an excellent reputation in the most demanding world rallies. This town laying on the foothills of the Strážovské vrchy Mts. has two Roman-Catholic churches, the originally Gothic **church of St. Nicolas** from the 15th century adapted in the Renaissance and Baroque style and the Classicist **church of the Most Holy Trinity** from 1802. Profane monuments include above all the Classicist **manor house** from 1817 in the local part Dolné Ozorovce.

Bánovce is today the ideal starting point for trips to the Strážovské vrchy Mts. in the area of Ponitrie. The villages in the environs of the town include **UHROVEC**, the native place of **Ľudovít Štúr,** the leading figure of Slovak national emancipation in the mid-19th century and that of **Alexander Dubček,** the representative of the Prague Spring of 1968 and the "Velvet Revolution" of 1989. It is remarkable that both of them were born in the same house, which is now **museum**. Apart from the originally Renaissance **manor house** from the beginning of the 17th century, later rebuilt and adapted, recreation area in the valley Strieborníca is also worth to mention. Fans of panoramic views will certainly invest time and forces in the short ascent to the Jankov vŕšok hill with the **monument of the Slovak National Uprising**, the Rokoš Mt. or the ruins of the medieval **Uhrovecký hrad** Castle from the 13th century in order to get a wonderful view of the Strážovské vrchy Mts. The extensive estate of the Castle was property of important noble Hungarian family of Zay. Some members of this family were successful businessmen who founded here tradition of glass manufacture and the lace-making craft in Uhrovec. As the Zay's maintained the castle, tourist can admire here one of the oldest and best-conserved castle architectures in Slovakia.

NITRA
(dial: 037-)

Information
- **Mestské a turistické informačné centrum - NISYS**, Štefánikova trieda 1, Nitra, ☎/fax 7410907, ☎ 16186, 7410906, info@nitra.sk, www.nitra.sk

Museums
- **Ponitrianske múzeum**, Štefánikova trieda 1, Nitra, ☎ 7419771, **Slovenské poľnohospodárske múzeum**, Dlhá 92, Nitra, ☎ 6523359, 6511305, **Mestské múzeum historických vozidiel**, Štúrova 33, Nitra, ☎ 7412054, **Misijný dom na Kalvárii**, Nitra, ☎ 7722183

Galleries
- **Nitrianska galéria**, Župné námestie, Nitra, ☎ 7721754, **Art-galéria**, Kupecká 7, Nitra, ☎ 7419360

Hotels
- **ZLATÝ KĽÚČIK******, Svätourbanská 27, Nitra, ☎ 6550289, **ZOBOR****, Štefánikova trieda 5, Nitra, ☎ 6525381-2, **OLYMPIA****, Tr. A. Hlinku 57, Nitra, ☎ 6536727-9, **AGROINŠTITÚT**, Akademická 4, Nitra, ☎ 6533361, **AGROKOMPLEX**, Vihorlatská 10, Nitra, ☎ 6534541

Restaurants
- **U SV. HUBERTA**, Kasalova 8, Nitra, ☎ 6516774, **MEXIKO**, Štefánikova trieda 5, Nitra, ☎ 6525381, **IZBA STAREJ MATERE**, Radlinského 8, Nitra, ☎ 6526016

ENVIRONS OF NITRA
(dial: 037-, 038-)

Information
- **TOP TIK**, Námestie M.R. Štefánika 30, Topoľčany, ☎ 038/5323048

Museums
- **Mestské múzeum - Migazziovský kaštieľ**, Námestie A. Hlinku, Zlaté Moravce, ☎ 037/6321470, **Zámok Topoľčianky**, Parková 1, Topoľčianky, ☎ 037/6301111, **Hipologické múzeum**, Parková ul., Topoľčianky, ☎ 037/6301613-4, **Tribečské múzeum**, Krušovská 291, Topoľčany, ☎ 038/5323253

Atractiveness
- **Arboretum Tesárske Mlyňany**, Vieska nad Žitavou, ☎ 037/6334573, **Game park**, Lovce, ☎ 037/6301232

Hotels
- **EMINENT*****, Bernolákova 1, Zlaté Moravce, ☎ 037/6321483, 6403150, **VION****, Továrenská 64, Zlaté Moravce, ☎ 037/6421405-6, **NÁRODNÝ DOM*****, Hlavná 122, Topoľčianky, ☎ 037/6301401-3, **ZÁMOK****, Parková 1, Topoľčianky, ☎ 037/6301111, **DOBYS****, Puškinova 1, Topoľčany, ☎ 038/5326001, **KOPAČKA**, Ul. Dr. Adámiho 1238, Topoľčany, ☎ 038/5320694

Restaurants
- **RADNIČNÁ REŠTAURÁCIA**, Ul. Cyrila a Metoda, Topoľčany, ☎ 038/5320181, **RIO**, Sládkovičova 37, Zlaté Moravce, ☎ 037/6421343

Upper NITRA
(dial: 038-, 046-)

Information
- **Turisticko-informačná kancelária Upper Nitra**, Nám. slobody 4, Prievidza, ☎ 046/16186, fax 046/5423135, tikprievidza@stonline.sk, www.prievidza.sk, **Turistická informačná kancelária**, Hurbanovo nám. 19, Bojnice, ☎ 046/5403251

Museums
- **Hornonitrianske múzeum**, Nová 4, Prievidza, ☎ 046/5423054, **Zámok Bojnice**, ☎ 046/5430624, 5430633, **Rodný dom Ľ. Štúra a Alexandra Dubčeka**, Uhrovec, ☎ 046/94247, **Múzeum A. S. Puškina**, Brodzany, ☎ 038/7487263-4

Atractiveness
- **ZOO**, Bojnice, ☎ 046/5402975, **Hornonitrianska hvezdáreň** observatory, Dolinky 177, Partizánske, ☎ 038/7497108

Hotels
- **MAGURA****, Námestie J. C. Hronského 2, Prievidza, ☎ 046/5192300, **SPOLOČENSKÝ DOM***, Partizánske, ☎ 038/7492542, **ARKÁDIA****, Jesenského 561/3, Bánovce nad Bebravou, ☎ 038/7607777, **LIPA**, Sládkovičova ulica, Bojnice, ☎ 046/5430308

Restaurants
- **SALAŠ VIGLAŠ**, Bojnice, ☎ 046/5430997, **RELAX**, Východná ulica 38, Prievidza, ☎ 046/5426440, **AFRODITA**, Nitrianska cesta 58, Partizánske, ☎ 038/749 58 92

POIPLIE

Levice and
its environs

Central Poiplie

Lučenec and
its environs

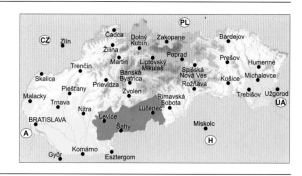

The region bears the name of the Ipeľ river, great part of which coincides with the frontier between the Slovak Republic and Hungary. The river, which springs in the mountain environment of the Slovenské rudohorie Mts. connects the harsh and hostile mountains with warmer and more fertile basin in the south before it flows into the Danube. In the past, Poiplie consisted of three historical regions. The eastern part of it was Novohrad and the central part belonged to the administration of the Hont while the region of Tekov covered the western part around Levice. Today, two districts Banská Bystrica and Nitra administer Poiplie, while for the purpose of this guide the districts of Levice, Krupina, Veľký Krtíš, Lučenec and Poltár were added to it.

The depressed parts of Poiplie are surrounded by volcanic mountain

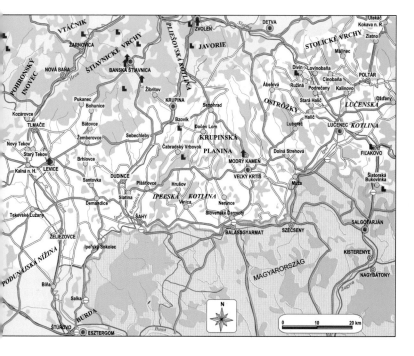

ranges. Although the last volcanoes extinguished a long time ago they have left great mineral wealth here. Apart from once famous mining towns like Krupina or Pukanec the region also boasts great amount of castle ruins and forts of anti-Turkish defence line. The long period of Turkish threat has left its traces as well. This southern corner of Slovakia has many old monasteries, manor houses and unique technical monuments set in wonderful landscape covered by vineyards.

Levice and its environs

The centre of the regions of lower Pohronie and western Poiplie is the district town **LEVICE** (population 36,550). It is situated in the eastern part of the

Left: At the Levický hrad Castle
Right: Museum of Tekov

Podunajská nížina lowland. The first written reference to Levice is from 1156. Existence of Levice and its history connected with its castle is also mentioned in the document from 1318. A new settlement Nové Levice was founded below the castle in the 14th century. The old Levice was a smaller settlement and existed independently from the new one until 1614. The expanding Nové Levice obtained the market and toll collection rights. However, the frequent and devastating Turkish raids brought about continuous suffering to its population. Many people were captured and the town repeatedly burnt. In spite of it, Levice flourished in the 17th century when it became the administrative and economic centre of the extensive estate of Tekov and it had a market place where craftsmen and merchants met every week. Prosperity of the town was also greatly helped by opening of the new railway track leading to Esztergom. Levice is now a modern town oriented above all to food industry. The town has its lively cultural and social milieu. The **"castle days"** in June and the fair of Levice in October are the most visited events in Levice.

The Roman Catholic sacral monuments of Levice include the Classicist parish **church of St. Michael** from 1780, the Baroque **church of St. Joseph** from the 17th century and the originally Franciscan **monastery**. The denominations are abundantly represented in Levice as there are the Classicist churches of Evangelicals and Calvinists from the 18th and 19th centuries. The oldest sacral architectural monument of the town is the Romanesque **church** from the 12th century in the urban district of **Kalinčiakovo**. The romantic Classicist building of **synagogue** from 1777 in the centre of the town commemorates the once large Jewish community living in the town. The Jewish **cemetery** is further in north. Profane monuments of Levice include the **town hall** from 1906 standing on the central Námestie hrdinov square, several **burgher houses** on the square, more than 100 years old building of teacher's institute and the Neo-Classical **manor house** in Kalinčiakovo.

The most important dominant of the town is the **Levický hrad** Castle from the end of the 13th century. It stands on top of volcanic rock protuberance above the swamps of the Hron river. It was the sentry fort guarding the road leading to central Slovakian mining towns. Its role was crucial in time of Turkish wars when the Turks occupied the territory south of Levice. It was then when the Levický hrad Castle was fortified, widened and the bulky Renaissance bastions were built. In summer 1664 the Turkish troops suffered a heavy defeat here which stopped their expansion

further to central parts of the country. This battle is known as the battle of Levice where the legendary hero of the Kingdom of Hungary, Štefan Koháry was killed. The Castle served the purpose until 1709 when its bastions were considerably damaged in the period of the Rebellion of Estates. Then it gradually lost importance as a military fort. Its conserved ruins and somewhat younger small fortified structures in the lower castle known as the **Dobóovský kaštiel'** (Manor House of Dobó) are the witnesses to the famous history of the Castle. The manor house of Dobó, two-storied Renaissance fortress bears the name of its owner, Count Štefan Dobó, one of the heroes of counter-Turkish wars. The manor house was built in the second half of the

16th century and it is the most extensive structure of the whole castle area. In the former unusually wide dike the castle park was planted. Today the Castle houses the **Tekovské múzeum** (Museum of Tekov) which contains archaeological, historic, ethnographic, and nature collections gathered in the region. The popular place in the Castle is its **tea room** located in one of the medieval bastions. The mysterious and reserved atmosphere of the place opened to public, which offers a varied assortment of exotic teas and drinks and the romantic silhouette of the Castle in background provide a pleasant experience to visitors.

One of the most interesting detached expositions of the Tekov Museum is situated several kilometres east of Levice, in the village **BRHLOVCE**. The complex of **rock dwellings** squeezed in tuff rocks, the **Monument Reserve of Folk Architecture**, is unique in the territory of Slovakia. Rock dwellings situated in the lane Šurda are from the 18th and 20th centuries. Some of them are still used for dwelling others serve as wine cellars. Exhibition of folk dwelling is situated in the house from 1932 and its backyard cut into the tuff rocks. Another interesting exhibition of the Tekov Museum is the **commemorative room of Franz Schubert** in town **ŽELIEZOVCE** (population 7,500). It is situated in what is referred to as Soví zámoček where this world-famous composer of early romanticism stayed twice, in 1818 and 1824. He was working here as the music teacher in noble family of Eszterházy and there is also the piano he played while composing. The house stands in the area of the Baroque **manor house** built in 1720 on the edge of an extensive park. It is under reconstruction now. The most important sacral building of the town is the Roman Catholic, originally Gothic, **church of St. James** from the beginning of the 14th century rebuilt in the

mid-20th century with conserved Gothic wall paintings, Gothic baptistery and Roman sarcophagus.

West of Levice the road passes through the village **KALNÁ NAD HRO-NOM**, lying on the bank of the Hron river, the symbol of this part of our territory with historic name of **Tekov**. The oldest seat of the County of Tekov was the disappeared Tekov Castle, which used to stand on top of a small volcanic hill next to the former free royal borough Tekov, now the village **STARÝ TEKOV**. Apart from its **folk traditions** and unusually colourful **folk costumes,** the village did not preserve much of its history. The neighbouring **NOVÝ TEKOV** is famous for horse breeding and the local **stud** founded in the second half of the 19th century. Further in north situated town **TLMAČE** (population 4,300) boasts rich history based on the Slav fort spreading on the right bank of the Hron river and the well-known archaeological locality

Kusá hora with a quarry. The quarry provides beautiful view of Tekov and Tlmače, which is now a prevailingly industrial town. Its environs are sought out by fans of canoeing who on their way down the **Hron** river most often stop at the roadhouse in the village **KOZÁROVCE** with preserved **folk architecture** from the 19th century.

Departing from Levice eastward the route continues in the undulated territory of the Ipeľská pahorkatina hill land with the Štiavnické vrchy Mts. in the north. This is the historical **County of Hont,** which once spread from the territory of Hungary to Banská Štiavnica in the north. Important settlement in this part of the region is **PUKANEC**, one of the seven free mining boroughs in central Slovakia. Pukanec was first mentioned as silver mine in 1321. **Burgher houses**, **town walls**, **pits**,

Left: Brhlovce
Right: Horses from Tekov

technical monuments, the Baroque-Classicist building of the former town hall and the Roman Catholic **church of St. Nicolas** from the 14th century are the reminders of its history. **BÁTOVCE** was also a mining settlement, originally populated by Slavs and resettled by German colonists in the 13th century. The County of Hont lacked a permanent administrative seat after Turkish raid in the 16th century and periodically arranged its meetings precisely in Bátovce. The Gothic **church** from the 14th century, Late Baroque **curia** and Toleration **church** from the end of the 18th century are its monuments. The preserved examples of the 19th century **folk architecture** are also interesting. North of **BOHUNICE** is the **water mill**, which belongs to the Museum of Tekov. The mill stands next to the Sikenica brook and in spite of the fact that it is

now power driven, the interior of the mill is original. Exhibitions of the Museum of Tekov in **ŽEMBEROVCE** situated in its Neo-Romanesque manor house show the original way of life of local people. However, since the manor house was privatised it is closed to public.

Vineyards coat the environs of Levice. The Ipeľská pahorkatina hill land is ideal for growing vine and wine production. The vineyards are sprinkled with small houses and cellars called here *hajlochy*. Most of them are in the locality of Stará hora near **SEBECHLEBY** on the southern foothills of the Štiavnické vrchy Mts. This type of folk architecture is protected and they are typical single or two-room **viticultural houses** with pillar porches and cellars carved into the tuff rock. There are more than hundred houses from the 18th and 19th centuries here. Original cellars, which along with the local **church** are part of the **Monument Reserve of Folk Architecture** can be seen. Visiting the cellars as for instance that of St. Urban you can taste the local wine accompanied by some speciality of the local cuisine. Sebechleby was one of important little towns in the 16th and 18th centuries and in the first half of the 18th century even the county administration seated here. Turkish raids heavily damaged the village in the 16th and 17th centuries. But the locals are known for their good humour and wit as testified to by the drama **Geľo Sebechlebský** written by Jozef Hollý. They also stick to their traditional costumes and do not seem to give up their old usage either.

The route continues from Levice in the direction of Šahy passing by the recreation area of **Margita-Ilona** with thermal pools and the car camping in the locality Kalinčiakovo. The road runs in slightly undulated landscape rich in mineral springs and travertine rock forms. The village **SANTOVKA** with spa history is the next stop. Although the spa disappeared at the beginning of the

Left: Sebechleby
Right: Dudince

20th century, the **travertine cascade** and thermal pool still attract visitors. The popular mineral water Santovka, familiar to Slovak consumers is bottled here, and the neighbouring village **SLATINA** produces the eponymous table mineral water of its own, which is likewise popular.

However, visitors mostly head to the spa of **DUDINCE** lying on the foothill of the Krupinská kotlina basin. Its good position and warm stable climate contribute to pleasant environment for relaxation, rehabilitation and therapy. The effects of the local thermal water were known as early as the Roman era when 32 **Roman baths** were carved here into the travertine rock. Temperature of thermal water in Dudince is 28.5 degrees of Celsius and it contains six critical mineral elements required by human body. The spa today is equipped by the most recent facilities and treats diseases of locomotion apparatus, cardiovascular and rheumatic disorders including hypertension, dermatological and gynaecological diseases. The effects of the local mineral water are also beneficial to digestive system. Visitors of the spa can make use of the public thermal pool opened from May to September.

Going from Dudince southward the route continues to the border town of **ŠAHY** (population 8,050) lying on the bank of the Ipeľ river. Šahy originated on the important medieval trade road, which leads from the royal seat of Esztergom over the Ipeľ to Banská Štiavnica and further to Poland. The first settlement in this territory developed around the Premonstratesian monastery from 1240, remains of which are still there. Premonstratesians also received the right to toll collection and their monastery was very important as a "trustworthy place" not only for the County of Hont, but also for those of Novohrad, Zvolen, Tekov and Gemer. Šahy received the statutes of town in

time of King Sigismund who granted it the right of fair in 1405 and that of sword two years later. In time of Turkish occupation of the Kingdom of Hungary, in 1546, the monastery was fortified. The Turks were there in the years 1552 to 1592 and from 1626 to 1686 when the Castle of Buda was re-conquered. Two years later Jesuits acquired the monastery, built new structures on its ruins and added to it a church in 1734. Šahy became the seat of the County of Hont at the beginning of the 19th century, which meant a new impetus for the economic and cultural development of the town. When it acquired the railway connection it became the administrative centre of the region. Šahy today is a busy boundary town visited above all during its **Hontianske kultúrne dni** (Cultural Days of Hont) and the Fair of Šahy held both in September.

The dominant of the town is the originally Gothic **church** from the 13th century, later rebuilt in the Baroque style. The pride of the town is the Baroque **pillar** from 1859 with the **statue of the Virgin Mary** on its top. The younger Evangelical **church** from the turn of the 19th and 20th centuries, **Calvary** and the former **monastery** complete the list of sacral monuments in Šahy. Profane monuments include the building of the former **County House** from 1857, the Late Classicist building

Left: Modrý Kameň
Right: Women from Hrušov

of the former **town hall** from 1888 and several **burgher houses**. Fans of arts and history will certainly use the occasion and visit the **Hontianské múzeum** or **Hontianska galéria**.

Central Poiplie

The central part of Poiplie consists of the picturesque Ipeľská kotlina basin and further in north lying Krupinská planina plateau. The largest town in this part of the region is **VEĽKÝ KRTÍŠ** (population 14,000) which was mentioned for the first time in the 13th century. In the past it developed in the framework of the Modrý Kameň estate. As it was sacked by Turkish troops in the 16th century, it was abandoned by population and later resettled by people from northern counties of the Kingdom of Hungary. Several yeoman and serf families came here from regions of Liptov, Orava and Turiec. Opening of coal mine Barbora and foundation of the mining society in the 19th century determined the modern history of the settlement. Intensive mining was the cause of further development of Veľký Krtíš in the 20th century when the housing estate was built here. Even after restructuring of the industry the mine Dolina is still operated. One of the few cultural or historical monuments of the town is the Late Renaissance **manor house** from the 17th century and the Evangelical **church** from the late 18th century built on the site of the former older Evangelical church.

The smallest town in Slovakia lies only several kilometres away in the northern direction. It is **MODRÝ KAMEŇ** (population 1,450). The settlement developed around the Gothic **castle** founded in 1137. The first known owner of the castle was Ditrich, the Count of Zvolen from the famous family of Knight Donč. Thanks to it, the settlement below the castle became the administrative centre of the western part of the Novohrad County, extensive territory reaching as far as Fiľakovo in the east while the larger part of it lied in what is now the territory of Hungary. The castle was one of the most important in the Kingdom of Hungary in its best times, as it was part of the anti-Turk defensive line. However, in the years 1575-1593 it was occupied and destroyed by the Turks. The family of Balašš had it repaired after the Turks left but it was destroyed again by the Turks and its upper castle is in ruins ever since. The Balašš had a **manor house** built in the Baroque style in the lower part of the castle area in 1730. Now the castle contains the **Museum of Puppets and Toys**, the only of its kind in Slovakia. Apart from this particular part, Museum also displays its collections concerning ethnography and history of the region. Another interesting cultural monument is the pilgrim place **Calvary** which forms together with the manor house and Castle a complex set in the tuff and sandstone rocks of the Calvary Hill.

East of Veľký Krtíš is **DOLNÁ STREHOVÁ** where in the local **manor house** from the 18th century in the Rococo-Classicist style surrounded by a large English park is the **Museum of Homeland Studies** with exhibition of the famous Hungarian writer **Imre Madách**. Wonderful landscape of Krupinská planina plateau on volcanic tuff rocks and with deeply incised valleys contrasting with high plains is situated west of Veľký Krtíš. Vineyards and chestnut groves, typical components of the local landscape coat sunny slopes of the plateau. The people living here are known as **producers of fine wines**, which were always much demanded by noble families in the Kingdom of Hungary. The assortment of wines including the ones produced in Veľký Krtíš, villages Nenince, Vinice, Plachtince and Čebovce includes such brands as the Burgundské biele, Tramín červený, and Cabernet Sauvignon. The local autumn **vintage feasts** and **folk festivals** held for instance in **HRUŠOV** attract the fans of this kind of fun. **Cellars** carved into the sandstone rocks above the village, imitation of the Neolithic settlement and the remains of **folk architecture** are also intriguing for visitors.

Remote history hovers above the village **ČABRADSKÝ VRBOVOK** with ruins of the **Čabraď** Castle. This originally sentry castle first mentioned in 1276 was built to guard the road leading to central Slovakian mining towns.

In the 16th century it was rebuilt to the counter-Turk fort which successfully resisted all Turkish raids. The Koháry family acquired the castle in the 17th century. They later moved into the more comfortable manor house in Sv. Anton and had the castle burned in 1812. The castle hill of Čabraď and its environs is now the National Nature Reserve with the most abundant **occurrence of reptiles** in Slovakia. The **fort** next to further in north lying **BZOVÍK** is another mute witness of history. This bulky structure originated by reconstruction of the Cistercian Abbey founded around 1130. Several decades later the Premonstratesian provostship moved here and became the largest feudal estate in the region of Hont. Its fort was repeatedly destroyed in the 15th century and ended up in hands of Sigismund Balassa who drove out the

monks and had the Romanesque monastery reconstructed to the Gothic-Renaissance castle with strong outer fortifications including four corner bastions and the dike. The fort was damaged at the end of the Second World War and reconstructed recently. Apart from fortifications and bastions the ruins of the former **monastery** and part of the Romanesque **church** in the courtyard survive.

Hiking path leads from the fort northward to another interesting monument from Turkish times, it is the former guard tower, now **view tower Vartovka** which was used in past by sentinels who announced the arrival of Turks. It was built in 1564 and its mission was to guard the town of Krupina. **KRUPINA** (population 8,000), one of the oldest towns of Slovakia lies below the tower. The oldest written reference to what was a mining settlement is from 1135. Rich deposits of copper and gold attracted German

Left: Fort of Bzovík
Right: Krupina

miners in the 12th and 13th centuries who later settled here. Although Tartars sacked it in 1241 it acquired the privileges of **free royal borough** several years after. Importance of Krupina increased in the 16th century when the town became one of the crucial points of counter-Turkish defence. They never conquered it. Rebellion of estates, Turkish wars and repeated fire in the 17th and 18th centuries slowed down development of the town but nevertheless it became the cultural, administrative, and economic centre of a wide area. The surviving parts of **town walls** built in the years 1551 to 1564 are also reminders of Turkish wars. The origin of **underground corridors** existing in the town, length and directions of which has not been yet determined, is not altogether clear. They were either used as escape ways or for storing wine. The medieval **Turkish wells** carved in rocks around the town are also mysterious. There are several Renaissance and Baroque burgher houses from the 17th and 18th centuries in the town. The dominant of the square is the **town hall** and the Baroque **Trinity Pillar** from 1752. Sacral monuments of Krupina are represented by the Roman Catholic church of **Nativity of the Virgin Mary,** the Romanesque three-nave basilica built in the first third of the 13th century with walls included in town fortifications. The Evangelical Classicist church from the end of the 18th century and the Baroque-Classicist **chapel of the Grieving Virgin Mary** from 1794 are among the most important historical monuments of the town. **Museum of Andrej Sládkovič** is dedicated to life and creative career of this famous Slovak poet, the local native. The Museum also contains **commemorative room** of another native lady writer M. Šoltésová. West of Krupina is the village **ŽIBRITOV** with preserved folk architecture and ruins of a small **fort**.

Lučenec and its environs

The centre of the eastern part of Poiplie and historical region of Novohrad is the district town **LUČENEC** (population 28,350) which was founded on the crossroads of old trade routes connecting Šahy with Rimavská Sobota and Fiľakovo with Zvolen. Old settlers left here numerous archaeological finds from the Neolithic period up to that of migration of nations. The find comprising swords in Opatová from the Lower Bronze Age is the most valuable. The oldest written reference to the town is the document of King Belo IV from 1247 where the name *Luchunch* is quoted for Lučenec. It was owned by an old Hungarian noble family of Lossonczy. The **Battle at Lučenec** in 1451 when the Hussite soldiers of Ján Jiskra won over the Hungarian troops of Ján Hunyady is the major event in the

town's history. It was then burnt. In the second half of the 16th century when the Castle of Fiľakovo was conquered, Turks occupied Lučenec and stayed until 1593. Population diminished in this period and in 1575 Lučenec was even described as abandoned and depopulated. During the Rebellion of Estates Lučenec was burnt twice while epidemics and fires accompanied it through the 18th century. Nevertheless, the town with its privilege to markets and fairs and a mail station in 1706 revived and developed. It was sacked and burnt again in the revolutionary years 1849. In the second half of the 19th century several industrial firms were opened in the town and by the end of the 20th century the plant producing agricultural machinery was founded here. Although the economic activities were poor during the inter-war period,

Left: The Golden Lane in Lučenec
Right: Belfry in Stará Halič

the business making of the modern Lučenec is considerable.

Due to numerous fires in the past the town is not rich in older monuments. Classicism and Art Nouveau styles are typically represented in Lučenec. The most interesting sacral monuments include the Baroque-Classicist Roman Catholic **church** from 1783, the Neo-Gothic Calvinist **church** with a 64-m tall tower from 1853, the Evangelical **church** from 1859, and the monumental Jewish **synagogue** built in 1925 in the Art Nouveau style with remarkable oriental details. The profane monuments consist of the Classicist building of **Reduta** from 1856, now cultural and commercial centre, the **town hall** (1894) and the complex of the burgher **houses** in the **Art Nouveau** style from the end of the 19th century. Those who are interested in history of the region of Novohrad should visit the **Novohradské múzeum** focused on folk ceramics and glass-making craft. Fans of fine arts will certainly stop in the **Novohradská galéria** (Gallery of Novohrad) which occupies one of the oldest buildings of the town. The symbol of flourishing business and commerce in Lučenec is **Zlatá ulička** or the Golden Lane, an exclusive place with attractive little shops. The people of Lučenec relax and recreate in the **Lučenské kúpele** spa and the **Ľadovo water reservoir**.

The route continues from Lučenec westward and passes through the village **HALIČ**, known for its Baroque, now rather abandoned, **manor house**, which is the result of the 18th century reconstruction of the former fort from the 17th century. Bellow the manor house are old structures of the estate offices including a wool-cloth producing plant, etc. The Roman Catholic church of **Promotion of the Holy Cross** from the 18th century also stands here. The dominant of the neighbouring village of **STARÁ HALIČ** is the precious Gothic **church of St. George** from the 14th century with conserved remnants of wall paintings. The wooden Renaissance **belfry** from the 17th century stands by the church. Ruins of the medieval **Divín** Castle can be seen above the village **DIVÍN** lying not far away. The Castle was built by the end of the 13th century and it played an important role as anti-Turkish fort in the 16th century. Its ill-famed owner Imrich Balassa, robber knight seated here in the 17th century and undertook assaults in its environs. After his death, the Castle was conquered by the Imperial troops in 1683 and fell in decay. Fortified and likewise abandoned Renaissance **manor house** from the 17th century stands below the Castle. During the Second World War it sheltered the field hospital and Partisan headquarters. This village has an original Gothic church later adapted in the Baroque style, the Roman Catholic **All Saints Church** from 1657 with Renaissance fortification and the Baroque building of parsonage with the oldest (1761) sun dial in region. The village together with the neighbouring **RUŽINÁ** is attractive for tourists above all in summer thanks to the **Ružiná water reservoir** with cottages and car-camping site. East of water reservoir is the village **LOVINOBAŇA**, history of which is connected with mining and production of magnesite materials. The principal attraction of the village where the Evangelical and Roman Catholic **churches** dominate is the competition in **gold washing** organised by the local club of gold-panners every year. The landmark of this territory is the Art Nouveau **manor house** from 1893 set in large park in the village **PODREČANY**, inspired in the French Baroque style.

The route continues from Lučenec north-eastward and this stretch is referred to as the "glass way" because the whole area of the Revúcka vrchovina upland is like Upper Novohrad linked to glass-making tradition. Tourists can buy glass ware decorated in gold in the

first village on the route **KALINOVO**. The most valuable monument of the village is the Evangelical church with the Romanesque core from the first half of the 13th century, widened and reconstructed in 1711. The centre of the region of the Upper Novohrad is the town **POLTÁR** (population 6,100) also known for manufacturing glass, cut class, and ceramics. Inhabitants of this settlement first mentioned in 1246 have suffered a lot from Turkish occupation in the second half of the 16th century. The stone bridge **Turecký most** over the Ipeľ river, the oldest of the kind in Slovakia, is the reminder of those hard times. The most important monument of the village is the Classicist **manor house** from 1782 rebuilt in 1865 and the Classicist Evangelical church from 1791. The **Mestské múzeum** (Town Museum) offers documents about history of the town, which was founded on the site of an old Slav settlement. It existed here in the 7th to 8th centuries and there are

still remains of the medieval fortress at Ceriny and the foundations of the Late Romanesque church at Kostolisko. Westerly situated **CINOBAŇA** thrived on mining, iron and glass production. The most important monuments of Cinobaňa are the originally gothic Evangelical **church** from the 15th century adapted in the Renaissance style in 1622 and the Roman Catholic **church of Holy Cross** from 1887 in local part Katarínska Huta.

The route continues northward following the "glass way" through the village **ZLATNO** also known as the glass-manufacturing community from the mid-19th century. Its famous native L. V. Pantoček was the pioneer and inventor in the area of glass craft and many of his technological procedures are still maintained. The environs of the further in north situated **KOKAVA NAD RI-**

Left: Fiľakovský hrad Castle. Šomoška Castle
Right: Stone Fall

MAVICOU are typical for scattered hamlets consisting of 54 settlements and isolated houses. Its living folklore traditions are displayed during the **folk festival Koliesko** held in summer. The last village on the glass way of the Upper Novohrad is **UTEKÁČ**. Apart from glass-making it is known by hikers as there are ideal conditions for their activities.

The easternmost town of regions of Poiplie and Novohrad is **FIĽAKOVO** (population 10,200). Its history is closely linked to that of its Fiľakovský hrad Castle. The serf village Fiľakovo was first mentioned in the mid-13th century as the settlement with toll station. It acquired town privileges in 1423. After its Castle was destroyed at the end of the 17th century instead of disappearing, the settlement thrived on crafts and farming. Several industrial firms were founded here in the 19th and 20th centuries. **Mestské múzeum** (Town Museum) of Fiľakovo contains numerous documents and artefacts, which convey the history of the place including Turkish arms and archaeological finds. The most conspicuous sacral monument of the town is the Baroque Roman Catholic Franciscan **church** built together with **monastery** in the years 1694 -1727 on older foundations.

The **Fiľakovský hrad** Castle is the dominant of the town, first referred to in 1246. It was rebuilt in the first half of the 15th century widened and fortified in the 16th century. It was conquered by the Turks in 1554 and occupied for forty years. It became the centre of the Turkish administrative district encompassing the whole of what is today the region of Poiplie. It was re-conquered only in 1593. The year 1682 was also fatal for the Castle as the rebellious troops of Imrich Thököly conquered and destroyed it. The fairly conserved pentagonal **Bebekova bašta** bastion stands next to the gate at the entrance of the Castle. In one of its walls there is a half-sunk bulky canon ball, reminiscent of the 1682 siege. Remains of palace, sentry tower and massive half-circle cannon bastion exist in the upper castle. The castle provides a wonderful view of the whole town and its environs. **Instructive path** runs around the castle hill with explanations of the history of the Castle and geology of the castle hill. It is in fact the remnant of the marginal tuff rampart of a volcano, typical element of the landscape of the **Cerová vrchovina** upland in the environs of Fiľakovo.

There is another remain of the past volcanic activity, the basalt rock in the administrative territory of the village **ŠIATORSKÁ BUKOVINKA** in the immediate vicinity of the Slovak-Hungarian frontier, with one of the most picturesque Slovak castle on top of it. It is the **Šomoška** Castle built of unconventional hexagonal basalt pillars. It is unique among the Slovak castles. It

was probably built in the later half of the 13th century after the Tartar invasion. After suppression of the Rákoczi's rebellion, the Emperor had several castles existing then in the environs pulled down but Šomoška was saved. However, it gradually decayed and the last tower burnt in 1826 when it was stricken by a lighting. Extensive conservation and partial reconstruction saved the castle in 1972. Visiting the Castle you will certainly notice the also unique natural phenomenon **Kamenný vodopád** (Stone Fall). It lies northeast of the castle hill and it consists of a fan of hexagonal basal pillars. Similar pillars occur in many places in the Cerová vrchovina upland but the small width (15 cm) and incredible regularity of these is rare. **Stone sea** is the large area in the middle of the wood nearby and it consists of a great amount of stones.

LEVICE AND ITS ENVIRONS
(dial: 036-, 045-)

Information
- **Turistická informačná kancelária DE-KAMPO**, Ul. sv. Michala 2, Levice, ☎/fax 036/6317898, ☎ 036/6222219, tiklv@isternet.sk

Museums
- **Tekovské múzeum**, Levice, ☎ 036/6312112, **Hontianske múzeum**, Rotaridesova 13, Šahy, ☎ 036/7412365

Galleries
- **Hontianska galéria**, Rotaridesova 13, Šahy, ☎ 036/7412365

Atractiveness
- **Levický hrad** Castle, Levice, ☎ 036/6312112, **Dudince** spa, Dudince, ☎ 045/5583411, **Rock dwellings**, Brhlovce, ☎ 036/6312112, **Water mill**, Bohunice, ☎ 036/6312112

Hotels
- **LEV*****, Čsl. armády 2, Levice, ☎ 036/6313064, **ATOM****, Ul. sv. Michala 4, Levice, ☎ 036/6312790, **BUČINÁR***, Kúpeľná 100, Dudince, ☎ 045/5583367, **MINERÁL***, Okružná 124, Dudince, ☎ 045/5583241, **PRAMEŇ***, K. Braxatorisa 8, Dudince, ☎ 045/5583184, **TEHLIAR***, Kúpeľná 101, Dudince, ☎ 045/5583131, **VILLA ROMAINE**, Hlavné nám. 13, Šahy, ☎ 036/7411283

Restaurants
- **SITNO**, SNP 3, Levice, ☎ 036/6223593, **U ZLATOKOPA**, Ul. sv. Michala 24, Levice, ☎ 036/6224064, **BLACK JACK**, Ul. sv. Michala 4, Levice, ☎ 036/6313071, **FAMILY RESTAURANT**, M. R. Štefánika, Levice, ☎ 036/6313054

CENTRAL POIPLIE
(dial: 045-, 047-)

Information
- **Informačné a komunikačné centrum**, Svätotrojičné nám. 15/15, Krupina, ☎/fax 045/5512000, ikc_ka@orangemail.sk, **Turistická a informačná kancelária Š-TEAM**, Slovenské Ďarmoty, ☎ 047/4876201

Museums
- **Múzeum bábkarských kultúr a hračiek**, Hrad Modrý Kameň, ☎ 047/4870194, **Múzeum Andreja Sládkoviča**, Sládkovičova 20, Krupina, ☎ 045/5521805, **Múzeum**, Dolná Strehová, ☎ 047/4897189

Atractiveness
- **Čabraď** Castle, Čabradský Vrbovok, ☎ 045/5597112, **Fort of Bzovík**, Bzovík, ☎ 045/5524183, **Modrý Kameň** Castle, Modrý Kameň, ☎ 047/4870194, **View tower Vartovka**, Bzovík

Hotels
- **DOLINA***, Škultétyho nám. 2, Veľký Krtíš, ☎ 047/4830012, **RÓZA***, Dolné Strháre, ☎ 047/4896428, **HONTSTAV**, Kuzmányho 22, Krupina, ☎ 045/5511496

Restaurants
- **JAKUB**, Nemocničná 31, Veľký Krtíš, ☎ 047/4831512, **KOALA**, Škultétyho nám. 4, Veľký Krtíš, ☎ 047/4831363, **ČERVENÉ VÍNO**, Jarmočná 310/7, Modrý Kameň, ☎ 047/4870025, **ROZVOJ**, Štefánikova 10, Krupina, ☎ 045/5521032

LUČENEC AND ITS ENVIRONS
(dial: 047-)

Information
- **Mestské informačné centrum**, Masarykova 14, Lučenec, ☎/fax 4331513

Museums
- **Novohradské múzeum**, Nám. Kubínyiho 3, Lučenec, ☎ 4332502, **Mestské múzeum**, Hlavná ul., Fiľakovo, ☎ 4382619, **Mestské múzeum**, Družby 43/45, Poltár, ☎ 4222270

Galleries
- **Novohradská galéria**, Nám. Kubínyiho 3, Lučenec, ☎ 4332397

Atractiveness
- **Church of St. George**, Stará Halič, **Divín** Castle, Divín, **Fiľakovský hrad** Castle, Fiľakovo, **Šomoška** Castle, Šiatorská Bukovinka, **Stone Fall**, Šiatorská Bukovinka

Hotels
- **REDUTA*****, Vajanského 2, Lučenec, ☎ 4331237, **P-7*****, Kármána 22/A, Lučenec, ☎ 4321255, **NOVOHRAD**, Novohradská 27, Lučenec, ☎ 4322206, **PELIKÁN**, Vajanského 2928, Lučenec, ☎ 4330871, **KRYŠTÁĽ**, Slobody, Poltár, ☎ 4223135

Restaurants
- **ZELENÝ DOM**, Železničná ul., Lučenec, tel. 4323749, **HVIEZDA**, Zvolenská cesta 2, Lučenec, ☎ 4326056

STREDNÉ POHRONIE

Zvolen and
its environs

Kremnica and
its environs

Banská Štiavnica and
its environs

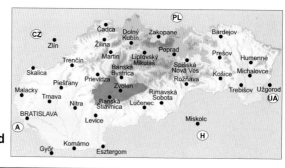

The axis of the central part of Pohronie is, as its name suggests (Pohronie in English is "the land along the Hron), the Hron river. The river flows here from the north-east and connects the area of Horehronie and Banská Bystrica, with what is now its twin town, Zvolen. In the past, central Pohronie was one of three historical regions with Zvolen County as its core. Today it is part of the administrative region of Banská Bystrica and contains the districts of Zvolen, Kremnica, Žiar nad Hronom, Žarnovica and Banská Štiavnica, as well as the picturesque area of Podpoľanie with the town Detva. In the south central Pohronie stretches as far as the Slovenská brána gate, a spot near Kozárovce, where the river Hron abandons the Carpathian Mts. and enters the territory of the Podunajská nížina low-

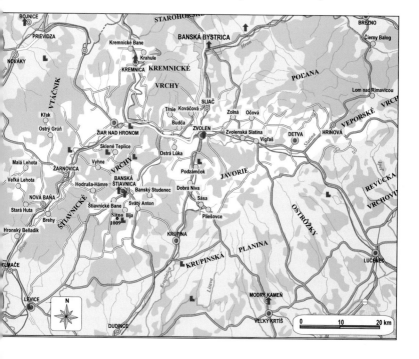

land. The middle reach of the river Hron forces its way through the volcanic mountain ranges of the Slovenské stredohorie Mts. The landscape surrounding it experienced volcanic eruptions of enormous magnitude in the Tertiary Age. The stratovolcano of Štiavnica with diameter of base amounting to more than 50 km was one of the largest in Europe. However, the last volcanoes extinguished here more than 130 thousand years ago and broke into the mosaic of mountain ranges and basins. The stream of the Hron and a series of narrow canyon-like valleys interconnect the basins. Volcanic heritage was exceptionally awarding for the inhabitants of the central Pohronie. The local mountains contain large mineral riches, iron, gold, silver, and copper deposits. One of the most important mining regions in Europe developed here in the Middle Ages, with famous mining towns Banská Štiav-

nica and Kremnica. The area though, also boasts ruins of romantic castles such as Revište, Šášov, and Dobrá Niva, the monastery of Hronský Beňadik and a great amount of unique technical monuments. All that is set amidst wonderful landscape with ideal conditions for hiking cycling or skiing.

Zvolen and its environs

The largest town of central Pohronie is **ZVOLEN** (population 43,800). Its situation is advantageous in terms of transport as it lies on the crossroads and railway routes of national importance. This advantage played the major role for the town and its development. It was the determining factor of the town, which always enjoyed great respect and importance in the upper part of the Kingdom of Hungary in the past. The territory squeezed between the riverbeds of the Hron and Slatina has been settled since primeval times. Finds from the Bronze Age are especially abun

Left: Zvolenský zámok Castle
Right: St. Elizabeth church in Zvolen

lant in its territory. In the period between the 7th and 12th centuries Slavs lived here in at least three settlements. The fortified site in the locality Priekopa near Môťová fulfilled the function of military and administrative centre of the Slav settlers. The County of Zvolen was separated from the County of Hont in the 12th century and the old castle of Zvolen called Pustý hrad Castle became the seat of the new county. The oldest written reference to the settlement of Zvolen existing below the castle is from 1243. The document issued by King Belo IV confirmed important self-administrative privileges to inhabitants of Zvolen, which they have been using already two years. More privileges conceded to colonists followed in 1254. Importance of Zvolen grew after the fortified royal castle was built in its vicinity in the years 1370-1382. Trade and crafts thrived in the little town including the guilds of shoe-makers, tailors and pottery-makers. In the second third of the 17th century the system of fortifications was built around Zvolen which determined the ground plan of the town including its unusually spacious rectangular square. Zvolen of today is a modern town with developed wood-processing industry, university and scientific institutions focused on forestry, wood-processing and environmental sciences.

The dominant and symbol of Zvolen is the **Zvolenský zámok** Castle. It was built in the second half of the 14th century for King Louis the Great of Kingdom of Hungary, fan of hunting in the surrounding Carpathian forests. The builders gave it the form of the Gothic hunting castle with rectangular ground plan following the Italian pattern. During the Renaissance reconstruction in 1548, to the originally two-storied building another storey and our corner towers were added. Building interventions made after 1590 did not alter its Renaissance appearance. They concentrated on small adjustments and adaptation of its interior. In the 18th century, the result of the remarkable Baroque reconstruction of the **large hall** in the western wing of the castle was a beautiful

panel **ceiling**. Seventy-eight panels bear portrays of the Roman emperors and the Habsburg rulers. Today the Zvolen Castle houses the **Slovak National Gallery** with a valuable collection of Gothic and modern art. Theatre shows called **Zvolenské zámocké hry** are held in its courtyard in summer.

North of the Castle is the **Námestie SNP square** with rectangular ground plan, one of the largest in Slovakia. Its dominant is the isolated building of the parish **church of St. Elizabeth** from the end of the 14th century. This originally Gothic single-nave building acquired its Renaissance dome in the 16th century. Considerably younger **Evangelical church** with a tall tower built in 1921-1923 stands nearby. Several old burgher houses with preserved original Renaissance and Baroque building elements stand around the square. The most interesting part of it is what is referred to as **small manor house** situated in the northern row of houses on the square. Its nice

Rococo facade is adorned by coat of arms. The building of **Finkova kúria** in the western row contains the collections of the **Lesnícke a drevárske múzeum** (Museum of Forestry and Wood Processing). The **armed train Hurban** situated in the eastern part of the town centre in the park between the Castle and railway station attracts the attention of visitor. It was made in 1944 in the railway workshops of Zvolen to help the rebellious Slovak troops in the Second World War.

If you want to see the oldest historical monument of Zvolen you have to abandon the centre and go to the area of **Pustý hrad** on the slope of the forested mountain in the Javorie mountain range. Pustý hrad (also known as the Old Castle of Zvolen) is surprisingly large. It can be compared with much more famous Spiš Castle. It occupies an area of almost 8 hectares. As its ruins are considerably

Left: Swimming pool in Kováčová. Poľana
Right: Waterfall of Bystré

damaged and hidden in forest, the monumentality of the Castle is not so obvious. The ongoing archaeological research was very successful. Traces of much older fortified settlement with stone walls from the Lower Bronze Age were found here. The royal castle, which later served as the seat of the County of Zvolen, was built in the 12th century. It consisted actually of two independent forts standing on top of two elevations connected by a stone ridge. Construction of this castle complex finished in the first half of the 14th century when Master Donč was the head of the County of Zvolen. The fighting between the followers of Ján Huňady and those of Ján Jiskra had considerably affected the castle in the 15th century and after a short revival by the end of the 16th century it definitely fell in decay.

The northern neighbour of Zvolen is the **SLIAČ** spa (population 4,700). The local mineral springs were mentioned as early as 1244. Therapeutic activities started in 1657. Today the spa of Sliač is equipped with modern therapeutic facilities for patients with heart diseases. The airport **Tri duby** which played an important role in time of the Slovak National Uprising in 1944 is situated in the vicinity of Sliač. On the opposite side of the valley of the Hron river, on the foothills of the Kremnické vrchy Mts. is the spa **KOVÁČOVÁ** specialised in therapy of locomotion apparatus and neurology. The local thermal swimming pool is the great attractiveness of the spa.

On the north-eastern edge of Zvolen, in urban district **Zolná** is the fortified Early Gothic church from the 13th century with precious medieval paintings in its interior. The church is built of volcanic sediments, which occur in the environs of Zvolen. Walking by the small training airport one will soon arrive at the village **OČOVÁ** known for its typical folk activities and as the birthplace of the famous scholar Matthias Bel (1684-1749). He has won the world fame with his *Notitia Hungariae novae historico-geographica*, the history of nation and nature of what was then territory of the Kingdom of Hungary in several volumes.

ZVOLENSKÁ SLATINA, which is not far away, also boasts several famous natives. Constructor of the first helicopter in the world, Ján Bahýľ was born here in 1856 followed by the lady-writer Terézia Vansová a year later. Composer Mikuláš Moyzes born in 1872 is also from Zvolenská Slatina. The factory producing the typical Slovak sheep cheese *bryndza* exists here since the 18th century. The village is also known for production of folk music instruments such as the typical shepherd flutes, pipes, bagpipes, etc.

The neighbouring village **VÍGĽAŠ** spreads below the **castle** bearing the same name, which seen from below is not conspicuous at all. But in fact the size of this old medieval building is surprising. It burnt during the fighting in 1945. Its history started in the 14th century. It was first referred to in 1393 as a newly built hunting castle owned by the king. Its importance increased in the 16th century

when it was reconstructed and fortified under the threat of Turkish raids. Its position within the system of fortified castles was a strategic one. After 1690 the aristocratic family of Eszterházy, which adapted it into a luxurious residence, owned it. They adorned the castle walls with stylish ornamentation at the end of the 19th century.

Hikers who continue eastward will arrive at the picturesque landscape called **Podpoľanie**. The huge silhouette of the extinguished Tertiary volcano **Poľana** (1,458 m) with a large depression in its centre, which geologists take for caldera, dominates it. The former forester's settlement **Kyslinky** lies nearby. Forest railway connected it with Vigľaš in the past. On the southern hillside of the Poľana Mt. is the **mountain hotel of Poľana**, accessible by road from Hriňová. It is a good starting point for hiking in the most elevated parts of the range and the 23 m tall waterfall of **Bystré**. There is also an excellent ski terrain around the hotel. The beautiful

mountain meadows of Poľana are especially attractive for tourists as they provide generous views encompassing a great portion of central Slovakia. The forests in turn, which preserved the character of virgin forests, are inhabited by abundant game. The local nature is protected in the framework of **CHKO** (Protected Landscape Area) **Poľana** administered in Zvolen. In 1990 it was included into the network of biosphere reserves of the international MaB Programme of UNESCO.

The centre of the Podpoľanie region is the comparatively young town of **DETVA** (population 15,000). Poet Andrej Sládkovič referred to Detva as "village" in one of his poems in the mid-19th century. Archaeological finds testify to settlement of this territory as early as Bronze Age. However, the community was founded in the first half of the 17th century. Shepherds and farmers inhabited it. The first

plant producing cheese in Slovakia was opened in Detva in 1787. Detva lost its rural agricultural character when a large plant of mechanical engineering accompanied by housing estates was built here after the Second World War. Fans of folklore and folk art visit Detva at the occasion of the popular **Podpolianske foklórne slávnosti** (Folk Festival of Podpoľanie) held here every year at the beginning of summer. It is one of the major events of the kind in Slovakia when visitors can admire the typical costume of local people and their captivating music or melodic dialect. This is the place where the Slovak language is most flattering to ear. Detva offers a charming natural setting suitable for undemanding trips on foot or bicycle. The town is surrounded by numerous **isolated farmsteads** inhabited by about a fifth of citizens of Detva. **HRIŇOVÁ** (population 8,300), the small town in vicinity of Detva with similar history and present, is also worth visiting for its wonderful setting.

Left: Folk Festival of Podpoľanie
Right: Dancers of Detva. Church in Kremnica

Kremnica and its environs

KREMNICA (population 5,900) situated in the western part of central Pohronie was one of the richest towns of the Kingdom of Hungary in the past. It gained its wealth from gold mining. The legend has that the king himself founded the town. While hunting in the local deep forests he shot a partridge. After grains of gold were discovered in his throat he ordered to search for the metal in the local streams. Golden vein was found and it was a good reason enough to found there the settlement called *Cremnychbana*, which obtained privileges of free royal and mining borough from King Charles Robert in 1328. Special privilege was that of coinage. The mint of Kremnica was founded by mint masters, invited here from Kutná Hora in Bohemia by the king of the Kingdom of Hungary. A year after its founding in 1329 the first Old Hungarian *groschen* coins were struck here. The mint of Kremnica also produced the ducats, which were highly praised for their quality and beauty and joined the most favourite coins in Europe. In the 16th century the craft involved in medal-making was also introduced. Commemorative coins, medals, and coins of different countries of the world are still struck in Kremnica today. The oldest part of Kremnica stretched on the mild slope of a short hill. It was referred to as *Alden Kamerhof* or the old mining yard. The German "guests" and colonists settled around the square called Ring. In 1405 the outer fortifications with town walls, bastions and three gates were also started. Privileges of King Matthias Corvinus from 1474 helped a lot to the development of trade in Kremnica. Bad times came in the 16th century as the result of Turkish threat, epidemic and fire including the Rebellion of Estates in the 17th century. The trend of decay did not stop in the 18th century either, though several nice Baroque buildings were built here in his time.

The central area of the town is the **Šte-fánikovo námestie** square with its dominant, which is the **town castle** and the Gothic **church of St. Catherine**, built in the 15th century on the site of older Romanesque church. The tower is accessible to public and it offers a splendid view of the town and its environs. The pride of the church is the old organ with wonderful sound appreciable above all during the traditional summer event **Kremnický hradný organ** (The Castle Organ of Kremnica). The oldest part of the castle and of the town in general is the **ossuary of St. Andrew** from the 13th century. Part of the castle is also the **Hodinová veža** (Clock Tower), remains of the former **town hall**, three bastions and the northern **Vežová brána** gate. The gem of the Štefánikovo námestie square is the bulky Baroque **Trinity Pillar**. It was built in the years 1765-1772 in memory of plague victims, which

swept death over Kremnica in 1710. D. Stanetti, the court sculptor of the mining towns of central Slovakia, made the statues of the pillar. In the western row of houses on the square is the **Franciscan church** and **monastery** built in the years 1653-1660 as the result of the massive counter-Reformation campaign of the Habsburgs. In the north-western corner of the square is the **building of mint**. It was originally a Gothic house from the 15th century which was later reconstructed. It had its own fortification and arsenal. The oldest part of the mint now is its south-eastern wing with surviving **treasury**. **Múzeum mincí a medailí** (Museum of coins and medals) situated in an old **burgher house** in the southern row of houses offers more information about the craft of coinage and its tradition in Kremnica. It was founded in 1890 as one of the first museums in Slovakia. There is another unique museum situated in the **barbican** of the **Dolná brána** gate, next to information bureau. It is the standing exhibi-

Left: Square in Kremnica
Right: Centre of Europe

tion of **history of skiing**. As a matter of fact, the name of Kremnica is closely linked with popularity of this wonderful sport in Slovakia. In its vicinity the traditional ski race **Biela stopa SNP** (The White Track of the Slovak National Uprising) is held every year and it is the Slovak analogue to famous Swedish cross-country ski race in Vass. In the eastern row of the square apart from several old burgher houses is also the building of the **new town hall**. The square becomes very lively in summer time when the festival of humour and satire **Kremnické gagy** (Gags of Kremnica) is held here.

Another attractiveness of Kremnica is the enticing environment of the Kremnické vrchy Mts. which offer numerous possibilities of nice walks, hiking and cycling trips. The old mining village of **KREMNICKÉ BANE** is situated in the saddle north of the town. The people of Kremnica founded it in the 14th century. The pilgrim **church of Svätojánsky** (St. John the Baptist church) stands outside the village. This place is especially interesting as it is the symbolical **centre of Europe**. It is marked by the monument in form of a large boulder placed next to the western wall of the church. Two important tourist centres with excellent ski and hiking conditions are situated in the central part of the range. It is **KRAHULE**, recreation settlement lying on high plain and the second is recreation area Skalka, known as the starting point for hiking in the most elevated parts of the Kremnické vrchy Mts.

On the eastern edge of the Žiarska kotlina basin is the district town **ŽIAR NAD HRONOM** (population 19,900). The oldest written reference to the settlement *Sancta Crux* (Holy Cross) appeared in the founding document of the Benedictine monastery in Hronský Beňadik in 1075. Thanks to the favoured position on the crossroads of trade routes it gradually developed into a small town. It has changed a lot after the Second World War when the testing manufacture of the **aluminium factory** was started. It is now one of the largest firms in Slovakia. The gigantic fac-

tory has attracted a lot of immigrants to the district of Žiar nad Hronom for which practically a new town was built. The most important monument of Žiar is the Renaissance-Baroque **manor house** built in 1631 for Archbishop Peter Pázmány. It was the summer residence of bishops of Banská Bystrica. In the years 1851-1869 the first chairman of Matica slovenská, **Štefan Moyzes** (1797-1869) lived in the manor house. His monument stands in the park next to it and Moyzes is buried in the crypt of the diocese bishops below the northern tower of the Classicist **church of Ascension of the Holy Cross** from 1813. Above the urban district **Šášovské Podhradie** are the ruins of the medieval castle Šášov. Historical sources assert that brothers Vančo built them in 1253, though the folk tradition offers a different explanation. According to a legend the lord of the Zvolen castle had it built for his court joker who saved him life during hunting. The task of the Šášov Castle was to guard the trade road and to collect toll.

It became royal property in the 14th century, and the part of the dowry of the royal wives. In 1490 the family of Dóczy bought it from Queen Beatrix and reconstructed it into the Renaissance fort. The Castle fell in decay after the Rebellion of Estates in 1708.

Banská Štiavnica and its environs

The gem among the towns of Slovakia is undoubtedly **BANSKÁ ŠTIAVNICA** (population 10,900) situated in the heart of the Štiavnické vrchy Mts. Its undeniable values and beauty caused that it is one of the first Slovak towns included into the List of the World Cultural Heritage of UNESCO in 1996. Extraction of precious metals in central part of the Štiavnické vrchy Mts. enjoys a very long history. The area was first mentioned in the document from

Left: The Trinity Pillar in Banská Štiavnica
Right: Banská Štiavnica

1156 as *terra banensium* or the land of miners. Silver ore prevailed among the mined metals and the town won the attribute of "silver". Several mining settlements existed here before the Tartar invasion. One of the oldest, referred to as *Bana* existed as early as the 10th century on top of the Glanzenberg Mt. (now the old part of the town). Banská Štiavnica acquired its first town privileges in 1238. The wealth stemming from the ore was transferred to building of a large and spectacular medieval town with luxurious houses of rich burghers called here *waldbürgers*, churches and public buildings. Banská Štiavnica progressively became the largest mining centre in the Monarchy in the 18th century. In the period between 1790 and 1863 the mountains surrounding the town yielded 490 tons of silver and 11 tons of gold. Mining schools and science also flourished in the town: the oldest mining school in the Kingdom of Hungary was founded in 1735. It was promoted to the **Banská akadémia** (Mining Academy) in 1762, the first superior mining school in Europe. Prosperity and fame returned to the town for some time and by the end of the 18th century Banská Štiavnica was the third largest town of the Kingdom of Hungary with 23 thousand inhabitants. But the development of the town reached the deadlock at the end of the 19th century when mining fell in decay. This trend also continued in the 20th century. The last pit was closed in the Štiavnické vrchy Mts. in 2001. However, Banská Štiavnica today is given special attention and it becomes the main Slovak centre of environmental research and schooling. Students brought life back to the town and they are the organisers of the **Salamander Days** every September with attractive cultural and artistic events including the night march through the town. The symbol of the event is the spotted little lizard which, as the local legend has, showed the miners the place where the deposits of silver and gold ore were. The town monument reserve of Banská Štiavnica comprises as much as 360 structures. Together they represent

the unique set of high cultural and historical value, which is set into the wonderful environment of the Štiavnické vrchy Mts. The dominant of the town centre is **Starý zámok ❶** (Old Castle) standing on the terrace west of the Trojičné námestie square. The oldest part of the Castle is the former parish **church of the Virgin Mary**. It was built together with the adjacent **ossuary of St. Michael** ín the 13th century as the three-nave Romanesque basilica. The fortifications added to the church in the 14th century formed foundations of the future town castle. A bastion and entrance gate with tower later equipped fortifications. Basilica was rebuilt into a Gothic church in the 16th century. The Turkish treat provoked the need of another reconstruction when the four-wing palace building with inner courtyard on the site of the central church nave as we know it today, originated. The 18th century Baroque adaptation concerned above all the original entrance tower. Today the Old Castle houses the **Slovenské banské múzeum** (Slovak Mining Museum). On the opposite hill **Nový zámok ❷** (New Castle) stands since 1571. It was built as the counter-Turkish fort in form of tower with four corner bastions. It also contains collections of the Slovak Mining Museum, and documents the counter-Turkish wars in Slovakia. In the vicinity of the New Castle is the Gothic **church of the Virgin Mary of Snow ❸** with the cemetery from 1512. **Piargska brána ❹**, the only surviving tower of the original five stands nearby. Walking on the road from the New Castle to the town centre passes one by **Klopačka ❺** or the Knocker. This tower-like structure built in 1681 was used for summoning miners to work by knocking on a wooden board.

The majority of monuments of Banská Štiavnica are concentrated into the area spreading between the Trojičné and Radničné námestie squares. Both squares are separated from each other by the Gothic **church of St. Catherine ❻** from the end of the 15th century and the building of **town hall ❼** with its slender clock tower.

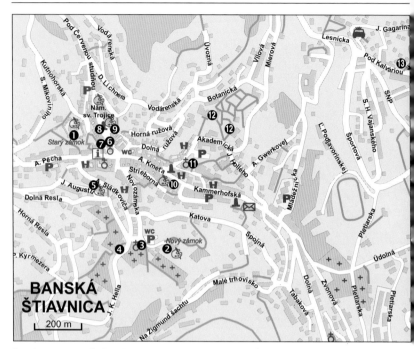

In the centre of the Trojičné námestie square skirted by old burgher houses and public buildings, the wonderful **Trinity Pillar ❽** stands erected here in piety for the victims of plague epidemic in 1711. The sculptor of Italian origin and native of Štiavnica, D. Stanetti, made the statues of the pillar. The masonry of K. Hobznecht, once considered the best central European artists of the craft is also worth seeing. The biggest building standing on the Trojičné námestie square is the **Hallenbach House ❾**, where the mining court yard seated. Today it contains the exhibits of the Slovenské banské múzeum. Another bulky building stands on the Kammerhofská ulica street which runs down from the town centre to the bus station. It is the building of **Kammerhof ❿** or Chamber Yard which originated in 1550 by adaptation of several Gothic houses. The main Chamber Count had resided here originally and officially supervised the

mining activities. The Count also acquired the office of director of the Mining Academy after 1864 and had its administration also moved to the building. On the corner of the Karmmerhofská and Akademická ulica streets stands the **church of Ascension of the Virgin Mary ⓫**. It was built as the three-nave basilica but later repeatedly reconstructed. Now its outer appearance is in Empirical style while its interior preserved the Baroque-Classicist elements. The Akademická ulica street leads to the trio of buildings of the **Banícka a lesnícka akadémia ⓬** (Academy of Mining and Forestry) built in the years 1892-1911. Formerly several burgher and public buildings in the town adapted to tuition served as parts of the oldest superior mining school in Europe. These buildings stand in the area of the **botanical garden** established in 1810 by the first professor of forestry in Slovakia, H. D. Wilkens. The cone-shaped hill **Kalvária ⓭** (Calvary) is the impressive dominant of the eastern part of Banská Štiavnica. Apart from the

Right: Open-air mining museum

beautiful view of the town it also offers a complete set of Baroque sacral monuments from the years 1744-1751. Between the upper church on top of the hill and the lower church on the western hillslope there are chapels by the path which symbolise the stops of the Cross Way. Further in the east is the **Arboretum Kysihýbeľ** utilised as research area where assimilation of imported wood species is studied.

SVÄTÝ ANTON (called Antol until 1996) is the village not far away from the town which is interesting for its monumental Baroque **manor house** with wonderful English park. It was built in 1744 on the site of an older castle for the Count of Hont and imperial general Andrej Koháry. Later the rich family of Coburg acquired the manor house. The former Bulgarian tsar Ferdinand Coburg lived there until the end of the Second World War. Architecture of the manor house represents the symbolic calendar. It has four entrances, 7 arcades, 12 chimneys, 52 rooms and 365 windows. Now it houses the **Poľovnícke múzeum** (Museum of Hunting). Apart from the wonderful interior with original furniture, the long corridor with great amount of hunting trophies intrigues visitors.

The tallest mountain of the Štiavnické vrchy Mts., **Sitno** (1,009 m), dominates the south-western horizon of Banská Štiavnica. with a fabulous view. The mountain is subject of numerous legends. One of the most popular of them talks about the knights hidden in the entrails of the mountain ready to intervene when the worst comes to worst for people of Slovakia. The top plain of the Sitno Mt. consists of erosion debris of andesite lava flow. Three faces of the mountain are steep almost inaccessible and on the forth side the Castle of **Sitno**, or its ruins, stands. It was built in the 13th century on the site of primeval fortified castle. It is in ruins since the 18th century. The best access to the Sitno Mt. is from the **Počúvadlianske jazero** lake on its western foothill. Its restored **view tower** from 1727 is now available to hikers. It also offers refreshment and basic information of

the Protected Landscape Area of **Štiavnické vrchy**. There are several beautiful mountain lakes along the road from the Počúvadlianske jazero lake through the old mining settlement **ŠTIAVNICKÉ BANE** to Banská Štiavnica referred to by locals as "tajchy". These artificial lakes constructed for the needs of mining are unique examples of efficient water management. The majority of them were founded in the course of the 18th century to design of two outstanding scholars from Banská Štiavnica, J. K. Hell and S. Mikovini. The ingenious system allowed for drawing the water through canals and tubes to the mines where it drove wheels, mills, pumps and ventilation. More than half of 60 lakes have been preserved until the present time. Today they serve to recreation, water sport, and fishing.

The **Banské múzeum** (Open Air Mining Museum) is on the road to Banská Štiavnica. Apart from the exhibits on surface there is also an attractive option to enter a pit. The tourists outfitted by helms

and macks enter the Bartholomew pit. The sightseeing trail is 1,300 m long and the deepest spot of the pit is 45 m under surface. The guide provide interesting information on the past of mining in Banská Štiavnica including the fact that gun powder was used here in 1627 for the first time. The deep forested valleys of the Štiavnické vrchy Mts. also offer an interesting and exciting experience to hikers. The spa **SKLENÉ TEPLICE**, with its mining and glass-production in the past is situated in the valley of the Teplá brook. Diseases of locomotion system are cured here. The local landmark is the **cave steam bath** known as early as the 16th century. Local **thermal springs** offer the water with temperatures of 53 degrees of Celsius. There is another **thermal swimming pool** in **VYHNE**, the village lying not far away from Sklené Teplice. This also is a mining settlement where iron ore was extracted

and melted in the local hammer mills. The dominant of the village now is the brewery, one of the oldest in Slovakia, which produces the Steiger beer.

HODRUŠA-HÁMRE, lying on the bottom of the deep valley of the Hodrušský potok brook consists of two old mining settlements where silver and gold were extracted in not so remote past. The local 12,149 m long **pit of Emperor Francis** is a remarkable mining structure. Several folk **mining houses** and the Renaissance tower-shaped *klopačka* or the **knocker** from the 17th century standing in the part Banská Hodruša opposite the parish Gothic **church of St. Nicholas** from 1387 are additional landmarks of the village. Silver processing factory **Sandrik** founded in 1892 is situated in the part called Dolné Hámre.

NOVÁ BAŇA (population 7,500) also boasts long and varied history of the mining town thriving on extraction of precious metals. The local gold-bearing veins brought prosperity and wealth to the settlement which was promoted to free royal borough in 1345. Nová Baňa was included among the seven richest mining towns in the Kingdom of Hungary in the second half of the 14th century. Development of the town stopped when Turks conquered it in 1664. Moreover, technical problems emerged caused flooding of the mines by groundwater. The pumping facility developed by English technician and constructor I. Potter in 1722 was used in order to save the pits. It was the first steam machine used outside the British Islands. It helped to renew the mining activity until 1887.

The historical centre of Nová Baňa contains several precious monuments. The dominant of the square is the **town hall**. It was built in 1353 as a royal house fulfilling the wish of King Charles Robert from 1335, which ordered every mining town to have houses referred to as royal house, in Latin *domus regiae*. Such house was the seat of royal clerk with title of mining count who collected the extracted metals from miners. They simultaneously ver-

Left: Nová Baňa
Right: Relief of St. Egidius basilica in H. Beňadik

ified their purity. The original Gothic appearance of the town hall was changed by Baroque adaptation made after fire in the first half of the 18th century. Now it houses the **Pohronské múzeum** (Museum of Pohronie). There are two Gothic churches and one new Classicist church in the town. Hinterland of Nová Baňa is exceptional for the arrangement of its settlements: there are scattered small hamlets called here *štále* around the larger settlements. Some of them are accessible from the village of **STARÁ HUTA,** where one of the oldest glass-producing factories of the Kingdom of Hungary was founded in 1630.

History of the northernmost situated town of the region **ŽARNOVICA** (population 6,600) started in the 14th century. The settlement, which was part of the estate of the Revište Castle, lied on the crossroads of trade routes where one lead to the rich town of Banská Štiavnica and another headed down the valley of the Hron river. Gothic castle was built here in the 15th century, which along with the town was plundered by the Turks in the 17th century in spite of its fortifications. Industries which developed in Žarnovica included processing of silver ore and processing of wood in the steam saw mill opened here in the 19th century. Fans of **motorcycling** know Žarnovica as it possesses the racetrack.

The ruins of the **Revište** Castle towering above the urban district **Revišťské Podzámčie** are set amidst a romantic environment. They stand on top of steep rock about 100 m above the floodplain of the Hron river. There is a wonderful meadow below the castle used by canoeist as a camping site. The castle was built in the 14th century as a part of protection of the central Slovakian mining towns and the trade route running along the Hron. Renaissance fortifications were added to the older Gothic part. At the end of the 15th century the castle became property of the Dóczy family who were protagonists of many bloody conflicts with their neighbours. Mercenaries of the rebellious magnate Imrich Thököly conquered the castle and converted it in ruins in 1678.

The bulky fortified **Benedictine monastery**, one of the oldest and most important architectural monuments of Slovakia, stands on the rocks above the village **HRONSKÝ BEŇADIK** south of Nová Baňa. Pursuing the historical documents King Gejza II decided to found the monastery in 1075. It was built with the aim to colonise the scarcely inhabited valley of the Hron river and promote the Christian ideas in the region. The King donated spacious lands to the Abbey. The oldest part of the monastic complex was the Romanesque basilica consecrated in the above-mentioned 1075. On its foundations the surviving Gothic **basilica of St. Egidius** was built in the years 1346-1375. The monastery was rebuilt into a fort supposed to resist Turkish raids in 1537. **Walls** and **canon bastions** were added then. However, construction of fortification also meant destruction of some of its Gothic parts. They reappeared in altered form during the period of Romanticism reconstruction carried out at the end of the 19th century.

ZVOLEN AND ITS ENVIRONS
(dial: 045-)

Information
– **Informačné centrum mesta Zvolen**, Trhová 4, Zvolen, ☎/fax 5429268, icko@zv.psg.sk, www.zvolen.sk, **Informačné centrum**, Nám. mieru 31, Detva, ☎/fax 5457692, cyklopolana@slovanet.sk, www.polana.slovanet.sk

Museums
– **Lesnícke a drevárske múzeum**, Nám. SNP 31, Zvolen, ☎ 5321886, **Podpolianske múzeum**, Partizánska 63, Detva, ☎ 5455212

Galleries
– **Slovenská národná galéria – Zvolenský zámok**, Nám. SNP, Zvolen, ☎ 5321903

Hotels
– **POĽANA*****, Nám. SNP 64/2, Zvolen, ☎ 5320124, **DETVA*****, Záhradná 22, Detva, ☎ 5456480, **B-éčko***, Bienska dolina 406, Kováčová, ☎ 5445329, **KRÁĽOVÁ**, 9. mája 8, Zvolen, 5333998, **MESTSKÝ HOTEL**, Trhová 4, Zvolen, ☎ 5325108, **LEONA**, Kúpeľná 233, Kováčová, ☎ 5445321, **SIELNICA**, Letecká 12, Sliač, ☎ 5442945

Restaurants
– **ACADEMIC**, Hviezdoslavova 13, Zvolen, ☎ 5322745, **CENTRUM**, Kozačeka 8, Zvolen, ☎ 5335036, **GURMÁN**, Masarykova 6, Zvolen, ☎ 5321821, **STRÁŽE NAD ZVOLENOM**, Strážska cesta 5, Zvolen, ☎ 5323060, **U RYTIERA**, Obrancov mieru 1, Detva, ☎ 5454934, **CENTRUM**, Hriňová, ☎ 5497407

KREMNICA AND ITS ENVIRONS
(dial: 045-)

Information
– **Informačné centrum mesta Kremnica**, Nám. M. R. Štefánika 35/44, Kremnica, ☎/fax 6742856, ☎ 6744388, infocentrum@kremnica.sk, www.kremnica.sk

Museums
– **Múzeum mincí a medailí**, Nám. M. R. Štefánika 10/19, Kremnica, ☎ 6742121, **Mestský hrad**, Zámocké nám. 1, Kremnica, ☎ 6743968

Galleries
– **Galéria**, Nám. M. R. Štefánika 33/40, ☎ 6743261

Thermal swimming pools
– **Termálne kúpalisko KATARÍNA**, Kremnica, ☎ 6742856, **Termálne kúpalisko**, Sklené Teplice, ☎ 6771070, **Termálne kúpalisko**, Vyhne, ☎ 6772185

Hotels
– **GOLFER*****, J. Horvátha 910/50, Kremnica, ☎ 6743767, **CENTRÁL****, Dolná 40/3, Kremnica, ☎ 6744210, **LUNA**, Nám. Matice slovenskej 2, Žiar nad Hronom, ☎ 6723219, **SKALKA**, Skalka 530, ☎ 6742236, **BLAUFUSS**, Krahule 59, ☎ 6744550

Restaurants
– **GOTIKA**, Nám. M. R. Štefánika, Kremnica, ☎ 6742077, **ZLATÝ SIVOŇ**, Langsfeldova 693/3, Kremnica ☎ 6744580, **TATRA**, SNP 52, Žiar nad Hronom, ☎ 6725994, **BIMARE**, SNP 121, Žiar nad Hronom, ☎ 6722403, **JELEŇ**, Dolná 74, Žiar nad Hronom, ☎ 6744105

BANSKÁ ŠTIAVNICA AND ITS ENVIRONS
(dial: 045-)

Information
– **Mestská turistická informačná kancelária**, Radničné nám. 1, Banská Štiavnica, ☎/fax 6911859, ☎ 16186, tikbs@banskastiavnica.sk, www.banskastiavnica.sk, **Informačné centrum mesta Nová Baňa**, Nám. slobody 2, Nová Baňa, ☎ 6856486, fax 6857888, info@novabana.sk, www.novabana.sk

Museums
– **Slovenské banské múzeum**, Kammerhofská 2, Banská Štiavnica, ☎ 6911544, **Banské múzeum v prírode**, J. K. Hella 12, Banská Štiavnica, ☎ 6912971, **Pohronské múzeum**, Bernolákova 2, Nová Baňa, ☎ 6855178, **Múzeum**, Svätý Anton, ☎ 6913932

Galleries
– **Galéria Jozefa Kollára**, Trojičné nám. 8, Banská Štiavnica, ☎ 6913765

Hotels
– **GRAND-MATEJ*****, Kammerhofská 5, Banská Štiavnica, ☎ 6913782, **HRON***, Nám. slobody 2, Nová Baňa, ☎ 6855560, **SITNO***, Vyhne 103, ☎ 6772187, **BRISTOL GARNI**, A. Kmeťa 11, Banská Štiavnica, ☎ 6911387

Restaurants
– **GALLERY**, Trojičné nám. 8, Banská Štiavnica, ☎ 6912735, **BANSKÝ DOM**, Radničné nám. 12, Banská Štiavnica, ☎ 6921258, **HUBERT**, Strieborná 4, Banská Štiavnica, ☎ 6913522, **HOŤAPO**, Nám. sv. Alžbety 102, Nová Baňa, ☎ 6856296, **NEZÁBUDKA**, Orovnica 136, ☎ 6856452, **KABINA**, Nám. SNP 12, Žarnovica, ☎ 6812305

HOREHRONIE

Banská Bystrica

Environs of
Banská Bystrica

Brezno and
its environs

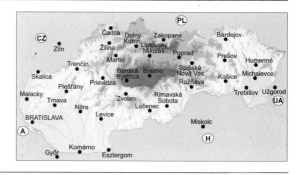

The river Hron, which gave the name to the territory this chapter is about, springs in the southern hillside of the majestic Kráľova hoľa Mt. It flows westward from this legendary mountain in the eastern end of the Nízke Tatry Mts., and continues through the centre of large depression between the Nízke Tatry Mts. in the north and the Slovenské rudohorie in the south. The beautiful landscape with typical villages around the upper reach of the Hron river lying almost in the heart of Slovakia was given the name Horehronie. The mountain barriers on both sides determined the way it is arranged. The main belt of settlements connected by road and railway in the east-west direction was formed here. Natural barrier in form of the massive ridge of the Low Tatras which comes down only in three points allowing

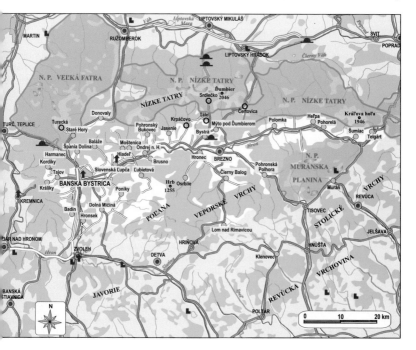

the passage to the region of Liptov by car is in its north.

And if one wants to leave the territory of Horehronie going south, the same thing occurs. There also are only three possibilities how to pass the mountain saddles over the Veporské vrchy Mts. and the Muránska planina plateau to the regions of Gemer, Malohont or Novohrad. Railway also leads over the sedlo Zbojská saddle to the south of Slovakia. Horehronie in its central part widens into the Breznianska kotlina basin. The Čierny Hron river accompanied by the romantic forest railway called Čiernohronská avoids it in its southern part and flows into the Hron river near iron works of Podbrezová. The Hron continues to the west. In Banská Bystrica it turns in almost perpendicular direction and flows to the south to the Zvolenská kotlina basin, around the volcanic mountain ranges of the Slovenské stredohorie.

Left: Námestie SNP square
Right: Municipal castle

Banská Bystrica

BANSKÁ BYSTRICA (population 83,100) lies in the north-west of the region of Banská Bystrica and the westernmost edge of Horehronie. Although the land next to the meander of the Hron river is rather narrow for Banská Bystrica of today, in Middle Ages it was an ideal area for founding a prosperous town. Two important trade routes crossed here, moreover the environs were rich in ores. Like many other Slovak towns, Banská Bystrica sprang from a little Slav settlement referred to as *Bystricia*, population of which grew larger with contribution of German colonists. In the oldest known document of King Belo IV from the 13th century the ruler gave the German "guests" the rights to extract gold, silver and other metals and provided them some privileges. The settlement gradually became the town *Novisolium* with Romanesque parish church. The main source of income of the medieval town was mining. Banská Bystrica was member of the exclusive trio of the richest central Slovakian mining towns along with Kremnica and "silver" Banská Štiavnica. Banská Bystrica's attribute was "copper" as this ore was extracted in the Staro-horské vrchy Mts. nearby the town in the 14th century. Colonists involved in mining enjoyed various privileges including those, which promoted the local settlements to boroughs, granted to them by ruler. The local feudal lords participated in extraction by a third of the profit.

The German banker and merchant Jacob Fugger of Augsburg and count Ján Thurzo of Spiš initiated their businesses in Banská Bystrica in the 15th century. Marriage contracted between their off-spring proved to be an extra successful business bond. The joint Thurzo-Fugger trade company invested in copper mines in the environs of Banská Bystrica and Špania Dolina. It was profitable because the new technology of smelting allowing for separation of metal from the ore was introduced. Such plants were kept in se-cret by Venetians who were the main buy-ers of copper from Banská Bystrica. Fug-ger and Thurzo became the principal pro-ducers of copper in the world after a short time and almost acquired a position of monopoly. The much demanded reddish metal was sold to many countries of the world. It was hauled down the valley of the Hron by heavy carts. Copper was then loaded in harbours and shipped to Venice, Antwerp, and Polish Gdansk or to Lisboa. Roofs of many churches all over Europe were made from Slovak copper and it was also used for production of sea ships trav-elling around the world.

However, in the 16th century the trade in central Slovakian metals started to de-cline under the heavy competition of over-seas ores. Moreover, the Thurzo-Fugger trade company fell in competency con-tentions with burghers of Banská Bystri-ca. The protests and discontent of miners were growing with deteriorating living conditions. Gradation of social tension culminated in May 1525 by rebellion of miners and the poor of the town, which

soon spread to all local mines. In Febru-ary 1526 also the colleagues of Kremnica and Banská Štiavnica joined the rebel-lious miners and in August only troops of royal army marching through the town on their way to south of the Kingdom to fight the Turks saved the town from the en-raged mob of armed rebels.

Raids of Turkish hordes into the northern parts of the Kingdom of Hungary were also aimed at Banská Bystrica, which could provide them copper for production of canyons. The town counsellors had the town castle rebuilt into a modern fort and the town walls fortified. But the Turks never directly threatened the town, fortu-nately. The strength of town walls of Ban-ská Bystrica had to be tried only in time of Rebellion of Estates in the 17th century.

Ideas of Reformation, which spread from Germany in the course of the 16th and 17th century, found response in the mining towns of central Slovakia and gained many followers. The reformed denominations prevailed in the town until 1620. The

largest insurrection against the German Nazi regime following the Yugoslav partisan war took place here. Although it was defeated it provided the Slovaks an honourable right to victorious countries over the bloodiest conflict in history of mankind. The second half of the 20th century brought great changes for Banská Bystrica. It expanded to a modern central Slovakian metropolis and became the sixth largest town of Slovakia.

The pride of Banská Bystrica is its central **Námestie SNP** square rebuilt into a throbbing pedestrian zone with an original charm and atmosphere. We can also admire its older equally attractive appearance as represented on paintings of **Dominik Skutecký** (1849-1921) who lived in Banská Bystrica for more than 30 years and also died there. His famous painting *Market in Banská Bystrica* from 1889 bears traces of impressionism.

The multicoloured area of the square can be best admired from the slender **Hodinová veža ❶** tower (The Clock Tower). It was built in 1552 as part of the town prison. The prison and torture rooms were in its basement. After the last reconstruction in the 18th century the top of the tower inclined by about 40 cm. The chapter **Church of St. František Xaverský ❷** is another tower-like building of the square. Jesuits had it built in the years 1695-1709 as the first Baroque building in the town. Its present appearance is owed to the Classicist reconstruction from 1844 and adjustments carried out in the 1880's in then fashionable historicising style.

The most beautiful building of the southern row of the square is **Thurzov dom ❸** (Thurzo's House) also called Mittelhaus in the past. Originally there were two Gothic houses where administration of the Thurzo-Fugger company seated in the years 1492-1540. They were joined into one by common Renaissance facade with graffito ornamentation in 1660. In the rear part of the house is the restored Zelená sieň (The Green Hall) adorned by the Late Gothic figural and ornamental wall paintings. The paintings represent the biblical motifs of

Counter-Reformation policy of Habsburgs though, sharpened the relations between the Catholics and Evangelicals and the churches of Banská Bystrica were passing from hands of one side to those of another. Economic structure of Banská Bystrica changed in the 18th century. Extraction of copper ore was replaced by extraction and processing of iron ore and the riches of forests surrounding the town were more intensively exploited. After the extensive fire in 1761 the town acquired a new, prevailingly Baroque appearance. In the 19th century Banská Bystrica played an important role in cultural and political life of the Slovak nation. The personality, which most contributed to the national emancipation efforts, was above all the Catholic bishop and the first chairman of Matica slovenská, Štefan Moyzes. In the mid-20th century the town entered the history when in August 1944 became the centre of the Slovak National Uprising. The second

---

Left: Church of St. František Xaverský

the *Last Judgement* and *Susan in Bath*. Today Thurzo's House is the seat of **Stredoslovenské múzeum** (Museum of Middle Slovakia). On the opposite side of the square stands **Beniczkého dom ❹** (Beniczky's House) which has got a lot of common with Thurzo's House. It too, is the result of reconstruction two older Gothic houses from around 1660 and its facade is also very interesting. It is easily discernible in the northern row of houses for its **loggia** with **arcades**. This element, so typical for the Italian Renaissance architecture suggests that the author of the building, Jacob di Pauli was Italian. On the Renaissance portal of the Beniczky's House is the **coat of arms** of Szentiványi family depicting a couple of miners wearing uniforms. It houses an exhibition hall at the first floor of the building. The third example of the Renaissance style at the Námestie SNP square is the **oriel** of the **Ebnerovský dom ❺** (Ebner House) in the northern row of houses.

At the corner of Námestie SNP square and Lazovná ulica street is the former

Biskupský palác ❻ (Bishop's Palace). Count Berchtold had it built in 1787. The **tablet** on its facade announces that in the second half of the 19th century the first chairman of Matica slovenská bishop Štefan Moyzes (1797-1869) resided in the building. Several famous natives of Banská Bystrica lived on Lazovná ulica street, including the poet and playwright Ján Botto and Gustáv Zechenter Laskomerský. In **house No. 11** Júlia Géczy known from the novel of Mór Jókai as the White Lady of Levoča lived more than two centuries ago. In the past the Lazovná ulica street headed to the stone town gate, which does not exist anymore because it was pulled down at the end of the 19th century. The wooden "articled" **Evangelical church** used to stand beyond the town gate. In its site the new Evangelical church stands since 1807. The **commemorative tablet** on its wall explains that the first vice-chairman of Matica slovenská Karol Kuzmány (1806-1966) lived in this house. **Literárno-hudobné múzeum** (Museum of Literature and

Music) is now in the neighbouring building of the former **Evangelical school**. In the cemetery behind the church several significant figures of Slovak culture such as Ján Botto, Terézia Vansová, Martin Rázus, Viliam Figuš Bystrický, and Alexander Matuška are buried.

The lower part of the Námestie SNP square tapers into the **Dolná ulica** street, which is the prolongation of the pedestrian zone. Among the houses of rich burghers of Bystrica the Bethlen's house from the 14th century is the most interesting one. The diet of the Kingdom of Hungary had its session here in 1620 and elected Prince Gabriel Bethlen of Transylvania for king. The great scholar and pride of the Kingdom of Hungary, **Mattias Bel** whose name bears the local **university** lived in house No. 47. At the lower end of the Dolná ulica street is the **church of St. Elizabeth ❼**. It was built around 1303 as part of hospital and burnt in 1605. It was the first Gothic building in the town, later rebuilt in the Baroque style. The remarkable thing about its interior is the **altar painting of St. Elizabeth paint-**

ed by the universally gifted **Jozef Murgaš**, native of Tajov which became famous not only as a painter but above all as inventor of wireless radiotelegraphy. The passage in the southern row of houses of the Námestie SNP square leads to the **Národná ulica** street heading to the Hron river. **Národný dom ❽** (National House) built in the years 1924-1929 pursuing the project of important Slovak architect, Emil Belluš, stands there. This multipurpose building also houses the opera of **Divadlo Jozefa Gregora Tajovského** theater.

Several ancient buildings on the Námestie Štefana Moyzesa square formed once the **town castle ❾**. The original appearance of the castle disappeared by removal of a substantial part of town walls that connected the isolated buildings into a whole. The castle built as intraurban defensive system was designed to serve the rich burgers of Bystrica as the occasional last refuge. The necessity of such system was proved by the rebellion of miners in the years 1525 and 1526. The town castle was built gradually. The parish church was

built as the first structure in the 13th century and fortifications were added to in the 15th century. Tall stone walls fortified by bastions and water dike replaced the original earth ramparts and palisades. In the 16th century Turkish threat called for further fortifications. Only a quarter of the original **town walls** and three bastions: **Farská** (Parish), **Banícka** (Mining), and **Pisárska** (Scrivener's) of the original four survive. The dominant architecture of the square is now the former **Barbican** with a **tower**. It used to be the entry gate of the castle with a bridge. Barbican acquired its present Baroque facade in the consequence of fire in 1751. The parish **church of the Virgin Mary** was started as early as 1255. Two windows of the tower and the northern wall of the nave are the evidence that its original style was Romanesque. In the course of the 14th and 15th centuries gradually Gothic parts widened the church. Its ground plan was expanded, and the Gothic chapels and oratory were built. The most valuable artistic work of its exterior is the relief of **Christ at Mount of Olives** from the beginning of the 16th century. In the interior, apart from other gems, the Late Gothic **wing altar of St. Barbara** from 1509 fashioned in the workshop of Majster Pavol of Levoča can be admired. Another castle church consecrated to the Holy Cross was built next to the northern walls of castle fortifications in 1492, which is sometimes also referred to as **Slovenský kostol** (Slovak church). Evangelicals owned it in the 17th century and made major building adjustments in it. Fire damaged it in 1782. The Late Gothic **Matejov dom** house was built in 1479 as a slender five-storied house squeezed inside the Banícka bastion. It served as the seat of the royal clerk supervising the mining activities. The name of the house (Mattias) relates to King Mattias Corvinus' coat of arms on its southern facade. The building of **Stará radnica** (Old Town Hall) with a tower also called **Praetorium** was built in 1500 and financed by the head of the Zvolen county, Vit Mühlstein, for the needs of the town council. The town hall was expanded in the 16th century by

loggia with arcades and reconstructed in the Baroque style in the 18th century.

Apart from town walls protecting the castle, Banská Bystrica also had **fortifications** that protected the town. When they were pulled down at the turn of the 19th and 20th centuries several segments with four bastions were spared. The best preserved section is the south-eastern one including the **Mäsiarska** and **Čižmárska brána** gates. The modern dominant, **Pamätník Slovenského národného povstania ⑩** (The Monument of the Slovak National Uprising), stands close to them. The monumental iron-concrete structure designed by architect Dušan Kuzma serves as a museum dedicated to one of the most important events of the modern history of Slovakia that took place in autumn 1944. The monument stands on the terrain

Left: Upper part of the Námestie SNP square.
Portal of Beniczký's House. Burgher house.
The Monument of the Slovak National Uprising
Right: Arkáda passage

now urban district of Banská Bystrica on the southern edge of the town is known for the events which took place here from November 1944 to February 1945 when it became witness to mass executions of partisans and innocent citizens including old people and children. In the memory of 747 victims of Nazi atrocities a monument was erected south of Kremnička in 1949.

Environs of Banská Bystrica

The calm and seducing rural landscape surrounding Banská Bystrica is only several kilometres away of the busy centre of the city. The villages situated west of it are ideal for recreation and in recent years they also became attractive localities for healthy living in countryside in close vicinity of the large town. Its famous native, writer Jozef Gregor Tajovský, described the village **TAJOV** as the most beautiful place in the world. It is still picturesque for its nice situation in the valley skirted by fresh forests. Tajov boasts also another famous native, Jozef Murgaš, the world famous inventor in the field of wireless radiotelegraphy. Thankful people of Tajov established commemorative rooms for both of them.

edge, which provides a nice view of the modern eastern part of Banská Bystrica with the building of **Lux Hotel**.

Life of Banská Bystrica is closely connected with famous **fairs of Radvaň**, which have always been an excellent opportunity for the craftsmen living in the region to display their products. Today they are also a pleasant refreshment of the cultural and social life of the citizens and visitors to Banská Bystrica. The urban district of **Radvaň** has got three remarkable manor houses. The oldest one, the Renaissance manor house of family Radvanský is from the 16th century. The Bárczy manor house from 1677 also contains the inn called Furmanská krčma, and Tihány manor house in the district of Kráľová exhibits part of natural-science collections of the **Stredoslovenské múzeum** (Museum of Middle Slovakia). Kremnička, independent village in the past,

KORDÍKY is situated higher. This former collier settlement lying on the plain below the foothills of the Kremnické vrchy Mts. is today a favourite centre of summer and winter tourism. Further to south situated **KRÁLIKY** is known to ski fans. It has the stadium of cross-country skiing with the final of the **Biela stopa SNP**, popular cross-country skiing competition, ski lifts, and maintained ski tracks. The mountain cottage **Chata nad Králikmi** is a good starting base for hiking in central part of the Kremnické vrchy Mts. The Farebný potok brook flowing beyond the village modelled the **Králická tiesňava** gorge in hard rocks. A bit farther the same brook falls down a 2 m tall rock step, called **Farebný vodopád** waterfall.

It is worthwhile to visit the national nature reserve **Badínsky prales** virgin for-

Left: Church tower in Tajov
Right: Chata nad Králikmi cottage. Virgin forest in Badín

est from the village **BADÍN** situated only several kilometres south of Banská Bystrica. It is one of the oldest protected areas of Slovakia designated as early as 1913. It is an especially valuable territory on the area of 30.7 hectares with surviving fir-beech woods with admixture of other broad-leaved species. Rare elm trees grow here, which inspired the British Prince Charles to visit it in 2000. Hikers who want to trace the route of the British crown prince can use the **instructive path** opened to public in 2001. As a matter of fact, instead of path, it is rather a passage through the virgin forest that requires in places crawling under or climbing over the fallen trees. Green marks painted on tree trunks should be followed.

The village **HRONSEK** is especially rich in historical monuments. It is situated on the left bank of the Hron river, south of Banská Bystrica. The **wooden "articled" church** from 1726 set in the wonderful environment of large lime trees is the most valuable of them. The member of the Štúr's literary group, romantic poet Andrej Sládkovič married in this church the local girl Júlia Senkovičová. The author· of the passionate love poem Marína died not far away from here, in the village of Radvaň. Side by side with church stands a nice **wooden belfry**. There are also two manor houses in Hronsek The older, Renaissance **manor house** was rebuilt from the Gothic water castle in 1576 and the other **manor house**

was built in the 18th century for the aristocratic family of Géczy.

The poet Samo Chalupka's verses about Turkish raid, perhaps known to all educated Slovaks mentioned the name of **PONIKY**, the village situated on the karstic high plain. In the past it was a prospering little town of miners who were working in the local gold mines. No wonder that the Turks were interested in Poniky. The village has the Gothic **church** with preserved medieval paintings in its interior from the 14th century. The lateral **altar of the Virgin Mary** is attributed to artists, which belonged to the group of Majster Pavol of Levoča. A hill with bulky Renaissance manor house with four oval corner towers above the village **DOLNÁ MIČINÁ**. It was built in the mid-16th century for the noble family of Beniczky. The road beyond the village passes by the travertine rocks of **Mičinské travertíny** with two mineral springs. More of such springs can be found in the region of Horehronie and the local people call such spring *medokýš*.

The busy road leading from Banská Bystrica to the north winds down the deep valley incised into the Starohorské vrchy Mts. Before it bends it enters the sedlo Donovaly saddle, nice mountain landscape offering numerous landmarks opens in front of the driver. Some of them are indeed worth to see. **ŠPANIA DOLINA** is especially· interesting. The former mining village lying in the side valley is undoubtedly one of the

most beautiful in Slovakia. Copper and silver ores were mined here in the past. Significance of the local deposits increased after the reserves of copper and other metals were exhausted in the Staré Hory Mts. not far away from here. While local men were involved in mining the women dedicated themselves to embroidery, a tradition which survives until now. The mining activities in Špania Dolina existed until the end of the 19th century. As the mines lost their profits they were closed in 1888. The village has been designated the **monument reserve of folk architecture** in 1979. It consists of a unique set of **miner houses** built from wood and stones. Many of them still possess shingle roofs. The greenery of the surrounding forests enhance the charm and originality of the place. In order to win the best view of Špania Dolina it is necessary to climb to the top of the extensive pit heaps. The tall tower built of the **church of**

Left: Špania Dolina
Right: Miner's house in Špania Dolina

Conversion of the Lord on Romanesque foundations dominates the wonderful panorama. In order to reach the fortified church built on steep slope it is necessary to climb 160 stairs of roofed staircase. The entrance is from a little park with the Renaissance building of former the klopačka or the knocker from the 16th century. The old water main, which carried water to the hammer mill in Špania Dolina from as far as the Prašivá Mt. in the Low Tatras is also a precious technical monument.

HARMANEC is the village lying in the valley of the Bystrica brook through which also the railway from Banská Bystrica to Vrútky leads. The section between Harmanec and Diviaky is one of the most beautiful pieces of landscape in Slovakia. The track running in the dissected relief between the Veľká Fatra Mts. and Kremnické vrchy Mts. passes through 22 tunnels. The longest of them is 4,498 m long. Harmanec today is widely known for production of paper. The local paper plant produces from 1829. **Vojenský kartografický ústav** (the

Institute of Military Cartography), the most important producer of tourist maps in Slovakia also seats here. Above Horný Harmanec is the **Harmanecká jaskyňa** cave. Its entrance is accessible after overcoming the altitude difference of 260 m. The cave known for occurrence of rare white soft sinter, tall pagodas and sinter lakes is open to public since 1950. The sight-seeing route is 720 m long. The entrance to the area of the cave called Izbica has been known since time immemorial and it provided shelter to loggers in bad weather. So far the explorers discovered 2,763 cave corridors. The local natural landmark of European importance is the natural growth of rare yew trees protected as the national nature reserve of **Harmanecká tisina**.

The wealth of the medieval Banská Bystrica had its origin in copper and silver mining in the environs of **STARÉ HORY**. Extracted ores were processed in the local foundries that operated until the mid-19th century. The dominant of the village is the Gothic **church of the Virgin Mary**. Pilgrims visit the precious statue of Madonna from the 16th century in its interior as Staré Hory is now a well-known pilgrim place. Staré Hory includes numerous hamlets in its environs. Small settlement of **Rybie** is in the side valley below the massive ridge of the Veľká Fatra Mts. Rybie was struck by an enormous snow avalanche in 1924 which slid down the slope of the **Krížna Mt.** (1,574 m) and killed 18 loggers. The settlement Turecká on the southern foothill of the Veľká Fatra Mts. is a well-known summer and winter tourist centre, it is also the venue of the world championship in cooking and eating the national meal of Slovaks "halušky" and competition in "krňačky", which is an ancient type of sled used in Slovakia in the past for timber skidding. **DONOVALY** is the village situated in an eponymous saddle (980 m) and it is also a well-known ski centre where the dog harness races are held every year. Slopes on both sides of Donovaly offer exquisite ski tracks with numerous ski lifts. The top of the dominant mountain of **Zvolen** (1,402 m) within the edge of the Veľká

Fatra Mts. is connected with the valley by **chair lift**. Hikers normally head to the eastern side where the westernmost part of the Nízke Tatry Mts. provides indeed ideal conditions for hiking, including the introductory part of the ridge tour in the Nízke Tatry Mts. The villages in the valleys of the right-side tributaries of the Hron river are also good starting points for hiking in high-mountain area of the Nízke Tatry Mts. **MOŠTENICA** and **HIADEĽ** with mineral springs Moštenická kyslá and Hiadeľská kyslá are the two most popular of them.

Above **SLOVENSKÁ ĽUPČA**, which is known for production of pharmacological drugs and is situated further in south, is one of the best preserved castles of Slovakia. The history of the **Ľupčiansky hrad** Castle is linked with the 13th century. The first written reference to the Castle is from 1306. The castle was part of dowry of queens of Kingdom of Hungary. Thanks to its position in the vicinity of extensive forests full of game, the ruler often visited it. In 1620 the castle became property of

the Széchy family. Marrying with Mária Széchy, Juraj Wesselényi, the Hungarian palatine won the castle. It survived the modern times in good condition. The castle though is closed to public.

The village **ĽUBIETOVÁ** in the side valley of the left tributary of the Hron river was also a prospering mining town in the Middle Ages. It acquired the town privileges as early as 1379. Apart from copper and gold also the rare mineral called libetenite (the name derived of the name of the locality), was extracted here. The landscape dominant of the environs of Ľubietová is the massive mountain of **Ľubietovský Vepor** (1,277 m) with its typical silhouette in form of large suitcase set on top of the mountain ridge and the mountain **Hrb** (1,255 m), often referred to as the geographic centre of Slovakia. The Hrb Mt. is easily accessible from the **Chata na Hrbe** cottage. In the quite atmosphere of the forested valley of

the Brusnianka brook will one find the spa of **BRUSNO**. The mineral water of the local spring discovered in 1829 is successfully used for therapy of diseases of digestive systems and metabolic disorders.

Brezno and its environs

The centre of the upper part of the Horehronie region is the town **BREZNO** (population 22,900). It lies in the part of the Horehronské podolie valley, which widens into a small basin. Mining settlement existed here in the 13th century, which received town privileges in 1380. The town situated on the crossroads of trade routes developed due to trade and crafts. In 1655 it was promoted to free royal borough. In the 18th and 19th centuries the employment in local ironworks became the main bread-winning activity of the locals. The villages Hronec, Valaská and Podbrezová maintained this tradition up to the present. The principal industry of Brezno is still mechanical engineering focused to

---

Left: Ľupčiansky hrad Castle. Brusno spa
Right: Museum of Horehronie in Brezno

production of bridge constructions and cranes. In the 19th century Brezno had a particular cultural milieu. Apart from other personalities, important Slovak playwright Janko Chalupka (1824-1871) lived here. The local theatre group bears his name.

The centre of Brezno consists of almost regular rectangular **square** with several originally Renaissance burgher houses. One of the most beautiful buildings is that of the former **town hall** from the second half of the 18th century, which now contains exhibition of the **Horehronské múzeum** (Museum of Horehronie). The tallest building on the square is the **town tower** built in 1830. The Baroque **Piarist monastery** from 1713, the Classicist Toleration church from the second half of the 18th century and the **Lady's Pillar** from 1741 are also interesting monuments of Brezno, which include the surviving remains of town walls.

The road from Brezno heading northward leads over the **Vagnár** saddle (733 m) to tallest part of the Nízke Tatry Mts. where

the beautiful view of the typical village **MÝTO POD ĎUMBIEROM** opens. In the past precious metals and iron ore were mined in this village which is now a popular down-hill ski centre. The road ascending to the sedlo **Čertovica** (1,232 m) in the main ridge of the Nízke Tatry Mts. passes through the village. It is one of the few possibilities how to get from Horehronie to the Liptov region by car. Čertovica also offers magnificent skiing in winter. On the southern end of the village **BYSTRÁ** is the entrance to the **Bystrianska jaskyňa** cave, which consists of two: the Stará and Nová jaskyňa caves. Its total length is 1,000 metres. The locals new about the existence of the cave long time before its proper exploration started in 1923. The cave, though without electric lighting, was opened to public in 1939. The present sightseeing route in the cave is 490 m long and it is used since 1968. Speleotherapy or therapy of the respiratory diseases is successfully applied in the part called Spodná partizánska sieň (the Lower Hall of Partisans).

The **Bystrianska dolina** valley is an ideal starting point if one wants to visit the very heart of the Nízke Tatry Mts. Use of this expression is not accidental as the road ascending up the valley ends at **Srdiečko** at the altitude of 1,216 m). **Chair lift** brings the hikers closer to the top of the Chopok Mt. (2,024 m). Then it is necessary to continue on foot from **Kosodrevina Hotel** (1,485 m). The usual route of ascent to the tallest mountain of the range, **Ďumbier** (2,043 m) leads up the dolina Trangoška valley. The **Chata gen. M. R. Štefánika** cottage (1,728 m) offers refreshment on the route and one can also visit the **Jaskyňa mŕtvych netopierov** cave (only with guide). In the lower part of the Bystrianska dolina valley is the favourite recreation centre **Tále** with natural bathing pool and ski slopes. **Krpáčovo**, situated nearby is another recreation centre.

With the aim to see the landscape of Horehronie south of Brezno it is possible to use the train of the **Čiernohronská lesná železnica** (forest railway) which connects Hronec, **ČIERNY BALOG** and the Vydrová valley. The first part of this narrow-gauge railway was built in 1908 and later it was prolonged to the total length of 113 km. Originally it served for hauling timber from remote forests, today tourists use it. Hundreds of young conservationists in summer camps participated in its restoration and in fact, salvation. The railway operates with regular schedule in summer season. The **Dobročský prales** virgin forest is situated beyond Čierny Balog. **Instructive path** leads the hikers through the almost intact Carpathian mixed forests with rare flora. Especially the firs of Dobroč are admired for their dimensions. The road heading southward from Čierny Balog ascends to the mountain saddle **Tlstý javor** (1,015 m) where an open and scarcely dissected landscape of the Sihlianska planina plateau opens in front of hiker. It is covered by

---

Left: Forest railway in Čierny Balog
Environs of the Bystrianska jaskyňa cave
Right: Band of Horehronie

small hamlets, including the village **LOM NAD RIMAVICIOU**, which is the highest situated village in Slovakia (1,015 m above sea level), except for the settlements in the High Tatras.

The railway connecting Brezno with Tisovec is also a remarkable technical monument. The extreme ascent to the **Zbojská** saddle (725 m) beyond the village **POHRONSKÁ POLHORA** required use of a rack in place between the rails until recently. The wide mountain of **Kráľova hoľa** (1,946 m) is undoubtedly the dominant of the local landscape which along with the Kriváň Mt. in the Tatras is considered the national mountain of Slovaks. Seen from any aspect, this wonderful mountain is majestic and bulky. No wonder it is mentioned in so many Slovak folk songs. The environs offer numerous spots for views of the Kráľova hoľa Mt. but the **Gindura Mt.** (1,098 m) which towers above the village **Pohorelská Maša** (part of larger village **POHORELÁ**) is perhaps the best. Asphalt road (closed to traffic) leads to the tower of TV transmitter at the top of the Kráľova hoľa Mt. but it is closed to public. If you do decide to climb it you have to walk and use the hiking paths starting in **ŠUMIAC** or **TELGÁRT**.

Panoramic view of an enormous piece of Slovakia including the peaks of Tatras is the reward for the demanding and lengthy ascent. Also other tops of the main ridge of this part of the Nízke Tatry Mts. are attractive. The shortest and quickest route of ascent to the **Homôlka Mt.** (1,660 m) is from the village **POLOMKA**, while the typical village **HEĽPA** with still living folk traditions and surviving folk architecture offers the access to the **Veľká Vápenica Mt.** (1,691 m). Závadka nad Hronom is the village which is used as starting point for the dolina Hronec valley which leads the hikers as far as below the Veľká and Malá Stožka Mts. in the centre of the National Park of **Muránska planina**. Wonderful karstic landscape with bizarre rocks and abysses has remained intact and still not discovered by mass tourism, though there is an instructive path leading through it.

BANSKÁ BYSTRICA
(dial: 048-)

Information
- **Kultúrne a informačné stredisko**, Nám. Š. Moyzesa 26, Banská Bystrica, ☎ 16186, 4155085, ☎/fax 4152272, kis@pkobb.sk, www.banskabystrica.sk

Museums
- **Stredoslovenské múzeum**, Nám. SNP 4, Banská Bystrica, ☎ 4125897, **Múzeum SNP**, Kapitulská 23, Banská Bystrica, ☎ 4123259, **Literárno-hudobné múzeum**, Lazovná 9, Banská Bystrica, ☎ 4123690, **Múzeum historických vozidiel**, Partizánska cesta 86, Banská Bystrica, ☎ 4141545, **Poštové múzeum**, Partizánska cesta 9, Banská Bystrica, ☎ 4339278

Galleries
- **Galéria Dominika Skuteckého**, Horná 55, Banská Bystrica, ☎ 4125450, **Štátna galéria**, Dolná 8, Banská Bystrica, ☎ 4124167, **TEO**, Národná 6, Banská Bystrica, ☎ 4125750

Atractiveness
- **Church of the Virgin Mary**, Banská Bystrica, **Clock tower**, Nám. SNP, Banská Bystrica, ☎ 4155085, **Observatory**, Banská Bystrica, ☎ 4156144

Hotels
- **DIXON*****, Švermova 32, Banská Bystrica, ☎ 4130808, **LUX*****, Nám. slobody 2, Banská Bystrica, ☎ 4144141-7, **NÁRODNÝ DOM****, Národná 11, Banská Bystrica, ☎ 4123737, **ARCADE****, Nám. SNP 5, Banská Bystrica, ☎ 4302111, **TURIST**, Tajovského ul., Banská Bystrica, ☎ 4138773

Restaurants
- **QUATRO**, Nám. Š. Moyzesa 7, Banská Bystrica, ☎ 4123304, **U KOMEDIANTOV**, Horná Strieborná 13, Banská Bystrica, ☎ 4153185, **BAŠTA**, Kapitulská 23, Banská Bystrica, ☎ 4126281, **ČERVENÝ RAK**, Nám. SNP 13, Banská Bystrica, ☎ 4153882

ENVIRONS OF BANSKÁ BYSTRICA
(dial: 048-)

Information
- **Informačná kancelária**, Nám. sv. Antona Paduánskeho 136, Donovaly, ☎ 4299055-7, fax 4299058, info@donovaly.sk, www.donovaly.sk

Atractiveness
- **Ľupčiansky hrad** Castle, Slovenská Ľup-

ča, ☎ 4196204, **Harmanecká jaskyňa** cave, Dolný Harmanec, ☎ 4198122, **Spa Brusno**, Brusno, ☎ 4194336-8, **Wooden articular church**, Hronsek, ☎ 4188165, **Badínsky prales** virgin forest, Badín, ☎ 4182601

Hotels
- **POĽANA*****, Brusno-kúpele, ☎ 4194336-8, **GALA KONGRES*****, Hronsecká cesta 1, Hronsek, ☎ 4188550-1, **ŠPORTHOTEL DONOVALY*****, Donovaly 15, ☎ 4199720, **DONOVALY****, Donovaly 287, ☎ 4199825, **VESEL**, Donovaly, ☎ 4199745, **POD ŠTURCOM**, Staré Hory 331, ☎ 4199180, **LESÁK**, Tajov 181, ☎ 4197226

Restaurants
- **KOLIBA PRI VLEKOCH**, Králiky, ☎ 4126056

BREZNO AND ITS ENVIRONS
(dial: 048-)

Information
- **Turisticko-informačná kancelária**, Nám. M. R. Štefánika 3, Brezno, ☎/fax 6114221, tikbr@brezno.sk, www.brezno.sk, **Turisticko-informačná kancelária**, Hlavná 56, Čierny Balog, ☎ 6191537, **Turisticko-informačná kancelária**, Lom nad Rimavicou, ☎ 6180100

Museums
- **Horehronské múzeum**, Nám. M. R. Štefánika 13, Brezno, ☎ 6112283, **Múzeum zvoncov**, Šumiac, ☎ 6181232

Atractiveness
- **Čiernohronská lesná železnica** forest railway, Hlavná 56, Čierny Balog, ☎ 6191537, **Bystrianska jaskyňa** cave, Bystrá, ☎ 6195133, **Jaskyňa mŕtvych netopierov** cave, Bystrá, ☎ 6175428

Hotels
- **PARTIZÁN*****, Tále, Brezno, ☎ 6170031-2, **APARTMÁN*****, Tále 528, Brezno, ☎ 6700028, **BYSTRÁ*****, Bystrá 119, ☎ 6195253, **MÝTO*****, Hlavná 492, Mýto pod Ďumbierom, ☎ 6195128, **GOLDEN FISH*****, Závadka nad Hronom, ☎ 6183909, **ĎUMBIER****, Nám. M. R. Štefánika 31/37, Brezno, ☎ 6112661, **KOSODREVINA****, Bystrá dolina, Brezno, ☎ 6170015, **BIOTIKA****, Krpáčovo, Dolná Lehota, ☎ 6170053

Restaurants
- **U RYTIERA**, Nám. M. R. Štefánika 38, Brezno, ☎ 6111673, **OMEGA**, Švermova 7, Brezno, ☎ 6115561, **U DRAKA**, Boženy Němcovej 6, Brezno, ☎ 6114491

LIPTOV

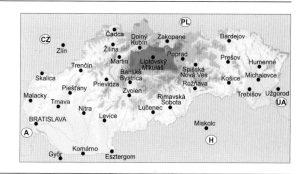

Central Liptov

Upper Liptov

Lower Liptov

The region of Liptov lies in the north of Slovakia and its north-eastern part borders on the Poland. The area of Liptov is 2,097 square kilometres and administratively it is the part of Žilina province. The districts constituting the region of Liptov are Ružomberok and Liptovský Mikuláš. The region is limited by the Šipska Fatra Mts., the ridge of the Chočské vrchy Mts. and the ridge of the West Tatras in the north. Its eastern border passes by the villages Štrba and Liptovská Teplička. Also the tourist villages in the Tatras, Podbanské, Tri studničky and Štrbské Pleso, today part of the municipal unit Vysoké Tatry, were once part of the Liptov region. Valaská Dubová is the village situated in the boundary of Liptov and Orava regions. The southern border of the region coincides with the ridge of the Low Tatras, and the western border is marked by the villages Liptovské Revúce, Ľubochňa and Stankovany.

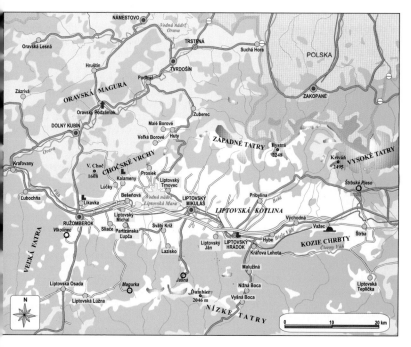

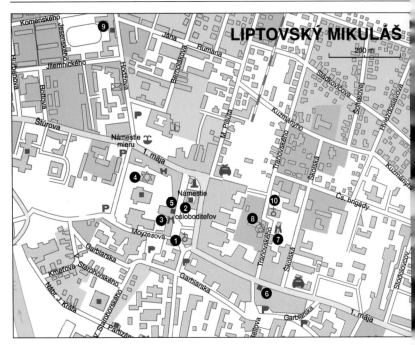

Central Liptov

The administrative, cultural, economic and tourist centre of the central Liptov region is the city of **LIPTOVSKÝ MIKULÁŠ** (population 33,000) stretching mostly on the right bank of the river Váh and in the middle of the Liptovská kotlina basin. Its situation on the eastern bank of the water dam Liptovská Mara and the vicinity of the Low Tatras, the Západné Tatry mountains, and the Chočské vrchy mountains have literally predetermined this city to become one of the most important tourist centres in Slovakia.

In 1677 the town became the seat of the Liptov province and provincial assemblies were held here regularly together with sessions of the provincial court of justice. Certainly a great deal of Slovaks are aware of the session of 1713 which sentenced to death the robber Juraj Jánošík who later became the Slovak folk hero. He

Right: Demänovská jaskyňa Slobody cave

was hung to death by his ribcage. Perhaps the most famous robber in the Kingdom of Hungary was born in 1688 in the north-western Slovakian village of Terchová. After a trial and torture he was executed in Liptovský Mikuláš on 18 March 1713. Juraj Jánošík became Slovakia's national folk hero and a legend in his own right which has been reflected in many literary, artistic and dramatic works.

Probably the most obvious start of the sightseeing tour is at the **Námestie osloboditeľov** (Liberators' Square), an historical nucleus of the city, the formation of which started in the 14th century. In its southern part is the dominating and oldest building, the Roman-Catholic **church of St. Nicholas ❶**. Originally a Gothic church it was built on the site of an older chapel in 1280. The Pongráczs' fortified the church and added little shops creating a compound of market halls. In the second half of the 15th century the church was expanded into the Gothic style and in the 18th century reconstructed in Baroque. In the opposite end of the square is another famous monument of the city, the former house of the province – **Župný dom** ❷, which is today the seat of the district office. Construction of the Late-Baroque building was started in 1713 and in the 18th century it was expanded and altered into the Classicist style. The last alteration in 1907 gave it its present face. In the late 17th and early 18th century the seat of the provincial administration was in the **Il-lésházy's curia** located at the western end of the square. Originally it was a Renaissance building characterised by a heavy triple arcade. In 1713 the legendary Slovak robber captain Juraj Jánošík was tried here. It was rebuilt in the second half of the 19th century and the beginning of the 20th century and at present it is the residence of the **Múzeum Janka Kráľa** (Museum of Janko Král) ❸. It originated in 1955 and bears the name of an important Slovak poet of the period of revolutionary Romanticism. Collections of the Museum contain mainly the items documenting the literary traditions and the history of the city. Right beside the Museum of Janko Král stands the oldest secular building of the town and the seat of the wealthiest family in Mikuláš, the **Pongrácz curia** ❺. Its origin dates back to the mid-15th century and it is remarkable for its irregular shape and the remains of the fortifications in the northern side of the yard. The central square of the city is skirted by a row of **burgher houses**, the majority of which had been built in Renaissance style, and restored after fires in the late 19th century. South-east of the square several **houses of tanners and dyers** built in 19th century are preserved. In the street of 1. mája is a National Cultural Monument, the building called **Čierny orol** (Black Eagle) ❻ where the first cultural events in the town were held. Later its name was changed to the Workers' House where in 1918 the first popular assembly was held, an occasion when the Slovaks declared their social and national requests. Today it houses the exposition of the **Liptov Museum** of Ružomberok. Near Čierny orol in the

building of the former Jesuit monastery is the seat of the **Slovenské múzeum ochrany prírody a jaskyniarstva** (The Slovak Museum of Nature Conservation and Speleology) ❼ opened in 1930. Next to the central square is the **Gallery of Peter Michal Bohúň** ❽. It was founded in 1955 and offers, besides the life-long work of the painter P. M. Bohúň (1822-1879), some older works of Slovak fine art from the 15th-18th century and the works of Slovak painters and sculptors from the 19th and 20th centuries. Among the most important secular cultural-historical monuments in the city centre are the monumental buildings of the grammar school **Gymnázium** ❾ built in the years 1914-1916 and that of **Tranoscius**, a publishing and book trading association founded in 1889. Sacral monuments in the central part of the city include the Roman-Catholic church of St. Nicholas and the Classicist Evangelical **church** ❿, with Neo-Romanesque facade, built in the years 1783-1785.

The most frequented tourist route in the environs of Liptovský Mikuláš is the one to the **Demänovská dolina** valley. It is also the one of the most favourite tourist and ski resorts in Slovakia. The most beautiful and most popular cave, not only in this region, but all over Slovakia is the **Demänovská jaskyňa Slobody**. It was discovered in 1921 and opened to the public in 1924. It consists of six floors and in the lowest of them flows the Demänovka stream. Its total length is more than 7 km, although the tourist circuit is shorter, about 2 km. The entrance to the cave, to which visitors are carried by a chair lift, is at the altitude of 870 m. Abundant dripstone ornamentation, with many lakes attracts many tourists and is the most frequently visited Slovak cave. The **Demänovská ľadová jaskyňa**, one of first such caves known around the world, is also attractive. Though the first reference to it is

Left: Church in Partizánska Ľupča
Right: Interior of the church in Svätý Kríž

from 1299 it was opened to the public only in the 1880's. It has four floors with a total length of 1.7 km. The entrance is at the altitude of 840 m with the tourist circuit being 650 m long. Especially charming is its lower part called "the freezer" with icicles and ice waterfalls.

The Demänovská dolina valley offers **ten marked routes** and a **dense network of footpaths** suitable also for more leisurely walkers. In the lower part of the valley the paths lead across forests and deep canyons interspersed with steep cliffs, contrasted by the upper part which is dominated by dwarf pine forests and alpine meadows. The majority of the routes are connected into circuits. Tourists in good physical condition almost always use the occasion to ascend to some of the Low Tatra peaks, like **Chopok** (2,024 m) or **Ďumbier** (2,043 m) providing a superb view of almost half of Slovakia. Skiers are well familiar with the community of Jasná situated at the lower station of the lift to Chopok. A number of funiculars, ski-lifts, and tracks in the localities of **Záhradky**, **Otupné**, and **Chopok-sever** provide skiers with excellent conditions for their much loved sport. Comfortable lodging of all categories and catering facilities have made Jasná an internationally renown ski resort, offering the most modern standards.

Communities **LAZISKO** and **SVÄTÝ KRÍŽ** are known to the locals for the **wooden articled Evangelical church**. One of the largest wooden buildings in the Central Europe was moved here in the years between 1974-1982 from Paludza and it stands on the boundary between the territories of Svätý Kríž and Lazisko. The ground plan of the church is in the shape of a 43 metre-long cross, admitting almost 6,000 people. The Baroque wooden furniture has an arousing emotional impact, together with the remarkable wooden Baroque altar from 1693 with the painting of Christ's Transformation. Also the pulpit standing on log foundations supported, as if by a Baroque angel, is both visually and acoustically unique. The altar and the pulpit were made by the

wood-carver J. Lerch of Kežmarok. The two-storeyed choir emporia in the interior of the church are adorned by Biblical paintings and along with a big chandelier of Venetian glass create a charming atmosphere. A harmonious part of the church is also an independently standing wooden tower serving as a belfry.

Historically more important is the community of **PARTIZÁNSKA ĽUPČA** the oldest and once the most famous town of the Liptov region. Around the 13th century "guests settlers" were invited to settle here. They were burghers from Krupina and Banská Štiavnica, mostly Germans who came here to look for gold, silver, and antimony. In the 14th-16th century Ľupča (called Nemecká Ľupča from the 14th century on) was the most important town in Liptov. In Partizánska Ľupča several architectural monuments commemorating the history of this famous town are conserved. In the centre is a rectangular **square**, formerly the site of the once famous cattle markets, with a stable

ground plan from the 14th century. The square is skirted by former Renaissance **burgher houses** which acquired in the course of the 18th and 19th centuries their present appearance. As the location of the town did not require construction of municipal fortifications the defensive function was fulfilled by the fortified Roman-Catholic **church of St. Matúš the Apostle** which has strong loopholed walls. A tower was also added, one of the tallest in northern Slovakia. The compound was modified in the Baroque style in the 18th century. Partizánska Ľupča is also the starting point for tourist trips to the almost 20 km long **Ľupčianska dolina** valley, remarkable for its continuous natural forests and abundance of game. There are several gamekeeper's lodges and hunting cottages in the area. The valley has numerous lateral branch routes, of which the most favourite is the Ďurková (blue-marked path) leading from the place called Tajch, with traces of a valley water reservoir, once used for float-

ing the timber to the small mountain community of **Magurka** (1,036 m). This old community originated in the 14th century around the gold, silver and later antimony and iron ore mines. Here are the remains of a ruined ore screening facility called *bašovňa*, pits, heaps of waste rock and a network of roads, which is today used by tourists. Tourists who lodge at Magurská Cottage frequently visit the community of **Železné** (970 m) accessible by the green-marked footpath. There used to be a **climatic spa** in the community in the 19th century used as a summer residence by writers, poets and artists. North-east of Partizánska Ľupča, on the opposite side of the railway track and motorway, stretches the largest summer holiday resort in the region – the water reservoir of **Liptovská Mara**. The reservoir, namesake of one of the flooded communities was built in the years 1970-1975. A

part of the population built new houses on the shores of the lake, but most of them moved to flats in Liptovský Mikuláš and Ružomberok.

Historically speaking the most remarkable community was Liptovská Mara, an important archaeological locality. The disclosure of stone barriers, palisade walls, tower gates, simple Celtic sacrificial altars and Celtic imitations of ancient coins in the locality of Havránok invoke the importance and the culture of the place. Also finds dating from the period of the Great Moravian settlements are unique. The Slavs made use of the Celtic fortifications with palisades, a ditch and a tower in Havránok and their traces (ceramics, ear rings) were also found in other places in the territory of the community of Liptovská Mara. The locality **Havránok** is at the present time an **open-air archaeological museum** and a National Cultural Monument. A part of the exposition are reconstructions of Celtic buildings and a medieval castle.

Left: The water reservoir of Liptovská Mara
Right: Prosiecka dolina valley

The most attractive community for tourists is **PROSIEK**. The community is generally known as a starting point for a trip to one of the most beautiful and most visited Slovak valleys – the **Prosiecka dolina** valley. This karst valley almost 4 km long is deeply embedded between the massive mountains of Lomné and Prosečné (1,372 m). Through the valley leads a blue-marked **educational path** with several wooden panels. Beyond the upper end of the valley is a grassy plain called Svorad crossed by a blue-marked path heading to the community of **VEĽKÉ BOROVÉ**. Together with another two communities, **MALÉ BOROVÉ** and **HUTY** this place indeed represents an oasis of peace and silence set in the heart of wonderful nature. It is situated in a relatively forgotten corner, isolated from traffic and the distant settlements. They are, however, holiday communities. Veľké Borové and Huty are popular as a tourist base for trips to the National Nature Reserve **Kvačianska dolina** valley. This canyon-type valley deeply cut into the dolomite and limestone rock between the Čierna hora (1,098 m) and Ostré (1,128 m) mountains runs parallel to the Prosiecka dolina valley. Both create a well-known one-day tourist circuit. The Kvačianska dolina valley has an **educational path** with numerous stops. The landmark in the upper part of the valley is called **Oblazy** – a unique and ancient **wooden water mill**. The most important summer holiday resort on the shores of the Liptovská Mara dam is the community of **LIPTOVSKÝ TRNOVEC**. A modern **car camping place** on the shore of the reservoir is visited by lovers of water sports. A nearby beach, the renting of sport equipment and excellent conditions for yachting and wind-surfing are the assets of this sought after holiday centre, offering also a good base for trips to the Chočské vrchy mountains and the Západné Tatry mountains.

The community of **ZÁVAŽNÁ PORUBA** became well-known among skiers and winter sport fans mainly because of its ski and cross-country tracks situated south of

the community. The entire area is known under the name of **Opalisko** and offers ski tracks and ski lifts for the keenest of sporty visitors. The final aim for most visitors though is **LIPTOVSKÝ JÁN**. At the present time there is an area of summer thermal **swimming pools** south of the community and an **in-door swimming pool** making use of the thermal water spring called Rudolf with temperature 28.5°C. Also a natural pool utilised for hip-bathing is available. The local springs are conducive for skin therapy and female diseases. Liptovský Ján is the point of departure for the **Jánska dolina** valley, one of the longest valleys in the Low Tatras.

Upper Liptov

LIPTOVSKÝ HRÁDOK (population 8,250), is the tourist and economic centre of the region of upper Liptov and is situated below the northern protuberances of the Nízke Tatry mountains and at the confluence of the Belá and Váh rivers. A pre-

decessor of the town was the community, Belsko, existing as early as the 13th century. Although it disappeared later, the continuity of the settlement of this territory was maintained by the castle **Hrádok** built on a small hill near the river Belá. Though several versions of a story narrating the origin of the castle exist, one thing is certain: The first reference to the castle is from 1341 as *novum castrum*. A castle was built on a five meter high limestone rock. It belonged to military buildings guarding an important trade route along the river Váh. One of the legends testifies that the castle was connected by underground passages to the fortifications near Liptovský Ján and even with the castle Liptovský hrad. Later it became the seat of administration of the castle estate. The castle was heavily damaged during the Rebellions of the Estates at the turn of the 17th and 18th century. After fire in 1803

only the manor house was restored as it was the seat of the administration of the estate in Likava and Hrádok. Further repairs to the building included an ethnographic museum completed in the 20th century but which is again in need of restoration. The symbols of wood and hammer are also in the coat of arms of the town. Its very favourable position near the Nízke Tatry mountains, at the confluence of two rivers, together with an attractive natural setting have, in addition, predestined Liptovský Hrádok to become a centre of water sports and tourism.

Only a few kilometres eastward near the confluence of Biely Váh and Čierny Váh rivers is the village of **KRÁĽOVA LEHOTA**. Kráľova Lehota provides an entry gate to the 35 kilometre long **valley of Čierny Váh**, the longest in the mountain range of the Nízke Tatry mountains. The river Čierny Váh springs from under the Kráľova hoľa mountain, at an altitude of 1,680 metres above sea level. In the valley there are two foresters' communities,

Left: Folk festival in Východná
Right: Natural amphitheatre in Východná

Svarín and Čierny Váh, known above all because of the water power station built on the river, the highest situated one in Slovakia. East of Liptovský Hrádok and south of the motorway bound for Poprad lies the famous community of **HYBE**. Hybe was originally a mining community and the local miners extracted gold in the Bocianska dolina valley until the mid-15th century. Since Hybe acquired the municipal rights it was referred to as a privileged royal town in historical acts. The town suffered a lot in the consequence of anti-Habsburg Estate rebellions as the enemy troops who passed through the country repeatedly damaged the property of Hybe. It was also one of the reasons why robbery as manifestation of the resistance on the side of serfs grew more predominant. One of the legend Hybe boasts of is a famous figure – the robber Pacho (a film was also made of the story). The protagonist and his adventures were mostly invented, though based on a true story as robbery was indeed a popular activity in the 17th

century. The 19th century was characterised by the activity of the local bricklayers and stone-masons who exported their skills also beyond the frontiers of Slovakia (namely in Budapest). There is a famous novel *A thousand year old bee* by the contemporary Slovak writer Peter Jaroš giving credit to the period with great mastery and art, describing the life of the Slovak bricklayers. Many of the crafts preserved up to the mid-20th century and find examples in the local population even today.

A well-known community, mainly because of its folk traditions is neighbouring **VÝCHODNÁ**. The local **natural amphitheatre** situated alongside the main road to Poprad is the pride of the village. The first weekend of July every year the national exhibition of the best folk ensembles under the title **Folk festival** Východná come here. Renowned ensembles and individuals from abroad are often invited to attend. No wonder then that the festival in Východná is a member of CIOFF, the in-

peasant wooden house with authentic interior furnishing is the part of the exposition. The most visited landmark of Važec is the National Nature Reserve the **Važecká jaskyňa** cave situated in the southern edge of the community. Remarkable is its drip-stone ornamentation of various colours and the underground little lakes. The Važecká jaskyňa cave is one of the best known in Europe for the discovery of the bones of the cave bear *Ursus speleaus* that lived here about 15,000 years ago. Its bones are to be seen mainly in the alluviums of the passage called Kostnica (Deposit of Bones). The community of **ŠTRBA** is located off the main road of Žilina to Poprad (16 km). The community of **Tatranská Štrba** with the highest located railway station for rapid trains also belongs to Štrba. It is connected to the Štrbské Pleso by the rack railway.

PRIBYLINA lies ten kilometres southwestward from Podbanské on the road from Liptovský Hrádok near the confluence of the Račkov potok brook and the river Belá. The most attractive landmark, however, is the **Museum of Liptov Village**, documenting the folk architecture of the Liptov region. The impetus behind the establishing of the museum arose out of extensive flooding west of Liptovský Mikuláš caused by the construction of the Liptovská Mara dam, whereupon the main task of the Museum was to save the most valuable monuments of the flooded area. The most important cultural monuments were moved from the eleven flooded communities which constitute the main exhibits in the museum. Original and even entire buildings were dismantled and moved to the museum which was opened to public in 1991. Precious samples of sacral and secular folk architecture are the Gothic-Renaissance **manor house** of Parížovce and an Early-Gothic **church of the Virgin Mary** from Liptovská Mara. Within the museum complex there is a training centre for folk crafts offering visitors samples of folk craft and arts (weaving, bobbin-lacing, wood, metal and leather-working, the manufacturing of

ternational association of folk festivals which are among the best events of their kind in the world. The amphitheatre with its wooden sculptures and regular expositions and accompanying events enhances the atmosphere of the festival.

A typical community of the Liptov region and an important ethnographic locality is also **VAŽEC**. Važec with its natural scenery, wooden peasant houses and distinctive people was highly attractive for artists. It was through the paintings of many artists that Važec became one of the most famous Slovak villages, a symbol of traditional rural life and culture. Eloquent evidence of the life and work of the great Czech painter Jan Hála is all gathered in the **commemorative house of Jan Hála**. It is a house-gallery where he lived and painted in the years between 1923-1959 and contains about 60 paintings. All of them depict the wooden houses, folk costumes and the village life. An original

Left: Environs of Važec

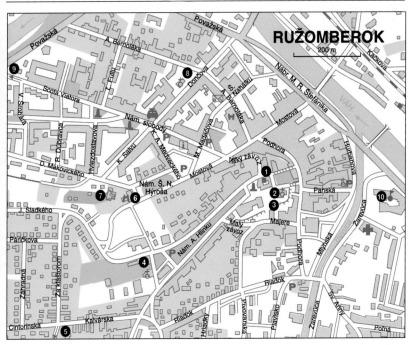

wicker or straw baskets, etc). as well as Liptov folk costumes.

Lower Liptov

The centre of the lower Liptov region, that is the westernmost part of the Liptov Basin, is the district city of **RUŽOMBEROK** (population 30,400). It extends almost exclusively along the left bank of the river Váh and both banks of its tributary, the Revúca. Its location on the eastern foothills of the Veľká Fatra mountains, the northwestern slopes of the Nízke Tatry mountains and the nearby south-western slopes of the Chočské vrchy mountains, creates the city's unique background – its three sides are enclosed by the mountains and the eastern side is open to the Liptovská kotlina basin. The fact that the city lies on the cross-roads of an ancient trade route leading form the Central Slovakian mining towns to Poland and the road along the river Váh from Košice and Spiš to Žilina, and further to Silesia, has strongly influ-

enced its economic and cultural development. The most important role in the history of the crafts in Ružomberok was played by paper manufacturing, a symbol of the city which is preserved until the present day. The best place to begin sightseeing in the city is the upper part called **Námestie A. Hlinku** (The Square of A. Hlinka), originally a quarter where the first German settlers arrived and founded the settlement Rosenberg. The "upper" part of the city is actually a copy of fort hills, common to other medieval cities. Because of the preserved **craftsmen's** and **burgher houses** in an original street structure from the 18th century, and numerous sacral and secular monuments, it was declared a monument reserve. Among the most valuable is the Late-Gothic Roman-Catholic **church of St. Andrew ❷**, built in 1585 in the eastern part of the square on the site of the former Gothic church. However, a Neo-Romanesque reconstruction of the church in 1902 considerably changed its original appearance. Next to the church a part of the

old fortifications is preserved and together with Tmavé schody (the Dark Stairs) it creates an impressive silhouette of the church. The secular landmark dominating the square is the **town hall** ❶ which stands beside the church. It was built in 1897 in Neo-Renaissance style. In its southern part there used to be a Roman-Catholic parsonage where A. Hlinka spent part of his life. His presence in the city is commemorated in the **mausoleum of A. Hlinka** ❸ located next to the southern nave of the St. Andrew church and set in the area of Veľké schody (the Big Stairs) with numerous balustrades. Other unique monuments in this part of the square are the **Lady's Pillar** of 1858 standing in front of the town hall, and at the opposite, western end of the square ❹ is a **piarist monastery**, the Roman-Catholic **church of Holy Cross** and the buildings of the **piarist secondary school**. Beyond the

square of A. Hlinka is another remarkable architectural monument – the **Calvary** ❺. It is the only Liptov Calvary and consists of the chapels of the Way of the Cross with 14 stations from the years 1858-1859 and a church from 1873. After seeing the upper part of the city visitors usually proceed to the lower part using one of the staircases (for instance the Dark, Big, Rose or Monastic Stairs) which emphasise the charm of the upper part of the city. A favourite old town street is called Podhora – the oldest street in the city, including several **burgher houses**. One of the liveliest streets of the city is the Mostová street (Bridge Street) which indeed symbolises the city's link between history and the present. The Mostová street ends in the square with a large park, and the building of **Liptovské múzeum** (The Liptov Museum) ❻. It was founded as an institution of the Liptov Museum Society and the museum now houses objects and documents of natural history, with branches all over the Liptov region. Not far away from the Museum is the

Left: Vlkolínec
Right: Likavský hrad Castle

building of the **Gallery of Ľudovít Fulla** ❼ which contains the lifetime work of this internationally known Slovak painter and illustrator Ľ. Fulla (1902-1980). Several **end-of-the-century buildings**, the Evangelic **church** ❽ of 1926 and the Roman-Catholic "workers'" **church of the Holy Family** (also called Fabrický) ❾ built in 1921 prevailingly for the employees of cotton manufacture are of interest. Also of fairly historicaly importance is a building which stands near the confluence of the rivers Revúca and Váh called the **mansion of St. Sophia** ❿. The purpose of this originally Gothic medieval building was that of a fort and it was first referred to as *castellum* in 1397. Presently its five buildings (70 rooms) and two court yards are under reconstruction.

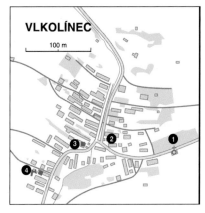

Biely Kostol is the salient point for the community of **Vlkolínec - a monument reserve of folk architecture** lying on southern foothill of the Sidorovo mountain. This extraordinary and remarkable oasis of folk architecture was included in 1993 in the List of the World Cultural and Nature Heritage of UNESCO. It is the place where time has stopped and one of the most frequently visited Slovak localities. The community was first referred to in 1376. It remained untouched by modern construction and represents a unique urbanistic compound of original folk buildings. Vlkolínec is a typical example of a two-line street pattern with long yards. Approximately in its centre the community divides into a street leading to the Baroque-Classicist brick Roman-Catholic **church of the Virgin Mary's Visitation** ❶ of 1875 and a street heading along a more steeper terrain to the foothills of the Sidorovo mountain (1,099 m). At the division of the streets stand the two most frequently photographed objects – a log two-storey **belfry** ❷ from 1770 on a stone stand and a **log well** ❸ from 1860. Amongst the protected buildings in the community are 45 log houses with farm yards, which consist mostly of three-roomed houses with an entrance chamber in the centre. The houses are covered by shingle saddle roofs and behind them are the farmsteads and stables. A typical example of a house in Vlkolínec is the **farmers' house** ❹ – a detached outdoor part of the expositions of the Liptov Museum. The house was built in 1886 and opened to public in 1991. Its well preserved original interior and furniture provide a true picture of the way of life of its ancient inhabitants from the end of the 19th and beginning of the 20th century. The remaining protected objects in the monument reserve are still inhabited, therefore the visitor can see only the exterior of the houses.

Visitors to Ružomberok generally concentrate on the Veľká Fatra mountain range and the massive **Malinné** (1,209 m). Under the top of Malinné is one of the most frequented ski resorts in Slovakia. In the north of Ružomberok are the Chočské vrchy mountains, that likewise offer beautiful corners for tourists. One of the most attractive views of the city's panorama is from the Čebrať mountain (1,054 m) and the Predný Čebrať mountain (945 m) accessible by a red-marked path from the city. The red-marked path also leads to the neigh-

bouring community of **LIKAVKA** located on the right bank of the river Váh, in the valley of the Likavka brook below which are the ruins of once famous **Likavský hrad** Castle. The Castle was referred to for the first time in 1315. Its construction started probably at the beginning of the 14th century with the intention to have a guarding point over the passage across the river Váh and the trade route from the Váh Basin to Orava and further to Poland. In the second half of the 17th century the Thökölys' eventually finished the entire fortification system though it was of no use as it did not prevent the disaster at the beginning of the 18th century when the retreating troops of František Rákoczi completely pulled down the castle in 1707. Folk traditions are held in the community in the form of a **children's folk festival** regularly held in an amphitheatre under the castle.

Visitors of this part of Liptov usually make the point of visiting the spa of **LÚČKY** situated under the impressing massive mountain of Veľký Choč. Its lower part consists of the old village and the upper part is the location of the spa. Lúčky is above all a **spa**. Mineral springs are known here from 1761. The spa has become important for the cure of gynaecological ailments. The decisive healing element here is the plaster-earthy carbonic mineral water of the spa spring with a water temperature of 32°C. The patients have the privilege of enjoying unique natural scenery and their walks often end in either of the two protected natural rarities: the **Lúčanský vodopád** waterfall – a cascading waterfall with water falling from the height of 12 m in two little lakes, and the **Lúčanské travertines** formed by two rocky walls (a well-known paleonthological and archaeological locality). Tourists will certainly use the occasion to ascend the majestic **Veľký Choč** mountain (1,611 m) – the highest summit of the Chočské

Left: Thermal swimming pool in Bešeňová
Right: Church in Liptovský Michal

vrchy mountains. Lúčky neighbours with **KALAMENY**. It originated in 1264 in the terrritory of Liptovská Teplá. The history of the community is closely linked to that of the **Liptovský hrad** Castle, ruins of which are accessible following a yellow-marked path. Liptovský castle also called Sielnický on the Sestrč mountain (1,000 m) belongs to the highest situated castles in the Central Europe. It was built in 1262 above an old trade route leading across the Sestrč valley and communicating the regions of Liptov and Orava with Poland and in 1340 it became the seat of provincial administration for the Liptov region. At the beginning of the 15th century it was repeatedly damaged by the fighting caused by king Sigismund of Luxembourg and later by those of the Hussites. Although the family Pongrác had the Castle repaired in 1447, the Old Hungarian king Matej Korvín ordered it to be demolished in his revenge against the former owner Komorovský who conspired against him. Today only one wall remains and the basement is overgrown by weeds.

Several kilometres south, on the right bank of the river Váh is **BEŠEŇOVÁ**. The community is today one of the most visited of the Liptov villages, because of its cultural monuments and nature. The Renaissance-Baroque **manor house** with towers dates back to the first half of the 17th century. It was rebuilt by the family Dvornik and 'Baroquised' in the second third of the 18th century. The most important monument of the community is the **chapel of the Most Holy Trinity** dating from 1890. However, most visitors come here because of the **thermal swimming pool** built on the site of thermal healing water springs from a depth of 1,980 m and reaching a temperature as much as 62°C. In five swimming pools the water temperature is between 30-40°C depending on the season. These mineral springs are proven to be beneficial to human health. The Protected Nature Area **Bešeňovské travertíny** north of the community is also interesting. Its area is 3.18 ha and consists of older travertine forma-

tions called the Travertine Field. Beside Bešeňová, on the other end of the motorway, is **LIPTOVSKÝ MICHAL**. Its most important monument is the Roman-Catholic, originally Gothic **church of St. Michael**, built in the 13th century. The church was rebuilt in the second half of the 19th century though the Gothic arches, windows and portals have been preserved. An interesting item of the exterior is a wooden **belfry** of the 17th century, originally built as the gate to the enclosure of the church yard.

On the way back to Ružomberok, there are several communities in the Liptovská kotlina basin, particularly in the part within the Low Tatras. The easternmost of them is **SLIAČE** with the originally Gothic Roman-Catholic **church of St. Simon and Jude** built in 1334. The tower and the defensive wall are from the 17th century. Lovers of folk architecture will find here log white-painted **granaries** and the **wooden belfry** from the beginning of the 19th century.

CENTRAL LIPTOV
(dial: 044-)

Information
– **Informačné centrum mesta Liptovský Mikuláš**, Námestie mieru 1, Liptovský Mikuláš, ☎ 16186, 5522418, fax 5514448, infolm@trynet.sk, www.icm.mikulas.sk, www.lmikulas.sk

Museums
– **Múzeum Janka Kráľa**, Nám. osloboditeľov 30, Liptovský Mikuláš, ☎ 5522554, **Synagóga**, Hollého 810/14, Liptovský Mikuláš, ☎ 5522554, **Slovenské múzeum ochrany prírody a jaskyniarstva**, Školská 4, Ul. 1. mája 38, Liptovský Mikuláš, ☎ 5522061, 5524558, **Archeologické múzeum v prírode**, Havránok, Bobrovník, ☎ 4322469

Galleries
– **Galéria P. M. Bohúňa**, Tranovského 3, Liptovský Mikuláš, ☎ 5522758

Atractiveness
– **Demänovská jaskyňa Slobody** cave, Demänovská Dolina, ☎ 5591673, **Demänovská ľadová jaskyňa** cave, Demänovská Dolina, ☎ 5548170, **Thermal swimming pool**, Liptovský Ján, ☎ 5208100, **Oblazy – water mill**, Kvačianska dolina valley, ☎ 5597392

Hotels
– **GRAND******, Demänovská Dolina, ☎ 5591441-4, **JUNIOR*****, Demänovská Dolina, ☎ 5591571-4, **LIPTOV****, Demänovská Dolina, ☎ 5591506-7, **BOCIAN****, Palučanská 38, Liptovský Mikuláš, ☎ 5541276, **SI****, Ul. 1. mája 117, Liptovský Mikuláš, ☎ 5522911, **MÁJ****, Liptovský Ján, ☎ 5208100, **ĎUMBIER****, Liptovský Ján, ☎ 5263232-3

Restaurants
– **LIPTOVSKÁ IZBA**, Nám. osloboditeľov 21, Liptovský Mikuláš, ☎ 5514853, **ATLAS**, Bellova 2, Liptovský Mikuláš, ☎ 5621916, **POD ŠIBENICOU**, Palúčanská 5, Liptovský Mikuláš, ☎ 5541130

UPPER LIPTOV
(dial: 044-)

Information
– **Informačné centrum**, SNP 311, Liptovský Hrádok, ☎ 5225060, fax 5225059, iclh@aprojekt.sk, www.iclh.sk

Museums
– **Múzeum liptovskej dediny**, Pribylina, ☎ 5293163

Atractiveness
– **Važecká jaskyňa** cave, Važec, ☎ 5294171, **Hrádok** Castle, Liptovský Hrádok, **Natural amphitheatre**, Východná

Hotels
– **BOROVÁ SIHOŤ****, Liptovský Hrádok, ☎ 5224039, **SMREK****, SNP 72, Liptovský Hrádok, ☎ 5222572, **ESPERANTO***, Pribylina, ☎ 5280640

Restaurants
– **POĽOVNÍCKA REŠTAURÁCIA**, J. D. Matejovie 591, Liptovský Hrádok, ☎ 5204201

LOWER LIPTOV
(dial: 044-)

Information
– **Kultúrne a informačné centrum**, Madačova 3, Ružomberok, ☎ 4321096, fax 4303684, kic.rbk@isternet.sk, www.ruzomberok.sk

Museums
– **Liptovské múzeum**, Š. Hýroša 10, Ružomberok, ☎ 4322468-9

Galleries
– **Galéria Ľudovíta Fullu**, Makovického 1, Ružomberok, ☎ 4324864

Atractiveness
– **Thermal swimming pool**, Bešeňová, ☎ 4392429, **Spa Korytnica**, Liptovská Osada, ☎ 4396917, **Spa**, Lúčky, ☎ 4392451, **Lúčasny vodopád** waterfall, Lúčky, **Vlkolínec**, Ružomberok, **Likavský hrad** Castle, Likavka, **Travertines of Sliače**, Sliače

Hotels
– **ÁČKO*****, Hrabovská cesta 34, Ružomberok, ☎ 4332485-7, **HRABOVO****, Hrabovská cesta 31, Ružomberok, ☎ 4328744-5, **MALINA**, Malinné, Ružomberok, ☎ 4325070

Restaurants
– **BIELY DOM**, Bystrická cesta 57, Ružomberok, ☎ 4321516, **PÁNSKY DOM**, Nám. A. Hlinku 43, Ružomberok, ☎ 4328206, **MODRANSKÁ REŠTAURÁCIA**, Podhora 23, Ružomberok, ☎ 4329178, **NOVÁ RUŽA**, Panská 1301, Ružomberok, ☎ 4322104, **HUBERTUS**, Likavka 247, ☎ 4322204

TATRAS

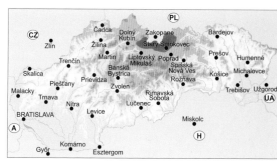

The High Tatras

The Belianske Tatras

The West Tatras

The Tatras are the most attractive tourist area of Slovakia. They are a boundary mountain range divided into the High, Belianske and West Tatras. Four fifths of the Tatras are in the Slovak territory. The Slovak-Polish frontier runs in the north of the Tatras. In the west the limits of the region coincide with mountain range of the Skorušinské vrchy Mts. In the south the Tatras abruptly pass to the Podtatranská kotlina basin. The contact zone between the basin and the mountain range and simultaneously the southern edge of the region are the foothills of the Tatras. The Podtatranská brázda furrow represents the northern or north-eastern limits of the Tatras. In the territory of the Tatras this elongated depression named Ždiarska brázda furrow separates the Belianske Tatras from the Spišská Magura Mts. The re-

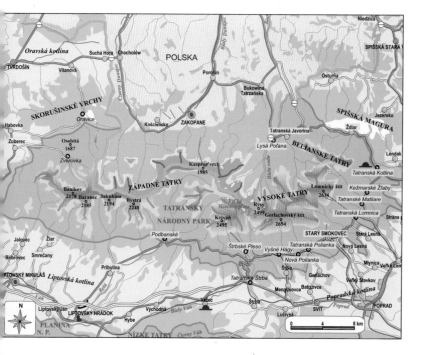

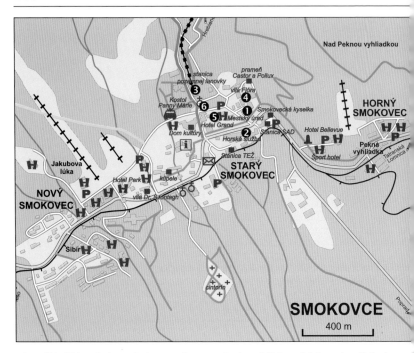

SMOKOVCE

400 m

gion of the Tatras belongs to two provinces – Prešov (district Poprad) and Žilina (districts Liptovský Mikuláš and Tvrdošín).

The High Tatras

STARÝ SMOKOVEC is the largest of the four original Tatra communities bearing the name Smokovec. They are all situated on the southern foothills of the Slavkovský štít peak and gradually merged into a common settlement with the exception of Dolný Smokovec, which has the statute of a town. Dolný Smokovec is the location of the municipal office administrating all High Tatra community seats, and is the main tourist centre of the Tatras, being an important communication crossroads. The name of the specific municipal body Starý Smokovec was changed to **VYSOKÉ TATRY** (High Tatras – population 5,400) in 1998. Roads from Štrbské Pleso (15 km), from Poprad (13

km) and Tatranská Lomnica (6 km) meet here. It is also a railway junction where the network of the Tatra tram branches into western, eastern and southern routes.

It is supposed that the spiritual father of the idea to found a summer holiday resort at the foothills of the Tatra mountains was the Evangelical pastor Tomáš T. Mauksch who belonged to a group commonly known as "the Tatra wanderers". He often set out to discover trips to his beloved Tatras from his parsonage in Veľký Slavkov in the summer. He shared the idea to found a summer resort in the Tatras with the landowner Štefan Csáky who in turn was a great lover of hunting in the Tatra estate belonging to his sister. After some persuasion the pastor finally convinced the count help construct the first building of the future Smokovec in 1793. It was originally a hunting lodge, a favourite destination for summer trips of the local aristocracy. The owner of the cottage was much appreciated for having invented this new form of social amusement. It encouraged him to

Right: Nový Smokovec

continue in the construction of other new buildings and facilities.

A hundred years of what was a premature holiday resort, when compared with other Tatra communities, was mainly due to its mineral water springs. The local water was used not only as a refreshing beverage but it was applied also in curative spa activities. Smokovec became the spa locality offering diverse varieties of water-curing. Climatic therapy was introduced several decades later. In spite of the pressure from the newer Tatra communities, Starý Smokovec maintained its conservative and old-fashioned character and its leading position as the principal High Tatra community. At the present time it is the seat of the **municipal office ❶**, an all-Tatra authority, and of the **Mountain Rescue Service ❷** (Horská služba TANAP-u).

The village of **NOVÝ SMOKOVEC** west of Starý Smokovec was also a spa centre, which continues up to the present time. **DOLNÝ SMOKOVEC** is the only one of the communities bearing the name Smokovec

which does not lie on the road Cesta Slobody, and which has not yet merged with the existing agglomeration. In the opposite direction **HORNÝ SMOKOVEC** merged with Starý Smokovec. Its name meaning "upper" is correct only in relation to Dolný Smokovec, as Starý and Horný Smokovec are situated above it. Horný Smokovec is the youngest of the four communities at the foothills of Slavkovský štít peak.

The oldest part of the Smokovce communities was situated between the amphitheatre and the **lower station of the rack railway ❸** in Starý Smokovec. Historic testimony, which is an example of the oldest architecture in the area is the villa **Flóra ❹** built in 1839. Originally a log house it is today used for cultural events. Behind the ostentatious building of the **Grand hotel ❺** of 1904, the work of the outstanding architect Guido Hoepfner, from Budapest, is that of a wooden Roman-Catholic **church of Immaculate Conception of the Virgin Mary ❻**. The church was designed by the architect

Gedeon Majunke of Spišská Sobota and built in 1894. Westbound roads and paths lead to the spa area of Nový Smokovec. The buildings of **Szontagh's sanatoriums and the sanatorium Palace** have been restored. The **Tokajík hotel** made from the former Szontagh's villa carries the family coat of arms. Its principal element is the sun, symbolising its curing properties used in climatic balneology.

Hrebienok (1,285 m) situated in the south-eastern end of the crest of Slavkovský štít peak has been one of the best attractions for visitors to the High Tatras for about one hundred years. Hrebienok is the traditional starting point for trips to the Veľká and Malá Studená dolina valleys, the Skalnaté pleso lake, the mountain hotel Sliezsky dom, and Slavkovský štít peak. Hrebienok itself offers a superb view of the Lomnický štít peak. The closest and at the same time, the most visited

landmark is the Vodopády Studeného potoka waterfalls. A part of the main Tatra tourist path connecting Hrebienok with Skalnaté pleso lake leads to it. A red-marked, comfortable path heads to the place where the thundering waters of the torrents flowing from the Veľká and Malá Studená dolina valleys join. At the end of the Veľká Studená dolina valley there used to stand the Kamzík cottage until quite recently, which was built in 1884. In the original Döller's project of Studenopotocké kúpele spa Kamzík cottage was to substitute an older tourist building sometime in the 1860's. The tourists visiting the Studené doliny valleys and the Lomnický štít peak used to stop at the cottage **Rainerova chata**. However, Kamzík cottage was finally built by its side and Rainerova chata cottage was transformed to a fuel store for its much bigger neighbour. This historical building was successfully reconstructed in 1983. After seeing **Vodopády Studeného potoka** waterfalls the return trip is possible either by the same track to Hrebienok and to Starý Smokovec or by continuing to Zbojnícka chata, the Téryho chata cottages or by *magistrála* to the Skalnaté pleso lake.

One of the most interesting all day trips from Hrebienok is the tour to **Slavkovský štít** peak (2,452 m). Its typical round top is an indivisible part of the mountain scenery around the Smokovce community. The majestic round peak was one of the first conquered by the mountaineers. Descent is possible only by the same route. Both, ascent and descent are much easier when the rack-railway to Hrebienok is used.

TATRANSKÁ POLIANKA is another hamlet situated on both sides of the road Cesta Slobody between Starý Smokovec (3 km) and Štrbské Pleso (11 km). One of the short trips starting in Tatranská Polianka is a walk to the place called **Veľká Žltá stena** (Big Yellow Wall). It is a remarkable geological and archaeological locality. The wall was originally about 60 m tall representing the highest geological rock exposure in Slovakia.

Left: Below the Slavkovský štít peak
Right: Gerlachovský štít peak

An all day trip from Tatranská Polianka is the ascent to the **Východná Vysoká Mt.**, an opportunity to see the very attractive Velická dolina valley with a singular view of the highest Tatra peak - the **Gerlachovský štít** peak (2,654 m). The route starts in Tatranská Polianka leading up to the Poľský hrebeň saddle by a green-marked footpath. Its lower section ending at the mountain hotel Sliezsky dom slightly ascends across a spruce forest. An excellent opportunity for a short rest and refreshment is offered by **Sliezsky dom** (1,670 m). This mountain hotel on the western shore of the Velické pleso lake is the largest high-mountain tourist facility in the Tatras. Immediately above the Velické pleso lake the first step of the terrace-shaped **Velická dolina** valley, with a beautiful 15 m tall **Velický vodopád** waterfall, is situated. A five and a half kilometre long glacier valley between the Gerlachovský štít peak and the ridge of Velické Granáty mountains has four steps. For its botanical diversity the valley terrace above the

Velický vodopád waterfall won the name Kvetnica (The Flower Garden). At an altitude of 1,929 m above sea level and located in the valley terraces over Kvetnica is the **Dlhé pleso** lake (The Long Lake). The tourist path over the Dlhé pleso lake bypasses the **Guľatý kopec Mt.** (2,125 m). The round rock elevation lying in the middle of the valley is an excellent example of the abrading and eroding activity of the glacier that once filled the Velická valley up to an altitude of two hundred metres. The path continues ascending by serpentines over debris fields to the saddle of **Poľský hrebeň** (2,220 m) where there is the possibility either to continue to the Bielovodská dolina valley or to ascend to the top of the Východná Vysoká Mt. The name of the saddle expresses the fact that it was used by Polish smugglers trafficking their goods out of and to Poland. A short but demanding ascent of the Poľský hrebeň saddle along the yellow-marked path to the **Východná Vysoká Mt.** (2,429 m) provides tourists with a wonderful panoramic sight of the

surrounding high-mountain landscape. The shortest conclusion of the tour is possible by descending along the same route to Tatranská Polianka. Longer alternatives are the ones along the tourist paths of the Bielovodská dolina valley (to Lysá Poľana) or the Veľká Studená dolina valley (to Hrebienok).

Closer to Vyšné Hágy at the foothills of the Gerlachovský štít peak is the small spa village of **NOVÁ POLIANKA**. The dominant building here is the one which serves as the military TBC sanatorium. **VYŠNÉ HÁGY** is one of the most important spa villages in the High Tatras. It is situated close to the point where the Batizovská dolina valley opens to the Popradská kotlina basin, on the Cesta Slobody road between Štrbské Pleso (7 km) and Starý Smokovec (8 km). The first patients of the then biggest sanatorium for tuberculosis

in Central Europe were admitted only on June 1, 1941. The equipment of the sanatorium allows for the performance of demanding surgery and scientific research.

TATRANSKÁ LOMNICA is the easternmost tourist centre of the three centres located on the southern foothills of the High Tatras. It is situated on the road Cesta slobody (Road of Freedom), 6 km north-east from another community, Starý Smokovec. It has a good road and railway communication with Poprad, 18 km away.

Tatranská Lomnica is today the principal centre of winter and summer sport in the eastern part of the High Tatras and offers a wide variety of choice. Besides hiking and mountaineering, it also offers downhill skiing, cross-country skiing, snowboarding, skating, swimming, tennis, minigolf and cycling.

A trip to **Lomnický štít** peak by chair lift is among the most attractive adventures for tourists and, indeed, enjoys the popularity of the public. It reaches in only a few minutes the differential height of

Left: Lomnický štít peak
Right: Meteorological station at the Lomnický štít peak

1,700 m and carries tourists to a height of 2,634 m above sea level. The only higher point in the Tatras, and the Carpathians as a whole, is the Gerlachovský štít peak (2,654 m) situated about 7 km south-east, which can be easily recognised for its unusually bevelled summit. In fine weather, on top of the Lomnický štít peak you can experience·a unique panoramic view over the whole area. If the visibility is good, one can see over the Belianske Tatras, the unending Polish plains, while in the opposite direction the human eye captures perhaps a fifth of the Slovak territory. But if the weather is not agreeable, and this is only too often at this altitude, the disappointed tourist will be surrounded by a milk-white mist, obscuring even the meteorological apparatuses placed right below the ledge. Regular meteorological measurements have been carried out at the Lomnický štít peak since 1940. The meteorological station is the highest located working place in Slovakia. Since the 1950's the meteorological station has been accompanied by a new building for astronomers, employed at the laboratory of physics of cosmic radiation and a coronal station of the Institute of Astronomy belonging to the Slovak Academy of Sciences.

The spruce forest over Tatranská Lomnica is ideal for agreeable and physically undemanding hiking, along the well maintained and marked footpaths. The blue-marked path leads tourists comfortably towards the **Vodopády Studeného potoka** waterfalls. These waterfalls are among the most frequently visited in the Tatras and form a complex system of multi-terraced cascades. The upper, called **Obrovský vodopád** (The Giant waterfall) is well visible from the bridge on the Tatra main tourist path. White-foamed water tumbles down the trough passing between two rocks into a 20 meter profusion. The name of the lower waterfall, **Trojitý vodopád**, in Hungarian and German languages is rather poetic - "the waterfall of artists". It is hidden deep in the forest and because of this is seldom visited. Below the confluence of the Veľký and Malý Studený potok brooks there are another four waterfalls. The tallest of them is the cascade of the **Malý vodopád** waterfall. At an altitude of 1,247 m there is the **Skrytý vodopád** waterfall and somewhat lower at 1,226 m above sea level is the lower end of the cascades of the **Veľký vodopád** waterfall. Its tallest cascade is 13 metres. The **Dlhý vodopád** waterfall is also on the Studený potok brook, immediately opposite the **Bilíkova chata** cottage in Hrebienok and is accessible by the yellow-marked path leading to the small community of Tatranská Lesná.

The majority of tourists try as quickly as possible to get above the upper timber line and to dedicate themselves to hiking passing the extensive dwarf pine growths and the rocky terrain. In Tatranská Lomnica there are two funiculars to the **Skalnaté pleso** lake (1,751 m). The National Nature Reserve **Skalnatá dolina** valley belongs to the smallest of the Tatra valleys, but as far as beauty is concerned it can compete with any of them. Its prin-

cipal assets are the peaks of Lomnický štít (left) and Kežmarský štít (right) and the notched top of the Vidly Mt. in the background. The highest rock terrace in the valley is called **Cmiter** (Cemetery). The majestic tranquillity of Cmiter is contrasted today with the noise brought by the "wind" from the Lomnické sedlo saddle, where every winter there are hundreds of skiers present until the late spring months.

The hiking part of the trip begins at the Skalnaté pleso lake. The route of the trip coincides at its first section with the red-marked arterial, or main tourist path *magistrála* in the direction of Hrebienok. The track first passes through the dwarf pine wood and maintains a south-easterly direction up to **Lomnická vyhliadka** (1,525 m), the spot with a wonderful view of the principal aim of the trip – the Veľká and Malá Studená dolina valleys. Later

Left: Zamkovského chata cottage
Right: View from the Lomnický štít peak

the path bends to the north-west and moderately descends into the forest. After more than an hour's walk it reaches the crossroads, where the blue-marked path is to be chosen. After several meters there is the first opportunity to take refreshment in **Zamkovského chata** cottage (1,475 m), the former Chata kapitána Nálepku cottage.

The not too distant **Malá Studená dolina** valley is the typical terrace-like glacial valley of the Tatras. It won the attribute Malá (small) mainly because it is smaller than its twin, the Veľká Studená dolina valley. The lower threshold of the Malá Studená dolina valley is 130 m high and is situated below the Zamkovského chata cottage and its name is Schodíky, over which the Obrovský vodopád waterfall flows. Above the cottage a low moraine ridge cuts the valley. The path between the cottages of Zamkovský and Téry ascends reaching a differential height of 540 m. An averagely fit tourist can make this section in about 2 hours. A typical U-shaped transversal cut in the valley is closed in by two high cleft mountain ridges. On the right side there is the Lomnický hrebeň ridge and on the left the Prostredný hrebeň ridge, forming a separate body between the two Studené doliny valleys. A reward for the tiresome ascent to Jazerná stena is refreshment taken in **Téryho chata** cottage (2,015 m), offering a fascinating view of the natural amphitheatre at the end of Malá Studená dolina valley.

A green and yellow-marked path proceeds from the Téryho chata cottage to a little basin under the Sedielko saddle and the Široká veža peak (2,461 m). Resting places along the serpentines provide opportune moments for contemplation of the lakes called **Päť Spišských plies**. The lakes are simply named by numbers (Five Spiš Lakes) and their situation, and all of them are typical cirque lakes. The largest is the Veľké Spišské pleso lake with an area of 3.48 ha. In the basin below the Sedielko saddle our route of ascent diverges from the green-marked path to

Sedielko, the highest (2,372 m) mountain saddle accessible to tourists in the Tatras. Beyond Sedielko the path continues across the Javorová dolina valley to Tatranská Javorina. The yellow-marked path leads over the screes and snow fields to the second highest situated saddle, **Priečne sedlo** (2,352 m). The ascent to the saddle from the Téryho chata cottage takes about one and a half hours. The final section of the path is equipped with safety chains facilitating the passage.

A partially limited view of the Priečne sedlo saddle, to the south-west, provides tourists, approaching from the other side, the first opportunity to see the **Veľká Studená dolina** valley. The descent to the **Zbojnícka chata** cottage (The Robber's Cottage – 1,960 m) takes about one and a half hours. The glacier filled the Veľká Studená dolina valley during the last Glacial period and left there numerous glacier trenches, bulging and smoothed by glacial stones and hollowed-out lake basins. Today numerous lakes fill these basins.

There are 26 small lakes in the Veľká Studená dolina valley, representing one sixth of the total number of lakes in the Tatras, the figure which relates to their number and not their volume of water, which is much lower. The area of the largest **Ľadové pleso** lake is 1.72 ha.

TATRANSKÉ MATLIARE is the first community on the road Cesta slobody, between Tatranská Lomnica and the Tatranská Kotlina. It is only 1.5 km away from its larger south-western neighbour Tatranská Lomnica. In 1928 the luxurious **Esplanade hotel** was opened, serving also as a sanatorium, and after the war the Esplanade became the central building of **military sanatoriums**. In 1956 treatment of pulmonary diseases moved to a new sanatorium in Nová Polianka, but Matliare still kept its role of providing therapeutic and medical service to the army. In the years between 1982 and 1985 Tatranské Matliare was expanded by the new trade union **convalescent homes**, the **Metalurg** and the **Hutník**. Both buildings are situat-

ed off the Cesta slobody road in a quiet neighbourhood of the **Loisch's spring**, a summer holiday resort, more than hundred years old, named after the founder of Tatranské Matliare. Tatranské Matliare offers similar possibilities to tourists as neighbouring Tatranská Lomnica, accessible on foot in about 20 minutes, starting near the Hutník Hotel (a yellow-marked path). The location of this community facilitates easier access to the valley of Dolina Kežmarskej Biele vody, to the cottage Chata pri Zelenom plese and the Jahňací štít peak (blue marked).

KEŽMARSKÉ ŽĽABY is a small holiday resort on the road Cesta slobody, about 4 km away from Tatranská Lomnica and 5 km from the Tatranská Kotlina. The first building erected here in 1885, was the gamekeeper's lodge available also for tourists. After three years a simple log hut hostel and several additional houses

Left: Chata pri Zelenom plese cottage
Right: Kežmarský štít peak

were built here. A part of the community burnt in 1933 and the preserved houses became part of the **recreation resort for young people Dukla**. The rather remote location of Kežmarské Žĺaby is the reason why it has remained such a small community.

About one kilometre before arriving in Kežmarské Žĺaby (from Tatranské Matliare) the Cesta Slobody road is cut by the Kežmarská Biela voda brook. The seclusion situated nearby is called **Biela Voda**. Biela Voda is the best starting point for the Dolina Kežmarskej Bielej vody valley. Starting at the bus stop Biela Voda the moderately ascending yellow-marked path leads across a forest. Where the path, or rather road, is wide enough it is used for supplying the cottage Chata pri Zelenom plese. After an hour of easy walking one reaches a water spring at **Šalviový prameň** (1,100 m). It took its name (Sage Spring) from the abundance of sage plants (*Salvia officinalis*) growing around the spring, which are said to grow only next to "sound" water. Passing the spring a yellow-marked path ascends a moderate slope preceding the **Kovalčíkova poľana** alpine meadow. The stony road ascends up to the dwarf-pine wood and offers a wonderful view over the Dolina of the Zelené pleso valley, the next stop of the trip. After a three hour walk from Biela Voda walkers can relax and enjoy the beauty of high-mountain nature with a cup of hot tea served in the **Chata pri Zelenom plese** cottage, which is 1,551 m above sea level. Many know the cottage under the name of Brnčalova chata cottage, which is approximately one hundred years old. The beautiful landscape around the cottage is enhanced by the picturesque **Zelené pleso** lake (1,545 m). With its area of 1.77 ha it is the largest lake in the easternmost part of the High Tatras. The name of the lake (zelené = green) is associated with the green spots produced by the water springs at the bottom of the lake.

Any view from the Zelené pleso lake is fascinating. Standing with your back turned to the **Jastrabia veža** peak

(2,137 m) you get a view of the huge rock face. Only by bending your head well back can you appreciate the highest perpendicular rock face of the Tatras on the northern side of the **Malý Kežmarský štít** peak (2,513 m). The height of the rock face measured from the bottom to the top is 900 m. A triangle-shaped granite monolith is transversally cut by an oblique rock ledge called the "German ladder". There are seven very difficult mountaineering tracks at the rock face. The most demanding of them is "superdiretissima", leading across the middle of the rock wall. West of the lake are the **Veľká** and **Malá Zmrzlá dolina** valleys. Both of them belong to the highest situated valleys in the Tatras.

TATRANSKÁ LESNÁ is a tiny holiday resort situated on the Cesta Slobody road near the point where it crosses the Studený potok brook. It lies about 2 km south-west of Tatranská Lomnica. The children's sanatorium recieved in turn the name **The Children's Paradise** and together with some additional buildings, constructed later, it became an **international centre of child recreation**. A group of cottages and hotels owned by various firms was constructed at the edge of the forest.

ŠTRBSKÉ PLESO (1,355 m) is the highest situated Tatra locality, existing around the lake bearing the same name, a product of the moraine pushed out into the mouth of the Mlynická dolina valley by a glacier in ancient times. Štrbské Pleso is 15 km away from Starý Smokovec and 17 km from Podbanské.

The initial walk to Štrbské Pleso may just as well start at the south-eastern shore of the lake near the **Solisko sanatorium**. Standing at the former railway station one gets the most beautiful view of the indented silhouette of the Tatra peaks, where the fourfold peak of the **Vysoká Mt.** (2,547 m), redolent of a royal crown, stands out. One cannot help noticing also the white slender ski-jump tower on a round hill nearby. In 1976 the triangular shaped **hotel Patria** joined this most frequently photographed Tatra view. There is a com-

fortable promenade, blue-marked path running around the whole lake and on the western shore the path passes by a "peninsula" with the **monument dedicated to partisans** who died in the war. The peninsula is the place where there is a nice view of the compound of the **Kriváň** and **Hviezdoslav** hotel buildings standing on the southern shore. Immediately behind the hotel Patria starts the red-marked Tatra main tourist footpath *(Tatranská magistrála)*. The route of the trip soon leaves the short section of the Tatra main tourist footpath and turns left tracing the road to **Areál snov**. This ski resort has received its unusual name (Dream Area) when the Chairman of the International Ski Federation noted with satisfaction that the area was "dream-like". It is dominated by two **ski-jumps**: the standard point of the smaller of them is 70 m and the higher was built for the world championships in 1970 for a

90 m long ski-jump. The performances of the courageous ski-jumpers can be watched by audiences of up to 60 thousand. A short ascent to the ski-jumps is rewarding, especially in fine weather, as it offers a wonderful view of the dark-blue water table of the Štrbské Pleso lake. A part of the area is also the **FIS hotel**, with its intriguing design imitating the shape of the Tatra peaks. The slope of the Solisko Mt., behind the Dream Area, is a ski paradise. In the lower part of the down-hill track, called the **Interski** slope, frequent exhibitions and races by acrobatic skiers and snow boarding events are held. The **chair lift** to Solisko Mt. exceeds a differential altitude of 438 m at a distance of 2,170 m. The sights of the Mlynická dolina valley on the right hand side are particularly splendid, and on the left, the belt of the down-hill skiing tracks on south-eastern slope of **Predné Solisko Mt.** (2,093 m), can be seen. It is precisely the place where the first ski lift in the Tatras was put into operation in 1943. Next to the upper station of the

Left: Štrbské pleso lake
Right: Vodopád Skok waterfall

chair lift, at an altitude of 1,840 m above sea level, is the cottage **Chata pod Soliskom**.

The Dream Area is the gateway to the National Nature Reserve **Mlynická dolina** valley. The valley, squeezed between the crests of the Solisko and Bašty mountains, is accessible by the yellow-marked path. Tourist path ends below the **Vodopád Skok** waterfall visible from the lake as a narrow white ribbon on the grey rocks. The total height of this cascading waterfall is 25 m and the best time to visit it is between spring and summer when it is most beautiful. The path leading from the Vodopád Skok waterfall to the Bystré sedlo saddle was built only in 1935 so that the Mlynická dolina valley was long spared of the damaging effects of tourism. There was never any tourist hotel or cottage, not even a mill that would give the origin to its name (mlyn = mill). The name of the valley derives of the Mlynica brook where there used to be some mills in the past, though not in the mountains, but down in the basin. The **Bystré sedlo** saddle (2,314 m) is the fourth highest pass of the Tatra crests accessible by a marked path. It provides a somewhat limited view of the Mlynická and Furkotská dolina valleys.

The National Nature Reserve **Furkotská dolina** valley is one of the five valleys descending southward, down to the Kriváň fork. Its length is about three and a half kilometres and it is the easternmost Tatra valley. Its streams flow first into the rivers Váh and Danube which end in the Black Sea, while the streams of the neighbouring Mlynická dolina valley end in the Baltic Sea. The attractiveness of the Furkotská dolina valley is enhanced by its lakes, the largest ones being the **Wahlenbergove plesá** lakes. The path proceeds left of the both Wahlenberg's lakes. Passing by the lake terraces the path still keeps to the left side of the Furkotská dolina valley where the noisy waters of the Furkotský potok brook can be heard. Visitors to the Furkotská dolina valley often go back to Štrbské Pleso using the Tatra main tourist path. There is also another option, using the

blue-marked path turning left into a dwarf pine forest in the direction towards the Chata pod Soliskom cottage.

The climb to **Kôprovský štít** peak offers the tourists an opportunity to see the whole of the eight kilometre long National Nature Reserve, Mengusovská dolina valley. The route starts on the eastern shore of the Štrbské pleso lake and heads north along the Tatra main tourist path. The moderately steep path leads to the top of the moraine rampart called **Trigan** (1,481 m). The moraine is the result of two neighbouring glaciers that once filled the Mlynická and Mengusovská dolina valleys. Beyond Trigan the path passes the slope of the Patria Mt. (2,203 m), the last peak in the massive Bašty crest. The section of *magistrála* between the Štrbské and Popradské pleso lakes is also called the "summer" road as it is open only in summer. In winter the Popradské pleso lake is accessible by the axis of the Mengusovská dolina valley (blue marked) on the last but one stop of the Tatra tram on

the route between Starý Smokovec and Štrbské Pleso. The summer road is threatened by frequent avalanches in winter that fall down the eastern slopes of the Bašty crest.

The **Mengusovská dolina** valley is one of the most frequently visited valleys in the Tatras. Interest in the valley rose in the second half of the 19th century when access to it was facilitated by the construction of comfortable footpaths leading to the Popradské pleso lake, starting in Štrbské Pleso and Mengusovská poľana (today the tram stop is called Popradské Pleso).

The **Popradské pleso** lake lies amid a forest at an altitude of 1,494 m. The lake, with an area of 6.88 hectares, contains about 450,000 m³ of water. As one of the few lakes where fish live it was called the Rybie pleso lake (Fish Lake). Its contemporary name is associated with the river Poprad flowing out of it. The first tourist facility on the shore of the Popradské pleso lake was built in 1879. The Popradská chata cottage, later named the Chata kapitána Morávka, underwent numerous adjustments. Its wooden structure completely collapsed under the weight of snow in 1961 and the result of the following reconstruction was the present **Chata pri Popradskom plese** (the cottage near the Popradské pleso lake).

The route continues from the Popradské pleso lake along the blue-marked path to the **Hincova dolina** valley. The valley Hincova dolina, allegedly named after the shepherd Hinco (a dialect for the name Ignác), has the largest and also deepest lake on the Slovak side of the Tatras. The area of the lake **Veľké Hincovo pleso** is 20.08 ha, it is 53 meters deep and contains almost 1,800,000 m³ of water. The lower situated lake, the **Malé Hincovo pleso**, is 9-fold smaller than its neighbour. At the end of the valley Hincova dolina there is a trio of peaks called the **Mengusovské štíty**, shadows of which

Left: Chata pri Popradskom plese cottage
Right: High-mountain carrier in the Tatras

fall on the opposite side, into a deep valley in Poland. Also the view from the southern, sun bathed faces of this proud Tatra triplet is very impressing. The highest peak is the Veľký Mengusovský štít (2,424 m). The path deviates left near the lake Veľké Hincovo pleso and ascends by serpentines to the saddle **Vyšné Kôprovské sedlo** (2,180 m). The climb continues from the saddle up to the top of the peak **Kôprovský štít** (2,363 m). Here there is a wonderful view of the Hincove plesá lakes, the Rysy and Vysoká mountains. After returning to the saddle the trip can be concluded either by a shorter way down, passing the valleys Hincova and Mengusovská dolina, to Štrbské Pleso using the same path, or there is a much longer option, to continue on the blue-marked path over the valleys Hlinská and Kôprová dolina to Podbanské or to Tri studničky.

One of the most frequently visited Tatra peaks is undoubtedly the **Rysy**. Its popularity is due to the collective ascents by tourists held annually from early August. This particular event very quickly acquired the mass appeal attracting as many as three thousand tourists in a season. After the "Velvet Revolution" the ascents to Rysy lost their political motivation. The route of the ascent is the same as the route to the peak of Kôprovský štít, up to the point of the crossroads in the lower part of the valley Hincova dolina, where an old Hincova hut used to stand. Then it turns right along a red-marked path ascending by numerous serpentines over a rock threshold of the valley **Žabia dolina**. Beyond the resting point at the lower terrace of the valley Žabia dolina the path again ascends to the next steep rock step where the most exposed sections are secured by iron chains. The path heads to a small valley under the Váha saddle where in the middle the cottage called **Chata pod Rysmi** stands. Its construction started in 1933 and it was accompanied by numerous adversities like snow blizzards and stone avalanches. In 1977 it was enlarged by adding a second floor. The cottage is at an altitude of 2,250 m

above sea level (the next higher place where a tourist can take a cup of tea is only on top of the peak Lomnický štít). In spite of technical progress and inventions such as helicopters, this highest situated cottage in the Tatras is supplied only by **high-mountain carriers**. It is quite common to meet strong men carrying huge loads on their backs on the tourist path between lake Popradské pleso and the cottage.

The saddle **Váha** (2,237 m) is situated on the Tatra ridge as tall as the contiguous Rysy Mt. The final ascent from the saddle Váha to the top of the **Rysy Mt.** (2,499 m) takes less than an hour. Originally the peak of Vyšný Žabí štít (2,259 m) was called Rysy and later the name was attributed to the peak within the main ridge. The name Rysy has probably nothing to do with our biggest predator lynx (in Slovak rys). It is rather more associated with the fact that the slopes of the peak are covered by troughs and grooves referred to by the Gorals as "grooved" or *porysované*.

The red-marked path from the Popradské pleso lake to the Batizovské pleso lake is a wonderful trip. Near the mountain hotel at Popradské pleso the yellow-marked path turns first to **Symbolický cintorín** (Symbolical Cemetery) which is worth visiting.

The route of the trip returns to the Tatra main tourist path – *magistrála*. It crosses, via a bridge, the Ľadový potok brook flowing from the valley called **Zlomiská**. There is a winding path from the Popradské pleso lake ascending to the saddle **Sedlo pod Ostrvou** (1,959 m). Similar to other serpentines, climbing from the cottage near the Zelené pleso lake, to the saddle under the Svišťovka peak, one encounters the main path which is very passable but also very exacting. The ascent with a differential altitude of 459 m requires a lot of effort. Luckily, the superb sight of the Popradské pleso lake, sur-

rounding the Tatra valleys, peaks, and crests improves the mood of tourists. The path crosses the massive edges of the slopes of the peaks Tupá and Končistá which were not affected by the activity of glaciers. There are no traces of glaciation in the small Štôlska dolina valley. Everywhere around only huge scree heaps can be seen. The dwarf pine trees are only sporadically seen near *magistrála*, their upper edge is normally situated several tens of meters lower. The way to the Batizovské pleso lake is full of enchanting views of the basins and the crests of the Low Tatras.

The National Nature Reserve **Batizovská dolina** valley is closed to public, as well as the valley Zlomiská. It is squeezed between the Končistá (2,537 m) and Gerlachovský štít peaks (2,654 m) – a singular rocky setting. In the middle of the valley stands a lonely mountain called **Kostolík** (Small Church – 2,261 m), reminding one of a little Gothic church. Leaving the picturesque Batizovské pleso lake it is possible to continue along the *magistrála* passing by the mountain hotel of Sliezsky dom.

PODBANSKÉ is the most westerly located of all the High Tatra communities, which lies at the crossroads of the Cesta Slobody (Road of Freedom) and the torrential river Belá. It is 16 km away from Štrbské Pleso and 15 km from Liptovský Hrádok. Podbanské is frequently used as the base for trips to the valleys of Tichá and Kôprová dolina and to the Bystrá Mt. The **Tichá dolina** valley is today indeed worthy of its name (tichá = silent). It is preferred above all by the tourists seeking a quiet natural environment. In its softer landscape, cloaked by rich meadows, the visitor is more likely to meet a herd of chamois than a group of noisy day trippers. The Tichá dolina valley with its length of 13.8 km and a total area of 52 square kilometres is the largest of its kind in the Tatras. Looking from the Liptovské kopy mountains there are another three lateral valleys ending in the Tichá dolina valley, the highest one being the **Špania dolina** valley. Under the big curve of the valley the crossroad board navigates the tourist in

Left: Symbolical Cemetery
Right: Podbanské

the direction of the **Tomanovská dolina** valley the name of which is related to the miner Toman. The red-marked footpath crossing the valley ends in Tomanovské sedlo saddle a deep, grassy saddle, which with its altitude of 1,680 m above sea level is the second lowest depression of the main Tatra mountain ridge. In the past it was frequently exploited by poachers, and from the path under the saddle the **Tomanovské plesá** lakes can be seen.

The upper section of the massive Tichá dolina valley has an unusual aspect. The bend of the valley causes that tourists loose their visual contact with the Liptovská kotlina basin and find themselves as if in the bottom of some volcanic crater, surrounded by high slopes covered by stones, meadows and dwarf pines. The view to the north is particularly interesting, where above the tops of the spruce trees one can see the silhouette of the **Červené vrchy Mts**. The Červené vrchy Mts., along with the Belianske Tatras, are the most important high-mountain karst areas in Slovakia with large lapies-fields and deep karst abysses. These karstificated slopes are not accessible to tourists and there is only one route to the boundary ridge of the Červené vrchy Mts. and only in summer. The end of the valley is called the **Zadná Tichá dolina** valley. In the past it was often frequented by the shepherds who crossed the Červené vrchy Mts. of Poland's Podhale. The initial slightly ascending footpath becomes steeper nearer to the tops of the westernmost part of the High Tatras, and leads to the **Závory** saddle (1,879 m). An additional 15 minute walk is needed to arrive to the higher situated **Hladké sedlo** saddle in the main mountain range. After the return to the Závory saddle tourists can take the same route to Podbanské or go back to the neighbouring Kôprová dolina valley.

The origin of the name of the National Nature Reserve **Kôprová dolina** valley is probably associated with the German word for copper, the subject of intense interest to the local miners. The trip to the Kôprová

dolina valley starts at the same point as the one to the Tichá dolina valley. At the cross-roads near the forester's cottage one has to turn to the green-marked path leading along the noisy Kôprovský potok brook. Looking west there is the wonderful view of the Liptovské kopy mountains, while the opposite side of the valley is adorned with substantially more dramatic curves of the cliff massif of Kriváň. Alpine dimensions are reached, above all, by the jagged **Rameno Kriváňa** (Arm of Kriváň). One of the jutting ridges has the same name as the giant K2 mountain in the Caracoram range. Behind it the **Nefcerka** valley opens out into the main valley.

The extraordinary beauty of the waterfall cascades flowing over the high threshold of this strictly protected valley can be observed only from a comparably long distance. This is also the case for the **Kmeťov vodopád** waterfall which is the champion

among the Tatra waterfalls with its height of 80 m. A real high-mountain climb starts only after the turn onto the green-marked footpath ascending to the Temnosmrečinská dolina valley. On the right side of the path is the **Vajanského vodopád** waterfall, one of the most beautiful Tatra waterfalls.

The **Temnosmrečinská dolina** valley looks like a wonderful natural amphitheatre. Its would-be auditorium is a high cliff with the jutting summit of the **Čubrina Mt.** (2,378 m). Where the stage would be is the flat bottom of the valley and its two large lakes, among the largest in the Slovak part of the High Tatras. The footpath ends near the bigger lake, called **Nižné Temnosmrečinské pleso**, with an area of 12 ha and 40 m deep. Another lake, **Vyšné Temnosmrečinské pleso** is situated higher and off the tourist path.

There are three alternatives how to end the hike, but each of them is quite demanding. The first, relatively the easiest one, is to return to Podbanské retracing the same route. More time and ener-

Left: Temnosmrečinská dolina valley with the lake
Right: Mountain Rescue Service

gy is required by the second option: the green-marked path to the **Kobylia dolina** valley. The name of the valley (kobyla = mare) is associated with the tradition of high-mountain horse breeding in this part of the Tatras. The path goes on from the saddle Závory down the Tichá dolina valley to Podbanské. Those who are interested in the third option of descent must go back to the blue-marked footpath and ascend up the **Hlinská dolina** valley to the **Vyšné Kôprovské sedlo** saddle (2,180 m). Leaving the saddle the track goes on down the Mengusovská dolina valley in Štrbské Pleso.

The route to Bystrá Mt. starts in Podbanské and goes on following the blue-marked path up the **Kamenistá dolina** valley. This seven kilometre long valley is special for not having any branches. Its slopes are mostly naked after an extensive fire in 1904. In the upper part of the valley there is a shallow glacier basin and the path ascends from this point to the **Pyšné sedlo** saddle (1,791 m). In this saddle the red-marked mountain ridge track over the West Tatras starts or ends the journey, as the case may be. Its route is the most demanding track in the Slovak Carpathians with a total variable elevation of about 2,800 m. The Pyšné sedlo saddle is 24 km from the opposite end of this track – the Hutianske sedlo saddle. The track follows the line of the crest only on the short section from the saddle Pyšné sedlo passing Blyšť Mt. (2,169 m) to the **Bystré sedlo** saddle (1,960 m) and goes on by the blue-marked footpath up to the top of the Bystrá Mt. **Bystrá Mt.** with an altitude of 2,248 m above sea level is the highest peak of the West Tatras. The cone-shaped summit offers a wonderful panoramic view, which in good weather encompasses the whole of the Liptov region, a part of Spiš and Podhalie. The shortest return trip from Bystrá Mt. is the yellow-marked footpath descending to the small but attractive **Bystrá dolina** valley. In the upper part of the path one can admire a group of four lakes called the Bystré plesá. The largest one of them is the **Vyšné Bystré pleso**

lake with an area of 0.86 ha. It is also the deepest lake in the West Tatras (12.5 m). At the point where the Bystrá dolina valley opens up into the Liptovská kotlina basin the yellow path crosses with the Tatra main tourist path leading to Podbanské.

Tri studničky (Three Wells – 1,140 m) is the landmark near Cesta slobody (the Road of Freedom) between Podbanské and Štrbské Pleso, in the lower edge of Podkrivánska poľana. The place was seasonally settled since the beginning of the 19th century. In 1806 a shelter was built here. The new cottage built in Tri studničky in 1961 was named **Chata kapitána Rašu**.

There is another possible trip from Tri studničky to the Jamské pleso lake – a pleasant and comfortable walk on the well maintained Tatra main footpath called in Slovak *Tatranská magistrála*. The route mostly proceeds through a spruce forest that occasionally retreats to offer an open view of the broad southern slope of the Kriváň Mt. The footpath brings the tourists to the southern shore of the **Jam-**

ské pleso lake (1,447 m), which is surrounded by spruce and pine forests. In 1936 the cottage called Krivánska chata was built here but it burned down seven years later. Near the western shore of the lake is the **limba pine grove** founded in the memory of the heroes and victims of the **Slovak National Uprising**. It is possible to go on from the Jamské pleso lake to Štrbské Pleso or to go back via the blue and green-marked paths to Tri studničky.

An exceptionally attractive climb is the ascent of the **Kriváň Mt.** (2,494 m) a stout peak in the western part of the High Tatras. This multiple winner of competitions for the most beautiful mountain in Slovakia is appropriately named when looked at from Liptov. It is easily recognisable for its conspicuously curved summit, which is the reason why it was called Kriváň (curved mount). The most comfortable and quick way to reach the top of

Left: Kriváň Mt. seen from Podbanské
Right: The ridge of the Belianske Tatras

Kriváň starts in Tri studničky. The first serpentines of the green-marked footpath bring the tourists to a place called **Grúnik**, which witnessed some bitter fighting between the partisans and the Nazi troops at the end of the Second World War. The path goes on from Grúnik crossing the slope of the Priehyba Mt. to a steep trough covered with falling debris from the Kriváň. Continuing from the cross-roads below the mountain the track joins the path from the Jamské pleso lake. At the **Daxnerovo sedlo** saddle, named after the Slovak writer and revivalist Š. M. Daxner (1823-1892) several dangerous snow fields last until advanced spring. The reward for a rather demanding ascent is a wonderful panoramic vista. The usual way back from the top of mount Kriváň is the one following the blue-marked path leading to the Jamské pleso lake. From there one can get either to Podbanské or to Štrbské Pleso.

The Belianske Tatras

ŽDIAR is a typical Goral community between the cliffs of the Belianske Tatras and the Spišská Magura Mts. Ždiar stretches over the Podtatranská brázda furrow, the Cesta slobody road of Tatranská Kotlina to Lysá Poľana and runs parallel to the axis of the community. The centre of the 6 km long community is about 13 km of the border crossing to Poland in Lysá Poľana and the shortest road of Ždiar to the district town of Poprad measures 34 km.

The four most valuable groups of folk buildings were in 1977 declared the **Monument Reserve of folk architecture**. Ždiar is famous for its **folk arts** and **traditions**. Until recently the villagers put on their folk costumes on Sundays or feast days. Today they can be seen only at the shows of the folk ensembles or in the museum called **Ždiarska izba.**

Opportunities for tourists coming to Ždiar are considerably limited at present as many of the marked footpaths in the Belianske Tatras are closed. The reason is the need to revive the disturbed ecological

balance in this particular area of the mountain range. In 1991 an area of 5,408 ha of this unique territory was declared the National Nature Reserve of the **Belianske Tatras**.

The only accessible path is the green-marked one tracing the edge of the reserve and continuing by the **instructive tourist path Monkova dolina** valley – **Kopské sedlo** saddle. The path was opened in the summer of 1993 and crosses the Belianske Tatras over a total length of 6 km reaching an elevation difference of about 900 m. It is accessible only in the summer season, in one-way direction of the bottom and subject to an entrance fee. There are six stops on the track presenting the sights and places of interests of the Belianske Tatras Information on the stops is provided by leaflets. However, lovers of hiking do not have to avoid Ždiar. There are some interesting walks to the opposite side, with an easily accessible mountain range of **Spišská Magura**. The ascent to the main ridge of the mountain range is worth it for

the unique view of the panorama of the Belianske Tatras over the typical community of Ždiar. Two of the marked footpaths crossing the main Magura ridge lead to the Jezerské jazero lake, or to the Veľké Osturnianske jazero lake in the Zamagurie region. Summer tourists lodged in Ždiar prefer the slopes of Spišská Magura Mts. as they offer the occasion to pick forest fruit. They are famous for blue-coloured "carpets" of blackberries. In turn the winter in the Spišská Magura Mts. means ideal conditions for cross-country skiing. Passes over the prolonged and rather flat Magura mountain ridges with slight different elevations are suitable also for less experienced skiers. Access to the main Magura ridge is facilitated by the **chair-lift** starting in the Bachledova dolina valley.

TATRANSKÁ KOTLINA is the easternmost and simultaneously the lowest situated Tatra community. It lies under the eastern end of the ridge of the Belianske Tatras, near the most pronounced curve of the Cesta Slobody road. Touristic

centre Tatranská Kotlina also took up the function of a spa. In the centre of the community there was the **Kúpeľný dom** providing patients with water-cures and for the time advanced physical therapy in the form of gymnastics. After the Second World War the buildings were expanded and modernised and today they serve to the patients as the **Specialised Therapeutic Institute of Respiratory Disorders**. Tourists can find accommodation in the local hostel Limba.

Also the trip to the Veľké Biele pleso lake, the final destination of the green-marked footpath, is interesting. The **Šumivý prameň** spring in a forest environment and 855 metres above sea level is the first stop. Near the brook Čierna voda a blue-marked path separates and leads to the Kežmarské Žľaby troughs. The green-marked path continues by moderately ascending serpentines to the easily accessible

Dolina Siedmich prameňov valley. This comparably small Tatra valley is preferred by the botanists and lovers of the Tatra flora. Due to the limestone base and the relative closeness of the valley that was not affected by glaciation, many rare endemic plant species grow here. An option for a short rest though without taking refreshment is offered by the **Plesnivec** cottage (1,209 m). Tourists are particularly attracted by the Dolina Siedmich prameňov valley ending in an amphitheatre of snow white limestone rock faces called **Skalné vráta**. The footpath traverses the southern side of the Bujačí vrch Mt. to the neighbouring Dolina Kežmarskej Bielej vody valley and heads to the end of the valley divided by several glacial cirques.

After crossing the Napájadlový potok brook in the valley of Predné Meďodoly the path ascends through dwarf pine forest and across the threshold of the Dolina Bielych plies valley bearing the curious name: Jerusalem. The landscape of the **Dolina Bielych plies** valley lying at the

Left: Veľké Biele pleso lake
Right: Environs of Tatranská Javorina

end of a valley system of the Kežmarská Biela voda is impressive. Under the cone-shaped Jahňací štít peak there are several lakes. The largest of them is the **Veľké Biele pleso** lake and until recently there was the Kežmarská chata cottage on its shore. Near the Veľké Biele pleso lake starts the longest Tatra main footpath, the famous **Tatranská magistrála**.

Tourists are often interested in the **Belianska jaskyňa** cave. It is the only one accessible to public in the Tatras and situated in the northern slope of the Kobylí vrch Mt. above the community of Tatranská Kotlina. The cave entrance is at an altitude of 885 metres above sea level. It was discovered by treasure-seekers in 1718 even though it is presumed that it was used as a dwelling for pre-historic people. At present sightseeing around the cave consists of a 1,001 m long track and the visitor can see more than a half of discovered cave corridors.

TATRANSKÁ JAVORINA is a small community amid huge forests in the northern foothills of the High Tatras. It is situated where the Javorová dolina valley opens to the shallow Podtatranská brázda furrow.

Trips to the northern part of the Tatras are quite different to the classic hiking tours in the south. Secluded valleys are visited by people looking for the majestic silence and sublime tranquillity of the area. In turn the tourists who do not like long ascents to high mountains of the distant ends of extremely long valleys try to avoid them. Such is also the **Javorová dolina** valley. The green-marked path leaves Tatranská Javorina which ascends along a 12.5 km long glacial valley up to its end. The most demanding is the final part of the ascent to the **Sedielko** saddle (2,372 m). The steep track ascends by serpentines up to the highest saddle, accessible to tourists, before reaching the Malá Studená dolina valley.

Tourists also enjoy the trip to the **Zadné Meďodoly** valley. The entire route coincides with the old poachers' path used for the traffic of goods from Old Hun-

gary to Poland. The first section of the track leads from Tatranská Javorina to Poľana under the Muráň Mt. along the green-marked path. Passing the cottage of the TANAP administration there is the blue-marked path turning left, taking the tourist to the Zadné Meďodoly valley. The ascent to the **Kopské sedlo** saddle (1,750 m) can be done by a path traversing several troughs and ribs sloping down from the ridge of the Belianske Tatras In a broad grassy saddle one can enjoy a wonderful view of the cliff tops of the Belianske Tatras and the High Tatras.

LYSÁ POĽANA is the last community on the Cesta Slobody road, in the direction of Poland. It lies 13 km away of Ždiar in the place where the Bielovodská dolina valley opens to the Podtatranská brázda furrow. The mighty Biela voda brook in Poland's Bialka divides the community into two parts – the Slovak Lysá Poľana and the Polish Łysa Polana. They are connected by a bridge and a border crossing in one. The origin of the name should be

sought on the Polish side where there is the 1,119 metres tall hill of Łysa Skalka. The small community has only the **administration buildings** of the **TANAP** and the **TNP**, two, today abandoned old customs offices and a new one common for both.

A good hiking opportunity is the National Nature Reserve **Bielovodská dolina** valley. This largest Tatra valley belongs indeed to the most attractive parts of the Tatras. The lower reaches of the glacial trough offer an occasion for pleasant and comfortable walks in a most peaceful natural setting where spruce woods alternate with fresh green mountain meadows.

More demanding tourists will certainly choose the pass over the High Tatras across the Poľský hrebeň ́saddle. The blue-marked path is part of the longest and most exacting transversal pass over the mountain range. The path follows the tor-

rent of the Biela voda. It alternatively crosses the forest and forest meadows. The part of the route near Poľana under the Vysoká Mt. provides impressive views of the rocky face of the **Mlynár** Mt. (2,170 m) with the most difficult climbing tracks in the Tatras. Rather difficult to ascend is the threshold of the Kačacia dolina valley with a wonderful 15 metres tall **Hviezdoslavov vodopád** waterfall. It is also called the Kačací vodopád waterfall. The **Kačacia dolina** valley is undoubtedly one of the most beautiful valleys in the Tatras. Its beauty is enhanced by a high rocky background of the northern faces between the Ganek and Litvorový štít peaks. The footpath passes by the Kačacia dolina valley and traverses to the neighbouring **Litvorová dolina** valley with an eponymous lake and peak above the valley. On the left side it passes by the higher situated **Zamrznuté pleso** lake. The water table of the lake is in a cool shadow of the northern faces of the Tatra mountain ridge at an altitude of 2,047 metres above sea level. The crossroads above

Left: Bielovodská dolina valley
Right: Museum of the Orava Village in Zuberec

the lake offers a choice of a shorter and a longer pass to the southern side of the High Tatras. The shorter route leads along the green-marked footpath across the **Poľský hrebeň** saddle (2,200 m) to the Velická dolina valley. The longer one continues by the blue-marked path to the **Prielom** saddle (2,288 m) which ends in the Veľká Studená dolina valley.

The West Tatras

The region of **ZUBEREC** (see page 182) spreads in the north-western part of the Tatra region occupying the Orava part of the West Tatras. Three kilometers from Zuberec, at Brestová, a unique **open-air Museum of the Orava Village** can be visited. Not far from the museum, at the foothills of Madajka mountain in the Studená dolina ˏvalley there is an interesting protected landscape – the cave of **Brestovská jaskyňa**. It is the largest cave in the Orava region and also the most important one in the West Tatras. The length of its underground space reaches up to 1.8 km. With its unique underground water labyrinth the cave is planned to be opened to public in the near future. Going south-eastward across the Studená dolina valley, the longest and most dissected valley of the Roháče Mts., we can see the protected landscape formation of the rocky **Mačie diery** (Cat Holes) on the left hand side, with extremely rare vegetation growing on a limestone base.

At the upper end of the Studená dolina valley at an altitude of 1,037 m above sea level extends a sunny mountain alpine meadow called **Zverovka**, the principal centre and natural starting point to all parts of the Roháče Mts. At the present time there are numerous options for accommodation in Zverovka available for the tourists, with well accessible high mountain hiking tours. One of them (the yellow marked path) leads across the **Látaná dolina** valley, an eastern prolongation of the the the Studená dolina valley. On the left side of the path there is the Nature Reserve of **Osobitá** bearing the same name

as the cliff peak Osobitá (1,687 m) among the most beautiful mountains of the Orava region. For the sake of protecting the rare flora at the summit, the Osobitá Mt. is not accessible to visitors.

At the end of the Látaná dolina valley, another favourite family walk is that to the National Nature Reserve of **Kotlový žľab**, a trough with original forestation in steep mountain terrain. Tourists who continue higher will get to **Sedlo Zábrať** saddle (1,656 m) which separates the valleys of Látaná dolina and Roháčska dolina, with the additional possibility to ascend even higher to the easiest accessible mountain of all the Roháče – **Rákoň** (1,879 m). Its peak is situated in the main ridge which forms part of the Slovak-Polish state border and offers wonderful views of the Roháčska kotlina basin and the Dolina Chochołowska valley in Poland.

South-east of Zverovka is the long **Roháčska dolina** valley with a paved road leading across it. As far as the scenery is concerned, this valley is the most remark-

able in the region. There are high quality cross-country ski tracks, excellent opportunities for walking and abundance of snow. The glacial origin of the Roháčska dolina valley is obvious for its numerous glacier relief manifestations.

The southern side of the Roháčska dolina valley has several projections which branch out into smaller valleys. The best known are the **Salatínska dolina** valley and the trough of **Spálený žľab**. They are popular centres of winter sports and downhill skiing with excellently treated tracks and artificial snow available when necessary. The **ski resort** has become the favourite and much frequented destination for all lovers of skiing.

Parallel to the Salatínska dolina valley are the valleys of **Zadná Spálená dolina** and **Spálená dolina** situated higher in the Roháčska dolina valley. The valley Spálená dolina is particularly attractive for tourists

because of its bizarre relief and rather wild nature. There are two routes for hiking, a yellow path (leading to the Baníkovské sedlo saddle – 2,045 m) and a blue-marked one (which leads to the Roháčske plesá lakes). The Spálená dolina valley, together with the higher situated Smutná dolina valley, in the upper part of the Roháčska dolina valley, and the contiguous peaks, form the National Nature Reserve of the **Roháčské plesá** lakes. It extends over an area of almost 452 hectares, which from a scenic and a scientific point of view, is one of the most valuable landscapes, not only in the Roháče Mts., but throughout the West Tatras. Visitors can familiarise themselves with it by using the **instructive path** with information boards, leading from the end of the Roháčska dolina valley to the Spálená dolina valley, which passes the lower part of the valley Smutná dolina beside the Roháčske plesá lakes and ends in the alpine meadow of Adamcuľa. The tour is not exacting and passes through the most interesting and most beautiful parts

Left: Roháčske plesá lakes
Right: Volovec Mt.

of the reserve. The instructive boards display the geomorphologic, climatologic, hydrological, botanical, zoologic and historical characteristics of the territory of Roháče Mts. The route begins at the point where the cottage Tatliakova chata used to stand (it burnt down in 1963) and where the Roháčska dolina valley passes over to the Smutná dolina valley. From here it continues along the Tatliakovo jazero lake to the **Roháčske plesá** lakes, remnants of the Glacial period in the Tatra territory. The first Roháčske pleso lake lies at an altitude of 1,563 m above sea level, its area is 2.22 ha, and its depth is 6.5 m. The second and the third Roháčske pleso lakes are at an altitude of 1,650 m and 1,653 m, above sea level, their areas are 0.21 and 0.61 ha, and are 1.3 m and 3.7 m deep respectively. The fourth Roháčske pleso lake is the highest situated at an altitude of 1,718 m, above sea level with an area of 1.45 ha, and it is 8.1 m deep. All lakes, partially silted by the remains of the moraines are situated in a kettle hollowed by the glacier.

More sturdy tourists usually continue to follow the blue path up the **Smutná dolina** valley to the **Smutné sedlo** saddle (1,965 m) in the main ridge of the West Tatras. The saddle provides the best possible passage between the north and south. Excellent skiers like to ski in the upper part of the Smutná dolina valley, but they have to carry their equipment on their backs. A tour tracing the ridge is possible in a north-easterly direction to the Volovec Mt. or by taking the north-western route to the Baníkov Mt. and the Baníkovské sedlo saddle.

The first peak of the main ridge of Roháče Mts., east of Smutné sedlo saddle, is the **Plačlivé Mt.** (2,126 m). It is a sharp and cliffy peak which was once also called Plačlivô or Plačlivý Roháč. Together with the **Ostrý Roháč Mt.** (2,084 m) they form the typical mountain silhouette of the Roháče Mts. and the West Tatras. The Ostrý Roháč Mt. is a double-top cliff peak, although its crumbling surface makes climbing possible only from the saddles of the Smutné sedlo

or the Jamnické sedlo (1,905 m). For the majority of visitors this is the final destination to the Roháče Mts., even though some sections of the track are rather exposed and secured by chains. But the rare prospect of seeing chamois and mountain marmot make the experience worthwhile. The third mountain of the Roháče triplet is the **Volovec Mt.** (2,063 m), a massive mountain which spreads over the Slovak-Polish border. It is, for the most part, a deforested, steep, dome-shaped mountain rendering perhaps the most exquisite view when compared to the rest of peaks in the West Tatras, and where one can see the valleys of Roháčska dolina, Jamnícka dolina and Dolina Chochołowska. The descent is possible by the Rákoň and Sedlo Zábrať saddles to the valleys of Roháčska dolina or Látaná dolina continuing on to Zverovka.

Departing from the Smutné sedlo saddle some sturdy tourists can undertake a

very exacting tour with several exposed points, secured by chains, to the Baníkovské sedlo saddle. The first ascent is to the tripple topped expanded rock formation (Prvá, Druhá and Tretia kopa) called the **Tri kopy Mt.** (2,154 m). In the north-east a rock projection called Zelené separates the kettle of the Roháčske plesá lakes from the Smutná dolina valley. The passage over the ridge from Tri kopy is demanding and not suitable for the casual and ill-equipped hiker. Alternately, the passage to the neighbouring **Hrubá kopa Mt.** (2,158 m) is easier and leads mostly through grassy slopes. Somewhat more difficult is the tour to the **Baníkov Mt.** (2,178 m), the highest peak of this part of the West Tatras ascending over awkward scales, which in places are secured by chains. From the point of view of landscape, the Baníkov Mt. is one of the most attractive peaks of the mountain range having on its slopes numerous well preserved surface formations of glacial activity and some rare plant species, such as *Ranunculus glacialis*. There is a panoramic view from the top of the mountain to all cardinal points. Below, in the west is the **Baníkovské sedlo** saddle (2,045 m) with the majority of ascending and descending routes oriented towards either the summit or to the valley.

The best start for the tour to the westernmost part of the West Tatras is the gamekeeper's lodge **Horáreň pod Bielou skalou**, situated several kilometres south of Zuberec, near the paved road to the city of Liptovský Mikuláš. The red marked path leads from the lodge to the forest, ascending to a steep slope and ending in a grassy saddle **Sedlo pod Bielou skalou** (1,316 m). The location offers a wonderful view of the Biela skala cliffs the tallest peak of the mountain range. A well-maintained path leads from Biela skala along a mountain ridge providing a magnificent view over the valleys of the Orava and Váh rivers and practically all of the Orava and Liptov regions. Some parts of the path are more exposed with various dolomite towers and fissures. This part of the tour is

Left: Mountain guide
Right: Žiarska dolina valley

called "Skalné mesto" (Rock City) and opens the way to the **Sivý vrch Mt.** (1,805 m). The ridge including its forks covers an area of almost 113 hectares Nature Reserve of Sivý vrch.

Advancing along the ridge of the West Tatras over the **Pálenica** saddle (1,570 m, an old historical route from Orava to Liptov) the red-marked path leads to the **Zuberec Mt.** (1,746 m) and further to the **Brestová Mt.** (1,902 m). From here one can descend from its summit following the blue-marked path to Zverovka, or for the more fitter hiker, there is the alternative treck south-east over the **Parichvost** saddle (1,870 m), along the ridge. There is also a moderately difficult ascent to the top of the **Salatín Mt.** (2,047 m) with steep faces on the northern and southern sides, followed by the pass over the **Skriniarky** ridge. This tour is considered the most exposed though also the most beautiful in the West Tatras. In the following peak of the **Spálená Mt.** (2,083 m) the main ridge bends from the east to the south-west towards the **Pachoľa** peak (2,166 m) which has a regular pyramidal shape and offers a splendid view of the surrounding landscape. The descent is comfortable and ends in the Baníkovské sedlo saddle or further in the valleys of Orava or Liptov.

ŽIAR and **SMREČANY** are situated north-east of Liptovský Mikuláš, not far away from the Žiarska dolina valley which opens out into the Liptovská kotlina basin. Visitors to Smrečany and Žiar usually pass through the communities in pursuit of snow or undertaking walks to higher situated places on the southern slopes of the West Tatras. Immediately beyond the community Žiar is a group of **holiday cottages** with two ski lifts and downhill skiing tracks for less demanding skiers. By taking the red-marked path towards Podbanské one gets to two short ski lifts placed two kilometres from the end of the Žiarska dolina valley at the point where it opens up to the Liptovská kotlina basin. However, the main aim of the tourists and skiers in the area is the seven kilometres long **Žiarska dolina** valley.

A favourite and sought-after resting place in the upper part of the valley is the tourist cottage **Žiarska chata** (1,300 m). Its position amid the mountains represents an excellent departing point for high-mountain tours to the surrounding peaks or passages over the saddles to the neighbouring valleys. North of the cottage and passing the dwarf pines are green and blue-marked footpaths which lead up to the bottom of the Prostredný grúň Mt. The blue track continues further up to the Smutné sedlo saddle (1,965 m) while the green-marked path deviates northeast up to a small wooden shelter about 450 m below the rocky **Žiarske sedlo** saddle (1,917 m) right below the top of Plačlivé Mt. It is possible to continue along the saddle observing the green mark to the Jamnícka dolina valley or the yellow one over a grassy ridge leading to the top of the Smrek Mt. (2,089 m). Smrek is usually only a stop on the ridge tour to the top of the **Baranec Mt.** (2,184 m) also called the Veľký vrch Mt. It is the

ier lakes – Bobrovecké plesá. The path goes on over the two lakes into a slope covered by dwarf pine trees and after a steep ascent it reaches the Pálenica saddle. From there one can continue northeast or south-west along the main ridge of the West Tatras.

PRIBYLINA lies ten kilometres southwestward from Podbanské on the road from Liptovský Hrádok near the confluence of the Račkov potok brook and the river Belá. The most attractive sight, however, is the **Museum of Liptov Village**, documenting the folk architecture of the Liptov region (see page 282).

Tourists know Pribylina mainly as a departing point for the **Račkova dolina** and **Jamnícka dolina** valleys. The road starting near the museum leads to the Račkova dolina valley. At its end opening up into the Liptovská kotlina basin there is a group of tourist cottages and a caravan camping regularly visited by natives and foreigners. Winter is the time for the fans of cross-country and downhill skiing as there are three ski lifts and well-maintained running tracks in the Račkova dolina valley. At the end of the valley there is an intersection of tourist routes. Tourist prefer the blue-marked path leading deeper into the Račkova dolina valley. The first two kilometres, common for both the Račkova and Jamnícka dolina valleys are called the **Úzka dolina** valley. It starts at 885 m above sea level and branches to the Račkova and Jamnícka valleys which are 960 m above sea level. From the point where the valley branches the yellow-marked footpath leads along the Račkova dolina valley. The first two thirds of the ascent up the valley is comparatively easy. The route continues across ever thickening woods to a large, almost flat alpine meadow called Prostredná poľana with an old log hut, testimony that there used to be pastures here in the past. Even further the remains of what was once the highest situated sheep dairy farm in Slovakia (1,600 m) can be found. Past this landmark one can turn to the **Gáborova dolina** valley.

third tallest peak of the West Tatras and offers a grandiose vista to all cardinal points.

Most tourists going to the main ridge of the West Tatras prefer the route leading across the **Jalovecká dolina** and **Bobrovecká dolina** valleys. This path continues in the northerly direction along the Jalovecký potok brook up to the steep slopes of **Lysec Mt.** (1,827 m). Its massive body represents the south-western fork of the Salatín Mt. It is called so because its summit is bare (lysý = bold). The valley under Lysec divides into two branches: the Bobrovecká dolina and Parichvost valleys. The Bobrovecká dolina valley stretches below the Sivý vrch Mt. up to the Brestová Mt. Its lower part is covered by forests and in its upper part dwarf pines and alpine meadows combine. The glacial activity left here distinctive forms of a modelled surface, as well as two glac-

Left: Sunday of compatriots in Pribylina
Right: The West Tatras seen from Pribylina

Ascending up the Gáborova dolina valley one can get to the main ridge and further to the Gáborovo sedlo (1,890 m) or the Bystré (1,960 m) saddles. But the most attractive destination for the tourists is the upper part of the Račkova dolina valley via the yellow-marked path. The stony path, crossing the dwarf pine forest is comparatively steep making the ascent difficult and straining, but the reward comes in the form of excellent sights of the surrounding peaks of Bystrá, Klin, Jakubiná and above all the romantic mountain scenery of **Račkove plesá** lakes at an altitude of 1,697 m above sea level which are set in a distinct glacier kettle. A winding path above the lakes leads further to the **Račkovo sedlo** saddle (1,956 m) situated in the main ridge of the West Tatras over which the top of **Končistá** peak (1,993 m) towers. From here one can ascend by a stony path (tracing the Slovak-Polish state borderline) to the very top of the **Hrubý vrch Mt.** (2,137 m) and enjoy the fine view of the Roháče Mts., the massive body of

Bystrá Mt. and the furthermost parts of the Račkova and Jamnícka dolina valleys. South of it is **Jakubiná Mt.** (2,194 m), the second tallest top of the West Tatras. Ascent to Jakubiná is very difficult.

But the most favourite track in this part of the West Tatras is the ascent along the Jamnícka dolina valley following the blue mark. It starts at an approximate altitude 960 m and ends in the end of the valley in the height 1,860 m. Jamnícka dolina valley is 6.5 km long and narrow. It widens in its end below the Ostrý Roháč Mt. and Žiarske sedlo saddle, called **Záhrady** alpine meadow. The blue mark continues along the Jamnícky potok brook up to the **Jamnícke plesá** lakes. Above, along the main ridge of Roháče Mts., a winding footpath leads up to **Jamnícke sedlo** saddle (1,908 m) which is situated between Ostrý Roháč and Volovec mountains. In upper part of the valley under Žiarske sedlo saddle, in the altitude 1,835 m another little lake is hidden. It is the **Žiarske pleso** lake. Its area is 0.11 hectares and depth only 0.8 m.

THE HIGH TATRAS
(dial: 052-)

Information
- Tatranská informačná kancelária, Dom služieb, P. O. Box 7, Starý Smokovec, ☎ 4423440, ☎/fax 4423127, zcr@sinet.sk, www.tatry.sk, Tatranská informačná kancelária, Štrbské Pleso, ☎ 4492391, Tatranská informačná kancelária, Tatranská Lomnica, ☎ 4468118-9

Museums
- Múzeum Tatranského národného parku (TANAP), Tatranská Lomnica, ☎ 4467951

Galleries
- Vila Flóra, Starý Smokovec, ☎ 4422818

Cottages
- Bilíkova chata, ☎ 4422439, Chata pod Rysmi, ☎ 4422314, Chata pod Soliskom, ☎ 4492221, Chata pri Popradskom plese, ☎ 4492177, Chata pri Zelenom plese, ☎ 4467420, Rainerova chata, ☎ 4524103, Skalnatá chata, ☎ 4467075, Sliezsky dom, ☎ 4425202, Téryho chata, ☎ 4425245, Zamkovského chata, ☎ 4422636, Zbojnícka chata, ☎ 0903/619000

Hotels
- GRAND***, Starý Smokovec, ☎ 4422154-5, SMOKOVEC**, Starý Smokovec 25, ☎ 4425191, PANDA***, Horný Smokovec II/13, ☎ 4422614, SOLISKO****, Štrbské Pleso, ☎ 4492138-40, FIS***, Štrbské Pleso, ☎ 4492221, PATRIA***, Štrbské Pleso, ☎ 4492591, PANORÁMA**, Štrbské Pleso, ☎ 4492111, PERMON****, Podbanské 18, ☎ 4710111, GRANDHOTEL PRAHA****, Tatranská Lomnica, ☎ 4467941, SLOVAKIA***, Tatranská Lomnica, ☎ 4467961, SLOVAN***, Tatranská Lomnica, ☎ 4467851, TATRANEC***, Tatranská Lomnica, ☎ 4467092, TATRY***, Tatranská Lomnica, ☎ 4467614, WILI***, Tatranská Lomnica, ☎ 4467761, HUBERT****, Gerlachov 302, ☎ 4780811, KONTAKT***, Stará Lesná, ☎ 4468185, ACADEMIA***, Stará Lesná, ☎ 4467464, NEZÁBUDKA***, Rekreačná 83, Tatranská Štrba, 4484838, MEANDER***, Rekreačná 42/9, Tatranská Štrba, ☎ 4781051-2, HUTNÍK I.**, Tatranské Matliare, ☎ 4467446, HUTNÍK II.**, Tatranské Matliare, ☎ 4467441

Restaurants
- TATRASPORT, Starý Smokovec, ☎ 4425241, SIBÍRANKA, Starý Smokovec, ☎ 4422001, POĽSKÁ KRČMA, Starý Smokovec, ☎ 4423171, ROGALO, Starý Smokovec, ☎ 4425043, SANTAL, Horný Smokovec, ☎ 4423271, JAVOR, Štrbské Pleso, ☎ 4492247, SLOVENSKÁ REŠTAURÁCIA, Štrbské Pleso, ☎ 4492192, FURMANSKÁ KRČMA, Štrbské Pleso, ☎ 4492251, JÚLIA, Tatranská Lomnica, ☎ 4467947, STARÁ MAMA, Tatranská Lomnica, ☎ 4467713, SLNEČNÝ DOM, Tatranská Lomnica, ☎ 4467046, LAVÍNA, Tatranská Lomnica, ☎ 4467203, VILA PARK, Tatranská Lomnica, ☎ 4780911

THE BELIANSKE TATRAS
(dial': 052-)

Museums
- Múzeum Ždiarsky dom, Ždiar, ☎ 4498142

Galleries
- Galéria Jána Zoričáka, Ždiar, ☎ 4498181

Cottages
- Chata Plesnivec, ☎ 0905/256722

Hotels
- MAGURA**, Ždiar, ☎ 4498121

Restaurants
- ŽDIARSKY DOM, Ždiar, ☎ 4498135, HUČAVA, Tatranská Kotlina, ☎ 4467759, KOLIBA, Tatranská Kotlina, ☎ 4468274

THE WEST TATRAS
(dial: 043-, 044-)

Information
- Turisticko-informačná kancelária Zuberec, Zuberec 289, ☎ 043/5320777, ☎/fax 043/5395197, tatrainfo@stonline.sk, www.zuberec.sk, www.tatrainfo.sk

Museums
- Múzeum oravskej dediny, Zuberec, ☎ 043/5395149, Múzeum liptovskej dediny, Pribylina, ☎ 044/5293163

Cottages
- Chata pod Náružím, Bobrovec, ☎ 044/5596964, Žiarska chata, ☎ 044/5591525, Chata Zverovka, Zuberec, ☎ 043/5395106

Hotels
- OSOBITÁ**, Roháčska dolina 378, Zuberec, ☎ 043/5395105, PRIMULA, Zuberec 373, ☎ 043/5395001, TATRAWEST, Zuberec, ☎ 043/5395210, MIER***, Račkova dolina, Pribylina, ☎ 044/5293121, ESPERANTO*, Pribylina, ☎ 044/5280640

Restaurants
- KOLIBA JOSU, Zuberec, ☎ 043/5395915, MILOTÍN, Zuberec, ☎ 043/5395113, ORAVSKÁ IZBA, Zuberec, ☎ 0907/852823, HOSTINEC HOREC, Zuberec, ☎ 043/5395192, KOLIBA, Zuberec, ☎ 043/5395855

SPIŠ

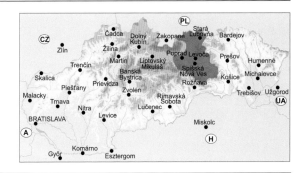

Central Spiš

Northern Spiš

Southern Spiš

Spiš is historical territory in the north of Slovakia. Its area is less than three and half thousand square kilometres. Spiš boasts of all basic natural attributes proper to the typical Carpathian landscape. It is arranged in varied mosaics while basins occupy the central position in this composition. Spiš consisted historically of three regions. Environs of Stará Ľubovňa along with Zamagurie form the northern Spiš, the Popradská

kotlina basin represents the central Spiš. The territory drained by the river Hornád and its tributaries constitutes the southern Spiš. Nevertheless, the new administrative and territorial division of Slovakia divided the territory of Spiš in two provinces in 1996. Districts of Poprad, Kežmarok, Levoča, and Stará Ľubovňa form the province Prešov. Districts of Spišská Nová Ves and Gelnica are now part of the province Košice.

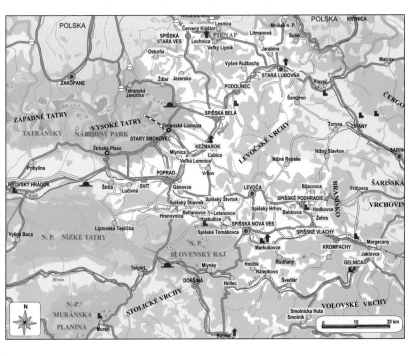

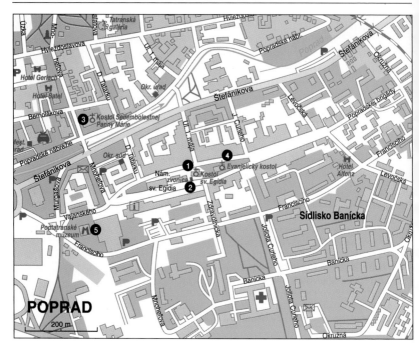

Central Spiš

POPRAD (population 55,150) lies south-east of the Popradská kotlina basin on both sides of the river Poprad. It is the main entrance "gate" to the High Tatras. Annually tens of thousands of tourists of Slovakia and from abroad pour in through the local airport, railways and roads to continue to Starý Smokovec or other Tatra communities.

Medieval Poprad was probably founded before the Tartar invasion. The oldest Slav community was strengthened by the German colonists invited here by the king in the mid-13th century. The present name of Poprad appears in the oldest known act of 1256. Initially Poprad did not develop as quickly as the neighbouring Veľká and Spišská Sobota communities. In spite of its favourable geographic situation Poprad only slowly changed from a farming com-

munity to a town of craftwork and trade. In the years between 1412-1772 it was included among 16 Spiš towns given as a forfeit to the Polish crown. Only in the 18th century did Poprad economically catch up with its contemporary towns. The principal driving force of the dynamic development of the town was finally the Košice-Bohumín railway track built in 1871. The dynamic growth 'of the town, to the detriment of Spišská Sobota and Veľká, gradually changed the hundreds of years' hierarchy of the settlements in the central Spiš region. After the First World War a plant producing railway cars was founded in Poprad and in its present form it represents the most important industry in the city. The growing interest of the tourists in the Tatras geared up intense cultural and social life in the city. Continuously growing, Poprad first swallowed its greatest rivals Spišská Sobota and Veľká, then in 1960 Stráže pod Tatrami were absorbed and the creation of the present "Large Poprad" was completed by annexing Matejovce in 1974.

Right: Wall paintings in St. Egidius church. Belfry

Poprad today with its large population is the largest city in the sub Tatra region, ranking tenth in the national scale.

The historical centre of Poprad is concentrated into the space around the spindle-shaped **square of St. Egidius**. The square is rimmed by a row of prevailingly Baroque and Classicist **burgher houses** from the 18th and 19th centuries. The city has an Early-Gothic Roman-Catholic **church of St. Egidius ❶** from the late 13th century. The local people know it as "the old church". In its interior the medieval wall paintings from the first half of the 15th century are preserved. One of the paintings by an unknown artist depicts the panorama of the Tatra peaks within a Biblical scene of Christ's resurrection. Alongside the old church stands a Renaissance **belfry ❷** from 1658. At present there is in Poprad a new Roman-Catholic **the Virgin Mary of Seven Grievances church ❸** built during the Second World War and the Classicist Evangelical **church ❹** was built in the years 1829-1834. The Poprad

synagogue is from 1830. Visitors to Poprad should not forget to visit the **Podtatranské múzeum ❺** which offers an abundant information about the region.

The municipal part of **Veľká** was already a wealthy little town in the 15th century. The medieval community Veľká grew around a wide square crossed by the Velický potok brook. In the eastern side of the square stands a fortified Early-Gothic Roman-Catholic **church of St. John the Evangelist**. Its oldest part is from the mid-13th century. A part of the prevailingly Baroque interior of the church is a valuable Gothic bronze baptistery from 1439 attributed to maestro J. Weygel of Spišská Nová Ves. The square is rimmed by original **burgher houses** in the Baroque or Classicist style.

Spišská Sobota was for centuries the wealthiest of the five Upper Spiš towns. From 1945 it has represented one of the municipal parts of large Poprad. The privileges endowed to the Saxon immigrants by the king contributed enormously to the

growth of Spišská Sobota and it quickly joined the important towns in the Spiš region, namely Levoča and Kežmarok. The period of culminating prosperity for the town were the 17th and 18th centuries when the craftsmen joined in guilds. The economic growth of the town reached the standstill in the 19th and 20th centuries. Its past rivalry with Poprad finally ended in favour of its economically stronger south-western neighbour. Spišská Sobota represents one of the best preserved medieval urban units in Slovakia declared in 1953 a **municipal monument reserve**. Its core is a triangle-shaped square bordered by a row of **burgher houses** built on narrow medieval plots. The typical trait of the burgher houses in Spišská Sobota are tall shingled roofs with massive shingled cornices. They can be seen, for instance, on the houses of the tanners at the north-eastern end of the square. Most of the burgher houses in this town were built in

Left: Burgher houses in Spišská Sobota
Right: Kežmarský hrad Castle

the period between the 15th to the 17th centuries in Gothic and Renaissance styles and later into the Baroque. Special attentions should be paid to several Gothic burgher houses from the second half of the 15th century. The Roman-Catholic **church of St. George** ❶ built before 1273 in the Late-Romanesque style, was rebuilt in the Gothic style in 1464 and at the beginning of the 16th century it was enlarged by the St. Anna chapel. In the 18th century a Baroque southern hallway was also added to it. The Late-Gothic wing altars of St. George and St. Anton were installed in the years between 1503 to 1520 in the workshop of Maestro Pavol of Levoča. Near the church stands a Renaissance **belfry** ❷ from 1598 and a Baroque statue of Immaculation from 1772. In a small park nearby a corn gauge can be seen as a single memory of the famous markets held in Spišská Sobota. The isolated building of the **town hall** ❸ was originally a Late-Baroque palace dating from the last third of the 18th century. The Evangelical **church** ❹ was included into the row of houses around the square in 1777.

SVIT (population 7,450) is the youngest of the sub Tatra towns, and following Starý Smokovec the second highest situated town in Slovakia (763 m). The town is typical for its red brick "**Baťa houses**" which exemplify the sofisticated social policy of its original owner, the businessman Baťa. South of Svit lies the sport and leisure centre for skiers called

Lopušná dolina valley equipped with ski-lifts and tourist accommodation facilities.

LUČIVNÁ lies on a subsidiary road between Svit and Štrba. In the early 18th century the community became the property of the family of Várady-Szatmáry, who built a climatic **spa** north of the community in 1872. In 1937 another modern, clinic specialising in children's therapy, was built in Lučivná. Today Lučivná has available three sanatoriums for non-specific respiratory diseases and children's allergies.

The sub Tatra community of **MLYNICA** originated probably after the Tartar invasion by German colonisation. The Roman-Catholic **church of St. Margita of Antiochia** built in the mid-13th century is one of the most precious ones in the sub Tatra region. In spite of repeated reconstruction its older features are recognisable in its architecture. The main **altar** consecrated to the patroness saint originated in 1515 and is allegedly created by the Maestro Pavol of Levoča. The former Evangelical **church** of Mlynica was used as a granary after the de-parture of the German citizens. In 1997 it was granted a new and interesting function when members of the Veteran Club of Poprad restored it and established here a remarkable Auto-moto museum.

The community of **GÁNOVCE** is known for its unique archaeological finds, especially the famous travertine cast of the brain of a Neanderthal man. Among the monuments in Gánovce the Early-Gothic Roman-Catholic **church of St. Michael the Archangel** built in the second half of the 13th century is of interest. In the presbytery and nave of the church some precious wall paintings from the 14th century can be seen. The Gothic bell from the 14th century is also of considerable value. The Classicist **curia** in Gánovce is from the mid-19th century. A natural landmark of Gánovce are the **travertine hills** declared in 1985 as a protected nature formation.

KEŽMAROK (population 17,400) lying in the middle of three district towns on the river Poprad (15 km from Poprad and 3 km from Stará Ľubovňa), is one of Slovakia's

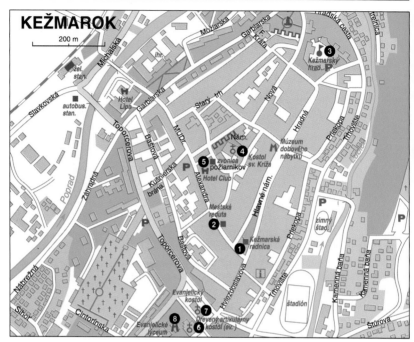

KEŽMAROK

200 m

historical towns. Medieval Kežmarok originated by merging of the main communities in one municipality. In 1269 it obtained proper municipal self-administration and up to 1348 it was protected by municipal walls. Kežmarok confirmed its economic and political position in the first half of the 15th century with additional privileges. On the downside of the economic development of the town was the on-going and often bloody disputes with the people of Levoča and the landlords of the newly built Kežmarok Castle. The further growth of Kežmarok benefited by the return of the Polish forfeit, and the favourable economic development of the town, by the end of the 17th century, is documented by the existence of 21 guilds. The first factory in Kežmarok, mechanical flax weaving manufacture, founded in 1860, only followed the long tradition of wool and linen making in Kežmarok, goods which were famous and sold as far as Greece and Albania. In 1884 an

other factory was built for flax processing, and in 1901 also cloth-production plant. Up to 1960 Kežmarok was the seat of district administration, the status which it regained following the implementation of the new territorial-administrative divisions of the Slovak Republic in 1996.

Along with Levoča, Kežmarok represents the most extensive and most compact compound of cultural and historical monuments in the region of Spiš, declared in 1950 a **Town Monument Reserve**. The walk around the town can start at the building of the **town hall ❶**, which dominates the **Hlavné námestie** (The Main Square). The first town hall on the site was built in 1461 by maestro Juraj of Spišská Sobota in the Gothic style. After the new town hall was damaged by fire in 1515, the mayor had the seat of his office built at the same place, in what was then the most recent Renaissance style. In 1799 the town hall was made higher by another floor and equipped with a tower which is today one

Right: Wooden church in Kežmarok

of the main landmarks of the town. Not far away from the town hall is the Classicist building of municipal **redoubt ❷** that originated in 1818 on the foundations of the former guard tower. The two oldest streets in Kežmarok start from the town hall, one heading to the north and other north-east. Both are skirted by ancient **burgher houses**. The best conserved Gothic-Renaissance houses on **Hradné námestie** (Castle Square) are from the first half of the 16ᵗʰ century.

Hradná ulica street leads eventually to the Hradné námestie square, which is dominated by the **Kežmarský hrad** Castle **❸**. The urban compound of the castle originated in 1462 on the site of the medieval community of Svätá Alžbeta (St. Elisabeth). Built originally by Imrich and Ján Zápoľský in the Gothic style, much stress was laid on the defensive nature of the castle building including thick walls and massive bastions. The castle gained its contemporary Renaissance form after extensive rebuilding, proceeding in various stages in the

years 1572, 1575, 1583, and 1624. In 1931 the first exposition of the **Museum of Kežmarok** was opened in a part of the castle compound. After general repairs to the castle between 1962 to 1985 its collections were expanded. The late Gothic Roman-Catholic **church of St. Cross ❹** is enclosed within the space of the fork formed by the main streets. It was built in the 14ᵗʰ century on the site of an older Romanesque chapel. Because of its dimensions it is one of the largest hall churches in Slovakia. There are wood carvings by artists who belonged to the circle around Maestro Pavol of Levoča. The church neighbours with the Renaissance **belfry ❺** of 1568, which is the oldest and certainly one of the most beautiful in the Spiš region.

The pride of Kežmarok is the Protestant wooden **articled church ❻** included in the list of national cultural monuments. This Protestant church was built in 1717 next to an older sacral stone building from 1593, which today is a sacristy. This unique wooden building made of yew and

red spruce wood was built without using a single metal component, and its ground plan is in the form of a Greek cross. The Baroque interior of the church is also made of wood. Of immense artistic value is also the church organ with wooden pipes. In 1898 the Protestants were granted a new **church ❼** built in a decorative Neo-Byzantine style. Next to the articled church is a building which is also included among the national cultural monuments, namely the **Evangelical Lyceé ❽**, built in 1775 with the approval of the ruler Maria Theresa herself. At present it houses an exposition of the literary traditions of the former lyceé placed here after a general reconstruction in 1975. It also contains the largest school library in Central Europe with about 150 thousand volumes, four thousand of them concerning Slovakia. A visit to Kežmarok can be concluded by a climb up the **Jeruzalemský vrch Mt.** at the eastern end

Left: Town walls in Podolínec
Right: Manor house in Strážky

of the town. It offers an excellent view of Kežmarok skirted by the charming frame of the Tatras' silhouette.

PODOLÍNEC (population 3,150) is an ancient Spiš town lying on the main road from Spišská Belá (10 km) to Stará Ľubovňa (14 km). Podolínec rapidly grew into a town obtaining some municipal privileges as early as 1292. In 1412 thanks to its promotion to the free royal borough, Podolínec reached the same status as Levoča or Kežmarok. In 1642 a Piarist order came to Podolínec and built a monastery and church in the north-eastern part of the town. The compound of the monastery became an important centre of education and culture in the Spiš region, as it had a secondary level school and a library. Fading out of economic growth, precisely at the time when many other Slovak towns greatly changed their original appearance, meant that Podolínec remained has it had done since the 16th and 17th centuries of the Renaissance period, and in 1990 was thus declared the **Town Monument Reserve**. Its ground plan is compact, typical for the Middle Ages, squeezed into a well-preserved **municipal fortification**. In the centre of the town is a picturesque square made of a widening out main street. In the middle of the square is the **church of the Virgin Mary's Ascension** of the late 13th century. Original one-nave Gothic building was later enlarged by an additional building of two lateral chapels and repeatedly adjusted. In the presbytery of the church are unique Gothic **wall paintings** in several layers of the years 1380-1430. In 1659 a nice Renaissance **belfry** was built beside the church with a rare bell of 1392. The square is skirted by the row of Renaissance **burgher houses**. Most of them originated in the early 17th century. Special attention deserves the **house no. 15** built in the 15th century. At the southern edge of the square stands the building of the **town hall** of 1903 when it originated by rebuilding an older object, very probably a part of the disappeared castle of Podolínec. At the northern suburb of the town is the monu-

mental building of the **Piaristic church** and **monastery**. The monastery compound was built in the years 1647 to 1651 in Renaissance style. Today it is an inseparable part of the town's beautiful silhouette. The best place for the view of it is the eastern end, i.e. the road bound for Lomnička. At the eastern edge of the monastic compound are the best preserved sections of **castle wall** with bastions. Interesting enough is the fact that the oldest building monument of Podolínec, the **chapel** of the 13th century, is situated out of its boundaries, at the local cemetery.

In the neighbouring town **SPIŠSKÁ BELÁ** (population 6,150) four important road communications meet: from Kežmarok, Stará Ľubovňa, Spišská Stará Ves and Lysá Poľana. The town acquired through a donation from king Štefan V in 1271 its first municipal rights and quickly became one of the richest towns organised by the Association of the Spiš Saxons. In the 18th and 19th centuries Spišská Belá became the largest sheep-raising

centre on the southern part of the Tatras. Its flocks could graze on extensive pastures of the Belianske Tatry Mts., over clearings of an area of 12 km².

The oldest, originally Late Renaissance and Baroque **burgher houses** in the centre of the town are from the 17th and 18th centuries. At the core of the spindle shaped square stand three buildings. The Roman-Catholic **church of St. Anton the Hermit** is the main dominant monument in the town. Of the original Late Romanesque building dating back to 1264 only the peripheral walls and the western portal are left. The interior of the church is recent, pseudo-historical. In the neigbourhood of the church the Renaissance **belfry** of the late 16th century stands. On the opposite side of the church is the **Museum of J. M. Petzval**. The museum was opened to public in 1964 in the former school building, where on January 6, 1807 the outstanding discoverer, mathematician and physicist Jozef Maximilián Petzval was born. Besides the documents about the creative life of

this famous Belá citizen the museum displays more than 600 artefacts illustrating the history of world photographic optics. There is also a famous daguerreotype apparatus with the revolutionary Petzval's lens that brought to its discoverer a world wide reputation.

The local part of Spišská Belá – **Strážky** today represents a complete compound of cultural and historical monuments, declared in 1970 a **Natural Cultural Monument**. The **manor house** in Strážky is a gem of Renaissance architecture in Slovakia. The original three-winged building was completed after a fire in 1708 creating a typical square-shaped ground plan with a square inner courtyard. The charm of the manor house is enhanced by an English park from the 19th century. Opposite the manor house stands the Roman-Catholic **church of St. Anna**, which was

Left: At the Ľubovniansky hrad Castle
Right: Open-air museum below the Ľubovniansky hrad Castle

built in the Gothic style by the end of the 15th century. Near the church a Renaissance **belfry** is adorned in 1629 by an original grafitto ornamentation of the facade.

The community of **ĽUBICA** lies 2 km east of the centre of Kežmarok. Examples of the past glory of the town are the originally Renaissance **burgher houses** and three valuable sacral buildings. The nucleus is formed by a triangle square with an Evangelic **church** built in 1786. In Ľubica are another two ancient Roman-Catholic churches from the 13th century. Even in spite of repeated reconstruction there are some Romanesque elements recognisable in the architecture of the **church of the Virgin Mary's Assumption**. The pride of the church is the **statue of Madonna** by the famous Maestro Pavol of Levoča. In the **Holy Spirit church** there used to be valuable Gothic altars, but they were carried away to Budapest before the First World War. The altars are replaced by copies today.

On the ancient road connecting Kežmarok with Spišský Štvrtok and Levoča is the community **VRBOV**. Vrbov attracted tourists mainly because of its **holiday resort** established south of the community. At the beginning there were only ponds around the Vrbovský potok brook, but following the discovery of a generous thermal water source in 1981 it soon had a system of **thermal swimming pools**.

Northern Spiš

STARÁ ĽUBOVŇA (population 16,250) lies together with Poprad and Kežmarok on the principal settlement axis of north-western Spiš, represented by the river Poprad. The oldest written reference from 1292 mentioning Ľubovňa exists in the historical documents belonging to the nearby community of Podolínec. Stará Ľubovňa received town privileges gradually. The town continued to flourish after 1412 when it was included among the 16 Spiš towns given by king Sigismond to the Polish crown as a guarantee on a loan. The final return of the towns to the lap of Old Hun-

gary in the time of Queen Mary Theresa did not favour Stará Ľubovňa. When the province of 16 Spiš town was established in 1778 the centre was located to Spišská Nová Ves and Stará Ľubovňa lost its privileged position dropping down to the level of the rest of the towns in the region. Later the impact of the industrial revolution came to the town at the beginning of the 20th century. Further industrialisation of Stará Ľubovňa came only after the Second World War when three industrial firms were set in operation.

The centre of Stará Ľubovňa is **Námestie sv. Mikuláša** (The Square of St. Nicholas) with a rectangular ground plan. It originated in 1346 by reconstructing an older spindle-shaped square. The majority of the contemporary houses in the square originated in the 17th and 18th century and underwent reconstruction which gave them Classicist or end-of-century facades. The most important building of the square besides the church is the arcade house of **Provinčný dom** (no. 12) once the seat of

the governor of the forfeited Spiš towns. This Renaissance house was reconstructed in 1639 and partially altered at the beginning of the 20th century. Attention should be paid to the Roman-Catholic **church of St. Nicholas**, built around the year 1280. The most valuable of them are the Late-Gothic baptistery of the 16th century, the Late-Gothic tomb slabs of the so-called "marmon" marble from the nearby quarry and the Gothic sculpture of the Madonna of Ľubovňa on a lateral altar.

On a limestone cliff over the local part called **Podsadek** stands **Ľubovniansky hrad** Castle. It originated at the turn of the 13th and 14th centuries as part of the system of boundary castles. Besides the protection of the former Polish-Old Hungarian border its task was to secure the important trade route passing along the valley of the Poprad river to Poland. In 1412 the historical meeting of the Old Hungarian ruler Sigismond of Luxembourg with the Polish king Vladislav II took place here. The castle remained property of the Old Hungarian

king but the captain of the castle fulfilled an important function of an administrator of the forfeited Spiš towns, of which there were 29 in all. After an extensive fire in 1557 Ľubovniansky hrad Castle obtained through reconstruction a more modern look with advanced artillery facilities and more comfortable housing. After the return of the Spiš towns to Old Hungary the role of the castle diminished and the castle itself fell into decay. Later the castle was successfully reconstructed and the castle museum collections were installed. In 1991 the castle chapel was reconstructed and again consecrated which today holds regular services. An independent collection is represented by an **open air folk architecture museum** in the area at the foot of the castle, which consists of a set of folk buildings collected in the surrounding villages forming, along with the castle, a unique and impressing composition. The group of country

houses forms a picturesque settlement around the castle. The most valuable item is the wooden Greek-Catholic **church of Matysová** of 1833. The wooden church is consecrated to St. Michael the Archangel.

Neigbouring **JARABINA** was founded in 14th century during the Wallachian colonisation by the Ruthenian people. Nearby the community is a large limestone quarry and next to it the Protected Nature Area, the well-known **Jarabinský prielom** gorge mentioned above. The Malý Lipník brook, which cuts deeply into the belt of cliffs, creates here a unique 200 m long gorge. The stream of five cascades has created beautiful giant pots, called by the local people "baďury".

LITMANOVÁ is a small boundary community and the highest situated one in the region of Stará Ľubovňa. It lies at the foothill of the highest mountain of the Ľubovnianska vrchovina highlands, the Eliášovka (1,023 m). The community of Litmanová became famous because of the alleged apparition of the Virgin Mary

Left: Vyšné Ružbachy spa
Right: Goral music band

which appeared before two girls in a place called Žvir. In commemoration of the event a Christian **pilgrimage** is held here, which is the reason why Litmanová is the most visited village in northern Slovakia.

The same mineral water springs made famous the neighbouring town **VYŠNÉ RUŽBACHY**. The curing effects of the earthy carbonate mineral water springs were also well known in the Middle Ages when the first spa was founded there. At present Vyšné Ružbachy is one of the most important **spa** and tourist centres in Slovakia, with nine types of mineral water springs of hydrocarbonate and calcareous-magnesian composition. The water temperature inside the springs is about 22˚C. The most productive spring, Izabela, feeds the outdoor swimming pool. At the centre of the swimming pool there is a small round island with greenery. The spa consists of therapeutic pools with mineral waters, tube baths, a sauna, gymnasium and massage rooms. In the summer season, besides swimming and bathing, hiking trips to the forest of the Spišská Magura mountains are a favourite pastime. In winter there are ideal conditions for down-hill skiing as there are four modern ski lifts. One of the principal attractions of Vyšné Ružbachy is the local **travertine quarry**. In the past travertine, as a decorative stone, was extracted here, but in 1964 the stonemasons were replaced by artists who changed the quarry into an interesting open air gallery of sculptures.

The pearl of the Spiš region is its north-western corner, called **Zamagurie**. It is one of the most attractive territories of Slovakia with the centre in **SPIŠSKÁ STARÁ VES** (population 2,350). As for the size of the population Spišská Stará Ves is the third smallest town in Slovakia. The village originated at the place, or near the older community quoted in old acts as *Antiqua Villa* or Old Village (Stará Ves). The village people exploited the position of their community which was located on an ancient trade road. The most important sacral monument of the town is the Roman-Catholic **church of the Virgin**

Mary's Ascension, built in the second half of the 14th century. After fire in 1760 it was reconstructed acquiring Baroque features and the damaged tower was shortened and strengthened by pillars. The main altar of 1765 is made in the Late-Baroque style. Among the secular monuments the **manor house Na tridsiatku** is of most interest, which was built in the 18th century.

In the valley of the Jezerský potok brook is the small community of **JEZER-SKO**. Its name is related to the nearby lake and was founded in 1610 by Polish refugees on the land of the landlords of the castle of Nedeca. Near the upper end of the village is the **Jezersko ski resort**, which has two ski lifts. In a lateral valley under the main ridge of the Spišská Magura mountains is the Nature Reserve of the **Jezerské jazero** lake.

Continuing westward the visitor arrives at **OSTURŇA**, a typical Goral village in a wide valley of the Osturniansky potok brook. It is probably the longest village extending over the banks of a brook in Slo-

vakia, measuring 7 km. There are many original buildings preserved in the community and protected as the **Folk Architectural Monument Reserve**. There are several natural lakes around Osturňa blocked by landslides with numerous rare varieties of plants, typical for swamps.

The most important tourist centre of Zamagurie is **ČERVENÝ KLÁŠTOR** which lies on the road between Spišská Stará Ves and Stará Ľubovňa. In 1319 master Kakaš donated the community of **LECHNICA** to the friars of Skala (today Kláštorisko) who built in the nearby valley of St. Anton a Carthusian **monastery**. Because the buildings of the monastery were built of red bricks the people began to call it Červený Kláštor (the Red Monastery). Soon a village sprung up around the monastery mentioned in historical acts of 1344 under the name *Uyvagas* (New village). In 1360 the construction of a

monastic church was initiated, as the Lechnica estate gradually expanded by adding new lands and properties. In 1563 the monastery was closed by Emperor Ferdinand and the Carthusians were obliged to move out of Červený Kláštor.

Carthusian friars were, due to the animosity of the Emperor, replaced by secular proprietors. In 1704 Červený Kláštor became again the church property, when bishop Ladislav Maťašovský, suffering from a serious illness, donated it to the Camaldolese Order of the Monte Corona Congregation. The monks of the order who came from Toscany in Italy repaired and rebuilt the monastic buildings in the Baroque style and added to it a church tower. They also founded there probably the oldest pharmacy in Slovakia. Because of the contribution of the enlightened Father Romuald Hadbavný (1714-1780) the monastery of the Camaldolese Order ultimately became an important cultural and national centre in the region. Hadbavný participated in the first translation of the Holy Script into the

Left: Červený Kláštor
Right: Rafters on the Dunajec river

Slovak language in 1750 and a compilation of the Latin-Slovak dictionary in 1763. This voluminous work of 942 pages contained also a brief grammar of the Slovak language, which can be considered the first attempt to codify the Slovak language.

The national cultural monument of **Červený Kláštor** is a unique cultural and historical relic set in the wonderful natural environment of Pieniny under the majestic mountain Tri koruny. The monastery was successfully restored in the years 1956-1966. The best building, from an architectural point of view, is the Gothic **church of St. Anton** from the end of the 14th century with one nave of unusual length restored in the Baroque style. The main altar is in the Baroque style, built in 1745. The **monastic buildings** are next to the church. In the Baroque building some older Gothic features are recognisable. The remains of the Late-Gothic paintings on the walls of the monastic refectory date back to 1520. In the building of the former monastery is a **museum** with ethnographic, pharmaceutical and historical collections.

In front of the entrance to the monastery is the park declared the Protected Area of **Pieninské lipy** in 1972. It protects 19 old and valuable lime trees. The community is the seat of administration of the **National Park of Pieniny**. The National Park of Pieniny was established on January 16, 1967 on an area of 2.125 hectares. Of its total area forests represent 928 ha while the rest is unique agricultural landscape with small fields, green meadows and pastures adorned in summer with stacks of sweet smelling newly mown hay, typical for Zamagurie. National Park of Pieniny is rich in rare species of plants with several local endemites. In the cliffs or forest pathways one can, for instance, meet a lynx or see an otter hunting in the water of the Dunajec river.

The most important sport event in Červený Kláštor is the **International Pieniny Water Slalom**, a competition held annually since 1954. The biggest attraction for tourists though, is rafting on the Dunajec river on wooden rafts.

The principal cultural event in Červený Kláštor is the **Folk Festival of Zamagurie**, which has been organised annually in June since 1976. The preface to the event is the passage down the Dunajec river on rafts, followed by a programme which takes place in an open-air amphitheatre for an audience of 7,000 people. It is situated on a beautiful green meadow with the familiar silhouette of the Tri koruny Mt. in the background.

A trip to the **Prielom Dunajca** (The Canyon of the Dunajec river) is one of the most beautiful in Slovakia. It starts in Červený Kláštor, continues on to the mouth of the Lesnický potok brook and further for quite a long while along the right bank of the meandering Dunajec. The red-marked pathway leads along the well-known **Pieninská cesta** road that used to connect Červený Kláštor with the Polish spa of Szczawnica in the 19th century. In this part the road passes over the National Nature Reserve of **Prielom Dunajca** declared as such in 1967, on an

area of 362.47 hectares. Thirteen stops along the **instructive footpath** provides tourists with more information about the Reserve.

The second section of the trip follows the blue-marked path across the Nature Reserve **Prielom of Lesnický potok brook – Kače** established in 1967. Its narrowest part is almost 300 m deep, on the right hand tributary of the Dunajec, locked in vertical dark grey limestone cliffs. The trip ends in **LESNICA**. It connects with Veľký Lipník by a 6 km log road passing the saddle in the ridge of Haligovské skaly rocks. Villagers can now, however, use a new border crossing for pedestrians to the Polish spa town of Szczawnica. The community has a Roman-Catholic **church of St. Michael the Archangel** from the first half of the 17th century.

Hiking along the ridge of the Haligovské skaly rocks is also another favourite trek. Starting from Červený Kláštor walkers

take the red-marked footpath leading along the conspicuous cliffy crest of Haligovské skaly. The National Nature Reserve of **Haligovské skaly** rocks was established in 1967 on an area of 80.80 ha. Impressive limestone cliffs with grey rock towers and walls are more than 300 m above the Lipník brook. The karst forms on the surface are modest but the underground karst is more interesting. The **Aksamitka** cave, at an altitude of 753 m, called in the past Mlečna džura, is known more for the occurrence of a rare species of bats and some valuable traces of the Stone Age settlement than for its drip-stone decoration.

Continuing eastward from Červený Kláštor one arrives at the community of **VEĽKÝ LIPNÍK**. The first colonists came here during period of the Sholtys colonisation in the 14th century. The community has a Baroque-Classicist Roman-Catholic **church of St. Michael the Archangel** built in 1794 and reconstructed in 1930. The tower of the church ends in a cupola in the Old Russian style. On the flanks of

Left: Haligovské skaly rocks

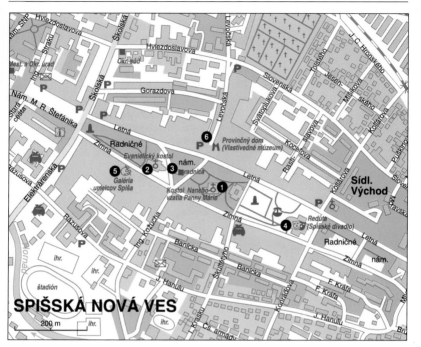

the nave, above the presbytery, are small
Baroque roof towers. The **Ikonostas**
placed on the main altar dates back to the
beginning of the 20th century. This valuable work of art is included in the list of
the national cultural monuments.

Southern Spiš

SPIŠSKÁ NOVÁ VES (population
39,200) is the metropolis of the southern
part of the Spiš region. The medieval town
originated on this river terrace in the course
of the 13th century. The name *villa Nova* –
New Village (Nová Ves) in an act of 1268 denoted a new community founded by German colonists beside an older Slavic community called *Iglov*. Its initial development
was stimulated by the privileges of the Saxons living in Spiš granted by king Štefan V
in 1271 and extended later by king Karol
Róbert. The most important right for
Spišská Nová Ves was the right to mine and
extract the ores that allowed its people to
use the rich deposits of copper, iron and sil-

ver ores found there. The first smelting
plants and hammer-mills originated in the
town and its environs during the 14th century, though it culminated only in the 18th
and the first half of the 19th centuries.

In the years 1412-1772 Spišská Nová
Ves was included in the forfeit of the Spiš
cities to the Polish ruler. After 1871 the
dynamic economic development of the city
was stimulated by the Košice-Bohumín
railway track. Numerous factories processing metals and wood, china and food
items were founded in the town, and its
rapid growth after the Second World War
manifested itself in the construction of
new municipal quarters and the up-dat-
ing of the industrial base was accompanied by a significant growth in population.

The historical core of Spišská Nová Ves
consists of the spindle-shaped **Radničné
námestie** (The Town Hall Square) tapering
in the western end to the Zimná street and
in the eastern side to the Letná street. Its
most conspicuous building is that of the
Roman-Catholic **church of the Virgin**

Mary's Ascension ❶. It was built in the second half of the 14th century on the site of an older church from the 13th century. In 1395 the still existing Gothic **chapel of St. Michael** was added to it. Baroque adaptations were subsequently made in the years between 1742-1772. Its massive basilica with three naves and **tower** at 87 m is the tallest in Slovakia. The interior of the church has plenty of valuable works of the old masters. The most precious of them is the group of the Calvary made in the workshop of Maestro Pavol of Levoča at the time around 1520 and the board paintings by maestro Martin painted in 1490.

The Classicist Evangelical **church ❷** was built in 1790-1796 as an independently standing hall in the centre of the square. In its original interior a precious altar painting of Jesus on the Mount of Olives by J. J. Stunder of 1797 is of considerable interest, as is the Classicist and detached building of

Left: Kláštorisko
Right: Prielom Hornádu canyon

the **town hall ❸** built in the years 1777-1779. Among the most important *fin-de-siécle* buildings in Slovakia is the building of **Reduta ❹** in Radničné námestie square. It originated in the years 1890-1905 after a project by the architect K. Gerster. Numerous **burgher houses** skirting the square have a Gothic core from the 15th century, and in a house on the Zimná St. is the dwelling of **Galéria umelcov Spiša ❺** (The Gallery of the Artists of Spiš Region). The conspicuous facade with rocaille ornamentation and allegorical reliefs of **provinčný dom ❻** (the Provincial House) on the Letná St. no. 50, the former seat of the provincial authorities, will certainly attract the attention of visitors. Today it functions as the **Vlastivedné múzeum** (Museum of Natural History) with a variety of general historical, natural historical, artistic, musicological and ethnographic collections. Tourists may also enjoy the annual event held in Spišská Nová Ves in July, the **Spišské výstavné trhy** (Spiš Fair) a follow-up to the city's famous market tradition.

Spišská Nová Ves is also the starting point for trips to the **National Park of Slovenský raj** (The Slovak Paradise), a wonderful landscape where deep forests alternate with karst plains, canyons and caves. The National Park of Slovenský raj occupying an area of 32,744 obtained a higher degree of protection. Approximately one fifth of the National Park is object of even stricter protection in form of 11 National Nature Reserves and 7 Nature Reserves. There are also individually protected Natural Phenomena Novoveská huta, Hranovnícke pleso lake, Dobšinská ľadová jaskyňa cave, and the protected area of Knola. The majority of Nature Reserves were established in 1964 with the principal aim to protect the most valuable gorges and valleys. The National Nature Reserve of Kyseľ calls attention with its area of 990 ha. Somewhat smaller National Nature Reserves Sokol (701 ha) and Stratená (679) protect the gorge-like valley of the Hnilec next to the village bearing the same name.

SPIŠSKÉ TOMÁŠOVCE is the best starting point for the north-eastern part of

Slovenský raj. Not far away from Spišské Tomášovce is **Čingov** (494 m), the biggest tourist centre of Slovenský raj lying above the left bank of the Hornád. The Sovia skala rock located east of the village provides a fine view of Čingov and the Prielom Hornádu gorge.

Čingov lies in the lower part of **Prielom Hornádu** canyon, one of the biggest tourist attractions of the Slovenský raj area. The narrow, canyon-like valley 16 kilometre long separated the marginal ridge culminating in **Tomášovský výhľad** view (667 m) from the mountain range. The ascent to the rock terrace facing south is worth the toil. The terrace provides a unique view of the lower part of the Prielom Hornádu canyon. In fine weather on the right side of the unique panorama also the curve of the High Tatras is visible. The rock faces of the terrace are much sought out targets of the mountaineers. In 1889 the first private mountaineer shelter was built on the Tomášovský výhľad view. On the marginal crest closer to Čingov there are two nice

rock formations called **Ihla** and **Kazateľnica**. Through the lower stretch of the valley of the Hornád river leads a 15 kilometre long route of **instructive path Prielom Hornádu** with eleven information boards.

In the village of **LETANOVCE** with a typical folklore starts the red-marked trial to Kláštorisko. Next to the **Letanovský mlyn** the path intersects the Prielom Hornádu canyon and ascends the slope of the Čertova sihoť Mt. (839 m). **Kláštorisko**, (790 m) the aim of the path, is the only tourist centre situated inside the Slovenský raj area accessible only on foot. It is located on a narrow eponymous plateau squeezed between the Prielom Hornádu canyon and the Kyseľ gorge. Judging from the foundation act from 1299 the Carthusians were granted permission to build a monastery beyond the western wall of the fort where there was also a church. Result of the common efforts of the researchers and conservationists is the remarkable site of the former **Carthusian monastery** amidst the wonderful karstic landscape, in

the six waterfalls is the 15 metre tall Okienkový vodopád waterfall.

West of Podlesok the river Veľká Biela voda mouths into the Hornád river. The **Dolina Veľkej Bielej vody** valley is one of the biggest in the Slovenský raj area. It is crossed by the forest road leading to the Dobšinská ľadová jaskyňa ice cave. Two gorges end in the valley. Next to the village Píla the yellow-marked path enters the **Piecky** gorge ascending to the western edge of the Glac plateau. Thanks to the 300 metre tall cliffs at the Glac plateau the gorge **Veľký Sokol** is quite impressive. In the place called **Kamenná brána** the slopes of the gorge leave only a metre wide gap.

Before October 5 1974 when the path called **Chodník Horskej služby Prielomom Hornádu** was ceremoniously opened to the public only the canoeists could enjoy the beauties of the gorge. It is equipped with numerous technical aids making possible easy and comfortable passage over obstacles: 374 metres of chains, 26 metre of ropes, 164 iron steps, 15 iron handles and 85 metres of footbridges secure the more than 4 kilometre long route. The sections where tourists climb the iron steps built-in the rock straight above the water of the Hornád are the most favourite ones. Exposure of the stretch in the narrowest part of the gorge called **Železná brána** squeezed between the almost vertical rock with only 10 metres of space between them makes the tourists stick closer to rock where the iron chain gives them some feeling of safety.

Only two kilometres west of Hrabušice is the community of **BETLANOVCE**, the birth place of the prominent Old Hungarian noble family Thurzo. Behind the originally Gothic Roman-Catholic **church of St. Kozma and Damián** from the early 14th century stands the major building in the community – the Renaissance **manor house**. The manor house, with an impressive arched attic gable along the roof, represents the first Renaissance building of its type without fortification and bastions.

SPIŠSKÝ ŠTIAVNIK extends along the bank of the river Hornád, 13 km west

many aspects similar to the romantic ruins of the medieval abbeys for instance in British Isles. The most interesting access road Kláštorisko comes from the north through the Kláštorská tiesňava gorge. It is the only one of the two gorges which ends directly in the Prielom Hornádu gorge.

At the Zelená hora Mt. (654 m) near the village of **HRABUŠICE** there are the remains of the medieval Castle **Marcelov hrad** from the 13th century. On the road connecting Hrabušice with Betlanovce pri Mýte is a turning to the well-known village of **Podlesok**, an ideal starting point for the trips to the gorges in the western part of the Slovenský raj and to the upper part of the Prielom Hornádu gorge. Immediately beyond Podlesok the **Suchá Belá** gorge ends in the Hornádska kotlina basin with the most beautiful part of the gorge – **Misové vodopády** waterfalls with wonderful eddies was made accessible. The tallest of

Left: Veľký Sokol gorge
Right: Manor house in Markušovce

of Spišský Štvrtok. The local Roman-Catholic **church of the Virgin Mary** was built by the end of the 14ᵗʰ century in Gothic style and in Spišský Štiavnik rebuilt in Baroque style in the 18ᵗʰ century. The Renaissance **manor house** stands on the left bank of the river, east of the community. Since 1669 the **chapel of Annunciation of the Virgin Mary** has also belonged to the manor house.

A little trip from Spišská Nová Ves down the stream of the Hornád river is what is needed to visit some remarkable places offering numerous historical and nature landmarks. **MARKUŠOVCE** is the community remarkable for its unusual concentration of historical monuments. In the western part of the community stands the **Markušovský hrad** Castle built in 1284. In the 14ᵗʰ century a Gothic palace and fortification were added to it. The continuous quarrels of the lords of the castle with the city of Levoča and other Spiš towns wounded up in the destruction of the castle in 1527. The most representative building in the village is the **manor house**, built in 1643 by František Máriássy. The original form of a Renaissance fort with round towers at the corners was changed during extensive reconstruction in 1773 when it acquired the Rococo flair. Shortly after, because of the expected arrival of emperor Josef II, the **summer residence Dardanely** was built in the garden. Even the most astute visitor will probably fail to realise that the lateral wings were finished only in the 1970's. The summer residence now houses the **Vlastivedné múzeum** (Museum of Natural History) containing, besides other objects of interest, an exposition of key musical instruments. The visit to Markušovce can be refreshed by a pleasant walk around the community. The yellow-marked footpath leads from the community to the **stone mushroom of Markušovce**.

SPIŠSKÉ VLACHY (population 3,500) is located 21 km east of Spišská Nová Ves. The medieval history of the town goes back to the mid-13ᵗʰ century. Until the 18ᵗʰ century copper ore was extracted here and carried to the local copper smelting plant. The

traders and craftsmen of Spišské Vlachy benefited from the town's favourable position on the road from the Gemer region to Poland. The spindle-shaped square is skirted by **burgher houses**, the oldest of which is from the 15ᵗʰ century. The square is dominated by the Roman Catholic **St. John the Baptist church**. Of the Romanesque buildings from around the middle of the 13ᵗʰ century very little is preserved. In 1434 the damaged church was pulled down and reconstructed in the Late-Gothic style. Among the most precious items in its interior is a crucifix made in the workshop of Maestro Pavol of Levoča around 1520. Perhaps the most attractive building in the town is the former Gothic **town hall** from the 15ᵗʰ century. Part of this remarkable architectural monument serves today as the Roman-Catholic **church of the Ascension of the Virgin Mary**. Also the **Lady's pillar** with the statue of the Immaculate of 1728 stands in the square. In the southern part of the square an Evangelical **church** was built in 1787.

standard amenities. Due to its supplies of artificial snow, ski tracks lit in the night and the high capacity of the ski lifts, Plejsy can successfully compete with the best ski resorts in Tatras.

On the shore of the water reservoir Ružín spreads the lowest situated village of the Spiš region, **MARGECANY**. Importance of this village with its past as the miners' and smelters' settlement considerably increased when the railway connected it with the rest of the world. Starting by the year 1936 the rapid trains going to Košice, Prague and Bratislava also stop at Margecany.

The city of **LEVOČA** (population 14,350) is often considered the brightest jewel in the Spiš crown. It was first mentioned in an act of 1249 as *Leucha*. The community, thriving on its advantageous position on the trade route *Via Magna*, rapidly grew into a town with numerous privileges. Shortly after, Levoča became the centre of German colonisation in the Spiš region and in 1271 it was even promoted to the capital of the Association of the Spiš Saxons, which eventually lost its influence and Levoča was declared the free royal borough in 1323. The biggest impact on the economic development of the town was the right to store the goods imported from Poland, Silesia, Germany, and Russia, which it enjoyed until 1321. The driving force of the Levoča's development was trade which gradually acquired an international dimension. The citizens of Levoča traded with Kraków, the Hanseatic towns and even with Venice. The craftsmen of Levoča produced not only for local consumption but also for the markets and fairs throughout Old Hungary and Poland. Later Levoča became the regional centre of the Renaissance and humanism in Old Hungary. Education and schooling thrived as well. The local Evangelical lycée became an important centre of the Slovak national revival in the 19th century. Unfavourable modern developments which affected Levoča culminated in the construction of the Košice-Bohumín railway track, which avoided the city and the epicentre of southern Spiš moved to

KROMPACHY (population 8,800) is following Spišská Nová Ves and Levoča the third biggest town of the southern Spiš. Smelting was the main industry in Krompachy since the 16th century. In the 19th century ironworks with a blast furnace and forge hearth existed there. The ironworks, property of the Rimamuránsko-salgótarjánska share holding company was the biggest in the region. It employed 3,000 persons. After the Second World War the situation improved as the production of copper was restored and a electromechanical plant and a power station were constructed there.

South of Krompachy, in the valley of the Slovinský potok brook, is the community of **SLOVINKY**, the former mining village. Krompachy and Slovinky are the starting points to **Plejsy**, an important ski resort. The ski slopes on the northern side of the Krompašský vrch Mt. (1,025 m) are very popular for their comparatively high

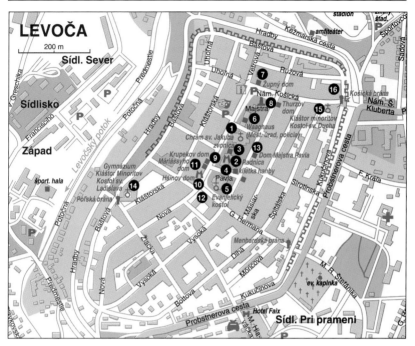

neighbouring Spišská Nová Ves. From 1996, almost after four decades, Levoča is again the seat of the district.

The **Town Monument Reserve** of **Levoča** represents a complete set of important cultural and historical monuments bordered by oblong municipal walls. The focus of ancient Levoča is the large **Námestie Majstra Pavla** (The square of Maestro Pavol). In its centre two big three-nave churches and a town hall stand. The Roman-Catholic **St. Jakub church ❶** is one of the most important sacral buildings in Slovakia and is the National Cultural Monument. Originally Gothic it was built during the 14th century on the site of an older church. The Gothic **St. George chapel** is of the same period. The tall slender tower of St. Jakub from the first half of the 19th century is the most distinct feature in the city's silhouette. Especially precious is the interior of the church, which is in fact a unique museum of medieval sacral art. The Late Gothic main **altar of St. Jakub** at a height of 18.6 m is the highest

of its kind in the world. Made of lime wood in 1507-1517 in the workshop of Maestro Pavol of Levoča the carving, by the maestro himself, is of extraordinary high artistic value, whilst the board paintings are attributed to the painter Hans. Part of them are based in the patterns of the wood carvings of Lucas Cranach. There are another thirteen lateral altars in the church, six Late-Gothic, one Late-Renaissance and three Baroque ones. Also the collection of Gothic liturgical objects and a Baroque monstrance by the Levoča goldsmith Ján Szilassy is of immense value.

The church neighbours with the arcaded building of the former **town hall ❷**, built after the fire in 1550 and is one of the finest buildings of secular Renaissance architecture in Slovakia. It houses the collections of the **Spišské múzeum** (Museum of Spiš) dedicated to the history of the city. Close to the town hall stands the Renaissance **belfry ❸**. The **cage of opprobrium ❹** is from the turn of the 16th and 17th centuries and was used in the past for the public humili-

ation of petty criminals. The Classicist Evangelical **church ❺** was built in the years between 1825-1837 in the southern part of the square on the site of an older wooden church. On the northern side of the square is a remarkable storehouse building – **Waaghouse ❻**. It originated in 1588 as what was referred to the building of the town scales. The merchants who came to Levoča in the past had to declare and store their goods at the store, which is today the municipal office. The neighbouring building of **Župný dom ❼** was built in the Empire style in the years between 1805-1831. It used to belong to one of the most representative buildings in Old Hungary. The central square is skirted by more than 50 remarkable burgher and patrician houses, many of which carry the name of their former owners. Of especial interest is **Thurzo's house ❽**, which acquired its Neo-Renaissance graffiti facade in 1904. Much older Renais-

sance facade paintings of the 16th century can be seen at the Late-Gothic **Krupek's house ❾**. **Hain's house ❿** was temporarily the seat of the Evangelical lycée. Today it houses the exposition of Fine Arts of Spiš, the Spišské múzeum in Levoča. One of the most beautiful houses in Levoča is **Mariássy's house ⓫** with an arcade courtyard. Similar arcade constructions used to surround the whole main square of Levoča before 1711. In a burgher house no. 26 the well-known **Breuer's printing office ⓬** is seated. The famous wood carving workshop of Maestro Pavol of Levoča has allegedly been located in the yard of **house no. 20 ⓭**. An exposition of the Spišské múzeum containing the material about the artist can be seen here.

In the side streets of Levoča another approximately 200 remarkable **burgher and craftsmen's houses** can be seen, many of which would grace any main square. In the neighbourhood of the Poľská brána gate stands the former **old monastery of Minorites** and the **St. Ladislav church ⓮**. The monastic buildings were built into the town walls in the course of the 14th century. After 1671 the monastery was rebuilt by Jesuits in the Baroque style. Near the Košická brána Gate is the **new monastery of Minorites** and the **Holy Spirit church ⓯** from 1753. The historical centre of Levoča is enclosed by the **town walls**. The oldest parts of fortifications originated back in the 13th century while the entire town was enclosed in 1410. The fortification consists of high inner and outer moat walls. There was an eastern **entrance gate** to the town called Menhardská brána and a southern one called **Košická brána ⓰**. A part of the southern fortification and the Dolná brána or Lower Gate were pulled down in the 19th century. Of the 2.5 km long original walls only about four fifths have been preserved. The Košická brána gate has now been converted into a restaurant and the polygonal bastion near the new monastery of Minorites provides shelter to the museum of the blind. Today the unique artefacts of this museum are included in the **Múzeum**

Left: Thurzo's house
Right: St. Jakub altar

špeciálneho školstva (the Museum of Special Education) located in a burgher house on the Maestro Pavol square. The Museum is unique in Slovakia. It introduces the visitor to Levoča's long tradition in the area of assistance to the blind.

High above the town is the **Mariánska hora Mt.** (781 m). Every year at the beginning of July Levoča becomes the meeting point of the largest pilgrimage in Slovakia. Thousands of pilgrims in long queues ascend to the mountain to render their gratitude to the Virgin Mary in the Neo-Gothic **church of the Virgin Mary's Visitation** from the beginning of the 20th century. In 1996 Pope John Paul II himself was one of the pilgrims.

The community of **SPIŠSKÝ ŠTVRTOK** in the western part of the Hornádska kotlina basin is the place where the roads of Poprad, Kežmarok, Levoča, Hrabušice

Left: Chapel of the Zápoľský family in Spišský Štvrtok
Right: St. Martin's Cathedral

and Spišská Nová Ves meet. The most remarkable landmark of the community is the Roman-Catholic **St. Ladislav church** from the late 13th century, impressive for its Gothic architecture with additional Romanesque and Baroque features. In its interior is a precious 13th century Early-Gothic baptistery, and in the following century a **chapel of the Zápoľský family** was added to the church, built for the head of the Spiš province and an Old Hungarian paladin and his family. The Early-Baroque building of the former **monastery of Minorites** built in 1688 is today an asylum for old people.

SPIŠSKÝ HRHOV is situated along the main road from Levoča to Spišské Podhradie. The most important monuments of Spišský Hrhov are the village church and a manor house. The Roman-Catholic **church of St. Šimon and Júda** was built in Early-Gothic style shortly after the Tartar invasion. Its prevailingly Baroque interior includes a precious painting of the Immaculate Conception. The Neo-Baroque **manor house** from the second half of the 19th century was built for the count Viktor Csáky and designed by the Vienna architect H. Adam.

Since ancient times the heart of the Spiš region was the eastern edge of the Hornádska kotlina basin. The land was ruled from behind the walls of Spiš Castle by the heads of the region and the ecclesiastical life was organised in Spišská Kapitula (The Spiš Chapter) by the bishops, provosts, and canonists. In a valley between these two centres of power the small town of **SPIŠSKÉ PODHRADIE** (population 3,800) originated probably as early as in the 11th century before the Tartar invasion. The streets and squares of the town are skirted by the originally Renaissance **burgher houses** sandwiched between houses of a later period. In the southern part of the Palešovo námestie square stands the Roman-Catholic **Birth of the Virgin Mary church**. Its contemporary Classicist form originated in 1829 on the site of a burnt down Gothic parsonage church of 1258. The most valuable items in

its interior include the Gothic wing altar of St. Barbora from around 1500 and Gothic baptistery made by Ján Weygel in the second half of the 15ᵗʰ century. The Baroque compound consisting of the **monastery of Charitable Brothers** and the **St. John of God church** originated in the years 1653-1658 by rebuilding of a medieval town spital of 1327 once administered by the Augustians. The Classicist Evangelical **church** was built in the years 1799-1808. In Mariánske square stands an originally Renaissance building of the old **town hall** from 1546 and the Baroque **Lady's Pillar** of 1726.

The **Town Monument Reserve of Spišská Kapitula** (The Spiš Chapter), extends on the hill west of Spišské Podhradie, administratively belonging to the community. It acquired the position of the ecclesiastical centre of the Spiš region way back in the 12ᵗʰ century. The religious setting evokes in the visitor a comparison of this small ecclesiastical townlet situated below the Spiš Castle to the Holy See. The

provostship in Kapitula initiated its activity in 1198 and shortly after also the Chapter was established here. Its destruction by the Tartars was soon followed by new construction and in 1245 the building of the cathedral was started and four years later the provost made use of the ruler's consent to build the provost palace. Since 1647 it was occupied by the Jesuits who built a monastery and gymnasium (secondary school) on the plot of the former workhouse. The gymnasium eventually moved together with Jesuits to Levoča in 1673. The provosts of Kapitula made a great effort to promote the provostship to a bishopric but always ran into strong resistance from the Ostrigom Archbishopric. Only in 1776 did Spišská Kapitula finally acquire the status of a bishopric the status of which it has kept until today.

The most important building of Spišská Kapitula is the Late-Romanesque **St. Martin's Cathedral**. It acquired its massive form of a three-nave building with two towers in the years between 1245-

1275. In 1382 a Corpus Christi chapel was added to it, though it was replaced by the contemporary one in the years 1488-1493. This **chapel of the Zápoľský family** imitates the French chapel of Saint Chapelle. Baroque traits were erased by reconstruction in the years 1873-1889 in an attempt to give it a medieval character in line with the taste of the period of Romanticism. In front of the Cathedral stands the **statue of St. Ján Nepomucký** built in 1732. The **Bishop's Palace** was built together with the Cathedral as a provost's palace, and from 1281 was the object of repeated Renaissance and Baroque reconstruction. Part of the palace is also a chapel. In the past there used to be a French park around the palace and its entrance was at the **Hodinová veža** (The Clock Tower) from 1739. On the grounds of a former inn stands the building of the former **seminary** from 1647. The original building of the Je-

suit monastery was rebuilt in Classicist style for the needs of the seminary between 1810-1815. In the eastern part of the Spiš Chapter on narrow Gothic plots the **Chapters** of the canonists are accessible only by one narrow lane. The **fortification** of this ecclesiastical townlet, with two entrance gates, was built in the 14th century and several times rebuilt. Its contemporary shape with two Late-Renaissance gates is from the second half of the 17th century, when Old Hungary was threatened by the Ottoman Empire. Fortunately, Spiš was spared the ignominy of Turkish occupation and other significant military assaults.

The eastern horizon of Spišské Podhradie is occupied by **Spiš Castle** standing on the land administered by the community of Žehra situated at the opposite side of the hill. As a National Cultural Monument Spiš Castle, with its area of more than 4 ha, and partially in ruins, is one of the largest castle compounds in Central Europe. Construction of the medieval castle on a travertine hill dates back to the

Left: Spiš Castle
Right: The Holy Spirit church in Žehra

beginning of the 12th century. The oldest written reference to the castle dates to 1120. At the beginning it was a boundary fort placed at the northern frontier of an Early Feudal Old Hungarian state. Afterwards it became the seat of the head of the Spiš region for many centuries. In the second half of the 15th century the reconstruction of the castle fell upon its new owner Štefan Zápoľský whose intention was to remake it into a stately aristocratic residence. The last building works at the Upper Castle were made under the orders of the Thurzos' and the Csákys'. In 1780 the castle compound was destroyed by fire and the proud Spiš Castle gradually fell into ruin. The total decay of the castle was prevented only through the intervention of conservationists who in 1970 got down to the difficult job of preserving the walls and palaces threatened by the instability of its rocky base. Their enormous effort was rewarded when Spiš Castle was included in the **UNESCO list of monuments** belonging **to the world cultural heritage** in 1993. At present there are

museum collections of the **Spišské múzeum** placed in the castle documenting its history, along with medieval arms and feudal jurisdiction.

The landscape around the community of Spišské Podhradie can be seen comfortably by using the **instructive footpath Sivá Brada – Dreveník**, which has eight information boards along its route apprising the visitor about the travertine hills and the significant natural phenomenon of this part of the region. Its length is 14.5 km. The footpath starts at a mineral water spring in **Sivá Brada**, where drivers travelling by car along the main road from Poprad to Prešov frequently prefer to stop. At the top of a low travertine hill stands a **pilgrim's chapel** of 1675.

South of Sivá Brada is the the community **BALDOVCE**. The water of the local mineral spring is filled in bottles and sold as a favourite table water called *Baldovská*. The instructive footpath heads eastward from Sivá brada towards the nature monument of **Jazierko na pažiti**, also a "living"

National Cultural Monuments. A simple single-nave building with a square presbytery has kept its original Early-Gothic form until the present time. The interior of the ancient church contains unique medieval **wall paintings** originating in different stages since the second half of the 13th century to the end of the 15th. The temple paintings in Žehrovce are remarkable for their artistic quality and unusual thematic diversity. They depict various Biblical stories and legends of the saints. The main altar is Early-Baroque dated 1656.

The community of **BIJACOVCE** also deserves the attention of the visitor to the southern part of Spiš. There is a valuable Romanesque **rotunda** and a large Rococo-Classicist **manor house** built by the Csákys', after Spiš Castle was burned down in 1780. The Roman-Catholic **church** standing beside the rotunda was built in 1260. Its interior is decorated by wonderful **wall paintings** from the 14th century. Experts classify them among the most beautiful specimens of the Gothic fine arts era in Slovakia.

The district town **GELNICA** (population 6,400) lies in the lower part of the Hnilecká dolina valley. Arrival of German colonists helped to Gelnica to develop from an old Slav village into a medieval town, which from the very beginning of its existence dominated this part of the Spiš region. The colonists were mostly miners. The town around the castle was promoted to the free royal mining town by king Sigismond. A number of workshops for production of iron ware with about two hundred blacksmiths worked in the town and its environs in the 19th century. The decay of Gelnica in the second half of the 19th century was largely caused by the exhaustion of the local ores and also the shift of the main developmental axis to the newly built railway line, which unfortunately avoided the valley of Hnilec. The urban buildings of the contemporary Gelnica skirt the rests of medieval **Gelnický hrad** Castle. The central square originated close to the road connecting the centre of the Spiš region and Smolník. The originally Early-Gothic **church of Assump-**

travertine hill. The nearby **St. John Chapel** of 1776 offers a magnificent view of the Chapter and the Spiš Castle. The path then passes by the walls of the Spiš Chapter and beyond Spišské Podhradie. It ascends to Spiš Castle standing on the highest travertine hill. The largest travertine form in Slovakia is the mountain **Dreveník** (609 m) above the community Žehra, which entered in the list of nature reserves in 1953. The thickness of its travertine reaches in places as much as 100 m. Travertine are subject to karstification and it is the reason why the karst phenomena – sinkholes, dolines, fissures and small caves occur here. The instructive footpath carries on along to the Baroque-Classicist **manor house** in **HODKOVCE** from the 17th century where it eventually ends.

The community of **ŽEHRA** is known for its precious local Roman-Catholic **Holy Spirit church** included in the list of

Left: Church in Smolník
Right: Square in Nálepkovo

tion of the Virgin Mary from the 13th century acquired its contemporary appearance in the Baroque style in 1769. The Evangelical **church** was built in 1787. In the building of the former town hall with a Baroque tower, which was built in the 18th century on the site of houses from time of the Renaissance, shelters today **Banícke múzeum** (The Mining Museum).

The southernmost situated community of Spiš, **SMOLNÍK**, hidden in the shadows of forested mountain ridges of the Volovské vrchy Mts., developed quickly above all due to the rich deposits of copper and silver ore. The mining village of German colonists was promoted to a free mining town in 1327 and immediately after the town joined the association of the Spiš mining towns, Smolník reached the peak of development in the 18th century. In 1754 the mining school was opened and Smolník was catching up with the much richer and proud town of Banská Štiavnica. Extraction of ores in the valley of Smolník intensified and consequently the capacity of the local metallurgical plants became short. It was the reason why in the village **SMOLNÍCKA HUTA** a modern copper processing plant was opened and equipped with new technology. The results of the 1785 census prove that Smolník was then the biggest town of Spiš county. Prosperous town had 915 houses and population 6,022. Its remote location and exhaustion of the mineral deposits though, were the causes of its decay in the 19th century. Today Smolník is an attractive tourist village with numerous cultural and historical monuments. There are the buildings dating to the most prosperous time, i.e. 18th century. They are the Roman-Catholic **church of St. Catherine of Alexandria**, the **town hall**, several **mining** and **burger houses** and the building of the **Mining Chamber**.

The mining village **ŠVEDLÁR**, founded in the 14th century on the left bank of the river Hnilec is squeezed between two dominating mountains of the Volovské vrchy Mts. It thrived on the production of copper in the 17th and 18th centuries. Remarkable in the village is the Roman-Catholic

church of St. Margita Antioch from the second half of the 14th century with a precious organ. The log roofed bridge over the river Hnilec is from the 19th century.

In the centre of the upper part of the Hnilecká dolina valley is the village **NÁLEPKOVO**. The medieval serf town Vondrišel, today Nálepkovo was developing until the end of the 15th century uninhibited thanks to abundance of iron and copper ore. Out of what was left let us mention the former Late-Baroque **town hall** from the end of the 18th century and two **churches** which were reconstructed and their original Baroque style was changed.

The main road climbs up the valley of Železný potok to small mining village **HNILČÍK**, which originated by joining three formerly independent villages. Beyond the point, where the valley tapers between Veľká Knola (1,266 m) and Babiná (1,277 m) is the village **MLYNKY** which originated by joining several hamlets in one. Today Mlynky is a favourite tourist centre open all the year round.

CENTRAL SPIŠ
(dial: 052-)

Information
– **Popradská informačná agentúra**, Nám. sv. Egídia 114, Poprad, ☎ 16186, 7721700, fax 7721394, infopp@pp.psg.sk, www.poprad.sk, **Kežmarské informačné centrum**, Hlavné nám. 46, Kežmarok, ☎/fax 4524047, infokk@sinet.sk, www.kezmarok.net

Museums
– **Podtatranské múzeum**, Vajanského 72/4, Poprad, ☎ 7721924, 7721868, **Múzeum**, Sobotské nám., Poprad-Spišská Sobota, ☎ 7721323, **Múzeum dopravy**, Mlynica, ☎ 7796567, **Múzeum – Kežmarský hrad**, Hradné nám. 42, Kežmarok, ☎ 4522618, **Múzeum J. M. Petzvala**, Petzvalova 3, Spišská Belá, ☎ 4591307, **Slovenská národná galéria – kaštieľ**, Medňanského 25, Spišská Belá-Strážky, ☎ 4581152

Galleries
– **Tatranská galéria**, Alžbetina 30, Poprad, ☎ 7721968, **Dom fotografie**, Nám. sv. Egídia 44, Poprad, ☎ 7723818, **Expozícia meštianskej bytovej kultúry**, Hlavné nám. 55, Kežmarok, ☎ 4522906, **Výstavná sieň Barónka**, Hlavné nám. 46, Kežmarok, ☎ 4523170

Hotels
– **POPRAD***, Partizánska 18, Poprad, ☎ 7721260, **SATEL***, Mnoheľova 826/5, Poprad, ☎ 7161111, **GERLACH***, Hviezdoslavova 2, Poprad, ☎ 7721945, **GARNI***, Karpatská 11, Poprad, ☎ 7763877, **MLADOSŤ***, Jilemnického 31, Svit, ☎ 7756641, **CLUB***, Dr. Alexandra 24, Kežmarok, ☎ 4524051-2, **HP**, Petzvalova 8, Spišská Belá, ☎ 4591338

Restaurants
– **EGÍDIUS**, Mnoheľova 18, Poprad, ☎ 7722898, **POD VEŽOU**, Nám. sv. Egídia 25, Poprad, ☎ 7726354, **SABATO**, Sobotské nám. 6, Poprad, ☎ 7769580, **U TROCH APOŠTOLOV**, Hlavné nám. 9, Kežmarok, ☎ 4523272, **KEŽMARSKÁ REŠTAURÁCIA**, Hradné nám. 33, Kežmarok, ☎ 4522933

NORTHERN SPIŠ
(dial: 052-)

Information
– **Informačné centrum mesta Stará Ľubovňa**, Nám. sv. Mikuláša 12, Stará Ľubovňa, ☎ 4231713, fax 4323033, mesto@sl.sinet.sk

Museums
– **Múzeum**, Ľubovniansky hrad, Stará Ľubovňa, ☎ 4322422, **Skanzen ľudovej architektúry**, Stará Ľubovňa, ☎ 4323982, **Múzeum**, Červený Kláštor, ☎ 4822955

Galleries
– **Provinčný dom**, Nám. sv. Mikuláša 12, Stará Ľubovňa, ☎ 4321413

Hotels
– **ĽUBOVŇA***, Ľubovnianske kúpele, Stará Ľubovňa, ☎ 4321751, **TRAVERTÍN***, Vyšné Ružbachy 48, ☎ 4398800, **KRÁTER***, Vyšné Ružbachy 243, ☎ 4398140, **CYPRIÁN***, 1. mája 302, Spišská Stará Ves, ☎ 4822342

Restaurants
– **GURMEN**, Nám. sv. Mikuláša 1, Stará Ľubovňa, ☎ 4281801, **U JELEŇA**, Nám. sv. Mikuláša 22, Stará Ľubovňa, ☎ 4321680, **EXKLUZÍV**, Letná 6, Stará Ľubovňa, ☎ 4321189

SOUTHERN SPIŠ
(dial: 053-)

Information
– **Turistické informačné centrum**, Letná 49, Spišská Nová Ves, ☎ 16186, 4298293, fax 4428292, brantner@spisnet.sk, www.slovenskyraj.sk, **Kultúrno-informačné centrum**, Nám. Majstra Pavla 58, Levoča, ☎ 16188, ☎/fax 4513763, tiklevoc@nextra.sk, www.levoca.sk, **Turistická informačná kancelária**, Hlavná 3, Gelnica, ☎/fax 4823001

Museums
– **Vlastivedné múzeum**, Provinčný dom, Letná 50, Spišská Nová Ves, ☎ 4423757, **Múzeum špeciálneho školstva**, Nám. Majstra Pavla 28, Levoča, ☎ 4512863, **Spišské múzeum**, Nám. Majstra Pavla 40, Levoča, ☎ 4512786, 4541336, **Vlastivedné múzeum**, Markušovce, ☎ 4498212, **Banícke múzeum**, Banícke nám., Gelnica, ☎ 4821468

Galleries
– **Galéria umelcov Spiša**, Zimná 47, Spišská Nová Ves, ☎ 4464259

Hotels
– **METROPOL***, Štefánikovo nám. 2, Spišská Nová Ves, ☎ 4422241, **ČINGOV***, Hradisko 8, Smižany, ☎ 4433663, **FLÓRA***, Čingov, Smižany, ☎ 4491131, **ARKÁDA***, Nám. Majstra Pavla 26, Levoča, ☎ 4512372, **BARBAKAN***, Košická 15, Levoča, ☎ 4513608, **SATEL***, Nám. Majstra Pavla 55, Levoča, ☎ 4512943, **RUNA****, Banícke nám. 6, Gelnica, ☎ 4821935

Restaurants
– **SONÁTA**, Radničné nám. 4, Spišská Nová Ves, ☎ 4428370, **RUDOLF**, Štefánikovo nám. 4, Spišská Nová Ves, ☎ 4425683, **BIELA PANI**, Nám. Majstra Pavla 36, Levoča, ☎ 4511586, **U JANUSA**, Kláštorská 22, Levoča, ☎ 4514592, **TATRAN**, Hlavná 60, Gelnica, ☎ 4822909

GEMER

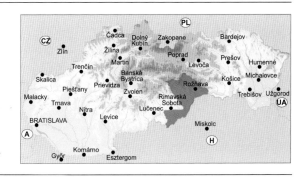

Eastern Gemer

Northern Gemer

Western Gemer

Southern Gemer

The territory of Gemer lies in the south of central Slovakia. The frontier between Hungary and Slovakia separates the southern (much smaller part) of the former Gemer County. The territory of this region is now covered by two districts out of which the district of Revúca is administered by the region of Banská Bystrica and district of Rožňava is part of region of Košice. The western border of the historical region of Gemer traces that of district

Revúca. The northern border coincides with the massive main ridge of the Volovské vrchy Mts. which separates Gemer from Spiš. Eastern border of our territory runs through the eastern edge of the Horný vrch plateau and the Slovak-Hungarian state frontier coincides with the southern edge of Gemer.

Unique natural assets of Gemer inspire the desire to know and see them. Part of the Nature Reserve of Slovenský

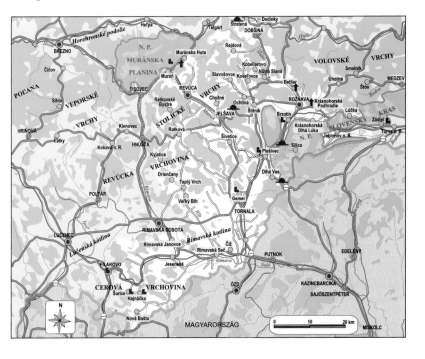

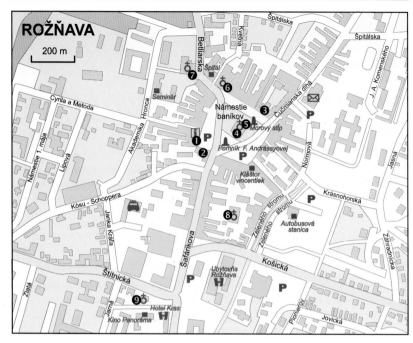

raj Mts. lies in the north of Gemer and neighbours with the National park of Muránska planina with uncountable threatened plant and animal species and unique karstic relief. The National Park of Slovenský kras situated in the southern and south-eastern parts of Gemer was designated in 2002. It is also included into the world network of biosphere reserves. Caves and abysses of the karst are inscribed in the UNESCO List of Natural Heritage.

Eastern Gemer

The largest town and natural centre of Gemer and simultaneously the starting point for trips to the Slovenský kras karst is **ROŽŇAVA** (population 19,250). It is situated on the bank of Slaná river in the small Rožňavská kotlina basin. The name of the town derives from the word for roses, which have always grown on sunny

Right: The town tower in Rožňava

southern slopes below the mountain Rákoš. Rose is also part of the coat of arms of Rožňava along with mining tools. The settlement *Rosnoubana* was first mentioned in the historical document from 1291, when King of Kingdom of Hungary, Ondrej III donated the settlement with its environs to the Archbishopric of Esztergom. Rožňava obtained the first privileges in 1340, which were followed by statutes of town in 1340, when it became the free mining borough.

History of Rožňava was always connected with **mining**. The best time of its development were the 14th and 15th centuries when iron, copper, and antimony, including precious metals like silver and gold were extracted from the ores in the town and its environs. The dramatic development of mining faded gradually from the mid-16th century as the Turks, who eventually sacked the town in 1555, threatened it.

The town built its fortifications with four gates at the end of the 16th century.

Crafts replaced mining in the 17th century. The town, where commerce and crafts dominated in the 18th century thrived above all on wool cloth production, tannery and fur-making. Historical milestone in life of its population was the establishment of the Roman Catholic bishopric in 1776, which assumed the function of the Archbishopric of Esztergom. Ranking of the town changed and Rožňava became the free bishop borough with lively economic activities.

The sightseeing walk around the town normally starts at the square-shaped **Námestie baníkov** square. This spacious part of the town was formed in the second half of the 13th century. Four roads start in the square, which once headed to the four town gates. When the Turks destroyed the outer fortifications in 1556, the square acquired its own gates which were closed in time of threat. **Burgher houses** on the square were built above the original pits of the medieval gold mines. The oldest surviving house is from the period around 1500. The **town hall ❶** from 1711 stands on the western side of the square. Another floor was added to this originally two-storied house and its facade reconstructed in the Neo-Classicist style in the 19th century. In the south-western corner of the square is the building of the former mining **chamber ❷** from the 17th century where at the turn of the years 1706-1707 the land council had its session. The mint also seated here in the same period. In the north-eastern part of the square is the Baroque-Classicist **Bishop's residence ❸** built in the years 1776-1778.

The dominant of the square and symbol of the whole town is the Late Renaissance **town tower ❹** standing in the middle of the square. It was built in the years 1643-1654 next to the original town hall, which disappeared and was later replaced by the Jesuit church. The tower was opened to public after a thorough reconstruction in the 1990's. Its terrace offers a nice panoramic view of the town and its environs. In the staircase of the tower an

exhibition instructing about the history of the tower and the town is installed. On the eastern side below the tower small shops survive which have been an interesting architectural element in the central part of the square since the Middle Ages. On the northern side of the tower is the originally Jesuit **church of St. František Xaverský ❺**. It is the Baroque building from 1658-1687 built by Jesuits in the centre of the square on the site of the old town hall and Protestant school. The Franciscan **church of St. Ann ❻** from the mid-18th century and the former Franciscan monastery from 1733 which now shelters the district archive stand on the north-western end of the square.

The most valuable sacral building of the town is the Catholic **church of Ascension of the Virgin Mary ❼**, which was originally a parish church. It is the bishop cathedral since 1776. It is the Gothic building from the beginning of the 14th century, which was finished in 1403. The Bakócz chapel was added to it during

reconstruction made at the turn of the 15th and 16th centuries. In the period when the bishopric was established in Rožňava the famous architect J. Mayer, native of Rožňava built the belfry here. In the interior of the church is the valuable painting of St. Ann from 1513. In the background of the picture the mining activities are represented and it is supposed that its author belonged to the group of artists around Majster Pavol of Levoča.

South of the square in the row of houses stands the Evangelical **church ➑** from the end of the 18th century. Pursuing the Toleration Patent of King Joseph II it had to be situated outside the square. This Classicist Toleration church lacking tower was built to design of J. Mayer. In its interior the Classicist altar with the relief of the Last Supper and Resurrection by J. Gode dominate. Further in south of square next to the Panorama cinema tow-

Left: Churches of Rožňava
Right: The manor house in Betliar

ers the Reformed **church ➒** from 1905. It is a brick building in the Art Nouveau style with Neo-Gothic elements designed by F. Weninger of Budapest. The building of **Banícke múzeum** or the Mining Museum from 1910 standing on the Šafárikova ulica St. is also in the Art Nouveau style. It houses the standing exposition dedicated to history of local mining and smelting. North of the square is **Calvary** from the mid-18th century with a chapel and the stops of the Way of Cross. **Observatory** is situated below the Calvary and offers the possibility to observe the Moon and other planets. Visitors to the town also like to stop at the **Gallery of Fine Arts** standing in the square.

Five kilometres north-west of Rožňava, in the valley of the Slaná river is the village **BETLIAR** often visited by tourists for its two-storied **manor house** surrounded by a wonderful English park. The area of the **park** (81 hectares) makes it one of the largest in Slovakia. The manor house inhabited by the noble family of Andrássy was built in the valley of the Betliarsky potok brook below the slopes of the Volovské vrchy Mts. on the site of the original Bebek castle from the 15th century. Part of material of this castle was used for building the Renaissance-Baroque single-storied building of manor house in the 17th-18th centuries. The appearance of the manor house as we know it now is from the end of the 19th century. One of the most remarkable things about the manor house is its library. Leopold Andrássy founded it in 1790. Furniture and interior of the library is from the same time. The library contains more than 20 thousand (some sources quote 30 thousand) volumes of theological, historical, geographical and philosophical literature of the 15th to 19th centuries, written in 15 different languages. The Andrássy family inhabited the manor house until 1945. It was nationalised after the Second World War but it conserves its original furniture and was converted to the **museum of dwelling culture**.

Rožňava is also the natural starting point for trips into its environs, including the **National Park of Slovenský kras**, the largest karstic area in Europe (440 square kilometres) with the densest concentration of underground forms (there is about 400 caves and abysses). Twelve of them are inscribed in the UNESCO List of the World Cultural and Natural Heritage. The most important and accessible caves lying south of Rožňava are the **Gombasecká jaskyňa** and **Domica** caves. Gombasecká jaskyňa was opened to public in 1955 and its total length is 285 m. Speleotherapy or therapy in cave was started in this cave for the first time in Slovakia in 1968 and respiratory diseases are successfully treated here since then. Green-marked hiking path leads around the Gombasecká jaskyňa cave. It heads eastward throughout the Silická planina plateau to Hrušov and westward to **PLEŠIVEC**. Among the monuments of the settlement is the **Plešivec** Castle located not far from the reformed church. The Castle was built around 1320 by the family of Bebek. Originally it was the water castle supervising toll collection next to the passage over the river. The ruins are all that is left of the Castle. The most valuable sacral monument is the local Reformed **church**, National Cultural Monument. The environs of the village are ideal for trips. Plešivec is also the starting point of the trips to three plateaux, which surround it. The blue-marked trail heads northward to the Plešivecká planina plateau and eastward to the Silická planina plateau. The green-marked trail connects the planina Koniar plateau with the Gombasecká jaskyňa cave and the Silická planina plateau.

South-east of Plešivec lies the village **DLHÁ VES**. Its greatest natural asset and attractiveness of national significance is the **Domica** cave, the National Nature Monument. It is situated in the south-western part of the Slovenský kras karst on the Silická planina plateau and its entrance is 339 m above sea level and 1,315 m of its length (including 140 m long un-

dergeround stream called Styx) is accessible to public since 1932. Domica is famous for spacious domes (in one of them the film based in folk fairy tale Salt More Precious than Gold was made). The cave boasts rich dripstone ornamentation, with cascaded lakes, onion-shaped stalactites and pagoda-shaped stalagmites. The interesting thing about this cave is that there live 16 different species of bats. This cave is one in the system of caves connected with the Baradla cave in the territory of Hungary. The whole cave system is about 25 km long and only a quarter of it falls in the territory of Slovakia. The **Instructive path Domica and its environs** leads around the cave. It is 4.5 km long and the elevation difference is 114 m.

The symbol of the village **KRÁSNO-HORSKÉ PODHRADIE** situated east of Rožňava is the **Krásna Hôrka** Castle, the National Cultural Monument. It stands on top of the conspicuous denuded mountain, which dominates in the Rožňavská kotlina basin. The original Gothic castle was built around 1320. The courtyard of

the upper castle of a rather small castle with triangle-shaped ground plan still survives. The castle acquired fortifications in time of the Turkish threat. The fortifications with three canon bastions and cannon terrace were made in the Renaissance style. It was when the interior of the castle was also made more habitable and when it acquired the form as we know it now. Three generations of the Andrássy family tried to obtain the castle and finally succeeded in 1642. In 1735 the area in front of the castle gates was adapted and the small Baroque **chapel of St. John Nepomuk** was built there. In the second half of the 18th century one of the bastions was rebuilt into the Baroque-Classicist **chapel of Nativity of the Virgin Mary**. There is the painting of black **Madonna** also referred to as the Virgin Mary of Krásna hôrka, the target of processions, on the main altar of the chapel. The castle houses the exhibition of the **Museum of Betliar** which illustrates the history and development of the castle, way of life of nobles in the past. The main attraction

though is the embalmed body of Sophia Andrássy-Serédy lying in the chapel. Writer Mór Jókai used the motif of the mummy in his novel *The White Lady of Levoča*. By the end of the 20th century an imitation of the medieval park was made next to the castle, where "the castle games" are staged every year.

East of the village by the road to Košice stands **Mausoleum of Andrássy** family finished in 1904. It is now one of the most valuable Art Nouveau buildings in Slovakia. The exterior of the building is made to the motifs of Egyptian and Byzantine architectures. Above the portal is the coat of arms of Andrássy's. In the interior two sarcophaguses with relieved portray of Františka Hablawcová and Dionýz Andrássy dominate. The **art gallery of the Andrássy's**, Art Nouveau building from 1908 decorated by pseudo-Renaissance relieves is also one of the monuments of this family. It has been opened to public recently.

The landmark of the administrative territory of our southernmost situated village **KRÁSNOHORSKÁ DLHÁ LÚKA** is the **Krásnohorská jaskyňa** cave, National Nature Monument. It was discovered comparatively recently (1964) by the potholers of Rožňava led by Š. Roda. The cave is 1,000 m long and in its rear part widens into several pot holes. Small groups of visitors led by a guide are allowed to enter the cave. The sightseeing route ends at **Kvapeľ rožňavských jaskyniarov** (The Dripstone of Potholers of Rožňava) which is a stalagmite 32.6 m tall, its base is 12 m wide. It is inscribed in the Guinness Book of Records as the largest in the world.

Krásnohorská Dlhá Lúka lies below the steep slopes of the **Silická planina** plateau, the most extensive karstic plateau in Slovakia. It stretches on an area of about 150 square kilometres and it is literally sprinkled with numerous deep sinkholes and lapies fields. The edges of the plateau end in steep slopes in some cases more than 400 m high and coated by karstic forests, Inside the plateau, in contrast, are deforested parts,

which provide wonderful views. Several deep abysses (Brázda, Silická ľadnica Veľká Bikfa, Veľký a Malý Žomboj) and caves (Domica, Gombasecká, Ardovská, Krásnohorská, and Silická) enhance the dramatic nature of the landscape.

The most popular spot in the easternmost part of the Slovenský kras karst is the National Nature Reserve of **Zádielská tiesňava** gorge, which is protected territory from 1954. Its area is 214.7 hectares. The length of the gorge is 2,200 m, it is 300 m deep and the narrowest stretches on its bottom are only 10 m wide. On its way through the narrow the brook falls from the altitude above sea level of 475 m to 270 m. Originally the main road connecting Košice and the Rožňavská kotlina basin led along the bottom of the narrow and a castle with bulky fortifications stood above it on the edge of the Zádielská

Left: Domica. Krásna Hôrka Castle. Castle Museum. Environs of Silická ľadnica Right: Krásnohorská jaskyňa cave

planina plateau. In remote past the **Zádielske hradisko** fort with an area of 100 hectares was one of the largest in the territory of Slovakia. Now only the remains of the northern rampart oriented perpendicularly to the eastern edge of the narrow exist. The 230 m long **Instruction path of Zádielská tiesňava** cuts the territory of the Nature Reserve.

However, the most important cultural monument of wide environs of the eastern part of Gemer are the **ruins** of the medieval fortified church from the 13th century standing above the village **LÚČKA**. The locals referred to the church as the "Hussite" church because Jiskra's troops seated in it. Its fortifications were built in the first half of the 15th century along with observation tower, which also served as a bellfry. Part of the walls of the church and a reduced fortifying wall with fragments of the tower is all that survived.

Left: Dobšiná
Right: Dobšinská ľadová jaskyňa cave

Northern Gemer

The centre of northern Gemer is the historical town of **DOBŠINÁ** (population 4,900). As a mining settlement, Dobšiná was first settled by Germans. The most valuable local product was copper extracted in the sites on the Zemberg Mt. Apart from copper, also iron, gold and silver were mined here. The Turks destroyed the town in the years 1582 and 1584. Fresh colonists from different parts of eastern and northern Slovakia, mostly miners, renewed it. The first blast furnace in Slovakia was built in Dobšiná in 1680. Cobalt was also extracted from the ores at the end of the 18th century, and the amount of cobalt mined here was then the greatest in the world. Mining activity gradually faded away towards the end of the 19th century and its past glory did no revive in the 20th century either. The centre of the town consists of the rectangular **square** skirted by prevailingly historic buildings, among them **burgher**

houses from the 19th century in the Classicist and Late Classicist styles. The most conspicuous of them is the Neo-Renaissance building of **town hall** finished in 1870. At the upper end of the square is the architectural dominant of the town - the Gothic Evangelical parish **church**, originally a single-nave Late Gothic building from 1480. It was built on the site of an older church from the beginning of the 14th century. The church was adapted in 1891 in the Late Gothic style. The second sacral building of the town is the Baroque-Classicist Roman Catholic **church of St. František Xaverský** from 1792. It stands on the site of wooden church and it was reconstructed in the years 1897 and 1960.

Lániho Huta is the settlement, which is part of Dobšiná now. One D. Fischer had the first blast furnace in the Kingdom of Hungary installed here in 1680. Famous swords for the royal army of King Matthias I Corvinus and sables for the revolutionaries of Francis Rákoczi were produced here, for instance. Lániho Huta is now a recreation settlement. The interesting technical structure of the area is the dam of Dobšiná, the first re-pumping water power station in Slovakia.

North of Dobšiná in the basin of the Hnilec river is the small village **STRATENÁ**, centre of tourism of the southern portion of the Slovenský raj Mts. and the starting point of the trips to the Stratenská dolina valley and to the **Dobšinská ľadová jaskyňa** cave. This 1,232 m long and 112 m deep cave with its entrance situated at the sea level altitude of 971 m is one of the largest ice caves in Europe. Except for the Alps, this is the only place in Europe with 110 thousand cubic metres of ice in places thicker than 25 m. The thickest layer of ice amounting to 26.5 m is in Veľká sieň (The Grand Hall) of the cave. The cave is also the lowest situated one in the world in terms of sea level altitude, which enhances its originality. Ice survives in the cave thanks to the form of the cave, which is similar to a

sack. As the cave is situated lower than its entrance, the cold air maintains in its bottom and its temperature never increases above zero. The cave was discovered by the mining engineer I. Ruffini in 1870 and opened to public a year after. It was also the first cave in the Kingdom of Hungary with electric lighting. The length of the sightseeing trail with elevation difference 43 m is 475 m and seeing it takes 45 minutes. The trail leading to the cave is simultaneously the 470 m long **instructive path**.

Not far from Stratená, in the same basin of the Hnilec river is the village **DEDINKY**. It is a typical tourist village lively the whole year round. Thanks to its situation on the shore of the **Palcmanská Maša** water reservoir, fans of water sport and bathing gather here. In winter it becomes a much visited ski resort. Environs of the village are ideal for hiking in summer and for cross-country skiing in winter.

Historic centre of the Štítnik basin, situated further in south is the village

ŠTÍTNIK. The first written reference to the settlement is from 1243. The first mine ever mentioned in the Kingdom of Hungary is the Ditrich iron mine located in the territory of this village. The record on use of water wheel for driving the hammer mill, also primacy in the Kingdom of Hungary, is from 1344. Production of iron developed along with crafts, as documented by the fact that there were 18 furnaces and 19 hammer mills in the area in the years 1804-1806. Among the oldest monuments of Štítnik the National Cultural Monument – Evangelical **church** with the oldest organ in Slovakia dominates. It was originally the Gothic building from the 14th century. The symbol of the past profane power is the **water castle**, or its remains, built on the former swamp in 1432. The castle resisted Turkish raids but was destroyed in the Rákoczi rebellion. Ruins of this castle can be seen. The Rococo-Classicist **palace** standing on the square of Štítnik, once seat of the Concord company trading in iron is also an important monument.

North-west of Štítnik on the bank of the eponymous river is the village **OCHTINÁ**. South-west of the village below the Hrádok Mt. (809 m) is the **Ochtinská aragonitová jaskyňa** (Aragonite Cave of Ochtiná) accessible by blue-marked hiking trail. This cave with aragonite dripstones is the only in central Europe while there are only several of them in the world. Rich and varied aragonite filling in the form of needle, spiral and kidney-shaped forms similar to those of coral occur here in unusually varied mixture of wonderful patterns. Out of the total length of 300 m 230 m are accessible to public since 1972. The originality of the snow-white "bushes" intrigues visitors.

The largest village on the upper reach of the Štítnik river is **SLAVOŠOVCE**, known for production of paper. In 1828 the most popular author of Slovak fairy tales, **Pavol Dobšinský** was born here. He published his life work, collection of 90 **folk Slovak legends and tales** close before his death.

Western Gemer

The largest town and simultaneously the district centre of the western part of Gemer is **REVÚCA** (population 13,450). For several centuries, the locals were involved in production of iron, competing with the adjacent town of Jelšava. In 1808 the first share-holding company producing iron in the Kingdom of Hungary was established in Revúca.

In the second half of the 19th century Revúca became the centre of the Slovak national and cultural life. The building of the first Slovak grammar school – **Slovenské evanjelické gymnázium**, the National Cultural Monument, established on 16 September 1862 commemorates this period. It was the only secondary school where tuition and final exams of all study subjects were given in the Slovak language until 1918. The second building of the school was built in the years 1871-1873 and when it was finished, the Evangelical priest Samo Tomášik consecrated

it. Both buildings were designated National Cultural Monuments in 1991. The older of them now shelters the **museum** with exhibits documenting the history of the school and Revúca in general. **Commemorative rooms** of the first Slovak grammar school were opened to public at the occasion of the 100th anniversary of its foundation in 1962.

Two important sacral buildings survive in the town. The older of them is the Roman Catholic **church of St. Vavrinec**, the Late Gothic building from the second half of the 15th century adapted in 1892. The Classicist Toleration Evangelical **church** was finished in 1785 and the tower was added to it three years later. In its interior the Rococo altar and pulpit for 1784 made by the wood-carver J. Reisiger of Jelšava dominate. Evangelical **parsonage** is also the National Cultural Monument. There is a **tablet** on its facade ded-

Left: Ochtinská aragonitová jaskyňa cave
Right: Revúca

icated to Samuel Reuss and his sons, founders of Slovak ethnology. Profane monuments of Revúca include the Classicist **town hall** from 1819, Cultural Monument and well conserved **burgher houses** from the second half of the 19ᵗʰ century.

Historically important place lying in the lower part of the Muránska dolina valley on the crossroads of the road from Tisovec, Revúca, and Červená skala is the village **MURÁŇ**. The first written reference to the castle in this locality is from 1271. The history of this village is closely related to that of the local castle. The **Muráň** Castle, one of the highest situated castles of Slovakia was built as the royal sentry castle on top of the Cigánka cliff at the height of 935 m in the 13ᵗʰ century. In the first half of the 16ᵗʰ century the castle fell in hands of the robber knight Matthias Baša who was executed in 1549. The castle thrived in time when it was owned by

Maria Széchy, famous for her beauty and referred to as the **Venus of Muráň**. The castle was then luxuriously restored and it became the meeting place of the nobility. It burnt twice in the 18ᵗʰ century and was abandoned. The Muráň Castle is now in ruins with preserved entrance gate and tower. The complex occupies the area of 360x96 m. Its Gothic palace, fragments of walls and several service buildings can be seen here. It is the favourite destination of trippers as it provides wonderful views of wide environs.

The village is an important centre of nature conservation and starting point for trips. The **National Park of Muránska planina** was designated in 1997 for the area of 20,318 hectares. Karstic plateau represents a considerable part of this protected territory, which also offers several valuable natural localities visited by tourists interested in unique natural phenomena. So far 38 karstic springs, more than 50 ponors, 150 caves and 15 abysses have been discovered here.

Left: Muráň
Right: Church in Chyžné. Church frescos

Canyons, rock towers, and rock windows refresh its relief. The world plant endemit, *Daphne arbuscula* also grows here.

The highest situated village of this area is **MURÁNSKA HUTA** lying next to the road from Muráň to Červená skala. In its part, called **Predná hora** stands the former **castle** of Francis I the Coburg, Bulgarian tsar, which is now sanatorium. The Neo-Baroque castle and its park were built at the beginning of the 20th century.

One of the stops of the **Gothic Way** which is the thematic route connecting the former counties of Spiš and Gemer is the highly valuable early Gothic Roman Catholic **church of the Virgin Mary** in the village of **CHYŽNÉ** from the first half of the 14th century, which was adapted in the Baroque style in the 18th century. The ceiling of the church is made from painted panels from 1745. The baptistery has original Gothic windows and at the eastern end of the nave is the Gothic portal. On the inner walls of the baptistery the medieval wall paintings from the second half of the 14th century dominate. The precious Late Gothic main altar from 1508 with a group of statues was made by Majster Pavol of Levoča.

Another important crossroads in the valley of the Muráň river where the roads from Rožňava to Hnúšťa and the road from Muráň to Tornaľa cross, is the town of **JELŠAVA** (population 3,300). In the 19th century deposits of magnesite were discovered and extracted here and the town became the centre of magnesite industry, which declined in the 1990's and the development of the town slowed down.

The dominant of the town is the **Coburg manor house** from the 16th century which was reconstructed in the years 1796-1801 in the Classicist style. It is the three-wing building added to an older Renaissance building from the 16th century. Originally there stood a monastery from the 13th century rebuilt to a castle in the 14th century. The manor house gradually assumed the role of the castle standing above the settlement. Out of the older buildings three Renaissance wings with square corner towers and details of Renaissance windows survive. Sacral monuments of the settlement consist of two churches. The Classicist Evangelical **church** is from 1784. Tower was added to it in 1834. The Classicist Roman Catholic **church of Sts. Peter and Paul the Apostles** was finished in 1838 and it is one of the few two-tower churches in the region of Gemer.

In the valley of Turiec river along the road from Jelšava to Hnúšťa lies the historic centre of the Revúcka vrchovina upland, **RATKOVÁ**. Its square is one of the most beautiful of the Slovak villages. It contains several historical buildings. The two-storied Classicist **house** from 1818 (former Evangelical school) and the Classicist building of the former **town hall** from 1827 are the most remarkable ones.

The village of **TEPLÝ VRCH** is interesting for its eponymous water reservoir. Also the adjacent village of **DRIENČANY** is worth to see for several caves situated in the **Drienčanský kras** karst, two of which were designated Natural Monuments in 1979. North of Drienčany is **KYJATICE**, important archaeological site. North-west

of the village is the archaeological **monument of people of Kyjatice culture** consisting of three burrows and two graves. The monument is the reminder of research of almost 200 graves from 1100 and 700 BC.

Southern Gemer

The largest and simultaneously the only town of southern Gemer is **TORNAĽA** (population 8,150) lying next to the river Slaná. The first written reference to the settlement on the territory of today's Tornaľa is from 1245. The settlement, which developed near it later, was the family seat of the Tornallya's. Tornaľa was an important mail station in the past and administrative centre of extensive agricultural area. It has maintained the farming character up to the present time. It has an interesting Reformed **church** from the 15th

century. Originally the Gothic church it was repeatedly adapted in the 18th and 19th century, its painted wooden ceiling is from 1768. Precious monuments of Tornaľa include two Classicist **curias** from the 19th century, the Roman Catholic **church** from the end of the 19th century and the Evangelical **church** from 1933.

Only 4 kilometres away from Tornaľa on the right bank of the Slaná river is an important site of the early history of the Gemer County, the village **GEMER**. It is one of the oldest in the area and its original administrative centre. The first castle was built here in time of arrival of the old Hungarian tribes to Gemer. At the end of the 14th century it was a royal castle and in the 16th century it was definitely destroyed. Now its site is overgrown by vegetation. One of the most important settlement of the region of Gemer was also **VEĽKÝ BLH** situated in the west. Its dissected relief with deep valleys and castle ruins is interesting for tourists. The first written reference to the castle is from

Left: The manor house in Tornaľa
Right: The Castle hill of Hajnáčka

1323. It was destroyed during the Thököly's and Rákoczi's rebellions. Centres of southern part of the region of Gemer were also the villages **RIMAVSKÉ JANOVCE** and **RIMAVSKÁ SEČ** where churches represent the most important monuments. The most valuable is the Romanesque church of St. John the Baptist from the 12th century in Rimavské Janovce, one of the oldest churches of Gemer. It is the simplified type of the Romanesque Basilica lacking side naves. The originally Gothic Reformed church in Rimavská Seč from 1332 with the Renaissance tower, which was finished in 1556 is also valuable. It was reconstructed in 1791 in the Classicist style.

East of Rimavská Seč lies what is perhaps the best known settlement of southern Gemer. It is **ČÍŽ**. In the past it was a small farming village but discovery of mineral springs changed its character. Iodide-bromine spa of national importance was opened here in 1889. It is indicated for the patients affected by nervous, skin and other chronic inflammatory diseases. Now also the diseases of locomotion and circulatory apparatuses are treated here. The **spa buildings** are from the end of the 19th century and their style imitates that of the Swiss spa architecture.

In the south-western part of Gemer is the village **ŠURICE** with the **Soví hrad** above it. It was designated the Natural Monument. Its area is of 2.8 hectares. Sovi hrad is a basalt vent from the Quaternary era when volcanic activity was fading away in this region. Hiking trail marked in yellow passes through the village and joins later the green-marked trail, which leads to the **Pohanský hrad**. It is also a basalt formation stretching on an area of 68 hectares. It is dissected into numerous, in places 30 m tall, cliffs. On top of one of them stood the fortified Slav site. The locality of Pohanský hrad is one

of the most valuable volcanic high plains in Slovakia.

The centre of the Cerová vrchovina upland is the village **HAJNÁČKA** situated in the narrow valley of the Gortva river. The name Hajnáčka refers to the rock and **castle** standing on top of it. The castle played an important role in the whole county of Gemer. It was royal castle and seat of estate, which owned 15 villages. Although it was fortified it did not resist the attacks of the Turks, which conquered it for a short time in the years 1546 and 1645. Its owners rebuilt it in the 17th century and improved its fortifications. But it burnt in 1703 and fell in decay. Its ruins provide a panoramic view of the environs. **Hajnáčsky hradný vrch** (The Castle hill of Hajnáčka) is the Nature Reserve with an interesting basalt cliff and thermophilous flora. The exposed layers of the top of the volcanic mountain display the Tertiary volcanic processes in the Cerová vrchovina upland. South of the village is the **Kostná dolina** valley. It is one of the richest archaeological localities in bones of the mammals from the Tertiary era in Europe. The village **NOVÁ BAŠTA** is also interesting as it was the centre of this part of Gemer in the past. Its dominant is the originally Romanesque Roman Catholic **church of St. Nicolas the Bishop** from 1397 which lost its original appearance because of repeated reconstruction.

EASTERN GEMER
(dial: 058-)

Information
– **Turistické informačné centrum**, Námestie baníkov 32, Rožňava, ☎ 7328101, fax 7324837, tic@roznava.sk, www.roznava.sk

Museums
– **Banícke múzeum - Historická expozícia**, Šafárikova 31, Rožňava, ☎ 7343710, **Banícke múzeum - Expozícia baníctva a hutníctva Gemera**, Šafárikova 41, Rožňava, ☎ 7344098, **Banícke múzeum - Expozícia prírody Slovenského krasu a priľahlých oblastí**, Šafárikova 43, Rožňava, ☎ 7344098, **Strážna veža**, Nám. baníkov, Rožňava, ☎ 7328101, **Mauzóleum Andrássyovcov**, Krásnohorské Podhradie, ☎ 7322034

Galleries
– **Banícke múzeum - Obrazáreň Andrássyovcov**, Lipová 122, Krásnohorské Podhradie, ☎ 7324258, 7323710, **Banícke múzeum – Expozícia výtvarného umenia**, Nám. baníkov 25, Rožňava, ☎ 7323041

Atractiveness
– **Manor house**, Betliar, ☎ 7983197, **Hrad Krásna Hôrka** Castle, Krásnohorské Podhradie, ☎ 7324769

Caves
– **Domica**, Dlhá Ves, ☎ 7882010, **Gombasecká jaskyňa**, Slavec, ☎ 7882020

Hotels
– **ČIERNY OROL****, Námestie baníkov 17, Rožňava, ☎ 7328186, **KRAS****, Šafárikova 52, Rožňava, ☎ 7324243

Restaurants
– **TRI RUŽE**, Námestie baníkov 32, Rožňava, ☎ 7344954, **ÁTRIUM**, Čučmianska dlhá 30, Rožňava, ☎ 0907/589901, **U ŽELEZNÉHO GRÓFA**, Rožňavská 635, Krásnohorské Podhradie, ☎ 7329980, **KOLIBA SOROŠKA**, Lipovník, ☎ 7971229

NORTHERN GEMER
(dial: 058-)

Information
– **Turistické informačné centrum**, SNP 567, Dobšiná, ☎ 7942159

Atractiveness
– **Evangelical church**, Štítnik, ☎ 7931342, **Evangelical church**, Dobšiná, ☎ 7941305

Caves
– **Dobšinská ľadová jaskyňa**, Stratená, ☎ 7881470, **Ochtinská aragonitová jaskyňa**, Ochtiná, ☎ 4481050

Hotels
– **RUFFÍNY****, Dobšinská Ľadová Jaskyňa, ☎ 7981277, **RAJ**, Dobšinská Maša 73, Dedinky, ☎ 7981213, **PRIEHRADA**, Dedinky 107, ☎ 7981212

Restaurants
– **ĽADOVÁ**, Dobšinská Ľadová Jaskyňa, ☎ 7981242

WESTERN GEMER
(dial: 058-)

Information
– **TRING s.r.o., cestovná agentúra a turisticko-informačná kancelária**, Daxnerova 5, Revúca, ☎ 4422159

Museums
– **Prvé slovenské gymnázium**, Muránska ul., Revúca, ☎ 4421644

Atractiveness
– **Muráň** Castle, Muráň, **Church of the Virgin Mary**, Chyžné, ☎ 4482210

Hotels
– **HRÁDOK*****, Jelšava, ☎ 4483986, 4482714, 4482458, **PYRAMÍDA***, Železničná 19, Revúca, ☎ 4421122

Restaurants
– **ROZKVET**, Jilemnického 97, Revúca, ☎ 4432860, 4426010, **U BOLKA**, Železničná 227, Revúca, ☎ 4423257, **BALATON**, Ormisova 562, Revúca, ☎ 4426043, **ŠARMAN**, Lubeník, ☎ 4493161

SOUTHERN GEMER
(dial: 047-)

Atractiveness
– **Spa Číž**, Číž-kúpele, ☎ 5593133, **Soví hrad**, Šurice, **Pohanský hrad**, Šurice, **The Castle hill of Hajnáčka**, Hajnáčka

Restaurants
– **CARMEN**, Odborárska 1, Tornaľa, ☎ 5523674

MALOHONT

Southern Malohont

Northern Malohont

Malohont is the historical territory stretching along the Rimava river and it is composed of the remains of what was probably the territorial unit owned by the old noble family of Hunt-Poznan. The name of the region, in English Small Hont suggests that it had some links with the adjacent county of Hont situated further in west. Malohont was part of it in the past and it obtained rather generous autonomy only in the end of the 17th centu-

ry. In the late 18th century Malohont joint the County of Gemer and existed as such until 1922.

The present western, northern and eastern borders of Malohont coincide with the administrative border of the district Rimavská Sobota. In the south it borders on the administrative territories of Ožďany and the town of Rimavská Sobota.

Southern Malohont

The administrative and economic centre of Malohont is the town of **RIMAVSKÁ SOBOTA** (population 25,090) situated on the fertile alluvial plain of the Rimava river. *Villa Stefani*, the name derived of King Stephen I was the primeval settlement, which originally existed here. Markets were held here every Saturday and this was why the name Sobota (Saturday) caught on. This name, written as *Rymona Zumbota* was first mentioned in the document from 1270. In the years 1441-1460 the town was occupied by Jan Jiskra of Brandýs whose soldiers built here the fort Sobôtka. The little town was the venue of several important historical events. In the years 1447, 1451, and 1452 the then rivals Ján Jiskra and Ján Hunyady negotiated and later concluded armistice in Rimavská Sobota. Fire destroyed the town in 1506. Two Turkish occupations affected the life of its people in the years 1553-1893 and in 1598-1686. The Turks seated at the Sobôtka fort, which is situated in the eponymous part of town. It was once an independent settlement first men-

tioned as *Zabadfalu* (Free Village) in 1341. After liberation, Rimavská Sobota was property of the Forgách and Koháry families. It became the free royal borough only by the end of the 18th century. In the years 1786-1790 and 1883 -1922 it was the seat of the County Gemer-Malohont.

During the Rebellion of Estates troops of Gabriel Bethlen (1626) and those of Juraj I Rákóczi (1645) camped near Rimavská Sobota. The Russian General Mikhail I. Kutuzov passed one night in Rimavská Sobota on this way back to Russia after the battle at Austerlitz. The people of the town had to take care after about 40 thousand soldiers and eight thousand horses and it certainly was not easy. The General himself expressed his thanks to the locals sending them a special letter. The town preserved its traditions in crafts and trades over the history. Thanks to fertile soil in its environs, agriculture was also an important activity in

Rimavská Sobota, which had about 27 guilds by the end of the 19th century. The traditions of food-processing industry survives - there is sugar refinery, brewery, dairy factory, and the meat-processing plant in the town.

Rimavská Sobota was the centre of education in the past, which was greatly influenced by its prevailingly Protestant population. Society of Scholars, which has positively influenced the development of the town, existed here in the past. The Protestant grammar school opened in Rimavská Sobota in 1853 contributed to the generally advanced level of education in the region. Several important figures of the Slovak or Hungarian science and culture were born or lived in Rimavská Sobota. The local **observatory** (1975) maintains the reputation of the town as centre of education and science. It is focused on observation of meteorites in Slovakia and the secretariat of the Slovak Union of Amateur Astronomers also seats there.

Left: Rimavská Sobota in the 18th century

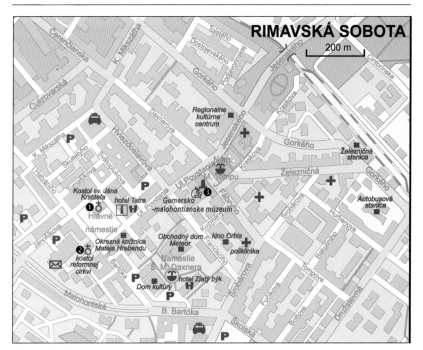

History and important position of the town in the past have left some traces in its architecture. The ground plan of the town is regular, but the town walls and older buildings did not survive. The dominant of its **Hlavné námestie**, the main square, now wonderfully reconstructed, is the Classicist Roman Catholic **church of St. John the Baptist ❶** built in the years 1774-1790 on the site of an old Gothic church, which was owned by Calvinists after Reformation. It was pulled down following the riots of 1771. The church is interesting above all for its Late Baroque interior and ceiling paintings from the end of the 18th century. The building of the Catholic **parsonage** was built in 1772-1775.

The Baroque-Classicist Evangelical **church** was built in the years 1784-1790 as the Toleration church, the tower was added to it in the years 1847-1856. It was adapted in 1898. Calvinist **church ❷** built in 1784 was enlarged by the end of the 19th century and its facade was later changed in the romantic style. Next to its tower is

the burial chapel of sculptor István Ferenczy, his own work. The local synagogue was also one of the important monuments of the town but it was pulled down. The development of Rimavská Sobota at the end of the 18th century and in the 19th century is documented by the Late Baroque building of the former grammar school from 1794, the former County House built in 1798 in the style of French Baroque, the former Classicist town hall from 1801 and the Classicist building of the Redoubt from 1840. All these buildings compose now the Town Monument Reserve.

The **Gemersko-malohontianske múzeum ❸** (The Museum of Gemer and Malohont) seats in the former military barracks and it contains precious collections of artefacts of natural history, ethnology and arts of the region. One of its exhibits is the Egyptian **female mummy**. The local lawyer I. S. Munkácsi donated it to the Museum. He brought it from Egypt. The woman whose name was Tasheritnetiakh lived in the Egyptian town Abusir-El-

Melek in the period of the 21st to 25th Egyptian dynasty (1087-664 BC). Her age (50-70 years) is remarkable for the period when the life expectancy of Egyptians was 40 years in average. The mommy of woman is one of the four Slovakia possesses. Apart from Museum in Rimavská Sobota there is also one mummy deposited in the manor house of Betliar. The Museum of Gemer and Malohont is one of the oldest in Slovakia. It contains more than 82 thousand items in its collections while the historical, archaeological and ethnological artefacts prevail. Historical books comprising more than 32 thousand volumes of old prints constitute part of its wealth.

Rimavská Sobota offers several types of accommodation and plenty opportunities for recreation. The town has its indoor and outdoor swimming pools, stadium

Left: Egyptian mummy in the museum of Rimavská Sobota
Right: Environs of Rimavská Sobota

and other cultural and social facilities. **Kurinec** is one of the favourite destinations of the tourists as it is the recreation area on the shore of the water reservoir situated south of the town. Accommodation and catering facilities, camping, sport grounds, minigolf, boating and fishing make it attractive for holidaymakers and trippers. On the shore of the reservoir is the Nature Reserve of **Kurinecká dubina** with protected oak wood as the example of lowland forests. Red-marked route referred to as the Road of Mária Széchy leads there from the town, and continues westward as far as Fiľakovo.

West of Rimavská Sobota on the road leading to Lučenec is the village **OŽĎANY**. The **castle** in this village is from the beginning of the 14th century. At the first half of the 15th century the troops of Ján Jiskra of Brandýs occupied it and the Imperial army burnt it in 1604. The remains of the castle were used for construction of the Renaissance **manor house** in the mid-17th century and this was rebuilt in the Baroque-Classicist style in the 18th century. Júlia Korponay, the White Lady of Levoča, is buried in its large park. In Ožďany was the seat of the renown Latin Lyceé in the 17th - 19th century, several important figures lived here including the geographer and historian L. Bartholomaeides, botanist J. Fábry, historian S. Kollár, etc. The secular monuments of Ožďany also include the yeoman **curia** from 1800. The Rococo Roman Catholic **church of St. Michael the Archangel** with furniture from the time when it was built (1768-1774) was repaired in the years 1732, 1895, and in the 20th century. The local Reformed **church** in the Neo-Classicist style is from 1825.

The main road from Rimavská Sobota to Tisovec ran through the valley of the Rimava river from the 9th century. It was the main transport route of the region, which connects the majority of the communities until the present. Further in north lying village **VEĽKÉ TERIAKOVCE** is situated next to this road. Among its monuments are the Baroque-Classicist Evangelical

church from 1790 with the Late Baroque altar and the Classicist building of the mill from 1800. But its most important monument situated in the local part **Malé Teriakovce** is the Gothic Evangelical **church** from the 15th century. Its interior, namely its panel ceiling, is very valuable. The oldest panels are from the 16th century. In its ornamentation the Renaissance elements prevail. Other parts of its interior, such as the pulpit and the Renaissance altar from the 17th century are also valuable. The fence of the church is also from the 17th century.

The yellow-marked hiking route leading around Maginhrad to Teplý vrch starts in Veľké Teriakovce. On top of the **Maginhrad Mt.** (430 m) was once the settlement from the Upper Bronze and Hallstadt periods. Later there was a medieval fort, which disappeared in the second half of the 15th century. Nothing remained of it.

The green-marked trail leads from Vyšná Pokoradza to the Maginhrad Mt. and ends in the village **NIŽNÝ SKÁLNIK**. The village was the seat of the **Čitateľská spoločnosť malohontská** (The Reader Society of Malohont) which existed here in the years 1808-1831 and of the **Malohontská učená spoločnosť** (The Society of Scholars of Malohont) in the years 1808-1842. The mission of both Societies was to promote science, administer the local library and to publish books. The historical monuments of Nižný Skálnik include the Classicist Evangelical **church** with the Baroque pulpit and organ from 1767 built on the site of a Gothic church in 1805.

The neighbouring village **VYŠNÝ SKÁLNIK** is known to public above all as the native place of the poet Ján Botto (1829-1881). There is the **commemorative tablet** on his native house. The local House of Culture also contains the **commemorative room of Ján Botto** and his **statue** stands in front of it.

Opposite Vyšný Skálnik, on the right bank of the Rimava river is **HRACHOVO**. It was a little town in the past as there existed the famous grammar school for children of noble families in the 17th and 18th century. There used to be also a castle in the village. It was the fort defending the frontiers against the Turks from the first half of the 15th century. It was pulled down in time of the Rákóczi rebellion. Part of the Late Gothic window of this castle was put into the wall of the Evangelical **church** standing next to it, which was built around 1800 in the Classicist style with Baroque elements. It was reconstructed in the years 1928 and 1946. Its Renaissance altar from 1629, baptistery and epitaphs were moved here from the former wooden Gothic church. The Classicist Roman Catholic **church of the Name of the Virgin Mary** is from 1808. Among secular monuments of the village, the originally Renaissance **manor house** from 1565 restored at the beginning of the 19th century and the Classicist **curia** from 1773 are of interest.

Left: Fields near Hrachovo
Right: Church in Rimavská Baňa

Further in north next to the confluence of the Rimava and Rimavica rivers
lies the village **RIMAVSKÁ BAŇA**, one of
the oldest in the region. On top of the hill
beyond the village stands the Late Romanesque Evangelical **church** from the
13th century, which was rebuilt in the
Gothic style in the 14th and 15th centuries
and restored in 1783. The building is
fenced with the Renaissance fortifications.
The interior of the church, which is the
National Cultural Monument, and part of
the Gothic Road contains very valuable
medieval Gothic **wall paintings** from the
14th century. The painting representing
what is referred to as the Ladislav's Legend can be seen on the wall of the triumphal arch or on the northern side of
the nave. Presumably the Early Gothic
stone baptistery in its interior is from the
time of construction of the church, the
painted panel ceiling is from 1783 and the
valuable Baroque furniture is from the
same year. Rimavská Baňa is the native
place of Juraj Palkovič (1769-1850) poet,

playwright, editor and professor of literature at the Lycée in Bratislava. His native
house burnt and for that reason the **commemorative tablet** dedicated to Palkovič
is situated on the wall of the local municipal office.

Up the stream of the Rimavica river is
the village **LEHOTA NAD RIMAVICOU**
that originated by joining two villages, Rimavica and Rimavská Lehota. The Classicist Evangelical **church** in this village is
from 1797. It was rebuilt in 1864. **Rimavica** is the older part of the village and it
was first mentioned as early as 1298.
Probably the gold miners founded this village. Iron processing workshops existed
here in the 19th century. The Toleration
Baroque-Classicist Evangelical **church**
was built in 1796. In its interior wooden
Baroque oratory from the same time is interesting. More villages, which were originally in the territory of Malohont lye on
the banks of the Rimavica river, they are
Kokava nad Rimavicou, Utekáč, Ďubáko-
vo and Šoltýska and are now part of the

district Poltár and villages Drábsko and Lom nad Rimavicou are administered by the district Brezno.

East of Rimavská Baňa is the village **KRASKOVO**. The most important dominant and the pride of the village is the old Early Gothic Evangelical **church** built on the site of an old church from the 13th century as the archaeological research confirmed. It is one of the National Cultural Monuments and part of the Gothic Road. On the walls of its presbytery and on the northern wall of the nave are the Gothic **wall paintings** from the 14th century. The church was fortified by wall and rebuilt in the 15th century. In 1555 Turks damaged it but it was restored again in the years 1814 and 1906. The paintings including the Ladislav's Legend and the church furniture were restored for the last time in 1985. The Renaissance altar and the pulpit carved in wood from 1668 were made

Left: Church in Kraskovo
Right: Municipal office in Hnúšťa

by the same artisan. The wooden panel ceiling from 1758 with folk paintings was adapted to the preserved fragments of older Renaissance ceiling from 1562. The stone baptistery with Romanesque elements is from the end of the 13th century and the Classicist organ is from 1818. The church was taken over by the Evangelicals after the Reformation. The wooden Renaissance **belfry** from 1657 stands next to the church

RIMAVSKÉ BREZOVO is situated further in north of Rimavská Baňa. The local people were mostly farmers and shepherds in the past. When iron works were established in the village, many villagers started to work as miners and steelworkers. Three hammer mills and smelting plants, which opened somewhat later, also offered additional work opportunities to the people of Rimavské Brezovo. The iron-producing traditions survive and the largest iron-working complex of Slovakia was founded precisely in Rimavské Brezovo. The most valuable his-

torical and cultural monument in the village is the originally Early Gothic Evangelical **church** built by the end of the 13th century and repaired in the years 1646, 1741, and 1827. It was enlarged in 1893. On the walls and the dome of the original presbytery there are valuable Gothic **wall paintings** from the 14th century restored in 1893. The Gothic stone baptistery is also from the 14th century and the Baroque altar and pulpit are from the second half of the 18th century. The church is the National Cultural Monument and part of the Gothic Road. There is also the originally Renaissance **County House** from the 17th century, which was later rebuilt. Today it houses the municipal office.

Northern Malohont

North of Rimavské Brezovo and next to the confluence of the Rimava and Klenovská Rimava rivers is the town **HNÚŠŤA** (population 7,560), the second to largest settlement of Malohont. The primeval community existed here probably in the last phase of the Slav settlement of this region. The medieval village originated by joining two settlements in the 12th or 13th century. The first written reference to it is from 1348. The development of Hnúšťa is connected with ironworks in the 18th century. At the beginning of the 19th century there was one blast furnace, three big and one smaller hammer mills. In 1900 more than half of the locals worked in iron works. In the 19th century also magnesite factory and the mill for processing talc were founded in Hnúšťa. The development of this industry also continued after the Second World War until 1990, when the majority of the local factories were closed under the impact of transformation of the national economy.

The town of Hnúšťa played an important role in the revolutionary years 1848 and 1849 when the local native, poet Ján Francisci, one of the most significant figures of the national revival gathered a troop of Slovak voluntaries. Due to high

concentration of workers the town became the centre of the workers' and later also communist movement. Situation was also aggravated by the fact that in high competition within the Czechoslovakia Republic the ironworks and furnaces were closed and people lost their jobs. After the Vienna Arbitrage Hnúšťa became part of Hungary and the seat of the district. During the Slovak National Uprising in the Second World War the town was one of its centres.

The most important native of Hnúšťa is the already mentioned co-founder of Matica Slovenská and in 1861 the chairman of the Slovak National Assembly in Martin Ján Francisci (1822-1905). Francisci, Š. M. Daxner and M. Bakulíni were the three men, referred to as "Three Falcons" who were imprisoned, sentenced to death, for their participation in the 1848 uprising, but eventually not executed.

The churches of Hnúšťa are its most important cultural and historical monuments. The Classicist Roman Catholic **church of Ascension of the Holy Cross** from 1802 was enlarged and the chapel was added to its western side in 1906. It also contains the Neo-Renaissance **chapel** with a crypt built in 1902. The Classicist Evangelical **church** was built in 1808 and in its interior the pseudo-Classicist altar from 1825 is interesting. The **monument** dedicated to Ján Francisci stands in the park of the Evangelical church, another **monument**, which commemorates the events of the Slovak National Uprising stands on the square and the **tablet** in memory of the railway workers who lost their lives in the Second World War is situated at the railway station.

The old part of the town is **Likier**, situated south of the centre. The first written mention of this settlement is from 1438 when it was property of the Hajnáč Castle. This old part of the town also thrived on iron industry, which was after all the main

Left: Sinec Mt.
Right: Klenovec

driving force of the development in the whole region in the past. The society Rimamuránsko-salgótarjánska spoločnost founded in 1881 supported the development of ironworks in the region and later the biggest ironwork in the Kingdom of Hungary in the 19th century. This joint-venture owned several mining and smelting plants.

The highest situated part of Hnúšťa is **Polom,** which lies in the north-east at the altitude of 694 m, about 7 kilometres away from the centre of the town. The settlement is in fact recreation community. The red-marked road referred to as **Cesta Márie Széchy** (Road of Mária Széchy) passes through it. It follows the old road from 1644, which connects Hnúšťa with Fiľakovský hrad Castle and the Muráň Castle. Hnúšťa represents a convenient salient point for the trips to the mountains of Slovenské rudohorie. The blue-marked trail leads westward to the mountain of **Sinec,** on top of which once stood the anti-Turkish fort. The green-marked trail heads to the north-east and connects Hnúšťa with the recreation area of Brezina.

If you start out of Hnúšťa north-westward up the stream of the Klenovská Rimava river, you will arrive at the typical village of **KLENOVEC**, which apart from its picturesque situation in a wonderful valley is interesting for its arrangement because its individual farmsteads are dispersed on the slopes of the surrounding hills. Klenovec in fact consists of 36 small settlements and farmsteads referred to in the local vernacular as "kolešne". It is an ideal place for holidaymaking in countryside. Klenovec is subject of many folk legends because it was in the local inn where the folk hero, the robber Jánošik, was captured. The Late Renaissance belfry also proves the famous history of Klenovec from the 17th century leaning of the wall of the Classicist Evangelical **church** from 1787. Klenovec was one of the revolutionary centres during the counter-Nazi resistance. The **monument** to the victims of the Uprising stands on the square of the village.

Excellent environment and tourist facilities in the environs of the village include the swimming pool, a hotel, tourist cottage with a ski lift in the settlement Čremoš. There is also a large drinking water reservoir above Klenovec, which is however not available for bathing or water sports. Klenovec serves as the starting base for the trips. The green-marked route heading to the **Klenovský Vepor Mt.** (1,338 m) joins the red-marked trail on its top. The environs of the Klenovský Vepor Mt. are protected as the National Nature Reserve with a varied mosaics of conserved forest vegetational associations. Andesite rocks on its top create a bizarre rocky relief. Below the mountain is the Nature Reserve of **Klenovské Blatá** with unique swamp flora and fauna.

At the end of the main road passing through the region of Malohont in its northernmost part stretches the third important town of this region. It is **TISOVEC** (population 4,200). Its origin dates to the 13th century. Its name, like the majority of local nomenclature, derives from those of tree species (*tis* means the yew tree in English). Tisovec was a serf village until the 16th century. In the mid-16th century it was mentioned as "oppidum" or the little town. The 17th and 18th centuries were the periods when various natural and man-caused disasters and calamities struck the town. Fire damaged part of the town in 1606, plague epidemic reduced its population in 1623 and 1711. In 1682, the town was sacked during the Thököly's uprising. All these events lead to its decay and Tisovec eventually lost its market right and town privileges and won in back only in time of Empress Maria Theresa's reign in 1780. The local people were mostly involved in iron processing There existed furnaces and hammer mill in Tisovec in the 16th century. In 1689 new factory was built here, which produced the arms for the rebels of Francis II Rákóczi who owned it after 1705. A large

Left: Veporské vrchy Mts.
Right: Tisovec

furnace driven by powerful water wheels was constructed in 1782. At the beginning of the 19th century Tisovské Hámre, the new mining settlement was founded near Tisovec, which later merged with the town. The ironworks developed further and in the mid-19th century the blast furnace in Tisovec was the most productive one in the Kingdom. The industry thrived until 1965 when it was moved to Košice. The remains of the two blast furnaces of Tisovec are now technical monuments.

At the end of the 1930's Tisovec was one of the places where the Slovak national life concentrated. Its leader was the Evangelical priest and bishop Pavol Jozeffy who lead the Slovak delegation in Vienna in 1842. The native of Tisovec, Štefan Marko Daxner (1822-1892) was one of the main protagonists of the revolutionary movement in the 19th century. Together with J. Francisci and M. Bakulíni he organised the Slovak voluntary corps during the 1948-1949 revolution. He was condemned to death but not executed. He was also the author of the Memorandum of the Slovak Nation from 1861, organiser of opening of the first Slovak grammar school in Revúca and co-founder of Matica slovenská. The house where he lived bears the **commemorative tablet** and his symbolical grave (he is in fact buried at the National Cemetery in Martin) is in the local cemetery. Samuel Daxner (1856-1949) founded the Slovenský spevokol ensamble of singers in Tisovec in 1877 (the oldest in Slovakia) which is still one of the best in the country. Another important native of Tisovec was the politician and journalist Vladimír Clementis (1902-1952). There is **commemorative tablet** on his native house, which is now **museum**. Tisovec was also one of the centres of the Slovak National Uprising where the military hospital was situated.

The important secular monument of the town is its **town hall,** the Classicist building from 1797, which was reconstructed in the years 1835-1845. The buildings of the municipal **mill** and **sawmill** are now technical monuments. The town has a well-

preserved **parsonage** with chapel from 1774, these originally Baroque structures were adapted in the 20th century. Two churches represent sacral monuments of the town. The Classicist Evangelical **church** was built in the years 1825-1832 on the site of an older church. The Late Classicist Roman Catholic **church of Ascension of the Virgin Mary** was built in 1845 and painted in 1863. On the site of an older disappeared church new Evangelical **church** in the Classicist style of Rimavská Sobota was built to design of architect Michal Martini in the years 1825-1832. Its interior stucco ornamentation, the altar and pulpit are the works of artisan István Ferenczy.

The locality **Rimavská Píla**, which lies between Hnúšťa and Tisovec south of the town centre exists here since the 16th century. It was mentioned in the document from 16th century. The wall of the Evangelical parsonage bears the **commemora-**

Left: The monument of Matej Hrebenda in Hačava
Right: Forests of the Muránska planina plateau

tive tablet of the lady-writer Terézia Vansová who lived and worked here in the years 1882-1911. The collector and promoter of Slovak and Czech literatures, Matej Hrebenda (1796-1880) was also born in Rimavská Píla. He is buried at the Hnúšťa-Hačava cemetery.

Tisovec offers several possibilities of recreation. There is the swimming pool right in the town and the mineral spring Šťavica near the town. The green-marked trail heading to north-east leads to the National Nature Reserve of Šarkanica. The yellow-marked route leaving the town and heading to the west leads to the limestone mountain **Hradová** with remains of **castle** from the 13th century. This castle was conquered by the troops of Ján Jiskra of Brandýs in the 15th century, Turks occupied it in the 16th century and eventually the Imperial army burnt and pulled in down in the end of the 17th century. The National Nature Reserve **Hradová** stretches in the immediate vicinity of the Castle on the area of 127 hectares. Numerous little caves, occurrence of several rare plant and animal species are of interest in this Reserve.

The blue-marked route leading along the main road to Brezno up the stream of the Furanec river passes by several protected territories of the **National Park of Muránska planina**. Above the road there is the National Nature Reserve of **Kášter** on the area of 58 hectares. Natural forest associations are protected here. In its neighbourhood is the Nature Reserve **Nad Furmancom**, important botanical locality with occurrence of relic Tertiary plants. Southwest of this locality is the Nature Reserve of **Suché doly** (257 hectares). It is the karstic territory with plenty sinkholes, springs, lapies fields and caves. It contains the most extensive group of karstic dolines in the Muránska planina plateau and there is also the deepest karstic abyss Michňová (105 m). Another Nature Reserve of **Hlboký jarok** with the meander of the Rejkovský potok brook, a deep gorge and several underground and surface karstic formations spread nearby on the area of the 34 hectares.

SOUTHERN MALOHONT
(dial: 047-)

Information
– **Turistické informačné centrum**, Hlavné nám. 2, Rimavská Sobota, ☎/fax 5623645, tic@rimavskasobota.sk, www.rimavskasobota.sk

Museums
– **Gemersko-malohontianske múzeum**, Nám. M. Tompu 24, Rimavská Sobota, ☎ 5632741

Galleries
– **Mestská galéria**, Hlavné nám. 5, Rimavská Sobota, ☎ 5624351

Atractiveness
– **Church of St. John the Baptist**, Hlavné nám. 29, Rimavská Sobota, ☎ 5631031, **Observatory**, Tomašovská 63, Rimavská Sobota, ☎ 5624709, **Female mummy**, Nám. M. Tompu 24, Rimavská Sobota, ☎ 5632741, **Recreation area of Kurinec**, Rimavská Sobota, ☎ 5631071, **National Nature Reserve Kurinecká dubina**, Rimavská Sobota, **Manor house**, Ožďany, ☎ 5694146, **Evangelical church**, Veľké Teriakovce, ☎ 5688149, **Commemorative room of Ján Botto**, Vyšný Skálnik, ☎ 5695440, **Evangelical church**, Rimavská Baňa, ☎ 5495229, **Evangelical church**, Kraskovo, ☎ 5690105, **Evangelical church**, Rimavské Brezovo, ☎ 5495420, **Evangelical church**, Žip, ☎ 5697285

Hotels
– **ZLATÝ BÝK*****, Nám. Š. M. Daxnera 1, Rimavská Sobota, ☎ 5632032-4, **ASTRA***, Kurinec, Rimavská Sobota, ☎ 5631017, **PENZIÓN**, Okružná 86, Rimavská Sobota, ☎ 5623381, **ORMET**, Teplý Vrch, ☎ 5696278, **DRIEŇOK**, Teplý Vrch, ☎ 5696119, **PENZIÓN POHANSKÝ HRAD**, Nová Bašta 259, ☎ 5691191

Restaurants
– **NATIRS**, Železničná 5, Rimavská Sobota, ☎ 5625775, **PICCOLO**, Cukrovarská 27, Rimavská Sobota, ☎ 5632276, **TAVERNA**, Čerenčianska 22, Rimavská Sobota, ☎ 5623707, **GASTRO**, Hlavné nám. 19, Rimavská Sobota, ☎ 5631952, **GOLDEN PARK**, Mestská záhrada 1909, Rimavská Sobota, ☎ 5622126, **HAM**, Hviezdoslavova 1, Rimavská Sobota, ☎ 5622595, **LAGÚNA**, Hviezdoslavova 1, Rimavská Sobota, ☎ 5627049, **MALOHONTSKÁ REŠTAURÁCIA**, Nám. Š. M. Daxnera 1, Rimavská Sobota, ☎ 5610125, **MOTOREST CIEĽ**, Čierna lúka, Rimavská Sobota, ☎ 5622912, **EURO MOTEL E50**, Košická cesta, Rimavská Sobota, ☎ 5622517

NORTHERN MALOHONT
(dial: 047-)

Information
– **Mestský úrad Tisovec**, Nám. Dr. Clementisa 1, Tisovec, ☎ 5493236

Museums
– **Mestské múzeum**, Nám. Dr. Clementisa 1, Tisovec, ☎ 5493236, **Rodný dom Dr. Vladimíra Clementisa**, Jozefyho 41, Tisovec, ☎ 5493236

Atractiveness
– **Swimming pool**, Klenovec, ☎ 5484302, **Belfry**, Klenovec, **Klenovský Vepor – National Nature Reserve**, Klenovec, **Nature Reserve Klenovské Blatá**, Klenovec, **Municipal mill and sawmill**, Tisovec, **National Nature Reserve Šarkanica**, Tisovec, **Hrad**, Tisovec, **National Nature Reserve Hradová**, Tisovec, **National Nature Reserve Kášter**, Tisovec, **Nature Reserve Nad Furmancom**, Tisovec, **Nature Reserve Suché doly**, Tisovec, **Nature Reserve Hlboký jarok**, Tisovec

Hotels
– **ROBOTNÍCKY DOM****, Hlavná 374, Hnúšťa, ☎ 5422579, **VEPOR**, Nám. Karola Salvu 61, Klenovec, ☎ 5484411, **CSM**, Daxnerova 957, Tisovec, ☎ 5494359

Restaurants
– **KAŠTIEĽ**, Klokočova 280, Hnúšťa, ☎ 5423048, **KOLIBA**, Hlavná ul., Hnúšťa, ☎ 5422040, **HRADOVÁ**, Štefánikova 626, Tisovec, ☎ 5493362, **DOLINA**, Daxnerova 734, Tisovec, ☎ 5494626, **ALSEX**, Muránska 494, Tisovec, ☎ 5494585

KOŠICE AND ITS ENVIRONS

Košice

Environs of Košice

The region of Košice and its environs is situated in the east of Slovakia. Its core is the L-shaped Košická kotlina basin. This fertile and densely populated basin is surrounded by mountain ranges, which offer excellent possibilities of hiking and recreation. Three mountain groups occupy its western end, part of the Slovenské rudohorie Mts. The river Hornád incised deeply into the massive of Čierna hora Mt.

in the north-western part of the region. The bulky and forested ridge of the Volovské vrchy Mts. culminates by its dominant and majestic Kojšovská hoľa Mt. The south-western part of the region is characterised by a special karstic landscape with plateaux of the Slovenský kras Mts. The eastern boundary of the region coincides with the Slanské vrchy Mts. volcanic mountain range from the Tertiary

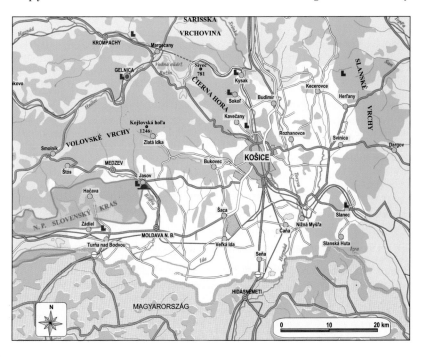

era. Now the mountains constitute a calm mountain barrier coated by forests.

In the past the territory of Košice and its environs was part of historical regions of the then existing Kingdom of Hungary – those of Abov and Turňa. They were separated from each other after 1918 and adjudicated respectively to Czechoslovakia and Hungary. Our territory of interest consists now of five districts. Four urban districts of Košice are surrounded by one of the largest Slovak districts, referred to as Košice-environs.

Košice

East of Slovakia is too far from Bratislava. This is the reason why **KOŠICE** (population 236,100) became the "centre of world" and unofficial metropolis for the Easterners. The city on the Hornád river

Left: Košice
Right: House in the Art-Nouveau style on the Hlavné námestie square

on the western edge of the Košická kotlina basins has a long and agitated history and its present is also dynamic. It has been the most important town of the region for centuries and a natural centre of trade, culture, and education. Today it is the second largest city of Slovakia. The life of the metropolis is closely connected with what was called the East Slovakian Iron Works now U. S. Steel which is one of the largest companies of Slovakia with an important share in gross domestic product of the country.

The territory where the Hornád river abandons the tight and closed Slovenské rudohorie mountain range and enters the Košická kotlina basin was settled since time immemorial. The archaeologists found here proofs that the area was settled as early as 40 thousand years ago by primeval people. Numerous finds from the periods such as the Neolithic up to the Middle Ages testify to permanent presence of advanced settlements. They include artistic ceramics, jewellery, arms found in the suburb Barca or not far away from it in

Nižná Myšľa. Among the numerous settlements built along the Hornád the old Slav fortified settlement situated in the territory of the urban district Krásna nad Hornádom stood out from the Roman times. By the end of the 11th century the Benedictine Abbey was built near it. It became the religious and cultural centre of the Above county. The power of the ruler of the young Kingdom of Hungary was represented here by the royal castle, the remains of which still survive on the forested slope of Hradová towering above the northern suburbs of Košice.

The medieval town of Košice was founded approximately on the middle way from the Abbey to the castle. The first written mention of its existence is from 1230. In the first historical documents it was referred to as *Villa Cassa*, later the in Latin *Cassovia*, German *Kaschau*, Hungarian *Kassa*, and the Slovak Košice. After the Tartar invasions in 1241 and 1242 German colonists occupied the sacked region. The arrival of colonists from the Lower Saxony in the second half of the 13th century brought about the period of development and prosperity when the majority of the Slovak towns were founded. The settlement on the right bank of the Hornád river expanded and became a fortified town inhabited by merchants and artisans. Their presence documents the oldest known document of the furrier guild of the Kingdom of Hungary. The burghers, inhabitants of Košice, of German origin had abundant contacts with the medieval Kraków and rich towns in the north and north-west.

The people of Košice applied successful diplomacy and also open fighting for self-government and privilege in the second half of the 13th and first half of the 14th centuries. Founding the parish of the St. Elisabeth church built in the middle of the central square meant that they became partially independent from the higher church hierarchy. The relationship of the thriving town to secular power was determined by the historical events, which took place at the beginning of the 14th century. In 1304 its people responded to the count

Omodej Aba who ruled over the extensive territory of what is today eastern Slovakia and together with its western ally, Matúš Čák they were the main opponents to royal crown held then by King Charles Robert of Anjou. The disliked lord was killed in 1311. After the victorious **battle at Rozhanovce** in 1312 the ruler appreciated the faithfulness of Košice and granted it privileges. The town citizens acquired important privileges of **royal borough** in 1342. The date of 7 May 1369 is especially important for the town because it received, as the first European town, the document of coat of arms signed by the king. Today it is celebrated as the "Day of Košice". Another four royal documents of coat of arms followed. The coat of arms of the town of Košice used now is from 1502.

The free royal borough of Košice lived a period of boom and prosperity until the first half of the 15th century. The town acquired the surrounding villages and forests, which were changed to fruitful vineyards. Many wonderful Gothic build-

In 1556 a large part of the town burnt. A new town in the Renaissance style was soon built on the ruins of the Gothic. The additional wave of refugees increased the size of Hungarian ethnicity living in the town and the followers of reformed churches above all of those of Luther and Calvin obtained the majority in the town. Košice became an almost unassailable fortress with three belts of walls, a water dike and bulky star-shaped citadel in front of the southern town gate. For the sake of better defence against the Turkish attacks the suburbs beyond the town walls were pulled down. But apart from Turkish wars the Rebellions of Estates also disturbed the life of the town. The crafts and trade were declining, population was shrinking. The imperial troops and the soldiers of the rebellious aristocracy alternatively conquered the town. One of the few positive features of the time was founding of the **Jesuit university** in 1657. The Bishop of Eger, Benedict Kišdy was the personality who greatly contributed to the founding of what was the easternmost situated university with three faculties in Europe. In 1776 it was transformed into Royal Academy.

ings were built and construction of the St. Elisabeth Church continued. The town walls were eventually finished and gave security to Košice's about four thousand inhabitants. Košice also reached some political success when it became of what was referred to as **Pentapolitana**, association of five east Slovakian towns. The peaceful and fertile period ended by the events of the first half of the 15th century connected with the fighting for the vacant throne of the Kingdom of Hungary. Košice after 1440 became the seat of Ján Jiskra of Brandýs with title of grand count of Šariš whose mercenaries undertook military assaults all over the territory of the Kingdom and in the neighbouring Poland. In the 15th century Košice with its 7 thousand inhabitants became the **second largest town of the Kingdom of Hungary** following Buda and followed by Bratislava.

Left: Jesuit church
Right: St. Elisabeth Cathedral

The calmer 18th century proceeded in the spirit of fierce re-Catolisation of until then firm bastion of reformed churches in the Kingdom of Hungary. Only the reforms of King Joseph II brought some more freedom to Evangelicals and Calvinists of Košice at the end of the century. Subcarpathian Jews and those from Halič also moved here. Establishment of the diocese in 1804 strengthened position of Košice. In the revolutionary years of 1948-49 Košice became one of the **principal centres** of Hungarian uprising against Vienna defeated by the Imperial troops with help of the Russian tsar's army. The second half of the 19th century was characterised by great changes caused by industrial revolution. Town walls were gradually pulled down and new residential and industrial quarters replaced them. Luxurious houses of well-to-do citizens of Košice sprang in the centre of the town. The first factories, which produced Eng-

lish porcelain, hats and wool cloth, were followed by invasion of industry. Development received a new stimulus in form of railway, which connected Košice with Budapest in 1960. The first steam engine started on the track between Bohumín and Košice ten years later.

The 20th century has dramatically changed the town of Košice although the motifs were mostly political. The town was included in new state formations: on the last day of 1918 it was included in the newly formed Czechoslovak Republic, in 1938 it was annexed by Horthy's Hungary for more than six years. In April 1945 the Czechoslovak Government met for the first time on homeland ground and issued the document known as the Košice Programme of the Government treating the after-war arrangement of the free Republic. However, some other attributes of Košice also changed, particularly its size, ethnic structure and its general appearance. Number of its citizens more than doubled after the Second World War. New housing estates

were constructed for immigrants of rural area. Today the majority of its inhabitants are Slovaks living here with Hungarian, Czech and Roma minorities. Východoslovenské železiarne (East Slovakian Iron Works) became the biggest company not only of Košice but also of the country.

Almost all monuments of Košice are concentrated in the historical core of the town, size of which makes it the largest **town monument reserve** of Slovakia. Spindle-shaped **Hlavné námestie** square of Košice is the heart of the town and rightly considered one of the most beautiful squares in Slovakia. It is closed to traffic and skirted by numerous wonderful historical buildings. The most valuable monuments are situated in its centre. The dominant of the square and the town is the monumental Gothic **Cathedral of Košice ❶** consecrated to the patron saint of the Kingdom of Hungary **St. Elisabeth**. This building rather isolated from the rest of the square, is the largest church of Slovakia and the easternmost situated Goth-

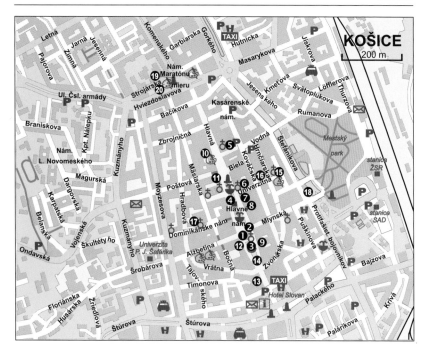

KOŠICE

|__200 m__|

ic cathedral of western type in Europe. Its longitudinal axis is 60.5 m and its transversal axis is 39.5 m long. The northern tower of the dome is 58.5 m tall. Construction of the church proceeded under the royal supervision in several stages from 1380 while some assert that it is still not finished. For its construction a special building plant was established in the town, which later enormously influenced Gothic constructions in eastern Slovakia. It was probably a branch of the Viennese company but the style of its work seems to bear signs of that proper to the constructors of the Prague St. Vít Cathedral. Originally, the church was designed as a five-nave basilica. Under the pressure of natural disasters and wars the resulting form was different; it became the five-nave dome with crossed nave. In spite of adjustments in new styles after fires and earthquakes in the 19th century the Cathedral of Košice preserved numerous original Gothic elements and valuable artistic features. They include, for example, the wonderful **northern portal** with the tympanum representing the Last Judgement. The medieval **gargoyle** in the south-western corner of the church is also interesting. It is supposed that it has a form of woman, in particular the wife of the famous royal constructor Stephan. This is how he allegedly punished his wife for drinking too much wine. Special attention must be paid to the **main altar of St Elisabeth** built in the years 1474-1477. It contains the largest European set of Gothic table paintings. Dutch and German influence on the sculptures and paintings is obvious. Liturgical objects include the most valuable works of important goldsmith J. Szilassy from the 18th century, which are classified as the national cultural monument. The **crypt of Francis II Rákóczi** stands in front of the church. The bones of the leader of the last Rebellion of Estates against the Habsburgs were deposited here in 1906. In front of the northern walls of the Cathedral of Košice stands what was originally **Urbanova veža** ❷ tower built in the 14ᵗʰ century. The bell in the belfry is the true copy of the bell called Urban made in the East Slovakian Iron Works. The fragments of the true Urban damaged by fire were gathered, the bell reconstructed and now it is exhibited in front of the church. On the walls of arcade corridor in the ground floor of the tower are the tombstones moved here from the Cathedral and the adjacent cemetery. The Urban's tower, the **chapel of St. Michael** ❸ from the end of the 14ᵗʰ century, which stands in front of the southern side of the Cathedral of St. Elisabeth forms together with it a complete Gothic set inscribed in the List of the National Cultural Monuments in Slovakia.

The building in of **Divadlo Janka Borodáča** ❹ (Theatre of Janko Borodáč) which bears the name of important Slovak actor and its first post-war director was built in the years 1897-1899 in historicizing style. The area between the Dome and theatre becomes a very lively place above all in summer. Its main attraction is the **font with music**. Intensity of water springing from the font changes in the rhythm of accompanying music.

In the eastern row of houses on the square apart from aristocratic palaces and burgher houses there are two churches. Further to north is situated the **Seminar church with monastery** ❺ built by the Franciscans at the beginning of the 15ᵗʰ century. It was originally a Gothic church but now it has got a nice Baroque facade. The building of the **University church** ❻ made of stone and with two towers from the 17ᵗʰ century stands nearer to the Cathedral. It is an important architectural monument with Renaissance and Baroque elements. Jesuits built it in 1681 in memory of **three martyrs of Košice**. The solemn sanctifying of the three men assassinated in the place where the sacristy stands now took place on 2 July 1992. The Pope John Paul II himself celebrated the ceremony. The former **Jesuit monastery** from 1654 used to be the seat of the University of Košice founded in 1657. The oldest surviving

house of the eastern row is **Levočský dom** ❼, or the house of Levoča from the 15ᵗʰ century. Merchant Alexis Thurso donated it to his native town. The building of the former **town hall** ❽ from the second half of the 18ᵗʰ century with a beautiful Classicist facade has got an interior of high artistic value. The former **county house** ❾ from 1779 where the first after was programme of Czechoslovakia known as the Košice Programme of the Government was read on 5 April 1945 is near the Cathedral. It also housed the seat of the grand county of Košice, today it is **Východoslovenská galéria Júliusa Jakobyho** (East-Slovakian Gallery of Július Jakoby).

The northernmost situated monument of the western row of the Hlavné námestie square tapers into the Hlavná ulica street is the Baroque-Classicist **Rákóczi Palace** ❿. It was originally a Gothic burgher house from the 13ᵗʰ century and repeatedly reconstructed. In 1654 it became the seat of

Right: Theatre of Janko Borodáč

the Košice Captaincy. Leader of the Rebellion of Estates dwelled in the palace in the years 1706-1707. Today the exhibits of the Slovak Technical Museum are exhibited here. This museum, unique of the kind, concentrates on the rare technical monuments, artistic products of blacksmith craft. Further in south is the Classicist **Csáky-Dessewffy Palace** ❶ from the first half of the 19th century. Former seat of the East-Slovakian Gallery now serves to the Constitutional Court of Justice of the Slovak Republic. Near the Dome is the **Bishop's Palace** ❷ from 1804 with a nice ceremonial hall with lavish stucco ornamentation. In the southern part of the row is the Empire **Forgách Palace** ❸ from the 19th century. What was originally an aristocratic residence was used as the seat of the head of the main Košice district after 1851. After the Second World War it was adjusted for

the needs of the Regional State Library with some valuable documents from the 16th century and it serves the purpose until the present time. In the southern part of the Hlavné námestie square is the first opportunity to see the medieval **town fortifications** of Košice. Entering the basement one can see reconstructed foundations of the **Dolná brána** ❹ gate, which is now used as an unconventional gallery and concert hall. Only fragments survived of what used to be the original 2,555 m long continuous fortification system. The best-conserved structure is that of **Katova bašta** ❺ bastion on the Hrčiarska ulica street which is now the seat of exhibition of natural history. The copy of **oriental house** in the Turkish town of Radošto, the refuge of the rebel magnate Francis II Rákóczi, stands on its courtyard. Walking beyond the reconstructed **town walls** one can see another **bastion** on the Krmanova ulica street.

The labyrinth of lanes and alleys of the historical centre of Košice is, apart from some exceptions, an oasis of silence and

Left: Horse tram
Right: Pedestrian zone. Statue of Marathon Runner on the Námestie Maratónu mieru square

tranquillity. Their atmosphere contrasts the throbbing noise of the Hlavné námestie square. The narrow and picturesque lane of **Vrátna ulica**, for example, provides some charming nooks. Likewise, **Hrnčiarska ulica** street in the east is often referred to as the street of historical crafts where the artisans exhibit their skills in front of passers-by. Not far away from is a remarkable medieval house from the 13th century known as **Miklušova väznica** ⑯ (Prison of Mikluš). The prison was established in this house in the 17th century, and it served the purpose until 1909. Now it is used as museum dedicated to the guilds of Košice. But there are also artefacts used by headman, swords, iron handcuffs and chains, and furniture of headman's house upstairs. On the western side the **Dominikánske námestie** square contains the monastery complex of the Dominican male order. The dominant building of this complex is the **church of Dominicans** ⑰ from the 13th century with a tall slender tower. It is the oldest sacral monument of the city. The

monastery, like the church, was considerably damaged by the 1556 devastating fire. Its present appearance is the result of reconstruction in the Baroque style from the 18th century. The **Alžbetina ulica** street is attractive because of the wonderful view of the Cathedral of Košice. Opposite to it the **Mlynská ulica** street on the eastern side of the square is a very busy communication with excluded traffic. It connects the centre of the city with railway station. It is the place of the first contact with the city for all that come here by train. The first monument one runs into is the Neo-Gothic **Jakab Palace** ⑱. Architect Arpád Jakab built it in 1899 as his private residence. For its construction he used the stones destined for reconstruction of the cathedral. The also attractive interior of the palace is used for solemn occasions celebrated by the town.

The Hlavná ulica street in the north has its outlet in the **Námestie Maratónu mieru** square. The **statue of Marathon Runner** ⑲ stands in the park and re-

en medals and golden chain more than 2 metres long. The overall weight of hoard is 11 kilograms. It was found in 1935 when the Rákóczi Palace on the Hlavné námestie square was reconstructed. The unique collection of golden coins consists of 81 mints of Europe, while the coins from Dutch towns are most abundantly represented (1,016 pieces). The majority of coins are from the 15th to 17th centuries. One coin is even from ancient Greece. **Wooden church** moved here from the village Kožuchovce, adorns the yard of the Museum since 1927.

Environs of Košice

The forested mountain ranges of eastern part of the Slovenské rudohorie Mts. provide excellent hinterland for recreation to almost quarter of million of Košice' s citizens. The tourists and trippers head to both near and farther situated centres. On the edge of the Čierna hora Mts. is the forested mountain of **Hradová** (466 m) with foundations of long disappeared medieval castle from the 14th century. The view tower opens the views over the forest to the environs of the Hradová. Not far away in **KAVEČANY** there are suitable conditions for winter and summer recreation, and the village has got its zoological garden. The tourist centre of **Bankov** on the edge of the Volovské vrchy Mts. is also well equipped with number of accommodation and sport facilities. The recreation centre of **Jahodná** is an important crossroads of hiking routes, which attracts citizens of Košice in winter and provides excellent conditions both for down-hill and cross-country skiing. The favourite spot for suburban recreation is the **Čermeľské údolie** valley with an attractive children train riding down the deep valley and pulled by steam engine called Katka. The 6 km long track connects the suburbs of Košice with the favourite picnic place of **Alpínka**.

minds that International Peace Marathon is organised in Košice every year in autumn since 1942. Below the inscription in Greek *Není khamen* (We have won) is the list of winners of this very popular race, one of the oldest in the world. The first runners started on the track 42,195 m long on 28 October of 1924. They ran from Košice to Turňa nad Bodvou. Today they turn in Šaca and run back to the centre of Košice. There is also the Neo-Renaissance building of **Východoslovenské múzeum** ⑳ (East-Slovakian Museum) on the square. It was built in the years 1896-1899. It offers and ideal opportunity to learn about history and culture of East Slovakia. Exhibition of coins, goldsmith's trade and jewel-making are especially interesting. One of the admired exhibits is the famous **Golden Hoard of Košice** consisting of 2,920 coins of pure gold, 3 gold-

The old trade road, which once led down the valley of the Hornád river over the Čierna Hora Mts. was guarded by two medieval castles. Both of them are in

Left: Wooden church and belfry in the East-Slovakian Museum
Right: Monastery complex in Jasov

ruins now. The remains of the Early Gothic castle from the 13th century are situated on the forested hillside above the village **SOKOĽ**. Another castle is built above the conspicuous bent of the Hornád valley near village **KYSAK**. Today Kysak is the entry gate to the region of Šariš and transferring railway station for passengers heading to Prešov. Two water reservoirs constructed on the river of Ida are in the environs of the village **BUKOVEC** west of Košice. The upper one of them is the reservoir of potable water while the lower reservoir is destined to sports and recreation. The mountain village of **ZLATÁ IDKA** lying further in the west was founded in the 14th century as a mining settlement next to the royal mines where gold and other metals were extracted. Copper was also extracted here from the 18th century. The mining activities terminated here before the First World War and Zlatá Idka today is above all the place for recreation. The village lies below the massive mountain of **Kojšovská hoľa** (1,246 m)

which dominates to the eastern part of the Volovské vrchy Mts. The access to the much sought for ski slopes is easy by **chair lift** on the southern slope of the mountain. On the western slope is the mountain hotel **Erika** with access to the top of the mountain with **meteorological station.** The view from the top is considered one of the most beautiful in Slovakia. One can even spot the peaks of the Tatras.

The road leading through the Čermeľské údolie valley will carry the hiker to the **Ružín** water reservoir. The river was dammed up near village of Ružín which is now covered by water, in order to raise the water level on a stretch of territory 14 km long and to obtain such an increase also in the tributaries of the river, the Hnilec and Belá. The depth of the lake with an area of 600 ha reaches in its deepest place 50 m. The best view of it gets one climbing the mountain of Sivec (781 m), a conspicuous dominant of the local landscape. The water from Ružín is used for industrial purposes by the firms of Košice and for recreation.

West of Košice two protuberances of the Košická kotlina basin reach the Slovenské rudohorie Mts. The first of them following the upper reach of the river Bodva separates the Volovské vrchy Mts. and the Slovenský kras Mts. from each other and the second deeply drives in between the karstic plateaux of the eastern part of the Slovenský kras Mts. The centre of this region, **MOLDAVA NAD BODVOU** (population 9,500), today the largest town in the environs of Košice, was founded in the 13th century on the estates of Turňa. The original settlement became royal borough in the 14th century, lost this favoured position in the following century and became the serf village of the town of Košice. The most important monument of the town is the Gothic **church** from the 15th century, which was adapted in Baroque style in the 18th century. Moving up the stream of the

Bodva it is possible to arrive at **JASOV**, which is undoubtedly one of the most attractive localities in the environs of Košice. It has got abundant natural and cultural appeals. In the western end of the villages with mining past the edge of the Jasovská planina plateau, the easternmost karstic plateau of the Slovenský kras Mts., is observable. Below the large rock, which provides a wonderful view of Jasov, is the entrance to the **Jasovská jaskyňa** cave, which is one of the four caves of the Slovenský kras Mts. accessible to public. Today the 550 m long circle consisting of 2,811 corridors is available to visitors. The Dome of Bats is used for speleoclimatic therapy. Jasov's history is documented from 1234. Jasov received the right to annual fairs in 1394 and became a market town. In the 18th century a metallurgical plant and iron works were put in operation here. The architectural gem of Jasov is the Baroque **monastery complex of the Premonstratesians** included among the national cultural monuments. This order ar-

Left: Turniansky hrad Castle
Right: Water hammer mill in Medzev.
Zádielska dolina valley

rived here in the 12ᵗʰ century before the Tartar invasion to the Kingdom of Hungary. The monastery existing here now was built on the site of an older Gothic building in 1766 pursuing the project of an outstanding architect Anton Pilgram. The lavishly ornamented interior of the monastic church in Baroque style, the library of monastery, and conserved French garden are especially valuable. Remains of the medieval **castle** from the 14ᵗʰ century are on the hill above the cave. The mercenaries of Ján Jiskra shortly occupied it in the 15ᵗʰ century. The castle is in decay from 1458.

MEDZEV (population 3,700) in the valley of the Bodva was a rich mining town with developed trades in the past. It originated by joining three settlements: Nižný and Vyšný Medzev, and Baňa Lucia. Local deposits of iron ore helped development of trades producing iron tools for farming. Part of the population sustained on colliery and shingle making. In the 19ᵗʰ century as much as 109 hammer mills worked in the town and its environs. The hammer mills of Medzev exploited energy of water collected in numerous small water reservoirs of abundant brooks existing in its environs. One of the surviving **water hammer mills** standing in the part Nižný Medzev is the protected technical monument. The local native, now President of Slovakia, Rudolf Schuster founded a tradition here. His invited top-level partners, presidents, kings or princes can forge a hoe or spade with their own hands here. The Gothic **church** from the 15ᵗʰ century is another valuable monument of

Medzev. Interesting thing about the town is that part of once a large enclave of Carpathian Germans who speak a specific **dialect** of German still lives here. In the upper part of the valley of the Bodva river is the village **ŠTÓS** that also was a mining town in the past. In the beautiful forests of the Volovské vrchy Mts. near the village is climatic spa where respiratory and occupational diseases are treated. The spa was founded in 1881. The park of the spa contains precious wood species.

The past of village **TURŇA NAD BODVOU** is more interesting than its present. It used to be the centre of the Turňa county, one of the smallest in the Kingdom of Hungary. Today its territory is divided between Slovakia and Hungary. The head of the county resided originally at the **Turniansky hrad** Castle, ruins of which stand on top of the conspicuous cone-shaped hill. Rare flora grows on its limestone slope including the local endemit *Onosma tornensis*. The aristocratic family of Turniansky built the castle at the turn of the 13ᵗʰ and

14th centuries. In spite of its fortifications reinforced in 16th century it was taken by the Turks in 1652. It fell in ruins after the fire in 1848. The county office moved to Turňa in the 19th century and resided in the still standing Classicist **County House**.

Beyond the village of **ZÁDIEL** is the **Zádielska dolina** valley, one of many bizarre gorges of Slovakia. The narrow skirted by limestone cliffs is 300 m deep. The dominant rock is the slender formation with a matching name Cukrová homoľa (Sugar Cone). Instructive path runs down the valley and in its rear part climbs to the edge of the plateau with beautiful views of the whole valley. The less known Hájska dolina valley with a road running through it to the picturesque village **HAČAVA** is equally beautiful.

The circle running around the Košická kotlina basin and Slanské vrchy Mts. can be started as well in the village of **ŠACA**,

which thanks to the vicinity of the iron works of Košice gained a more or less urban character. It has a smart Rococo **manor house** from 1776. The beauty of the originally Renaissance **manor house** from 1688 in the adjacent **VEĽKÁ IDA** is enhanced by extensive park with a little lake. The landmark of the village **SEŇA** on the main road from Košice to Hungary is the rare Early Gothic **church** from the 13th century. The favourite centre of summer recreation and fishing is at the **Čanianske jazerá** lakes next to the village of **ČAŇA**. On the right bank of the Hornád river is the village **NIŽNÁ MYŠĽA**. It became known for numerous archaeological finds. Especially important was the discovery of settlement and burial place of the Ottoman culture from the Bronze Age. The area is being now adjusted to **archaeological park** in order to make it more attractive for visitors.

SLANEC is the village situated in the distinctly sank part of the ridge of the Slanské vrchy Mts. with castle hill towering above it. The ruins of an old medieval

Left: Waterfalls in the Hájska dolina valley
Right: Geyser of Herľany

castle are on top of it. The document from 1230 mentions it as the castle, which guarded the salt stores. Following its first owner, family of Aba, it fell in hands of the Druget family who built here the central cylinder-shaped tower in the 14th century, which is still the dominant feature of castle ruins. During the Thököly uprising in 1679 the Imperial troops pulled the castle down. Its last owners, the family of Forgách tried to restore the castle and had a family museum established in it in the 19th century. The museum was destroyed during the Second World War. The wonderful natural lake **Izra** is accessible from the village of **SLANSKÁ HUTA** by a forest road. This lake blocked by a landslide lies amidst wonderful beech forest on the eastern slope of the frontier mountain of **Veľký Milič** (895 m).

Below the Dargovský priesmyk pass which is the second largest depression of the mountain barrier of the Slanské vrchy Mts. is the village **SVINICA**. The ancient Late Romanesque **church** from the 13th century, national cultural monument, is its dominant. In its interior medieval wall paintings survive. The favourite destination in the environs of Košice is undoubtedly **HERĽANY**. The landmark of this former spa is the famous **Geyser of Herľany**. In the 1970's artesian well was drilled here in pursue of another source of mineral water for the expanding spa. The 404.5 m deep probe brought up a strong spring of mineral gas water. Now the periodicity of emanation is about 32-34 hours. The water springs for about 20-30 minutes to the height of maximum 15 metres. The yield of one eruption is about 600 hl of water. As this unique natural scene occurs approximately every one and a half days the best thing is to enquire by phone at the local post office. Herľany is also the starting point for nice trips to its environs including the one to **Rankovské skaly** rocks (790 m) in the Slanské vrchy Mts. In the village of **KECEROVCE** stands a very old **manor house** built by the end of the 15th century in the Late Gothic style and it is one of the oldest in Slovakia. There is another 16th

century **manor house** this time in Renaissance style. Lost in the forest of the Slanské vrchy Mts. east of the village are the remains of medieval **Lipovec** castle. The village of **BUDIMÍR** situated on the right bank of the Torysa river is also rich in aristocratic residences. Family of Aba had probably built the older Gothic **manor house** while the second substantially younger **manor house** with strikingly smart Rococo architecture is set in a looked after French garden and English park. Today it temporarily shelters exhibition of the **Slovak Technical Museum**. The last stop of the circle around Košice is the village of **ROZHANOVCE**. It is know for one of the most famous **battles** in history of Slovakia, which took place not far from it. On 15 June 1312 the troops of Omodej and Matúš Čák against those of King Charles Robert of Anjou fought here. King's victory definitely concluded expansion of the powerful Lord of the Váh and the Tatras from the Castle of Trenčín and its allies and the ruler's power was confirmed.

KOŠICE
(dial: 055-)

Information
– **Informačné centrum mesta Košice**, Hlavná 59, Košice, ☎ 6258888, ☎/fax 6254502, icmk@ke.sanet.sk, www.kosice.sk/icmk, www.kosice.sk, **Mestské informačné centrum**, Štúrova 1, Košice, ☎ 16186, fax 6436541, mic@pangea.sk, www.pangea.sk, www.kosice.sk

Museums
– **Slovenské technické múzeum**, Hlavná 88, Košice, ☎ 6224035-6, **Východoslovenské múzeum**, Hviezdoslavova 3, Košice, ☎ 6220309, **Expozícia numizmatiky, zlatníctva a šperkárstva**, Nám. Maratónu mieru 2, Košice, ☎ 6220309, **Prírodovedná expozícia – Katova bašta**, Hrnčiarska 7, Košice, ☎ 6220309, **Múzeum – Miklušova väznica**, Pri Miklušovej väznici 10, Košice, ☎ 6220309, **Múzeum Vojtecha Löfflera**, Alžbetina 20, Košice, ☎ 6223073, **Múzeum letectva**, Areál letiska, Košice, ☎ 6224035

Galleries
– **Východoslovenská galéria Júliusa Jakobyho**, Hlavná 27, Košice, ☎ 6221187, **Galéria – Dolná brána**, Hlavná ul., Košice, ☎ 6228393, **DECOR ART**, Hlavná 49, Košice, ☎ 0905/556939, **Antika**, Alžbetina 3, Košice, ☎ 6231239, **Fotogaléria Nova**, Hlavná 48, Košice, ☎ 6223291, **Galéria Dr. Živaga**, Dominikánske nám. 8, Košice, ☎ 6253508

Atractiveness
– **St. Elisabeth Cathedral**, Hlavná ul., Košice, ☎ 6227625, **Urbanova veža** tower, Hlavná ul., Košice, **Prison of Mikluš**, Pri Miklušovej väznici 10, Košice, ☎ 6220309, Church of **Dominicans**, Dominikánske nám., Košice, **Golden Hoard of Košice**, Nám. Maratónu mieru 2, Košice, ☎ 6220309, **Botanical garden**, Mánesova 23, Košice, ☎ 6331556

Hotels
– **SLOVAN****, Hlavná 1, Košice, ☎ 6227378-80, **BANKOV****, Dolný Bankov 2, Košice, 6334522-4, **CENTRUM***, Južná trieda 2/A, Košice, ☎ 6783101-2, **ALESSANDRIA***, Jiskrova 3, Košice, ☎ 6225903, **FERUM***, Železiarenská 49, Košice, ☎ 6841342-5, **GLORIA PALACE***, Bottova 1, Košice, ☎ 6257327-30, **DÁLIA***, Löfflerova 1, Košice, ☎ 7994321-2, **AMBASSADOR***, Hlavná 101, Košice, ☎

7203720, **AKADÉMIA****, Južná trieda 10, Košice, ☎ 7260700, **HUTNÍK****, Tyršovo nábr. 1, Košice, ☎ 6003296, **KOHAL****, Trieda SNP 61, Košice, ☎ 6425572, **RANČ****, Šebastovská 4, Košice, ☎ 6783003, **ŠTADIÓN***, Čermeľská 1, Košice, ☎ 6330814, **METAL***, Železiarenská 11, Košice, ☎ 6842531, **ALI**, Alejová 2, Košice, ☎ 6433862

Restaurants
– **U VODNÁRA**, Hrnčiarska 25, Košice, ☎ 6228991, **U LEONARDA**, Komenského 39, Košice, ☎ 6223765, **LAMPÁREŇ**, Hlavná 115, Košice, ☎ 6224995, **LAGÚNA**, Masarykova 2, Košice, ☎ 6005166, **BOMBA KLUB**, Hlavná 5, Košice, ☎ 6233430, **GAZDOVSKÁ PIVNICA**, Čajkovského 4, Košice, ☎ 6227930, **KLEOPATRA**, Hlavná 24, Košice, ☎ 6252137, **LEVOČSKÝ DOM**, Hlavná 65, Košice, ☎ 6222372, **SEDLIACKY DVOR**, Biela 3, Košice, ☎ 6220402, **GOLDEN ROYAL**, Vodná 8, Košice, ☎ 6223658, **ZLATÝ ZVON**, Zvonárska 4, Košice, ☎ 6225689, **CARAVELLA**, Orlia 4, Košice, ☎ 6230378, **HYCONT CLUB**, Lomená 1, Košice, ☎ 6831301, **ROKOKO**, Gorkého 9, Košice, ☎ 6332731, **AJVEGA**, Orlia 10, Košice, ☎ 6220452

ENVIRONS OF KOŠICE
(dial: 055-)

Atractiveness
– **ZOO**, Košice-Kavečany, ☎ 6331517, **Spa**, Štós-kúpele 235, Štós, ☎ 4667524, 4667532, **Jasovská jaskyňa** cave, Jasov, ☎ 4664165, **Monastery complex of Premonstratesians**, Jasov, ☎ 4664224, **Water hammer mills**, Medzev, ☎ 4663105, **Geyser of Herľany**, Herľany, ☎ 6964122, **Manor house**, Budimír, ☎ 6958294, **Turniansky hrad** Castle, Turňa nad Bodvou, **Zádielska dolina** valley, Zádiel

Hotels
– **HRABINA***, Bukovec, ☎ 6853152, **PLÁŽ***, Rekreačná 1, Čaňa, ☎ 6200457, **SPOLOČENSKÝ DOM***, Školská 5, Moldava nad Bodvou, ☎ 4602708-9

Restaurants
– **U MEDVEĎA**, Budanova 6, Košice-Kavečany, ☎ 6325224, **FERDINAND**, Okružná 20, Moldava nad Bodvou, ☎ 4898811, **ROSSI**, Hviezdoslavova 2, Moldava nad Bodvou, ☎ 4603929, **CONDOR CLUB**, Kováčska 89, Medzev, ☎ 0905/709127, **RANČ ŠUGOV**, Šugovská dolina, Medzev, ☎ 4667638-9

ŠARIŠ

Prešov

Environs of Prešov

Bardejov and
its environs

Svidník and
its environs

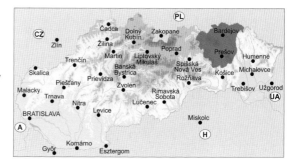

Apart from being the trademark of popular beer, Šariš is also a historical region in the north of eastern Slovakia replenished with tourist destinations. Historical towns of Prešov, Bardejov, and Sabinov and unique technical monuments such as the salt mines in Solivar or the mines of Dubník, which yielded unusually beautiful opals are its pride. Šariš is also the place where most of Slovakia's old wooden churches are concentrated, it boasts the world famous spa of Bardejov, where also Empress Elisabeth nicknamed Sissy experienced the hospitality and excellent service of the locals. By the way, the locals speak their typical colourful dialect with charm and naturalness, which contributes to the overall impression of freshness and novelty of this area.

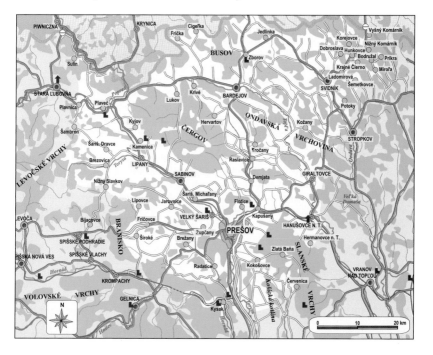

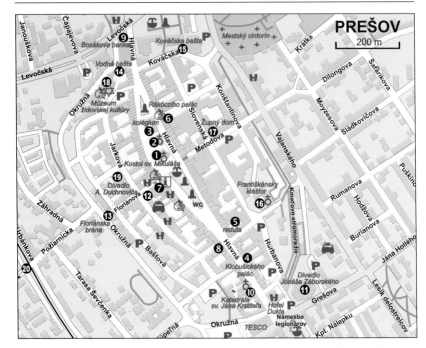

Šariš is situated in the northern part of eastern Slovakia. In the west and north-west it borders on the region of Spiš, in the west it stretches as far as the northern parts of region of Zemplín. In the south-east it neighbours with the region of Abov. Šariš is moderately mountainous and the depressions regularly alternate with mountain ranges. The southern part of its territory is occupied by the Košická kotlina basin connected with the territory next to the Black Sea and the countries lying on the shore of the Baltic Sea by an old trade route called *Via regale* (the Royal Road). Mining and trade in salt was one of the main sources of income of this area in the past.

Prešov

PREŠOV (population 92,800), the metropolis of Šariš is the third biggest town of Slovakia. It has been the rival of Košice and Bardejov, each of them trying to win the

Right: St. Nicholas church

dominance in eastern Slovakia. Rich archaeological finds in the north of the Košická kotlina basin testify to very old settlement of this territory. People of what the scientists refer to as the beech-mountain culture founded the first permanent settlements here in the Neolithic Age. In Roman era farming settlements with specific types of houses denominated the Prešov type of dwelling existed here. Old Slavic settlements, which were included into the Great Moravian Empire in the 9th century, existed on the banks of the Torysa river. In the 11th and 12th centuries side by side with the Slav settlements Magyar immigrants, and finally in the 13th century German colonists invited here from German Saxony settled in several villages, which later became parts of the medieval town.

Prešov strengthened its autonomous position in 1342 when it acquired exemption from the rule of the count of Šariš. When it obtained more royal privileges in 1370, Prešov became **free royal borough** and later in 1480 member of what was referred to as *Pentapolitana*, association of five eastern-Slovakian towns. In the 16th and 17th centuries Reformation found its followers in Prešov which became the bastion of the reformed denominations in the Kingdom of Hungary. Leaders of the Rebellion of Estates against the Catholic rulers, the Habsburgs, leaned on the position of Prešov, which had to face the attacks of Imperial troops several times. Suppression of the Imrich Thököly's rebellion in 1687 meant especially cruel consequences for the town. Imperial General Antonio Caraffa punished the town by hard economic sanctions and beheaded 24 noblemen and burghers of Prešov. This sad event has entered the history of the town as the *Bloodshed of Prešov.*

Apart from progressing trade and crafts, culture and education also successfully developed in the town. The seat of the Šariš county was moved here in 1647 and in 1667 Evangelical college was founded. After a short period of economic stagnation in the first half of the 18th century, activities, which brought back to Prešov its privileged position as the centre of the region, revived. Prešov avoided decline which affected the towns of Kežmarok or Levoča by construction of railway. A section the Košice-Bohumín railway deviating from Kysak to Prešov was constructed and the first train passed through the town on 1 September 1870. Two years later prolongation of the track to Plaveč and in 1893 to Bardejov was made. Shortly after the first World War Prešov experienced the attempt to establish a communist state inspired by the Bolshevik revolution in Russia. Establishment of the **Slovenská republika rád** (The Slovak Republic of Councils) was announced from the windows of the Prešov's town hall on 16 June 1919. Its existence though, was very short. In the years of the Second World War position of Prešov was partially improved by the fact that the town assumed several competencies and institutions moved here from Košice, which was occupied by Hungary then. The industrial development continued after the war and number of its population was steadily increasing.

The monuments of Prešov are concentrated into its historical core stretching around **Hlavná ulica** street, which widens into the spindle-shaped square. The dominant here is the parish **church of St. Nicholas ❶** from the mid-14th century with tall tower reconstructed in Gothic style. The construction of the Gothic church was finished in 1515. Despite of repeated modifications and fire in 1788 many Gothic elements have been preserved in its architecture: domes, windows and portals. The Gothic and Baroque styles alternate on the main altar of St. Nicholas from 1696. Statues of angels from the beginning of the 16th century made in workshop of Master Pavol of Levoča are Gothic, for example. North of the parish church stands the Evangelical **church of the Holy Trinity ❷** built in the years 1642-1647 in the Late Renaissance style. It was built for the Hungarian Evangelicals living in the town. Beside it another important building of Evangelicals in Prešov classified as the national cultural monument stands. It is the originally Re-

naissance building of the former Evangelical **college** ❸ from the second half of the 17th century. This school of superior type founded in 1667 was the centre, which propagated the ideas of reforming humanism. The fresh graduates of German universities taught here. The Bishop's Office of the Eastern District of the Evangelical church of Augsburg Confession in Slovakia seats in the building now.

The fire afflicted the row of houses on the Hlavná ulica street in 1887 and destroyed a large portion of the town. Originally Late Gothic, Renaissance and Baroque burgher houses were reconstructed in new style. The majority of them possess the attic gables typical for Prešov with lavish graffito ornamentation. The four-wing **Klobušický Palace** ❹ in the southern part of the eastern row is a nice example. It was built in 1756. Only the arbour survived from the French park situated behind the

palace. Further north in the eastern row of houses is the building of the **town redout** ❺. In 1562 aldermen of the town had a municipal inn constructed here and on its yard the first theatre building in Prešov was built in 1833. In the rear part the Neo-Classicist building known as **Čierny orol** (The Black Eagle) with large dancing and concert hall ornamented by wall paintings was built in 1884. The most valuable building of the eastern row of houses is the **Rákózci Palace** ❻. This building standing near the parish church is the result of the 16th century reconstruction of older burgher houses into the seat of aristocrat Žigmund Rákóczi of Transylvania. Its facade has got an attic with rich ornamentation. During the last reconstruction the original Renaissance graffito ornamentation with plant motifs was restored. Today it houses **Vlastivedné Museum**. Part of it is an interesting exhibition of firemen history in Slovakia. One of few houses, which preserved the Renaissance style, is the **burgher house No. 115** situated in the northern part of the western row. It contains three-storied basement with a well. Two other interesting buildings of the western row are easy to find. Next to the **Neptun's fountain** in a small park on the square is the building of **town hall** ❼. It stands here since 1520. It acquired the present appearance after two major modifications realised in the years 1788 and 1887. At the beginning it was used as the town tavern now it is the private **Museum of Wines**. The second building with passage through it is in the southern part of the western row. It is the **burgher house No. 23** ❽ with Classicist facade ornamented in stucco.

If you want to see what is perhaps the most interesting monument of Prešov you have to go to the northern end of the Hlavná ulica street. It is the Art Nouveau building of **Bosákova banka** ❾ from 1954. It contains statues on its facade and a corner dome. Sightseeing on the Hlavná ulica street finishes at its southern end. The most valuable structure here is the Greek-Catholic **Cathedral of St. John the Baptist** ❿ from the 18th century, which forms

Left: Burgher house
Right: Neptun's fountain

one common structure with the **Bishop Palace** and the **Greek-Catholic Theological Faculty**. The complex was built at the site of the former town hospital and the Carmelite church of the Virgin Mary from 1429. In 1686 the Minor male order seated here. The remains of the convent built by them are now built-in the body of the Bishop Palace. The church was promoted to cathedral when the Greek-Catholic bishopric was established in Prešov in 1881. The single-nave Baroque Building has got a beautiful Rococo facade with stucco ornamentation and statues. The Hlavná ulica street ends in the **Námestie legionárov** square where the modern building of the **Divadlo Jonáša Záborského** ⓫ theatre opened in 1990 dominates.

The side streets of the historical core of Prešov also contain interesting monuments. Walking through the passage of the town hall you will reach the Floriánova ulica street with **Caraffov dom** ⓬ house, the former town prison. The building is in fact the reconstructed Gothic house from 1624. In 1687 the Imperial General Caraffa held prisoners and tortured the rebels before their execution. The Floriánska ulica street ends by the **Floriánova brána** ⓭ gate, which is part of a small fragment of surviving town walls. In its prolongation northward is the **Vodná bašta** ⓮ bastion. It formed the corner of the walls. Its vernacular name *Kumšt* (corruption of German word for art *Kunst*) relates to the special hydraulic facility used for water pumping in the water dike. In the north-eastern bent of the town wall is the **Kováčska bašta** ⓯ bastion from the 16th century. It stands between the houses of the Kováčska ulica street. The former name of the bastion Pekárska (Baker) suited it better because the baker's guild was entrusted its defence. Another fragment of town walls is also on the south-eastern side of the historical core, near the originally Gothic **Franciscan monastic complex** ⓰ built around 1380. Its church and the monastery were thoroughly rebuilt at the beginning of the 18th century and its style displays the traces of

influence of architecture applied to the Roman church of Il Gesú. On the Slovenská ulica street stands the building of the former **Župný dom** (County House). It was built for the office of the Šariš County in Rococo-Classicist style in 1790. In the southern part of the town is the Orthodox **church of Alexander Nevský** with typical onion-shaped domes. The Jewish community has in Prešov one of the most beautiful **synagogues** in Slovakia, which stands on the northern side of the historical core. The Moorish style with oriental ornamentation of the synagogue from 1898 is very impressive. In its interior it contains a valuable collection of Jewish artefacts collected by E. Barkány. The Jarkova ulica street leads to the **Pulský Palace** built around 1750. Originally it was surrounded by gardens and noble D. Pulský owned it. Now it houses the theatre **Divadlo Alexandra**

Duchnoviča . The last landmark of Prešov is situated on the opposite bank of the Torysa river. West of the centre is the **Calvary** with a set of sacral monuments from the 18th and 19th centuries. The **church of the Holy Cross** offers a wonderful view of the town surrounded by the volcanic mountains in the northern horizon.

Environs of Prešov

In **Solivar**, once independent village, now part of Prešov situated on its southeastern edge is a remarkable complex of technical monuments   related with the local mining of stone salt. For centuries water of salty springs was captured in place referred to as *Sauuvar*. Salt was extracted from this water by cooking and it was later hauled all over the Kingdom of Hungary and to Poland. The prospering settlement near the springs was referred to as a little town in 1417. As the King of Hungary could not claim any rights on salt in form of solution, his experts started to search for deposits of solid salt. After successful exploration its mining could be started in 1572. The miners carried broken pieces of salt out of underground while the salt water from the springs was still cooked. In 1752 a flow of water flooded the pits and created a large underground salt lake. For a long time it seemed that it was an end to mining in Solivar. Only in the 19th century a solution was found. A simple pumping gadget driven by four pairs of horses or oxen, called here "gápeľ" was built above the pit

Left: Cathedral of St. John the Baptist. "Gápeľ" in Solivar
Right: Opal of Dubník. Entrance to the pit Viliam

Leopold. Large sacks made of oxen hide were dipped into the salt lake in the depth of 135 metres pulled out and poured into wooden troughs. Salty solution flowed further into warmed up metal vessels. The water evaporated unit white crystals of salt appeared in their bottoms.

Gápeľ above the pit Leopold is the only mining structure open to public in Solivar. Utilities like the tanks for salt solution, "čerentne" are to be seen in the **cooking structure František**, **"the knocker"** used to summon the miners and the **chapel of St. Rochus** can be also contemplated in Solivar. The salt store with tower is in ruins. Since 1946 salt solution is extracted from deep probes situated on the hill east of Solivar. The present capacity of production is almost 100,000 metric tons of salt a year.

East of Solivar, in the territory of the Slanské vrchy Mts. between the villages **ZLATÁ BAŇA** and **ČERVENICA** are the famous **opal mines of Dubník**. For long they were the most important deposits of precious opals in the world until opals in Australia were discovered. Opals of Dubník are highly appreciated in the world markets for their unique characteristics. Their striking property is what is referred to as the opalescence or perfect play of colours. They originated by hydrothermal transformation of the local Tertiary volcanic rocks. The beginnings of mining in Dubník consisted of search for stones on surface and sporadic illegal mining only. When Empress Maria Theresa ruled, approximately in the mid-18th century, the

territory was guarded and authorised lessees carried out mining.

The boom of the opal mines in Dubník came in the years 1845-1880 when their lessee was the Viennese jeweller Solomon Johan Nepomuk Goldschmidt and his heirs. The family of Goldschmidt introduced the opals at the world market and made them famous all over the world. But the best stones were found a little earlier. The **opal Harlequin** from Dubník found in the bed of the brook Oľšavka in 1775 is the largest in the world. It is 23 cm long and its weight is 594 grams (2,970 carats). It is one of the precious exhibits of the Museum of Natural Science in Vienna where it is exhibited in an armed crystal case. Its price is estimated at a half a million dollars. The **opal Burning of Troy**, part of the French crown hoard, is also famous. It used to belong to Napoleon's wife, Empress Josephine. The opal mines in Dubník were closed after the First World War in 1922, but today their reopening is seriously considered. Only one house is left from the for-

mer mining settlement of **Dubník**. The manor house of the Goldschmidt family was burnt by Germans in the Second World War. Only the names given to the individual pits which coincide with those of his wife and ten children and the monument erected above the settlement dedicated to the widow Emily Goldschmidt remind the family of Goldschmidt. Apart from reopening of mining also building of the open-air museum which will comprise the preserved fragments of mines are considered. Forest road leads to the portal of the **pit Viliam** where in 1889 a nest of opals called *Gizelina kaplnka* (Gizela's Chapel) was discovered. The nest contained an incredible amount of 200 kg of precious stones.

In the south-east the region of Šariš reaches as far as the little town **HANUŠOVCE NAD TOPĽOU** (population 3,600) with a bulky fortified **manor house**

Left: Ruins of the Šarišský hrad Castle
Right: Wooden church in Brežany. Church of Beheading of St. John the Baptist in Sabinov

from the 17th century, now **museum of nature science**. Interesting technical monument of the town is the **viaduct of Hanušovce**, one of the largest railway bridges in central Europe. The picturesque valley called **Údolie obrov** guarded by the the bizarre andesite **Hermanovské skaly** rocks on one side and the forested **Oblík Mt.** (925 m) with round top on the other is accessible from the village **HERMANOVCE**.

The medieval power centre of Šariš was the **Šarišský hrad** Castle, the ruins of which are on the top plain of a distinct elevation above the town **VEĽKÝ ŠARIŠ** (population 4,000) situated north-west of Prešov. Its history started in the 12th century and it was one of the largest castles in Slovakia until 1660 when explosion of gun powder stored in castle destroyed it. The ruins testify to its bulkiness so as the old pictures of castle do. Veľký Šariš is now popular because of beer Šariš that is brewed in the local **brewery**. The **castle hill of Šariš** (570 m) forms together with the surrounding volcanic mountains a

group of landscape dominants in the environs of Prešov. In order to see a nice example of Classicist **manor house** from the 19th century one has to travel westward from Prešov to the village **ŽUPČANY** where also the Slovak writer and playwright Jonáš Záborský is buried. If you continue on the road from Prešov to Levoča, you will arrive at the village **FRIČOVCE** with interesting **manor house** from the 17th century. Its building with remarkable attic is one of the most significant Renaissance monuments of eastern Slovakia.

Side road leads northward from Fričovce to the picturesque mountain village of **LIPOVCE**. It is the starting point for the trip to interesting and bizarre **Lačnovský kaňon** canyon with the 60 m tall rock tower **Mojžišov stĺp**. Below the village is a **mineral spring** and its alkaline water is filled in bottles and sold under the wide known trademark **Salvator**. In the village **BREŽANY** in the Šarišská vrchovina Mts. stands precious Baroque **wooden church** from 1727. It is the only in the district of Prešov. Wandering in the environs of Prešov can be finished in the southern suburb of Prešov **Haniska**. The top of the mountain **Furča** (309 m) on the edge of the Šarišská vrchovina Mts. stands the **monument dedicated to the east-Slovakian peasant rebellion** in 1831.

The picturesque town **SABINOV** (population 12,300) boasts a long and rich history of free royal borough with numerous interesting monuments. In modern times Sabinov was not able to compete with substantially stronger Prešov and lived in its shadow. However, retardation of its devel-

opment has also its positive side, because the ancient character of the town has been preserved. Sabinov, like Prešov or Košice has a central lent-shaped **square** skirted by burgher houses. In its centre stands the parish church of **Beheading of St. John the Baptist**. This originally Gothic church which was started at the beginning of the 14th century was enriched by the Renaissance elements in the following reconstruction. The copies of the original medieval paintings of the interior are now deposited in Budapest. However, several precious Gothic **statues** from the workshop of Majster Pavol of Levoča are still in its interior. Beside the parish church is the Renaissance building of the former **Lycée** founded in 1530. It was later adapted for the needs of the Piarist College. Apart from the parish church Sabinov has also two Evangelical churches of Toleration type and the Greek-Catholic church. Remains of **town walls** and eight out of original 13 bastions survive here. Sabinov is the starting point for recreation area of **Drienica-Lysá** with excellent ski tracks.

Not far away from Sabinov is **ŠARIŠSKÉ MICHAĽANY**, known as the centre of pharmaceutical industry – vaccines, infusions and drugs are produced here. If you continue from Sabinov in the contrary direction you will arrive at the little town of **LIPANY** (population 6,150). Its history reaches back to 1312. It was a yeoman town in the 14th century and part of the Kamenica Castle estate. In the revolutionary year of 1849 the battle between the Hungarian revolutionaries and the Russian tsarist army took place near Lipany.

The most important monument of the town is the Gothic **church of St. Martin the Bishop** from the first half of the 14ᵗʰ century with valuable interior. The landscape around Lipany is unusually attractive. The belt of small cliffs of different forms enhances its beauty. The ones near the village **KYJOV** are referred to as **Kyjovské bradlá**. On one of them, above the village **KAMENICA**, remains of the medieval **Kamenický hrad** Castle from the 13ᵗʰ century are to be seen. The top of the castle hill offers a wonderful view of wide environs including the forested massive range of **Čergov** with the tallest mountain **Minčol** (1,157 m). The saddle **Pusté pole** (595 m) lies on the main European water divide. Beyond it is the basin of the Poprad river, which flows in the catching area of the Baltic Sea. This is the westernmost part of the regions of Šariš. Several kilometres beyond the village **PLAVEČ** the re-

Left: St. Egidius church in Bardejov
Right: Town hall of Bardejov

gion of Spiš starts. The ruins of the **Plaveč** Castle from the 13ᵗʰ century adorn the top of the hill towering above the wide valley of the Poprad river and again it is an ideal place for unique views.

Bardejov and its environs

The ancient town of **BARDEJOV** (population 33,250) is undoubtedly one of the most beautiful towns in Slovakia. It was rightly awarded the European award, gold medal of ICOMOS Foundation of UNESCO in 1986 and inscribed into the List of the World Cultural Heritage of the same organisation in 2001. The town was referred to in *ipatievsky* annals as the market settlement of *Bardouev*. Another, six year younger document, mentions that in the territory of *Bardha* was Cistercian monastery. Arrival of German colonists after the Tartar invasion gave impetus to development of a prospering and flourishing town. Royal privileges and above all decision of Louis I of 1376 to promote Bardejov to **free royal borough** accelerated its further development. Bardejov lived its best times in the 15ᵗʰ century. The driving force of its prosperity was trade and crafts, which classified it among the most important towns of the Kingdom of Hungary. The town opened itself to modern ideas in the field of culture and education in the 16ᵗʰ century. The representatives of the Renaissance and reformation humanism imported here from Germany brought them. The tumultuous 17ᵗʰ century tortured by the series of Rebellions of Estates caused that Bardejov started to decline and was overshadowed by more successful Prešov.

Bardejov is spoken of as the "most Gothic town in Slovakia". Its centre consists of a set of historical buildings arranged in the area of pear-shaped ground plan limited by almost continuous belt of town fortifications. The principal area of the historical core is the rectangular **Radničné námestie** square skirted by rows of antique burgher houses with typi-

cal gable facades. In the centre of the square is the building of the former **town hall ❶** from the 16th century. This wonderful solitary building is a splendid example of harmony of the fading out Gothic and the early transalpine Renaissance styles. The interior of the town hall contains the most valuable exhibits of the **Šarišské múzeum ❷** (Museum of Šariš). More expositions of this Museum are exhibited in the originally Gothic burgher house **Gantzughof ❸** with Renaissance arcade, which stands in the south-western corner of the square. Among the numerous architectural and artistic details the wooden Renaissance panel ceiling with paintings in the main hall, portals, decoration of gables and staircase are worth seeing. In the southern row of the square the Gothic **burgher house** with impressive Baroque figural painting on its facade calls attention.

The most important monument of the square is the parish **church of St. Egidius ❹** standing in its northern part. Like town hall, it is the national cultural monument.

Its construction started at the beginning of the 15th century probably at the site of the Cistercian monastery. It was conceived as a majestic Gothic basilica with three naves. The main nave and the church as a whole were finished in the years 1513-1518. The generally simple architecture of the church contains many valuable details and artistic works. In the set of 11 Late Gothic wing altars built in the period between 1460 and 1520 the side **altar of Nativity of the Lord**, attributed to the circle of artists around the Krakow workshop of W. Stwosz is considered the most valuable. The statue **The Chair of Mercy** on the **altar of St. Barbara** made probably in the workshop of Majster Pavol of Levoča is considered the top woodcarving work in Slovakia. The top of the New Gothic **church tower** offers a unique view of the town. Behind the parish church is the Renaissance building of the former town **humanistic school ❺**, the centre of culture and education in the 16th century known in the whole Kingdom of Hungary and even beyond its frontiers. For instance,

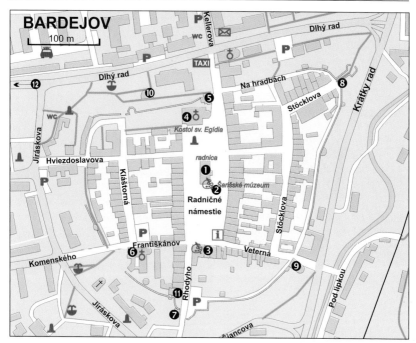

Luther's student and follower Leonard Stöckel referred to sometimes as the "teacher of the Kingdom of Hungary" taught here. Today **musical school** seats in this building, which bears the name of composer Vojtech Keller. The tablet on the wall of the school commemorates the fact that in what is now the Gutgesell's print house the first book in Slovakia written in Biblical Czech languages was printed. It was Luther's *Catechism*.

The **Franciscan monastery** with the **church of St. John the Baptist ➎** was built in the Gothic style and in mid-17th century adapted in Renaissance style in the western part of the town after 1460. The interesting architectural detail of the complex is the monastic corridor with the Renaissance cross vault. The monastery stands near the **town walls**, the best preserved medieval fortification system in Slovakia. Apart from the stone walls two gates and four

bastions survive here. The historical core of the town is accessible from the south by the **Horná brána ➐** (Upper Gate) with stone bridge and in the north-eastern corner of the walls is the **Dolná Brána ➑** (Lower Gate) with barbican. The best-preserved bastions are the **Hrubá bašta ➒** bastion in the east, **Archívna bašta ➓** bastion in the north and the **Štvorhranná bašta ⓫** bastion next to the Horná brána in the south. Outside the historical centre of Bardejov (on Mlynská ulica street) stretches the **Jewish suburb ⓬**, a set consisting of the Jewish bath, synagogue, cemetery, houses and different service structures.

Attractiveness of Bardejov is enhanced by pleasant landscape with numerous landmarks. In the calm valley of the Bardejovský potok brook on the south-eastern foothill of the Flysch mountain of Busov the **spa of Bardejov** is located. The town administers it. Diseases of gastrointestinal system, not specified diseases of respiratory system and occupational diseases are treated here. The local medicinal springs

Right: Burgher houses. Sanatorium Astória.
Town walls of Bardejov. Spa park

were mentioned as early as 1247 in the document of King of Hungry Belo IV, which donated them together with plots to Bardejov. The first spa buildings were built prevailingly of wood in the 17ᵗʰ century. The spa flourished in the 19ᵗʰ century. Perhaps the most famous guest who visited the spa of Bardejov was Empress Elisabeth of Austria known as Sissy. At the end of the 19ᵗʰ century the capacity of spa amounted to 5,000 guests. Today the spa area consists of a set of older and modern buildings set in the oldest spa park in Slovakia. **Astória** is perhaps the most beautiful building with Art Nouveau elements and the liveliest place is the **spa colonnade**. The spa has total of 17 springs and **Hercules** is the one that yields 2.5 litres per second, it is one of the richest in Slovakia. **Múzeum ľudovej architektúry** (Museum of folk architecture), situated on the edge of the spa, concentrates 28 folk buildings gathered in the upper part of the Spiš and north of Zemplín. **Two wooden churches** moved here from the villages Zboj and Mikulášov in the Bukovské vrchy Mts. dominate in this open-air museum.

The environs of Bardejov offer good opportunity to see the examples of folk architecture. Seven wonderful wooden churches included among the national cultural monuments can be admired here. The oldest of them is in the village **HERVARTOV** on the northern foothill of the Čergov Mt. It was build around 1500 in Gothic style. West of Bardejov are three wooden churches in the villages **KRIVÉ**, **FRIČKA**, and **LUKOV**. Near Frička is the village **CIGEĽKA** known for the local **mineral water** with typical salty taste, which is indicated for the therapy of stomach, intestinal or metabolic disorders. It was also exported to the USA in the past. On the way to another Orthodox **wooden church** from 1763 in the village **JEDLINKA** one can stop in the village **ZBOROV**. Heavy fighting took place here between the Austrian-Hungarian and Russian armies during the First World War. The victims are buried in the local **cemetery**. On the forested hill above the village are the comparatively extensive ruins of the **Zborov Castle**. Its beginnings fall to the 11ᵗʰ cen-

tury. The Gothic castle was rebuilt to a large Renaissance fort in the 16th century. It fell in decay after it was conquered by the Imperial troops in 1684. The **ski centre Regetovka** is situated nearby. The two remaining wooden churches stand on the edge of the district of Bardejov. One of them in the village of **KOŽANY** lies a bit farther from the main roads and the wooden Greek-Catholic **church** from 1739 is accessible by a short detour to **TROČANY** from the main road communication between Bardejov and Prešov.

Svidník and its environs

Since 1964 **SVIDNÍK** (population 12,450) is the centre of the area. The **Múzeum materiálnej a duchovnej kultúry Ukrajincov** (Museum of material and spiritual culture of Ukrainians and Ruthenians) documents creativity of local people. Its ex-

hibits are to be seen in open-air exhibition at the hilly locality of Kochanovský breh. It contains a complete set of folk buildings including the **precious wooden church** from 1766 moved here from the village Nová Polianka. In the centre of what is now a modern town is the **Duklianske Museum** built in shape of the anti-tank mine. Documents of different forms contained in it present the history of war operation, one of the largest in the European fronts of the Second World War, which took place not far away from here. **Exposition of arms**, which were used in this operation, is displayed on an open area behind the Museum. The **Monument to the Soviet Army** built in honour of 84,000 dead soldiers of the Red Army and 6,500 members of the Czecho-Slovak Army in autumn 1944 is the third part of this complex. In common graves 9,000 war victims are buried.

The monuments of folk architecture and war operations of the Second World War are concentrated in a small area around Svidník. The road from Svidník

Left: Wooden church in Kožany
Right: Interior of the wooden church in Frička

heading northward will take you to cross-roads "guarded" by two tanks. The road digresses here to the village **KAPIŠOVÁ** and ascends up the valley with matching name **Údolie smrti** (The Death Valley). The hardest battle of tanks took place here in autumn 1944. The war front stopped here for long weeks and every foot of ground, soaked with blood of soldiers, was heavily fought for. But the central commemorative place of the Second World War fighting is the pass **Dukliansky priesmyk** (502 m). The area around this saddle in the main ridge of the Nízke Beskydy Mts. with border crossing to Poland has been adapted to the open-air **Vojenské prírodné múzeum karpatsko-duklianskej operácie** (Military Museum of Carpathian Dukla Operation). The dominant of the area is the monument in form of 28 m tall pylon. The venue of the battle can be seen from the 49 m tall **view tower**, which stands at the site of the observation point of General Ludvík Svoboda, commander of the 1st Czecho-Slovakian army.

Only about a fifth of more than 330 **wooden churches**, which existed once in the northern and eastern Slovakia survive. They are mostly concentrated in the district of Svidník. There are 13 wooden churches classified as national cultural monuments. The churches normally stand on top of hills surrounded by greenery. They were built of spruce or yew wood and their architecture is simple. The Catholic churches are older and usually with a single tower bearing signs of Gothic style. The churches of so-called eastern ritual possess three towers with step-like roofs ending in onion-shaped domes typical for churches of oriental provenience. Their interiors contain valuable and ornamented icons. The later described type of churches prevails in the district of Svidník. They are to be seen in the villages **DOBROSLAVA, LADOMÍROVÁ, ŠEMETKOVCE, KRAJNÉ ČIERNO** (two churches), **HUNKOVCE, KOREJOVCE, NIŽNÝ** and **VYŠNÝ KOMÁRNIK, PRÍKRA, BODRUŽAL, MIROĽA** and **POTOKY**. The village Príkra is also the smallest in Slovakia. At the time of 2001 population census only 7 inhabitants lived here.

The town of **STROPKOV** (population 10,900) has a much longer and richer history than Svidník and also possesses more monuments. An Old Slav settlement existed here as early as before the 13th century. In 1404 it was mentioned as *oppidum*, or little town. Its prosperity was based on the right to markets and annual fairs. The most important monument of Stropkov is the **manor house** built after 1711 by reconstruction of medieval castle, lords of which owned as much as 51 villages. The parish **church of the Most Holy Christ's Body** was built in Gothic style in the 14th century. The Baroque **church and monastery of the Minor order** that came to the town around the 17th century is another dominant of the town. Stropkov, like the town **GIRALTOVCE** situated nearby thrives on tourism, which concentrates to the water reservoir **Veľká Domaša,** built on the river Ondava in 1966. Bathing in its water can be a pleasant conclusion to the trip around the picturesque landscape of Šariš.

PREŠOV
(dial: 051-)

Information
- **Mestské informačné centrum**, Hlavná 67, Prešov, ☎ 16186, ☎/fax 7731113, mic@pis.sk, www.pis.sk, www.presov.sk

Museums
- **Vlastivedné múzeum**, Hlavná 86, Prešov, ☎ 7734708, **Múzeum židovskej kultúry**, Okružná 32, Prešov, ☎ 7731638, **Múzeum vín**, Floriánova ul., Prešov, ☎ 7733108

Galleries
- **Šarišská galéria**, Hlavná 51, Prešov, ☎ 7725423, **AG Gallery**, Hlavná 66, Prešov, ☎ 0907/932001

Atractiveness
- **Church of St. Nicholas**, Hlavná ul., Prešov, ☎ 7725425, **Planetarium and observatory**, Dilongova 17, Prešov, ☎ 7722065

Hotels
- **DUKLA*****, Nám. legionárov 2, Prešov, ☎ 7722741, **SENÁTOR*****, Hlavná 67, Prešov, ☎ 7731186, **ŠARIŠ***, Sabinovská 1, Prešov, 7716351, **MESTSKÁ HALA**, Športová 12, Prešov, ☎ 7734572

Restaurants
- **ČIERNY MOST**, Masarykova 18, Prešov, ☎ 7733858, **LEONARDO**, Hlavná 144, Prešov, ☎ 7720602, **PLATAN**, Požiarnická 4, Prešov, ☎ 7734629, **SLOVENSKÁ REŠTAURÁCIA**, Hlavná 13, Prešov, ☎ 7724827, **TRATTORIA**, Tkáčska 5, Prešov, ☎ 7721588

ENVIRONS OF PREŠOV
(dial: 051-)

Museums
- **Slovenské technické múzeum – Solivar**, Zborovská 2/A, Prešov, ☎ 7757427, **Mestské múzeum**, Nám. slobody 100, Sabinov, ☎ 4521413, **Literárne múzeum**, Župčany, ☎ 7717500

Hotels
- **JAVORNÁ****, Drienica 501, ☎ 4891200, **ŠPORT**, Drienica, ☎ 4584271, **ZDRAVOTNÍK****, Dubovica-Žliabky 366, Lipany, ☎ 4574475, **HOLCIJA***, Dubovica-Žliabky, Lipany, ☎ 4572291, **CANYON***, Lipovce 158, ☎ 7918231, **KAMENNÁ BABA**, Lipovce 1, ☎ 7918229

Restaurants
- **JONATÁN**, SNP 14, Sabinov, ☎ 4523487, **DIMATEX**, Nám. slobody 63/65, Sabinov, ☎ 4892300

BARDEJOV AND ITS ENVIRONS
(dial: 054-)

Information
- **Turisticko-informačná kancelária – SPIRIT**, Radničné nám. 21, Bardejov, ☎/fax 4726273, spirit@spirit-travel.sk, www.spirit-travel.sk, www.bardejov.sk

Museums
- **Šarišské múzeum**, Radničné nám. 13, Bardejov, ☎ 4724966, **Múzeum ikon**, Rhódyho 6, Bardejov, ☎ 4722009, **Radnica**, Radničné nám. 48, Bardejov, ☎ 4746038, **Prírodovedné múzeum**, Rhódyho 4, Bardejov, ☎ 4722630, **Múzeum ľudovej architektúry**, Bardejovské Kúpele, ☎ 4722072, **Villa Rákóczi**, Bardejovské Kúpele, ☎ 4722072

Atractiveness
- **Church of St. Egidius**, Radničné nám., Bardejov, **Spa**, Bardejovské Kúpele, ☎ 4774245

Hotels
- **BELLEVUE*****, Miháľov, Bardejov, ☎ 4728404, **ŠPORTHOTEL***, Kutuzovova 34, Bardejov, ☎ 4724949, **MIER****, Bardejovské Kúpele, ☎ 4774023, **SATEL MINERÁL****, Bardejovské Kúpele, ☎ 4724122

Restaurants
- **HUBERT**, Radničné nám. 6, Bardejov, ☎ 4742603, **ROLLAND**, Radničné nám. 12, Bardejov, ☎ 4729220, **U ZLATEJ KORUNY**, Bardejov, ☎ 4725310

SVIDNÍK AND ITS ENVIRONS
(dial: 054-)

Information
- **Mestské informačné centrum**, Sovietskych hrdinov 38, Svidník, ☎ 7522394

Museums
- **Múzeum ukrajinsko-rusínskej kultúry**, Centrálna 258, Svidník, ☎ 7521569, 7522271, 7522952, **Vojenské múzeum**, Bardejovská 14, Svidník, ☎ 7521398

Galleries
- **Galéria D. Millyho**, Svidník, ☎ 7521684

Hotels
- **DUKLA SENIOR***, Sovietskych hrdinov 96, Svidník, ☎ 7523388, **RUBÍN***, Centrálna ul., Svidník, ☎ 7524210, **ALFA**, Duklianska 71, Giraltovce, ☎ 7322322, **WHITE HORSE**, Chotčianska 168, Stropkov, ☎ 7424200, **JAMI**, Domaša-Valkov, Turany nad Ondavou, ☎ 0905/973861, **ZIPPKA**, Domaša-Valkov, Turany nad Ondavou, ☎ 7491334

ZEMPLÍN

Lower Zemplín Ⓐ

Upper Zemplín

Zemplín for its varied natural assets is one of the most beautiful parts of eastern Slovakia. In the north of the region the typical Carpathian landscape with original virgin forest and rare fauna spreads. It offers intact nature, extensive oasis of silence with far-reaching views and picturesque little villages. Numerous Orthodox and Greek Catholic wooden temples of high cultural and historic value adorn the region. The southern part of Zemplín is characterised by wide lowlands with many water bodies, river nooks and meanders, excellent Tokaj wine and specialities of Eastern Slovakian cuisine. Most of the territory is filled by flat land, prevailingly deforested landscape of the Eastern Slovakian plain. The most visited localities are the Zemplínska Šírava and Domaša water reservoirs, as well as the National Park of Pieniny and Protected Landscape Areas of Vihorlat and Východné Karpaty.

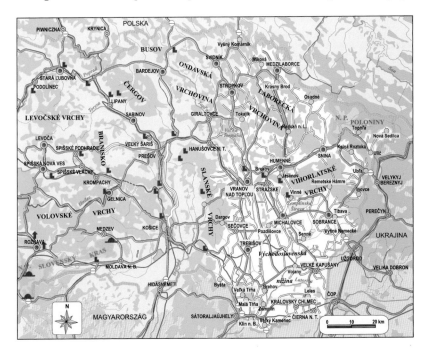

The region adopted the name of the Zemplínsky hrad Castle built long before the Tartar invasion on the site of the former Old Slave fortified settlement. The region was always periphery to any historical forms it belonged to. The result is its comparative economic underdevelopment. Now Zemplín consists of seven administrative units: districts of Michalovce, Trebišov, Sobrance, Humenné, Medzilaborce, Snina, and part of the district of Vranov nad Topľou. Population of about 4,000 lives on a comparatively large area of five thousand square kilometres.

Lower Zemplín

MICHALOVCE (population 40,000) is the economic and cultural centre of the Lower Zemplín. The town lies in the northern part of the Východoslovenská

Left: Manor house in Michalovce
Right: Zemplínska šírava

nížina lowland watered by the middle reach of the Laborec river. Two forested mountains rise beyond the town: it is the characteristic dominant Hrádok (193 m) and the bulkier Biela hora (159 m). Archaeological finds collected in the territory of the town prove almost a continuous settlement of the area from the Stone Age. The first written reference to the town is from 1244. Somewhat later also German colonist settled side by side the Slavs. The old Michalovce was the seat of the royal estate administered by the settlers of the water sentry castle standing next to the Laborec river on important trade route comprising 20 villages. In the Middle Ages Michalovce was a little serf town and it also became victim of wars and fighting between the followers of different religions. Peasant rebellion took place here in the 19th century. Railway facilitated development of trade in agricultural products and the associated industry after 1871. Those of textile, machinery and other later widened the scale of industries. Michalovce today is a modern town with animated cultural and social life. The most visited event its the **Zemplínske slávnosti tancov a piesní** (Folk Festival of Dance and Song of Zemplín).

The most attractive cultural monument of the town is its **manor house**. It stands in the middle of the town on the bank of the Laborec river, on the site of the old water castle, which protected the territory against the enemy assaults. Originally, it was a Gothic building with corner towers guarding the road and the bridge over the Laborec river. The Renaissance reconstruction followed by the Baroque adaptations changed the overall appearance of the manor house and the Classicist style was applied giving it the final touch in the 19th century. In its park the easternmost situated rotunda in Slovakia from the time of the Great Moravian Empire was discovered. The manor house now gives shelter to the **Zemplínske múzeum** (Museum of Zemplín), which documents the developments of nature, society and arts of the region since the oldest time to the present. Natural-historical exhibits from the area of Nature Reserve of Senné are particularly interesting and archaeological collections contain golden jewellery, the oldest proof of gold-work in Slovakia. Another very valuable and unique item is the Bronze amphora with the oldest picture of a two-wheel cart in Europe. Ethnographic collection displays the products of Pozdišov pottery. Among sacral monuments of the town is the Roman Catholic **church of Nativity of the Virgin Mary** from the 18th century and two Greek Catholic **churches**, that of **Nativity of the Virgin Mary** from 1772 and the **Holy Spirit church** from 1934.

Michalovce is the place sought out by tourists for its water reservoir **Zemplínska šírava**. It was constructed in the 1960's and it is situated on the bottom of a large depression. Its is comparatively shallow, its depth reaches only the maximum of 3.5 metres and the area of

its surface is between 22 and 35 square kilometres. Due to the very favourable local climate, above all in summer (high mean air and water temperatures and abundance of sunshine), it is intensively used for recreation. Accommodation and catering facilities are situated mostly on its northern waterside. The eastern and shallower part of the reservoir (about one fifth of its total area) is the protected **ornithological reserve**, the largest of the kind in eastern Slovakia. Almost 100 species of waterfowl including some highly rare ones were identified here.

Environs of the reservoir, especially the Vihorlatské vrchy Mts. are also interesting above all for hikers. On its southern side, north-west of the village **VINNÉ** on top of the hill is the **Viniansky hrad** Castle. It dates to the second half of the 13th century and like other castles in region (Brekov, Jasenov, Kamenec, Streda nad Bodrogom, Čičava, Tibava, Parič) it served as sentry castle on the *Via Magna*, old trade road

leading from the region of Potisie to Poland. All of them were pulled down during the Rebellion of Estates. Ruins of the Viniansky hrad Castle offer a nice view of the Východoslovenská nížina lowland.

The **Vihorlatské vrchy Mts**. is among the most densely forested ranges in Slovakia with common occurrence of the West Carpathian, East Carpathian and Pannonian flora. The range includes the Protected Area of **Vihorlat**, the smallest in Slovakia. It covers several small protected territories including virgin forests in the Motrogon Reserve and **Morské oko**, the unique lake that originated by landslide. It lies amidst the forests of the Vihorlatské vrchy Mts. at 618 m above sea level. The water level of this flow-through lake fed by pristine clear water of the brooks oscillates considerably throughout the year. Its area is 14 ha and it is about 25 m deep. As it is protected, no water sports are admitted here, but on the other side you can ob-

serve trout and crabs living in its water. The **instructive path Morské oko lake - Sninský kameň - Sninské rybníky ponds** provides a nice walk around the locality. The Sninský kameň Mt. (1,005 m) is a fairly conspicuous dominant and provides a wonderful panoramic view of its environs. Some parts though, such as the top of the Vihorlat Mt. are not accessible to hikers.

Iron ore was mined in the northwestern foothill of the Sninský kameň Mt. from the beginning of the 19th century. Heaps of waste rock are visible from the instructive path. Ore was also extracted in the locality near the village **REMETSKÉ HÁMRE** (on the southern side of the range not far away from the Zemplínska Šírava water reservoir) where iron processing plants were constructed after 1864.

Further in south situated **SOBRANCE** (population 6,300) developed in the Middle Ages as the agricultural yeoman town with market and fair

rights. Vineyards were always the typical landscape trait for this little town. Its attractiveness is the **Gitarové múzeum** (Museum of Guitars), which displays more than 200 guitars and historical technology of sound reproduction. Part of the town is the **Sobranecké kúpele** spa with medicinal springs indicated for the diseases of digestive system, those of skin and for rheumatic disorders. The local springs were first mentioned as early as 1336 and the spa is one of the oldest in Slovakia. The village **TIBAVA** represents together with Sobrance the core of the viticultural region. Sand and clay soils are ideal for growing vine and sorts such as Rizling vlašský, Rulandské biele, and Zweigeltrebe. The village is also known for its archaeological site where golden jewellery and pieces of golden sheets similar to coins from the time of Middle Neolithic (4000 to 3600 years BC) were found. Their age is the same as that of the oldest golden objects from Mesopotamia. The **Senianske ryb-**

níky ponds represent another interesting landmark. Some of them are included under the National Ornithological Reserve. Its well-conserved natural setting provides what is referred to as the relaxation zone for the migrating fowl before they cross the Carpathian mountains on their way to the south. Some species also nest here.

POZDIŠOVCE is situated only several kilometres south-west of Michalovce. It is an important ethnographic locality, typical for the region. It is known above all for its ceramics. The oldest written reference to the craft is from 1416. The pottery-makers settled at the local part called Vislok and their houses are different from the rest. They contain historical kilns in form of caves dug into the slopes or field kilns situated behind their houses, normally used by several artisans. Products of the local potters have won in-

Left: Morské oko lake in Vihorlat
Right: Vineyards of Tibava

ternational recognition (for instance, at the 1958 World Exhibition in Brussels) and it is now exported to many countries of the world. Few visitors resist the captivating and tasteful beauty of the local pottery, which is among of the most appreciated types made in Slovakia.

The town of **TREBIŠOV** (population 22,300) is another important centre of the Lower Zemplín with developed food industry. The first written mention of the settlement is from 1254. Despite receiving limited town privileges in the 15th century, Trebišov developed as a serf town. In the centre of the large town English park stand the ruins of the **Parič** Castle (known as castrum Paris from the 13th century) and it is one of the oldest historical monuments of the region. This lowland fort was blown by the Thököly's troops in the 17th century during the Rebellion of Estates. The Csáky

family had the rest of it pulled down and used the stone for building the **manor house** standing nearby by the end of the 18th century. This originally Baroque manor house, later adapted in the Classicist style is also in the town park, the favourite place of the town citizens. The manor house is now the seat of **Vlastivedné múzeum** (Museum of Homeland Studies) with interesting exhibits from farming and viticultural history of eastern Slovakia. The noble family of Andrássy has here a remarkable Neo Gothic **mausoleum** from 1893 with sarcophagus of the last Prime Minister of Austria-Hungary, Count Július Andrássy. The most important sacral monuments of the town include the foundations of the **church of Holy Spirit** from the 13th century and originally Gothic Roman Catholic **Visitation of the Virgin Mary church** from the 15th century, later rebuilt in the Baroque style.

Further in north lying **SEČOVCE** (population 7,800) developed in the Middle Ages as the yeoman town with right to fairs and was also known for its markets and crafts. The famous assembly of the counties of Zemplín and Above where the Bocskay rebellion was announced was held in Sečovce in 1601. The military history of this town also symbolised the **Dargovský priesmyk** pass where one of the heaviest fighting of the Second World War with the final balance of twenty-two thousand casualties took place. Visitors interested in this part of history should walk down the **instructive path** with information panels and exhibited reconstructed war technology.

The exclusive and the youngest **viticultural region** of Slovakia, that **of Tokaj** spreads on the south-western protuberance of the Zemplínske vrchy Mts. south of Trebišov. The name Tokaj derives from the Old Slav word *tokaj* for confluence. This region, together with the part lying over the frontier in Hungary, is one of the few in the world where grapes used for production of naturally

Left: The Andrássy mausoleum
Right: Wine cellars of Tokaj. Tokaj wine

sweet wines are grown. It is said to be *the king of wines and the wine of kings* as it was always served to rulers in the past. In favourable years, that is with during long and dry autumns under the effect of *Botrytis cenerea*, a kind of mould, the grapes change into raisins which give the wine its particular taste, colour and aroma. As the climate of the region is ideal for growing vine, it is one of the best quality wines in Slovakia. In some years there are as much as 2,200 hours of sunshine in the area of Tokaj. Vine was grown here since the Roman period, when the region was part of Pannonia. In the 13th century the Tartars completely destroyed its vineyards and people fled. King Matthias Corvinus greatly helped to revival of

vine growing. The majority of existing wine cellars in the region are from the time of Turkish wars when they were built to serve also as hiding places. Some of them are dug into the volcanic substrate in the depth of 8 to 16 m. The total length of the medieval underground corridors in the village Viničky is 1.2 kilometres. The viticultural region of Tokaj with its centres in the villages **MALÁ TŔŇA** and **VEĽKÁ TŔŇA** now offers 10 sorts of wine.

The Zemplinske vrchy Mts. are surrounded by the Východoslovenská rovina plain, which is an extensive landscape unit with monotonous relief. In the administrative territory of **KLIN NAD BODROGOM,** at the point where the Bodrog river leaves the

territory of Slovakia is the lowest situated spot (94.3 metres above sea level) in Slovakia. Bulky river sediments are the huge stores of groundwater. The typical **weighted beam wells** and sand dunes sporadically animate the monotony of the landscape. They are observable near the village **LELES** (the oldest settlement of the east Slovakia region mentioned in documents in 1190). The dominant of Leles is the Renaissance **monastic complex** (originally the monastery of the Premonstratesian Provostship from the end of the 12th century) situated in the historical part of the community, on an elevated spot, on top of a sand dune. Similar dunes are also near the town **KRÁ-ĽOVSKÝ CHLMEC** (population 8,000) with its landmark – the **ruins** of the Pustý hrad Castle from the 16th century. Vintage festival held in this town every second year attracts visitors. Several

kilometres eastward from Kráľovský Chlmec is a much younger town, function of which is predominantly connected with transports. **ČIERNA NAD TISOU** (population 4,600) was founded only in 1947 as the terminal of combined transport. As the width of railway gauge on the Slovak and Ukraine sides of the frontier is different, all goods passing over the frontier must be submitted to rather demanding manipulation, which is carried out precisely in Čierna nad Tisou. Development of another small town lying nearby **VEĽKÉ KAPUŠANY** (population 9,700) is also connected with transport of ores and coal for the largest classical thermal power station of Slovakia situated in **Vojany** or for what is now the US Steel works in Košice. The Classicist Roman Catholic **church of Sts. Simon and Jude** from 1807 and the Baroque-Classicist Calvinist **church** from 1784 represent the cultural and historical monuments of the town.

Left: Next to the Tisa river
Right: Manor house in Humenné

Upper Zemplín

The most important centre of the Upper Zemplín is **HUMENNÉ** (population 35,000). The town developed from an old Slav settlement mentioned for the first time in the 13th century. The 14th century brought about the first privileges to the town including that of toll collection. In the Middle Ages it was the centre of an extensive feudal estate owned first by the Drugeth family and later by the families Andrássy and Csáky. As it lay on the road connecting the Kingdom of Hungary and Poland, the town also acquired the right to fairs and consequently the town flourished in the 17th and 18th centuries. Humenné today is a modern town, as its old houses were almost entirely destroyed during the Second World War. The character of the town completely changed after the war and its life concentrates around the local chemical plant producing synthetic fibres.

The town is situated on the middle reach of the Laborec river and the originally Renaissance **manor house** from 1610 surrounded by modern urban fabric is rather a surprise. The manor house was reconstructed in the Baroque style, which imitated French architecture in the 19th century. The powerful family Drugeth built it on the site of an old Gothic castle and for centuries it was the seat of one of the largest feudal estates in Slovakia. Now it houses the **Vihorlatské múzeum** (Museum of the region of Vihorlat) with collections of art, history and natural history. In the garden of the manor house is the **open-air museum** exhibiting folk architecture. One of its exhibits is the National Cultural Monument, the wooden **church of St. Michael the Archangel** from 1754 with Baroque interior and icons, which was moved here from the village Nová Sedlica. There is also an observatory and the dendrological reserve with more than 100 species of rare trees in the park. The

Roman Catholic Gothic Franciscan **church** from the 14th century, adapted in the 17th and 18th centuries with interesting stained windows is also worth to see. Nearby stands the Franciscan **monastery**, the Gothic building from the 17th century which was adapted to a stately residence in the Renaissance style. As there live several religious denominations in the town, correspondingly it has several different churches including the synagogue from the late 18th century.

North of Humenné in the valley Hubková is the popular recreation zone of the town. Going southward of the town one can visit the Nature Reserve of **Humenský Sokol** with the 3.5 km long instructive path informing about the interesting and unique specimen of fauna and flora living here. Fans of history will perhaps prefer the ascent to the ruins of

Left: Jasenov Castle
Right: Water reservoir Domaša

the **Brekov** Castle rising above the town on top of the andesite rock with a nice view of the environs, including the towns of Humenné and Strážske. The Brekov Castle is from the 13th century when it was built on the site of an older fort from the Great Moravian period. In time of the Rebellion of Estates in the 17th century one or anther fighting party repeatedly damaged it. It decayed in the late 17th century and only part of its walls and some domes survive. South of Humenné in the wonderful setting of woods of the Humenské vrchy Mts. are the ruins of another castle called **Jasenov** from the 13th century. The Jasenov Castle is known for the particularity that the Drugeth family stroke false coins in it in the mid-16th century. After repeated complaints of nobles from Poland and the Kingdom of Hungary the royal chamber ordered punishment of forgers. Master Mikuláš, who was in charge of the castle workshop was also imprisoned and later beheaded on the square of Prešov. The Castle was occupied and heavily damaged by the rebellious Rákoczi's troops in the mid-17th century. It is in decay ever since.

Not far away from Humenné, in the northern part of the Východoslovenská nižina lowland is **STRÁŽSKE** (population 4,500). It was founded at the beginning of the 12th century as sentry settlement on important trade route connecting the Baltic Sea with the Balkans. In the mid-14th century the settlement lost its strategic purpose because a whole series of sentry castles was built in the region of Zemplín and assumed the protecting function. Construction of railway track in 1871 was the crucial event for the after-war development of this little town as it rendered connection with Michaľany, Humenné and Michalovce and continued to Poland. Dynamics of it development was enhanced by construction of the large chemical factory Chemko. The Greek Catholic **church** from 1794 and the Roman Catholic **church** from 1821 represent sacral monuments of the town. Well-maintained **park** and dendrological reserve with bulkiest poplar and plane trees in Slovakia in the neighbourhood of the Art Nouveau manor house from 1901 are also worth to see.

East of Strážske spreads the one of the oldest towns of Zemplín, **VRANOV NAD TOPĽOU** (population 23,000), first mentioned in historical documents in 1270. It used to be the centre of the Čičava estate in the past and developed as a serf town with the Franciscan monastery. Vranov nad Topľou with its environs became the centre of the eastern Slovakian peasant rebellion in 1831 when the most dramatic events concentrated precisely here. The former agricultural and trade-oriented town was industrialised in the second half of the 20th century when the timber processing factory Bukóza and textile plants were opened here. The most valuable sacral monument of the town is the originally Gothic Roman Catholic **church of the Nativity of the Virgin Mary** from the 16th century with precious interior, an example of the Late Gothic monumental sacral building. The church of Vranov possesses a precious liturgical set made by J. Szilaši, the gold-smith of Levoča. The Pauline **monastery** was built next the northern wall of the church in the 17th century. Jewish **tombstones** from the 16th to 18th centuries can be contemplated at the local Jewish cemetery. Sacral monuments also include the Roman Catholic **Francis of Assisi church**, the Evangelical pseudo-Gothic **church**, and the Greek Catholic **church**. The Classicist **manor house** was built by the end of the 18th century on the ruins of an old castle, which is popular because it was there where the ill-famed Alžbeta Bátory, the "bloody countess" of Čachtice married František Nádašdy in 1575. **Catacombs**, parts of town fortifications from the 15th to 18th centuries were discovered under the town recently.

Hikers use Vranov nad Topľou as the starting point for trips to the Do-

maša water reservoir. The way leads below the ruins of the **Čičava** Castle from the 13th century. The Castle did not survive the last Rákoczi's rebellion in 1711 when it was damaged. The Castle is known for its "Book of Lies and Liars" held here in the 16th and 17th centuries, also referred to as the Book of Čičava - in which curious lies and names of liars were noted. The still used Slovak idiom "it should be entered in the Čičava Book" in case to some outrageous lie refers to the famous book, then known in the whole of Slovakia. The water reservoir of **Domaša** is situated in the mountain setting of the Ondavská vrchovina upland. The warm local climate makes pleasant the bathing and water sports in recreation centres (such as Poľany, Nová Kelča, and Dobrá) situated on its shores.

In the vicinity of the Polish frontiers in the northern part of the Nízke Beskydy Mts. is the town **MEDZILABORCE** (population 6,700), important centre of the Ruthenian and Ukraine ethnicities living

in Slovakia. The oldest written reference to Medzilaborce as a serf village is from 1557. Thanks to its position on the old trade road from Potisie to Halič in Poland it developed into a little town. It was almost destroyed in the two world wars for it is situated next to important mountain passes over the ridge of the Beskydy Mts. Sacral monuments of the town are represented by the Greek Catholic **church** from the end of the 18ᵗʰ century and the Orthodox **church** standing on an elevated spot. The latter mentioned church built in the old Russian style is one of the town dominants. It is dedicated to the victims of the world wars. Visitors to the town like to stop at the **Múzeum moderného umenia rodiny Warholovcov** (Museum of Modern Art of the Warhol Family). Parents of **Andy Warhol**, famous American pop art painter are natives from the village Miková, situated near Medzi-

laborce and the Museum displays 18 of its paintings plus valuable authentic material of different kind documenting his life and work. The cultural event attracting lovers of folklore is the **Festival of the Ruthenian and Ukraine Culture** held every year.

The neighbouring **KRÁSNY BROD** is one of the old settlements of eastern Slovakia first mentioned at the beginning of the 13ᵗʰ century. Approximately in the later half of the 14ᵗʰ century about forty thousand Ukrainians moved here and their *monastyr*, wooden **monastery** from the beginning of the 15ᵗʰ century, became their spiritual and cultural centre. A special chronicle giving details of lives of the Ukrainian minority was kept in the monastery. The monastery existed until 1914 and now in is in ruins. South of the village are the ruins of the pilgrim monastery and the church from the end of the 19ᵗʰ century, destroyed during the First World War and the Baroque **chapel** which was restored.

Left: Museum of the Warhol family
Right: Meadows "poloniny"

One of the easternmost situated towns of Slovakia is **SNINA** (population 21,000). Woods of the Nízke Beskydy and the Vihorlat Mts. surround it. Its history was influenced by discovery of iron ore deposits at the beginning of the 19th century. The Dutch magnate Joseph Rholl founded in the Jozefova dolina valley the iron processing plant and foundry. The statue of Hercules standing on the courtyard of the manor house in Snina was also made there. At the beginning of the 20th century the plant closed and the locals concentrated on farming, colliery and work in forests. Construction of the railway track between Humenné, Snina and Stakčín in the years 1909-1912 was another important event, which contributed to the development of the town. Textile and machinery industry established here after the Second World War gave employment to many locals. The sacral dominant of Snina is the Roman Catholic **church** from 1736 reconstructed in 1992, while the Classicist **manor house** of the Rholl family with remains of English **park** from the end of the 18th century is its most important profane historical building. Its past glory is symbolised by the courtyard with a well and the **statue of Hercules** fighting the dragon. World famous **art gallery MIRO,** one of the three private galleries (one in Prague and another in Berlin) also seats in Snina and contains several gems of the world and Slovak fine arts. The Gallery actively participates in different cultural events organised in international context. The town of Snina was granted the 2000 Art Prize of the European Union.

The region of Upper Zemplín is that with the highest concentration of the Ukraine and Ruthenian minorities. Despite of prevalence of the Slovak population the Ruthenians and Ukrainians are the representatives of the local picturesque folklore and specific features of this region. Ruthenians are defined as an independent nation among the east Slav nations. They arrived at the territory of Slovakia between the 14th and 17th centuries. At the turn of the 19th and 20th centuries many of them emigrated to America pursuing jobs and better life. The period after 1948 brought about hard times for this ethnicity. The communist government prohibited their Greek Catholic church and the believers were obliged to convert and adopt the Orthodox confession. Ruthenian ethnicity was not tolerated after 1952 and Ruthenians were officially considered members of the Ukraine ethnicity. One of the things democracy offers to the locals is reviving of their ethnic and religious community in the territory of Slovakia. The 2001 census revealed that 24 thousand and 11 thousand citizens adhere to the Ruthenian and Ukraine ethnicities respectively. They are mostly members of the Greek Catholics and Orthodox churches.

Wooden churches are important manifestations of local culture in this re-

gion. They dominate in the landscape not only for their size but also position, as they usually stand isolated on top of the hill or on the edge of the village. Normally they are fenced complexes consisting of church (*cerkva*), belfry and cemetery. Abundant forests existing in the area provided building material for such structures. Older churches were often built without a single iron nail. They generally date back to the 17th or 18th centuries though there are also some younger churches built recently. In the area of Upper Zemplín there are nine churches surviving on their original sites: **Kalná Roztoka, Topoľa, Ruský Potok, Ruská Bystrá, Uličské Krivé, Hrabová Roztoka, Jalová, Šmigovec,** and **Inovce**. Churches of **Zboj** and **Nová Sedlica** were moved to the open-air museum of folk architecture in Bardejov and Humenné. The common feature of

churches is the interior ornamentation with great taste and sense for harmony. The dominant functional and artistic element of their interior are the icons.

The remotest part of the region, and as a matter fact of Slovakia, is becoming ever more attractive for tourists. They can visit here the **National Park of Poloniny**, which was added to the list of National Parks of Slovakia in 1997. It is situated at the point where three frontiers meet: Slovak, Polish and Ukrainian. The Park immediately neighbours with the Polish Bieszczadski Park Narodowy, also National Park. The territory is part of the Východné Karpaty Mts. The mountain area where the Park was established is also known under the Slovak name, the Bukovské vrchy Mts. The name of the Park derives from the Slovak term for special and unique alpine meadows spreading here above the upper timberline called by the locals ***poloniny***. The most beautiful are those around Pľaša, Ďurkovec, Riaba skala,

Left: Wooden church in Uličské Krivé
Right: Poloniny - the Stužica virgin forest

and Kamenná lúka. Almost 80 per cent of the forest area consist of rounded ridges and waterlogged valleys. Sharp stones such as Oreničova skala rock or the continuous long strip of sandstone rocks in administrative territory of Runina village are less frequent. Particularities of the territory is the occurrence of the largest complexes of original, in places virgin, beech-fir woods in Europe and the rare concentration of threatened animal and plant species. The densest concentration of natural woods and virgin forests in Slovakia is precisely in the territory of this National Park. The Park contains several small Protected Areas among them are the most frequently visited Stužica, Jarabá skala, Rožok, Pľaša, Stinská, and Havešová. The plant and animal species living in the Park including several endemits are of the type typical for the Východné Karpaty (East Carpathian) Mts. Occurrence of game, including all carnivorous mammals and sporadic visits of the European bison and reindeer coming here from Poland are the prides of the Park.

The UNESCO in the framework of the Man and Biosphere Programme defines the territory as the **Biosphere Reserve Východné Karpaty.** Its area is more than 40 thousand hectares. Together with reserves of the same type in the territory of Poland and Ukraine, the International Biosphere Reserve of Východné Karpaty forms an area of more than 165 thousand hectares. The whole area is rich in pure surface water, lakes and water reservoirs. The starting point for the trips to the eastern part of the National Park is the easternmost situated village of Slovakia, **NOVÁ SEDLICA.** Its environs are indeed interesting for hikers for their intact natural environment. There is the Nature Reserve of **Stužica** near the village, considered the most beautiful example of virgin forest in Slovakia with huge fir and beech trees. The ascent to the tallest mountain of the Bukovské vrchy Mts. the **Kremenec Mt.** (1,221 m) standing close to the frontiers separating the three countries also starts in this village. While the eastern part of the National Park preserved the impressive character similar to that of Ukraine, its western part is almost unpopulated. Construction of the **Starina water reservoir** in the 1980's required important changes including flooding of seven villages on the upper reach of the Cirocha river in order to protect the high quality water in the dam as it supplies the drinking water to the whole region of Eastern Slovakia.

LOWER ZEMPLÍN
(dial: 056-)

Information
- **Mestské informačné centrum Michalovce**, Nám. osloboditeľov 77, Michalovce, ☎ 6423555, fax 6420020, mic@ba.telecom.sk, www.zemplininfo.sk

Museums
- **Zemplínske múzeum**, Kostolné nám. 1, Michalovce, ☎ 6441093, **Vlastivedné múzeum**, M. R. Štefánika 257/61, Trebišov, ☎ 6722234, **Gitarové múzeum**, Sobrance, ☎ 6522210, **Cirkevné múzeum Pavla Horova**, Bánovce n/O, ☎ 6883411

Atractiveness
- **Sobranecké kúpele** spa, Sobrance, ☎ 6522359, **Viniansky hrad** Castle, Vinné, **Parič** Castle, Trebišov, **Pustý hrad** Castle, Kráľovský Chlmec

Hotels
- **JALTA****, Nám. osloboditeľov 70, Michalovce, ☎ 6426086-8, **DRUŽBA***, Hollého 1, Michalovce, ☎ 6420452-4, **ŠÍRAVA***, Zemplínska šírava – Kamenec, Kaluža, ☎ 6492556-9, **VOJENSKÁ ZOTAVOVŇA**, Medvedia hora – Zemplínska šírava, Kaluža, ☎ 6492571-2, **POŠTÁR**, Zemplínska šírava, Kaluža, ☎ 6492350, **CHEMES**, Zemplínska šírava, Kaluža, ☎ 6492101, **TOKAJ***, M. R. Štefánika 171/37, Trebišov, ☎ 6722431, **ZEMPLÍN***, M. R. Štefánika 861/230, Trebišov, ☎ 6722950, **ŠPORTCLUB**, Ul. J. Kostru, Trebišov, ☎ 6723288, **MINERÁL***, Kúpele Byšta 73, Kazimír, ☎ 6701838, **KORZO***, Ul. Dargovských hrdinov, Sečovce, ☎ 6783979, **MAŇA***, Štefánikova 1, Sobrance, ☎ 6522364

Restaurants
- **SLOVENSKÁ REŠTAURÁCIA**, Masarykova ul., Michalovce, ☎ 6431244, **AMADEUS**, M. R. Štefánika 50, Trebišov, ☎ 6727526, **SALAŠ**, Medvedia hora, Kaluža, ☎ 6492120

UPPER ZEMPLÍN
(dial: 057-)

Information
- **Turisticko-informačné centrum pri CK UNITUR**, Strojárska 102, Snina, ☎ 16186, 7685735, fax 7682285, unitur@stonline.sk

Museums
- **Vihorlatské múzeum**, Nám. slobody 1, Humenné, ☎ 7752240, **Skanzen**, Nám. slobody 1, Humenné, ☎ 7752240, **Vlastivedné múzeum**, Zámocká 160/5, Hanušovce n/T, ☎ 4452371, **Múzeum moderného umenia Andyho Warhola**, A. Warhola 749, Medzilaborce, ☎ 7321059

Galleries
- **Galéria MIRO**, Centrum OD, Snina, ☎ 7622864

Atractiveness
- **Church of St. Michael the Archangel**, Humenné, ☎ 7752240, **Observatory**, Humenné, **Brekov** Castle, Humenné, **Jasenov** Castle, Humenné, **Čičava** Castle, Vranov n/T, **Wooden churches** – Kalná Roztoka, ☎ 7696148, Topoľa, ☎ 7698119, Ruský Potok, ☎ 7698121, Ruská Bystrá, ☎ 056/6584071, Uličské Krivé, ☎ 7694181, Hrabová Roztoka, ☎ 7693087, Jalová, ☎ 7692358, Šmigovec, ☎ 7693052, Inovce, ☎ 056/6582522

Hotels
- **ARMALES***, Duchnovičova 282/1, Stakčín, ☎ 7674247-8, **KAMEI***, Sninské rybníky, Snina, ☎ 7682187, 7682605, **VIHORLAT***, Strojárska 2206, Snina, ☎ 7622707, **ROZKVET**, Nám. slobody 3, Vranov n/T, ☎ 4421747, 4422586, **CHEMES**, Nám. slobody 51, Humenné, ☎ 7762546, **KARPATIA**, Čsl. armády 1377, Humenné, ☎ 7752037, **SECON**, Mierová 1439/5, Humenné, ☎ 7752597, **LABOREC**, A. Warhola 195/30, Medzilaborce, ☎ 7321307

Restaurants
- **PLZEŇSKÁ REŠTAURÁCIA**, Ul. osloboditeľov, Humenné, ☎ 7757697, **CAFE AMADEUS**, Nám. slobody, Humenné, ☎ 7762461, **KRIVÁŇ**, Študentská 1, Snina, ☎ 7622396, **MIKOS**, Staničná 1021, Snina, ☎ 7685864, **ZLATÝ BAŽANT**, Strojárska 104, Snina, ☎ 7685318, **U KRIŠTOFA**, Strojárska 2206/97, Snina, ☎ 7581070, **TEMPER**, Kolárska 1317, Snina, ☎ 7580900, **MARGARETT**, Mierová 289/2, Medzilaborce, ☎ 7322291, **MODRÁ PERLA**, Soľ 268, ☎ 4880560

Holiday in Slovakia

Hiking and mountaineering

Slovakia compared to the rest of Europe, possesses a dense network of hiking trails. This network provides abundant opportunities for combination of hiking routes of different grade and length. Standard tourist signs in four colours: red, blue, green, and yellow, mark the routes. Road signs stand at important crossroads and contain the data on sign colour, direction and distance of destinations. The distance is measured by time it takes to reach the aim of the trip.

The most attractive territory of Slovakia for tourists is that of the **High Tatras**. But the Roháče Mts. in the West Tatras, the Demänovská dolina valley in the Low Tatras Mts. Slovenský raj Mts., Pieniny Mts., Vrátna valley in the Malá Fatra Mts., southern part of the Veľká Fatra Mts., environs of Banská Štiavnica, Kremnica, and Bratislava with its landscape part are also frequently visited by fans of hiking.

There are numerous collective events organised for tourists which enjoy great popularity; among them are the passages over the ridges of Low Tatras, Veľká Fatra and Malá Fatra Mts. and the inhabitants of Bratislava interested in hiking take part in the passage over the ridge of the Malé Karpaty Mts.

Cycling is also winning increasing popularity. So far though, the special trails for cyclists in Slovakia are still missing and for this kind of tourism the subsidiary and not too busy roads are used. Many cyclists frequent the **International Danube Cyclotourist Route** leading through Bratislava and further along the dike of the Gabčíkovo Dam.

The High Tatras are the paradise for mountaineers, which can be in this sense compared to the Austrian Alps. Many tourist cottages in the Tatras serve as the base for mountaineering trips deeper into the range. Other mountain ranges also

Right: The ridge of the Malá Fatra Mts.

offer suitable conditions for practising this sport. There are numerous rocks dispersed all over Slovakia used by the mountaineers for training or competitions.

Winter sports and tourism

In winter there are good conditions for skiing almost in the whole territory of Slovakia. Ski tracks with lifts are in all mountain ranges from the Malé Karpaty Mts. to the High Tatras. Use of artificial snow has now equalled the differences that previously existed in the duration of ski seasons between the high-mountain and sub-mountain ski centres. Many ski tracks are also lighted in the night.

The most sought after ski centres in Slovakia are: **Solisko** and **Skalnaté Pleso** in the High Tatras, Spálený žľab in the Roháče Mts., northern and southern slopes of the Chopok Mt. in the Low Tatras, Čertovica in the Low Tatras, Dono-

valy on the boundary between the Low Tatras and Veľká Fatra Mts., Malinné and Turecká in the Veľká Fatra Mts., Vrátna valley, and the Martinské hole in the Malá Fatra Mts., Dedinky in the Slovenský raj Mts., Skalka and Krahule in the Kremnické vrchy Mts., Kojšovská hoľa in the Volovské vrchy Mts., and Kubínska hoľa in the Oravská Magura Mts. Among the recently opened ski centres Litmanová in the Ľubovnianska vrchovina highland, Bachledova dolina valley and Jezerské in the Spišská Magura Mts., **Plejsy** near Krompachy, Podháj-Háj in the Stolické vrchy Mts., Veľká Rača in the Kysucké Beskydy Mts., Lopušná dolina valley near Svit, Valčianska dolina valley in the Malá Fatra Mts., Jasenská dolina in the Veľká Fatra Mts., and Regetovka near Bardejov have won reputation among skiers.

The lower mountain regions are ideal for cross-country skiing. Maintained tracks though, are available only in selected winter sport resorts such as **Štrbské Pleso**, Donovaly, Skalka or Osrblie. Sports in higher mountains require ski-alpine outfit because of higher probability of injury in highly dissected and forested terrain. There are good conditions for ski-alpinism in the High Tatras and West Tatras mountain ranges.

Water sports and bathing places

Although Slovakia has no sea and the natural lakes are not numerous either, it can offer water bodies for bathing and water sports. There are many artificial water reservoirs, which were made by blocking rivers or after extraction of gravel and sand. The majority of dams in Slovakia, with exception of reservoirs of drinking water, were also adapted for bathing and recreation. There are dams of Orava and Liptovská Mara in northern Slovakia, Veľká Domaša, Zemplínska Šírava, Bukovec and Ružín in eastern Slovakia. In central Slovakia people bath at Teplý vrch, Ružiná or Palcmanská Maša. The Gabčíkovo dam offers ideal conditions for water sports at the locality Hrušov, and there are also some wonderful sun

Left: Mountaineer in icefall
Right: Swimming pool in Patince

bathed water reservoirs in south-western Slovakia such as Sĺňava near the spa of Piešťany and in Kráľová near Sereď. In the environs of Bratislava there are several artificial lakes adapted to bathing and water sports – **Slnečné jazerá** in Senec, Zlaté piesky in outskirts of Bratislava and in Rovinka near Bratislava. The region of Záhorie also offers nice lakes. The citizens of Košice in turn prefer the lakes in Čaňa. Those in the Štiavnické vrchy Mts. called "tajchy" are also very popular.

There is abundance of swimming pools in Slovakia. Many of them are fed by natural thermal and often medicinal water. The best known and very popular are the swimming pools in the **Podunajská nížina** lowland, such as those in Veľký Meder, Dunajská Streda, Štúrovo, Podhájska, Santovka and Dudince. In the Carpathians there are several thermal swimming pools and the most popular are the open-door and indoor swimming pools in Piešťany, Trenčianske Teplice, Rajecké Teplice, Bojnice, Kováčová, Oravice,

Bešeňová, Vrbov and Vyšné Ružbachy. Some of them are opened the whole year round.

Spas and mineral springs

People knew about the mineral springs in Slovakia since the time immemorial and soon discovered their medicinal effects. Many of these springs gave rise to spas and some of them became important therapeutic centres with the most recent and modern equipment for therapy of varied diseases and health problems. The spas of Bardejov, Piešťany, Trenčianske Teplice, Sliač or Vyšné Ružbachy are recognised world-wide and their clientele is from different countries of the world. Slovakia also offers the possibility of therapy in climatic spas on the southern foothills of the High Tatras. Only minor part of the mineral waters existing in Slovakia is bottled. If all water of the mineral springs available in Slovakia was exploited, Slovakia could supply this precious gift of nature to all countries of Eu-

rope. The most popular mineral waters are sold under the trademarks of Baldovská, Salvator, Fatra, Kláštorná, Budiš, and Slatina.

Caves and karstic landscapes

There is an unusually varied scale of different karstic phenomena in Slovakia. The water, which penetrates into the entrails of limestone mountain ranges and plateaux, is the force, which created an extra rich underground world. The branched labyrinth of cave corridors, domes and halls is adorned by a wide choice of multicoloured ornamentation of dripstones of amazing and surprising beauty. This world submerged in eternal dark was progressively discovered by Slovak potholers. They have invested thousands of hours into exploration and mapped tens of kilometres of corridors of the complicated cave systems.

The largest known cave system in Slovakia is in the **Demänovská dolina** valley on the northern foothills of the Low Tatras that is 30 km long. In the adjacent Jánska dolina valley is the deepest Slovak cave of Starý hrad. Between its lowest and highest situated parts is the difference of 432 metres. The area of the Slovenský kras Mts. is especially rich in surface karst. It spreads in the Slovak-Hungarian boundary.

Total 12 caves have been made accessible to public in Slovakia. The **Demänovská jaskyňa slobody** cave is remarkable for its dripstones while the **Dobšinská ľadová jaskyňa** cave boasts magnificent and bulky ice filling, and the unusual beauty of aragonite ornamentation can be admired in the **Ochtinská aragonitová jaskyňa** cave. Some other caves can be visited in company of specialised guides. Above all the visit to the Krásnohorská jaskyňa cave in the area of Slovenský kras is an exciting experience.

*Left: The Hamman bath in Trenčianske Teplice
Right: Silická planina plateau in the Slovenský kras Mts.*

Car-camping in Dedinky

General information from A to Z

A – Autoopravovne – Car repair

There is a network of car repair stations all over Slovakia, with one in every town providing general repairs and emergency services for virtually every model of vehicle. The opening hours during the tourist season are longer. Private workshops also offer, in smaller communities, a part-time service.

B – Bezpečnosť – Safety

A network of police stations in towns and bigger communities provides for the public order and safety of local citizens and visitors. In the event of any danger, loss or theft of personal belongings in the territory of the Slovak Republic call the phone number **158**.

C – Cestná a železničná sieť – The road and railway networks

The road network of Slovakia is dense and fairly well maintained. It consists of motorways, state roads of the 1st and 2nd class and side roads. Out of the total of 18,000 kilometres of public road communications the 1st class roads represent about 17 per cent. The current 200 km of motorway network is being continuously expanded. The continuous motorway system running from Bratislava to Košice is now under construction. Apart from Prague, Bratislava will have the direct motorway to Vienna and Budapest in near future. Use of motorways is paid through purchase of **motorway stamps**, normally sold at the frontiers, petrol stations and post offices. The roads running transversally from south to north are a bit more demanding for drivers as they pass through mountain ranges. The road mountain passes of Donovaly, Veľký Šturec or Čertovnica are the most frequented ones. Snow is normal in winter and it requires the appropriate equipment such as winter tires and snow chains. **Car rentals** are not numerous and it is advisable to order this service before arriving at Slovakia through travel agency. The majority of Slovak towns have their public transports that observe a fixed schedule.

The railway network of Slovakia with density of 74 km per square kilometre and the length 3,600 km connects the majority of the Slovak towns. The sole owner of the company **Železnice Slovenskej republiky** or ŽSR is still the State. Slovakia is one of the European states with best developed domestic bus transport. Buses of the **Slovenská autobusová doprava** (SAD) carry the passengers to almost all Slovak towns and villages. Most of them start in Bratislava from Autobusová stanica Mlynské Nivy (Bus Terminal on the Mlynské Nivy St.) or in Nitra and Košice. The bus drivers normally sell bus tickets but they

Railway station in Stratená

can be also purchased in advance with the place card at bus stations in every larger town. This is also true in case of international lines that are frequently sold out several days before departure of the bus. It is advisable to inquire on occasional discounts at information desks in the stations. Return tickets are not subject to discounts.

C – Cestovné kancelárie – Travel agencies

Tourism and travel is serviced by a network of numerous travel agencies in every town and tourist resort offering attractive half-day, all-day and longer trips to the most interesting parts of Slovakia.

C – Colné predpisy – Customs provisions

Custom-free import to Slovakia concerns items for personal use and consumption. Custom free export of items is permitted if their value does not exceed 3,000 Sk (only 1 litre of spirit and 2 litres of wine and 200 cigarettes per person are exempt from customs duty). Goods exceeding this limit are subject to custom surcharges. More detailed information on custom provisions are provided at every border crossing. Please read the leaflets updating the custom tariffs, or the list of the items with the limited export or import duty.

Č – Čas – Time

CET - Central European Time i.e. one hour ahead of Greenwich Mean Time is valid in Slovakia. Central European Summer Time is introduced for the summer season (six months) in the majority of European states, i.e. 2 hours ahead of the Greenwich time.

Boat traffic on the Danube river

D – Doprava – Transport

Slovakia is accessible by plane, train, bus, car, and by boat. There are airports in Bratislava, Košice, Piešťany, Sliač, and Poprad. The majority of foreign visitors prefer the Viennese airport Schwechat that is only 50 kilometres away from Bratislava and buses connect it. International trains come to Bratislava from Prague over Kúty (CZ/SK) and continue to Štúrovo (SK/H). Five railway tracks connect Slovakia with the neighbouring Czech Republic. The comparatively frequent connection of Bratislava with Vienna can be interesting for overseas visitors.

There are bus connections with several European cities, such as London, Paris, Munich, Stockholm, Brussels, Prague, etc. There are 49 road border crossings for car drivers (15 CZ, 5 A, 16 H, 2 UA, 11 PL). Two of them are on motorways (Kúty CZ/SK and Jarovce (A/SK). Some border crossings serve only to the local cross-frontier contacts which means that only the citizens of the neighbouring countries can make use of them. The border crossing Jarovce-Kitsee is an exception and all EU visitors can use it. Boat is an attractive option of transport to Slovakia. The personal port on the Danube in Bratislava offers regular boat lines to Vienna, Hainburg, Budapest and other river ports on the Danube.

D – Dopravné predpisy – Traffic rules

All traffic signs agree with European standards. Use of safety belts is obligatory. In accordance with other countries there is a ban on the drinking of alcohol whilst driving. A speed limit of 60 km in the communities and 90 km outside the communities is to be observed. The speed limit on motorways and fast roads is 130 km/hour. Essential car equipment must include a first aid box, a tow rope, a warning triangle and a spare wheel. Children below 12 and pets must not sit in the front seats.

E – Elektrická energia – Electric power

Electric installations are as a rule adjusted to 220 V of alternate current (AC). Sockets corresponding to European standards are available for general use.

G – Gastronómia – Food

Bryndzové halušky means for the Slovaks the same as sushi for the Japanese or pizza for the Italians. This Slovak national meal consists of dumplings made of potato dough mixed with a special kind of soft and salty sheep cheese. Baked bacon chopped in tiny pieces is added to the ready meal, which makes it especially tasty. The traditional beverage to accompany the meal is sour milk or whey. Annual competition in cooking and eating of this traditional meal is organised in the little mountain village of Turecká at the foothills of the Veľká Fatra Mts. where fans of "halušky" from all over the world meet.

After an exhausting ascent to one of the mountain tourist cottages or mountain hotels it is recommendable to have a glass of the typical distillate. The Demänovka liqueur, which contains an extract of medicinal herbs, is a good choice, for instance. Apart from distillates, beer is very popular. Slovak beers are of good quality and the brands like Zlatý bažant, Smädný mních or Topvar are comparable to excellent Czech beers. High quality wines are also produced in Slovakia where vine is grown since the Roman era. The Frankovka of Rača is one of the typical west-Slovakian red wines while in the east it is advisable to taste **Tokaj**.

I – Informácie – Information
Information on travel and tourism is provided by some bureaux of travel information and promotion in certain areas. Information concerning other regions is provided by the travel agencies.

J – Jazyk – Language
Slovak is the official language in the territory of Slovakia. In cities and popular tourist resorts and in the majority of hotels a reasonable level of German and English

"Bryndzové halušky"

is spoken. In hotels, public institutions, travel agencies and banks English, German, and to a limited extent, French, Russian, and Italian are spoken.

L – Lekárska pomoc – Medical care
In all Slovak towns medical care is provided for in hospitals or clinics. Larger communities also have their medical centres. In the event of serious accidents or a sudden deterioration of health emergency services are available on phone number **155**. Before travelling to Slovakia health insurance enquiries are advisable.

M – Mapy – Maps
Whilst travelling around Slovakia use a road map of Slovakia on a scale of 1 : 100 000, or a car atlas on a scale of 1 : 200 000 available in book shops or road border crossings.

N – Nákupy a suveníry – Shopping and souvenirs
Foreigners most often buy objects of folk arts, which may be a puppet dressed in the traditional folk costume, embroidery, folk garments, glass, wire or wooden art objects, and the like. Typical pottery of Modra or Pozdišovce can also be a nice souvenir.

O – Otváracie hodiny – Opening hours
Shops are open from 9:00 to 18:00h, some grocery shops open at 6:00h and close late at night. On Saturdays and Sundays the majority of shops close at 13:00h. Pharmacies open from 8:00 to 18:00h, and there is always one or two emergency pharmacies open during the night and during holidays. Banks open from 8:00 to 15:00h with

Market hall in Bratislava

a lunch break and are closed on Sundays and Saturdays. Banking automats are available. Museums open as a rule from 9:00 or 10:00h to 17:00h with closing days on Monday or Tuesday, with regional variation. See other opening hours included in other entries.

P – Parkovanie – Parking

Parking in town centres is possible only in limited locations. In big cities parking cards are used. They must be made visible in the car and are sold in newspaper stands or tobacco shops. The parking of cars in prohibited places is subject to a fine, or clamping and towing away.

P – Peniaze – Money

The Slovak currency unit is the Slovak crown (1 Sk = 100 haliers). Bank notes are in the nominal value of 20, 50, 100, 200, 500, 1000, and 5000 Sk, the coins are in the nominal value of 10, 20, 50 haliers and 1, 2, 5, and 10 Sk. The Slovak crown is not a free exchangeable currency, and the exchange rate moderately oscillates. The import of foreign currency to Slovakia is optional and the export of the Slovak crown and foreign currency from Slovakia is limited. Banks, hotels, top restaurants, car rental shops and some retail shops mostly accept the majority of international credit cards. In towns and tourist centres the banking automats which accept international cards, and cards issued by Slovak banks are available.

P – Pohonné hmoty – Fuel

The prices of petrol and motor oil are lower in Slovakia than the European average. All over the Slovak territories a dense network of petrol stations is available. In Slovakia the petrol SUPER (95), ŠPECIÁL (91), lead-free petrol NATURAL (95 and 98) and motor oil are sold. The export of fuel in an amount exceeding 10 litres is prohibited. In the towns and on the motorways and main roads some petrol stations are open 24 hours per day.

P – Pošta – Post offices

Post offices are open Mon-Fri 8:00-18:00h, Saturdays they close at 13:00h. Some main offices and telegraph service in towns and tourist centres operate 24 hours per day. The international dial number of the Slovak Republic is 00421.

T – Telefóny – Telephone

Telephone Information Service:
Telephone numbers in the territory of the SR: 1181
Telephone numbers abroad: 12149
Railways: 02 50 58 45 65
Buses: 0984 22 22 22

Dialing codes of selected Slovak towns:

Banská Bystrica	048
Bardejov	054
Bratislava	02
Dunajská Streda	031
Komárno	035
Košice	055
Levice	036
Liptovský Mikuláš	044
Lučenec	047
Martin	043
Michalovce	056
Nitra	037
Poprad	052
Prešov	051
Prievidza	046
Trenčín	032
Trnava	033
Žilina	041

Slovak bank notes

R – Reštaurácie – Restaurants

The opening hours in the majority of restaurants are generally from 10:00 to 22:00h in bigger towns and tourist centres night clubs exist. Tipping roughly represents the percentage comparable to European countries, and where no service charge is included in the bill a tip generally expresses the recognition of the service.

S – Sviatky – The state holidays

- January 1– Declaration of the Slovak Republic
- January 6 – Three Magi day
- Good Friday
- Easter Monday
- May 1 – May Day
- May 8 – Victory over Fascism Day
- July 5 – The Day of the Slovak Messengers of Faith - Constantine and Method
- August 29 – The Anniversary of the Slovak National Uprising
- September 1 – The Day of the Slovak Constitution
- September 15 – The Virgin Mary of Seven Grievances
- November 1 – All Saints' Day
- November 17 – Day of Fight for Freedom and Democracy
- December 24 – Christmas
- December 25 – The First Christmas Holiday
- December 26 – The Second Christmas Holiday

T – Taxi

Taxi services are available in all towns and tourist centres in Slovakia. The tourist tariff per 1 km within the municipal limits is approx. 20 Sk.

Hotel Forum in Bratislava

T – Tiesňové volanie – Emergency numbers
Police: 158
Municipal police: 159
Fire and rescue service: 150
Rapid medical assistance: 155, 16155
Car driver's assistance: 0124, 124 *55 (handy)
Tow truck service: 16116

U – Ubytovanie – Accommodation
Luxurious hotels are available only in Bratislava at the moment, though some spas and some hotels in the High Tatras also offer excellent and expensive accommodation choice. Such hotels are for instance the Forum, Holiday Inn, Devín and Danube in Bratislava. Bratislava can also accommodate its visitors in boat hotels on the Danube. In the High Tatras the Hubert hotel near Gerlachov enjoys very good reputation.

In last years many small boarding houses have been opened and accommodation in private houses can be also quite comfortable. It should be noted though that in high summer or winter season they are all full. Above all tourists coming from Poland and Czech Republic prefer this kind of accommodation. In case if you have no reservation try first information centres where the data on vacancies concentrate. Young people can make use of accommodation offered by student residencies in summer holidays. About a hundred of car camping sites with standard amenities are opened in summer. The largest is the FICC Camping in Tatranská Lomnica (the High Tatras). Apart from caravans and tents the camping sites offer accommodation in tourist huts and bungalows.

Mountain tourist cottages and mountain hotels serve to hikers along their tours. Camping outside the places especially indicated for the purpose is prohibited.

V – Veľvyslanectvá – Embassies
Embassy of the Kingdom of Belgium
F. Kráľa 5, 811 05 Bratislava,
☎ 02/5249 1338
Embassy of the Czech Republic
Panenská 33, 810 00 Bratislava,
☎ 02/5293 1204, 5293 1205
General Honorary Consulate of the Kingdom of Denmark
Ventúrska 12, 815 16 Bratislava,
☎ 02/5441 8470-1
Embassy of the Republic of France
Hlavné nám. 7, 812 83 Bratislava,
☎ 02/5934 7111
Embassy of Greece
Panská 14, 811 01 Bratislava,
☎ 02/5443 4143
Embassy of the Kingdom of Holland
Fraňa Kráľa 5, 811 05 Bratislava,
☎ 02/5249 1577
Consulate of the Canadian embassy for technical co-operation
Mišíkova 28/D, 811 03 Bratislava,
☎ 02/5244 2175

Chata pod Suchým cottage in the Malá Fatra Mts.

Honorary Consulate of the Grand Duchy of Luxembourg
Bajkalská 25, 827 18 Bratislava, ☎ 02/5341 8585
Embassy of the Republic of Hungary
Sedlárska 3, 814 25 Bratislava, ☎ 02/5443 0544
Embassy of the Republic of Poland
Hummelova 4, 811 01 Bratislava, ☎ 02/5441 3196
Embassy of the Republic of Austria
Ventúrska 10, 811 03 Bratislava, ☎ 02/5443 2985
Embassy of the Republic of Romania
Fraňa Kráľa 11, 811 05 Bratislava, ☎ 02/5249 1665, 5249 3562
Embassy of the Russian Federation
Godrova 4, 811 06 Bratislava, ☎ 02/5441 5823
Embassy of the United Kingdom of Great Britain and Northern Ireland
Panská 16, 811 01 Bratislava, ☎ 02/5441 9632, 5441 9633, 5441 7689
Embassy of the United States of America
Hviezdoslavovo nám. 4, 811 02 Bratislava, ☎ 02/5443 3338
Embassy of the Federal Republic Germany
Hviezdoslavovo nám. 10, 813 03 Bratislava, ☎ 02/5441 9640, 5441 9634
Embassy of the Kingdom of Spain
Prepoštská 10, 811 01 Bratislava, ☎ 02/5441 5726
General Honorary Consulate of Sweden
Lermontovova 15, 811 05 Bratislava, ☎ 02/5443 3900, 5411 5462
Embassy of the Republic of Italy
Červeňova 19, 811 03 Bratislava, ☎ 02/5441 3195

Obchodná ulica St. in Bratislava

Z – Zmenárne, banky – Foreign exchange, banks

In all towns and tourist centres a network of state-owned and private foreign exchange establishments are available. The opening hours on work days are as a rule from 8:00 to 16:00h, in bigger centres some of them open also on holidays or open longer hours. The use of the foreign exchange service at border crossings when entering Slovakia, and banking automats placed next to some banks in the biggest Slovak towns and holiday centres, are recommended. For your personal safety the exchange of foreign currencies in the banks and exchange points found in all hotels, tourist agencies and shops is recommended. Producing a bank receipt also the reverse purchase of the previously exchanged currency is possible.

Important:

- change your money in banks and official foreign exchange points only, never in the street
- do not leave your money, cameras and valuable objects in a parked car
- do not carry on you large sums of money
- leave your money, jewellery and valuable objects in a hotel locker
- when taking a taxi observe whether the taximeter is on or ask for a receipt beforehand
- if possible, park your car in guarded parking lot

Index of interesting items

The UNESCO list of the World Cultural and Natural Heritage:
Banská Štiavnica 250
Spišský hrad Castle and the monuments in its environs (Spišské Podhradie) 348
Vlkolínec (Ružomberok) 285
Caves of the Slovenský a Aggteleg karsts 357
Bardejov 410

The most interesting destinations of tourists:
●●● extra interesting
●● very interesting
● interesting

Index of towns and villages

Matúšovo kráľovstvo, 916 22 Podolie 510
tel: 033/7740548 e-mail:spravcamk@nextra.sk, www.matusovo-kralovstvo.sk

Pozývame Vás na návštevu Matúšovho kráľovstva. Leží v západnej časti Slovenska a nachádza sa v ňom 53 malebných hradov, zámkov a kaštieľov. Ak radi spoznávate históriu, hľadáte tajomné a nespoznané, tak máte šancu stretnúť sa s množstvom duchov a strašidiel, ktoré u nás sídlia. Môžete sa pokochať ďalekými výhľadmi po Matúšovej krajine, vystúpiť na tajuplné hradné zrúcaniny, spoznať povesti a legendy k nim sa viažúce. A ak máte trochu fantázie, možno nájdete i ukryté poklady bývalých hradných pánov a vládcov. V podhradí sa nachádza množstvo Hlások, kde dostanete informácie o dianí v kráľovstve a môžete si zakúpiť viaceré suveníry. Po dlhom putovaní vám istotne padne vhod navštíviť Pútnické miesta Matúšovho kráľovstva, kde vás prichýlia a postarajú sa o všetkých hladných, smädných a unavených pútnikov. Zadovážte si pas Matúšovho kráľovstva, staňte sa jeho občanom, putujte po jeho 9 džavách a získajte pečiatky pasových kontrol 53 hradných panstiev a viac ako 100 pútnických miest!

We would like to invite you to visit the Matheus's Kingdom. It lies in the western part of Slovakia and there are 53 picturesque castles, chateaux and manor houses. If you like to discover history, to look for mysterious and unknown things, you have the chance to meet with a number of ghosts and spectres that reside at our place. You can feast your eyes on alluring views of the Matheus's country, ascend mystery castle ruins, learn about myths and legends connected with them. And if you have a touch of imagination you might even find hidden treasures of former castle lords and rulers. Situated at the foot of the castle hills is a number of Watchposts, where you can get information about events in the Kingdom and buy many souvenirs. After a long journey it will be convenient for you to visit the Pilgrim Places of the Matheus's Kingdom, where you are given a warm reception and they take care of all hungry, thirsty and exhausted pilgrims. Get the passport of the Matheus's Kingdom, become its citizen, travel through its 9 domains and acquire the stamps of passport controls of 53 castle demesnes and more than 100 Pilgrim Places!

599

alpinus

⊘ SCARPA®

CampuS

STYL GRAND®

OUTDOOR COMPANY